Advances in Pattern Recognition

AF889520

For futher volumes:
http://www.springer.com/series/4205

Nanning Zheng · Jianru Xue

Statistical Learning and Pattern Analysis for Image and Video Processing

Springer

Prof. Nanning Zheng
Xi'an Jiaotong University
Inst. Artificial Intelligence &
Robotics
28 Xianningxilu, Xi'an, 710049
China, People's Republic
nnzheng@mail.xjtu.edu.cn

Prof. Jianru Xue
Xi'an Jiaotong University
Inst. Artificial Intelligence &
Robotics
28 Xianningxilu, Xi'an, 710049
China, People's Republic
jrxue@mail.xjtu.edu.cn

Series editor
Professor Sameer Singh, PhD
Research School of Informatics
Loughborough University
Loughborough, UK

ISSN 1617-7916
ISBN 978-1-4471-2673-7 e-ISBN 978-1-84882-312-9
DOI 10.1007/978-1-84882-312-9
Springer Dordrecht Heidelberg London New York

British Library Cataloguing in Publication Data
A catalogue record for this book is available from the British Library

© Springer-Verlag London Limited 2009
Softcover reprint of the hardcover 1st edition 2009
Apart from any fair dealing for the purposes of research or private study, or criticism or review, as permitted under the Copyright, Designs and Patents Act 1988, this publication may only be reproduced, stored or transmitted, in any form or by any means, with the prior permission in writing of the publishers, or in the case of reprographic reproduction in accordance with the terms of licenses issued by the Copyright Licensing Agency. Enquiries concerning reproduction outside those terms should be sent to the publishers.
The use of registered names, trademarks, etc., in this publication does not imply, even in the absence of a specific statement, that such names are exempt from the relevant laws and regulations and therefore free for general use.
The publisher makes no representation, express or implied, with regard to the accuracy of the information contained in this book and cannot accept any legal responsibility or liability for any errors or omissions that may be made.

Printed on acid-free paper

Springer is part of Springer Science+Business Media (www.springer.com)

Preface

Why are We Writing This Book?

Visual data (graphical, image, video, and visualized data) affect every aspect of modern society. The cheap collection, storage, and transmission of vast amounts of visual data have revolutionized the practice of science, technology, and business. Innovations from various disciplines have been developed and applied to the task of designing intelligent machines that can automatically detect and exploit useful regularities (patterns) in visual data. One such approach to machine intelligence is statistical learning and pattern analysis for visual data.

Over the past two decades, rapid advances have been made throughout the field of visual pattern analysis. Some fundamental problems, including perceptual grouping, image segmentation, stereo matching, object detection and recognition, and motion analysis and visual tracking, have become hot research topics and test beds in multiple areas of specialization, including mathematics, neuron-biometry, and cognition. A great diversity of models and algorithms stemming from these disciplines has been proposed. To address the issues of ill-posed problems and uncertainties in visual pattern modeling and computing, researchers have developed rich toolkits based on pattern analysis theory, harmonic analysis and partial differential equations, geometry and group theory, graph matching, and graph grammars.

Among these technologies involved in intelligent visual information processing, statistical learning and pattern analysis is undoubtedly the most popular and important approach, and it is also one of the most rapidly developing fields, with many achievements in recent years. Above all, it provides a unifying theoretical framework for intelligent visual information processing applications.

The main topics of this book are the modeling and computing of visual patterns in image sequences and the methods required to construct intelligent video analysis systems. For visual pattern modeling, we apply statistical learning and statistical pattern analysis to extract semantic visual objects. In our view, such models can be learned efficiently to emulate complex scenes in the image sequence. For video analysis system building, the methods presented here are based on techniques of statistical computing, such as motion analysis, inferring underlying states of objects of interest, and reducing the dimensionality of video data while preserving useful information as much as possible.

How the Book is Organized

This book provides a comprehensive overview of theories, methodologies, and recent developments in the field of statistical learning and statistical analysis for visual pattern modeling and computing. We had three objectives in selecting topics to cover. We wish to 1) describe a solid theoretical foundation, 2) provide a comprehensive summary of the latest advances of recent years, and 3) present typical issues to be considered in making a real system for visual information processing. We have tried to achieve a balance between these three objectives. The rest of this book is organized as follows:

Chapter 1 is devoted to constructing the theoretic basis for pattern analysis and statistical learning. The fundamentals of statistical pattern recognition and statistical learning are presented via introducing the general framework of a statistical pattern recognition system. We also discuss pattern representation and classification, two important components of such a system, as well as concepts involved in three main approaches to statistical learning: supervised learning, semistatistical learning, and unsupervised learning. This introduction leads to the development of three parts of the whole book.

In the first part, we focus on the unsupervised learning of visual pattern representational models for objects in images, which covers through Chapters 2 to 5. Usually, what a vision algorithm can accomplish depends crucially on how much it knows about content of the visual scenes. This knowledge can be mathematically represented by simple but general models that can realistically characterize visual patterns in the ensemble of visual data. Representation and computation are thus two principal problems in visual computing. We provide a comprehensive survey of recent advances in statistical learning and pattern analysis with respect to these two problems. Chapter 2 discusses cluster analysis and perceptual grouping algorithms used in unsupervised visual pattern analysis. The systematic approaches for deriving these models are also illustrated step by step. Chapters 3 through 5 focus on representing and learning visual patterns in both spatial and temporal domains. Chapter 3 describes component analysis approaches, which are used to find hidden components via visual data analysis techniques. Chapter 4 discusses the manifold learning perspective on visual pattern representation, dimensionality reduction, and classification problems. Chapter 5 presents a review of recent advances in the adaptive wavelet transform for image and video coding.

In the second part, we introduce the supervised learning of visual patterns in images, which is covered in Chapter 6. We focus on supervised statistical pattern analysis and introduce concepts and major techniques in feature extraction and selection as well as classifier design. Especially, we introduce statistical machine learning techniques by examining the support vector machine and AdaBoost classifier.

In the third part, we focus on the visual pattern analysis in video, which covers through Chapters 7 to 11. In this part, we discuss methodologies for building intelligent video analysis systems such as object detection, tracking, and recognition in video. Chapter 7 focuses on the critical aspects of motion analysis, including statistical optical flow, model-based motion analysis, and joint motion estimation and segmentation. For the object-level motion analysis, we first introduce the sequential Bayesian estimation framework in Chapter 8, which acts as the theoretic basis for visual tracking, and then present approaches to constructing a representation model of specific objects. Then, in Chapter 9, we present a probabilistic fusion framework for robust tracking. Chapters 10 and 11 offer a multitarget tracking in video (MTTV) formulation that exploits a Markov network whose solution is arrived at using Monte Carlo-based belief propagation. Using this approach, problems including occlusion and various number of objects in MTTV are addressed.

Finally, in Chapter 12, we make an in-depth discussion of visual data processing in the cognitive process. A new scheme of association memory and new architecture of artificial intelligent system with attractors of chaos are also addressed. We argue that to make a breakthrough in current research on intelligent visual data processing, people should pay great attention to the mechanism of cognition and selective attention.

Acknowledgments

First, we thank the National Science Foundation of China (Grant Nos. 608750081 and 60635050) for their continuing support of our research in the image and video processing field. Our interest in statistical learning and pattern analysis approaches to image and video processing could not have developed to the point of writing this book without their funding.

We also thank Xi'an Jiaotong University, for their support of our efforts in writing this book, and Wayne Wheeler, Senior editor of Springer-Verlag, for his suggestion in writing this book. Another major source of stimulation for this effort comes from our former graduate students, who have provided a continuing stream of new ideas and insights. Those who have made contributions directly reflected in this book include Mr. Xiaoping Zhong, Dr. Weixiang Liu, and Dr. Zaide Liu.

A special thanks goes to Dr. Clayton McMillan, who read the first draft very carefully and made numerous corrections for improvements. We also thank Dr. Shaoyi Du and Dr. Gaofeng Meng for their dedication and patience in preparing drafts and writing Chapter 6. The second author would like to thank Prof. Songchun Zhu for the hosting of his visiting in the Center for Image and Vision Science in University of California, Los Angeles, when he was writing this book.

Last but not least, we are greatly indebted to our families: our parents and our wives and children for their unconditional support, encouragement, and continuing love throughout our research work.

Contents

Chapter 1
Pattern Analysis and Statistical Learning

Abstract This chapter presents the fundamentals of statistical pattern recognition and statistical learning. First, we present the general framework of a statistical pattern recognition system and discuss pattern representation and classification, two important components of such a system. Second, we introduce the concept of statistical learning and examine the three main approaches to statistical learning: supervised learning, semi-supervised learning, and unsupervised learning.

1.1 Introduction

In the communities of artificial intelligence, one of ultimate goals is to build a vision machine that can make sense of the world by discovering meaningful visual patterns from the light falls on its image sensors. Visual pattern analysis plays an important role in pursuing this goal. Visual pattern can be roughly defined as the repeatable components of an image, and image (or image sequence) always contain an overwhelming number of visual patterns. The purpose of visual pattern analysis is to compute a hierarchy of increasingly abstract interpretations of the observed images (or image sequence) and this has also been one of the most important topics in the field of vision, biologic and machine.

Two facts make the problem of visual pattern analysis complicated. Firstly, visual pattern analysis is considered to be a general data collection and analysis problem, where existing concepts and methods in statistical theory and information theory can in principle be used to model and interpret the image data. Secondly, visual pattern analysis also proves to be a highly specialized data collection and analysis task. We must understand the special characteristics of the nature image data in order to develop realistic models and efficient algorithms for representing and recognizing the wide variety of natural image patterns. Taking the image parsing problem as an example, depending on the types of visual patterns that a visual task is interested in, the image parsing problem is called (1) perceptual grouping on the pixel level, (2) image segmentation on the region level, and (3) object recognition on the object

N. Zheng, J. Xue, *Statistical Learning and Pattern Analysis for Image and Video Processing*, Advances in Pattern Recognition, DOI 10.1007/978-1-84882-312-9_1,
© Springer-Verlag London Limited 2009

level, respectively. This requests a common and mathematically sound framework for visual pattern analysis.

The idea of establishing a unifying theory for the various concepts and models encountered in visual pattern analysis is not new. Visual pattern has been studied in four directions (Zhu 2003): (1) studying natural image statistics, in which the natural images are studied from the perspective of image coding and redundancy reduction, or are used to predict or explain the neuron response; (2) analyzing natural image components, in which image is transformed into a superposition of image components for the purposes of variable decoupling and dimension reduction; (3) grouping natural image elements, in which the global perception of images is achieved by grouping local elements according to Gestalt laws; and (4) modeling visual patterns, in which explicit models for the visual patterns have been developed.

In recent years, modeling visual pattern stochastically and making inference statistically become more and more obvious trend in visual pattern analysis. In this line of thinking, a visual pattern is defined as an abstraction of some properties decided by a certain vision tasks. These properties can be featured as statistical computing from either raw image data or some hidden descriptions inferred from raw image data. In both ways, a visual pattern is equalized to a set of observable signals governed by a statistical model. There are two major research areas in this trend: statistical pattern recognition, pattern theory. In the following, we present a historic overview of them.

1.1.1 Statistical Pattern Recognition

The term pattern recognition can be traced back to the work of Nobel Laureate Herbert Simon, in which the central observation is that pattern recognition is critical in most human decision-making tasks. Simon stated that "the more relevant the patterns at your disposal, the better your decision will be." This motivates the belief that pattern recognition is the best possible way to utilize existing sensors, processors, and domain knowledge to make decisions automatically. Rapidly growing and readily available computing power, while enabling faster processing of huge data sets, has facilitated the use of elaborate and diverse methods for data analysis and classification. At the same time, demands on automatic pattern recognition systems are rising enormously due to the availability of large databases and stringent performance requirements (speed, accuracy, and cost). Driven by the above trends, the automatic recognition, description, classification, and grouping of patterns are important problems in a variety of engineering and scientific disciplines such as biology, psychology, medicine, marketing, computer vision, artificial intelligence, and remote sensing.

Pattern recognition aims to classify data (patterns) based on either a priori knowledge or statistical information extracted from the patterns. The patterns to be classified are usually groups of measurements or observations, defining points in an appropriate multidimensional space. This is different to the pattern matching, where the pattern is rigidly specified. Given a pattern, its recognition problem usually is being posed as a classification or categorization task, where the classes are either defined by the system designer (in supervised classification) or learned based on the similarity of patterns (in unsupervised classification). Even in some literatures, recognition and categorization are different recognition tasks. However, they are similar in representing different trade-offs between specificity and invariance. The main computational difficulty is the problem of variability. A vision system needs to generalize across huge variations in the appearance of an object such as a face, for instance due to viewpoint, illumination, or occlusions. At the same time, the system needs to maintain specificity. It is important here to note that an object can be recognized at a variety of levels of specificity: a cat can be recognized as my cat on the individual level or more broadly on the categorical level as cat, mammal, animal, and so forth.

Statistical pattern recognition is based on statistical characterizations of patterns, assuming that the patterns are generated by a stochastic process. Take the supervised classification problem as an example, the recognition problem can be stated as follows: given training data $\{(\mathbf{x}_1, y_1), \ldots, (\mathbf{x}_n, y_n)\}$ produce a classifier C: $\mathscr{X} \to \mathscr{Y}$, which maps a pattern $\mathbf{x} \in \mathscr{X}$ to its classification label $y \in \mathscr{Y}$. The observations (or measurements) of the patterns to be classified are assumed to have a probability density or mass (depending on whether they are continuous or discrete) function conditioned on the pattern class. Thus a pattern x belonging to class y_i is viewed as an observation drawn randomly from the class-conditional probability function $p(x|y_i)$. A wide range of algorithms including the Bayes estimation, the maximum likelihood estimation (which can be viewed as a particular case of the Bayes rule), and the Neyman–Pearson rule are utilized to establish decision boundaries between pattern classes.

A complete pattern recognition system, as shown in Fig. 1.1, consists of (1) a sensor that gathers the observations to be classified or described, (2) the processing module that segments, removes noise, normalizes the pattern, and any other operation which will contribute in defining a compact representation of the pattern, (3) a feature extraction mechanism that computes numeric or symbolic information from the observations, and (4) a classification or description scheme that does the actual job of classifying or describing observations, relying on the extracted features. In the training mode, the feature extraction/selection module finds the appropriate features for representing the input patterns, and the classifier is trained for partitioning the feature space. In the classification mode, the trained classifier assigns the input pattern to one of the pattern classes under consideration based on the measured features.

The problem domain dictates the choice of sensor(s), preprocessing technique, representation scheme, and the decision-making model. In general, a well-definedand sufficiently constrained recognition problem will lead to a representation of compact pattern and a simple decision-making strategy. Usually, a pattern is represented in terms of d features or measurements and is viewed as a point in a d-dimensional space. The goal is to choose those features that allow pattern vectors belonging to different categories to occupy compact and disjoint regions in a d-dimensional feature space. While the classification or description scheme is usually based on the

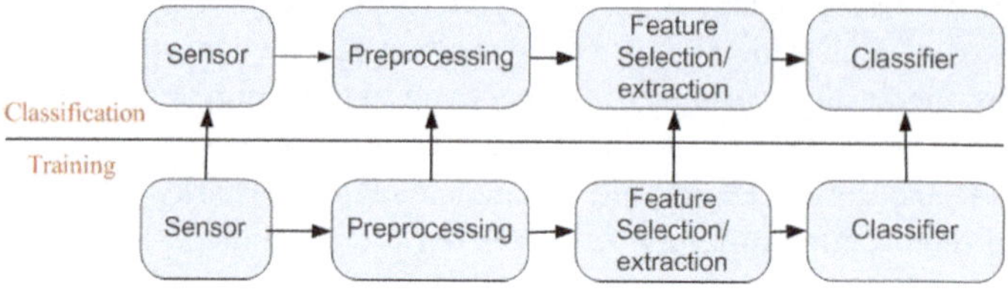

Fig. 1.1 The architecture of a complete pattern recognition system

availability of a set of patterns that have already been classified or described. This set of patterns is termed the training set, and the resulting learning strategy is characterized as supervised learning. Learning can also be unsupervised, in the sense that the system is not given an a priori labeling of patterns, instead it itself establishes the classes based on the statistical regularities of the patterns.

A good recognition systems relies on its generalization ability, that is, the ability to correctly classify test samples which are likely to be different from the training samples. Therefore, optimizing a classifier to maximize its performance on the training set may not always result in the desired performance on a test set. A poor generalization of a classifier can be attributed to any one of the following factors: (1) the number of features is too large relative to the number of training samples (curse of dimensionality), (2) the number of unknown parameters associated with the classifier is large, and (3) a classifier is too intensively optimized on training set (overtraining).

In addition to the statistical pattern recognition, there are also three optional approaches for visual pattern analysis: (1) template matching, (2) syntactic or structural matching, and (3) neural networks. These methods are not necessarily independent and sometimes the same pattern recognition methods exist with different interpretations. For details of these three approaches, please refer to an outstanding survey written by Jain et al. (2000).

1.1.2 Pattern Theory

Different from that statistical pattern recognition begins by prescribing algorithms and machinery to recognize and classify patterns. Pattern theory, formulated by Grenander and Miller (2007), defines a vocabulary to articulate and recast visual pattern concepts in precise language and provides a mathematical formalism to represent visual knowledge. The visual knowledge includes two parts: (1) mathematical definitions and models of various visual patterns, and (2) effective inference of the visual patterns and models.

Pattern theory follows the Bayesian framework and develops explicit models for visual patterns. For the purpose of visual pattern analysis, there are three ingredients in the Bayesian framework: (a) a set of random variables, some of which describe the observed images and some hidden variables describing visual patterns in the world which are causing the images; (b) a class of stochastic models allow one to express the variability of the pattern and the noise present in the images; and (c) specific parameters for the one stochastic model in this class best describes the class of images we are trying to interpret. More formally, we assume that we have a set $\mathbf{x} = (\mathbf{x}_o, \mathbf{x}_h)$ of observed and hidden random variables, which may have real values or discrete values in some finite or countable sets, a set Θ of parameters and a class of probability models $P(\mathbf{x}|\Theta)$ on the $\mathbf{x}$'s for each set of values of the Θ's. It is usual to factor these probability distributions:

$$P(\mathbf{x}|\Theta) = P(\mathbf{x}_o|\mathbf{x}_h)P(\mathbf{x}_h|\Theta) \tag{1.1}$$

where the first factor, describing the likelihood of the observations from the hidden variables, is called the imaging model and the second, giving probabilities on the hidden variables, is called the prior. In the full Bayesian setting, one has an even stronger prior, a full probability model $P(\mathbf{x}_h, \Theta)$, including the parameters.

Accordingly, there are three related problems in the perception of images using pattern theory:

1. Crafting or learning of the model $P(\mathbf{x}|\Theta)$. In pattern theory, a Gibbs-like graph model is often used. In the graph, the prior distributions for hidden variables and models for the observed variables form the vertices. And then the randomness and variability of these graphs are studied.
2. Estimating the values of the parameters Θ, which give the best stochastic model of the pattern. This often means that we have some set of observations (or measurements) $\{\mathbf{x}_o^{(i)}\}_{i=1}^N$ and seek the values of Θ, which maximizes their likelihood $\prod_i P(x_o^{(i)}|\Theta)$. If the hidden variables as well as observations are known, this is called supervised learning; if the hidden variables are not known, then it is unsupervised and one may maximize, for instance, $\prod_i \sum_{\mathbf{x}_h} P(x_o^{(i)}, \mathbf{x}_h|\Theta)$. Furthermore, if one has a prior on the Θ's, one can also estimate them from the mean or mode of the full posterior $P(\Theta|\{\mathbf{x}_o^{(i)}\})$.
3. Using this machinery to actually perceive images. In this situation, we want to use the measured specific values $\mathbf{x}_o = \hat{\mathbf{x}}_o$ to infer the values of the hidden variables $\mathbf{x}_h$. By Bayes' rule, the hidden variables are distributed by the posterior distribution:

$$P(\mathbf{x}_h|\hat{\mathbf{x}}_o, \Theta) = \frac{P(\hat{\mathbf{x}}_o|\mathbf{x}_h, \Theta)P(\mathbf{x}_h|\Theta)}{P(\hat{\mathbf{x}_o}|\Theta)} \tag{1.2}$$

More insight into the second problem, one will find a more challenging problem: how many parameters Θ to include. This depends on how much data one has: for any set of data, models with too few parameters distort the information the data contains, and models with too many parameters overfit the accidents of this data set. There are two approaches to this issue. One is cross-validation: holds back parts of the data, train the model to have the maximum likelihood on the training set, and test it by checking the likelihood of the held out data. There is also a beautiful theoretical analysis of the problem principally due to Vapnik (2000) and involving the VC dimension of the models – the size of the the largest set of data which can be split in all possible ways into more and less likely parts by different choices of Θ. A useful test for a class of models is to synthesize from it, i.e., choose random samples according to this probability measure and see how well they resemble the images we are accustomed to observing in the world.

In the rest of this chapter, we will present basics for statistical classification and pattern recognition in Section 3.1.2. The feature extraction/selection and classifier design, two major components of a statistical pattern recognition system, are discussed in Sections 1.2.1 and 1.2.2, respectively. Sections 1.3 and 1.4 are devoted to the problems of pattern representation and learning in pattern theory, respectively.

1.2 Statistical Classification

Statistical classification is at the core of a statistical pattern recognition system, in which individual items are placed into groups based on quantitative information on one or more characteristics inherent in the items (referred to as traits, variables, characters, etc.) and based on a training set of previously labeled items.

The distinction between recognition and categorization is mostly semantic. The difficulty depends on parameters such as the size and composition of training set and how much of the variability required for generalization is covered by the training examples. However, they share a same system architecture as shown in Fig. 1.1, feature extraction/seclection and classifying scheme are two of their major components. We discuss each of them one by one in the following.

1.2.1 Feature Extraction and Selection

Feature extraction and selection aims to achieve a compact pattern representation and which also leads to the decrease of measurement cost and the increase of the classification accuracy. Consequently, the resulting classifier will be faster and will use less memory.

Usually, feature extraction takes the form of transformation (Due Trier et al. 1996). New features, created by transforming the raw data or combination of the original data sets, determine an appropriate subspace of dimensionality m in the original data space of dimensionality d, and usually, $m \leq d$. Feature selection follows feature extraction and can be defined as follows: given a set of d features, select a subset of size $n (n \leq m)$ to the smallest classification error. Ideally, we hope that some of the extracted features with low discrimination ability are discarded. However, in real applications, this goal cannot always be achieved successfully.

The algorithm design for feature extraction and feature selection depends on the application domain and specific training data one has. One of the most difficult challenges in developing a general theory which is capable of dealing with every kind of patterns without requiring any a priori knowledge of the specific application domain. Often, for a large spectrum of applications, the best performing approaches were designed by using specific knowledge and by manually selecting the best-suited features or the most appropriate representation structure. This caused the proliferation of a huge number of application-dependent techniques which cannot be successfully applied outside their typical environment. However, the view of "let the data speak for itself" in the statistical learning leads to a set of useful tools for constructing representations for a visual pattern and this will be discussed in the subsequent chapters of this book.

1.2.2 Classifier

The trained classifier defines a boundary between the positive samples and the negative samples with the training set. Classification is a process that the classifier assigns a class label to an input, or equivalently, identifying the probabilistic source of a measurement. The only statistical model needed here is the conditional model of the class variable given by the measurement. Once a feature selection or classification procedure finds a proper representation, a classifier can be designed using a number of possible approaches.

A comprehensive review Jain et al. (2000) identifies three main approaches to design a classifier.

- Similarity-based approach: Similar patterns should be assigned to the same class. So, once a good metric has been established to define similarity, patterns can be classified by template matching or the minimum distance classifier using a few prototypes per class. The choice of metric and the prototypes is crucial to the success of this approach. The K-nearest neighbor decision rule and the nearest mean classifier belong to this category.
- Probabilistic approach: The optimal Bayes decision rule assigns a pattern to the class with the maximum posterior probability. This rule can be modified to take into account costs associated with different types of misclassifications. For known class conditional densities, the Bayes decision rule gives the optimum classifier, in the sense that, for given prior probabilities, loss function and class-conditional densities, no other decision rule will have a lower risk.
- Constructing decision boundaries: This category of classifiers constructs decision boundaries directly by optimizing certain error criteria. While this approach depends on the chosen metric, sometimes classifiers of this type may approximate the Bayes classifier asymptotically. The driving force of the training procedure is the minimization of a criterion such as apparent classification error or the mean squared error (MSE) between the classifier output and some preset target

value. Well known classifier of this category includes Fisher's linear discriminant, single-layer perceptron.

In addition to the above-mentioned classifiers, decision trees and support vector machines are also widely used for the purposes of classification. A decision tree is trained by an iterative selection of individual features that are most salient at each node of the tree. The criteria for feature selection and tree generation include the information content, the node purity, or the Fisher's criterion. During classification, only those features that are needed for the test pattern are considered, so feature selection is implicitly built-in. The optimization criterion for the support vector machine is the margin between the classes, i.e., the empty area around the decision boundary defined by the distance to the nearest training patterns. These patterns, called support vectors, ultimately define the classification function. Their number is minimized by maximizing the margin.

Classifier combination is also an important approach in designing a classifier. We may have different feature sets, different training sets, different classification methods, or different training sessions, all resulting in a set of classifiers whose outputs may be combined, with the hope of improving overall classification accuracy. A typical combination scheme consists of a set of individual classifiers and a combiner that combines the results of the individual classifiers to make the final decision. When the individual classifiers should be invoked or how they should interact with each other is determined by the architecture of the combination scheme. AdaBoost is one of the most well-known algorithms for classifier combination, which we will introduce in Chapter 6.

1.3 Visual Pattern Representation

In pattern theory, explicit models are needed for the pattern representation. However, what is a quantitative definition of a visual pattern? For example, what is a "human face" or a "pedestrian"? A pattern is an abstraction of some properties that are relevant with respect to a certain "recognition purpose." These properties are feature statistics computed from either raw signals or some hidden descriptions inferred from raw signals. In either case, a pattern in statistical pattern analysis is equalized to a set of observable signals governed by a statistical model and the statistical model forms an intrinsic representation of visual knowledge and image regularities.

Modeling the visual pattern requires that the pattern must first be converted into a mathematical object, some vector in $\mathbb{R}^n$. The dimensionality of the visual pattern, n, affects through the rest of the representation problem including how many observations (measurements) should be collected for learning the parameters of the representation model and how is the generalization ability of the learned model. The n of a visual pattern is always larger than the number of training samples available. This caused the curse of dimensionality.

1.3.1 The Curse of Dimensionality

Inappropriate choices of n possibly lead to the curse of dimensionality. The performance of a classifier depends upon the interrelationship between sample sizes, number of features, and classifier complexity. A simple table-lookup technique, which partitions the feature space into cells and associates a class label with each cell, requires that the number of training data points be an exponential function of the feature dimension. This phenomenon is termed the "curse of dimensionality." The curse of dimensionality leads to the so-called "peaking phenomenon" which is a paradoxical behavior in which the added features may actually degrade the performance of a classifier if the number of training samples that are used to design the classifier is small relative to the number of features.

All of the commonly used classifiers can suffer from the curse of dimensionality. However, an exact relationship between the probability of misclassification, the number of training samples, the number of features, and the true parameters of the class-conditional densities is very difficult to establish. A generally accepted rule is that the more complex the classifier, the larger the ratio of sample size to dimensionality should be, in order to avoid the curse of dimensionality. This suggests that a system designer should try to select only a small number of salient features when confronted with a limited training set.

In summary, the curse of dimensionality dictates that a system designer should keep the dimensionality of the pattern representation as small as possible. A limited yet salient feature set simplifies both the pattern representation and the classifiers that are built on the selected representation. Moreover, a small number of features can alleviate the curse of dimensionality when the number of training samples is limited. And feature extraction and selection are two essential steps in developing an effective representation of a pattern.

1.3.2 Dimensionality Reduction Techniques

For visual pattern analysis, a wealth of models for pattern representation have been proposed in the literature. We briefly review three main techniques to reduce the dimensionality in archiving compact representation of visual pattern: (1) component analysis, (2) manifold learning, and (3) functional analysis.

- **Learning components for a pattern**: Natural images consist of an overwhelming number of visual patterns generated by very diverse stochastic processes. For example, an image usually contains a number of different objects, parts, or features and these components can occur in different configurations to form many distinct images. Identifying the underlying components that are combined to form images is thus essential for learning the perceptual representations necessary for performing object recognition. Chapter 3 presents a survey of this line of research.

- **Manifold Learning**: Visual patterns contained in observed images may not be as complicated as they appear. Often, however, these observations result from changes to only a few degrees of freedom, lending a predictable structure to the high-dimensional data. Algorithms for finding this underlying structure within the data are collectively referred to by the term "manifold learning." More details can be found in Chapter 4.
- **Functional Approximation**: If one treats an image as a continuous 2D function, then it can be shown that some classes of functionals (such as Sobölev, Holder, Besov spaces) can be decomposed into bases, for example, Fourier, wavelets, and more recently, wedgelets and ridgelets. It has been proved that the Fourier, wavelet, and ridgelet bases are independent components of various functional spaces (Do and Vetterli 2003). More details can be found in Chapter 5. With an overcomplete basis, an image may be reconstructed by a small (sparse) number of bases. This often leads to a 10- to 100-fold reduction in dimension.

1.4 Statistical Learning

Learning plays an important role in both the statistical pattern recognition and the pattern theory, since many problems in pattern analysis can be formally stated as the problem of real-valued or binary function estimation from noisy examples. More formally, a statistical learning method is an algorithm that estimates an unknown mapping (dependency) between system's inputs and outputs, from the available data, i.e., known (input, output) samples. Once such a dependency has been estimated, it can be used for prediction of system outputs from the input values.

The key point of learning techniques is that the trained function from examples should be predictive, e.g., how well it estimates the outputs for previously unseen inputs. The prediction accuracy, also known as generalization, is a central concern in designing a learning system. A generic statistical learning system consists of the following:

- A generator of random input vectors $\mathbf{x}$, drawn from a fixed (unknown) probability distribution $P(\mathbf{x})$.
- A system which returns an output value y for every input vector $\mathbf{x}$ according to the fixed conditional distribution $P(y|\mathbf{x})$, which is also unknown.
- A learning machine, which is capable of implementing a set of approximating functions $f(\mathbf{x}, w)$, $w \in \Omega$, where Ω is a set of parameters of an arbitrary nature.

The goal of learning is to select a function (from this set) which best approximates the system's response. In a typical scenario, we have an outcome measurement, usually quantitative or categorical, upon which we wish to predict based upon a set of features (properties of the patterns of interest). We have a training set of samples, in which we observe the outcome y and feature measurements $\mathbf{x}$ of samples. Using this data, we build a prediction model or learner $f(\mathbf{x})$, which will enable us to predict the outcome for new, unseen data. A good learner is one that accurately predicts such an outcome. The distinction in the outcome type has led to a naming convention for the prediction tasks: *regression* when we predict quantitative output, and *classification* when we predict qualitative outcomes. In fact, these two tasks have a lot in in common, and in particular both can be viewed as a task in function approximation.

1.4.1 Prediction Risk

In a regression formulation, the goal of learning is to estimate an unknown function $g(\mathbf{x})$ in the relationship: $y = g(\mathbf{x}) + \varepsilon$, where the random error ε is zero mean, $\mathbf{x}$ is a d-dimensional vector, and y is a scalar output. A learning method (of the estimation procedure) selects the "best" model $f(\mathbf{x}, w_0)$ from a set of approximating functions $f(\mathbf{x}, w)$ that are specified a priori, where the quality of an approximation is measured by the loss or discrepancy measure $L(y, f(\mathbf{x}, w))$.

A common loss function for regression is the squared error. Thus, learning is the problem of finding the function $f(\mathbf{x}, w_0)$ that minimizes the prediction risk function

$$R(w) = \int (y - f(\mathbf{x}, w))^2 p(\mathbf{x}, y) d\mathbf{x} dy \tag{1.3}$$

using only the training data $(\mathbf{x}_i, y_i)$, $i = 1, ..., n$, generated according to some (unknown) joint probability density function (PDF) $p(\mathbf{x}, y) = p(\mathbf{x})p(y|\mathbf{x})$. A prediction risk function measures the accuracy of the learning method's predictions of the unknown target function $g(\mathbf{x})$.

The learning problem above is ill-posed, since the prediction risk is unknown. Most learning methods implement an idea known as "empirical risk minimization" (ERM), which attempts to choose the model that minimizes the empirical risk, or the average loss for the training data:

$$R_{ERM}(w) = \frac{1}{n} \sum_{i=1}^{n} (y_i - f(\mathbf{x}_i, y))^2 \tag{1.4}$$

The ERM approach is only appropriate under parametric settings, i.e., when the parametric form of an unknown dependency is known. Under such an approach, the unknown dependency is assumed to belong to a narrow class of functions (specified by a given parametric form). In most practical applications, parametric assumptions do not hold true, and the unknown dependency is estimated in a wide class of possible models of varying complexity. This is achieved by choosing a model of optimal complexity corresponding to the smallest prediction error for future data.

Nonasymptotic (guaranteed) bounds on the prediction risk for finite-sample settings have been proposed in the VC theory. All approximation theory results are aiming at deriving accurate estimates of risk, since the goal of risk estimation is equivalent to complexity control when the number of samples is large. However, there is a subtle but important difference between the goal of accurate estimation of prediction risk and using these estimates for model complexity control with finite samples. That is, a model selection criterion can provide poor estimates of prediction risk, yet differences between its risk estimates may yield accurate model selection.

There are two general approaches for estimating prediction risk for learning problems with finite data: analytical and data-driven. Analytical methods use analytic estimates of the prediction risk as a function of the empirical risk, penalized by some measure of model complexity. Once an accurate estimate of the prediction risk is found, it can be used for model selection by choosing the model complexity. These estimates take the form of

$$R_{est} = r\left(\frac{d}{n}\right)\frac{1}{n}\sum_{i=1}^{n}(y_i - \hat{y}_i) \tag{1.5}$$

where r is a monotonically increasing function of the ratio of model complexity d (the number of degrees of freedom) and the training sample size n. $r(\cdot)$ is often called a penalization factor, because it inflates the average residual sum of squares for increasingly complex models.

Statistical learning theory provides analytic upper bounds on the prediction risk (Vapnik 2000). This results in the penalization factor $r(p,n)$, called the Vapnik's measure (VM).

$$r(p,n) = \left(1 - \sqrt{(p - p\ln p + \frac{\ln n}{2n})}\right)_{+}^{-1} \tag{1.6}$$

where $p = h/n$, h denotes the VC dimension of a model and $(\cdot)_{+} = 0$, for $x < 0$. In statistical learning theory, R_{est} in Eq. (7.27) is obtained by substituting $r(p,n)$ for $r(d/n)$. For linear estimators with m degrees of freedom, the VC dimension is $h = m + 1$. For a given training data set, selection of the "best" model from several parametric models corresponds to choosing the model providing the minimum bound on prediction risk (7.27), with a penalization factor given by Eq. (1.6).

1.4.2 Supervised, Unsupervised, and Others

A classifier in a statistical pattern recognition system is also a learner and can be obtained by *supervised learning* (labeled training samples), *semi-supervised learning* (partially labeled training samples), *unsupervised learning* (with unlabeled training samples). The label of a training sample represents the category to which that pattern belongs. In an unsupervised learning problem, sometimes the number of classes must be learned along with the structure of each class.

More specifically, consider a machine which receives a sequence of inputs $x_1, x_2, \ldots$, where x_t is the sensory data at time t. This input, which we will often call the sample or the data, could correspond to an image, a sound waveform, or less obviously sensory data, for example, the words in a text. Now we discuss the three different kinds of machine learning techniques.

1. In supervised learning, the machine is also given a sequence of labels $y_1, y_2, \ldots$ corresponding to the category the input belongs, and the goal of the machine is to learn to produce the correct output given by a new input.
2. In unsupervised learning, the machine simply receives inputs $x_1, x_2, \ldots$, but obtains neither supervised target outputs nor rewards from its environment. The machine's goal here is to build representations of the input that can be used for decision-making, predicting future inputs, efficiently communicating the inputs to another machine, etc. In a sense, unsupervised learning can be thought of as finding patterns in the input data and beyond what would be considered pure unstructured noise. Two very simple classic examples of unsupervised learning are clustering and dimensionality reduction. We discuss these in the next chapter.
3. Semi-supervised learning is a new area of study in machine learning. Traditional classifiers use only labeled data to train, e.g., the supervised learning methods. However, labeled instances are often difficult, expensive, or time consuming to obtain as they require the efforts of experienced human annotators. Meanwhile unlabeled data may be relatively easy to collect, but there have been few ways to use them. Semi-supervised learning addresses this problem by using large amounts of unlabeled data, together with the labeled data, to build better classifiers.

In addition to the statistical learning mentioned above, reinforcement learning is also a kind of machine learning technique. In reinforcement learning, the machine interacts with its environment by producing actions $a_1, a_2, \ldots$. These actions affect the state of the environment, which in turn results in the machine receiving some scalar rewards (or punishment) $r_1, r_2, \ldots$. The goal of the machine is to learn to behave in a way that maximizes the future rewards it receives (or minimizes the punishments) over its lifetime. Reinforcement learning is closely related to the fields of decision theory and control theory. Since we focus on the statistical learning method in this book, extent discussion of the reinforcement learning is beyond the scope. Interested reader can refer to Kaelbling et al. (1996) for more detailed information.

In the last decades, local photometric descriptors computed for interest regions have proved to be very successful in applications such as wide baseline matching, object recognition, texture recognition (Mikolajczyk and Schmid 2005). Recent work has concentrated on making these descriptors invariant to image transformations. The idea is to detect image regions invariant to a class of transformations, which are then used as support regions to compute invariant descriptors. Given invariant region detectors, the remaining questions are which descriptor is the most appropriate to characterize the regions and whether the choice of the descriptor depends on the region detector. There is a large number of possible descriptors and associated distance measures which emphasize different image properties like pixel intensities, color, texture, edges, etc. The evaluation of the descriptors has been performed in the context of matching and recognition of a same scene or object observed under different viewing conditions (Mikolajczyk and Schmid 2005).

1.5 Summary

Pattern analysis is a highly interdisciplinary field, which borrows and builds upon ideas from statistics, computer science, engineering, cognitive science, optimization theory, and many other disciplines of science and mathematics. In this chapter, we have presented a high-level overview of pattern analysis and statistical learning, and paint a picture of the concepts and terminologies that are common in this field. The rest of this book will turn to statistical learning approaches in image and video processing.

References

Do M, Vetterli M (2003) The finite ridgelet transform for image representation. IEEE Transactions on Image Processing 12(1):16–28

Due Trier, Jain A, Taxt T (1996) Feature extraction methods for character recognition - a survey. Pattern Recognition 29(4):641–662

Grenander U, Miller M (2007) Pattern theory: from representation to inference. Oxford University Press, USA

Jain A, Duin R, Mao J (2000) Statistical pattern recognition: a review. IEEE Transactions on Pattern Analysis and Machine Intelligence 22(1):4–37

Kaelbling L, Littman M, Moore A (1996) Reinforcement learning: a survey. Journal of Artificial Intelligence 4:237–285

Mikolajczyk K, Schmid C (2005) A performance evaluation of local descriptors. IEEE Transactions on Pattern Analysis and Machine Intelligence 27:1615–1630

Vapnik V (2000) The nature of statistical learning theory. Springer, New York

Zhu S (2003) Statistical modeling and conceptualization of visual patterns. IEEE Transactions on Pattern Analysis and Machine Intelligence 25:691–712

Chapter 2
Unsupervised Learning for Visual Pattern Analysis

Abstract This chapter presents an overview of topics and major concepts in unsupervised learning for visual pattern analysis. Cluster analysis and dimensionality are two important topics in unsupervised learning. Clustering relates to the grouping of similar objects in visual perception, while dimensionality reduction is essential for the compact representation of visual patterns. In this chapter, we focus on clustering techniques, offering first a theoretical basis, then a look at some applications in visual pattern analysis. With respect to the former, we introduce both concepts and algorithms. With respect to the latter, we discuss visual perceptual grouping. In particular, the problem of image segmentation is discussed in terms of contour and region grouping. Finally, we present a brief introduction to learning visual pattern representations, which serves as a prelude to the following chapters.

2.1 Introduction

2.1.1 Unsupervised Learning

The problem of unsupervised learning or "learning without a teacher" can be formulated as follows: given a set of N observations $(x_1, x_2, ..., x_N)$ of a random p-vector $\mathbf{x}$ having joint density $P(\mathbf{x})$, the goal is to directly infer the properties of this probability density without the help of a supervisor or teacher providing correct answers or degree-of-error for each observation.

Unsupervised learning methods can be generally divided into three categories. First, in low-dimensional problems ($p \leq 3$), there are a variety of effective non-parametric methods for directly estimating the density $P(\mathbf{x})$ for each value in $\mathbf{x}$ (Silverman 1986). However, these methods fail in high dimensions due to the curse of dimensionality. One must settle for estimating rather crude global models, such as Gaussian mixtures or various simple descriptive statistics that characterize $P(\mathbf{x})$. Generally, these descriptive statistics attempt to characterize $\mathbf{x}$-values, or collections

N. Zheng, J. Xue, *Statistical Learning and Pattern Analysis for Image and Video Processing*, Advances in Pattern Recognition, DOI 10.1007/978-1-84882-312-9_2,
© Springer-Verlag London Limited 2009

of such values, where $P(\mathbf{x})$ is relatively large. Second, methods including principal components analysis (Jolliffe 1986), multidimensional scaling (Kruskal and Wish 1978), and principle curves (Banfield and Raftery 1992), for example, attempt to identify low-dimensional subspaces within the $\mathbf{x}$-space that represents $P(\mathbf{x})$. This provides information about the relationships between the variables and whether or not they can be considered as functions of a small set of "latent" variables. Third, cluster analysis attempts to find multiple convex regions of the $\mathbf{x}$-space that contain modes of $P(\mathbf{x})$. This can indicate whether or not $P(\mathbf{x})$ can be characterized by a mixture of simple densities representing distinct types or classes of observations. Mixture modeling has a similar goal.

There is no direct measure of success in unsupervised learning, and it is difficult to ascertain the validity of inferences drawn from the output of most unsupervised learning algorithms. One must resort to heuristic arguments not only for motivating the algorithms, but also for judgments as to the quality of the results. This situation has led to heavy proliferation of proposed methods, since effectiveness is a matter of opinion and cannot be verified directly.

2.1.2 Visual Pattern Analysis

With the viewpoint of statistical learning, we can think that natural images consist of an overwhelming number of visual patterns generated by very diverse stochastic processes in nature (Tu et al. 2005). One important objective of image analysis is then to parse generic images into their constituent patterns based upon properties of these stochastic processes. Depending on the types of patterns of interest to a particular task, the image-parsing problem is respectively referred to as (1) perceptual grouping of local features, such as points, lines, and curves, (2) image segmentation for regions, and (3) object recognition for high-level objects. Unsupervised learning plays an important role in all three levels of the parsing problem, and has been used widely in mathematical definitions and models of visual data segmentation (image/video segmentation) and in constructing representational models of objects for the purposes of detection and recognition.

Almost all these techniques can be viewed as learning an underlying probabilistic model that generates the observed data. For example, in perceptual grouping, we compute the posterior probability ratio of "grouping" versus "ungrouping" based on local features. In image segmentation, we assign labels to each pixel by computing its fitness to the models competing to explain various visual patterns in an image. Such visual patterns include flat regions, clutter, texture, and smooth shading. In object recognition, we learn the underlying probability distribution of the object. Even when the machine is given no supervision or reward, it may make sense for it to estimate a model that represents the probability distribution for a new input x_t, given previous inputs $x_1, \ldots, x_{t-1}$.

In general, the true distribution of the visual data is unknown, but we can learn a model of this distribution. The KL divergence is usually used to measure how the learned distribution approximates the true distribution. If we denote the true probability distribution and estimated distribution as $P(x)$ and $Q(x)$, respectively, the KL divergence is defined as

$$KL(P||Q) = \sum_{x} P(x) log \frac{P(x)}{Q(x)} \tag{2.1}$$

The KL divergence is non-negative and zero if and only if $P = Q$. It measures the coding inefficiency in bits by using a model Q to compress the true data distribution P. Therefore, the better our model of the data, the more efficiently we can compress and communicate new data.

2.1.3 Outline

In this chapter, we present those unsupervised learning techniques that are among the most commonly used in visual pattern analysis. Among them, cluster analysis and dimensionality reduction are two well-known examples. We focus only on cluster analysis in this chapter, i.e., on how the clustering techniques are used in perceptual grouping and segmentation of visual data. A discussion of techniques for dimensionality reduction appears in Chapters 3–5.

The rest of this chapter is organized as follows: In Section 2.2, we discuss cluster analysis, an unsupervised classifying technique. Section 2.3 presents several representative clustering algorithms. Section 2.4 focuses on the problem of perceptual grouping in visual data segmentation, which includes image segmentation as well as video segmentation. Finally, in Section 2.5, we present the basic idea of unsupervised learning for visual pattern representation, which provides an exordium for the following chapters on dimensionality reduction techniques.

2.2 Cluster Analysis

In statistical pattern recognition, clustering can also be viewed as the unsupervised classification of patterns. The pattern is usually represented as a vector of measurements, described by its relation to other patterns, or just a point in a multidimensional space. The goal of cluster analysis is the grouping or segmenting of a collection of patterns into subsets or "clusters," such that those patterns within a cluster are more closely related to one another than those assigned to different clusters (Aldenderfer and Blashfield 1984) (Jain et al. 1999) (Hastie et al. 2001).

In such clustering problems, there is often little prior information (e.g., statistical models) available about the patterns, and the decision-maker must make as few assumptions about the patterns as possible. It is under these restrictions that a clustering methodology is particularly appropriate for the exploration of interrelationships among the data points to make an assessment of their structure. Sometimes, clustering is even expected to arrange the clusters into a natural hierarchy. This involves successively grouping the clusters themselves so that at each level of the hierarchy, clusters within the same group are more similar to each other than those in different groups.

Cluster analysis is also used to form descriptive statistics to ascertain whether or not the data consists of a set of distinct subgroups, each group representing objects with substantially different properties. This latter goal requires an assessment of the degree of difference between the patterns assigned to the respective clusters.

Figure 2.1 shows some simulated data clustered into three groups via the K-means algorithm. The K-means clustering algorithm starts with initial estimates of the centers of three clusters. Then it alternates the following steps until convergence:

1. for each data point, the label of the nearest cluster center (in Euclidean distance) is assigned;
2. each cluster center is replaced by the coordinate-wise average of all data points that are nearest to it.

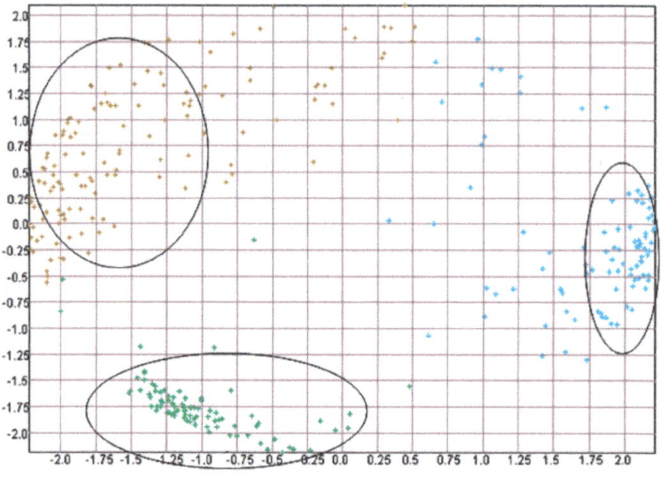

Fig. 2.1 Simulated data in the plane are clustered into three groups by the K-means clustering algorithm. The three colors indicate the cluster memberships

The variety of techniques for representing data, measuring proximity (similarity) between data elements, and grouping data elements has produced a rich assortment of clustering methods. Fundamental to all clustering techniques is the choice of distance or similarity measure between two patterns (Hastie et al. 2001). In other words, a clustering method attempts to group the patterns based on the definition of similarity supplied to it. In the following, we first discuss distance measures before describing a variety of algorithms for clustering.

Because of the variety of feature types and scales, the distance measures must be chosen carefully. It is most common to calculate the dissimilarity between two patterns using a distance measure defined on the feature space. We will focus on three levels of distance measures in this section: proximity matrices, dissimilarities based on attributes, and pattern dissimilarity.

The proximity matrix is used for measuring distance between patterns that are represented directly in terms of the proximity (a likeness or affinity). It can be either similarities or dissimilarities (difference or lack of affinity), and can be represented by an $N \times N$ matrix $\mathbf{D}$, where N is the number of patterns, and each element d_{ij} records the proximity between the ith and the jth pattern. The matrix $\mathbf{D}$ is called a proximity matrix. Most algorithms presume a proximity matrix with nonnegative entries: $d_{ij} > 0$ for $i \neq j$, and $d_{ii} = 0$. This matrix is then provided as an input to the clustering algorithm. Also, most algorithms assume symmetric dissimilarity matrices, so if the original matrix $\mathbf{D}$ is not symmetric it must be replaced by $(\mathbf{D}+\mathbf{D}^T)/2$.

Dissimilarities based on attributes are used for patterns with attributes. For patterns with measurements x_{ij} for $i = 1,2,...,N$, on variables $j = 1,...,p$ (also called attributes), the dissimilarity matrix is constructed by defining pair-wise dissimilarities between patterns first. In most common cases, we define a dissimilarity $d_j(x_{ij},x_{i'j})$ between values of the jth attribute, and then define

$$D(x_i,x_{i'}) = \sum_{j=1}^{p} d_j(x_{ij},x_{i'j}) \tag{2.2}$$

as the dissimilarity between patterns i and i'. By far, the most common choice is the squared distance

$$d_j(x_{ij},x_{i'j}) = (x_{ij} - x_{i'j})^2 \tag{2.3}$$

In addition to the squared distance in Eq. (2.3), other choices are possible, and can lead to potentially different results. For non-quantitative attributes, squared distance may not be appropriate. In addition, it is sometimes desirable to weight attributes differently rather than giving them equal weight as in Eq. (2.2).

There are alternatives in terms of the attribute type:

- If the attributes are represented by continuous real-valued numbers, then it is natural to define the "error" between them as a monotonically increasing function of their absolute difference $d(x_i,x_{i'}) = l(|x_i - x_{i'}|)$. Besides the squared-error loss $(x_i - x_{i'})^2$, a common choice is the identity measure. The former places more emphasis on larger differences than smaller ones.
- Clustering can also be based on the correlation

$$\rho(x_i, x_{i'}) = \frac{\sum_j (x_{ij} - \bar{x}_i)(x_{i'j} - \bar{x}_{i'})}{\sqrt{(\sum_j (x_{ij} - \bar{x}_i)^2 \sum_j (x_{i'j} - \bar{x}_{i'}))^2}} \tag{2.4}$$

with $\bar{x}_i = \sum_j (x_{ij}/p)$. Note this is averaged over attributes, not observations. Clustering based on correlations (similarity) is equivalent to that based on squared distance (dissimilarity).

Pattern dissimilarity combines the p-individual attribute dissimilarities $d_j(x_{ij}, x_{i'j}), j = 1, ..., p$ into a single overall measure of dissimilarity $D(x_i, x_{i'})$ between two patterns or observations $(x_i, x_{i'})$ possessing the respective attribute values. This is nearly always done by means of a weighted average (convex combination)

$$D(x_i, x_{i'}) = \sum_{j=1}^{p} w_j \cdot d_j(x_{ij}, x_{x'j}); \ \sum_{j=1}^{p} w_j = 1 \tag{2.5}$$

where w_j is a weight assigned to the jth attribute regulating the relative influence of that variable in determining the overall dissimilarity between patterns. This choice should be based on subject matter considerations.

However, setting the weight w_j to the same value for each attribute does not necessarily give all attributes equal influence (Hastie et al. 2001). The influence of the jth attribute on pattern dissimilarity $D(x_i, x_{i'})$ depends on its relative contribution to the average pattern dissimilarity measure over all pairs of observations in the data set. This can be calculated as follows:

$$\bar{D} = \frac{1}{N^2} \sum_{i=1}^{N} \sum_{i'=1}^{N} D(x_i, x_{i'}) = \sum_{j=1}^{p} w_j \cdot \bar{d}_j \tag{2.6}$$

with

$$\bar{d}_j = \frac{1}{N^2} \sum_{i=1}^{N} \sum_{i'=1}^{N} d_j(x_{ij}, x_{i'j}) \tag{2.7}$$

being the average dissimilarity on the jth attribute. Thus the relative influence of the jth variables is $w_j \cdot \bar{d}_j$, and setting $w_j = 1/\bar{d}_j$ would give all attributes equal influence in characterizing the overall dissimilarity between patterns. Although this may seem reasonable, it can be highly counterproductive. If the goal is to segment the data into groups of similar patterns, all attributes may contribute equally to the notion of dissimilarity between patterns. Some attribute value differences may reflect greater actual pattern dissimilarity in the context of the problem domain. Attributes that are more relevant in separating the groups should be assigned a higher influence in defining pattern dissimilarity. Specifying an appropriate dissimilarity measure is far more important in obtaining success with clustering than is the choice of clustering algorithm. However, there is no substitute for careful thought in the context of each individual problem, since it depends on the specifics of domain knowledge and is less amenable to general research.

2.3 Clustering Algorithms

Cluster analysis aims to partition the observations into groups so that the pair-wise dissimilarities between those assigned to the same cluster tend to be smaller than those in different clusters. There exists a rich literature on clustering techniques (Jain et al. 1999) (Ng and Han 1994) (Hastie et al. 2001). The hierarchy shown in Figure 2.2 provides a helpful taxonomy of these clustering algorithms. At the top level, there is a distinction between hierarchical and partitional approaches (hierarchical methods produce a nested series of partitions, while partitional methods produce only one).

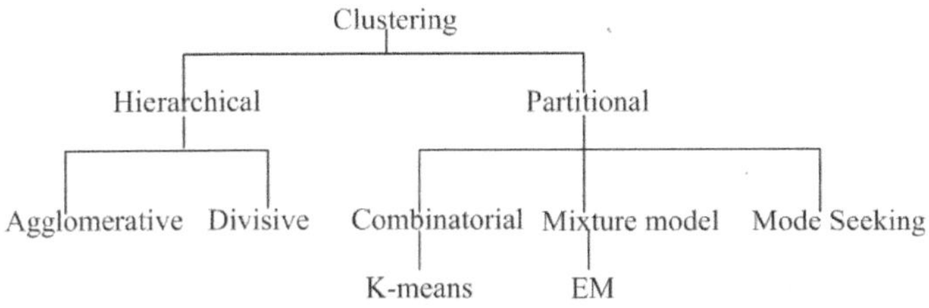

Fig. 2.2 A taxonomy of clustering algorithms

A partitional algorithm obtains a single partition of the data. Before applying the partitional algorithm, the choice of the number of desired output clusters should be specified. Then the partitional techniques usually produce clusters by optimizing a criterion function defined either locally (on a subset of the patterns) or globally (defined over all of the patterns).

Hierarchical clustering methods do not require any specification of the number of clusters to be searched or a starting configuration assignment. Instead, they require the user to specify a measure of dissimilarity between groups of patterns, based on the pair-wise dissimilarities between the patterns in the two groups. As the name suggests, these methods produce hierarchical representations in which the clusters at each level of the hierarchy are created by merging clusters at the next lower level. At the lowest level, each cluster contains a single pattern. At the highest level, there is only one cluster, containing all of the data.

2.3.1 Partitional Clustering

Partitional clustering algorithms fall into three distinct types: combinatorial algorithms, mixture modeling, and mode seeking. Combinatorial algorithms work directly on the observed data with no direct reference to an underlying probability model. Mixture modeling supposes that data are independent identical distribution (i.i.d.). samples from some population described by a probability density function. This density function is characterized by a parametric model taken to be a mixture of component density functions; each component density describes one of the clusters. This model is then fit to the data by maximum likelihood or corresponding Bayesian approaches. A mode seeker takes a nonparametric perspective, attempting to directly estimate distinct modes of the probability density function. Observations "closest" to each respective mode then define the individual clusters.

In partitional clustering, each pattern is only assigned one cluster. These assignments of clustering can be characterized by a many-to-one mapping $k = C(i)$ that assigns the ith pattern to the kth cluster, where $i \in 1,...,N$, and $k \in 1,...,K$. A prespecified number of clusters $K < N$ is postulated, and each pattern is assigned to one and only one cluster. One seeks the particular mapping $C^*(i)$ that optimizes the criterion function, based on the dissimilarities $d_(x_i, x_{i'})$ between every pair of patterns. The partitional clustering algorithms usually produce clusters by optimizing the criterion function defined either locally (on a subset of patterns) or globally (defined over all of the patterns).

2.3.1.1 Combinatorial Algorithms

Combinatorial clustering algorithms directly assign each observation to a group or cluster without regard to a probability model describing the data. This is usually done by directly specifying a mathematical loss function and minimizing it through some combinatorial optimization algorithm. Two loss functions are available in the literature:

- Within-cluster point scatter: $W(C) = \frac{1}{2}\sum_{k=1}^{K}\sum_{C(i)=k}\sum_{C(i')=k} d_(x_i, x_{i'})$. This criterion characterizes the extent to which patterns assigned to the same cluster tend to be close to one another.
- Between-cluster point scatter: $B(C) = \frac{1}{2}\sum_{k=1}^{K}\sum_{C(i)=k}\sum_{C(i')\neq k} d_(x_i, x_{i'})$. This criterion tends to be large when patterns assigned to different clusters are far apart.

The total point scatter: $T = \frac{1}{2}\sum_{k=1}^{K}\sum_{C(i)=k}\left(\sum_{C(i')\neq k} d_(x_i, x_{i'}) + \sum_{C(i')\neq k} d_(x_i, x_{i'})\right)$ or $T = W(C) + B(C)$, is constant given the data, independent of cluster assignment. Thus, one has $W(C) = T - B(C)$, and minimizing $W(C)$ is equivalent to maximizing $B(C)$.

In principle, one simply minimizes W or equivalently maximizes B over all possible assignments of the N points to K clusters. However, such a combinatorial search of the set of possible assignments is feasible only for very small data sets. The number of distinct assignments (Jain et al. 1999) is

$$S(N,K) = \frac{1}{K!}\sum_{k=1}^{K}(-1)^{K-k}\binom{K}{k}k^N \tag{2.8}$$

For this reason, practical clustering algorithms are able to examine only a very small fraction of all possible assignments. The goal is to identify a small subset that is likely to contain the optimal one, or at least a good suboptimal partition.

The K-means algorithm is one of the most popular iterative descent-clustering methods among combinatorial algorithms, in which the squared Euclidean distance is chosen as the dissimilarity measure.

$$d(x_i, x_{i'}) = \sum_{j=1}^{p} (x_{ij} - x_{i'j})^2 = ||x_i - x_{i'}||^2 \tag{2.9}$$

The within-cluster point scatter can be written as

$$W(C) = \frac{1}{2} \sum_{k=1}^{K} \sum_{C(i)=k} \sum_{C(i')=k} ||x_i - x_{i'}||^2 = \sum_{k=1}^{K} N_k \sum_{C(i)=k} ||x_i - \bar{x}_k||^2 \tag{2.10}$$

where $\bar{x}_k = (\bar{x}_{1k}, \ldots, \bar{x}_{pk})$ is the mean vector associated with the kth cluster, and $N_k = \sum_{i=1}^{N} I(C(i) = k)$. Thus, the criterion is minimized by assigning the N observations to the K clusters in such a way that within each cluster the average dissimilarity of the patterns from the cluster mean, as defined by the points in that cluster, is minimized.

K-means is an iterative descent algorithm for solving

$$C* = \min_C \sum_{k=1}^{K} N_k \sum_{C(i)=k} ||x_i - \bar{x}_k||^2 \tag{2.11}$$

This can be minimized by an alternating optimization procedure as follows:

1. Choose K cluster centers to coincide with K randomly chosen patterns or K randomly defined points inside the hypervolume containing the patter set.
2. Assign each pattern to the closet cluster center.
3. Recompute the cluster centers using the current cluster memberships.
4. If a convergence criterion is not met, go to step 2. Typical convergence criteria are no (or minimal) reassignment of patterns to new cluster centers, or minimal decrease in $W(C)$.

Each of steps 2 and 3 reduces the value of $W(C)$, so that convergence is assured. However, the result may represent a suboptimal local minimum. Thus, one should start the algorithm with many different random choices for the starting means, and choose the solution having the smallest value of the objective function.

Several variants of the K-means algorithm have been reported in the literature (Jain et al. 1999). Some of them attempt to select a good initial partition so that the algorithm is more likely to find the global minimum. The well-known ISODATA (Dunn 1973) permits splitting and merging of the resulting clusters. Typically, a cluster is split when its variance is above a prespecified threshold, and two clusters are merged when the distance between their centroids is below another prespecified threshold. Using this variant, it is possible to obtain the optimal partition, provided proper threshold values are specified. The dynamic clustering algorithm (Zamir and Etzioni 1999) involves selecting a different criterion function altogether. It permits representations other than the centroid for each cluster.

2.3.1.2 Mixture Modeling

The mixture modeling approach to cluster analysis has been addressed in a number of ways. Most of the work in this area assumes that the individual components of the mixture density are Gaussian, and in this case the parameters of the individual Gaussians are to be estimated by the procedure. Traditional approaches to this problem involve obtaining (iteratively) a maximum likelihood estimate of the parameter vectors of the component densities.

Let $\mathbf{Y} = [Y_1,...,Y_d]^T$ be a d-dimensional random variable, with $\mathbf{y} = [y_1,...,y_d]^T$ representing one particular outcome of $\mathbf{Y}$. In the mixture modeling approach to cluster analysis, it is said that $\mathbf{Y}$ follows a k-component finite mixture distribution if its probability density function can be written as

$$p(\mathbf{y}|\theta) = \sum_{m=1}^{k} \alpha_m p(\mathbf{y}|\theta_m) \tag{2.12}$$

where $\alpha_1,...,\alpha_k$ are the mixing probabilities, each θ_m is the set of parameters defining the mth component, and $\theta \equiv \{\theta_1,...,\theta_k,\alpha_1,...,\alpha_k\}$ is the complete set of parameters needed to specify the mixture. Of course, being probabilities, the α_m must satisfy

$$\alpha_m \geq 0,\ m = 1,...,k, \text{and} \sum_{m=1}^{k} \alpha_m = 1 \tag{2.13}$$

Here we assume that all the components have the same functional form (for example, they are all d-variate Gaussian), each one being thus fully characterized by the parameter vector θ_m.

Given a set of n independent and *i.i.d.* samples $\mathcal{Y} = \{\mathbf{y}^{(1)},...,\mathbf{y}^{(n)}\}$, the log-likelihood corresponding to a k-component mixture is

$$logp(\mathcal{Y}|\theta) = log\prod_{i=1}^{n} p(\mathbf{y}^{(i)}|\theta) = \sum_{i=1}^{n} log \sum_{k=1}^{m} \alpha_m p(\mathbf{y}^{(i)}|\theta_m) \tag{2.14}$$

It is well known that the *maximum likelihood* (ML) estimate

$$\hat{\theta}_{ML} = \arg\max_{\theta}\{logp(\mathcal{Y}|\theta)\} \tag{2.15}$$

cannot be found analytically. The same is true for the Bayesian maximum a posterior (MAP) criterion,

$$\hat{\theta}_{MAP} = \arg\max_{\theta}\{logp(\mathcal{Y}|\theta) + logp(\theta)\} \tag{2.16}$$

given some prior $p(\theta)$ on the parameters. Additionally, the maximizations defining the ML or MAP estimates must satisfy the constraints in Eq. (2.13).

The usual choice for obtaining ML or MAP estimates of the mixture parameters is the EM algorithm (Bilmes 1998). EM is an iterative procedure which finds local maxima of $logp(\mathscr{Y}|\theta)$ or $logp(\mathscr{Y}|\theta)+logp(\theta)$. It is based on the interpretation of $\mathscr{Y}$ as incomplete data. For mixtures, the missing part is a set of n labels $\mathscr{Z} = \{\mathbf{z}^{(1)},...,\mathbf{z}^{(n)}\}$ associated with the n samples, indicating which component produced each sample. Each label is a binary vector $\mathbf{z}^{(i)} = [z_1^{(i)},...,z_k^{(i)}]$, where $z_m^{(i)} = 1$ and $z_p^{(i)} = 0$, for $p \neq m$, indicating that sample $\mathbf{y}^{(i)}$ was produced by the mth component. The complete log-likelihood is

$$logp(\mathscr{Y},\mathscr{Z}|\theta) = \sum_{i=1}^{n}\sum_{m=1}^{k} z_m^{(i)} log[\alpha_m p(\mathbf{y}^{(i)})|\theta_m] \tag{2.17}$$

The EM algorithm produces a sequence of estimates $\{\hat{\theta}(t), t = 0,1,2,...\}$ by alternately applying two steps until some convergence criterion is met:

- **E-step**: compute the conditional expectation of the complete log-likelihood, given $\mathscr{Y}$ and the current estimate $\hat{\theta}(t)$. Since $logp(\mathscr{Y},\mathscr{Z}|\theta)$ is linear with respect to the missing $\mathscr{Z}$, we simply have to compute the conditional expectation $\hat{Z} \equiv E[\mathscr{Z}|\mathscr{Y},\hat{\theta(t)}]$ and plug it into $logp(\mathscr{Y},\mathscr{Z}|\theta)$. This results in the so-called Q-function:

$$Q(\theta,\hat{\theta}(t)) = E[logp(\mathscr{Y},\mathscr{Z}|\theta)|\mathscr{Y},\hat{\theta}(t)] = logp(\mathscr{Y},\hat{Z}|\theta) \tag{2.18}$$

Since the elements of $\mathscr{Z}$ are binary, their conditional expectations are given by

$$\hat{z}_m^{(i)} = E[z_m^{(i)}|\mathscr{Y},\hat{\theta}(t)] = Pr[z_m^{(i)} = 1|y^{(i)},\hat{\theta}(t)] = \frac{\hat{\alpha}_m p(\mathbf{y}^{(i)}|\hat{\theta}_m(t))}{\sum_{j=1}^{k}\hat{\alpha}_j p(\mathbf{y}^{(i)}|\hat{\theta}_j(t))} \tag{2.19}$$

- **M-step**: update the parameter estimates by maximizing the expectation computed in the first step.

$$\hat{\theta}(t+1) = \arg\max_{\theta}\{Q(\theta,\hat{\theta}(t)) + logp(\theta)\} \tag{2.20}$$

in the case of MAP estimation, or

$$\hat{\theta}(t+1) = \arg\max_{\theta} Q(\theta,\hat{\theta}(t)) \tag{2.21}$$

for the ML criterion, in both cases, under the constraints in Eq. (2.13).

For some distributions, it is possible to arrive at analytical expressions for θ_m as functions of everything else. For example, if we assume d-dimensional Gaussian component distributions with mean μ and covariance matrix Σ, i.e., $\theta = (\mu,\Sigma)$, then

$$p(\mathbf{y}|\theta_m) = \frac{1}{(2\pi)^{d/2}|\Sigma_m|^{1/2}} e^{-\frac{1}{2}(\mathbf{y}-\mu_m)^T \Sigma_m^{(-1)}(\mathbf{y}-\mu_m)} \tag{2.22}$$

After derivations with the ML criterion, the estimates of the new parameters in terms of the old parameters $\hat{\theta}(t-1) = \{\alpha_m(t-1), \mu_m(t-1), \Sigma_m(t-1)\}_{m=1}^{k}$ can be summarized as follows:

$$\alpha_m(t) = \frac{1}{N}\sum_{i=1}^{n} p(m|\mathbf{y}^{(i)}, \hat{\theta}(t-1)) \tag{2.23}$$

$$\mu_m(t) = \frac{\sum_{i=1}^{n} \mathbf{y}^{(i)} p(m|\mathbf{y}^{(i)}, \hat{\theta}(t-1))}{\sum_{i=1}^{n} p(m|\mathbf{y}^{(i)}, \hat{\theta}(t-1))} \tag{2.24}$$

$$\Sigma_m(t) = \frac{\sum_{i=1}^{n} p(m|\mathbf{y}^{(i)}, \hat{\theta}(t-1))(\mathbf{y}^{(i)} - \mu_m(t))(\mathbf{y}^{(i)} - \mu_m(t))^T}{\sum_{i=1}^{n} p(m|\mathbf{y}^{(i)}, \hat{\theta}(t-1))} \tag{2.25}$$

Figure 2.3 illustrates the use of the EM algorithm to fit a mixture of Gaussians to a data set by maximum likelihood. The data set consists of 40 data points in a 2-dimensional space, generated by sampling from a mixture of two Gaussian distributions. We create and initialize a mixture model consisting of a mixture of two Gaussians having "spherical" covariance matrices. The Gaussian component is displayed on the same plot as the data by drawing a contour of constant probability density for each component having radius equal to the corresponding standard deviation. Component 1 is colored red and component 2 is colored blue. We adapt the parameters of the mixture model iteratively using the EM algorithm. Each cycle of the EM algorithm consists of an E-step followed by an M-step. We start with the E-step, which involves the evaluation of the posterior probabilities (responsibilities) that the two components have for each of the data points. In the M-step, we replace the centroids of the component Gaussians by the corresponding weighted means of the data. Thus, the centroid of the red component is replaced by the mean of the data set, in which each data point is weighted according to the amount of red (corresponding to the responsibility of component 1 for explaining that data point). The variances and mixing proportions of the two components are similarly re-estimated.

2.3.1.3 Mode Seeking

Modes are important characteristics of a data set and can be used to delineate the underlying distribution structure. In the context of clustering, if the density represents the distribution of the input data in a given problem, then the modes may be taken as representatives of clusters. Usually, mode-seeking algorithms search for bins with large counts in a multidimensional histogram of the input pattern set. The space of the patterns is regarded as the empirical probability density function (PDF) of the represented parameter. Dense regions in the space thus correspond to local maxima of the PDF, that is, to the modes of the unknown density. Once the location of the mode is determined, the cluster associated with it is delineated based on the local structure of the space. This can be depicted as in Fig. 2.4.

Mean shift is one well known mode-seeking algorithm. It is a nonparametric, iterative procedure seeking the mode of a density function represented by a set of samples. It was first introduced by Fukunaga and Hostertler (1975), and then revisited and generalized by Cheng (1995). Recently, the mean shift procedure has met with great attention in the computer vision community. Applications range from image segmentation and discontinuity-preservation smoothing (Comaniciu and Meer 2002), to higher level tasks like appearance-based clustering (Georgescu et al. 2003) and blob tracking (Comaniciu and Meer 2002).

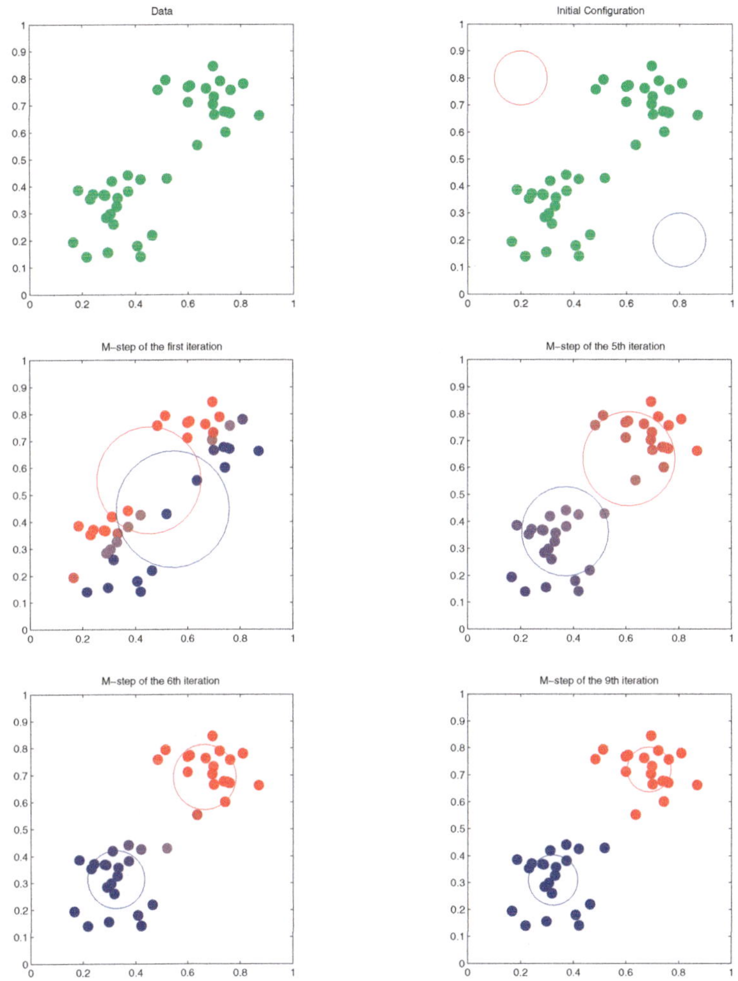

Fig. 2.3 Mixture model estimated via the EM algorithm: the *first row* of graphs show the initial configuration and initialization of the parameters of the GMM. In the *second row*, the *left* graph shows the estimated components after the first EM iteration, and the *right* graph shows the results after the 5th iteration. The graphs in the *third row* show the results of the 6th and 9th iterations, respectively

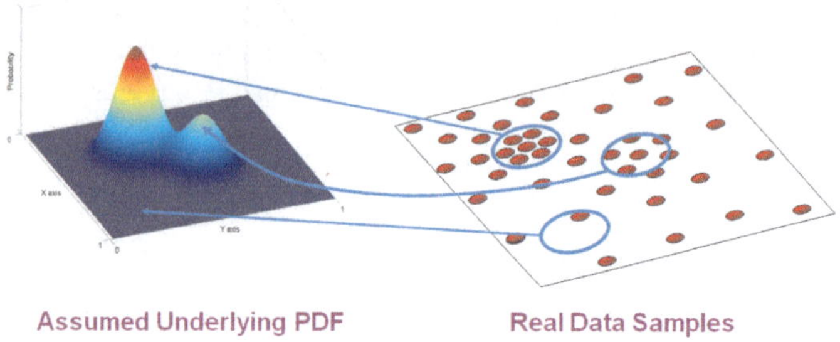

Fig. 2.4 Intuition of modes of an underlying density

Conventionally, mean shift is defined in terms of a kernel. Let $\mathbf{x}$ be a d-variate in $\mathbb{R}^d$. The function $K : \mathbb{R}^d \mapsto \mathbb{R}$ is said to be a kernel if there exists a profile $k : [0, \infty] \mapsto \mathbb{R}$, such that $K(\mathbf{x}) = k(||\mathbf{x}||^2)$, where k is nonnegative, nonincreasing, and piecewise continuous. The kernel $K(\mathbf{x})$ is a bounded function with compact support satisfying

$$\int_{\mathbb{R}^d} K(\mathbf{x})d\mathbf{x} = 1$$
$$\lim_{||\mathbf{x}|| \to \infty} ||\mathbf{x}||^d K(\mathbf{x}) = 0$$
$$\int_{\mathbb{R}^d} \mathbf{x}K(\mathbf{x})d\mathbf{x} = 0$$
$$\int_{\mathbb{R}^d} \mathbf{x}\mathbf{x}^T K(\mathbf{x})d\mathbf{x} = c_K \mathbf{I}$$

where c_K is a constant. In practice, the d-variate kernel $K(\mathbf{x})$ often takes the form $K(\mathbf{x}) = c\prod_{i=1}^{d} k(x_i)$ or $K(x) = ck(||\mathbf{x}||)$. The Epanechnikov kernel, Uniform kernel, and Normal kernel (see Fig. 2.5) are the three most widely used kernel functions in literature.

With the definition of kernel function given above, the mean shift can then be given as: Let S be a set of n data points $\mathbf{x}_i$, $i = 1, ..., n$ in the d-dimensional space $\mathbb{R}^d$. With a kernel K and a weight $w : \mathbf{x} \mapsto (0, \infty)$ at $\mathbf{x}$, the sample mean is defined as

$$\mathbf{m}(\mathbf{x}) = \frac{\sum_{i=1}^{n} K(\mathbf{x}_i - \mathbf{x})w(\mathbf{x}_i)\mathbf{x}_i}{\sum_{i=1}^{n} K(\mathbf{x}_i - \mathbf{x})w(\mathbf{x}_i)} \tag{2.26}$$

Let $T \subset \mathbb{R}^d$ be a finite set (the cluster centers) and $M(T) = \{\mathbf{m}(\mathbf{t}) : t \in T\}$. One iteration of mean shift is given by $T \leftarrow M(T)$. The full mean shift procedure iterates until it finds a fixed point $T = M(T)$. The weight $w(\cdot)$ can be either fixed throughout

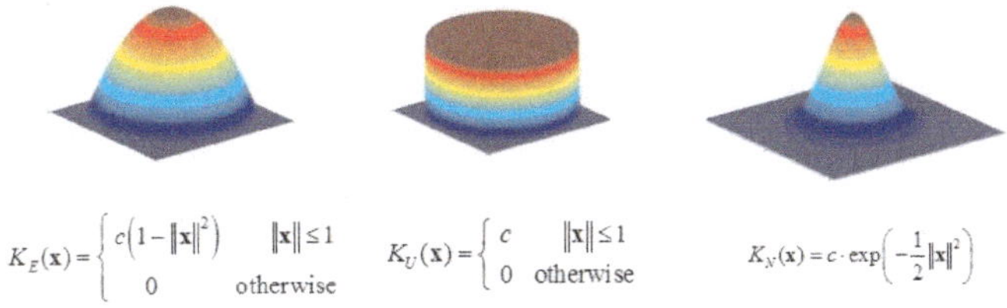

Fig. 2.5 Kernel functions. *Left:* Normal kernel. *Middle:* Uniform kernel. *Right:* Epanechnikov kernel.

the process or re-evaluated after each iteration. It may also be a function of the current T.

Mean shift is a deterministic process, and its iteration gives rise to natural clustering algorithms. When T is initialized to S, the final configuration of T is a local maximum of the underlying density. The number and distribution of these local maxima depend only on the kernel, the dimensionality of the space, and the data size. This characterizes the mean shift as differing from the aforementioned clustering algorithms. Many clustering algorithms are treated as means for optimizing certain measures about the partition. For example, the K-means clustering algorithm attempts to minimize the within-group sum of squared errors, and mixture modeling methods attempt to maximize the likelihood function or the a posterior probability.

More importantly, mean shift is an adaptive gradient ascent algorithm. It has an automatic convergence speed. The mean shift vector size depends on the gradient itself. When near maxima, the steps are small and refined. Convergence is guaranteed for infinitesimal steps only. This means it is infinitely convergent (therefore setting a lower bound). With a uniform Kernel, convergence is achieved in a finite number of steps. A normal kernel exhibits a smooth trajectory, but the convergence speed is slower than using a uniform kernel.

To find all the modes in a set of sample points that is assumed to be sampled from an underlying density, one needs an updated mean shift procedure:

- Find all modes using the simple mean shift procedure.
- Prune modes by perturbing them (find saddle points and plateaus).
- Prune nearby modes by taking the highest mode in the window.

Figure 2.6 shows immediate results of the updated mean shift procedure for clustering.

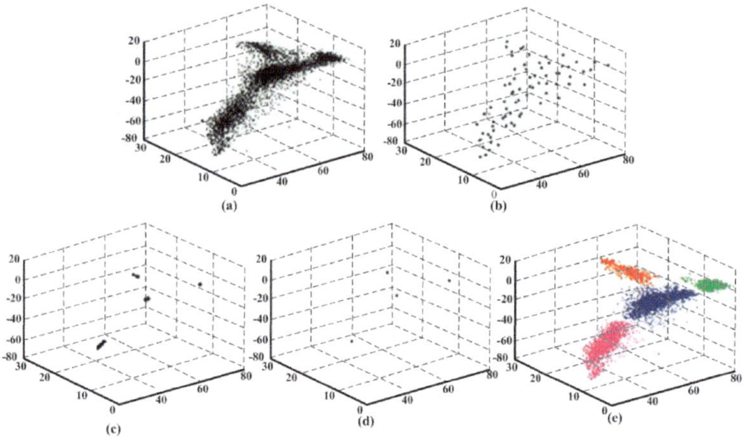

Fig. 2.6 The updated mean shift procedure. (a) the original data set, (b) initial window centers, (c) modes found, (d) pruning nearby modes, (e) final clusters

2.3.2 Hierarchical Clustering

Strategies for hierarchical clustering can be divided into two basic paradigms: agglomerative (*bottom-up*) and divisive (*top-down*). Agglomerative strategies start at the bottom and at each level recursively merge a selected pair of clusters into a single cluster. This produces a grouping at the next higher level with fewer clusters. The pair chosen for merging consists of the two groups with the smallest intergroup dissimilarity. Divisive methods start at the top and at each level recursively split one of the existing clusters at that level into two new clusters. The split is chosen so as to produce two new groups with the largest between-group dissimilarity. With both paradigms there are $N-1$ levels in the hierarchy.

Each level of the hierarchy represents a particular grouping of the data into disjoint clusters of observations. The entire hierarchy represents an ordered sequence of such groupings. It is up to the user to decide which level (if any) actually represents a "natural" clustering in the sense that patterns within each of its groups are sufficiently more similar to each other than to patterns assigned to other groups at that level.

Hierarchical clustering may be represented by a two-dimensional diagram known as dendrogram which graphically illustrates the binary splitting/agglomerations made at each successive stage of analysis. A dendrogram provides a highly interpretable, complete description of the hierarchical clustering. One can think the dendrogram as a rooted binary tree. The nodes of the tree represent groups. The root node represents the entire data set. The N terminal nodes each represent one of the individual patterns (singleton clusters). Each nonterminal node ("parent") has two daughter nodes. For divisive clustering the two daughters represent the two groups resulting from the split of the parent; for agglomerative clustering the daughters represent the two groups that were merged to form the parent. The dissimilarity between merged clusters is monotonically increasing with the level of the merger. Thus, the binary tree can be plotted so that the height of each node is proportional to the value of the intergroup dissimilarity between its two daughters. The terminal nodes representing individual patterns are all plotted at zero height.

2.3.2.1 Agglomerative Clustering

Agglomerative clustering algorithms begin with every observation representing a singleton cluster. At each of the $N-1$ steps the closest two (least dissimilar) clusters are merged into a single cluster, producing one less cluster at the next higher level. Therefore, a measure of dissimilarity between two clusters (groups of patterns) must be defined.

Let G and H denote two such groups. The dissimilarity $d(G,H)$ between G and H is computed from the set of pairwise pattern dissimilarities $d_{ij}, i \in G$, and $j \in H$. Although there are many proposals for defining the intergroup dissimilarity, we choose to introduce the three most commonly used proposals: single linkage, complete linkage, and group average. Figure 2.7 shows the three definitions of intergroup dissimilarity. Accordingly, agglomerative clustering algorithms can be subdivided into single linkage agglomerative clustering, complete linkage agglomerative clustering, and group average clustering algorithms.

- In single linkage agglomerative clustering, the intergroup dissimilarity is that of the closest (least dissimilar) pair $d_{SL}(G,H) = \min_{\{i \in G, j \in H\}} d_{ij}$, which is also often called the nearest-neighbor technique.
- Complete linkage agglomerative clustering takes the intergroup dissimilarity to be that of the furthest pair $d_{CL}(G,H) = \max_{\{i \in G, j \in H\}} d_{ij}$.
- The group average clustering algorithm uses the average dissimilarity between the groups $d_{GA}(G,H) = \frac{1}{N_G N_H} \sum_{i \in G} \sum_{j \in H} d_{ij}$, where N_G and N_H are the respective number of patterns in each group.

If the data dissimilarities $\{d_{ij}\}$ exhibit a strong clustering tendency, with each of the clusters being compact and well separated from the others, then all three methods produce similar results. If this is not the case, results will differ. If we define the diameter D_G of a group of patterns as the largest dissimilarity among its members, $D_G = \max_{i \in G, j \in G} d_{ij}$, then the single linkage can produce clusters with very large diameters. These clusters can violate the compactness property that all patterns within each cluster tend to be similar to one another, based on the supplied d_{ij}. At the same time, complete linkage represents the opposite extreme. Clusters produced by complete linkage may violate the closeness property, in that patterns assigned to a cluster can be much closer to members of other clusters than they are to some members of their own cluster. The group average clustering represents a

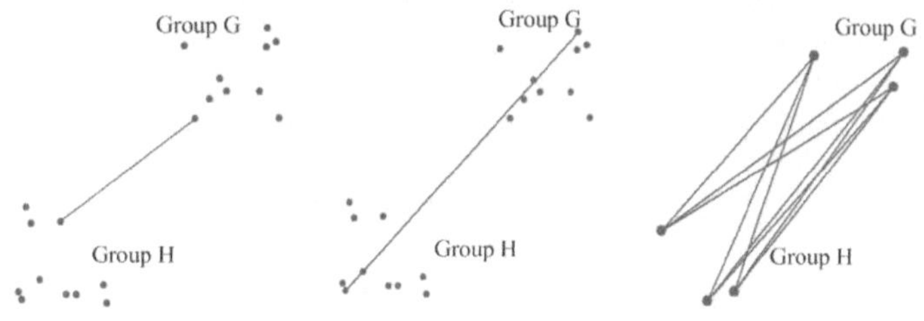

Fig. 2.7 Definitions for the intergroup dissimilarity: d_{SL}, d_{CL}, and d_{GA}

compromise between the two extremes of single and complete linkage. It attempts to produce relatively compact clusters that are relatively far apart.

2.3.2.2 Divisive Clustering

Divisive clustering algorithms begin with the entire data set as a single cluster, and recursively divide one of the existing clusters into two daughter clusters at each iteration in a top-down fashion. This approach has not been studied nearly as extensively as agglomerative methods in the clustering literature. In the clustering setting, a potential advantage of divisive over agglomerative methods can occur when interest is focused on partitioning the data into a relatively small number of clusters.

The divisive paradigm can be employed by recursively applying any of the combinatorial methods, for example, K-means, with $K = 2$, to perform the splits at each iteration. However, such an approach would depend on the starting configuration specified at each step. In addition, it would not necessarily produce a splitting sequence that possessed the monotonicity property required for the dendrogram representation.

To avoid these problems, Macnaughton Smith et al. (1964) proposed an alternative divisive algorithm. It begins by placing all patterns in a single cluster G. It then chooses that pattern whose average dissimilarity from all the other patterns is largest. This pattern forms the first member of a second cluster H. At each successive step that pattern in G whose average distance from those in H, minus that for the remaining patterns in G is largest, is transferred to H. This continues until the corresponding difference in averages becomes negative. That is, there are no longer any patterns in G that are, on average, closer to those in H. The result is a split of the original cluster into two daughter clusters, the patterns transferred to H, and those remaining in G. These two clusters represent the second level of the hierarchy. Each successive level is produced by applying this splitting procedure to one of the clusters at the previous level.

2.4 Perceptual Grouping

The human visual system can detect many classes of patterns and statistically significant arrangements of image elements. Perceptual grouping refers to the human visual ability to extract significant image relations from lower-level primitive image features without any knowledge of the image content and group them to obtain meaningful higher-level structure.

In the field of pattern recognition, clustering is often seen as the partitioning of data without label information, while classification is regarded as the partitioning of data with label information. The term perceptual grouping is sometimes used as a general term for all kinds of clustering and classification processes. Even this definition sometimes causes ambiguity. In the context of computer vision, perceptual grouping can be classified as a mid-level process directed toward closing the gap between what is produced by the state-of-the-art low-level algorithms (such as edge detectors, local image descriptors) and what is desired as input to high level algorithms (such as perfect contours, absence of noise, absence of fragmentation).

In this section, we first introduce hierarchical perceptual grouping principles (in Section 2.4.1) from their origins in vision research (in Section 2.4.2), and then we study how this can be integrated with clustering techniques for the purpose of segmenting visual data (for example, the problems of contour grouping in Section 2.4.3 and region grouping in Section 2.4.4).

2.4.1 Hierarchical Perceptual Grouping

The objective of grouping is to derive a kind of hierarchic tree as shown in Fig. 2.8. This can be seen as an inverse process of the organization of image features into higher-level structures. The grouping of low-level features provides the basis for discovering a higher-level structure. Higher-level structures, in turn, may be further combined to yield yet another level of higher-level structures. The process may be repeated until a meaningful semantic representation is achieved that may be used by a higher-level reasoning process. For example, how should an image of a tiger standing in the grass be grouped? As shown in Fig. 2.9, the image is first grouped into smooth contours, regions, and junctions. Then each contour is assigned to one of two abutting regions, after which shape analysis and object recognition occur.

Accordingly, we divide the perceptual grouping of an image into three levels: (1) Low-level vision, which focuses on the determination of local image properties including smoothing/diffusion, edge detection, color, and texture, (2) Middle-level vision, which converts low-level data into objects and scene description, the goal being to represent the image in terms of boundaries, regions, surfaces, and objects, and (3) High-level vision, which includes making inferences of scene description, scene analysis, and interpretation. Computer vision algorithms in all three levels employ gestalt principles explicitly or implicitly. Figure 2.10 illustrates an example of the procedure for hierarchical grouping of an object, explicitly or implicitly.

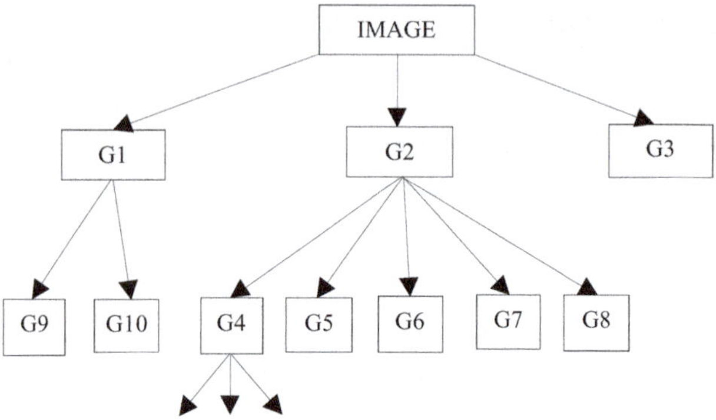

Fig. 2.8 Hierarchical tree: visual grouping image components

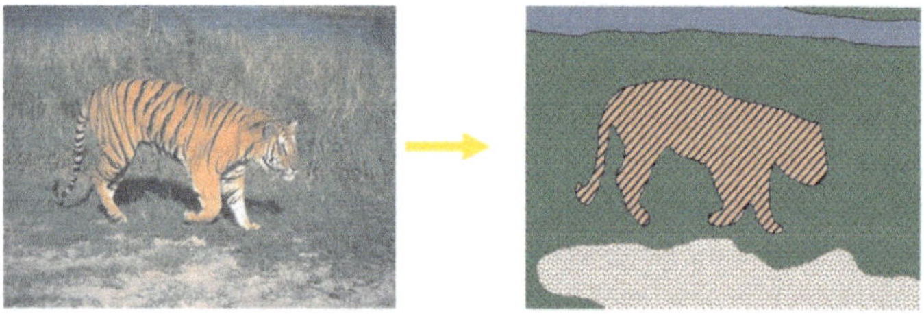

Fig. 2.9 An example of grouping

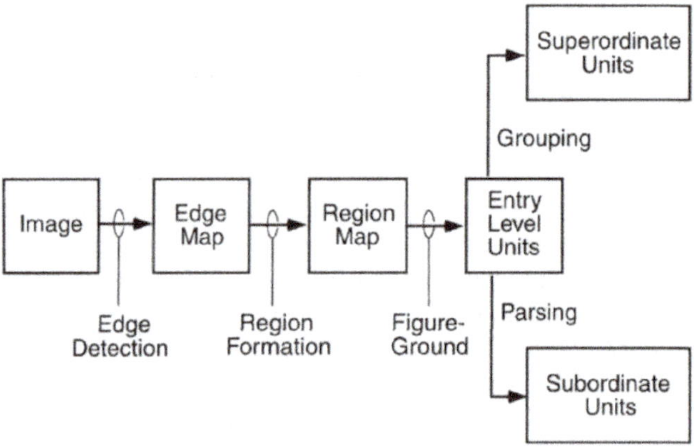

Fig. 2.10 The procedure of hierarchical grouping

In practice, certain scene structures will always produce images with discernable features regardless of viewpoint, while other scene structures virtually never do. This correlation between salience and invariance suggests that the perceptual salience of viewpoint invariance is due to the leverage it provides for inferring geometric properties of objects and scenes. It has been noted that many of the perceptually salient image properties identified by Gestalt psychologists such as collinearity, parallelism, and good continuation, are viewpoint invariant. To discover and describe structure, the visual system uses a wide array of perceptual grouping mechanisms. These range from the relatively low-level mechanisms that underlie the simplest principles of grouping and segregation, which include similarity, continuation, and proximity, to relatively high-level mechanisms such as figure and ground, or symmetry, in which complex learned associations guide the discovery of structure. Perceptual grouping generally results in highly compact representations of images, facilitating later processing, storage, and retrieval.

2.4.2 Gestalt Grouping Principles

Research in perceptual grouping began in the 1920s with Gestalt psychologists, whose goal was to discover the underlying principles that would unify the various grouping phenomena of human perception. Gestalt psychologists observed the tendency of the human visual system to perceive configurational wholes, using rules that govern the uniformity of psychological grouping for perception and recognition, as opposed to recognition by analysis of discrete primitive image features. The hierarchical grouping principles proposed by Gestalt psychologists embodied such concepts as grouping by similarity, continuation, closure, proximity, and figure and ground.

- Similarity occurs when objects look similar to one another. People often perceive them as a group or pattern. The figures in Fig. 2.11 all appear as a single unit because all of the shapes have similarity. Unity occurs because these four parts of each figure look similar. When similarity occurs, an object can be emphasized if it is dissimilar to the others. This is called anomaly, and it can explain why the figure on the far right becomes a focal point: it is dissimilar to the other shapes.

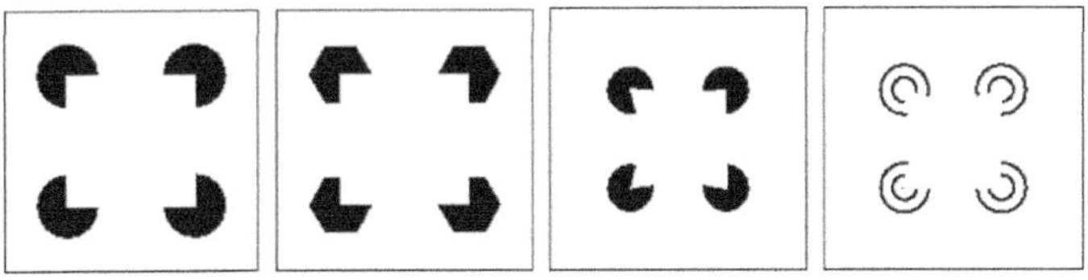

Fig. 2.11 Gestalt principle: similarity. Similarity occurs when objects look similar to one another, while the figure on the far *right* becomes a focal point because it is dissimilar to the other shapes

- Continuation occurs when the eye is compelled to move through one object and continue to another object. Continuation occurs in Fig. 2.12, because the viewer's eye will naturally follow a line or curve. The smooth flowing crossbar of the "H" leads the eye directly to the maple leaf.
- Closure occurs when an object is incomplete or a space is not completely enclosed. If enough of the shape is indicated, people perceive the whole by filling in the missing information. As shown in the image of a panda in Fig. 2.12, although the animal is not complete, enough is present for the eye to complete the shape. When the viewer's perception completes a shape, closure occurs.

Fig. 2.12 Gestalt principle: continuation and closure. *Left:* the smooth flowing crossbar of the "H" leads the eye directly to the maple leaf

- Proximity occurs when elements are placed close together. They tend to be perceived as a group. The nine squares in the left of Fig. 2.13 are placed without proximity. They are perceived as separate shapes. As shown in the right of Fig. 2.13, when the squares are given close proximity, unity occurs. While they continue to be separate shapes, they are now perceived as one group.

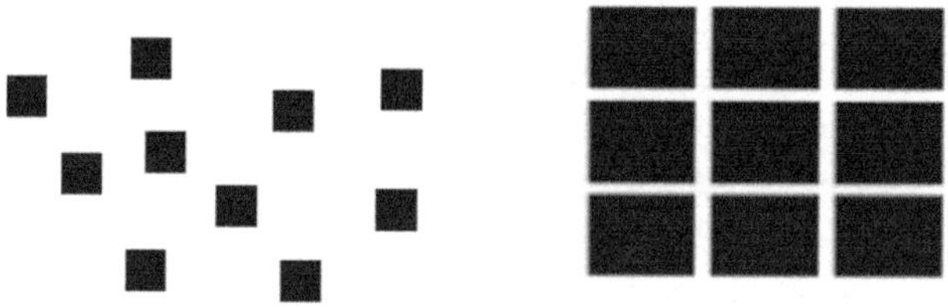

Fig. 2.13 Gestalt principle: proximity. *Left:* the nine squares above are placed without proximity. *Right:* The squares are given close proximity, unity occurs

- Figure and ground denotes the human vision's ability to separate elements based upon contrast. The eye differentiates an object from its surrounding area. A form, silhouette, or shape is naturally perceived as a figure (*object*), while the surrounding area is perceived as ground (*background*). Balancing figure and ground can make the perceived image clearer. Using unusual figure/ground relationships can add interest and subtlety to an image. Figure 2.14 shows complex figure/ground relationships that change as the viewer perceives leaves, water, and a tree trunk.

Fig. 2.14 Gestalt principle: figure/ground. This image uses complex figure/ground relationships that change upon perceiving leaves, water, and tree trunk

Many Computer Vision methods attempt to compute the above-mentioned gestalt concepts explicitly. The idea is to use various cues to partition an image into groups. Organizing the overwhelming data of an image into simple, coherent groups requires us to represent these cues in terms of image statistics. As a comparison with the aforementioned gestalt concepts, we list the cues commonly used in computer vision.

- Similarity: Various features determine the similarity of two areas: brightness, texture, motion, and stereo disparity or depth.
- Proximity: Grouping by proximity is based on the idea that objects that project to nearby points on the image are usually close to each other in the world. One could probably consider this another form of similarity. In grouping visual data, similarity (or proximity) always takes the form of the proximity matrices discussed in Section 2.2.
- Contour continuation: Here we concentrate on the contour or boundary of a group. In particular, images in Fig. 2.15 show the concept of boundaries, which are not apparent from changes in image intensity. In fact, the apparent region formed by these contours could not be separated by any of the similarity clues above. These apparent boundaries are called subjective contours, illusory contours, imagined boundaries, or gradient-less edges. Figures 2.15(a), 2.15(b), and 2.15(c) show examples of subjective contours and are taken from a paper by Kanizsa (1979). For the purpose of grouping visual data, we prefer to explain

contour continuation in terms of image statistics. Snake (Kass et al. 1988) is a well-known example that provides a unified account of subjective contours.

Fig. 2.15 Illusory contours

- Closure: The physical world consists of objects that are usually seen in images as closed contours. It therefore makes sense for there to be a preference for perceiving contours which close a region. In order to infer shape from contour, the human visual system must selectively integrate fragments projecting from a common object while keeping fragments from different objects separate. Contour closure has a strong influence on the speed of this process. One widely used closure measure is proposed by Elder et al. (1994), which is based on a sum of squares of the lengths of contour gaps, and has the form:

$$C = 1 - \frac{1}{l}\sqrt{\left(\sum_{i=1}^{n} g_i^2\right)} \tag{2.27}$$

  where C is the closure measure, g_i is the length of the ith gap in the figure, and l is the total arc-length of the boundary. This closure measure is considered to be an extremely compressed representation of a fragmented figure, which predicts the effects of the fragmentation on the speed of the shape perception.
- Symmetry and parallelism: Many shapes in the physical world are somewhat asymmetric, most notably surfaces of revolution. As a result, their outlines have a bilateral symmetry. Bilateral symmetry is a symmetrical arrangement of an outline or part of an outline along a central axis, so that the outline or part can be divided into two equal halves.
- Familiar configuration: Faces are a good example. Dark regions for the eyes and mouth, and a shadow for the nose or nostril form a familiar configuration.
- T-junctions: Actually, other junctions can give you information about figure/ground relationships, but, as shown in Fig. 2.16, T-junctions often indicate which object is in front. At the same time, the snake shows how this may not be the case. There the T-junctions result from texture on the figure, not occlusion.
- Increasing texture gradient: For textured objects, at an apparent boundary that does not result from occlusion, the texture becomes denser as it is foreshortened. This can give information about which object is not occluded and therefore closer. These same boundaries can result in T-junctions as shown before, and if

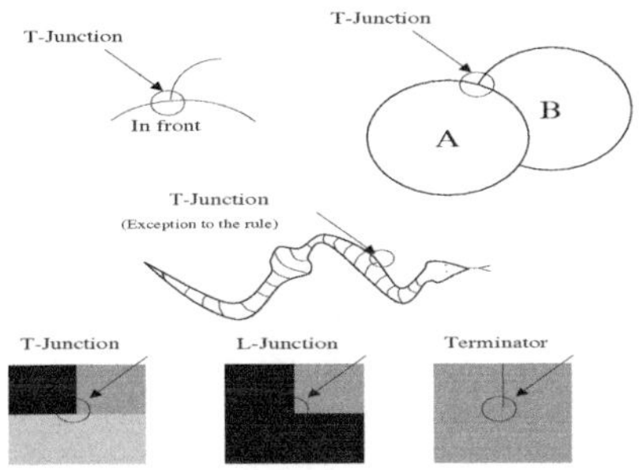

Fig. 2.16 Various junctions

the background color of the object matches that of the surface behind it, terminators result.

- Convexity: What makes a closed contour look like the outline of a small object instead of a small hole in a very large object? We can operationalize this preference by locally assuming that the convex side of a curve is the foreground.

However, many computer vision systems still implicitly use some aspects of processing that can be directly related to the perceptual grouping processes of the human visual system. Frequently, however, no claim is made about the pertinence or adequacy of the digital models, as embodied by computer algorithms, with respect to a proper model of human visual perception. Edge-linking and region-segmentation, which are used as structuring processes for object recognition, are seldom considered to be part of an overall attempt to structure the image. This enigmatic situation arises because research and development in computer vision is often considered quite separate from research into the functioning of human vision. A fact that is generally ignored is that biological vision is currently the only measure of the incompleteness of the current stage of computer vision, and illustrates that the problem is still open to solution. Furthermore, the gestalt principles tend to supply conflicting explanations to many stimuli. This makes the computational implementation of such principles nontrivial.

2.4.3 Contour Grouping

When we look at images, certain salient structures often attract our immediate attention without requiring a systematic scan of the entire image. In subsequent stages, processing resources can be allocated preferentially to these salient structures. Accordingly, contour grouping in an image involves two subproblems. First, saliency requires identifying contour elements that "stand out." Second, grouping attempts to gather contour elements together into curves, which can require, for instance, making choices about how a curve continues through junctions. In the following, we show how the gestalt principles guide the process of grouping through two examples: inferring salient curves from an image and grouping contours from local features.

2.4.3.1 Inferring Salient Structure

One well-known approach to extracting salient curves from an image while performing gap completion is the saliency network proposed by Ullman and Shaashua (1988). In the following, based on the saliency network, we first discuss saliency detection, which shifts our attention to salient structures, and then we talk about a method for grouping contour fragments.

In Shaashua and Ullman (1988), the saliency of curves is defined via properties measured along them. The input image is represented by a network of $n \times n$ grid points, where each point represents a specific x, y location in the image. At each point P there are k orientation elements coming into P from neighboring points, and the same number of orientation elements leaving P to nearby points. Each orientation element p_i responds to an input image by signaling the presence of the corresponding line segment in the image, so that those elements that do not have an underlying line segment are associated with an empty area or gap in the image. There is also a connected sequence of orientation elements $p_i, \ldots, p_{i+N}$, each element representing a line-segment or a gap, as a curve of length N (note that the curves may be continuous or contain any number of gaps). The saliency of such a curve is defined as monotonically increasing with the length of the evaluated curve while decreasing monotonically with its energy (the total squared curvature). The saliency map of an image is an image in which the intensity value of each pixel is proportional to the score of the most salient curve starting from that pixel.

Thus, the creation of the saliency map is formulated as an optimization problem with the above problem configuration. Let $\Phi(\cdot)$ be a measure of saliency associated with each location in the image. The optimization problem is formulated as maximizing Φ_N over all curves of length N starting from p_i:

$$\max_{(p_{i+1},\ldots,p_{i+N})\in\delta^N(p_i)} \Phi_N(p_i, \ldots, p_{i+N}) \tag{2.28}$$

where $\delta^N(p_i)$ is the set of all possible curves of length N starting from p_i.

For a certain class of measures $\Phi(\cdot)$, the computation of Φ_N can be obtained by iterating a simple local computation:

$$\max_{\delta^N(p_i)} \Phi_N(p_i, \ldots, p_{i+N}) = \max_{p_{i+1}\in\delta(p_i)} \Phi_1(p_i, \max_{\delta^{N-1}(p_{i+1})} \Phi^{N-1}(p_{i+1}, \ldots, p_{i+N})) \tag{2.29}$$

where $\delta(p_i)$ stands for $\delta^1(p_i)$. In this manner, the search space needed for each curve of length N starting from p_i is reduced to the size of kN instead of the k^N

needed for the naive approach. The family of functions that obey the principle in Eq. (2.29) is referred to as extensible functions.

There are two important factors in the measure of saliency: the length of the curve and the shape of the curve. Given a curve Γ composed of the $N+1$ orientation elements $p_i, p_{i+1}, \ldots, p_{i+N}$, the saliency of Γ is defined by

$$\Phi(\Gamma) = \sum_{j=i}^{i+N} \sigma_j \rho_{ij} C_{ij} \tag{2.30}$$

with

$$\sigma_j = \begin{cases} 1 & \text{if } p_j \text{ is actual} \\ 0 & \text{if } p_j \text{ is virtual} \end{cases} \tag{2.31}$$

and

$$\rho_{ij} = \rho^{g_{ij}} \tag{2.32}$$

where $\rho_{ii} = 1$ and where ρ is some constant in the range $[0, 1]$. σ_j ensures that only actual elements will contribute to the saliency measure, g_{ij} is the number of gaps between p_i and p_j, and ρ_{ij} reduces the contribution of an element according to the total length of the gaps up to that element. Further,

$$C_{ij} = e^{-K_{ij}}, K_{ij} = \int_{p_i}^{p_j} \kappa^2(s)ds \tag{2.33}$$

where $\kappa(s)$ is the curvature at position s. K_{ij} reduces the contribution of elements according to the accumulated squared curvature from the beginning of the curve.

The saliency of an element p_i is defined to be the maximum saliency over all curves emanating from p_i:

$$\Phi(i) = \max_{\Gamma \in \mathscr{C}(i)} \Phi(\Gamma) \tag{2.34}$$

where $\mathscr{C}(i)$ denotes the set of curves emanating from p_i. $\Phi(i)$ is computed via a network of locally connected elements. Since the measure $\Phi_N(i)$ satisfies

$$\Phi_N(i) = \max_{p_j \in \mathscr{N}(i)} F(i, j, \Phi_{N-1}(j)) \tag{2.35}$$

where $\mathscr{N}(i)$ is the set of all neighboring elements of p_i, and where $F(\cdot)$ is a function of $\Phi_{N-1}()$ and constants stored at elements p_i and p_j:

$$F(i, j, \Phi_{N-1}(j)) = \sigma_i + \rho_i C_{ij} \Phi_{N-1}(j) \tag{2.36}$$

which gives

$$\Phi_N(i) = \sigma_i + \rho_i \max_{p_j \in \mathscr{N}(i)} C_{ij} \Phi_{N-1}(j) \tag{2.37}$$

The saliency network computes, for every element, the saliency of the most salient curve emerging from that element. For grouping, the algorithm tends to recover the curves that made those locations salient. The method is simple: at each iteration each element p_i selects the neighbor p_j that contributes the most to its saliency. The information regarding local preference can be used to trace a linked curve starting from p_i in a recursive manner, namely, p_j is the second element in the curve, p_j's preferred neighbor is the third element, etc. Given a conspicuous element as a starting point, the algorithm extracts the curve that is optimal according to Eq. (2.30). That is, to extract the optimal (most salient) curve emerging from an element, during the computation, one has to store for every element p a single pointer $\pi(p)$ which points to the second element on the optimal curve emerging from p. At the end of the computation, the best curve from p can be retrieved by tracing these pointers starting from p. To obtain the most salient curve in the image, the algorithm traces from the most salient element. Figure 2.17 presents one example of the curves.

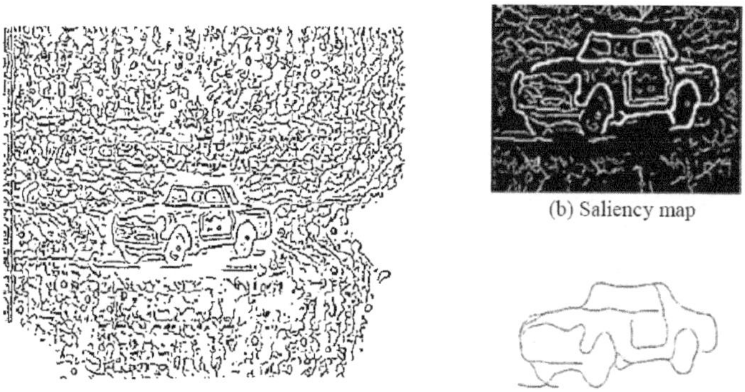

(a) Input image

(b) Saliency map

(c) The 5 most salient curves

Fig. 2.17 Contour grouping results from Shashua and Ullman's saliency network (Shaashua and Ullman 1988)

2.4.3.2 Contour Grouping from Local Features

The physical evidence extracted locally from images (e.g., through edge detectors) is in many cases ambiguous and does not correspond to the expected perception of the image. Determining groups in a given set of such pieces of evidence can be a very expensive computational task. Not only does one need to consider all possible subsets for grouping [a complexity of $O(2^n)$, where n is the number of local features], but the actual measurement of compatibility of a subset is not well defined. Using global perceptual considerations when attempting to connect fragmented edge images can alleviate this problem. In the following, we introduce another algorithm capable of highlighting features due to co-curvilinearity and proximity (Guy and Medioni 1996).

The input of the algorithm can be a set of oriented features, as produced by a typical edge-detector, as well as features with an associated direction uncertainty, and even edges with no associated orientation (dot formation). The algorithm outputs a set of oriented features, with an associated strength reflecting its saliency, and an uncertainty of orientation. The core of the algorithm is designing the mapping function that links perceived features and the measured features extracted by local operators. For example, in edge detection, we extract edges and assign position, orientation, and strength based on the local physical measurements. However, the relationship between the strength of the perceived edges and the strength of the measured signal is not straightforward. To solve this problem, a vector field is generated by each segment, and a function over the whole space determines points of saliency. A subsequent step links areas of high saliency to produce a description in terms of curves and junctions.

In order to define saliency qualitatively, four perceptual constraints are adopted: (1) co-curvilinearity, (2) constancy of curvature, (3) preference of low curvature over large, and (4) proximity. To implement these constraints in grouping with measured local features such as edges, each measured feature is associated with an extension field. The extension field is a maximum likelihood directional vector field describing the contribution of a single unit-length edge element to its neighborhood in terms of length and direction. In other words, the extension field votes on the preferred direction and the likelihood of the existence of a relationship between every point in space and the original segment.

The design of the extension field needs to account for the shape of the field, the orientation at each site, and the strength at each site. The field direction at a given point in space is chosen to be tangent to the osculating circle passing through the edge segment and that point, while its strength is proportional to the radius of that circle. The choice of a circular extension agrees with the constraint of smallest total curvature. In addition, the strength decays with the distance from the origin as well as the higher curvature. The strength has an analytical function

$$EF(x,y) = \begin{cases} e^{-Ax^2}(1,0)^T & y=0 \\ e^{-Ax^2+B\arctan(|y|,|x|)^2}(\frac{x}{R},\frac{y}{R}-1)^T & y\neq 0 \end{cases} \tag{2.38}$$

where $R(x,y) = \frac{x^2+y^2}{2y}$. The parameter A controls the proximity decay, while B controls the decay due to higher curvature. The parameters A, B are selected empirically based on the above-mentioned constraint.

The computation of the saliency map is via a defined directional convolution. That is, a pixel receives a vote from all sites whose field overlaps this pixel, and each vote has the form of a vector, given by its strength (length) and orientation. For each voting site, the algorithm aligns the appropriate extension field with the direction of the site, center the field at the site, and compute the vector contribution at each location covered by the field. This is repeated for all input sites. These accumulated vector votes are well approximated by the best fit ellipse representing the moments of these votes. More mathematical details are given as following.

The output of the directional convolution, $O(i,j)$ is in the form of a variance-covariance matrix for each point in space.

$$O(i,j) = m_{uv}^{i,j} = \begin{bmatrix} m_{20}^{i,j} & m_{11}^{i,j} \\ m_{11}^{i,j} & m_{02}^{i,j} \end{bmatrix} \tag{2.39}$$

The directional convolution operator $EF \bigoplus I = O$ of a vector field EF with an input field I is defined

$$m_{uv}^{x,y} = \sum_j \sum_i ||I_{i,j}||^2 \cdot \left[(R_{\bar{I}_{i,j}} \cdot T_{i,j} \cdot EF)_x^{x,y} \right]^u \cdot \left[(R_{\bar{I}_{i,j}} \cdot T_{i,j} \cdot EF)_y^{x,y} \right]^v \tag{2.40}$$

where $0 \le u, u \le 1$ and $u + v = 1$. This define all elements in $O(x,y)$.

T and R in Eq. (2.40) are translation and rotation operators to translate and rotate an arbitrary vector field V, respectively. For T, we have

$$T_{\Delta x, \Delta Y} \cdot \bar{V}(i,j) = \bar{V}(i + \Delta x, j + \Delta y) \tag{2.41}$$

which simply translates the indices of the target vector field. For R, we have

$$R_{a,b} \cdot \bar{V}(i,j) = M_{a,b} \cdot \bar{V}(M_{a,b} \cdot \{i,j\}^T) \tag{2.42}$$

where $M_{a,b}$ is a rotation matrix, which brings the unit vector $\{0,1\}^T$ to any given unit vector $\{a,b\}^T$. Such matrices always exist, but may not be unique. When the input field is a scalar field, the rotation operator becomes the identity operator, and has no effect.

At each pixel location, we approximate the vector vote $O_{i,j}$ in the form of an ellipse $(\lambda_{max}, \lambda_{min}, \theta)$.

$$\begin{bmatrix} m_{20} & m_{11} \\ m_{11} & m_{02} \end{bmatrix} = \begin{bmatrix} EV_{min} \\ EV_{min} \end{bmatrix} \begin{bmatrix} \lambda_{min} & 0 \\ 0 & \lambda_{max} \end{bmatrix} \begin{bmatrix} EV_{min}^T & EV_{max}^T \end{bmatrix} \tag{2.43}$$

λ_{max} is chosen as the raw saliency measure as it relates to the number of votes collected. λ_{min} creates a junction saliency map, which means that the largest non-eccentric sites are good candidates for junctions. By finding all local maxima of the junction map we localize junctions. $\lambda_{max} - \lambda_{min}$ is chosen as the enhanced saliency measure since it considers both the number of vote and the eccentricity.

In summary, the algorithm discussed above provides a unified way to extract perceptual features from an edge map. The scheme is threshold-free and non-iterative. It is especially suitable for parallel implementation, since computations of the saliency maps are independent for each site.

One common characteristic between the saliency network (Shaashua and Ullman 1988) and the extension field-based algorithm (Guy and Medioni 1996) is that they both follow a traditional edge detection-edge, thinning-edge sorting sequence. The snake model, an active contour model based on variational computing by Kass et al. (1988), provides an alternative to the contour grouping. It uses energy minimization as a framework. The local minima of the designed energy function comprise the set of alternative solutions available to high-level processes. In the active contour model, factors such as connectivity of the contours and the presence of corners are incorporated into the model by adding suitable energy terms to the minimization. The result is an active model that falls into the desired contour when placed near it.

2.4.4 Region Grouping

Region grouping approaches attempt to partition image pixels into sets corresponding to coherent image properties such as brightness, color, and texture. This is important for a number of reasons: (1) surfaces are the natural units of perception; (2) one can design texture/color descriptors for each region, which is necessary for applications such as content-based image querying and compression. On the other hand, region grouping is a challenging problem in computer vision. Since there are many possible partitions of the domain of an image into subsets, how do we pick the right one? Two aspects of the problem are that the partition is not unique and that the partition is inherently hierarchical, respectively. Therefore, it is more appropriate to think of returning a tree structure corresponding to a hierarchical partition rather than a single flat partition.

The discussions above relate the problem of region grouping to the agglomerative and divisive algorithms in the clustering community. In particular, the hierarchical divisive approach produces a tree, the dendrogram. This motivates region-merging/splitting techniques. In region-merging techniques, the input image is first tessellated into a set of homogeneous primitive regions, then, using an iterative merging process, similar neighboring regions are merged according to certain decision rules. In splitting techniques, the entire image is initially considered as one rectangular region. In each step, each heterogeneous image region of the image is divided into for rectangular segments and the process is terminated when all regions are homogeneous. In split-and-merge techniques, after the splitting stage, a merging process is applied for unifying the resulting similar neighboring regions. However, the splitting technique tends to produce boundaries consisting of long horizontal and vertical segments. The heart of the above techniques is the region homogeneity test, usually formulated as a hypothesis testing problem.

The 1980s brought in the use of Markov random fields (Geman and Geman 1987) and variational formulations (Morel and Solimini 1995) in region grouping. The true image is assumed to be a realization of a Markov or Gibbs random field with a distribution that captures the spatial context of the scene. Given the prior distribution of the true image and the observed noisy one, grouping is formulated as an optimization problem. The commonly used estimation principles are MAP estimation, maximization of the marginal probabilities (ICM) and maximization of the posterior marginals. However, these methods require fairly accurate knowledge of the prior true image distribution and most of them are quite expensive. In the variational formulation, energy minimization is used as the framework. The local minima of the designed energy function comprise the set of alternative solutions. With such a formulation, factors such as compactness, homogeneity, or histogram can be incorporated into the model by adding suitable energy terms to the minimization. Similar to MRF-based methods, two basic questions are exposed: what is the criterion that one wants to optimize, and is there an efficient algorithm for carrying out the optimization?

Spectral clustering has been applied widely in region grouping (Shi and Malik 2000) (Ng et al. 2002), which is most related to graph theoretic formulation of grouping. The set of points in an arbitrary feature space are represented as a weighted undirected graph $G = (V, E)$, where the nodes of the graph are the points in the feature space, and an edge is formed between every pair of nodes. The weight on each edge, $w(i, j)$ is a function of the similarity between nodes i and j. In grouping, the algorithm seeks to partition the set of vertices into disjoint sets $\mathbf{V}_1, \ldots, \mathbf{V}_m$, where, by some measure the similarity among the vertices in a set $\mathbf{V}_i$ is high, and across different sets $\mathbf{V}_i$ and $\mathbf{V}_j$ it is low. To achieve this goal, the algorithm partitions the rows of the Laplacian matrix according to their components in the top few singular vectors of the matrix.

The discussion above leads to one core problem in region grouping: what is the optimal measure of disassociation between sub-regions? Obviously, region grouping based on low-level cues can not and should not aim to produce a complete, final correct segmentation. The objective should instead be to use the low-level coherence of brightness, color, texture, or motion attributes to sequentially come up with hierarchical partitions. Mid- and high-level knowledge can be used either to confirm these groups or select some for further attention. This attention could result in further repartition. On the other side of the coin, recent work has demonstrated that learning and graph partitioning can be effectively combined to form larger groups of edge features enhanced with photometric information (Kaufhold and Hoogs 2004). Tu et al. (2005) have derived a probabilistic learning framework for segmentation and detection that incorporates various image models, including smooth regions, contours, texture, and classes of objects. Similarly, Borenstein and Ullman (2002) learn which image fragments are salient for segmenting known classes of objects. In contrast to traditional perceptual grouping approaches that focus on edges, properties of regions have been used to learn a common set of image features that is optimal for general image segmentation (Kaufhold and Hoogs 2004). These Gestalt perceptual characteristics of closure/common region, compactness, colinearity, constant curvature, and parallelism are very useful features. Figure 2.18 shows the Gestalt characteristics based on region.

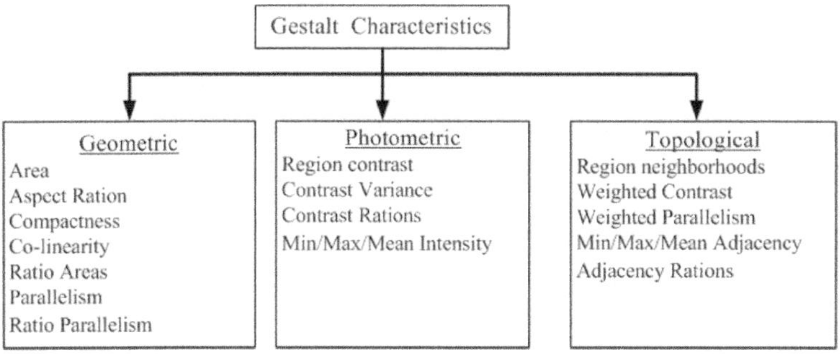

Fig. 2.18 Gestalt characteristics based on region

2.5 Learning Representational Models for Visual Patterns

In traditional computational approaches to vision, the perception of an image can be thought of as a process of computing a hierarchy of increasingly abstract interpretations of the observed images (or image sequences). Therefore, it is of fundamental importance to know what the pattern representations used at each level of interpretation are. For example, the framework for extracting 3-D shape information from images, which is suggested by Marr (1982), consists of representations in three levels: (1) The primal sketch, which makes explicit the intensity changes and local two-dimensional geometry of an image, (2) The $2\frac{1}{2}$-D sketch, which is a viewer-centered representation of the depth, orientation, and discontinuities of the visible surface, and (3) The 3-D model representation, which allows an object-centered description of the 3-D structure and organization of a viewed shape. Each of the three levels of representation will have its places in the eventual understanding of perceptual information processing, and of course there are logical and causal relations among them.

The problem of visual pattern representation, one of the most important problems in computer vision, can be considered to be a data collection and analysis problem, where existing concepts and methods in statistical theory and information theory can be used to model and interpret the visual data. However, visual pattern representation proves to be a highly specialized data collection and analysis task, since visual data is known to be very different from other kinds of data. Thus, constructing a representational model for visual pattern requires that we must understand the special characteristics of the visual data in order to develop realistic models and efficient algorithms for representing and recognizing the wide variety of visual patterns.

Learning from example provides an efficient and direct approach to solving the pattern representation problem. It makes it possible for recognition and detection to directly depend on images and avoids the use of intermediate three-dimensional models. In addition, this image representation allows the use of learning techniques for the analysis of images as well as for the synthesis of images. Almost all work in unsupervised learning can be viewed in terms of learning a probabilistic model of the pattern from the observed data. Even when the machine is given no supervision or reward, it may make sense for it to estimate a model that represents the probability distribution for a new input x_t given previous inputs $x_1,...,x_{t-1}$. In the following three chapters (Chapters 3–5), we discuss how unsupervised learning techniques are applied for visual pattern representation.

2.6 Summary

We have provided an overview of unsupervised learning techniques for visual pattern analysis in this chapter. The application of unsupervised learning can be classified into two categories: (1) applying clustering techniques in order to group visual patterns perceptually and (2) applying dimensionality reduction to achieve compact representations of visual patterns. This chapter focused on the visual grouping problem, and both the theoretic basis and applications of clustering have been highlighted. In particular, the problem of image segmentation was discussed in terms of contour grouping and region grouping.

Appendix

Curvature: For a plane curve C, the mathematical definition of curvature uses a parametric representation of C with respect to the arc length parametrization. Let $\gamma(s)$ be a regular parametric curve, where s is the arc length, or natural parameter. This determines the unit tangent vector T, the unit normal vector N, the curvature $\kappa(s)$, the signed curvature $\kappa(s)$, and the radius of curvature at each point: $T(s) = \kappa^{'}(s)$,$T'(s) = \kappa^{'}(s) = k(s)N(s)$, $\kappa(s) = ||\kappa^{''}(s)|| = |k(s)|$, $R(s) = \frac{1}{\kappa(s)}$.

References

Aldenderfer M, Blashfield R (1984) Cluster Analysis. Sage, Beverly Hills.

Banfield J, Raftery A (1992) Ice floe identification in satellite images using mathematical morphology and clustering about principal curves. Journal of the American Statistical Association 87(417):7–16

Bilmes J (1998) A gentle tutorial of the EM algorithm and its application to parameter estimation for Gaussian mixture and hidden Markov models. International Computer Science Institute 4

Borenstein E, Ullman S (2002) Class-specific, top-down segmentation. European Conference on Computer Vision 2:109–122

Cheng Y (1995) Mean shift, mode seeking, and clustering. IEEE Trasactions on Pattern Analysis and Machine Intelligence 17:790–799

Comaniciu D, Meer P (2002) Mean shift: A robust approach toward feature space analysis. IEEE Trasactions on Pattern Analysis and Machine Intelligence 24:603–619

Dunn J (1973) A fuzzy relative of the ISODATA process and its use in detecting compact well-separated clusters. Journal of Cybernetics 3(3):32–57

Elder J, Zucker S (1994) A measure of closure. Vision Research 34:3361–3361

Fukunaga K, Hostetler L (1975) The estimation of the gradient of a density function, with applications in pattern recognition. IEEE Transactions on Information Theory 21(1):32–40

Geman S, Geman D (1987) Stochastic relaxation, Gibbs distributions and the Bayesian restoration of images. Readings in Computer Vision: Issues, Problems, Principles, and Paradigms pp 564–584

Georgescu B, Shimshoni I, Meer P (2003) Mean shift based clustering in high dimensions: a texture classification example. Proceedings of IEEE Conference on Computer Vision pp 456–463

Guy G, Medioni G (1996) Inferring global perceptual contours from local features. International Journal of Computer Vision 20(1):113–133

Hastie T, Tibshirani R, Friedman J (2001) The Elements of Statistical Learning: Data Mining, Inference, and Prediction. Springer

Jain A, Murty M, Flynn P (1999) Data clustering: a review. ACM Computing Surveys (CSUR) 31(3):264–323

Jolliffe I (1986) Principal component analysis. Springer, New York

Kanizsa G (1979) Organization in Vision: Essays on Gestalt Perception. Praeger, New York

Kass M, Witkin A, Terzopoulos D (1988) Snakes: Active contour models. International Journal of Computer Vision 1(4):321–331

Kaufhold J, Hoogs A (2004) Learning to segment images using region-based perceptual features. Proceedings of IEEE Conference on Computer Vision and Pattern Recognition 2:954–961

Kruskal J, Wish M (1978) Multidimensional Scaling. Sage Publications, California.

Macnaughton-Smith P, Williams W, Dale M, Mockett L (1964) Dissimilarity analysis: A new technique of hierarchical sub-divison. Nature 202(4936):1034–1035

Marr D (1982) Vision: A Computational Investigation into the Human Representation and Processing of Visual Information. Henry Holt and Co., Inc., New York

Morel J, Solimini S (1995) Variational methods in image segmentation. Progress in Nonlinear Differential Equations and their Applications 14, Birkhauser, Boston

Ng A, Jordan M, Weiss Y (2002) On spectral clustering: analysis and an algorithm. Advances in Neural Information Processing Systems, MIT Press, Cambridge

Ng R, Han J (1994) Efficient and effective clustering methods for spatial data mining. Proceedings of the 20th International Conference on Very Large Data Bases pp 144–155

Shaashua A, Ullman S (1988) Structural Saliency: the detection of globally salient structures using a locally connected network. Proceedings of International Conference on Computer Vision 1

Shi J, Malik J (2000) Normalized cuts and image segmentation. IEEE Transactions on Pattern Analysis and Machine Intelligence 22:888–905

Silverman B (1986) Density Estimation for Statistics and Data Analysis. Chapman & Hall/CRC, London

Tu Z, Chen X, Yuille A, Zhu S (2005) Image parsing: unifying segmentation, detection, and recognition. International Journal of Computer Vision 63(2):113–140

Zamir O, Etzioni O (1999) Grouper: a dynamic clustering interface to web search results. Computer Networks 31(11):1361–1374

Chapter 3
Component Analysis

Abstract Researchers in the visual information processing community are regularly confronted with the problem of finding meaningful low-dimensional structures hidden in images or videos, in order to achieve a compact or simplified representation for further processing. In this chapter and the two subsequent chapters, we present a thorough survey of recent research advances in dimensionality reduction for visual pattern representation. We summarize approaches to this problem into three major categories: (1) component analysis (CA), (2) manifold learning, and (3) functional analysis (FA). This chapter focuses on the first category—CA. CA aims to find hidden components by applying data analysis techniques including principal component analysis (PCA), independent component analysis (ICA), and so on. These data analysis techniques are discussed, as well as the underlying models and assumptions that they employed. Additionally, we also discuss interrelationships between these methods.

3.1 Introduction

Dimensionality reduction is the transformation of high-dimensional data into a meaningful representation of reduced dimensionality. Developing appropriate representations for visual pattern is one central problem in visual data analysis. Researchers in this community are regularly confronted with the problem of finding meaningful low-dimensional structures hidden in images or videos for the purposes of developing a compact or simplified representation for use in further high-level processing tasks.

In traditional statistical data analysis, we think of taking observations of instances of a particular phenomenon. These observations can be represented as a vector of values measured on several variables and one assumes many observations and a few, well-chosen variables. The trend today is toward more observations but even more so, toward radically larger numbers of variables—the voracious, automatic, systematic collection of hyper-informative detail about each observed instance. We

N. Zheng, J. Xue, *Statistical Learning and Pattern Analysis for Image and Video Processing*, Advances in Pattern Recognition, DOI 10.1007/978-1-84882-312-9_3,
© Springer-Verlag London Limited 2009

are seeing examples where the observations gathered on individual instances are curves, spectra, images, or even movies, so that a single observation has dimensions in the thousands or billions, while there are only tens or hundreds of instances available for study. Accordingly, there arises the curse and blessing of dimensionality.

The curse of dimensionality refers to the apparent intractability of systematically searching through a high-dimensional space, the apparent intractability of accurately approximating a general high-dimensional function, the apparent intractability of integrating a high-dimensional function. The blessings of dimensionality are less widely noted, but they include the concentration of measurable phenomena (so-called in the geometry of Banach spaces) that certain random fluctuations are very well controlled in high dimensions. They also include the success of asymptotic methods, used widely in mathematical statistics and statistical physics. This implies that although operations in moderate dimensions may be too complex, it does not automatically follow that very high-dimensional settings are also intractable. Indeed, research suggests that the opposite may be true.

Classical methods are simply not designed to cope with this kind of explosive growth of dimensionality in the observation vector. To meet the huge needs of high-dimensional data analysis, many completely new methods for dimensionality reduction have been developed in recent years. Generally, there are three research streams for the purpose of dimensionality reduction: (1) component analysis (CA), (2) manifold learning, and (3) functional analysis (FA). Figure 3.1 presents an overview of dimensionality reduction methods belonging to these three different categories.

CA approaches try to find hidden components via data analysis techniques. According to the models and assumptions employed, CA methods could be further divided into three classes using: (1) generative models. Methods in this class include principal component analysis (PCA) (Jolliffe 2002), nonnegative matrix factorization (NMF) (Lee and Seung 1999), and independent component analysis (ICA) (Hyvarinen et al. 2000); (2) discriminative models. Methods in this class include linear discriminant analysis (LDA) (Chan et al. 1995), oriented component analysis (OCA) (De la Torre et al. 2005), canonical correlation analysis (CCA) (Hardoon et al. 2004), and relevant component analysis (RCA) (Shental et al. 2002); and (3) standard extensions of linear models (Hardin and Hilbe 2001). This class includes latent variable models, tensor factorization, and kernel methods. CA is appealing because many visual data analysis problems can be solved as generalized eigenvalue problems or alternated least squares procedures, for which there exist extremely efficiently and numerically stable algorithms. These spectral approaches offer a potential for solving linear and nonlinear estimation/learning problems efficiently and without local minima.

Functional analysis and manifold learning are two other important methods for dimensionality reduction. The functional analysis methods are based upon treating an image as a continuous function and rely upon recent advances in harmonic analysis. Methods in this category attempt to develop new forms of functional rep-

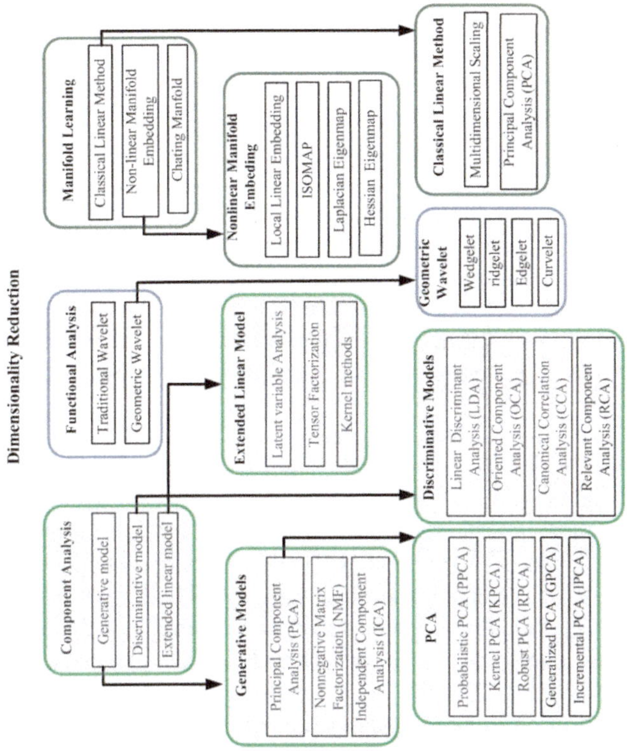

Fig. 3.1 The overview of the dimensionality reduction methods covered in this book

resentations for images and video, and they aim to find an optimal dictionary in order to achieve an optimal sparse representation by atomic decomposition. On the other hand, manifold methods attempt to construct a representation of data lying on a low-dimensional manifold embedded in a high-dimensional space, modeling the local geometry of the data by constructing a graph.

This chapter focuses on CA methods, and manifold learning and functional analysis are discussed in the next two chapters. The rest of this chapter is organized as follows: we first present a general overview of CA methods in Section 3.2, and then classify CA methods into three categories: generative model-based methods in Section 3.3, discriminative model based methods in Section 3.4, and the standard extensions of linear models in Section 3.5. Finally, a summary concludes this chapter.

3.2 Overview of Component Analysis

We can view N gray images as an $N \times D$ data matrix, where D denotes the number of pixels of each image. Each image gives rise to an observation, different images are then different individuals. In studying such an $N-by-D$ data matrix, we often refer to it as D-dimensional because we look at the matrix as representing N points (the images) in a D-dimensional space (the resolution of each image). If the image is n by n, then we have $D=n^2$ variables. With so many different dimensions, it is difficult to comprehend or even visualize the patterns of association among them. The process is further complicated by the fact that there is often substantial redundancy among dimensions, leading to high levels of correlation and multicollinearity.

Having defined the problem of high-dimensional data analysis, we now turn to a description of the methods used for the purpose of analysis. In describing these methods, we rely on three characteristics: (1) whether the technique is used principally for the analysis of interdependence or the analysis of dependence, (2) whether the technique is used mainly for the purpose of exploration or for the purpose of confirmation and testing, and (3) whether the technique is designed to be used with metric data or nonmetric data. All these approaches differ in their noise assumptions, the use of prior information, and the underlying statistical models, but all of them are directly or indirectly related to linear or bilinear regression.

Three statistical models are generally used in component analysis: generative model, discriminative models, and standard extensions of the linear models. Accordingly, CA methods can be classified into three classes according to their characteristics and underlying statistical model. Section 3.3 focuses on generative models, and covers methods primarily concerned with the analysis of interdependence. These techniques include PCA, NMF, ICA, and use generative models to analyze the interdependence among variables (PCA) or objects (NMF and ICA). Section 3.4 pays attention to discriminative models, and covers methods primarily concerned with the analysis of dependence—that is, using one set of variables (called independent variables) to explain the variation observed in another set of variables (called dependent variables). Methods using discriminative models include linear discriminative analysis (LDA), oriented component analysis (OCA), canonical correlation analysis (CCA), and relevant component analysis (RCA). Section 3.5 is devoted to standard extensions of the linear models. For each of these methods, we discuss not only the special case involving one dependent variable, but also the more general case involving more than one dependent variable.

3.3 Generative Models

A generative model is a model for randomly generating observable data, typically given some hidden parameters. It introduces hidden (latent) variables to account for the underlying process. For example, given a set of observed images $\mathscr{I} = \{\mathbf{I}_1, ..., \mathbf{I}_N\}$, where $\mathbf{I}_n, n = 1, ..., N$, are considered as realizations of some underlying stochastic process governed by $f(\mathbf{I})$, then a generative model $p(\mathbf{I})$ is chosen from a family of probability distributions that share the same statistics as $\mathscr{I}$. The generative model $p(\mathbf{I})$ approaches $f(\mathbf{I})$ by minimizing a defined distance from f to p. Well-known examples of generative models include Gaussian distribution, Gaussian mixture model, multinomial distribution, hidden Markov model, Naive Bayes, and Latent Dirichlet allocation.

For component analysis, a generative model postulates hidden variables as the cause for the complicated dependencies in raw data. The hidden variables employed to represent or generate the observed image usually follow very simple models, for example, a linear additive model where an image $\mathbf{I}$ is the result of linear superposition of some components ψ_i from a dictionary $\mathscr{D}$, $i = 1, ..., K$, plus a Gaussian noise process $\mathbf{n}$.

$$\mathbf{I} = \sum_{i=1}^{K} \alpha_i \cdot \psi_i + \mathbf{n}, \psi_i \in \mathscr{D}, \forall i \tag{3.1}$$

where α_i, $i = 1, ..., K$ are the coefficients, and $\{\psi_i \in \mathscr{D}\}$ are the eigenvectors in PCA, nonnegative matrix factors in NMF, or independent components in ICA. The hidden variables are the K coefficients of the components, $\{\alpha_i\}_{i=1}^{K}$, plus the noise $\mathbf{n}$.

In the following sections, we discuss three well-known component analysis techniques: PCA, NMF, and ICA, as well as their variants. They are all generative model-based component analysis methods.

3.3.1 Principal Component Analysis

Principal component analysis (PCA) (Jolliffe 2002) is a well-known method that can be used to reduce the dimensionality of multivariate data. It allows researchers to re-express the data, by taking linear combinations of the original variables, so that the first few resulting new variables (called *components*) account for as much of the available information as possible. If substantial redundancy is presented in the data set, then it may be possible to account for most of the information in the original data set with a relatively small number of components. This dimension reduction makes visualization of the data more straightforward and subsequent data analysis more manageable. In application, user must decide how many principal components to retain for subsequent analysis, trading off simplicity (i.e., a small number of dimension, which is easier to manage) against completeness (i.e., a large number of dimensions, which captures a greater amount of the available information).

The most common derivation of PCA is given in terms of a standardized linear projection, which maximizes the variance in the projected space. Let $\mathbf{D} = [\mathbf{d}_1, \mathbf{d}_2, ..., \mathbf{d}_n]$ be a matrix $\mathbf{D} \in \mathscr{R}^{d \times n}$, where each column $\mathbf{d}_i$ is a data sample (or image), n is the number of the training images, and d is the number of pixels in each image. Previous formulations assume the data is zero mean. In the least-squares case, this can be achieved by subtracting the mean of the entire data set from each column $\mathbf{d}_i$.

The first k principal components of $\mathbf{D}$, $\mathbf{B} = [\mathbf{b}_1, ..., \mathbf{b}_k] \in \mathscr{R}^{d \times k}$, define k orthonormal axes onto which the retained variance under projection is maximal. Figure 3.2 shows four samples and the corresponding reconstructed images using the first 8 principal components. The columns of $\mathbf{B}$ form an orthonormal basis that spans the principal subspace. It can be shown that the vectors $\{\mathbf{b}_i\}_{i=1}^k$ are given by the k dominant eigenvectors of the sample covariance matrix Γ, where $\Gamma = \mathbf{D}\mathbf{D}^T = \sum_i \mathbf{d}_i\mathbf{d}_i^T$ is the covariance matrix. $\{\mathbf{b}_i\}_{i=1}^k$ are also the directions of maximum variation within the data, which maximize $\sum_{i=1}^n \parallel \mathbf{B}^T \Gamma \mathbf{B} \parallel_p$, with the constraints $\mathbf{B}^T\mathbf{B} = \mathbf{I}$, where $||A||_F$ denotes the p norm of matrix A (e.g., p can be taken value as 1 or 2).

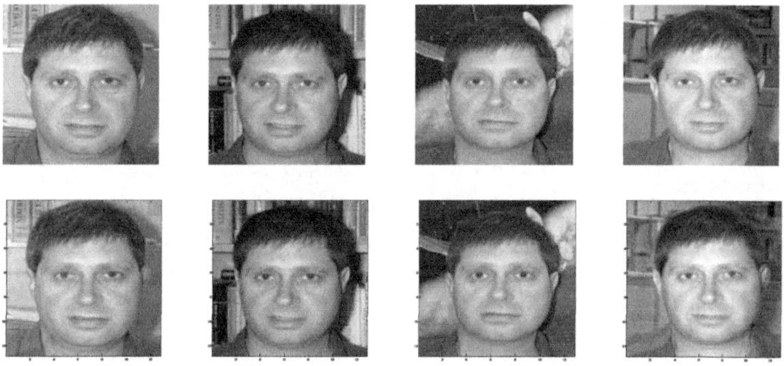

Fig. 3.2 PCA results. *Top row*: original image samples; *Bottom row*: from *left* to *right* shows reconstructed images using first 8 principal components. These images are download from http://www.cs.unimaas.nl/l.vandermaaten/dr/download.php.

If the effective rank of $\mathbf{D}$ is much less than d, then we can approximate the column space of $\mathbf{D}$ with $k \ll d$ principal components. The data $\mathbf{d}_i$ can be approximated as a linear combination of the principal components as $\mathbf{d}_i^{rec} = \mathbf{B}\mathbf{B}^T\mathbf{d}_i$, where $\mathbf{B}^T\mathbf{d}_i = \mathbf{c}_i$ are the linear coefficients obtained by projecting the training data onto the principal subspace; that is, $\mathbf{C} = [\mathbf{c}_1, ..., \mathbf{c}_n] = \mathbf{B}^T\mathbf{D}$.

The most widely used method for calculating principal components in the statistics and neural network community formulates PCA as the least-square estimation of the basis images $\mathbf{B}$ that maximize:

$$E_{pca}(\mathbf{B}) = \sum_{i=1}^{n} e_p ca(\mathbf{e}_i) = \sum_{i=1}^{n} \| \mathbf{d}_i - \mathbf{B}\mathbf{B}^T\mathbf{d}_i \|_2^2 = \sum_{i=1}^{n}\sum_{p=1}^{d} (d_{pi} - \sum_{j=1}^{k} b_{pj}c_{ji})^2 \quad (3.2)$$

where $c_{ji} = \sum_{t=1}^{d} b_{tj}d_{ti}$, $\mathbf{B}^T\mathbf{B} = \mathbf{I}$. $\| \cdot \|$ denotes the L_2 norm, $\mathbf{e}_i = \mathbf{d}_i - \mathbf{B}\mathbf{B}^T\mathbf{d}_i$ is the reconstruction error vector, and $e_{pca}(\mathbf{e}_i) = \mathbf{e}_i^T\mathbf{e}_i$ is the reconstruction error of $\mathbf{d}_i$.

Although Eq. (3.2) has a "closed-form" solution in terms of an eigen-equation (the base $\mathbf{B}$ are eigenvectors of the covariance matrix $\mathbf{D}\mathbf{D}^T$), for high-dimensional data the EM approach (Bilmes 1998) can be more efficient in space and time. The EM algorithm for Eq. (3.2) uses the following equations:

$$\begin{aligned} \mathbf{B}^T\mathbf{B}\mathbf{C} &= \mathbf{B}^T\mathbf{D} \qquad \text{(E-Step)} \\ \mathbf{B}\mathbf{C}\mathbf{C}^T &= \mathbf{D}\mathbf{C}^T \qquad \text{(M-Step)} \end{aligned} \quad (3.3)$$

The algorithm alternates between solving for linear coefficients $\mathbf{C}$ and solving for the base $\mathbf{B}$.

3.3.1.1 Probabilistic PCA (PPCA)

In addition to the algebraic–geometric interpretation, PCA can also be understood in a probabilistic manner. More specifically, PCA can be rewritten in a probabilistic framework, the probabilistic PCA (PPCA) (Tipping and Bishop 1999), allowing for the implementation of PCA as an EM algorithm.

PPCA demonstrates how the principal axes of a set of observed data vectors may be determined through the maximum-likelihood estimation of parameters in a latent model (which is closely related to factor analysis). The latent variable model seeks to relate a d-dimensional observation vector $\mathbf{d}$ to a corresponding q-dimensional vector of latent variables $\mathbf{x}$.

$$\mathbf{d} = \mathbf{W}\mathbf{x} + \mu + \varepsilon \quad (3.4)$$

The $d \times q$ matrix $\mathbf{W}$ relates two sets of variables, while the parameter vector μ permits the model to have nonzero mean. The motivation is that, with $q < d$, the latent variables will offer a more parsimonious representation of the dependencies between the observations. Conventionally, $\mathbf{x} \sim \mathcal{N}(\mathbf{0}, \mathbf{I})$, and the latent variables are defined to be independent and Gaussian with unit variance. By additionally specifying the error, or noise to be likewise Gaussian, Eq. (3.4) induces a corresponding Gaussian distribution for the observation: $\mathbf{d} \sim \mathcal{N}(\mu, \mathbf{W}\mathbf{W}^T + \psi)$.

The model parameters may thus be determined by maximum-likelihood, although because there is no closed-form analytic solution for $\mathbf{W}$ and ψ, their values must be obtained via an iterative procedure. By constraining the error covariance ψ to be a diagonal matrix whose elements ψ_i are usually estimated from the data, the observed $\mathbf{d}_i$ are conditionally independent given the values of the latent variables $\mathbf{x}$. These latent variables are thus intended to explain the correlations between $\mathbf{d}_i$, while ε_i represents the variability unique to a particular $\mathbf{d}_i$. This is where factor analysis fundamentally differs from standard PCA, which effectively treats covariance and variance identically.

Because of the distinction made between variance and covariance in standard factor analysis modeling, the subspace defined by the maximum-likelihood estimate of the columns of $\mathbf{W}$ will generally not correspond to the principal subspace of the observed data. However, certain links between the two methods have been previously established, and such connections center on the special case of an isotropic error model, where the residual variances $\varepsilon_i = \sigma^2$ are constrained to be equal.

The use of the isotropic Gaussian model $\mathcal{N}(0, \sigma^2\mathbf{I})$ for ε in conjunction with Eq. (3.4) implies that the $\mathbf{x}$-conditional probability distribution over $\mathbf{d}$-space is given by

$$p(\mathbf{d}|\mathbf{x}) = \mathcal{N}(\mathbf{W}\mathbf{x} + \mu, \sigma^2\mathbf{I}) \tag{3.5}$$

With the marginal distribution over the latent variables is also Gaussian and conventionally defined by $\mathbf{x} \sim \mathcal{N}(\mathbf{0}, \mathbf{I})$, the marginal distribution for the observed data $\mathbf{d}$ is readily obtained by integrating out the latent variables and is likewise Gaussian.

$$d \sim \mathcal{N}(\mu, \mathbf{C}) \tag{3.6}$$

where the observation covariance model is specified by $\mathbf{C} = \mathbf{W}\mathbf{W}^T + \sigma^2\mathbf{I}$. The corresponding log-likelihood is then

$$\mathcal{L} = -(N/2)\{dln(2\pi) + ln|\mathbf{C}| + tr(\mathbf{C}^{-1}\mathbf{S})\} \tag{3.7}$$

where $S = (1/N)\sum_{n=1}^{N}(\mathbf{d} - \mu)(\mathbf{d} - \mu)^T$. The maximum-likelihood estimator for μ is given by the mean of the data, in which case $\mathbf{S}$ is the sample covariance matrix of the observations $\mathbf{d}_n$. Estimations for $\mathbf{W}$ and σ^2 may be obtained by iterative maximization of $\mathcal{L}$, for example, by using the EM algorithm. Then we have

$$p(\mathbf{x}|\mathbf{d}) \sim \mathcal{N}(\mathbf{M}^{-1}\mathbf{W}^T(\mathbf{d} - \mu), \sigma^2\mathbf{M}^{-1}), \tag{3.8}$$

where $\mathbf{M}$ is defined as $\mathbf{M} = \mathbf{W}^T\mathbf{W} + \sigma^2\mathbf{M}^{-1}$, and it is of size of $q \times q$ while $\mathbf{C}$ is $d \times d$.

In EM, we consider the latent variables $\{\mathbf{x}_n\}$ to be "missing" data, which together with these latent variables comprise the observations. The corresponding complete data log-likelihood is then

$$\mathcal{L}_c = \sum_{n=1}^{N} ln\{p(\mathbf{d}_n, \mathbf{x}_n)\} \tag{3.9}$$

$$p(\mathbf{d}_n, \mathbf{x}_n) = (2\pi\sigma^2)^{-d/2} e^{\{-\frac{\|\mathbf{d}_n - \mathbf{W}\mathbf{x}_n - \mu\|^2}{2\sigma^2}\}} \times (2\pi)^{\frac{-q}{2}} e^{\{-\frac{\|\mathbf{x}_n\|^2}{2}\}} \tag{3.10}$$

In the E-step, we take the expectation of $\mathscr{L}_c$ with respect to the distribution $p(\mathbf{x}_n | \mathbf{d}_n, \mathbf{W}, \sigma^2)$.

$$\langle \mathscr{L}_c \rangle = \sum_{n=1}^{N} \{ \frac{d}{2} ln\sigma^2 + \frac{1}{2} tr(\langle \mathbf{x}_n \mathbf{x}_n^T \rangle) + \frac{1}{2\sigma^2} (\mathbf{d}_n - \mu)^T (\mathbf{d}_n - \mu) - \frac{1}{\sigma^2} \langle \mathbf{x}_n \rangle^T \mathbf{W}^T (\mathbf{d}_n - \mu) + \frac{1}{\sigma^2} tr(\mathbf{W}^T \mathbf{W}) \langle \mathbf{x}_n \mathbf{x}_n^T \rangle \} \tag{3.11}$$

where we omit terms independent of the model parameters and

$$\langle \mathbf{x}_n \rangle = \mathbf{M}^{-1} \mathbf{W}^T (\mathbf{d}_n - \mu)$$

$$\langle \mathbf{x}_n \mathbf{x}_n^T \rangle = \sigma^2 M^{-1} + \langle \mathbf{x}_n \rangle \langle \mathbf{x}_n \rangle^T \tag{3.12}$$

In the M-step, $\langle \mathscr{L}_c \rangle$ is maximized with respect to $\mathbf{W}$ and σ^2 giving new parameter estimates.

$$\tilde{\mathbf{W}} = [\sum_n (\mathbf{d}_n - \mu \langle \mathbf{x}_n \rangle^T)][\sum_n \langle \mathbf{x}_n \mathbf{x}_n^T \rangle]^{-1}$$

$$\tilde{\sigma^2} = \frac{1}{Nd} \sum_{n=1} N\{\| \mathbf{d}_n - \mu \|^2 - 2\langle \mathbf{x}_n \rangle^T \tilde{\mathbf{W}}^T (\mathbf{d}_n - \mu) + tr(\langle \mathbf{x}_n \mathbf{x}_n^T \rangle) \tilde{\mathbf{W}}^T \tilde{\mathbf{W}} \} \tag{3.13}$$

To maximize the likelihood then, the sufficient statistics of the conditional distributions are calculated from Eq. (3.12), after which revised estimates for the parameters are obtained from Eq. (3.13). These four equations are iterated in sequence until the algorithm is judged to have converged.

It should be noted that in PPCA, the noises are assumed to be independent samples drawn from an unknown distribution, and theproblem becomes one that identifies the subspace and the parameters of the distribution in a maximum likelihood sense. When the underlying noise distribution is Gaussian, the algebraic-geometric and probabilistic interpretations coincide (Collins et al. 2002). However, when the underlying distribution is non-Gaussian the solution to PPCA is no longer linear.

3.3.1.2 Robust PCA (RPCA)

The traditional PCA approach constructs the rank k subspace approximation to the zero-mean training data that is optimal in a least-squares sense. However, in real applications, training data may contain undesirable artifacts due to occlusion (e.g., a hand in front of a face), illumination (e.g., specular reflections), noise (e.g., from scanning archival data), or errors from the underlying data generation method (e.g., incorrect optical flow vectors). Least-squares techniques are not robust in these cases, and such outlying observations (or measurements) can arbitrarily skew the outcome from the desired solution. Loosely, the term "outlier" refers to data that does not conform to the assumed statistical model. A "robust" estimation method is one that can tolerate some percentage of outlying data without resulting in and arbitrarily skewed solution.

These difficulties motivate the research being done in robust principal component analysis (RPCA). In the following, we introduce an efficient RPCA techniques (De la Torre and Black 2003) that views the above-mentioned artifacts as statistical outliers, which are dealt with by using robust M-estimation techniques of the statistics community. Its goal is to recover the solution (i.e., the learned model) that best fits the majority of the data, and to detect and down-weight "outlying" data.

Problem formulation

Let $\mathbf{D} = [\mathbf{d}_1 \mathbf{d}_2 ... \mathbf{d}_n]$ be a matrix $\mathbf{D} \in \mathbb{R}^{d \times n}$, where each column $\mathbf{d}_i$ is a data sample (or image), n is the number of training images, and d is the number of pixels in each image. Let the first k principal components of $\mathbf{D}$ be $\mathbf{B} = [\mathbf{b}_1, ..., \mathbf{b}_k]$. The columns of $\mathbf{B}$ are the directions of maximum variation within the data. The principal components maximize $max_{\mathbf{B}} \sum_{i=1}^{n} ||\mathbf{B}^T \mathbf{d}_i||_2^2 = ||\mathbf{B}^T \mathbf{P} \mathbf{B}||_F$, with the constraint $\mathbf{B}^T \mathbf{B} = \mathbf{I}$, where $\mathbf{P} = \mathbf{D}\mathbf{D}^T = \sum_i \mathbf{d}_i \mathbf{d}_i^T$ is the covariance matrix. $\mathbf{C} = [\mathbf{c}_1 \mathbf{c}_2 ... \mathbf{c}_n] = \mathbf{B}^T \mathbf{D}$ is the linear coefficient matrix obtained by projecting the training data onto the principal subspace.

RPCA extends previous work on robust PCA methods by adding an intra-sample outlier process motivated by the necessity of dealing with the type of outliers that typically occur in images. The outlier process has computational advantages and is related to robust M-estimation. More specifically, it addresses the general problem of learning both the basis vectors and linear coefficients robustly, and learns the PCA model from the observed data by minimizing the following energy function.

$$E_{rpca}(\mathbf{B}, \mathbf{C}, \mu, \mathbf{L}) = \sum_{i=1}^{n} \sum_{p=1}^{d} [L_{pi}(\frac{\tilde{e}_{pi}^2}{\sigma_p^2}) + P(L_{pi})] \tag{3.14}$$

where μ is the mean. In the robust case, outliers are defined with respect to the error in the reconstructed images which include the mean. Thus μ can no longer be computed directly, but must be estimated (robustly), analogously to the other bases. $0 \leq L_{pi} \leq 1$ is an analog outlier process that depends on both images and pixel locations, and $P(L_{pi})$ is a penalty function. The error $\tilde{e}_{pi} = d_{pi} - \mu_p - \sum_{j=1}^{k} b_{pj} c_{ji}$ and $\sigma = [\sigma_1, \sigma_2, ..., \sigma_d]^T$ specifies a "scale" parameter for each of the d pixel locations.

By exploring the relationship between outlier processes and the robust statistics (Black and Rangarajan 1996), one finds that minimizing Eq. (3.14) is equivalent to minimizing the robust energy function (3.15) for a particular class of robust ρ-functions.

$$E_{rpca}(\mathbf{B},\mathbf{C},\mu,\sigma) = \sum_{i=1}^{n} e_{rpca}(\mathbf{d}_i - \mu - \mathbf{B}\mathbf{c}_i, \sigma) \qquad (3.15)$$
$$= \sum_{i=1}^{n}\sum_{p=1}^{d} \rho(d_{pi} - \mu_p - \sum_{j=1}^{k} b_{pj}c_{ji}, \sigma_p)$$

where μ_p is the $p-$th pixel of the mean image.

The robust magnitude of a vector $\mathbf{x}$ is defined as the sum of the robust error values for each component; that is, $e_{rpca}(\mathbf{x},\sigma) = \sum_{p=1}^{d} \rho(x_p, \sigma_p)$, where $\mathbf{x} = [x_1, x_2, ..., x_d]^T$ and $\rho(x,\sigma_p) = \frac{x^2}{x^2+\sigma_p^2}$, σ_p is a "scale" parameter that controls the convexity of the robust function and is used for deterministic annealing in the optimization process. This robust ρ-function corresponds to the penalty term $P(L_{pi}) = (\sqrt{L_{pi}} - 1)^2$ in Eq. (3.14). It should be noted that there are many other choices for the robust ρ-function, but the function used here has been used widely and has been shown to work well. Additionally, unlike some other ρ-functions, it is twice differentiable, which is useful for optimization methods based on gradient descent.

Computational Issues

Now we consider how to compute the mean and the subspace spanned by the first k principal components. The minimization of Eq. (3.15) can be formulated as a weighted least squares problem and be solved by using iteratively re-weighted least squares (IRLS). For an iteration of IRLS, Eq. (3.15) can be transformed into a weighted least-squares problem and rewritten as Eq. (3.16).

$$E(\mathbf{B},\mathbf{C},\mu,\mathbf{W})_{wpca} = \sum_{i=1}^{n} (\mathbf{d}_i - \mu - \mathbf{B}\mathbf{c}_i)^T \mathbf{W}_i (\mathbf{d}_i - \mu - \mathbf{B}\mathbf{c}_i) \qquad (3.16)$$
$$= \sum_{p=1}^{d} (\mathbf{d}^p - \mu_d \mathbf{1}_n - \mathbf{C}^T\mathbf{b}^p)^T \mathbf{W}^p (\mathbf{d}^p - \mu_d \mathbf{1}_n - \mathbf{C}^T\mathbf{b}^p) \qquad (3.17)$$

where the $\mathbf{W}_i \in \mathscr{R}^{d\times d} = diag(\mathbf{w}_i)$ are diagonal matrices containing the positive weighting coefficients for the data sample $\mathbf{d}_i$, and $\mathbf{w}_i$ denotes the ith column of $\mathbf{W}$. $\mathbf{W}^p \in \mathscr{R}^{n\times n} = diag(\mathbf{w}_p)$ are diagonal matrices containing the weighting factors for the pth pixel over the whole training set. $\mathbf{d}_i$ represents the ith column of the data matrix $\mathbf{D}$ and $\mathbf{d}^p$ is a column vector which contains the pth row.

In order to find a solution to $E(\mathbf{B},\mathbf{C},\mu,\mathbf{W})_{wpca}$, we differentiate the first line of Eq. (3.16) with respect to $\mathbf{c}_i$ and μ and differentiate the second line with respect to $\mathbf{b}^p$ to find necessary, but not sufficient conditions for the minimum. From these conditions, we derive the following coupled system of equations.

$$\mu = (\sum_{i=1}^{n} \mathbf{W}_i^{-1}) \sum_{i=1}^{n} \mathbf{W}_i(\mathbf{d}_i - \mathbf{B}\mathbf{c}_i) \qquad (3.18)$$

$$(\mathbf{B}^T\mathbf{W}_i\mathbf{B})\mathbf{c}_i = \mathbf{B}^T\mathbf{W}_i(\mathbf{d}_i - \mu)\forall i = 1,...,n \qquad (3.19)$$

$$(\mathbf{C})(\mathbf{W}^j\mathbf{C}^T)\mathbf{b}_j = \mathbf{C}\mathbf{W}^j(\mathbf{d}^j - \mu_d\mathbf{1}_n)\forall j = 1,...,d \qquad (3.20)$$

Given these updates of the parameters, an approximation algorithm for minimizing Eq. (3.15) can employ a two-step method that minimizes $E(\mathbf{B},\mathbf{C},\mu)$ using alternated least squares. The most computationally expensive part of the algorithm involves computing the three coupled system of equations. The computational cost of one iteration is $O(nk^2d)+O(nk^3)+O(nkd)$ for $\mathbf{C}$ and $O(nk^2d)+O(dk^3)+O(nkd)$ for $\mathbf{B}$. Typically $d \gg n \gg k$ and, for example, estimating the basis $\mathbf{B}$ involves computing the solution of d systems of $k \times k$ equations, which for large d is computationally expensive.

Rather than directly solving d systems of $k \times k$ equations for $\mathbf{B}$ and n systems of $k \times k$ equations for $\mathbf{C}$, RPCA performs gradient descent with a local quadratic approximation to determine an approximation of the step sizes, to solve for $\mathbf{B}$,$\mathbf{C}$, and μ. The robust learning rules for updating successively B, C, and μ are as follows:

$$\mathbf{B}^{n+1} = \mathbf{B}^{n} - [\mathbf{H_b}].^{-1} \circ \frac{\partial E_{rpca}}{\partial \mathbf{B}} \tag{3.21}$$

$$\mathbf{C}^{n+1} = \mathbf{C}^{n} - [\mathbf{H_c}].^{-1} \circ \frac{\partial E_{rpca}}{\partial \mathbf{C}} \tag{3.22}$$

$$\mu^{n+1} = \mu^{n} - [\mathbf{H}_\mu].^{-1} \circ \frac{\partial E_{rpca}}{\partial \mu} \tag{3.23}$$

The partial derivatives with respect to the parameters are

$$\frac{\partial E_{rpca}}{\partial \mathbf{B}} = -\psi(\tilde{\mathbf{E}},\sigma)\mathbf{C}^T \tag{3.24}$$

$$\frac{\partial E_{rpca}}{\partial \mathbf{C}} = -\mathbf{B}^T\psi(\tilde{\mathbf{E}},\sigma) \tag{3.25}$$

$$\frac{\partial E_{rpca}}{\partial \mu} = -\psi(\tilde{\mathbf{E}},\sigma)\mathbf{1_n} \tag{3.26}$$

where $\tilde{\mathbf{E}}$ is the reconstruction error which can be denoted in matrix form as $\tilde{\mathbf{E}} = \mathbf{D} - \mu\mathbf{1}_n^T - \mathbf{BC}$, and an estimate of the step size is given by:

$$\mathbf{H_b} = \xi(\tilde{\mathbf{E}},\sigma)(\mathbf{C}\circ\mathbf{C})^T,\ \mathbf{h}_{\mathbf{b}_i} = maxdiag\left(\frac{\partial^2 E_{rpca}}{\partial \mathbf{b}_i \partial \mathbf{b}_i^T}\right) \tag{3.27}$$

$$\mathbf{H_c} = (\mathbf{B}\circ\mathbf{B})^T\xi(\tilde{\mathbf{E}},\sigma),\ \mathbf{h}_{\mathbf{c}_i} = maxdiag\left(\frac{\partial^2 E_{rpca}}{\partial \mathbf{c}_i \partial \mathbf{c}_i^T}\right) \tag{3.28}$$

$$\mathbf{H}_\mu = \xi(\tilde{\mathbf{E}},\sigma)\mathbf{1}_n,\ \mathbf{h}_{\mu_i} = maxdiag\left(\frac{\partial^2 E_{rpca}}{\partial \mu_i \partial \mu_i^T}\right) \tag{3.29}$$

where $\frac{\partial E_{rpca}}{\partial \mathbf{B}} \in \mathscr{R}^{d\times k}$ is the derivative of E_{rpca} with respect to $\mathbf{B}$, and similarly for $\frac{\partial E_{rpca}}{\partial \mathbf{C}} \in \mathscr{R}^{k\times n}$ and $\frac{\partial E_{rpca}}{\partial \mu} \in \mathscr{R}^{d\times 1}$. $\psi(\tilde{\mathbf{E}},\sigma)$ is a matrix that contains the derivatives of the robust function; that is, $\psi(\tilde{e}_{pi},\sigma_p) = \frac{\partial\rho(\tilde{e}_{pi},\sigma_p)}{\partial\rho(\tilde{e}_{pi}} = \frac{2\tilde{e}_{pi}\sigma_p^2}{(\tilde{e}_{pi}+\sigma_p^2)^2}$. $\mathbf{H_b} \in \mathscr{R}^{d\times k}$ is a matrix in which every component ij is an upper bound of the second derivative; that is, $h_{ij} \geq \frac{\partial^2 E_{rpca}}{\partial b_{ij}^2}$ and, similarly, $\mathbf{H_c} \in \mathscr{R}^{n \times k}$ and $\mathbf{H}_\mu \in \mathscr{R}^{d \times 1}$. Each element p_i of the matrix $\xi(\tilde{\mathbf{E}}, \sigma) \in \mathscr{R}^{d \times n}$ contains the maximum of the second derivative of the ρ-function; that is $\xi_{pi} = max_{\tilde{e}_{pi}} \frac{\partial^2(\tilde{e}_{pi}, \sigma_p)}{\partial \tilde{(e)}_{pi}^2} = \frac{2}{\sigma_p^2}$.

Observe that now the computational cost of one iteration of the learning rules is $O(ndk)$. After each update of (B, C), or μ, the error $\tilde{\mathbf{E}}$ is updated.

Implemention issues

The scale parameter σ controls the shape of the robust ρ-function and hence determines what residual errors are treated as outliers. When the absolute value of the robust error $|\tilde{e}_{pi}|$ is larger than $\frac{\sigma_p}{\sqrt{(3)}}$, the ρ-function used here begins reducing the influence of the pixel p in image i on the solution. The scale parameter σ_p for each pixel p is estimated automatically using the local median absolute deviation (MAD) of the pixel. The MAD can be viewed as a robust statistical estimate of the standard deviation, and can be computed as:

$$\sigma_p = \beta max(1.4826 med_R(|\mathbf{e}^p - med_R(|\mathbf{e}^p|)|), \sigma_{min}) \tag{3.30}$$

where med_R indicates that the median is taken over a region, R, around pixel p and σ_{min} is the MAD over the whole image. β is a constant factor that sets the outlier σ_p to be between 2 and 2.5 times the estimated standard deviation. For calculating the MAD, an initial error $\mathbf{e}_p$ is needed, and it can be obtained as follows: compute the standard PCA on the data, and calculate the number of bases that preserve 55% of the energy E_{pca}. This is achieved when the ratio between the energy of the reconstructed vectors and the original vectors is larger than 0.55. With this number of bases, the least-squares reconstruction error $\mathbf{E}$ can be computed, and then be used to obtain a robust estimate of σ.

Since the aforementioned computation is an iterative process, an initial guess for the parameters $\mathbf{B}$ and $\mathbf{C}$ and μ has to be given. An initial estimate of μ is given by the robust mean which can be found by minimizing $\sum_i e_{rpca}(\mathbf{d}_i - \bar{\mathbf{x}}, \sigma)$. Alternatively, simply taking the median or mean is often sufficient. We can take the standard PCA as an initial guess for $\mathbf{B}$. The parameter $\mathbf{C}$ is just the solution of the linear system of equations which minimize $min_{\mathbf{C}}||\mathbf{D} - \mu \mathbf{1}_n^T - \mathbf{BC}||_2$. With these parameters and σ we can calculate $\mathbf{W}$ and start the process.

In summary, the whole optimization process is described as follows:

- Compute the robust mean, $\mu^{(0)}$, and standard PCA solution. Calculate the residuals, initialize $\mathbf{B}^0$, $\mathbf{C}^0$ and select the initial number of bases.
- Calculate the scale parameter σ using Eq. (3.30); this is the final scaling σ_{fin}. Multiply it by a constant, so all pixels are initially treated as inliers, that is, $\sigma_{fin} = K * \sigma_{init}$.
- Until the principal angle between $\mathbf{B}^n$ and $\mathbf{B}^{n+1}$ is less than a chosen ε:
  - Compute an estimation of the step size (Eq. (3.27–3.29)).
  - Compute the partial derivatives with respect to the parameters.
  - Update the parameters (Eq. (3.21–3.72)).

  – Lower σ according to the annealing schedule if it is bigger than σ_{fin}.

- Additionally, compute $\mathbf{W}*$ by thresholding the weight matrix $\mathbf{W}$. Keep adding bases and solving for $\mathbf{B}$, $\mathbf{C}$, and μ while $\zeta = \frac{\sum_{i=1}^{n}(\mathbf{Bc}_i)^T \mathbf{W}_i^* (\mathbf{Bc}_i}{\sum_{i=1}^{n}(\mathbf{d}_i-\mu)^T \mathbf{W}_i^* (\mathbf{d}_i-\mu)}$ is less than 0.9.

3.3.1.3 Generalized PCA (GPCA)

GPCA considers the problem of clustering data lying on multiple subspaces of unknown and possibly different dimensions (Vidal et al. 2005). Given a set of sample points $X = \{x^j \in \mathscr{R}^K\}_{j=1}^N$ drawn from $n > 1$ different linear subspaces $\{S_i \subseteq \mathscr{R}^K\}_{i=1}^n$ of dimension $k_i = dim(S_i)$, $0 < k_i < K$, identify each subspace S_i without knowing which points belong to which subspace. There are three issues related to the identification of the subspaces: (1) identify the number of subspaces n and their dimensions $\{k_i\}_{i=1}^n$; (2) identify a basis (or a set of principal components) for each subspace S_i (or equivalently $S_i^{\perp}$), and (3) group or segment the given N data points into the subspace to which they belong.

Based on an algebraic geometric approach, GPCA eliminates the data segmentation portion of problem algebraically and then solves the model estimation portion directly, using all data and without having to iterate between data segmentation and model estimation as is required with other models discussed previously. The algebraic elimination of the data segmentation portion of the problem is achieved by finding algebraic equations that are segmentation independent, that is equations that are satisfied by all the data regardless of the group or model associated with each point. For the classes of problems considered in this section, such segmentation-independent constraints are polynomials of a certain degree in several variables. The degree of the polynomials corresponds to the number of groups and the factors of the polynomials encode the model parameters associated with each group. The problem is then reduced to

- Computing the number of groups from the data: this question is answered by looking for polynomials with the smallest possible degree that fit all the data points. This leads to simple rank constraints on the data from which one can estimate the number of groups after embedding the data into a higher-dimensional linear space;
- Estimating from the data the polynomials representing each group: this question is trivially answered by showing that the coefficients of the polynomials representing the data lie in the null space of the embedded data matrix;
- Factoring such polynomials to obtain the model for each group: this question is answered with a novel polynomial factorization technique based on computing roots of univariate polynomials, plus a combination of linear algebra and multivariate polynomial differentiation and division. The solution can be obtained in closed form if and only if the number of groups is less than or equal to four.

To achieve the above goals, GPCA models the collection of subspaces as an algebraic set represented by a collection of homogeneous polynomials in several variables. Then the set of vectors normal to each subspace is obtained by evaluating the derivatives of these polynomials at any point lying on the subspace. Since all the polynomials can be retrieved linearly from the data, this reduces subspace clustering to the problem of classifying one point per subspace. When these points are given (e.g., in semi-supervised learning), this means that in order to learn the mixture of subspaces, it is sufficient to have one positive example per class. When the data is unlabeled (e.g., in unsupervised learning), a simple algorithm is needed to choose points in the data set that minimize the distance to the algebraic set, hence dealing automatically with noise in the data. A basis for the complement of each subspace is then obtained by applying standard PCA to the set of derivatives at these points.

GPCA is applicable to segmentation problems in which the data have a piecewise constant, a piecewise linear, or piecewise bilinear structure, and is well motivated by various problems in computer vision, robotics, and control. Data are often piecewise constant in the segmentation of static scenes based upon different cues such as intensity, texture, and motion. Piecewise linear data occur in computer vision problems such as detection of vanishing points, clustering of faces under varying illumination, and segmentation of dynamic scenes with linearly moving objects. This also occurs in control problems such as the identification of linear hybrid systems. Piecewise bilinear data occur in the multibody structure inherent in the problem of motion in computer vision, that is, the problem of segmenting dynamic scenes with multiple rigidly moving objects. Experimental results indicate that GPCA is efficient on low-dimensional data.

3.3.1.4 Incremental PCA

A well-known computational approach to PCA involves solving an eigensystem problem, that is, computing the eigenvectors and eigenvalues of the sample covariance matrix, using a numerical method such as the power method or the QR method (Ye and Li 2005). This approach requires that all training images be available before the principal components can be estimated, a methodology known as batch training. Batch training, however, fails to satisfy a growing new trend in computer vision research, in which all visual filters are incrementally derived from very long online real-time video streams, motivated by the example of animal vision systems. Online development of visual filters requires that the system perform while new sensory signals flow in. Further, when the dimension of the image is high, both the computation and storage complexity grow dramatically. Thus, using an incremental method requires computing the principal components of observations that are arriving sequentially, such that the principal components estimation is updated by each arriving observation vector. The estimation of a covariance matrix as an intermediate result is not allowed. There is evidence that biological neural networks use an incremental method to perform various learning tasks, for example, Hebbian learning (Song et al. 2000).

Several IPCA techniques have been proposed to compute principal components without the covariance matrix (Oja 1983) (Oja and Karhuen 1985). However, these have encountered convergence problems in the face of high-dimensional image vectors. To overcome these convergence problems, a covariance-free IPCA (CCIPCA) algorithm (Weng et al. 2003) is proposed, which is motivated by a well-known statistical concept called efficient estimation. In CCIPCA, an amnesic average technique is used to dynamically determine the retaining rate of the old and new data, instead of a fixed learning rate. In the following, we present a brief summary of the algorithm.

- Compute the first k dominant eigenvectors, $v_1(n), v_2(n), ..., v_k(n)$, directly from samples $u(n), n = 1, 2, ...$.
- For $n = 1, 2, ...$, do the followings steps,
  - $u_1(n) = u(n)$.
  - For $i = 1, 2, ..., min\{k, n\}$, do
    - If $i = n$, initialize the *ith* eigenvector as $v_i(n) = u_i(n)$
    - Otherwise
      $v_i(n) = \frac{n-1-l}{n} v_i(n-1) + \frac{1+l}{n} u_i(n) u_i^T(n) \frac{v_i(n-1)}{||v_i(n-1)||}$
      $u_{i+1}(n) = u_i(n) - u_i^T(n) \frac{v_i(n)}{||v_i(n)||} \frac{v_i(n)}{||v_i(n)||}$

A mathematical proof of the convergence of CCIPCA can be found in (Weng et al. 2003).

3.3.2 Nonnegative Matrix Factorization

Matrix factorization is an efficient tool for large-scale data processing and analysis. The nonnegative matrix factorization (NMF) method, which decomposes the nonnegative matrix into two nonnegative factor matrices, provides a new way for matrix factorization. In recent years, NMF becomes an important technique in intelligent information processing and pattern recognition.

Lee and Seung first proposed NMF in *Nature* in 1999 (Lee and Seung 1999). The method decomposes the nonnegative matrix into two nonnegative factor matrices. From a computational viewpoint, negative values are admissible; however, they lose their physical meaning in practice. NMF has attracted increasing attention because of its many advantages. Among these are a simple, yet efficient decomposition algorithm, the ability to provide definite physical meaning without negative values, and lower storage requirements. From the viewpoint of signal decomposition, NMF is a linear signal decomposition method that provides base depend upon data.

Definition

NMF is, in fact, a kind of multivariate data analysis. Let matrix $X_{n\times m}$ be a data matrix with m samples in an n-dimensional space and let all elements of the matrix be nonnegative ($X > 0$).The matrix can be linearly decomposed into

$$X_{n\times m} \approx B_{n\times r}C_{r\times n} \tag{3.31}$$

where $B_{n\times r}$ is called the basis matrix and $C_{r\times n}$ is called the coefficient matrix. When using r smaller than n and when the coefficients are considered to be new features, this approach leads to dimensionality reduction and to lower storage and computational resources. From the standpoint of the encoding, one can consider the basis matrix to represent a code book and the coefficient matrix to represent the corresponding encoding coefficients. See reference (Lee and Seung 1999) for a further discussion of PCA, vector quantization, ICA, and NMF in terms of matrix factorization.

NMF Algorithms

In order to implement NMF, it is necessary to define a loss function to quantify the approximation error, and then to solve it with nonnegative constraints. Here we discuss some possible loss functions and iterative algorithms for NMF. The earliest NMF approaches adopted a traditional gradient descent method with additive updates (Paatero and Tapper 1994). The methods in Lee and Seung (1999, 2001), which employ multiplicative updates, are more suitable to property of nonnegative data. In the case of additive updates, nonnegativity can only be maintained through forced steps that set negative values to zero, whereas in the case of multiplicative updates, nonnegativity is preserved well by simply enforcing the nonnegative initialization of the data.

3.3.2.1 The Probabilistic Model of NMF

In the context of the linear mixture model with additive noise, we discuss the loss functions of NMF and the relationship between multiplicative updates and additive updates. We consider matrix factorization in the context of the following linear mixture model with additive noise.

$$X_{n\times m} = B_{n\times r}C_{r\times m} + E_{n\times m} \tag{3.32}$$

where $E_{n\times m}$ is the noise matrix. Furthermore, Eq. (3.32) can be represented as

$$X_{ij} = (BC)_{ij} + E_{ij} \tag{3.33}$$

In order to derive the factor matrices B and C, we can consider the following maximum likelihood resolution:

$$\begin{aligned} \{B,C\} &= argmax_{B,C}\, p(X|B,C) \\ &= argmin_{B,C}[-log p(X|B,C)] \end{aligned} \tag{3.34}$$

Supposing that the noise obeys different probability distributions, we can obtain different loss functions. For example, let the noise be Gaussian, that is

$$p(X_{ij}|B,C) = \exp\left\{-\frac{1}{2}[\frac{X_{ij}-(BC)_{ij}}{\sigma_{ij}}]^2\right\}/(\sqrt{(2\pi)}\,\sigma_{ij}) \tag{3.35}$$

where σ_{ij} is the weight for each observation. Let

$$p(X|B,C) = \prod_{ij} p(X_{ij}|B,C) \tag{3.36}$$

Then the maximum likelihood resolution is equivalent to the minimization of the following loss function.

$$L(B,C) = \frac{1}{2}\sum_{ij}[X_{ij}-(BC)_{ij}]^2/\sigma_{ij}^2 + \sum_{ij} log(\sqrt{(2\pi)})\sigma_{ij}) \tag{3.37}$$

Set $\sigma_{ij} = 1$ and omit factor $1/2$ and constant term $log(\sqrt{(2\pi)})\sigma_{ij}$, and we can obtain $L_{ED}(B,C) = \sum_{ij}[X_{ij}-(BC)_{ij}]^2$.

By traditional gradient methods, differentiating $L_{ED}(B,C)$ yields the following rule:

$$\begin{aligned}\frac{\partial L_{ED}}{\partial B_{ik}} &= -2[(XC^T)_{ik} - (BCC^T)_{ik}] \\ \frac{\partial L_{ED}}{\partial C_{kj}} &= -2[(B^TX)_{kj} - (B^TBC)_{kj}]\end{aligned} \tag{3.38}$$

As a result, we obtain the following additive update rules:

$$\begin{aligned}B_{ik} &\leftarrow B_{ik} + \phi_{ik}[(XC^T)_{ik} - (BCC^T)_{ik}] \\ C_{kj} &\leftarrow C_{kj} + \varphi_{kj}[(B^TX)_{kj} - (B^TBC)_{kj}]\end{aligned} \tag{3.39}$$

Setting $\phi_{ik} = \frac{B_{ik}}{(BCC^T)_{ik}}, \varphi_{kj} = \frac{C_{kj}}{(B^TBC)_{kj}}$, the additive updates above become multiplicative updates $B_{ik} \leftarrow B_{ik}\frac{(XC^T)_{ik}}{(BCC^T)_{ik}}$, $C_{kj} \leftarrow C_{kj}\frac{(B^TX)_{kj}}{(B^TBC)_{kj}}$.

If one considers the noise as having a Poisson distribution, then $p(X_{ij}|B,C) = \frac{BC_{ij}^{X_{ij}}}{X_{ij}!}exp[-(BC)_{ij}]$. Similarly, maximization of likelihood is equivalent to minimization of the following loss function.

$$L(B,C) = \sum_{ij}[X_{ij}log(BC)_{ij} - (BC)_{ij} - log(X_{ij}!)] \tag{3.40}$$

In fact, minimization of Eq. (3.40) is equivalent to maximizing $L_{KL}(BC) = \sum_{ij}(X_{ij}log\frac{X_{ij}}{(BC)_{ij}} - X_{ij} + (BC)_{ij})$. Using gradient descent, we can obtain the following additive updates:

$$B_{ik} \leftarrow B_{ik} + \phi_{ik}[\sum_j C_{kj}\frac{X_{ij}}{(BC)_{ij}} - \sum_j C_{kj}]$$
$$C_{kj} \leftarrow C_{kj} + \varphi_{kj}[\sum_i B_{ik}\frac{X_{ij}}{(BC)_{ij}} - \sum_i B_{ik}] \tag{3.41}$$

If $\phi_{ik} = \frac{B_{ik}}{\sum_j C_{kj}}, \varphi_{kj} = \frac{C_{kj}}{\sum_i B_{ik}}$, then the update rule in Eq. (3.41) can be rewritten as $B_{ik} \leftarrow B_{ik}\frac{\sum_j C_{kj}X_{ij}/(BC)_{ij}}{\sum_j C_{kj}}$, $C_{kj} \leftarrow C_{kj}\frac{\sum_i B_{ik}X_{ij}/(BC)_{ij}}{\sum_i B_{ik}}$.

From the above discussion, we can see that different noise models lead to different loss functions. If we consider the case in which the noise is Laplacian and derive a new loss function, the likelihood becomes

$$p(X_{ij}|B,C) = exp\{-|\frac{X_{ij} - (BC)_{ij}}{\sigma_{ij}}|\}/2\sigma_{ij} \tag{3.42}$$

and the loss function is $L_1(B,C) = \sum_{ij}|\frac{X_{ij}-(BC)_{ij}}{\sigma_{ij}}|$. Linear programming method can also be used to solve Eq. (3.66). However, since the loss function is not continuously differentiable, it is usually approximated via

$$L_{app}(B,C) = \sum_{ij} log\{cosh[\gamma(\frac{X_{ij} - (BC)_{ij}}{\sigma_{ij}})]\} \tag{3.43}$$

where $\gamma \gg 1$.

In summary, we can formulate NMF as the following constrained optimization problem.

$$min f(B,C)$$
$$s.t. B \geq 0, C \geq 0 \tag{3.44}$$

where $f(B,C)$ is the loss function. During the iterative update procedure, it is necessary to normalize the basis matrix. For example, in (Lee and Seung 1999), the basis vector is normalized according to $1 - norm$, that is, $\sum_i B_{ik} = 1, \forall k$ and the corresponding multiplicative rules are

$$B_{ik} \leftarrow B_{ik}\sum_j C_{kj}X_{ij}/(BC)_{ij} \tag{3.45}$$

$$B_{ik} \leftarrow \frac{B_{ik}}{\sum_l(B_{lk})} \tag{3.46}$$

$$C_{kj} = C_{kj}\sum_i B_{ik}X_{ij}/(BC)_{ij} \tag{3.47}$$

Additionally, the basis vectors can be normalized according to $p-norm$, as investigated in (Liu et al. 2006).

3.3.2.2 Local NMF

In the above discussion, NMF only requires that the factor matrices be nonnegative. However, the NMF algorithm can be improved by adding more constraints according to real applications. Inspired by this notion, Li et al. proposed a local NMF algorithm (Feng et al. 2002), in which the following three constraints are observed: (1) the components of one basis vector cannot be decomposed further, and the number of the basis vectors which represent the original data should be as small as possible; (2) different basis vectors are approximately orthogonal; and (3) components containing important information should be preserved. Actually, the Li NMF approach transforms modifies the original NMF problem into the following constrained optimization problem.

$$
\begin{aligned}
minL_{LNMF}(B,C) = \Sigma_{ij}(X_{ij}log\frac{X_{ij}}{(BC)_{ij}} - X_{ij} + (BC)_{ij}) + \alpha\Sigma_{ij}U_{ij} - \beta\Sigma_i V_{ii} \\
s.t. B \geq 0; C \geq 0; \Sigma_i B_{ij} = 1, \forall k
\end{aligned}
\tag{3.48}
$$

where $U = B^T B, V = CC^T$. The multiplicative updates are

$$
B_{ik} \leftarrow B_{ik}\frac{\Sigma_j C_{kj}X_{ij}/(BC)_{ij}}{\Sigma_j C_{kj}} \tag{3.49}
$$

$$
B_{ik} \leftarrow \frac{B_{ik}}{\Sigma_l B_{lk}} \tag{3.50}
$$

$$
C_{kj} \leftarrow \sqrt{C_{kj}\sum_i B_{ik}X_{ij}/(BC)_{ij}} \tag{3.51}
$$

The use of the regulation parameters α and β is replaced in the updates by approximation methods. Thus, this method really requires further investigation to demonstrate its soundness.

3.3.2.3 Nonnegative Sparse Coding

Following principles of sparse coding (Hoyer 2004), Hoyer has proposed a nonnegative sparse coding approach (NNSC), which requires a certain sparsity in the coefficients, and is equivalent to resolving of the following constrained optimization problem.

$$
\begin{aligned}
minL_{NNSC}(B,C) = \Sigma_{ij}[X_{ij} - (BC)_{ij}]^2 + \lambda\Sigma_{ij}C_{kj} \\
s.t. B \geq 0; C \geq 0; \Sigma_i B_{ik}^2 = 1, \forall k
\end{aligned}
\tag{3.52}
$$

The iterative algorithm is summarized as

$$B \leftarrow B - \eta(BC - X)C^T$$

$$B_{ik} \leftarrow 0, if B_{ik} < 0 \tag{3.53}$$

$$B_{ik} \leftarrow \frac{B_{ik}}{\sqrt{(\sum_i B_{ik}^2)}} \tag{3.54}$$

$$C \leftarrow C. * (B^T X)./(B^T BC + \lambda) \tag{3.55}$$

where η is the learning rate. This algorithm has some disadvantages: the update for learning the basis is additive and it does not preserve nonnegativity, so negative values must be set to zero. Hoyer (2004) used NNSC to model receptive fields in vision research.

To overcome the limitations of the original NNSC, we have proposed a sparse NMF (Liu and Zheng, 2004)

$$minL_{NNSC}(B,C) = \sum_{ij}(X_{ij} log \frac{X_{ij}}{(BC)_{ij}} - X_{ij} + (BC)_{ij}) + \beta \sum_{ij} C_{kj}$$

$$s.t. B \geq 0; C \geq 0; \sum_i B_{ik}^2 = 1, \forall k \tag{3.56}$$

where the iterative updates are made as follows:

$$B_{ik} \leftarrow B_{ik} \sum_j C_{kj} X_{ij}/(BC)_{ij}$$

$$B_{ik} \leftarrow \frac{B_{ik}}{\sum_l B_{lk}} \tag{3.57}$$

$$C_{kj} \leftarrow \frac{C_{kj} \sum_i B_{ij} X_{ij}/(BC)_{ij}}{1 + \beta} \tag{3.58}$$

In contrast to NNSC, the sparse NMF adopts multiplicative rules and can consistently maintain nonnegativity. Readers can refer to Hoyer (2004) for more details about sparse constrained of NMF.

3.3.2.4 Other NMF Algorithms

NMF can be viewed as a kind of optimization problem with nonnegative constraints. Based on this perspective, some new or modified algorithms are proposed in addition to the algorithms mentioned above: weighted NMF (Guillamet et al. 2003), multilinear engine (Lin 2007), positive tensor factorization (Welling and Weber 2001), Wang's fisher NMF (Wang et al. 2005), and Ahn's multilayer networks of NMF (Cichocki and Zdunek 2007).

3.3.3 Independent Component Analysis

Independent component analysis (ICA) was originally developed to deal with problems that are closely related to the *cocktail-party problem*: Imagine that you are in a room where two people are speaking simultaneously. You have two microphones, which you hold in different locations. The microphones give you two recorded time series signals. Each of these recorded signals is a weighted sum of the speech signals emitted by the two speakers. It would be very useful if you could now estimate the two original speech signals, using only the recorded signals. This is called the cocktail-party problem.

Definition

To rigorously define ICA, we can use a statistical "latent variables" model. Assume that we observe n linear mixtures $x_1, ..., x_n$ of independent components

$$x_j = a_{j1}s_1 + a_{j2}s_2 + ... + a_{jn}s_n, for \ \forall j \tag{3.59}$$

We assume that each mixture x_j as well as each independent component s_k is a random variable. The observed values x_j are then a sample of this random variable. Without loss of generality, we can assume that both the mixture variables and the independent components have zero means: If this is not true, then the observable variables x_i can always be centered by subtracting the sample mean, which makes the model zero-mean.

Let $\mathbf{x}$ denote the random vector whose elements are the mixtures $x_1, ..., x_n$, and likewise by $\mathbf{s}$ the random vector with elements $s_1, ..., s_n$. Let $\mathbf{A}$ denote the matrix with elements a_{ij}. Assume all vectors are column vectors; thus $\mathbf{x}^T$, or the transpose of $\mathbf{x}$, is a row vector. Using this vector-matrix notation, the above mixture model is written as

$$\mathbf{x} = \mathbf{A}\mathbf{s} \tag{3.60}$$

The statistical model in Eq. (3.60) is called independent component analysis, or the ICA model. The ICA model is a generative model, which means that it describes how the observed data are generated by a process of mixing the components s_i. The independent components are latent variables, meaning that they cannot be directly observed. Also the mixing matrix is assumed to be unknown. All we observe is the random vector $\mathbf{x}$, and we must estimate both $\mathbf{A}$ and $\mathbf{s}$ using it. This must be done on assumptions that are as general as possible.

The starting point for ICA is the very simple assumption that the components s_i are statistically independent. It is also assumed that the independent components must have non-Gaussian distributions. However, in the basic model we do not assume these distributions are known. For simplicity, we also assume that the unknown mixing matrix is square, but this assumption can sometimes be relaxed. After estimating the matrix $\mathbf{A}$, we can compute its inverse, say $\mathbf{W}$, and obtain the independent component simply by:

$$\mathbf{s} = \mathbf{W}\mathbf{x} \tag{3.61}$$

It should be noted that there exist two ambiguities in the ICA model: (1) we cannot determine the variance of the independent components, and (2) we cannot determine the order of the independent components. The main reason is that since both $\mathbf{s}$ and $\mathbf{A}$ are unknown, any scalar multiplier in one of the sources s_i can always be canceled by dividing the corresponding column $\mathbf{a}_i$ of $\mathbf{A}$ by the same scalar. Secondly, we can freely change the order of the terms in the independent components and call any of them the first one. Since a permutation matrix $\mathbf{P}$ and its inverse can be substituted in the model to give $\mathbf{x} = \mathbf{AP}^{-1}\mathbf{Ps}$, the elements of $\mathbf{Ps}$ are the original independent variables s_j, but in another order.

Principles of ICA estimation

The fundamental restriction in ICA is that the independent components must be non-Gaussian for ICA to be possible. More rigorously, one can prove that the distribution of any orthogonal transformation of the Gaussian has exactly the Gaussian distribution. Thus, in the case of Gaussian variables, we can only estimate the ICA model up to an orthogonal transformation. In other words, the matrix $\mathbf{A}$ is not identifiable for Gaussian-independent components.

To use non-Gaussianity in ICA estimation, we must have a quantitative measure of non-Gaussianity of a random variable. There are many optimization criteria:

- Minimize the high order moments, for example, Kurtosis.
  Kurtosis is a classical measure of non-Gaussianity. For a random variable y, its kurtosis is defined by

$$kurt(y) = E\{y^4\} - 3(E\{y^2\}) \tag{3.62}$$

  Kurtosis can be both positive and negative. Random variables that have negative kurtosis are called sub-Gaussian, and those with positive kurtosis are called supergaussian. Typically non-Gaussianity is measured by the absolute value of kurtosis.
- Maximize the negentropy.
  A fundamental conclusion in information theory is that *a Gaussian variable has the largest entropy among all random variables of equal variance*. To obtain a measure of nongaussianity that is zero for a gaussian variable and always nonnegative, the negentropy J is defined as follows.

$$J(\mathbf{y}) = H(\mathbf{y}_{gaussian}) - H(\mathbf{y}) \tag{3.63}$$

  where $\mathbf{y}_{gaussian}$ is a Gaussian random variable of the same covariance matrix as $\mathbf{y}$. Actually, negentropy is based on the information-theoretic quantity of (differential) entropy, and it has the additional interesting property that it is invariant for invertible linear transformations.
- Minimization of mutual information
  The mutual information I between m random variables, $y_i, i = 1, ..., m$ is defined as follows

$$I(y_1, y_2, ..., y_m) = \sum_{i=1}^{m} H(y_i) - H(\mathbf{y}) \tag{3.64}$$

Mutual information is a natural measure of the dependence between random variables. In fact, it is equivalent to the well-known Kullback-Leibler divergence between the joint density $f(\mathbf{y})$ and the product of its marginal densities. It is always nonnegative and zero if and only if the variables are statistically independent. We define the ICA of a random vector $\mathbf{x}$ as an invertible transformation $\mathbf{s} = \mathbf{W}\mathbf{x}$, thus, we have

$$I(s_1, ..., s_n) = \sum_i H(s_i) - H(\mathbf{x}) - log|det\mathbf{W}| \tag{3.65}$$

where the matrix $\mathbf{W}$ is determined so that the mutual information of the transformed components s_i is minimized.

- Maximum likelihood estimation.
  It is possible to formulate directly the likelihood in the noise-free ICA model, and then estimate the model by a maximum likelihood method. Denoting by $\mathbf{W} = (\mathbf{w}_1, ..., \mathbf{w}_n)^T$ the matrix $\mathbf{A}^{-1}$, the log-likelihood takes the form:

$$L = \sum_{t=1}^{T}\sum_{i=1}^{n} logf_i(\mathbf{w}_i^T\mathbf{x}(t)) + Tlog|det\mathbf{W}| \tag{3.66}$$

  where the f_i are the density functions of the s_i, and the $\mathbf{x}(t), t = 1, ..., T$ are the realizations of $\mathbf{x}$. The term $Tlog|det\mathbf{W}|$ in the likelihood comes from the classical rule for transforming random variables and their density: in general, for any random vector $\mathbf{x}$ with density p_x and for any matrix $\mathbf{W}$, the density of $\mathbf{y} = \mathbf{W}\mathbf{x}$ is given by $p_x(\mathbf{W}\mathbf{x})|det\mathbf{W}|$.

Preprocessing

Before applying an ICA algorithm on the data, it is usually very useful to do some preprocessing. Here we discuss some preprocessing techniques that make the problem of ICA estimation simpler and better conditioned.

- Centering: the most basic and necessary preprocessing is to center $\mathbf{x}$, i.e., subtract its mean vector $\mathbf{m} = E\{\mathbf{x}\}$ so as to make $\mathbf{x}$ a zero-mean variable. This implies that $\mathbf{s}$ is zero-mean as well. After estimating the mixing matrix $\mathbf{A}$ with centered data, we can complete the estimation by adding the mean vector of $\mathbf{s}$ back into the centered estimates of $\mathbf{s}$. The mean vector of $\mathbf{s}$ is given by $\mathbf{A}^{-1}\mathbf{m}$.
- Whitening: before the application of the ICA algorithm, we transform the observed vector $\mathbf{x}$ linearly so that we obtain a new vector $\tilde{\mathbf{x}}$ which is white, that is, its components are uncorrelated and their variances equal unity. One popular method for whitening is to use the eigenvalue decomposition (EVD) of the covariance matrix $E\{\mathbf{x}\mathbf{x}^T\} = \mathbf{E}\mathbf{D}\mathbf{E}^T$, where $\mathbf{E}$ is the orthogonal matrix of eigenvectors of $E\{\mathbf{x}\mathbf{x}^T\}$ and $\mathbf{D}$ is the diagonal matrix of its eigenvalues. Whitening can now be done by $\tilde{\mathbf{x}} = \mathbf{E}\mathbf{D}^{-1/2}\mathbf{E}^T\mathbf{x}$. Whitening transforms the mixing matrix into a new matrix $\tilde{\mathbf{A}}$. The utility of whitening resides in the fact the $\tilde{\mathbf{A}}$ is orthogonal, and this reduces the number of parameters to be estimated. An orthogonal matrix contains $n(n-1)/2$ degrees of freedom.

- Other preprocessing: The success of ICA for a given data set may depend crucially on performing some application-dependent preprocessing steps. For example, if the data consists of time-signals, some band-pass filtering may be very useful.

3.3.3.1 ICA Algorithms

In the preceding sections, we introduced different measures of non-Gaussianity, that is, objective functions for ICA estimation. In practice, one also needs an algorithm to maximize the objective function. Here, we introduce the FastICA, an efficient method of maximization suited for this task. It is here assumed that the data is preprocessed by centering and whitening.

FastICA is based on a fixed-point iteration scheme for finding a maximum of the non-Gaussianity of $\mathbf{w}^T\mathbf{x}$ as measured in the negentropy $J(y)$. $J(y)$ is approximated as $J(y) \propto [E\{G_(y)\} - E\{G_(v)\}]^2$, where G is one nonquadratic function, v is a Gaussian variable of zero mean and unit variance. The variable y is assumed to be of zero mean and unit variance. In particular, choosing a G that does not grow too fast, one obtains a more robust estimator. The following choices of G have proved very useful:

$$G_1(u) = \frac{1}{a_1} logcosha_1u \tag{3.67}$$

$$G_2(u) = -exp(-u^2/2) \tag{3.68}$$

where $1 \leq a1 \leq 2$ is some suitable constant.

Let g denote the derivative of the nonquadratic function G; for example, the derivatives of the functions in Eqs. (3.67) and (3.68) are $g_1(u) = tanh(a_1u$ and $g_2(u) = uexp(-u^2/2)$. Thus, the basic form of the FastICA algorithm is as follows:

1. Choose an initial weight vector $\mathbf{w}$.
2. Let $\mathbf{w}^+ = E\{\mathbf{x}g(\mathbf{w}^T\mathbf{x})\} - E\{g'(\mathbf{w}^T\mathbf{x})\}$.
3. Let $\mathbf{w} = \mathbf{w}^+/||\mathbf{w}^+||$.
4. If not converged, go back to 2.

The above algorithm estimates just one of the independent components. To estimate several independent components, we need to run the FastICA algorithm using several units with weight vectors $\mathbf{w}_1, \mathbf{w}_2, ..., \mathbf{w}_n$. To prevent different vectors from converging to the same maxima we must decorrelate the outputs $\mathbf{w}_1^T\mathbf{x}, \mathbf{w}_2^T\mathbf{x}, ..., \mathbf{w}_n^T\mathbf{x}$ after every iteration. A simple method to achieve this is as follows:

1. Let $\mathbf{W} = \mathbf{W}/\sqrt{(}||\mathbf{W}\mathbf{W}^T||)$.
2. Repeat doing $\mathbf{W} = \frac{3}{2}\mathbf{W} - \frac{1}{2}\mathbf{W}\mathbf{W}^T\mathbf{W}$, until convergence.

3.4 Discriminative Models

Discriminative models are a class of models used in machine learning to model the dependence of a unobservable variable x on an observed variable y. Within a statistical framework, this is done by modeling the conditional probability distribution $P(y|x)$, which can be used for predicting y from x. Discriminative models differ from generative models in that they do not allow one to generate samples from the joint distribution of x and y.

The purpose of discriminative analysis is to classify objects into one of two or more groups based on a set of features that describe the objects. In general, we assign an object to one of the number of predetermined groups based on observations made on the object. In discriminative analysis, the dependent variable x is the group and the independent variables y are the object features that might describe the group. Furthermore, if we can assume that the groups are linearly separable, we can use a linear discriminant model (LAD) to distinguish between the groups. Linear separability suggests that the groups can be separated by a linear combination of features that describes the object.

3.4.1 Linear Discriminative Analysis

Linear discriminative analysis (LDA) and the related Fisher's linear discriminant are methods used in statistics and machine learning to find the linear combination of features which best separates two or more classes of objects or events. The resulting combination may be used as a linear classifier, or, more commonly, for dimensionality reduction for later classification.

3.4.1.1 Classical LDA

Definition

Given a data matrix $X \in \mathbb{R}^{n\times N}$, the LDA seeks to find a linear transformation $G \in \mathbb{R}^{n\times l}$ that maps each column $\mathbf{x}_i$ of X, for $1 \leq i \leq N$, in an *n-dimensional* space to a vector $\mathbf{y}_i$ in an *l-dimensional* space as follows: $y_i = G^T\mathbf{x}_i \in \mathbb{R}^l (l < n)$. Assume that the original data in X is partitioned into k classes $X = [X_1, ..., X_k]$. Classical LDA aims to find the optimal transformation G such that the structure of the original high-dimensional space is preserved in the low-dimensional space.

From the definition, LDA is closely related to PCA in that both look for linear combinations of variables that best explain the data. LDA explicitly attempts to model the difference between the classes of data. PCA on the other hand does not take into account any difference in classes and as such does not include label information on the data. LDA works when the measurements made on each observation are continuous quantities and utilizes the label information in finding informative projections.

Classical LDA considers maximizing the following objective:

$$J(G) = \frac{G^T S_B G}{G^T S_W G} \tag{3.69}$$

where S_B is the "between classes scatter matrix" and S_W is the "within classes scatter matrix." Note that due to the fact that scatter matrices are proportional to covariance matrices we could have defined J using covariance matrices—the proportionality constant would have no effect on the solution. The definitions of the scatter matrices are:

$$S_B = \sum_c N_c(\mu_c - \bar{\mathbf{x}})(\mu_c - \bar{\mathbf{x}})^T \tag{3.70}$$

$$S_W = \sum_c \sum_{i \in c} (\mathbf{x}_i - \mu_c)(\mathbf{x}_i - \mu_c)^T \tag{3.71}$$

where,

$$\mu_c = \frac{1}{N_c} \sum_{i \in c} \mathbf{x}_i \tag{3.72}$$

$$\bar{\mathbf{x}} = \frac{1}{N} \sum_i \mathbf{x}_i = \frac{1}{N} N_c \mu_c \tag{3.73}$$

and N_c is the number of samples in class $c, c = 1, \ldots, k$. Since the total scatter $S_T = \sum_i (\mathbf{x}_i - \bar{\mathbf{x}})(\mathbf{x}_i - \bar{\mathbf{x}})^T$ is given by $S_T = S_W + S_B$, the objective can be rewritten as

$$J(G) = \frac{G^T S_T G}{G^T S_W G} - 1 \tag{3.74}$$

and hence can be interpreted as maximizing the total scatter of the data while minimizing the within scatter of the classes.

Since J is invariant with respect to rescaling of the matrix $G \rightarrow \alpha G$, the problem of maximizing J can be transformed into the following constrained optimization problem,

$$\begin{aligned} &min_G - \tfrac{1}{2} G^T S_B G \\ &s.t. G^T S_W G = 1 \end{aligned}$$

It also corresponds to the Lagrangian

$$L_P = -\frac{1}{2} G^T S_B G + \frac{1}{2} \lambda (1 - G^T S_W G) \tag{3.75}$$

The KKT conditions tell us that the following equation needs to hold at the solution.

$$S_B G = \lambda S_W G \Rightarrow S_W^{-1} S_B G = \lambda G \tag{3.76}$$

The solution can be obtained by applying an eigen-decomposition to the matrix $S_W^{-1} S_B$, if S_W is nonsingular, or, $S_B^{-1} S_W$, if S_B is nonsingular. There are at most $k-1$ eigenvectors corresponding to nonzero eigenvalues since the rank of the matrix S_B is bounded above by $k-1$. Therefore, the number of retained dimensions in classical LDA is at most $k-1$.

3.4.1.2 LDA via QR Decomposition

Traditional LDA methods maximize the between-class distance and minimize the within-class distance simultaneously by applying SVD or GSVD. But they are not only computationally expensive but also not very scalable. An intrinsic limitation of classical LDA is that its objective function requires that one of the scatter matrices be nonsingular. Ye and Li proposes an LDA method via QR decomposition in (Ye and Li 2005). By applying QR decomposition, the LDA method proposed first maximizes the between-class distance, and then minimizes the within-class distance. It is this two-step procedure that leads to scalability and low computational cost.

The first stage of LDA/QR aims to compute the optimal transformation matrix G that solves the following optimization problem:

$$G = argmax_{G^T G = I_t} trace(G^T S_B G) \tag{3.77}$$

Note that this optimization problem only addresses the issue of maximizing between-class distance.

To solve this problem, we define the precursors H_b and H_w of the between-class and within-class scatter matrices as follows.

$$H_b = \frac{1}{\sqrt{N}}[\sqrt{(}N_1)(\mu_1 - \bar{\mathbf{x}}), ..., \sqrt{(}N_k)(\mu_k - \bar{\mathbf{x}})] \tag{3.78}$$

$$H_b = \frac{1}{\sqrt{N}}[X_1 - \mu_1 \cdot e_1^T, ..., X_k - \mu_1 \cdot e_k^T] \tag{3.79}$$

The solution to Eq. (3.77) can be obtained through QR decomposition with column pivoting on H_b. More specifically, let $H_b = QR\Pi$ be the QR decomposition of H_b with column pivoting, where $Q \in \mathbb{R}^{n \times t}$ has orthonormal columns, $R \in \mathbb{R}^{t \times k}$ is upper triangular, $\Pi \in \mathbb{R}^{k \times k}$ is a permutation matrix, and $t = rank(H_b)$; then, $G = QW$, for any orthogonal matrix $W \in \mathbb{R}^{t \times t}$, solving the optimization problem.

The second stage of LDA/QR refines the first stage by addressing the issue of within-class distance. It incorporates within-class scatter information by applying a relaxation scheme to W. Since

$$G^T S_B G = W^T (Q^T S_B Q) W \tag{3.80}$$

$$G^T S_W G = W^T (Q^T S_W Q) W \tag{3.81}$$

The original optimization problem of finding the optimal G is equivalent to finding the optimal W, with $\tilde{S}_B = Q^T S_B Q$ and $\tilde{S}_W = Q^T S_W Q$ as the "reduced" between-class and within-class scatter matrices, respectively.

The optimal W can be computed by solving the following optimization problem:

$$W = argmin_W trace((W^T \tilde{S}_B W)^{-1}(W^T \tilde{S}_W W)) \tag{3.82}$$

Note that $\tilde{S}_B$ is nonsingular and has much smaller size than the original scatter matrix S_B. Thus, we can compute the optimal W by applying the eigen-decomposition to $\tilde{S}_B^{-1} S_W$.

3.4.2 Oriented Component Analysis

If a second-order statistical descriptor of the signal of interest is provided, Σ_x, the oriented component analysis (OCA) maximizes the signal-to-signal ratio between two random vectors, **x** and **n**.

$$max_{\mathbf{B}} \frac{\mathbf{B}^T \Sigma_x \mathbf{B}}{\mathbf{B}^T \Sigma_n \mathbf{B}} \tag{3.83}$$

where $\Sigma_\mathbf{x}$ and $\Sigma_\mathbf{n}$ are covariance or correlation matrices. The optimal **B** will preserve the directions of maximum variation of **x**, which do not have high projections in the **n** directions. A closed form solution is given by the following generalized eigenvalue problem.

$$\Sigma_x \mathbf{B} = \Sigma_n \mathbf{B} \Lambda \tag{3.84}$$

This generalized eigenvalue problem is equivalent to a joint diagonalization, that is, finding a common basis **B** that simultaneously diagonalizes both matrices Σ_x and Σ_n (i.e., $\mathbf{B}^T \Sigma \mathbf{B} = \mathbf{I}$ and $\mathbf{B}^T \Sigma_x \mathbf{B} = \Lambda$).

To understand the usage of OCA in dimension reduction, we apply OCA to the problem of face recognition as an example. Let $\mathbf{D} \in \mathbb{R}^{d \times n}$ be a data matrix, such that each column $\mathbf{d}_i$ is a vectorized image. Let $\mathbf{G} \in \mathbb{R}^{n \times c}$ be a dummy indicator matrix such that $\sum_j g_{ij} = 1$, $g_{ij} \in 0, 1$, and $g_{ij} = 1$, meaning that $\mathbf{d}_i$ belongs to class j. The symbol c denotes the number of classes and n denotes the number of images in the gallery set. For each class i, OCA will design a basis $\mathbf{B}_i$, which maximizes Eq. (3.84), where $\Sigma_x^i = \mathbf{D}\mathbf{g}_i\mathbf{g}_i^T\mathbf{D}^T$ contains the autocorrelation matrix of the sample in class i and $\Sigma_i^n = \frac{1}{n-1}\mathbf{D}(\mathbf{G}\mathbf{G}^T - \mathbf{g}_i\mathbf{g}_i^T)\mathbf{D}^T$ the extra class variation.

3.4.3 Canonical Correlation Analysis

Canonical correlation analysis (CCA) is a way of measuring the linear relationship between two multidimensional variables (Hardoon et al. 2004). It finds two bases, one for each variable, that are optimal with respect to their correlations, and at the same time, it finds the corresponding correlations. In other words, it finds the two bases in which the correlation matrix between the variables is diagonal and the correlations on the diagonal are maximized. The dimensionality of these new bases is equal to or less than the smallest dimensionality of the two variables. An important property of canonical correlations is that they are invariant with respect to affine transformations of the variables. This is the most important difference between CCA and ordinary correlation analysis, which is highly dependent upon the basis in which the variables are described.

Definition

Canonical correlation analysis can be defined as the problem of finding two sets of basis vectors, one for **x** and the other for **y**, such that the correlations between the projections of the variables onto these basis vectors are mutually maximized.

Take the case where only one pair of basis vectors is sought, namely the pair corresponding to the largest canonical correlation. Consider the linear combinations $x = \mathbf{x}^T \mathbf{w}_x$ and $y = \mathbf{y}^T \mathbf{w}_y$ of the two variables respectively. According to the definition of CCA, the function to be maximized is

$$\begin{aligned}\rho &= \frac{E[xy]}{\sqrt{E[x^2]E[y^2]}} = \frac{E[\mathbf{w}_x^T \mathbf{x}\mathbf{y}^T \mathbf{w}_y]}{\sqrt{E[\mathbf{w}_x^T \mathbf{x}\mathbf{x}^T \mathbf{w}_x]E[\mathbf{w}_y^T \mathbf{y}\mathbf{y}^T \mathbf{w}_y]}} \\ &= \frac{\mathbf{w}_\mathbf{x}^T \mathbf{C}_{xy}\mathbf{w}_y}{\sqrt{\mathbf{w}_x^T \mathbf{C}_{xx}\mathbf{w}_x\mathbf{w}_y^T \mathbf{C}_{yy}\mathbf{w}_y}}\end{aligned} \tag{3.85}$$

The maximization of ρ with respect to $\mathbf{w}_x$ and $\mathbf{w}_y$ is the maximum canonical correlation. The subsequent canonical correlations are uncorrelated for different solutions, that is, $E[x_i x_j] = 0$, $E[y_i y_j] = 0$, $E[x_i y_j] = 0$, $\forall i \neq j$. The projections onto $\mathbf{w}_x$ and $\mathbf{w}_y$, that is, x and y, are called canonical variates.

Calculation

Consider two random variables **x** and **y** with zero mean. The total covariance matrix

$$\mathbf{C} = \begin{bmatrix} \mathbf{C}_{xx} & \mathbf{C}_{xy} \\ \mathbf{C}_{yx} & \mathbf{C}_{yy} \end{bmatrix} \tag{3.86}$$

is a block matrix where $\mathbf{C}_{xx}$ and $\mathbf{C}_{yy}$ are the within-sets covariance matrices of **x** and **y** respectively and $\mathbf{C}_{xy} = \mathbf{C}_{yx}^T$ is the between-sets covariance. The canonical correlations between **x** and **y** can be found by solving the eigen-value equations

$$\begin{aligned}\mathbf{C}_{xx}^{-1}\mathbf{C}_{xy}\mathbf{C}_{yy}^{-1}\mathbf{C}_{yx}\mathbf{w}_x &= \rho^2 \mathbf{w}_x \\ \mathbf{C}_{yy}^{-1}\mathbf{C}_{yx}\mathbf{C}_{xx}^{-1}\mathbf{C}_{xy}\mathbf{w}_y &= \rho^2 \mathbf{w}_y\end{aligned} \tag{3.87}$$

where the eigenvalues ρ^2 are the squared canonical correlations and the eigenvectors $\mathbf{w}_x$ and $\mathbf{w}_y$ are the normalized canonical correlation basis vectors. The number of nonzero solutions to these equations is limited to the smallest dimensionality of **x** and **y**. Only one of the eigenvalue equations needs to be solved since the solutions are related by

$$\begin{aligned}\mathbf{C}_{xy}\mathbf{w}_y &= \rho\lambda_x \mathbf{C}_{xx}\mathbf{w}_x \\ \mathbf{C}_{yx}\mathbf{w}_x &= \rho\lambda_y \mathbf{C}_{yy}\mathbf{w}_y\end{aligned} \tag{3.88}$$

where $\lambda_x = \lambda_y^{-1} = \sqrt{\frac{\mathbf{w}_y^T \mathbf{C}_{yy}\mathbf{w}_y}{\mathbf{w}_x^T \mathbf{C}_{xx}\mathbf{w}_x}}$.

Ordinary correlation analysis is dependent upon the coordinate system in which the variables are described. This means that even if there is a very strong linear relationship between two multidimensional signals, this relationship may not be visible in an ordinary correlation analysis if one coordinate system is used, while in another coordinate system this linear relationship would have a very high correlation. CCA finds the coordinate system that is optimal for correlation analysis, and the eigenvectors of Eq. (3.4) defines this coordinate system.

3.4.4 Relevant Component Analysis

Relevant component analysis (RCA) is motivated by a frequently encountered problem, namely that there is variability in the original data representation that is not relevant to the task. Left unaccounted for, this will reduce the quality of the results. Intuitively, in a task where irrelevant variability is large, performance using the general and indiscriminating pre-determined distance measure can be poor.

RCA is an unsupervised adjustment scheme, which will modify the distance so as to enhance its discriminative capabilities on a given set of test data. For this purpose, it identifies and uses a relatively small set of data points, in which the class label is constant, but unknown. These small sets of data points are called chunklets. Specifically, assuming that the data is represented as vectors of features, RCA modifies the feature representation of the data space by a linear transformation W, such that the Euclidean distance in the transformed space is less affected by irrelevant variability. Effectively, the Euclidean distance in the transformed space is equivalent to the Mahalanobis distance in the original data space with weight matrix W^TW. The transformation W is called *the rescaling transformation.*

Similar to PCA, which compresses the description of the data along the dimensions of smallest variability, RCA compresses the description of the data along the dimensions of highest irrelevant variability. Specifically, in RCA we modify the data space by a transformation matrix W, which assigns large weights to "relevant dimensions" and small weights to "irrelevant dimensions." Thus we maintain concurrently as much relevant variability as possible and as little irrelevant variability as possible within the given data set.

The Whitening Transformation

Let $x \in \Omega$ denote the sampled data, and $|\Omega|$ denote the size of the sample. Similarly, let $|\Omega_m|$ denote the size of the sample from class m, where $\bigcup \Omega_m = \Omega$. Let the random variable $\mathbf{C}_m$ denote the distribution of the m-th class, and M denote the number of classes. For simplicity, we also assume that $\mathbf{C}_m$ is distributed normally, that is, $\mathbf{C}_m \sim N(\mu_m, \Sigma_m)$. Let S_W denote the within-class variability of the data set. Assume first that the covariance matrix of all classes is identical, that is, $\Sigma_m = \Sigma, \forall m$. In this case, the optimal rescaling transformation is the whitening transformation defined as $W = V\Lambda^{-1/2}$, where V is the orthogonal matrix of eigenvectors of S_W, and Λ is its corresponding matrix of singular values.

Irrelevant Variability

Irrelevant variability assumes that the observed data depends not only on the class label, but also on environmental conditions and sensory characteristics. Thus, for class m, the distribution of the observed measurements is

$$\mathbf{X}_{observable} = \mathbf{C}_m + \mathbf{G} \tag{3.89}$$

where $\mathbf{G}$ is a random variable that denotes the additive contribution of features due to the global environment and sensor characteristics. Furthermore, we assume that $\mathbf{G}$ is additive with a zero mean and nonisotropic covariance, and more specifically, $\mathbf{G} \sim N(0, \Sigma_G)$ and $\Sigma_G \neq \mathbf{I}$; $\mathbf{G}$ is independent of $\mathbf{C}_m, \forall m$, and has an identical effect on all classes; the variability in $\mathbf{G}$ is relatively large compared to $\mathbf{C}_m$, that is, $\Sigma_G > \Sigma_m, \forall m$.

Chunklet Approximation

Without access to labeled data, we cannot compute S_W directly. Chunklets are used to approximate S_W. First, each chunklet is shifted so that its mean (centroid) coincides with the origin. Then, the shifted chunklets are superimposed, defining a distribution of points around the origin whose covariance matrix approximates S_W.

More specifically, let H_n denote the sample of the nth chunklet where $\cup_{n=1}^{N} H_n = \Omega$. We assume that the number of chunklets N is much larger than the number of classes M. We further assume $\forall n, H_n \subseteq \mathbf{C}_m$ for some unknown label m. Let $\hat{\mu}_n$ denote the chunklet H_n, $\hat{\mu}_n = \frac{1}{|H_n|} \sum_{\mathbf{x}} \in H_n \mathbf{x}$, where $|H_n|$ is the size of the n-th chunklet. We define the chunklet scatter matrix S_{ch} as:

$$S_{ch} = \frac{1}{|\Omega|} \sum_{n=1}^{N} |H_n| Cov(H_n) = \frac{1}{|\Omega|} \sum_{n=1}^{N} \sum_{j=1}^{|H_n|} (\mathbf{x}_n^j - \hat{\mu}_n)(\mathbf{x}_n^j - \hat{\mu}_n)^T \tag{3.90}$$

Under ideal conditions, in which each chunklet is chosen randomly from the appropriate class and is large enough, it can be shown that $Cov(H_n)$ approaches $\Sigma_{m_n} + \Sigma_G$, where m_n is the class label of chunklet H_n. In this case $S_{ch} = S_W$. In reality, however, data points in the same chunklet tend to have a stochastic dependency, and therefore we cannot assume that they were independently sampled from the data with a distribution identical to the corresponding class distribution.

RCA Algorithm

The RCA algorithm is defined as follows:

1. Compute S_{ch} as in Eq. (3.90); let r denote its effective rank.
2. Compute the total covariance matrix of the original data S_T, and project the data using PCA to its r largest dimensions.
3. Project S_{ch} onto the reduced dimension space, and compute the corresponding whitening transformation W.
4. Apply W to the original data (in the reduced space).

Step 2 is meant to insure that while the whitening transformation rescales the variability in all directions so as to equalize them, it will not rescale directions whose corresponding eigenvalues are effectively zero.

3.5 Standard Extensions of the Linear Model

3.5.1 Latent Variable Analysis

Latent variable analysis is a statistical tool for describing and modeling the underlying structure in multivariate data. The analysis is widely used in situations where observed variables can be explained by a small number of unobservable factors and where underlying theoretical quantities cannot be measured directly.

3.5.2 Kernel Method

Kernel representation offers an alternative learning paradigm to nonlinear functions by projecting the data into a high-dimensional feature space to increase the computational power of linear learning machines, though this still leaves open the issue of how to choose the features or the kernel function such that performance will be improved.

Kernel PCA (KPCA)

Another extension of PCA is nonlinear principal component analysis (NLPCA) or kernel PCA (KPCA), which is the problem of identifying a nonlinear manifold from sample data points. The standard solution to NLPCA (Scholkopf 1998) is based upon first embedding the data into a higher-dimensional feature space F and then applying standard PCA to the embedded data. That is, one assumes that there exists an embedding of the data such that the embedded data points lie on a linear subspace of a higher-dimensional space. Since in practice the dimension of F can be large, a more practical solution is obtained from the eigenvalue decomposition of the so-called kernel matrix, hence the name KPCA. One of the disadvantages of KPCA is that it is unclear what kernel to use for a given problem, since the choice of the kernel naturally depends on the nonlinear structure of the manifold to be identified. In fact, learning kernels is an active topic of research in the KPCA community.

3.6 Summary

In this chapter, we present a thorough survey of recent research advances in component analysis (CA). CA aims to find hidden components by applying data analysis techniques including principal component analysis (PCA), independent component analysis (ICA), and so on. These data analysis techniques are discussed, as well as the underlying models and assumptions that they employed. Additionally, we also discuss interrelationships between these methods.

References

Cichocki and Zdunck (2007) Multi-layer nonnegative matrix factorization using projected gradient approaches. International Journal of Neural System 17(6):431–446

Bilmes J (1998) A gentle tutorial of the EM algorithm and its application to parameter Estimation for Gaussian mixture and hidden Markov models. International Computer Science Institute 4

Black M, Rangarajan A (1996) On the unification of line processes, outlier rejection, and robust statistics with applications in early vision. International Journal of Computer Vision 19(1):57–91

Chan H, Wei D, Helvie M, Sahiner B, Adler D, Goodsitt M, Petrick N (1995) Computer aided classification of mammographic masses and normal tissue: linear discriminant analysis in texture feature space. Physics in Medicine and Biology 40:476, 857

Collins M, Dasgupta S, Schapire R (2002) A generalization of principal component analysis to the exponential family. Advances in Neural Information Processing Systems 14

Feng T, Li S, Shum H, Zhang H (2002) Local non-negative matrix factorization as a visual representation. The 2nd International Conference on Development and Learning pp 178–183

Guillamet D, Vitrif J, Schiele B (2003) Introducing a weighted non-negative matrix factorization for image classification. Pattern Recognition Letters 24(14):2447–2454

Hardin J, Hilbe J (2001) Generalized Linear Models and Extensions. Stata Press, College Station

Hardoon D, Szedmak S, Shawetaylor J (2004) Canonical correlation analysis: an overview with application to learning methods. Neural Computation 16: 2639–2664

Hoyer P (2004) Non-negative matrix factorization with sparseness constraints. The Journal of Machine Learning Research 5:1457–1469

Hyvarinen A, Karhunen J, Oja E (2000) Independent component analysis. IEEE Transactions on Biomedical Engineering 14:21–30

Jolliffe I (2002) Principal component analysis. Springer, New York

Lee D, Seung H (1999) Learning the parts of objects by non-negative matrix factorization. Nature 401(6755):788–791

Lee D, Seung H (2001) Algorithms for non-negative matrix factorization. Advances in Neural Information Processing Systems 13:556–562

Lin C (2007) Projected gradient methods for nonnegative matrix factorization. Neural Computation 19(10):2756–2779

Liu W, Zheng N (2004) Learning sparse features for classification by mixture models. Pattern Recognition Letters 25(2):155–161

Liu W, Zheng N, You Q (2006) Nonnegative matrix factorization and its applications in pattern recognition. Chinese Science Bulletin 51(1):7–18

Oja E, Karhuen J (1985) On stochastic approximation of the eigenvectors and eigenvalues of the expectation of a random matrix. Journal of mathematical analysis and applications 106(1):69–84

Oja E (1983) Subspace Methods of Pattern Recognition. Research Studies Press England

Paatero P, Tapper U (1994) Positive matrix factorization: a non-negative factor model with optimal utilization of error estimates of data values. Environmetrics 5(2):111–126

Scholkopf B (1998) Nonlinear Component Analysis as a Kernel Eigenvalue Problem. Neural Computation 10(5):1299–1319

Shental N, Hertz T, Weinshall D, Pavel M (2002) Adjustment learning and relevant component analysis. Lecture Notes in Computer Science, pp 776–792

Song S, Miller K, Abbott L (2000) Competitive Hebbian learning through spike-timing-dependent synaptic plasticity. Nature Neuroscience 3:919–926

Tipping M, Bishop C (1999) Probabilistic principal component analysis. Journal of the Royal Statistical Society Series B (Statistical Methodology) 61(3):611–622

De la Torre F, Black M (2003) A Framework for robust subspace learning. International Journal of Computer Vision 54(1):117–142

De la Torre F, Gross R, Baker S, Kumar B (2005) Representational oriented component analysis (ROCA) for face recognition with one sample image per training class. In: IEEE Conference on Computer Vision and Pattern Recognition, IEEE Computer Society; 1999, vol 2, p 266

Vidal R, Ma Y, Sastry S (2005) Generalized principal component analysis (GPCA). IEEE Transactions on Pattern Analysis and Machine Intelligence 27(12):1945–1959

Wang Y, Jia Y, Hu C, Turk M (2005) Non-negative matrix factorization framework for face recognition. International Journal of Pattern Recognition and Artificial Intelligence 19(4):495–511

Welling M, Weber M (2001) Positive tensor factorization. Pattern Recognition Letters 22(12):1255–1261

Weng J, Zhang Y, Hwang W (2003) Candid covariance-free incremental principal component analysis. IEEE Transactions on Pattern Analysis and Machine Intelligence 25(8):1034–1040

Ye J, Li Q (2005) A two-stage linear discriminant analysis via QR-Decomposition. IEEE Transactions on Pattern Analysis and Machine Intelligence 27:929–941

Chapter 4
Manifold Learning

Abstract Manifold learning methods are one of the most exciting developments in machine learning in recent years. The central idea underlying these methods is that although natural data is typically represented in very high-dimensional spaces, the process generating the data is often thought to have relatively few degrees of freedom. A natural mathematical characterization of this intuition is to model the data as lying on or near a low-dimensional manifold embedded in a higher dimensional space.

Recently, manifold learning has also been applied in utilizing both labeled and unlabeled data for classification, that is, semi-supervised learning. For example, once the manifold is estimated, then the Laplace–Beltrami operator may be used to provide a basis for maps intrinsically defined on this manifold and then the appropriate classifier (map) is estimated on the basis of the labeled examples.

In this chapter, we will discuss the manifold perspective of visual pattern representation, dimensionality reduction, and classification problems, as well as a survey that includes manifold learning concepts, technical mechanisms, and algorithms.

4.1 Introduction

In this chapter, we discuss the problem of nonlinear dimensionality reduction (NLDR): the task of recovering meaningful low-dimensional structures hidden in high-dimensional data. In many cases of interest, the observed data are found to lie on an embedded submanifold of the high-dimensional space, e.g., images generated by different views of the same three-dimensional (3D) object. Intuitively, the human brain confronts the same problem in everyday perception, extracting from $30,000$ auditory nerve cells or 10^6 optic nerve fibers, i.e., from very high-dimensional sensory inputs, a manageably small number of perceptually relevant features. Coherent structures in the real world lead to strong correlations between inputs (such as between neighboring pixels in images), generating observations that lie on or close to a smooth low-dimensional manifold. To compare

N. Zheng, J. Xue, *Statistical Learning and Pattern Analysis for Image and Video Processing*, Advances in Pattern Recognition, DOI 10.1007/978-1-84882-312-9_4,
© Springer-Verlag London Limited 2009

and classify such observations, in effect, to reason about the world depends crucially upon the ability to model the nonlinear geometry of these low-dimensional manifolds. The degrees of freedom along this submanifold correspond to the underlying variables. In this form, the NLDR problem is known as "manifold learning."

In the classical approaches to dimensionality reduction discussed in Chapter 3, various methods that generate linear/nonlinear maps were considered. Most of them set up an optimization problem whose solution is typically obtained by gradient descent, which is only guaranteed to produce a local optimum – and in which the global optimum is difficult to attain by efficient means. Kernel-based extensions such as the kernel principal component analysis (KPCA) (Schoelkopf et al. 1997) and kernel Fisher discriminant (KFD) analysis (Mika et al. 1999) provide new means to perform PCA and LDA in an implicitly higher dimensional feature space. Most of these methods do not explicitly consider the structure of the manifold on which the data may possibly reside.

In contrast to CA methods discussed in Chapter 3, manifold learning methods address the dimensionality reduction problem by uncovering the intrinsic low-dimensional geometric structure hidden in their high-dimensional observations. More specially, the generic problem addressed by manifold learning is as follows: given a set $\mathbf{x}_1,...,\mathbf{x}_k$ of k points in $\mathbb{R}^D$, find a set of points $\mathbf{y}_1,...,\mathbf{y}_k$ in $\mathbb{R}^d(d \ll D)$ such that $\mathbf{y}_i$ "represents" $\mathbf{x}_i$. Manifold learning methods assume the special case where $\mathbf{x}_1,...,\mathbf{x}_k \in \mathbb{M}$ and $\mathbb{M}$ is a manifold embedded in $\mathbb{R}^D$, such that the algorithms consider constructing a representative $\mathbf{y}_i \in \mathbb{R}^d$, where $d \ll D$.

Manifold learning algorithms find the intrinsic structure of high-dimensional visual patterns by constructing a representation of the data lying on a low-dimensional manifold. The representational map generated by the computation may be viewed as a discrete approximation to a continuous map that naturally arises from certain properties of the manifold. Isometric feature mapping (Isomap) (Balasubramanian et al. 2002), for example, tries to preserve geodesic distances. Locally linear embedding (LLE) (Roweis and Saul 2000) embeds data points in a low-dimensional space by finding the optimal linear reconstruction in a small neighborhood. Laplacian eigenmaps (Belkin and Niyogi 2003) restate the nonlinear mapping problem as an embedding of vertices in a graph and uses the graph Laplacian to derive a smooth mapping. Semidefinite embedding (Weinberger and Saul 2006) first unrolls the manifold onto a flat hyper-plane before applying PCA. Manifold charting (Brand 2003), local tangent space alignment (LTSA) (Zhang and Zha 2002), diffusion maps (Coifman et al. 2005), and conformal eigenmaps (Sha and Saul 2005) combine multiple local coordinate systems in the manifold in a consistent manner.

Each of these above-mentioned manifold algorithms attempts to preserve a different geometrical property of the underlying manifold and they vary in the embedding type, preservation of local or global geometry, and in their computing complexity. In general, these algorithms come in three flavors: local, global, and hybrid. Table 4.1 lists these algorithms according to the chronology of their development.

Local methods such as LLE, diffusion map, Laplacian eigenmaps, and Hessian LLE (Donoho and Grimes 2003) aim to preserve the local geometry of the data by building a graph that incorporates neighborhood information in the data set, then use the Laplacian or Hessian of the graph to compute a low-dimensional representation of the data set that optimally preserves neighborhood information in a certain sense. Essentially, they seek to accurately characterize the local geometry of manifolds, but they break down at the global level. These methods are also known as spectral embedding methods (Belkin and Niyogi 2002) since they reduce the low-dimensional embedding to solve a sparse eigenvalue problem under a unit covariance constraint. However, due to this imposed constraint, the aspect ratio is lost and the global shape of the embedded data cannot reflect the underlying manifold.

In contrast to the local methods, global methods such as the Isomap aim to preserve the metrics at all scales, hence giving a more faithful embedding. However, an Isomap, which is based on the rigid constraint of isometric mapping, can only be applied to intrinsically flat manifolds, for example, 2D developable surfaces (cylinders, cones, and tangent surfaces). Since the distance computation and (MDS) (Borg and Groenen 2003) in an Isomap are computationally expensive, algorithms such as multidimensional scaling conformal Isomap (C-Isomap) (de Silva and Tenenbaum 2003) and L-Isomap (de Silva and Tenenbaum 2003) are proposed to improve the Isomap algorithm. Alternatively, incremental Isomap (Law and Jain 2006) is proposed to satisfy sequential data sets.

Hybrid methods make use of both local and global properties of the manifold. For example, manifold charting and (LTSA) try to integrate the ability of global methods to render a faithful representation with the computational efficiency and representational capacity of local methods. They combine multiple local coordinate systems in the manifold in a consistent manner. Specifically, the LTSA estimates the tangent space at each point, and then these tangent spaces are aligned to find global coordinates for the points. The alignment is computed by minimizing a cost function that allows any linear transformation of each local coordinate space. The same idea can also be found in manifold charting and Riemannian manifold learning (Lin et al. 2006).

In addition, manifold learning has been developed to address the problem of classifying a semi-supervised learning problem with a partially labeled data set (Belkin and Niyogi 2004). This line of research exploits the intrinsic structure of the data to improve classification by using unlabeled examples to estimate the manifold, and using the labeled examples to specify a classifier defined on that manifold. To classify, the classifier must equate all data points from the same manifold but distinguish between data points from different manifolds. More formally, the semi-supervised learning problem can be stated as follows. Given a set of labeled examples $((\mathbf{x}_i, y_i); \mathbf{x}_i \in \mathbb{R}^D, y_i \in Y)$ and a set of unlabeled examples $\mathbf{x}_j \in \mathbb{R}^D$, the normal impulse is to seek a classifier $f\colon \mathbb{R}^D \rightarrow Y$. Since D is very large, this immediately leads to difficulties due to the "curse of dimensionality." Instead, by exploiting the fact that all $\mathbf{x}_k \in \mathbb{M}$ where $\mathbb{M}$ is a low-dimensional manifold, we can turn to

Table 4.1 Major Manifold Learning Algorithms

Author	Algorithm	Embedding type	Approach type	Description
Roweis and Saul 2000	LLE	Linear reconstruction weights	Local	Computes the reconstruction weights for each point, and then minimizes the embedding by solving as an eigenvalue problem
Balasubramanian et al. 2002	Isomap	Isometric mapping	Global	Computes the geodesic distance, and then uses MDS
de Silva and Tenenbaum 2003	C-Isomap	Conformal mapping	Hybrid	Preserves angles
	L-Isomap	Isometric mapping	Global	Approximates the original Isomap by choosing a small number of landmark points
Belkin and Niyogi 2003	Laplacian eigenmaps	Locality preserving	Local	Minimizes the squared gradient of an embedding map (equivalent to finding the eigenfunctions of the Laplace-Beltrami operator)
Donoho and Grimes 2003	Hessian eigenmaps	Locally isometric	Local	Substitutes the Hessian for the Laplacian to generate a variant of the Laplacian eigenmap
Brand 2003	Manifold charting	Preserving local variance and neighborhood	Hybrid	Decomposes the input data into locally linear patches, and then merges these patches into a single low-dimensional coordinate system by using affine transformations
Zhang and Zha 2002	Local tangent space alignment	Minimized the reconstruction error	Hybrid	First constructs the tangent space at each data point, and then aligns these tangent spaces with a global coordinate system
Weinberger and Saul 2006	Semdefinite embedding	Local isometry	Local	Maximizes the variance of the outputs, subject to the constraints of zero mean and local isometry
Coifman et al. 2005	Diffusion maps	Preserving diffusion distances	Hybrid	Given a Markov random walk on the data, constructs a diffusion map ucted based on the first few eigenvalues and eigenvectors of the transition matrix
Sha and Saul 2005	Conformal eigenmaps	Angle-preserving embedding	Hybrid	Maximizes the similarity of triangles in each neighborhood
Roweis et al. 2002	Global alignment of local linear model	Global probabilistically two-way mapping	Hybrid	Constructs a probabilistic mixture of factor analyzers to model the density of the images sampled from the manifold and then recovers the global parameterizations of the manifold.
Law and Jain 2006	Incremental Isomap	Isometric mapping	Global	Collects data sequentially, and updates all-pair shortest path distances, then solves an incremental eigenvalue problem.
Lin et al. 2006	Riemannian manifold learning	Coordinate charts	Global	Estimates the neighborhood size and the intrinsic dimension based on the reconstruction of the manifold, then computes the normal coordinates for the mapping.

constructing classifiers of the form f: $\mathbb{M} \rightarrow Y$. These are the intuitions formalized in the semi-supervised learning on Riemannian manifolds.

The rest of this chapter is organized as follows. First, basic concepts related to manifold learning are introduced in Section 4.2. Then local and global approaches to manifold learning are presented in Sections 4.3, and 4.4, respectively. A discussion of local approaches vs. global approaches is presented in Section 4.5. Finally, Section 4.6 summarizes this chapter.

4.2 Mathematical Preliminaries

In this section, we briefly review some necessary concepts in manifold and graph theory, which are important in understanding the principles of the algorithms introduced in this chapter.

4.2.1 Manifold Related Terminologies

Loosely, manifolds are topological spaces that locally resemble an Euclidean space. More precisely, it is a space that can be identified locally within an Euclidean space such that the two topological spaces are compatible on overlaps. Consider the curve in Fig. 4.1. Note that the curve is in $\mathbb{R}^3$, with zero area. The extrinsic dimensionality "3" is somewhat misleading since the curve can be parameterized by a single variable. One way of formalizing this intuition is via the idea of a manifold: the curve is a 1D manifold because it locally looks like a copy of $\mathbb{R}^1$. In the following, let us review some basic terminology from geometry and topology in order to crystallize this notion of dimensionality.

Fig. 4.1 Manifold examples. Left: A curve in $\mathbb{R}^3$ can be considered as a 1D manifold embedded in the 3D Euclidean space. Middle: the set of points sampled from Swiss roll manifold. The set of points sampled from S-shaped manifold

Homomorphism: a map from one algebraic structure to another of the same type that preserves all the relevant structure. For example, if one considers two sets X and Y with a single binary operation defined on them (an algebraic structure), a homomorphism is a map $\Phi: X \to Y$ such that $\Phi(u \cdot v) = \Phi(u) \circ \Phi(v)$ where "$\cdot$" is the operation on X and "$\circ$" is the operation on Y, $\forall u, v \in X$ and $\Phi(u), \Phi(v) \in Y$.

There are several types of homomorphisms. Among them, isomorphism is the one most often used in manifold learning.

Diffeomorphism: given two manifolds $\mathbb{M}$ and $\mathbb{P}$, a bijective map f from $\mathbb{M}$ to $\mathbb{P}$ is called a diffeomorphism if both f and its inverse f^{-1} are differentiable. Two manifolds $\mathbb{M}$ and $\mathbb{P}$ are diffeomorphic if there is a diffeomorphism f from $\mathbb{M}$ to $\mathbb{P}$.

Isomorphism: a bijective map f such that both f and its inverse f^{-1} are homomorphic, i.e., Structure-preserving mappings. Isometry is a relation between manifolds. Two manifolds are said to be isometric if there is a diffeomorphism such that the metric on one pulls back to the metric on the other.

Manifold: A d-dimensional manifold $\mathbb{M}$ has the property that it is locally homeomorphic with respect to $\mathbb{R}^d$. That is, for each $x \in \mathbb{R}^d$, there is an open neighborhood around x, N_x, and a homeomorphism $f: N_x \to \mathbb{R}^d$. These neighborhoods are referred to as coordinate patches, and the map is referred to as a coordinate chart. The image of the coordinate chart is referred to as the parameter space.

In this chapter, we will be interested only in the case where $\mathbb{M}$ is a subset of $\mathbb{R}^D$, where $D \gg d$. In other words, the manifold will lie in a high-dimensional space $\mathbb{R}^D$, but will be homeomorphic with a low-dimensional space $\mathbb{R}^d$.

Riemanian manifold: a real differentiable manifold $\mathbb{M}$ in which each tangent space is equipped with an inner product g in a manner which varies smoothly from point to point.

Embedding: an embedding of a manifold $\mathbb{M}$ into $\mathbb{R}^D$ is a smooth homeomorphism from $\mathbb{M}$ to a subset of $\mathbb{R}^D$. The algorithms discussed in this chapter find embeddings of discrete point sets, by which we simply mean a mapping of the point set into another space (typically a lower dimensional Euclidean space). An embedding of a dissimilarity matrix into $\mathbb{R}^D$ is a configuration of points whose interpoint distances match those given in the matrix.

4.2.2 Graph Related Terminologies

In manifold learning, the graph, a mathematical structure, is often used to model pairwise geometrical relations between data points from a manifold. A "graph" $G = (V, E)$ in this context refers to a collection of vertices V or "nodes" (data points) and a collection of edges E that connect pairs of vertices. A graph may be undirected, meaning there is no distinction between the two vertices associated with each edge, or its edge may be directed from one vertex to another. In the following, we introduce some common terminology from the manifold learning literature (Fig. 4.2).

Adjacent matrix: an $n \times n$ matrix W, where n is the number of the vertices in the graph. If there is an edge from vertex i to vertex j, then the element w_{ij} has value 1 (a weight in a weighted graph), otherwise it is 0.

Degree: the degree of a vertex is the number of edges incident to the vertex (the sum of weights associated with edges incident to the vertex in the weighted graph).

Volume: the volume of a set of vertices is the sum of the degree of all vertices of the set.

Laplacian matrix: a matrix representation of a graph. The Laplacian matrix **L** of a graph is defined as $\mathbf{L} = \mathbf{D} - \mathbf{W}$, where **D** is a diagonal matrix holding the degree of each vertex.

Cut: a partition of the vertices V of a graph $G = (V, E)$ into two sets S and T. Any edge $(u, v) \in E$ with $u \in S$ and $v \in S$ is said to cross the cut and is a cut edge. The size of the cut is the total number of edges crossing the cut. In weighted graphs, the size of a cut is defined as the sum of the weights of the edges that cross the cut.

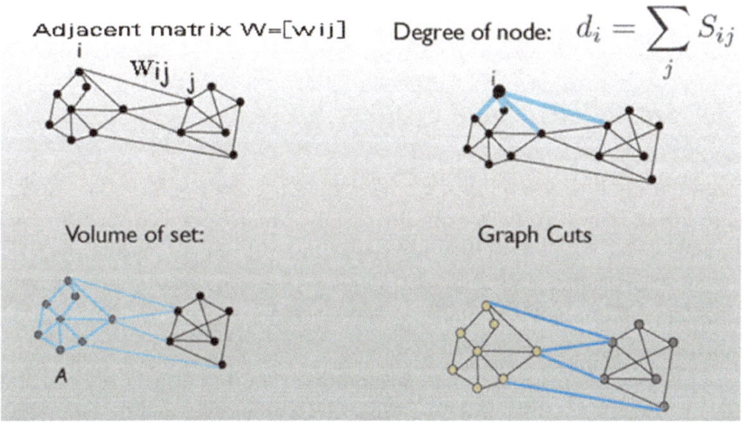

Fig. 4.2 Graph-related terminologies: adjacent matrix W, the degree of node i, the volume of vertex set A, and the cut between two disjoint sets of nodes.

Graph embedding: the embedding of a graph G on a surface $\mathbb{M}$ is a representation of G on $\mathbb{M}$ in which the points of $\mathbb{M}$ are associated with vertices and simple arcs (homeomorphic images of [0,1]) and are associated with edges in such a way that:

- the end points of the arc associated with an edge e are the points associated with the end vertices of e;
- an arc includes no points associated with other vertices;
- two arcs never intersect at a point which is interior to either of the arcs.

Here a surface is a compact, connected two-manifold. Informally, the embedding of a graph into a surface can be thought of as a drawing of the graph on the surface in such a way that its edges may intersect only at their end points.

4.3 Global Methods

The goal of manifold learning algorithms is to map a given set of high-dimensional data points onto a surrogate low-dimensional space. In their implementations, global methods such as MDS and Isomap aim to preserve metrics at all scales, thus giving a more faithful embedding. Moreover, their metric-preserving properties are better understood theoretically. Local methods, such as LLE, Laplacian eigenmaps, on the other hand, aim to preserve proximity relationships within the data.

In this section, we focus on manifold learning algorithms belonging to the category of global methods. We choose to present the ideas and key techniques of several representative algorithms including MDS, Isomap, and variants of the Isomap algorithm.

4.3.1 Multidimensional Scaling

Given data points $\mathbf{X} = [\mathbf{x}_1, ..., \mathbf{x}_k]$ with $\mathbf{x}_i \in \mathbb{R}^D, i = 1, ..., k$, MDS is the problem of finding a mapping from $\mathbf{X}$ with the distance matrix $\mathbf{D}$ to a low-dimensional set of points $\mathbf{Y} = [\mathbf{y}_1, ..., \mathbf{y}_k]$ which preserves $\mathbf{D}$ under the cost function $\rho(\mathbf{D}, \mathbf{D}')$, where $\mathbf{D}'$ denotes the distances between the points $\mathbf{y}_i, i = 1, ..., k \in \mathbb{R}^d$, and $d \ll D$. Note that in this formulation, MDS places no requirements on the form or complexity of the transformation.

For a general cost function ρ, MDS is a difficult nonlinear optimization problem. Various selections of ρ have given rise to a wealth of research. One very convenient form for ρ is given by

$$\rho_{MDS}(\mathbf{D}, \mathbf{D}') = ||\mathbf{J}^T(\mathbf{D} - \mathbf{D}'^2)\mathbf{J}||_F^2 \tag{4.1}$$

where $\mathbf{D}^2$ is the matrix of squared distance (element-wise product), $||\cdot||_F^2$ is the Frobenius norm, and $\mathbf{J}$ is the centering matrix, which is defined as $\mathbf{J} = \mathbf{I}_k - 1/k\mathbf{1}\mathbf{1}^T$. Here, $\mathbf{I}_k$ is the $k \times k$ identity matrix, $\mathbf{1}$ is the k-dimensioanal column vector made by all 1s. This criterion, also called the "STRAIN" criterion, is intended to match variations in distance rather than the values themselves. This makes the criterion invariant to the addition of a constant to all distances, or to all distances from a given datum, a potentially useful characteristic given the perceptual nature of the dissimilarity values from psychometry.

The STRAIN criterion is also called classical MDS. The closed form solution of Eq. (4.1) is given by the eigen structure of $-1/2\mathbf{J}^T\mathbf{D}^2\mathbf{J}$. The top d eigenvectors of the covariance matrix of $\mathbf{X}$, $\Sigma = \mathbf{X}\mathbf{J}\mathbf{J}^T\mathbf{X}^T$, capture the largest components of variations in $\mathbf{J}^T\mathbf{D}^2\mathbf{J}$, and thus give the coordinates of the solution $\mathbf{Y}$. This technique is closely related to that of PCA.

Other criteria for MDS have also been studied, for example, the STRESS and SSTRESS given by $||\mathbf{D} - \mathbf{D}'||_F^2$ and $||\mathbf{D}^2 - \mathbf{D}'^2||_F^2$, respectively. However, the available algorithms for minimizing these cost functions lack the same globally optimal convergence properties that accompany STRAIN.

The main problem in applying any of the above formulations of MDS to nonlinear manifold learning, however, is their direct use of, and reconstruction based upon Euclidean distance. These formulations treat all pairwise Euclidean distance measurements equally; yet for a manifold which has been nonlinearly embedded in a high-dimensional space, many of these distances do not respect the topology of the manifold and are thus unsuitable for use in determining the nonlinear relationship.

4.3.2 Isometric Feature Mapping

As stated previously, inclusion of Euclidean distances in the optimization means that classical MDS fails to recover the planar nature of the data. An Isomap works on a different principle from MDS: given a set of distances $\mathbf{D}$, classical MDS recovers a set of locations which best approximate those distances in a Euclidean space $\mathbb{R}^d$. However, for a nonlinearly embedded manifold, the distances $\mathbf{D}$ used in the Isomap is not the Euclidean distances between each data pair but rather the shortest curve length which respects the geometry of the data (geodesic). In a short, an Isomap builds on classical MDS but seeks to preserve the intrinsic geometry of the data, as captured in the geodesic manifold distances between all pairs of data points.

In the Isomap algorithm, the local quantities computed are the distance between neighboring data points. For each pair of non-neighboring data points, the Isomap finds the shortest path through the data set connecting the two points, subject to the constraint that the path must hop from neighbor to neighbor. The length of this path is an approximation of the distance between its end points, as measured within the underlying manifold. Finally, the classical method of MDS is used to find a set of low-dimensional points with similar pairwise distances. The key point here is estimating the geodesic distance between faraway points, given only input-space distances. For neighboring points, input-space distance provides a good approximation to geodesic distance. For faraway points, geodesic distance can be approximated by adding up a sequence of "short hop" between neighboring points. These approximations are computed efficiently by finding shortest paths in a graph with edges connecting neighboring data points.

The complete isometric feature mapping algorithm, or Isomap has three steps, which are detailed as follows.

1. Find the neighborhood for each point $\mathbf{x}_i$.
2. Compute the shortest path distance between all pairs of points using Dijkstra's or Floyd's algorithm, and store the squares of these distances in a matrix.
3. Apply classical MDS to the distance matrix.

The first step determines which points are neighbors on the manifold $\mathbb{M}$, based on the distance $d_{\mathbf{X}}(i,j)$ between pairs of points i,j in the input space $\mathbf{X}$.

These neighborhood relationships are presented as a weighted graph G over the data points, with edges of weight $d_{\mathbf{X}}(i,j)$. Figure 4.3 shows two simple methods to find neighbors.

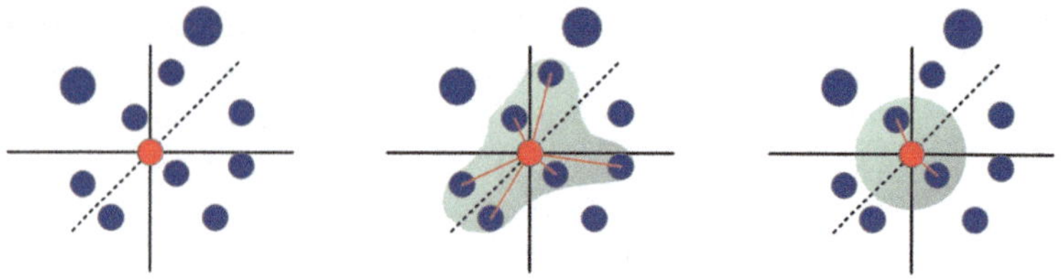

Fig. 4.3 Adjacency graph construction. Left: the data points. Middle: the K nearest neighbors. Right: the ε-neighboring

The second step estimates the geodesic distance $d_{\mathbb{M}}$ between all pairs of points on the manifold $\mathbb{M}$ by computing their shortest path distances $d_G(i,j)$ in the graph. It first initializes $d_G(i,j) = d_{\mathbf{X}}(i,j)$ if i,j are linked by an edge; or set $d_G(i,j) = \infty$ otherwise. Then for each value of $m = 1,...,k$ in turn, replace all entries $d_G(i,j)$ with $min\{d_G(i,j), d_G(i,m) + d_G(m,j)\}$. Finally, the matrix $\mathbf{D}_G = d_G(i,j)$ will contain the shortest path distances between all pairs of points in G.

The third step applies classical MDS to the matrix $\mathbf{D}_G$ to obtain the embedding of the data in a d-dimensional Euclidean space $\mathbf{Y}$ that best preserves the manifold's estimated intrinsic geometry. This is achieved by setting the coordinates $\mathbf{y}_i$ to the top d eigenvectors of the matrix $\tau(\mathbf{D}_G)$, where the operator τ is defined by $\tau(\mathbf{D}) = -\mathbf{HSH}/2$, where $\mathbf{S}$ is the matrix of squared distances (with $S_{ij} = D_{ij}^2$), and $\mathbf{H}$ is the centering matrix (with $H_{ij} = \delta_{ij} - 1/k$). This operator converts distances to inner products, which uniquely characterize the geometry of the data in a form that supports efficient optimization.

An Isomap is guaranteed asymptotically to recover the true dimensionality and geometric structure of a strictly large class of nonlinear manifolds. Figure 4.4 illustrates a two-dimensional embedding recovered by the Isomap in step three and shows that the residual variance decreases as the dimensionality d is increased. This indicates that the Isomap algorithm recovers the true dimensionality of the manifold since reduction of the residual variance stops at dimensionality $d = 2$. In the experiment, the neighborhood size is 7.

4.3.3 Variants of the Isomap

4.3.3.1 Conformal Isomap

To improve the computational efficiency and representational capacity of the Isomap, de Silva and Tenenbaum (2003) propose the C-Isomap which extends the Isomap by making a uniform sampling assumption about the data.

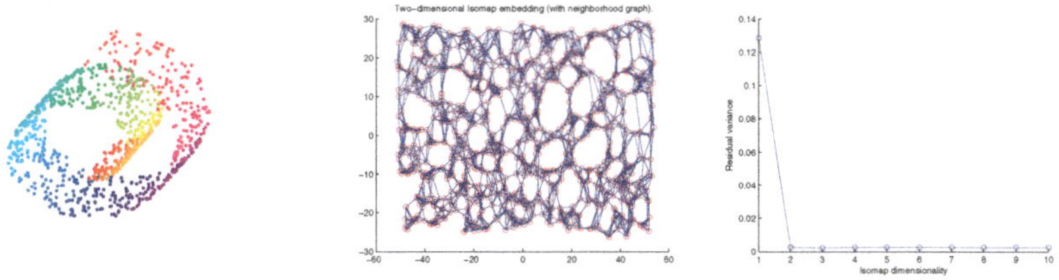

Fig. 4.4 The Swiss roll data set, illustrating the 2D embedding recovered by the Isomap in step three, and how the residual variance decreases as the dimensionality d is increased. Left: the true manifold; middle: the 2D embedding recovered by the Isomap with neighborhood graph overlaid; right: the residual variance decreases as dimensionality increases

In the C-Isomap algorithm, the problem of manifold learning is formulated as follows: let $\mathbf{Y}$ be a d-dimensional domain contained in the Euclidean space $\mathbb{R}^d$, and let $f: Y \mapsto \mathbb{R}^D$ be a smooth embedding, for some $D > d$. Hidden data $\{\mathbf{y}_i\}$ are generated randomly in $\mathbf{Y}$, and are then mapped by f to become the observed data $\{\mathbf{x}_i = f(\mathbf{y}_i)\}$. The object of manifold learning is to recover $\mathbf{Y}$ and f based upon a given observation set $\{\mathbf{x}_i \in \mathbb{R}^D\}$.

The problem as stated is ill-posed: some constraints are needed on f if we are to relate the observed geometry of the data to the structure of the hidden variables $\mathbf{y}_i$ and to $\mathbf{Y}$ itself. There are two kinds of constraints. The first is that f is an isometric embedding in the sense of Riemannian geometry, and f preserves infinitesimal lengths and angles. The Isomap exploits this idea by constructing the geodesic metric for $f(\mathbf{Y})$ approximately as a matrix, using the observed data alone. The second constraint is that f is a conformal embedding that preserves angles but not lengths. At each point $\mathbf{y} \in \mathbf{Y}$ there is a scalar $s(\mathbf{y}) > 0$ such that infinitesimal vectors at $\mathbf{y}$ get magnified in length by a factor $s(\mathbf{y})$.

The C-Isomap estimates $s(\mathbf{y})$ at each point $f(\mathbf{y})$ in the observed data by first rescaling to restore the original metric structure of the data, and then processing as with the Isomap. A conformal map f rescales local volumes in $\mathbf{Y}$ by a factor $s(\mathbf{y})^d$. Hence the local density of the observed data will be $1/s(\mathbf{y})^d$ if the hidden data is sampled uniformly in $\mathbf{Y}$. It follows that the conformal factor $s(\mathbf{y})$ can be estimated in terms of the observed local data density, provided that the original sampling is uniform.

In implementation, the C-Isomap is a simple variation of the Isomap. Specifically, the C-Isomap uses the nearest-neighbors method to determine a neighborhood graph and replaces the second step of the Isomap algorithm with the following:

- Compute the shortest paths in the graph for all pairs of data points. Each edge i, j in the graph is weighted by $|\mathbf{x}_i - \mathbf{x}_j|/\sqrt{M(i)M(j)}$, where $M(i)$ is the mean distance of $\mathbf{x}_i$ to its K nearest neighbors.

The C-Isomap algorithm requires a large sample size since it depends on two approximations – local data density and geodesic distance. In the special case where the conformal embedding is actually an isometry, it is preferable to use the Isomap rather than the C-Isomap.

4.3.3.2 Landmark Isomap

One drawback of the original Isomap is its quadraic memory requirement: the geodesic distance matrix is dense, of order $O(n^2)$, making the Isomap infeasible for large data sets. The landmark Isomap (L-Isomap) was proposed by (de Silva and Tenenbaum 2003) to reduce the memory requirement while at the same time lowering the computation cost.

Instead of computing $\mathbf{D}_{k\times k}$, the L-Isomap designates n data points to be landmark points, where $n \ll k$, and computes the $n \times k$ matrix $\mathbf{D}_{n\times k}$ of distances from each data point to the landmark points only. Using Landmark MDS (LMDS), which is presented in the following, one can find a Euclidean embedding of the data using $\mathbf{D}_{n\times k}$.

LMDS consists of three stages. In the first stage, classical MDS is applied to the landmark-only distance matrix $\mathbf{D}_{n\times k}$. The procedure is as follows. First, construct a matrix $\mathbf{B}_n = -\mathbf{J}_n\mathbf{H}_n\mathbf{J}_n/2$, where $\mathbf{H}_n$ is the matrix of squared distance, and $\mathbf{J}_n$ is the centering matrix with elements $(\mathbf{H}_n)_{ij} = \delta_{ij} - 1/n$. Secondly, find the eigenvalues and eigenvectors of $\mathbf{B}_n$. Let λ_i denote the eigenvalue (labeled so that $\lambda_1 \geq \lambda_2 \geq \cdots \geq \lambda_d$) and $\mathbf{v}_i$ be the corresponding eigenvector. Non-positive eigenvalues are ignored. Thirdly, for $l \leq d$ the required optimal l-dimensional embedding vectors are given as the columns of the matrix $\mathbf{L}$:

$$\mathbf{L} = \begin{pmatrix} \sqrt{\lambda_1}\mathbf{v}_1 \\ \sqrt{\lambda_2}\mathbf{v}_2 \\ \cdots \\ \sqrt{\lambda_l}\mathbf{v}_l \end{pmatrix}$$

If $\mathbf{B}_n$ has no negative eigenvalues, then the l-dimensional embedding is perfect. Otherwise, there is no exact Euclidean embedding.

The second stage of LMDS embeds the remaining points with respect to the landmark points. Let $H_{\mathbf{x}}$ denote the column vector of squared distances between a data point $\mathbf{x}$ and the landmark points. The embedding vector $\overrightarrow{x}$ of $\mathbf{x}$ is related linearly to $H_{\mathbf{x}}$ by

$$\overrightarrow{x} = \frac{1}{2}\tilde{\mathbf{L}}(\bar{H}_{\mathbf{x}} - H_{\mathbf{x}}) \tag{4.2}$$

where $\bar{H}_{\mathbf{x}}$ is the column mean of $H_{\mathbf{x}}$, and $\tilde{\mathbf{L}}$ is the pseudoinverse transpose of $\mathbf{L}$

$$\tilde{\mathbf{L}} = \begin{pmatrix} \mathbf{v}_1/\sqrt{\lambda_1} \\ \mathbf{v}_2/\sqrt{\lambda_2} \\ \cdots \\ \mathbf{v}_l/\sqrt{\lambda_l} \end{pmatrix}$$

The final stage is to use PCA to realign the data with the coordinate axes. Figure 4.5 shows the results of testing the L-Isomap on the Swiss roll data. The neighborhood size is 7. Compared with the results of the ordinary Isomap in Fig. 4.4, the L-Isomap recovers an embedding that closely approximates the Isomap embedding. The experiment also indicates that the L-Isomap is stable over a wide range of the number of landmarks. However, it should be noted that the landmark points should be chosen at random, or affine distortion may arise if the landmark points lie too close to a subspace.

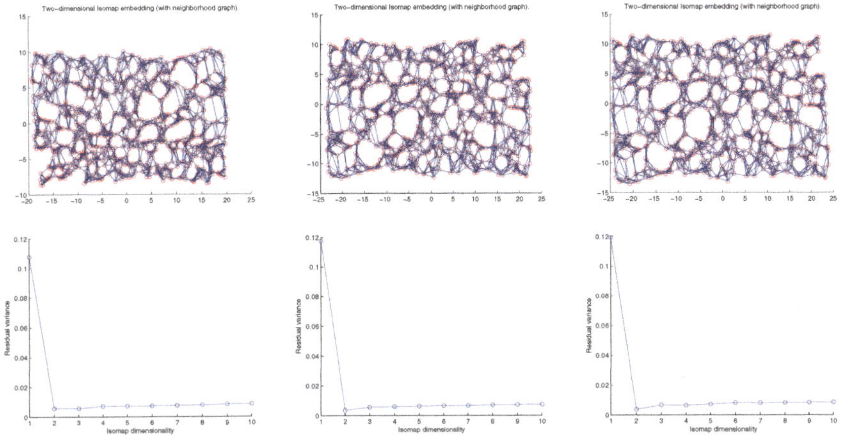

Fig. 4.5 The L-Isomap is stable over a wide range of values for the number of landmarks. The first row shows the recovered 2D embedding of the Swiss roll data, and the second row shows that the residual variances decrease as dimensionality increases

4.3.3.3 Incremental Isomap

Most manifold learning algorithms operate in a batch mode, meaning that all data points need to be available during training. These algorithms cannot be efficiently applied when data are collected sequentially. Here we introduce an incremental version of the Isomap (I-Isomap) (Law and Jain 2006).

The problem to be solved by the I-Isomap is stated as follows: assume that the low-dimensional coordinates $\mathbf{y}_i$ of $\mathbf{x}_i$ for the first n points are given. The new sample $\mathbf{x}_{n+1}$ is observed. How should we update the existing set of $\mathbf{y}_i$ and find $\mathbf{y}_{n+1}$? The solution consists of three stages: (1) the geodesic distances g_{ij} are updated first in view of the change in the neighborhood graph due to the new node v_{n+1}; (2) the geodesic distances of the new point to the existing points are then used to estimate $\mathbf{x}_{n+1}$; (3) all $\mathbf{y}_i$ are updated in view of the change in g_{ij}.

In the implementation of the I-Isomap, there are too many technical details to cover here and these can be easily found in the literature (Law and Jain 2006), thus we restrict our discussion to the basic idea. It should be noted that one interesting aspect of the I-Isomap is that the gradual changes in the data manifold can be visualized. As more and more data points are obtained, the evolution of the data manifold can reveal interesting properties of the data stream. The algorithm can then adjust the manifold in the presence of the drifting of data characteristics.

4.3.3.4 Discussion

The Isomap is intuitive, well understood, and produces good mapping results. Furthermore, there are theoretical studies supporting the use of the Isomap, such as its convergence proof, (Bengio et al. 2004) and the conditions for successful recovery of coordinates (Salzmann et al. 2007).

However, the Isomap still suffers from the following problems in applications:

- The graph must be fully connected.
- Neighborhood size and sample size affect the results greatly (short circuits). (This problem has been addressed by Efros et al. "Convex flows embedding.")
- Holes are NOT addressed (shortest paths go around).
- Global isometry C does not deal with local distortions (This problem has been fixed by de Silva and Tenenbaum's normalization of distances locally.)
- Shortest paths are expensive to compute.

4.4 Local Methods

In this section, we present several representative manifold learning algorithms which take into account the preserving of the local geometry of the data. Again consider the general dimensionality reduction problem: given a set of high-dimensional data points $\mathbf{x}_1, \ldots, \mathbf{x}_k$ in a high-dimensional space $\mathbb{R}^D$, the goal is to find a low-dimensional representation $\mathbf{y}_1, \ldots, \mathbf{y}_k \in \mathbb{R}^d, d \ll D$. Algorithms falling into the category of local methods seek to map nearby points on the manifold to nearby points in the low-dimensional representation. In these algorithms, weighted graphs are usually employed to represent a notion of geometry based on the local similarity or interaction between the data points. Then, the low-dimensional embedding is computed from the eigenvectors of an appropriately constructed matrix. We refer these approaches as spectral embedding algorithms.

More specifically, spectral embedding algorithms have their roots in spectral graph theory, which studies the properties of a graph in relationship to the characteristics of its adjacency matrix or Laplacian matrix, such as its polynomiality, eigenvalues, and eigenvectors. An eigenvalue of a graph is defined as an eigenvalue of the graph's adjacency matrix or of the graph's Laplacian matrix. The set of eigenvalues of the Laplacian matrix is usually called the spectrum of the matrix, which captures fundamental properties of the graph. For example, the magnitude of the second smallest eigenvalue of a graph is a measure of how well connected the graph is. To enhance understanding of the basic idea of spectral embedding algorithms, we review several important manifold learning algorithms in the following section.

4.4.1 Locally Linear Embedding

Roweis et al. proposed the locally linear embedding (LLE) algorithm in 2000 (Roweis and Saul 2000). They assume that the data lie on or near a smooth nonlinear manifold of lower dimensionality $d \ll D$. They further assume that each data point and its neighbors lie on or close to a locally linear patch of the manifold, and that this characterizes the local linear geometry of these patches by using linear coefficients (i.e., reconstruction weights), which reconstruct each data point from its neighbors. To a good approximation then, there exists a linear mapping – consisting of a translation, rotation, and rescaling – that maps the high-dimensional coordinates of each neighborhood to global internal coordinates on the manifold. By design, the reconstruction weights reflect the intrinsic geometric properties of the data that are invariant to exactly such transformations. They expect the characterization of local geometry by the reconstruction weights in the original data space to be equally valid for local patches on the manifold. In particular, the same weights that reconstruct the ith data point in the D dimensions should also reconstruct its embedding manifold coordinates in d dimensions.

The details of the LLE algorithm consist of three steps:

1. Discover the adjacency information: for each data point $\mathbf{x}_i$, find its n neighbors in the data set, $\mathbf{x}_{i1}, \mathbf{x}_{i2}, \ldots, \mathbf{x}_{in}$. Alternately, $\mathbf{x}_{i_1}, \mathbf{x}_{i_2}, \ldots, \mathbf{x}_{i_n}$ could be data points contained in an ε-ball around $\mathbf{x}_i$.
2. Construct the approximation matrix: let w_{ij} be such that $\sum_j w_{i_j}\mathbf{x}_{ij}$ is equal to the orthogonal projection of $\mathbf{x}_i$ onto the affine linear span of $\mathbf{x}_{i_j}$'s. w_{ij} is found by minimizing $\sum_{i=1}^{l} ||\mathbf{x}_i - \sum_{j=1}^{n} w_{ij}\mathbf{x}_{i_j}||^2$
3. Compute the embedding: compute the embedding by taking eigenvectors corresponding to the d lowest eigenvalues of the matrix $\mathbf{E} = (\mathbf{I}-\mathbf{W})^T(\mathbf{I}-\mathbf{W})$, where $\mathbf{W} = \{w_{ij}\}$.

The first step involves the determination of the neighborhood size. In implementation, the K nearest neighbors are measured by Euclidean distance or normalized dot products, where K, the number of the neighbors, is the only free parameter of this algorithm. Once neighbors are chosen, the optimal weights w_{ij} and coordinates $\mathbf{y}_i$ are computed by standard methods in linear algebra. The algorithm involves a single pass through the three steps in Fig. 4.6.

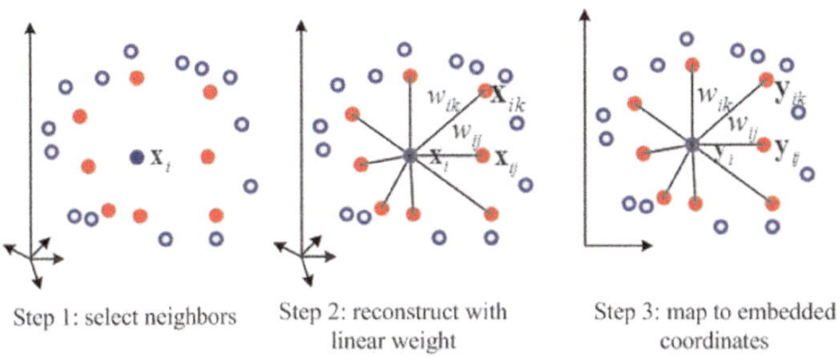

Fig. 4.6 Steps in locally linear embedding, from (Roweis and Saul 2000)

In the second step, the weight w_{ij} summarizes the contribution of the jth data point to the ith reconstruction. The minimization is subject to two constraints: first, $w_{ij} = 0$ if $\mathbf{x}_{i_j}$ does not belong to the set of neighbors of $\mathbf{x}_i$; second, the rows of the weight matrix sum to one, $\sum_j w_{ij} = 1$. Weight w_{ij} subject to these constraints can be found by solving a least-squares problem. The obtained reconstruction weights obey an important symmetry and characterize intrinsic geometric properties of each neighborhood.

In the final step of the algorithm, each high-dimensional observation $\mathbf{x}_i$ is mapped to a low-dimensional vector $\mathbf{y}_i$ representing global internal coordinates on the manifold. This is done by choosing d-dimensional coordinates $\mathbf{y}_i$ to minimize the embedding cost function $\Phi(\mathbf{Y}) = \sum_i |\mathbf{y}_i - \sum_j w_{ij}\mathbf{y}_j|^2$. This cost function, like the previous one, is based on locally linear reconstruction errors, but here the weights w_{ij} are fixed while optimizing the coordinates $\mathbf{y}_i$. The embedding cost $\Phi(\mathbf{Y})$ defines a quadratic form in the vectors $\mathbf{y}_i$. Subject to constraints that make the problem well posed, it can be minimized by solving a sparse eigenvalue problem, i.e., the eigenvalue of $\mathbf{E}$.

In LLE, the neighborhood size n and the intrinsic dimension d reflect the topological properties of the underlying manifold $\mathbb{M}$. An appropriately chosen neighborhood size is the key to the success of the algorithm. Choosing a too large neighborhood may introduce "short-circuit" edges between two separating branches, which can drastically alter the original topological connectivity. On the other hand, choosing a too small neighborhood may fragment the manifold into a large number of disconnected components. Figure 4.7 shows embeddings obtained by choosing different neighborhood sizes.

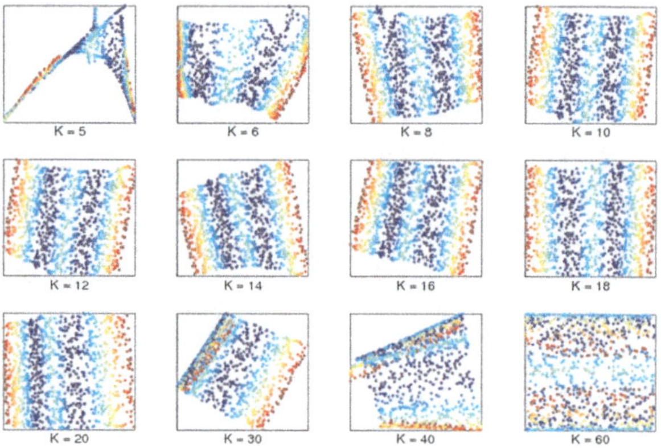

Fig. 4.7 S-shaped data mapped into the embedding space described by the first two coordinates of LLE. It shows effects of the embedding caused by choosing different neighborhood size

LLE scales well with the intrinsic manifold dimensionality, d, and does not require a discretized gridding of the embedding space. As more dimensions are added to the embedding space, the existing dimensions do not change, so that LLE does not have to be returned to compute higher dimensional embeddings. However, estimating the intrinsic dimensionality is a classical problem in pattern recognition. LLE does not provide an answer to this problem. Lin et al. (2006) proposed to determine the neighborhood size by first constructing the edges and then reconstructing the underlying manifold as a simple complex. The dimension of this complex serves as a reliable estimation of the intrinsic dimension of the manifold.

4.4.2 Laplacian Eigenmaps

Belkin and Niyogi (2002) proposed the Laplacian eigenmaps algorithm. This work establishes both a unified approach to dimension reduction and a new connection to spectral theory. Laplacian eigenmaps are the predecessor of next method Hessian eigenmaps (Donoho and Grimes 2003), which overcome the convexity limitation of Laplacian eigenmaps.

4.4.2.1 Laplacian Eigenmap for Discrete Data

We first describe the Laplacian eigenmap for discrete data. Its relevant theorem in the continuum will be discussed in Section 4.4.2.2. Given a set of data points in $\mathbb{R}^D$, the algorithm first builds a graph incorporating neighborhood information, and then uses the graph Laplacian to compute a low-dimensional representation while preserving local neighborhood information. For a graph with a matrix of edge weights, $\mathbf{W}$, the graph Laplacian is defined as $\mathbf{L} \triangleq \mathbf{D} - \mathbf{W}$, where $\mathbf{D}$ is the diagonal matrix with elements $D_{ii} = \sum_j w_{ij}$. The eigenvalues and eigenvectors of the Laplacian reveal a wealth of information about the graph such as whether it is complete or connected. The embedding map is then provided by computing the eigenvectors of the graph Laplacian. The algorithmic procedure is formally stated as follows.

1. Constructing the adjacency graph: put an edge between nodes i and j if $\mathbf{x}_i$ and $\mathbf{x}_j$ are "close". This can be done by either of two ways: (1) ε-neighborhoods ($\varepsilon \in \mathbb{R}$). Node i and j are connected if $||\mathbf{x}_i - \mathbf{x}_j||^2 < \varepsilon$ where the norm is the usual Euclidean norm in $\mathbb{R}^D$; (2) K nearest neighbors ($K \in \mathbb{N}$). Node i and j are connected if $\mathbf{x}_i$ is among K nearest neighbors of $\mathbf{x}_j$ or vice versa. Figure 4.3 shows these two ways to construct the adjacency graph.
2. Choosing the weights: there are also alternative methods to determine the weights of an edge. (1) Heat kernel, in which the weight is set as $w_{ij} = e^{-\frac{||\mathbf{x}_i - \mathbf{x}_j||^2}{t}}$ if there is an edge between node i and j, and (2) $w_{ij} = 1$ if and only if nodes i and j are connected.
3. Computing Eigenmaps: with the assumption that the graph G constructed above is connected, compute eigenvalues and eigenvectors for the generalized eigenvector problem $\mathbf{Lf} = \lambda \mathbf{Df}$ component. Leave out the eigenvector corresponding to eigenvalue 0 and use the eigenvectors corresponding to the d smallest eigenvalues for embedding in a d-dimensional Euclidean space.

The Laplacian eigenmaps algorithm is based upon the standard graph spectral theory. It uses the similarity matrix $\mathbf{W}$ to find points $\mathbf{y}_1, \ldots, \mathbf{y}_k \in \mathbb{R}^d$ that are the low-dimensional analogues of $\mathbf{x}_1, \ldots, \mathbf{x}_n$. Similar to the intrinsic dimensionality problem with LLE, d is also a parameter of the algorithm, but it can be automatically estimated by using conformal Eigenmaps as a post-processor.

Intuitively, if $\mathbf{x}_i$ and $\mathbf{x}_k$ have a high degree of similarity, as measured by $\mathbf{W}$, then they lie very near to one another on the manifold. Thus, $\mathbf{y}_i$ and $\mathbf{y}_j$ should be near to one another. The problem now becomes mapping a connected and weighted graph $G = (V,E)$ into a d-dimensional Euclidean space. This embedding is given by the $k \times d$ matrix $\mathbf{F} = [\mathbf{f}_1, \mathbf{f}_2, ...\mathbf{f}_d]$ where the ith row provides the embedding coordinates of the ith vertex. Thus, a reasonable criterion for choosing a "good" map is to minimize the following objective function

$$\sum_{i,j} ||\mathbf{y}^{(i)} - \mathbf{y}^{(j)}||^2 w_{ij} = tr(\mathbf{F}^T \mathbf{L} \mathbf{F}) \tag{4.3}$$

where $\mathbf{y}^{(i)} = [\mathbf{f}_1(i), ..., \mathbf{f}_d(i)]^T$ is the d-dimensional representation of the ith vertex. This reduces to finding $argmin_{\mathbf{F}^T\mathbf{DF}=\mathbf{I}} tr(\mathbf{F}^T \mathbf{L} \mathbf{F})$. The value $\mathbf{F}^T \mathbf{D} \mathbf{F} = \mathbf{I}$ constrains $\mathbf{F}$ so that we do not end up with a solution with dimensionality less than d. The solution is then provided by the eigenvectors of the corresponding smallest eigenvalues of the generalized eigenvalue problem $\mathbf{L}\mathbf{f} = \lambda \mathbf{D}\mathbf{f}$.

There are two free parameters in this algorithm: the heat kernel parameter t and the number of nearest neighbors K. Figure 4.8 shows 2D Laplacian eigenmaps of the Swiss roll data obtained from different parameter settings. From left to right of each row, we fix t, and increase K from 5 to 20; from top to bottom of each column, we fix K and increase t from 5 to 15. It is clear that t has little impact on the embedding, while K, the neighborhood size, impacts the embedding in a significant way. This is similar to that of LLE algorithm.

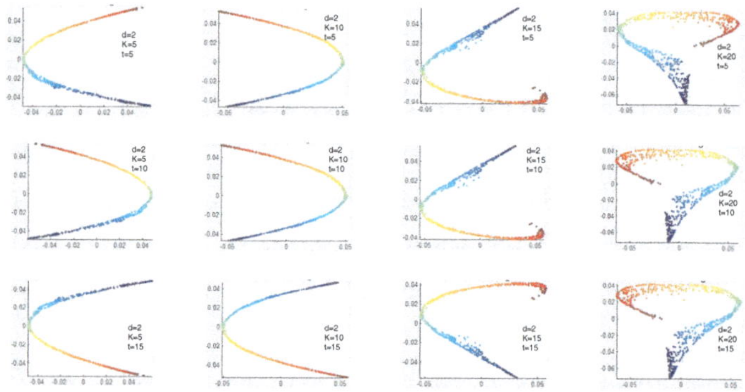

Fig. 4.8 2D embedding of the Swiss roll data by Laplacian Eigenmaps algorithm. From left to right of each row, we fix t, and increase K from 5 to 20; from top to bottom of each column, we fix K and increase t from 5 to 15

4.4.2.2 Laplace–Beltrami operator

Let $\mathbb{M}$ be a smooth, compact, d-dimensional Riemannian manifold. Let f be a map from the manifold $\mathbb{M}$ to the real line $\mathbb{R}$ such that points close together on the manifold get mapped close together on the line. Assume that $f : \mathbb{M} \rightarrow \mathbb{R}$ is twice differentiable.

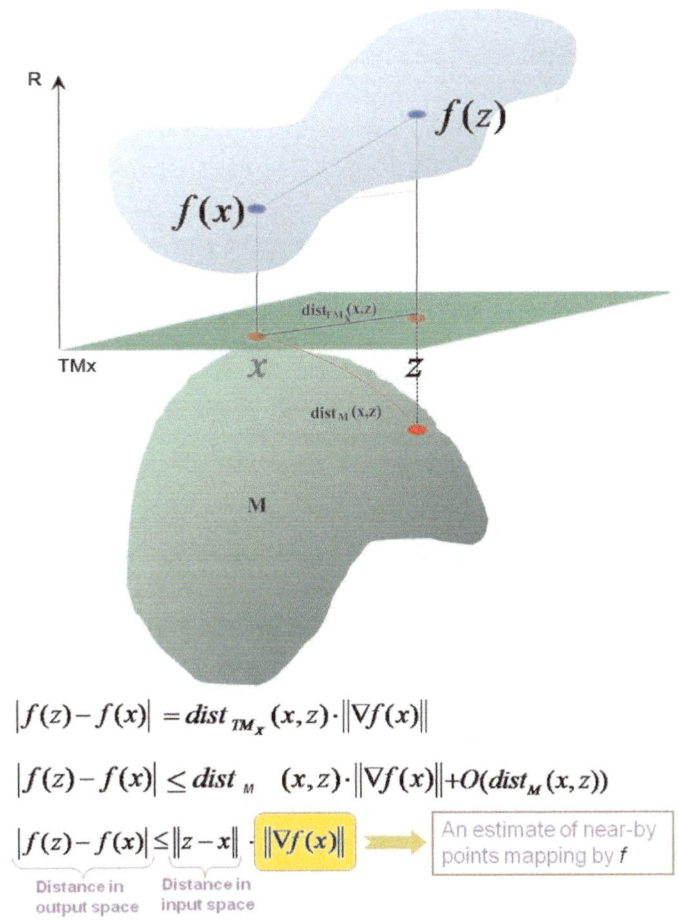

Fig. 4.9 The Laplace–Beltrami operator

Figure 4.9 interprets the Beltrami operator geometrically. First, given two neighboring points $\mathbf{x}, \mathbf{y} \in \mathbb{M}$, which are mapped to $f(\mathbf{x})$ and $f(\mathbf{z})$, respectively, we have

$$|f(\mathbf{z}) - f(\mathbf{x})| = dist_{TM_x}(\mathbf{x}, \mathbf{z}) \cdot ||\nabla f(\mathbf{x})|| \tag{4.4}$$

where $\nabla f(\mathbf{x})$ is a vector in the tangent space TM_x. By using the geodesic distance defined in $\mathbb{M}$ replace the $dist_{TM_x}(\mathbf{x}, \mathbf{z})$, we then obtain

$$|f(\mathbf{z}) - f(\mathbf{x})| = dist_{\mathbb{M}}(\mathbf{x},\mathbf{z}) \cdot ||\nabla f(\mathbf{x})|| + o(dist_{\mathbb{M}}(\mathbf{x},\mathbf{z})) \tag{4.5}$$

Next, by assuming that $\mathbb{M}$ is isometrically embedded in $\mathbb{R}^D$, we have $dist_{\mathbb{M}} = ||\mathbf{x}-\mathbf{z}||_{\mathbb{R}^D} + o(||\mathbf{x}-\mathbf{z}||_{\mathbb{R}^D})$ and

$$|f(\mathbf{z}) - f(\mathbf{x})| \leq ||\nabla f(\mathbf{x})||||\mathbf{z}-\mathbf{x}|| + o(||\mathbf{z}-\mathbf{x}||) \tag{4.6}$$

Thus, it is clear that $||\nabla f||$ provides a measure of how far apart f maps nearby points in $\mathbb{R}^D$ to those in $\mathbb{M}$. We therefore look for a map that best preserves average locality by trying to find

$$argmin_{||f||_{L^2(\mathbb{M})}=1} \int_{\mathbb{M}} ||\nabla f(\mathbf{x})||^2 \tag{4.7}$$

where the integral is taken with respect to the standard measure on a Riemannian manifold. Note that minimizing $\int_{\mathbb{M}} ||\nabla f(\mathbf{x})||^2$ corresponds directly to minimizing $L\mathbf{f} = 1/2\sum_{i,j}(f_i - f_j)^2 W_{ij}$ on a graph.

Since

$$\int_{\mathbb{M}} ||\nabla f||^2 = \int_{\mathbb{M}} \mathscr{L}(f)f \tag{4.8}$$

It turns out that minimizing $\int_{\mathbb{M}} ||\nabla f(\mathbf{x})||^2$ reduces to finding eigenfunctions (for more details about the eigenfunction, see Appendix) of the Laplace–Beltrami operator $\mathscr{L}$, where $\mathscr{L}$ is defined as $\mathscr{L} = -div\nabla(f)$.

The spectrum of $\mathscr{L}$ on a compact manifold $\mathbb{M}$ is known to be discrete. Let the eigenvalues (in increasing order) be $\lambda_0 \leq \lambda_1 \leq ...$ and let f_i be the eigenfunction corresponding to eigenvalue λ_i. To avoid the situation in which the constant function f_0 maps $\mathbb{M}$ to a single point, it is required that the embedding map f be orthogonal to f_0. The optimal d-dimensional embedding is provided by

$$\mathbf{x} \rightarrow (f_1(\mathbf{x}), ..., f_d(\mathbf{x})) \tag{4.9}$$

4.4.2.3 Relationship to LLE

As discussed earlier, the first and third steps of the Laplacian eigenmaps algorithm are essentially equivalent to LLE. They differ only in choice of weight matrix $\mathbf{W}$. Let $\mathbf{W}$ be the weight matrix estimated by LLE. Using a Taylor approximation, one can show that at each point $\mathbf{x}$

$$(\mathbf{I} - \mathbf{W})f(\mathbf{x})|_{\mathbf{x}=\mathbf{x}_i} \approx -\frac{1}{2} \sum_{j \in N(i)} w_{ij}(\mathbf{x}_i - \mathbf{x}_j)^T H_i(\mathbf{x}_i - \mathbf{x}_j) \tag{4.10}$$

where $N(i)$ denotes the neighbors of i, H_i denotes the Hessian of f at $\mathbf{x}_i$. If vectors to neighboring points $\sqrt{w_{ij}}(\mathbf{x}_i - \mathbf{x}_j)$ form an orthonormal basis of the tangent space at $\mathbf{x}_i$, it follows immediately that

$$\sum_{j \in N(i)} w_{ij}(\mathbf{x}_i - \mathbf{x}_j)^T H_i(\mathbf{x}_i - \mathbf{x}_j) = trace(H_i) = \nabla(f) \tag{4.11}$$

More generally, if neighboring points are uniformly distributed on any sphere centered at $\mathbf{x}_i$, the expectation of Eq. (4.11) is proportional to $\nabla(f)$.

4.4.3 Hessian Eigenmaps

The Hessian eigenmap framework (Donoho and Grimes 2003) draws on the Laplacian eigenmap theory discussed in Section 4.4.2. However, by replacing the Laplacian operator with the Hessian, one can correct a key deficiency of the Laplacian cost functional (4.7), producing an algorithm which is guaranteed to asympotically recover the true manifold under fairly broad assumptions.

4.4.3.1 Asymptotic Convergence Guarantee

Let $d_{\mathbb{M}}$ denote the distance of the shortest path between $\mathbf{x}, \mathbf{x}' \in \mathbb{M}$ which lies entirely within the manifold $\mathbb{M}$. Then, assuming an infinite number of data points are drawn from a positive distribution over the manifold, the Isomap algorithm will recover the true coordinates of the manifold by finding the mapping $f\colon \mathbb{M} \to \mathscr{Y}$ (up to a rigid transformation) under the following assumptions:

- Isometry: for all pairs of points on the manifold, the manifold distance is equal to the Euclidean distance between their corresponding coordinates: $d_{\mathbb{M}}(\mathbf{x}, \mathbf{x}') = ||\mathbf{y} - \mathbf{y}'||, \forall \mathbf{x} = f(\mathbf{y})$ and $\mathbf{x}' = f(\mathbf{y}')$.
- Convexity: the coordinate space $\mathbb{Y}$ is a convex subset of $\mathbb{R}^d$.

Donoho and Grimes (2003) have investigated the validity of these two assumptions in the context of families of images. They argue that while istometry is often a reasonable assumption, the convexity requirement is frequently violated. Their Hessian eigenmaps framework leads to the Hessian LLE algorithm, which provides the same convergence guaranties under the following weaker assumptions.

- Local isometry: for points $\mathbf{x}' \in \mathbb{M}$ in a sufficiently small neighborhood around each point $\mathbf{x} \in \mathbb{M}$, geodesic distances $d_{\mathbb{M}}(\mathbf{x}, \mathbf{x}')$ are identical to Euclidean distances ——**y-y'**—— between their corresponding coordinates.
- Connectedness: the coordinate space $\mathbb{Y}$ is an open connected subset of $\mathbb{R}^d$.

In such a setting, the original assumptions of the Isomap are violated, and the algorithm itself fails to recover the manifold, while Hessian LLE can.

4.4.3.2 Theoretical Framework

Donoho and Grimes (2003) found that by minimizing $\mathscr{H}(f)$, the convexity condition in the previous approaches (Isomap and Laplacian Eigenmaps) can be relaxed to a weaker constraint connectedness.

Hessian LLE revolves around a quadratic form $\mathscr{H}(f) = \int_{\mathbb{M}} ||H_f(x)||_F^2 dx$ defined on functions $f\colon \mathbb{M} \to \mathbb{R}$, where H_f denotes the Hessian of f, and $\mathscr{H}(f)$ averages the Frobenius norm (see Appendix for more details) of the Hessian over $\mathbb{M}$. The key observation is that if $\mathbb{M}$ truly is locally isometric to an open connected subset of $\mathbb{R}^d$, then $\mathscr{H}(f)$ has a $(d+1)$-dimensional null space (see Appendix for definition) consisting of the constant functions and a d-dimensional space of functions spanned by the original isometric coordinates. Hence, the isometric coordinates can be recovered up to a linear isometry.

In the following, we provide a definition of $\mathscr{H}(f)$. It involves first estimating the H_f, i.e., the *tangent Hessian*, and then defining the quadratic form $\mathscr{H}(f)$.

First, at each point $\mathbf{x} \in \mathbb{M}$, we can use the tangent coordinates and differentiate f in the coordinate system. Suppose that $\mathbb{M}$ is a smooth manifold, so that the tangent space $T_{\mathbf{x}}(\mathbb{M})$ is well defined at each point $\mathbf{x} \in \mathbb{M}$. Thinking of the tangent space as a subspace of $\mathbb{R}^D$, each such tangent space $T(\mathbb{M})$ can be associated with an orthonormal coordinate system using the inner product inherited from $\mathbb{R}^D$. There is a neighborhood $N_{\mathbf{x}}$ of $\mathbf{x}$ such that each point $\mathbf{x}' \in N_{\mathbf{x}}$ has a unique closest point $\mathbf{z}' \in T_{\mathbf{x}}(\mathbb{M})$ and such that the implied mapping $\mathbf{x}' \mapsto \mathbf{z}'$ is smooth. The point in $T(\mathbb{M})$ has coordinates given by the choice of orthonormal coordinates for $T(\mathbb{M})$. In this way, the local coordinates for a neighborhood $N_{\mathbf{x}}$ of $\mathbf{x} \in \mathbb{M}$ can be obtained.

With the obtained local coordinates, the Hessian of the function $f\colon \mathbb{M} \to \mathbb{R}$, which is C^2 near $\mathbf{x}$, can be defined. Suppose that $\mathbf{x}' \in N_{\mathbf{x}}$ has a local coordinate z'. Then the rule $g(\mathbf{z}') = f(\mathbf{x}')$ defines a function $g\colon U \mapsto U$, where U is a neighborhood of 0 in $\mathbb{R}^d$. Since the mapping $\mathbf{x}' \mapsto \mathbf{z}'$ is smooth, the function g is C^2. The Hessian of f at $\mathbf{x}$ in tangent coordinates is the ordinary Hessian of g

$$(H_f(\mathbf{x}))_{i,j} = \frac{\partial}{\partial x_i}\frac{\partial}{\partial x_j} g(\mathbf{x})|_{x=0} \tag{4.12}$$

However, there is some ambiguity in the above definition of the Hessian, because the entries in the Hessian matrix H_f depend on the choice of coordinate system on the underlying tangent space $T_{\mathbf{x}}(\mathbb{M})$.

Secondly, in order to extract invariant information about f, the Frobenius norm of H_f is introduced, and then a quadratic form defined on C^2 functions is considered

$$\mathscr{H}(f) = \int_{\mathbb{M}} ||H_f(\mathbf{x})||_F^2 d\mathbf{x} \tag{4.13}$$

where $d\mathbf{x}$ stands for a probability measure on $\mathbb{M}$ which has strictly positive density everywhere on the interior of $\mathbb{M}$. $\mathscr{H}(f)$ measures the average curviness of f over the manifold $\mathbb{M}$.

4.4.3.3 ALgorithm: Hessian LLE

The Hessian LLE algorithm adapts the basic structure of LLE to estimate the null space of the functional $\mathscr{H}(f)$. The algorithm has three stages:

1. Find nearest neighbors: this stage is identical to LLE (nonsymmetric neighborhoods are allowed).
2. Estimate tangent Hessians: for each data point $\mathbf{x}_i$, perform a PCA of the neighboring points to find the best fitting d-dimensional linear subspace. Project the local

neighborhood to this subspace, and use the result to construct a least-squares estimate of the local Hessian matrix H_i.
3. Compute embedding from estimated $\mathscr{H}$ functional: using the discretization implied by the data points, and the local Hessian estimates H_i, construct a sparse matrix that approximates the continuous operator $\mathscr{H}$. Then choose $\mathbf{Y}$ to be the eigenvectors corresponding to the d smallest eigenvalues, excluding the constant eigenvector.

4.4.3.4 Comparison to LLE/Laplacian Eigenmaps

Hessian LLE bears a substantial resemblance to the LLE procedure proposed by Roweis and Saul (2000). The theoretical framework we have described also bears a considerable resemblance to the Laplacian eigenmap framework, only with the Hessian replacing the Laplacian.

Table 4.2 gives a comparison of the Laplacian eigenmap and the Hessian eigenmap. See Section 4.4.2.3 for a discussion of the relationship between LLE and the Laplacian eigenmap.

Laplacian eigenmaps	Hessian eigenmaps
Sparse problem	Guaranteed to recover the manifold asymptotically
Rooted in Spectral Graph Theory	Can handle non-convex sets
Not independent of the choice of coordinate frame results; distorted embedding	Assumes all points lie exactly on the manifold
Nonlinear functions with zero Laplacian	Requires estimate of second order data, which is noisy
Sensitive to neighborhood size	Sensitive to neighborhood size

Table 4.2 Pros and Cons of Laplacian eigenmaps and Hessian eigenmaps

Figure 4.10 shows the learned manifold by using the Isomap algorithm, regular LLE, and Hessian LLE, respectively. The data are generated by the random sampling of 600 points in three dimensions. The results show the dramatic effect that non-convexity can have on the resulting embeddings. In the case of Laplacian eigenmaps, the effects of a missing sampling region make the resulting embedding functions asymmetric and nonlinear with respect to the original parameterization. In the case of the Isomap, non-convexity causes a strong dilation of the missing region, warping the rest of the embedding. Hessian LLE, in contrast, embeds the result almost perfectly into 2D space.

4.4.4 Diffusion Maps

The use of the first few eigenvectors of the normalized eigenvalue problem, either as a low-dimensional representation of data or as good coordinates for clustering purposes, is typically justified with heuristic arguments or as a relaxation of a discrete clustering problem (Boykov and Jolly 2001). For example, in the Laplacian

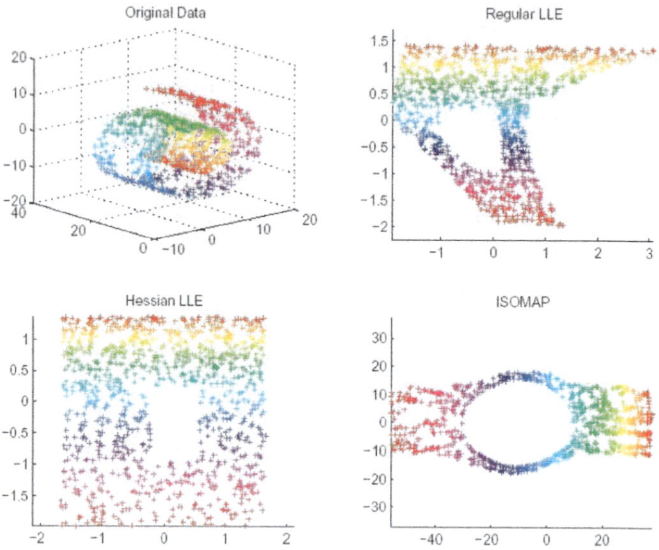

Fig. 4.10 Top left: original data. Top right: LLE embedding (neighborhood size: 12); Bottom left: Hessian eigenmaps (neighborhood size: 12); Bottom right: Isomap (neighborhood size: 7). From Donoho and Grimes (2003)

eigenmap, the first few eigenvectors of the Laplacian matrix are discrete approximations of the eigenfunctions of the Laplace–Beltrami operator on the manifold, thus providing a mathematical justification for their use in manifold learning.

In this section, we introduce diffusion maps, which provide a diffusion-based probabilistic interpretation of spectral clustering and dimensionality reduction algorithms that use the eigenvectors of the normalized graph Laplacian. Diffusion maps define a system of coordinates with an explicit metric that reflects the connectivity of a given data set and that is robust to noise. This construction is based upon a Markov random walk on the data and offers a general scheme for simultaneously reorganizing and subsampling the graph and arbitrarily shaped data sets in high dimensions using intrinsic geometry.

4.4.4.1 Random Walk on a Graph

The spectral embedding algorithms discussed so far are, in general, based on the analysis of the dominant eigenvectors of a suitably normalized weight matrix. Usually, a graph $G = (V, E)$ of the data set $\mathbf{X} = \{\mathbf{x}_i \in \mathbb{R}^D\}_{i=1}^n$ is constructed first. The weights on the edges in the graph constitute a prior definition of the local geometry of **X**, and since a given kernel will capture a specific feature of the data set, its choice should be guided by the application that one has in mind. Here, we choose a Gaussian kernel as an example, and the weights lead to a matrix **W** with entries

$$w_{ij} = \exp - \frac{-||\mathbf{x}_i - \mathbf{x}_j||^2}{2\varepsilon} \tag{4.14}$$

$$D = Diag([D_1, ...D_n]) \text{ with } D_i = \sum_{j=1}^{n} w_{ij} \tag{4.15}$$

where ε denotes the variance of the Gaussian. Subsequently, normalization of the matrix **W** is performed in such a way that its rows add up to 1.

In the framework of diffusion maps, if the weight function satisfies certain conditions (symmetry and point - wise positivity), the pairwise similarities are interpreted as edge flows in a Markov random walk on the graph. Thus, from the graph defined by $(\mathbf{X}, \mathbf{W})$, one can construct a reversible Markov chain on **X**, with the transition matrix **T** of entries

$$p(\mathbf{x}^{t+\Delta} = \mathbf{x}_j | \mathbf{x}^t = \mathbf{x}_i) = T(i,j) = \frac{w_{ij}}{\sum_{k \in V} w_{ik}} \tag{4.16}$$

where Δ denotes the time step size. Indeed, the transition directly reflects the local geometry defined by the immediate neighbors of each node in the graph of the data. In other words, each entry represents the probability of the transition in one time step from node i to node j and it is proportional to the edge weight w_{ij}.

For $t \geq 0$, the probability of a transition from i to j in t times is given by $T^t(ij)$, the kernel of the tth power of **T**. Thus, running the chain forward in time, or equivalently, taking a larger power of **T**, will allow us to integrate the local geometry and therefore reveal relevant geometric structures of **X** at different scales. For example, if one starts a random walk from location $\mathbf{x}_i$, the probability of landing in location **y** after r time steps is given by

$$p(t = r\Delta, \mathbf{y}|\mathbf{x}_i) = p(\mathbf{x}^t = \mathbf{y}|\mathbf{x}^0 = \mathbf{x}_i) = \mathbf{e}_i \mathbf{T}^r \tag{4.17}$$

where $\mathbf{e}_i$ is a row vector with all zeros, except that ith position is equal to 1.

For large Δ, all points in the graph are connected $(T_{ij} > 0)$, and the eigenvalues of **T** are as follows

$$\lambda_0 = 1 \geq \lambda_1 ... \lambda_{n-1} \geq 0 \tag{4.18}$$

Then, regardless the initial starting point **x**, we have the straightforward result

$$\lim_{t \longrightarrow \infty} p(t, \mathbf{y}|\mathbf{x}_i) = \lim_{r \longrightarrow \infty} \mathbf{e}_i \mathbf{T}^r = \phi_0(\mathbf{y}) \tag{4.19}$$

where $\phi_0(\mathbf{y})$ is the left eigenvector of **T** with the eigenvalue $\lambda_0 = 1$, explicitly given by

$$\phi_0(\mathbf{x}_i) = \frac{D_i}{\sum_{j=1}^{n} D_j} \tag{4.20}$$

The eigenvector $\phi_0(\mathbf{x})$ has a dual representation. The first is that it is the stationary probability distribution on the graph, while the second is that it is the density estimate at location $\mathbf{x}$.

For any finite time t, the probability distribution $p(t,\mathbf{y}|\mathbf{x})$ can be decomposed in the eigenbasis $\{\phi_j\}$

$$p(t,\mathbf{y}|\mathbf{x}) = \phi_0(\mathbf{y}) + \sum_{j=1}^{n-1} \varphi_j(\mathbf{x})\lambda_k^r \phi_j(\mathbf{y}) \tag{4.21}$$

where φ_j and ϕ_j are the right and left eigenvectors of $\mathbf{T}$, and λ_j^r is the jth eigenvalue of $\mathbf{T}^r$.

4.4.4.2 Diffusion Distance and Diffusion Map

Given this definition of a random walk on the graph, the diffusion distance is defined as the distance measure at time t between two points

$$Dis_t^2(\mathbf{x}_i,\mathbf{x}_j) = \sum_{\mathbf{y}=\mathbf{x}_1}^{\mathbf{x}_n} (p(t,\mathbf{y}|\mathbf{x}_i) - p(t,\mathbf{y}|\mathbf{x}_j))^2/\phi_0(\mathbf{y}) \tag{4.22}$$

The key idea behind the diffusion distance is that it is based on many paths through the graph. This makes the diffusion distance more robust to noise than, e.g., the geodesic distance.

The mapping between the original space and the first d eigenvectors is defined as the diffusion map

$$\Psi_t(\mathbf{x}) = (\lambda_1^t \psi_1(\mathbf{x}), \lambda_2^t \psi_2(\mathbf{x}), \ldots, \lambda_d^t \psi_d(\mathbf{x})) \tag{4.23}$$

The diffusion distance relates to the diffusion map as follows

$$D_t^2(\mathbf{x}_0,\mathbf{x}_1) = \sum_{j=1}^{n-1} \lambda_j^{2t} (\phi(\mathbf{x})_0 - \phi(\mathbf{x})_1)^2 = ||\Psi_t(\mathbf{x}_0) - \Psi_t(\mathbf{x}_0)|| \tag{4.24}$$

This means that the diffusion distance is equal to the Euclidean distance in the diffusion map space with all $n-1$ eigenvectors. It also provides a justification for using Euclidean distance in the diffusion map space for the purposes of spectral clustering. Therefore, geometry in the diffusion space is meaningful and can be interpreted in terms of a Markov chain.

4.4.4.3 Dimensionality Reduction and Parameterization of Data by Diffusion Maps

The eigenvectors of $\mathbf{T}$ also provide a low-dimensional representation for the original data set while preserving their diffusion distances. In many practical applications the spectrum of the matrix $\mathbf{T}$ has a spectral gap with only a few eigenvalues close to one, and therefore the diffusion distance at a large enough time t can be well approximated by only the first few k eigenvectors $\psi_1(\mathbf{x}), ..., \psi_k(\mathbf{x})$, with a negligible error of the order of $O((\lambda_{k+1}/\lambda_k)^t)$. That is, the optimal k-dimensional approximation is given by the truncated sum under a mean squared error criterion.

$$\hat{p}(t, \mathbf{y}|\mathbf{x}) = \phi_0(\mathbf{y}) + \sum_{j=1}^{k} \lambda_j^t \varphi_j(\mathbf{x}) \phi_j(\mathbf{y}) \tag{4.25}$$

The mapping $\Psi_t : \mathbb{R}^D \mapsto \mathbb{R}^d$ provides a parametrization of the data set $\mathbf{X}$, or equivalently, a realization of the graph G as a cloud of points in a low-dimensional space $\mathbb{R}^d$, where the rescaled eigenvectors are the coordinates. The dimensionality reduction and the weighting of the relevant eigenvectors are dictated by both the time t of the random walk and the spectral fall off of the eigenvalues. Moreover, Ψ_t embeds the entire data set in the low-dimensional space in such a way that the Euclidean distance is an approximation of the diffusion distance, which is quite different from other eigenmap methods.

4.5 Hybrid Methods: Global Alignment of Local Models

The global structure of a perceptual manifold tends to be highly nonlinear. However, despite their complicated global structure, we can usually characterize these manifolds as locally smooth. This is the starting point of hybrid methods for manifold learning. In building models of high-dimensional data points sampled from such manifolds, hybrid methods focus on (i) modeling the density of data sampled from such manifolds and (ii) recovering global parameterizations of these manifolds in an unsupervised manner. Furthermore, this globally nonlinear probabilistic mapping between coordinates on the manifold to raw data points and vice versa is obtained by combining several locally valid linear/nonlinear mappings.

In this section, we introduce three manifold learning algorithms that ascribe to this line of thinking: global coordination of local linear models (Roweis et al. 2002), charting of a manifold (Brand 2003), and local tangent space alignment (Zhang and Zha 2002). We refer to them as hybrid methods since they learn a manifold effectively with local and global consistency, and more importantly, they also provide an efficient approach to improve global and local manifold learning algorithms.

4.5.1 Global Coordination of Local Linear Models

Roweis and Ghahramani (1999) propose using a mixture of factors analyzer (MFA) (Ghahramani and Hinton 1997) to describe high-dimensional data that lies on or near a low-dimensional manifold. The MFA model assumes that data are sampled from different neighbors on the manifold with prior probabilities, and that within each neighborhood, the data's coordinates are normally distributed, while the model's global coordinates on the manifold as latent variables. The data's high- and low-dimensional coordinates are then related to each other by linear processes parameterized by the properties of the neighborhood.

MFA parameterizes a joint distribution over observed and hidden variables:

$$p(\mathbf{x}, s, \mathbf{z}_s) = P(\mathbf{x}|s, \mathbf{z}_s)P(\mathbf{z}_s|s)P(s) \tag{4.26}$$

where the observed variables, $\mathbf{x} \in \mathbb{R}^D$, denote the high-dimensional data; the discrete hidden variables, $s \in \{1, 2, ..., S\}$, index different neighborhoods on the manifold; and the continuous hidden variables, $\mathbf{z}_s \in \mathbb{R}^d$, denote low-dimensional local coordinates. The model assumes that $\mathbf{x}$ is sampled from different neighborhoods on the manifold with prior probabilities $P(s) = p_s$, and the data's local coordinates $\mathbf{z}_s$ are distributed as

$$P(\mathbf{z}_s|s) = (2\pi)^{-\frac{d}{2}} \exp\left\{-\frac{1}{2}\mathbf{z}_s^T \mathbf{z}_s\right\} \tag{4.27}$$

The data's high- and low-dimensional coordinates are related by a linear process

$$P(\mathbf{x}|s, \mathbf{z}_s) = |2\pi\Psi_s|^{-\frac{1}{2}} \exp\left\{-\frac{1}{2}[\mathbf{x} - \mu_s - \Lambda_s\mathbf{z}_s]^T \Psi_s^{-1}[\mathbf{x} - \mu_s - \Lambda_s\mathbf{z}_s]\right\} \tag{4.28}$$

The marginal data distribution $P(\mathbf{x})$ can then be obtained by summing/integrating out the model's discrete and continuous latent variables. This results in a mixture of Gaussian distributions of the following form

$$P(\mathbf{x}) = \sum_s p_s|2\pi(\Lambda_s\Lambda_s^T + \Psi_s)|^{\frac{1}{2}} \exp\left\{-\frac{1}{2}[\mathbf{x} - \mu_s]^T(\Lambda_s\Lambda_s^T + \Psi_s)^{-1}[\mathbf{x} - \mu_s]\right\} \tag{4.29}$$

The learning problem for $P(\mathbf{x})$ is to estimate the center μ_s, transformations Λ_s, and noise levels Ψ_s of these linear processes, as well as the prior probabilities p_s of sampling data from different parts of the manifold. This problem can be solved by the EM algorithm that maximizes the log-probability, averaged over training examples.

However, the parameter space of this model exhibits an invariance: arbitrary rotations and reflections of the local coordinates in each linear model do not change the marginal distribution. Thus, maximum likelihood estimation in MFA does not favor any particular alignment; instead, it produces models whose internal representations change unpredictably as one traverses connected paths on the manifold.

To deal with this problem, global coordination is needed. This can be accomplished by treating the coordinates $\mathbf{g}$ as unobserved variables and incorporating them into the probabilistic model $P(\mathbf{g}|s, \mathbf{z}_s) = \delta(\mathbf{g} - A_s\mathbf{z}_s - \kappa_s)$, where the global coordinates relate to the local coordinates of different neighborhoods via a linear transformation $g(s, \mathbf{z}_s) = A_s\mathbf{z}_s + \kappa_s$. With this probabilistic model, it is appealing to make another useful inference. In particular.

$$P(\mathbf{g}|\mathbf{x}_n, s) = \int d\mathbf{z}_s P(\mathbf{g}|s, \mathbf{z}_s)P(\mathbf{z}_s|s, \mathbf{x}_n) \tag{4.30}$$

$$P(\mathbf{g}|\mathbf{x}_n) = \sum_s P(s|\mathbf{x}_n)P(\mathbf{g}|\mathbf{x}_n, s) \tag{4.31}$$

A regularizing term is then added to the standard maximum likelihood objective function. This regularization breaks a degeneracy in the mixture model's parameter space, favoring local models whose internal coordinate systems are aligned in a consistent way. As a result, the internal coordinates change smoothly and continuously as one traverses a connected path on the manifold. More specifically, the new objective function consists of two terms: (i) the term that computes the log-probability of the data and, (ii) the term that computes a sum of Kullback–Leibler (KL) divergence. These two terms are designed to penalize MFAs whose posterior distribution over the global coordinates is not unimodal.

$$\Omega = \sum_n logP(\mathbf{x}_n) - \lambda \sum_{ns} \int \mathbf{dg} Q(\mathbf{g}, s|\mathbf{x}_n) log \left[\frac{Q(\mathbf{g}, s|\mathbf{x}_n)}{P(\mathbf{g}, s|\mathbf{x}_n)} \right] \quad (4.32)$$

where $\mathbf{g}$ is the set of global coordinates which parameterize the manifold everywhere. $P(\mathbf{g}, s|\mathbf{x}_n)$ is the posterior distribution over both $\mathbf{g}$ and s, which can be derived easily according to Eq. (4.33) and (4.31).

$Q(\mathbf{g}, s|\mathbf{x}_n)$ represents a family of unimodal distributions factorized via a Gaussian density and a multinomial:

$$Q(\mathbf{g}, s|\mathbf{x}_n) = Q(\mathbf{g}|\mathbf{x}_n) Q(s|\mathbf{x}_n) \quad (4.33)$$

where $Q(\mathbf{g}|\mathbf{x}_n) \sim N(g_n, \Sigma_n)$, and $Q(s|\mathbf{x}_n) = q_{ns}$. At each iteration of learning, the means $\mathbf{g}_n$, covariance matrices Σ_n, and the mixture weights q_{ns} are determined separately for each data point $\mathbf{x}_n$, so as to maximize the objective function.

4.5.2 Charting a Manifold

In addition to the diffusion maps, the framework we have discussed thus far is purely deterministic, in that it assumes that the observed data points lie exactly on the manifold of interest. However, for most real data sets, we can at best hope that the data are "close" (in a probabilistic sense) to some manifold. Furthermore, although these algorithms rely on the empirical estimates of differential operators, they do not consider the noise introduced into these estimates by a sparse, nonhomogeneous sampling of the manifold.

The charting algorithm (Brand 2003) addresses these problems by casting manifold learning as a density estimation problem. In particular, charting first fits a mixture of Gaussian densities to the data and then coordinates the local coordinates implied by each Gaussian's covariance into a single global system. The density model underlying charting naturally provides a function mapping of all coordinates to the high-dimensional manifold rather than an embedding of the given data.

The charting algorithm retains LLE's basic three-step structure, including an attractive property that the optimal solution to each stage may be computed in closed form.

1. Soft nearest neighbor assignment: for each $\mathbf{x}_i$, assign a weight w_{ij} to each $\mathbf{x}_j, j \neq i$, according to a Gaussian kernel centered at $\mathbf{x}_i$ as in the Laplacian eigenmap framework. The bandwidth of the kernel should be chosen as $\sigma \approx r/2$, where r is the radius over which the manifold is expected to be locally linear. An interesting heuristic for automatically estimating r can be found in Brand (2003).
2. Fit the Gaussian mixture model: let $N(\mathbf{x};\mu,\Lambda)$ denote a Gaussian density with mean μ and covariance Λ, evaluated at the point $\mathbf{x}$. In charting, the high-dimensional data space is modeled by an n-component Gaussian mixture, where the component means are set to the observed data points $\mathbf{x}_i$

$$p(\mathbf{x}|\Lambda) = \frac{1}{n}\sum_{i=1}^{n} N(\mathbf{x};\mathbf{x}_i,\Lambda_i) \tag{4.34}$$

here, Λ_i denotes the covariances Λ_i placed around the n data points. Left to its own devices, the maximum likelihood covariance estimate shrinks all of the covariance Λ_i to zero. To avoid this degenerate solution, charting places the following prior on the local covariances:

$$p(\Lambda) = \alpha \exp\left\{-\sum_{i\neq j} w_{ij} KL(N(\mathbf{x};\mathbf{x}_i,\Lambda_i)||N(\mathbf{x};\mathbf{x}_j,\Lambda_j))\right\} \tag{4.35}$$

where $KL(p||q)$ denotes the Kullback–Leibler divergence. This prior encourages neighboring Gaussian densities, as determined by the weights w_{ij}, to span similar subspaces. The maximum of a posterior (MAP) covariance estimate may be determined in the closed form by solving a coupled set of linear equations. This estimate brings nonlocal information into the estimation of the local coordinate frames defined by the Λ_i matrices, ensuring that neighboring coordinates span similar subspaces.
3. Connect local charts: suppose that we wish to find an embedding in $\mathbb{R}^d$. For the kth mixture component $N(\mathbf{x};\mathbf{x}_k,\Lambda_k)$, let $U_k = [u_{k1},...,u_{kn}]$ denote the projection of the n data points onto the d-dimensional subspace spanned by the d dominant eigenvectors of $\Lambda - k$. For each chart, we would like to determine a low-dimensional affine projection $G_k \in \mathbb{R}^{d\times d+1}$ that maps these points into the global coordinate frame. We couple these projections by requiring them to agree on data points for which they share responsibility, as encoded by the following objective:

$$\Phi_{chart}(G) = \sum_{k\neq j}\sum_{i=1}^{n} p_k(\mathbf{x}_i)p_j(\mathbf{x}_i)\left|\left|G_k\begin{bmatrix}u_{ki}\\1\end{bmatrix} - G_j\begin{bmatrix}u_{ji}\\1\end{bmatrix}\right|\right|_F^2 \tag{4.36}$$

where $p_k(\mathbf{x}_i)$ is the posterior probability (as defined by the mixture model selected in step 2) that $\mathbf{x}_i$ was sampled from $N(\mathbf{x};\mathbf{x}_k,\Lambda_k)$. The objective function can also be rewritten as

$$\Phi_{chart}(G) = trace(GQQ^TG^T) \tag{4.37}$$

for an appropriate matrix Q. Thus, as with LLE, the optimal embedding may be found by finding the bottom eigenvectors of an $n \times n$ symmetric matrix. This matrix may be made sparse by approximating very small posterior probabilities $p_k(\mathbf{x}_i)$ to be zero.

Examples in Brand (2003) show that charting performs well on sparsely sampled manifolds which cause problems for other methods like LLE.

4.5.3 Local Tangent Space Alignment

The LTSA represents the local geometry of the underlying manifold using tangent spaces learned by fitting an affine subspace in a neighborhood of each data points. These tangent spaces are then aligned to calculate the internal global coordinates of the data points with respect to the manifold, by way of partial eigen decomposition of the neighborhood connection matrix.

LTSA algorithm is summarized as follows. Given a set of high-dimensional data points $\{\mathbf{x}_i \in \mathbb{R}^D\}_{i=1}^N$ sampled possibly with noise from an underlying d-dimensional manifold, the algorithm produces N d-dimensional coordinates $T \in \mathbb{R}^{d \times N}$ for the manifold constructed from k local nearest neighbors.

1. Extracting local information: for each $i = 1, ..., N$,
   a. Determine the k nearest neighbors $\mathbf{x}_j$ of $\mathbf{x}_i$, $j = 1, ..., k$
   b. Compute the d largest eigenvectors $g_1, ..., g_d$ of the correlation matrix $(X_i - \mathbf{x}_i e^T)^T (X_i - \mathbf{x}_i e^T)$, and set $G_i = [e/\sqrt(k), g_1, ..., g_d]$
2. Construct the alignment matrix: form the alignment matrix Φ by locally summation if a direct eigen-solver will be used. Otherwise implement a routine that computes the matrix-vector multiplication $B\mu$ for an arbitrary vector μ.
3. Compute global coordinates: compute the $d+1$ smallest eigenvectors of Φ and pick up the eigenvector matrix $[\mu_2, ..., \mu_{d+1}]$ corresponding to the second to $d+$ 1st smallest eigenvalue and set $T = [\mu_2, ..., \mu_{d+1}]$.

4.6 Summary

This chapter presents a survey of recent advances in the manifold learning. We introduce basic concepts, as well as details of three main approaches to manifold learning: local, global, and hybrid approaches. These methods uncover the intrinsic geometric structure of a manifold embedded in the underlying space of possible patterns in order to construct representations, invariant maps, and ultimately learning algorithms. We have also discussed the manifold perspective of visual pattern representation, dimensionality reduction, and classification problems, as well as basic concepts, technical mechanisms, and algorithms.

Appendix

Eigenfunction

In mathematics, an eigenfunction of a linear operator, **A**, defined on some function space is any nonzero function f in that space that returns from the operator exactly as is, except for a multiplicative scaling factor. More precisely, $\mathbf{A}f = \lambda f$ for some scalar, λ, the corresponding eigenvalue. The solution of the differential eigenvalue problem also depends on any boundary conditions required of f.

Null Space

If T is a linear transformation of $\mathbb{R}^n$, then the null space $Null(T)$, also called the kernel $Ker(T)$, is the set of all vectors $\mathbf{X} \in \mathbb{R}^n$ such that $T(\mathbf{X}) = 0$, i.e. $Null(T) \equiv \{\mathbf{X} : T(\mathbf{X}) = 0\}$.

Affine space

Let **V** be a vector space over a field **K**, and let **A** be a nonempty set. Now define addition $\mathbf{p} + \mathbf{a} \in \mathbf{A}$ for any vector $\mathbf{a} \in \mathbf{A}$ and element $p \in \mathbf{A}$ subject to the conditions:

1. $\mathbf{p} + \mathbf{0} = \mathbf{p}$
2. $(\mathbf{p} + \mathbf{a}) + \mathbf{b} = \mathbf{p} + (\mathbf{a} + \mathbf{b})$
3. For any $\mathbf{q} \in \mathbf{A}$, there exists a unique vector $\mathbf{a} \in \mathbf{A}$ such that $\mathbf{q} = \mathbf{p} + \mathbf{a}$

Here, $\mathbf{a}, \mathbf{b} \in \mathbf{A}$. Then **A** is an affine space and **K** is called the coefficient field. In an affine space, it is possible to fix a point and coordinate axis such that every point in the space can be represented as an n-tuple of its coordinates. Every ordered pair of points **A** and **B** in an affine space is then associated with a vector **A, B**.

Frobenius Norm

The Frobenius norm, sometimes also called the Euclidean norm (which may cause confusion with the vector L^2-norm, which is also sometimes known as the Euclidean norm), is a matrix norm of an $m \times n$ matrix **A** defined as the square root of the sum of the absolute squares of its elements.

$$||\mathbf{A}||_F = \sqrt{\sum_{i=1}^{m} \sum_{j=1}^{n} |a_{ij}|^2} \tag{4.38}$$

The Frobenius norm can also be considered to be a vector norm. It too is equal to the square root of the matrix trace of $\mathbf{AA}^H$, where $\mathbf{A}^H$ is the conjugate transpose, i.e., $||\mathbf{A}||_F = \sqrt{Tr(\mathbf{AA}^H)}$.

References

Balasubramanian M, Schwartz E, Tenenbaum J, de Silva V, Langford J (2002) The isomap algorithm and topological stability. Science 295:7

Belkin M, Niyogi P (2002) Laplacian Eigenmaps and spectral techniques for embedding and clustering. Advances in Neural Information Processing Systems 1:585–592

Belkin M, Niyogi P (2003) Laplacian eigenmaps for dimensionality reduction and data representation. Neural Computation 15:1373–1396

Belkin M, Niyogi P (2004) Semi-supervised learning on Riemannian manifolds. Machine Learning 56(1):209–239

Bengio Y, Paiement J, Vincent P, Delalleau O, Le Roux N, Ouimet M (2004) Out-of-sample extensions for LLE, Isomap, MDS, eigenmaps, and spectral clustering. In: Advances in Neural Information Processing Systems 16:177–186. MIT Press, Bradford Book

Borg I, Groenen P (2003) Modern multidimensional scaling: theory and applications. Journal of Educational Measurement 40(3):277–280

Boykov Y, Jolly M (2001) Interactive graph cuts for optimal boundary and region segmentation of objects in N-Dimages. In: International Conference on Computer Vision, Vancouver, BC, Canada, vol 1, pp 105–112

Brand M (2003) Charting a manifold. Advances in Neural Information Processing Systems 15:985–992. MIT Press, Cambridge

Coifman R, Lafon S, Lee A, Maggioni M, Nadler B, Warner F, Zucker S (2005) Geometric diffusions as a tool for harmonic analysis and structure definition of data: diffusion maps. Proceedings of the National Academy of Sciences 102(21):7426–7431

Donoho D, Grimes C (2003) Hessian eigenmaps: locally linear embedding techniques for high-dimensional data. Proceedings of the National Academy of Sciences 100(10):5591–5596

Efros A, Isler V, Shi J, Visontai M (2005) Seeing through water. In: Advances in Neural Information Processing Systems, MIT Press, Cambridge

Ghahramani Z, Hinton G (1997) The EM Algorithm for Mixtures of Factor Analyzers. University of Toronto Technical Report CRG-TR-96-1

Law M, Jain A (2006) Incremental nonlinear dimensionality reduction by manifold learning. IEEE Transactions on Pattern Analysis and Machine Intelligence 28:377–391

Lin T, Zha H, Lee S (2006) Riemannian manifold learning for nonlinear dimensionality reduction. Lecture Notes in Computer Science 3951:44

Mika S, Ratsch G, Weston J, Scholkopf B, Mullers K (1999) Fisher discriminant analysis with kernels. In: Neural Networks for Signal Processing IX, IEEE Signal Processing Society Workshop, pp 41–48

Roweis S, Ghahramani Z (1999) A Unifying review of linear gaussian models. Neural Computation 11(2):305–345

Roweis S, Saul L (2000) Nonlinear dimensionality reduction by locally linear embedding Science 290:2323–2326

Roweis S, Saul L, Hinton G (2002) Global Coordination of Local Linear Models. In: Advances in Neural Information Processing Systems, MIT Press

Salzmann M, Pilet J, Ilic S, Fua P (2007) Surface deformation models for nonrigid 3D shape recovery. IEEE Transactions on Pattern Analysis and Machine Intelligence 29:1481–1487

Schoelkopf B, Smola A, Mueller K (1997) Kernel principal component analysis. Lecture Notes in Computer Science, Springer, Berline, pp 583–588

Sha F, Saul L (2005) Analysis and extension of spectral methods for nonlinear dimensionality reduction. In: International Workshop on Machine Learning, vol 22

de Silva V, Tenenbaum J (2003) Global versus local methods in nonlinear dimensionality reduction. In: Advances in Neural Information Processing Systems 15:721–728. MIT Press, Cambridge

Weinberger K, Saul L (2006) Unsupervised learning of image manifolds by semidefinite programming. International Journal of Computer Vision 70(1):77–90

Zhang Z, Zha H (2002) Principal manifolds and nonlinear dimension reduction via local tangent space alignment. Arxiv preprint csLG/0212008

Chapter 5
Functional Approximation

Abstract This chapter presents a review of recent advances in the adaptive wavelet transform applied to image and video coding. We focus on research to improve the properties of the wavelet transform rather than on the entire encoder. These advances include enhancements to the construction of an adaptive wavelet transform that results in fewer wavelet coefficients and improvements in motion-compensated temporal filtering that achieve temporal scalability for video compression. These nonlinear wavelet transforms provide added flexibility for image and video representations and accomplish higher compression efficiency than traditional wavelets. The authors also discuss several future research directions in the summary.

5.1 Introduction

Intense research is being carried out to make image and video compression algorithms more efficient, flexible, and robust against bit and packet errors. Designing a complete or over-complete expansion that allows for the compact representation of visual data (including images and videos) is a central problem in visual data compression.

Achieving a compact representation requires an intimate knowledge of the features in visual data. The knowledge can be mathematically represented by general and parsimonious models that realistically characterize the visual data source. This in turn can be useful for many other important tasks, including classification, denoising, interpolation, and segmentation. The main function of modeling is to convey the real scene and the image one obtains, or similarly, to describe the changes between consecutive images of a video sequence in terms of object motion and other effects, such as illumination variations and camera motion. Such models describe the assumptions that one makes about the real world. Depending on the selected model, one is then able to describe the real world with more or less detail and precision. For example, in order to relate changes in the real world to those in a video sequence, one needs parametric models that describe the real world and the

N. Zheng, J. Xue, *Statistical Learning and Pattern Analysis for Image and Video Processing*, Advances in Pattern Recognition, DOI 10.1007/978-1-84882-312-9_5,
© Springer-Verlag London Limited 2009

corresponding image generation process. Using image analysis tools, the parameters of a parametric mode are estimated from a video sequence of images of the real model. Using the parametric model and its estimated parameters, a model world, that is an approximation of the real world, can be reconstructed.

However, an accurate model for visual data would be of potentially overwhelming complexity, because images and video are naturally infinite-dimensional phenomena. They take place in a continuum, and in principle, the recording of an image or a video sequence cannot be constrained by a finite number of parameters. Effective compression of images and video depends on exploiting tendencies of pixels to be similar to their neighbors or to differ in partially predictable ways. Yet, the most general way to utilize the probable relationships between pixels is infeasible for larger numbers of such pixels. To overcome such compression problem, transform coding, as embodied in state-of-the-art lossy compressors, divides the encoding operation into a sequence of three relatively simple steps: (1) the computation of a linear transformation of the data designed primarily to produce uncorrelated coefficients, (2) separate quantization of each scalar coefficient, and (3) entropy coding.

From a computational analysis point of view, one can say that the transformation in transform coding is to build a dictionary $D = \{f_i\}_{i \in I}$ of elementary functions (e.g., f_i) that can well approximate any signal in a given function class F with the superposition of a few of its elements. The design of a dictionary with good approximation properties is not the only important element. Together with D, one also needs to find a fast algorithm that can efficiently find the sparse representation of any signal $g \in F$ in terms of the elements of D. It is well known that wavelets are optimal for representing unidimensional signals with a finite number of discontinuities (Vetterli 2001), in the sense that the mean squared error (MSE) of a nonlinear approximation (NLA) from the k maximal wavelet coefficients decreases in $O(k^{-1})$. Wavelet-based image/video codecs (Antonini et al. 1992), such as EZW (Shapiro et al. 1993), SPIHT (Kim and Pearlman 1997), and EBCOT (Taubman 2000), are successful examples of transform coding.

Wavelets are used in the latest image/video coders (JPEG2000 and the coming scalable video coding standard (SVC) (Reichel et al. 2005)) because of their efficient NLA properties for in processing a piecewise smooth function in one dimension (Vetterli 2001). In 1D, wavelets derive their efficient NLA behavior from their vanishing moment properties, and the question now is to see how these properties carry through in the 2D or 3D scenario. Even if good approximation properties are necessary for efficient compression, they may not be sufficient in NLA because the indexing and individual compression of wavelet coefficients might be inefficient. It has been shown in (Vetterli 2001) that, even in 1D, wavelet-based schemes perform suboptimally because they fail to precisely model singularities. In the 2D scenario, this is because the situation is much worse. The reason is that wavelets in 2D are obtained by a tensor product of 1D wavelets, and therefore they are adapted only to point singularities and cannot efficiently model the higher order singularities, such as curvilinear singularities, which are abundant in images.

This suggests that wavelets might have some limitations for image/video processing applications, especially for compression. To understand the magnitude of this limitation, consider a simple 2D function that is composed of two 2D polynomials separated by a linear boundary. Assume that one applies the wavelet transform with enough vanishing moments on this function. Then at level j, the number of significant wavelet coefficients corresponding to 2D polynomial regions is bounded by a constant, but the number of significant wavelet coefficients representing linear boundaries grows exponentially at a rate of 2^j. Even if the linear singularities can be represented by only two parameters, namely, the slope and intercept, the wavelet-based scheme models end up using an exponentially growing number of wavelet coefficients.

Obviously, despite scale invariance and other useful properties of wavelets, they do not provide an explicit representation of the geometric structures found in images, because these geometric features are nonlinearly related to the pixel intensities. Wavelets cannot efficiently model singularities along lines or curves. Edges in an image exhibit a certain degree of smoothness, that is, wavelet-based schemes fail to explore the geometric structure that is so typical in the smooth edges of images. However, geometric features, like edges, represent some of the most important perceptual and objective information in an image. It might be of interest to have a transform that overcomes these drawbacks by filtering along the image contours. In short, the precise modeling of geometric information is very crucial in image/video compression, and new schemes capable of exploiting geometric information present in images are needed.

We investigate the problem of coding images and video via wavelets in this article and focus on research for improving the properties of the transform rather than the encoder. More precisely, we present a review of recent advances in constructing an adaptive wavelet transform, which results in fewer wavelet coefficients. Such nonlinear wavelet transforms provide added flexibility for image and video representations. This survey is meant to be as structured as possible. It emphasizes the underlying ideas, concepts, and assumptions of the methods, rather than particular implementations for specific applications. This should help the reader to understand not only how these methods work but also their pros and cons.

The authors hope that this survey reveals the interrelationships among various methods well. However, the reader should keep in mind that many such statements are based on the authors' personal views and preference, and are not always accurate or unbiased, although a good deal of effort has been made toward that goal. In addition to such discussions, a considerable amount of material included in this survey has not appeared elsewhere, including a significant number of open problems and ideas for further research. Furthermore, more recent results are discussed in greater detail.

The remainder of this chapter is organized as follows. After a brief systematic overview of each major research problem in the field of image/video coding in Section 5.2, the basics of wavelets are reviewed and their lifting scheme (LS) is introduced in Section 5.3. Then, in Section 5.4, an overview of recent advances in the optimization of the integer wavelet transform (IWT) is discussed. In Section 5.5, the underlying ideas, concepts, and assumptions in introducing adaptivity into wavelet transforms are discussed. Section 5.6 first presents an overview of the implementation of adaptive wavelets via a lifting structure and then discusses two main approaches. In Section 5.7, the directional adaptive wavelet is discussed. Section 5.8 introduces motion-compensated temporal filtering (MCTF), which is a key technology in the coming SVC standard. Finally, Section 5.9 concludes this chapter.

5.2 Modeling and Approximating the Visual Data

At present, there is no mechanical way to characterize the structure of images and video. The true underlying mechanism of visual data is markedly non-Gaussian, and highly nonstationary (Simoncelli and Olshausen 2001). In the zero-mean Gaussian case, all behavior can be deduced from properties of the countable sequence of eigenvalues of the covariance kernel (Berger 1971). Outside of the Gaussian case, very little is known about characterizing infinite-dimensional probability distributions, which would be immediately helpful in modeling image and video.

Thus, a great challenge facing the disciplines of both theoretical and practical visual data compression is how to exploit knowledge about the modeling and approximation of the visual data source (Donoho et al. 1998). This challenge has three facets: (1) obtaining accurate models of visual data (image/video), (2) obtaining "optimal representations" of such models, and (3) rapidly computing such "optimal representations". It is obvious that current compression methods might be very far away from the ultimate limits imposed by the underlying structure of visual data sources and efforts to improve upon current methods, particularly image and video processing, are likely to pay off.

There are two prevailing mathematical theories of image modeling. The first one is the descriptive Markov random field (MRF) theory, which originated from statistical mechanics. It represents a visual pattern by pooling the responses of a bank of filters over space. The statistics of the responses define a so-called Julesz ensemble (Wu et al. 2000): a perceptual equivalence class, which is in turn equivalent to the MRF models (Geman and Geman 1984). The second theory is that of a generative wavelet/sparse coding, which originated from harmonic analysis. This theory represents images with elements selected from a dictionary of image bases (primitives or tokens) (Olshausen and Field 1997) such as wavelets (Antonini et al. 1992) and ridgelets (Candes 1999), etc.

The following is a summary of recent efforts made to push forward the modeling of the underlying structure of images/video in these two modeling regimes. Issues related to the problems of approximation and compression are also discussed.

5.2.1 On Statistical Analysis

Over the last decade, studies of the statistics of natural images/video have repeatedly shown their non-Gaussian character (Simoncelli and Olshausen 2001; Hyvärinen et al. 2003). Empirical studies of wavelet transforms of images using histograms of coefficients that fall into a common subband have uncovered a markedly non-Gaussian structure (Simoncelli and Olshausen 2001; Field 1987; Olshausen and Field 1996). Simoncelli reported the generalized Gaussian model $C \cdot exp\{-|u|^{\alpha}\}$, where the exponent α is 2 when the Gaussian is applied (Simoncelli and Olshausen 2001). Field proposed that the wavelet transform of images offered probability distribution that is "sparse" (Olshausen and Field 1996). A simple probability density with such a sparse character is the Gaussian scale mixture $(1-\varepsilon)\Phi(x/\delta)/\delta+\varepsilon\phi(x)$ (Field 1987).

To replicate some of the known empirical structure of images, particularly the sparse histogram structure of wavelet subbands, one can consider a simple model of random piecewise smooth functions in 1D. In this model, the piece boundaries are thrown down at random by, for example a Poisson process. The pieces are realizations of (different) Gaussian processes (possibly stationary) and discontinuities are allowed across the boundaries of the pieces.

If one takes Shannon's $R(D)$ theory literally and applies the abstract $R(D)$ principle, determining the best way to code an image or a video sequence would require one to solve a mutual information problem involving probability distributions defined on an infinite-dimensional space. Unfortunately, it is not clear whether one can obtain a clear intellectual description of such probability distributions in a form that would make it possible to actually state the problem coherently, much less solve it.

Regrettably, outside the domain of Gaussian models, the ability to compute $R(D)$ is lost. Instead, one begins to operate heuristically. Suppose, for example, a conditionally Gaussian model is employed. Conditionally, Gaussian models offer an attractive way to maintain ties with the Gaussian case, while exhibiting globally non-Gaussian behavior. There is no general solution for $R(D)$ for such a class, but it appears reasonable that the two-stage structure of the model gives clues about the optimal coding. One might assume that an effective coder should factor in a component that adapts to the apparent segmentation structure of the image and a component that acts in a traditional way conditional on that structure. In such models, image function takes place in two stages. An initial random experiment lays down regions separately by edges, and in subsequent stages, each region is assigned a Gaussian random field. In this model, discontinuities must be well represented as well. It seems natural that one attempt should be made to identify an empirically accurate segmentation and then to adaptively code that piece. MRFs (Geman and Geman 1984) represent one such type of model, used widely to capture the characteristics of local dependencies among different regions of the image.

5.2.2 On Harmonic Analysis

Rather than considering an image to be compressed as numerical arrays with an integer index u, we consider the objects of interest as function-functions of a space $f(x,y)$ or spatial-temporal functions $f(x,y,t)$. This point of view is clearly the one in Shannon's 1948 introduction to the optimization problem underlying $R(D)$ theory, but it is seen less frequently today because many practical compression systems start with sampled data.

Assume we have a space of function $\mathbf{S}$ and wish to represent an element $f \in \mathbf{S}$. The space $\mathbf{S}$ can be, for example, composed of integrable functions on the interval $[0,1]$ with a finite square integral $\int_0^1 |f(t)|^2 dt < \infty$, which is denoted by $L_2(0,1)$. The first question is then to find a basis for $\mathbf{S}$; that is, a set of basis functions $\{\phi_i\}_{i\in I}$ in $\mathbf{S}$ such that any element $f \in \mathbf{S}$ can be written as a linear combination.

$$f = \sum_{i\in I} \alpha_i \phi_i \tag{5.1}$$

A question of immediate concern is in what sense (5.1) is actually true. Consider $\hat{f}_N(t)$ as the approximation using N terms and a norm to measure the approximation error.

$$\|f(t) - \hat{f}_N(t)\|_p = (\int_{-\infty}^{\infty} |f(t) - \hat{f}_N(t)|^p dt)^{1/p} \tag{5.2}$$

$$\lim_{n\to\infty} \|f(t) - \hat{f}_N(t)\|_p = 0 \tag{5.3}$$

If one has a set of functions $\{\phi_i\}_{i\in I}$, such that all functions in $\mathbf{S}$ can be approximated arbitrarily precisely as in (5.3), then one can say that the set is complete in $\mathbf{S}$. If furthermore, the elements are linearly independent, then $\{\phi_i\}_{i\in I}$ is a basis for $\mathbf{S}$. Among all possible bases, the basis functions or basis vectors are all mutually orthogonal. Normalizing their norm to 1, or $\|\phi_i\| = 1, i \in I$, an orthonormal set of vectors satisfies $<\phi_i, \phi_j> = \delta_{ij}$, where $< \cdot >$ is the inner product.

For orthonormal bases, the expansion formula becomes

$$f = \sum_{i\in I} <\phi_i, f> \phi_i \tag{5.4}$$

This is a representation formula for f in the orthonormal basis $\{\phi_i\}_{i\in I}$. Given the representation of f in an orthonormal basis as in (5.4), its orthogonal projection onto a fixed subspace of dimension N spanned by $\{\phi_n\}_{n=0,\ldots,N-1}$ is denoted as $\hat{f}_N(t)$.

$$\hat{f}_N = \sum_{n=0}^{N} <\phi_n, f> \phi_n \tag{5.5}$$

Thus, one is led to the approximation problem. Given objects of interest and spaces in which they are embedded, one wishes to know how fast an N-term approximation converges. Examples of this applicability include the appearance of the fast cosine transform in the JPEG standard and the consideration of the fast wavelet transform for the JPEG-2000 standard.

This immediately raises other questions. Different bases can give different rates of approximation. There are various ways to choose the N-terms used in the approximation. A fixed subset (e.g., the first N-terms) leads to a linear subspace approximation, as in Eq. (5.5). Adaptive schemes, to be discussed later, are nonlinear. Will different choices of the subject lead to different rates of approximation? Regarding the visual data compression, this involves not only the approximation quality but also the description complexity. These issues are discussed in the next subsection.

5.2.3 Issues of Approximation and Compression

Approximation: How can one obtain a good approximation with few terms? Which bases lead to fast linear/NLA? An efficient transform-based representation requires sparsity, that is, a large amount of information has to be constrained in a small portion of transform coefficients. As discussed earlier, the design of a dictionary $\mathscr{G} = \{\phi_i, i \in \mathscr{I}\}$ with efficient approximation properties is not the only consideration. Together with $\mathscr{G}$, fast algorithms need to be developed to efficiently find the sparsest representation of any signal $g \in \mathscr{F}$ in terms of the elements of $\mathscr{G}$. When $\mathscr{G} = \{\phi_i, i \in \mathscr{I}\}$ is a basis, there is a unique way to express g as a linear combination of the ϕ_is, and this representation can be easily found by computing the inner products between g and duals of ϕ_is. Despite this efficient property, over-complete dictionaries are often preferred to basis expansions. They are more flexible and can adapt better to the characteristics of the signal of interest and this allows for sparser signal representation. However, it is more difficult to develop fast algorithms that find the right sparse representation of a signal in $\mathscr{F}$. Because the elements of $\mathscr{G}$ are linearly dependent, there are infinitely many ways to express g as a linear combination of the ϕ_is. Generally, the search for the sparsest signal representation is an NP-complete problem (Davis 1994).

Frames and bases: The image/video is a difficult-to-understand class of functions in a functional space. However, it has a characterization as a superposition of "atoms" of a more or less concrete form. From the point of view of approximation theory, one can say that the problem is to build a dictionary of elementary functions that can approximate any signal in a given functional class with the superposition of few of its elements. Research work in this respect ranges from Fourier transform, Karhunen–Loeve transform, and wavelets, to current research works on new, non-separable bases, even frames. This body of work has grown gradually over 100 years and shows fruitful analogies in the discrete-time setting of practical image/video coders. Corresponding to the theoretical developments, today one has fast Fourier transform, fast discrete cosine transform (DCT), and fast wavelet transform. Transform coding has become a very popular compression method for lossy still image and video coding in the past two decades. However, finding a sparse representation even in the presence of 1D discontinuities, like edges or contours, is still a challenging research topic in the community of visual data coding.

Rate Distortion: Data compression involves not only the quality of an approximation but also the complexity of the description. There is a cost associated with describing the approximated function f, and this cost depends on the approximation method. The performance of a lossy coder is measured by its operational Rate distortion (R-D) function, denoted by $R(D)$, which describes the bit rate R required to achieve a given distortion D, for given source characteristics. The R-D theorem (Berger 1971) establishes the bound on the minimal rate required among all possible coders. During the last 50 years, R-D theory has been actively studied in the information theory literature, mainly focusing on performance bounds, including asymptotic analysis and high rate approximation. It should be noted that theoretical analysis and analytical R-D performance bounds are likely to be found only for simple sources and simple encoding schemes. For complicated sources, such as 2D images and 3D videos, and sophisticated compression systems, such as JPEG and JPEG2000 image coding, MPEG-2/4, H.263, and H.264 video encoding, this type of theoretical performance analysis is often infeasible (Ortego and Ramchandran 1998). The difficulty of mathematically modeling both source characteristics and compression systems creates a significant gap between the information-theoretical R-D analysis and practices in rate control and quality optimization. To fill this gap, a set of R-D analysis techniques, rate control, and quality optimization algorithms for practical video compression have been developed (He and Mitra 2005).

Quality Assessment: In the transform coding of image and videos, the two most important factors are the coding bit rate and the picture quality. The coding bit rate, denoted by R, determines the channel bandwidth or storage space required to transmit or store the coded visual data. One direct and widely used measure for the picture quality is the MSE. The MSE is the L_2 norm of the arithmetic difference between the original signal g and the reconstructed signal $\hat{g}$. However, the correlation between MSE and human judgment of quality is not tight enough for most applications, and the goal of quality assessment over the past three decades has been to improve upon the MSE. Recently, modeling of the human visual system (HVS) has been regarded as the most suitable paradigm for achieving better quality predictions (Wang et al. 2004). Other researchers have explored signal fidelity criteria that are not based on the assumptions of HVS models but that are motivated by the need to capture the loss of *structure* in the signal, structure that the HVS hypothetically extracts for cognitive understanding (Sheikh and Bovik 2006).

5.3 Wavelet Transform and Lifting Scheme

5.3.1 Wavelet Transform

Wavelets are mathematical functions that decompose the data into different frequency components and then study each component with a resolution matched to its scale. They have advantages over traditional Fourier methods in analyzing physical situations where the signal contains discontinuities and sharp spikes.

The wavelet analysis procedure is to adopt a wavelet prototype function, called an analyzing wavelet or mother wavelet. Temporal analysis is performed with a contracted high-frequency version of the prototype wavelet, whereas frequency analysis is performed with a dilated, low-frequency version of the same wavelet. Because the original signal or function can be represented in terms of a wavelet expansion (using coefficients in a linear combination of the wavelet functions), data operations can be performed using just the corresponding wavelet coefficients. If one further chooses the wavelets best adapted to the data, or truncate the coefficients below a threshold, the data are sparsely represented. This sparse coding makes wavelets an excellent tool in the field of data compression.

More mathematically, the discrete wavelet transform represents a signal $f(x)$ in terms of shifts and dilations of a low-pass scaling function $\Phi(t)$ and a bandpass wavelet function $\Psi(t)$, as presented in Eq. (5.6). The transform is multi-scale, in that it creates a set of coefficients that represents signal information at the lowest scale and a set of detailed coefficients with increasingly finer resolution. The wavelet acts as a singularity detector, with a precise behavior across scales; whereas a scaling function produces polynomial behavior, it captures the trend in a signal.

$$f(x) = \sum_{j=0}^{n-1}\sum_{k=0}^{2^j-1} c_{jk}\Phi(x) + \sum_{j=0}^{n-1}\sum_{k=0}^{2^j-1} d_{jk}\Psi(x) \tag{5.6}$$

There also exist two important relations between $\Phi(x)$ and $\Psi(x)$. They are the duality Eq. (5.7) and the wavelet Eq. (5.8).

$$\Phi(x) = \sum_{k=-N}^{N} h_k \Phi(2x-k) \tag{5.7}$$

$$\Psi(x) = \sum_{k=-N}^{N} g_k \Phi(2x-k) \tag{5.8}$$

where $x \in [-N+1, N-1]$, $N \in \mathbf{Z}$, $\{h_k\}_{k\in\mathbf{Z}} \in l^1$, and $\{g_k\}_{k\in\mathbf{Z}} \in l^1$ are real-valued series with finite length, corresponding to the analysis's low-pass filter and high-pass filter, respectively, in the implementation of the wavelet transform as a filter bank (FB).

By taking the zeta transform to $\{h_k\}_{k\in\mathbf{Z}} \in l^1$ and $\{g_k\}_{k\in\mathbf{Z}} \in l^1$, one obtains the analysis's low-pass filter $H(z)$ and high-pass filter $G(z)$. In a typical wavelet transform, the input image is decomposed into a coarse image and a high-pass image containing detailed information by convoluting it with $H(z)$ and $G(z)$, followed by subsampling, as shown in Fig. 5.1. The inverse transform uses upsampling, followed by a synthesis low-pass filter $\tilde{H}(z)$ and high-pass filter $\tilde{G}(z)$, as shown in Fig. 5.2. The transform is iterated on the output of the low-pass band ($c[n]$) to create a series of detailed coefficients at different scales.

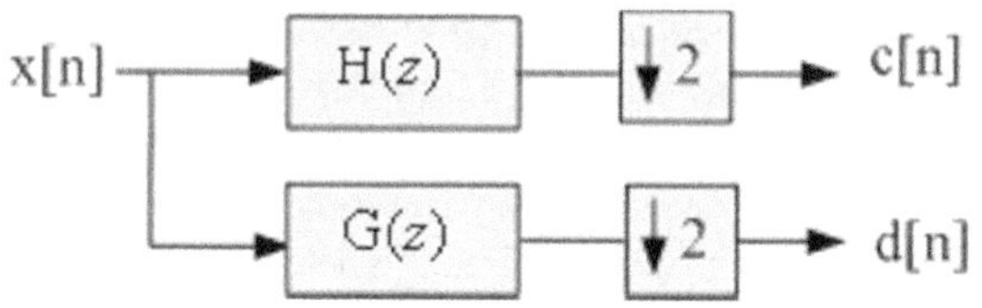

Fig. 5.1 Wavelet filter bank. H and G are the analysis's low-pass/high-pass pair. $c[n]$ and $d[n]$ are the scaling and wavelet coefficients, respectively

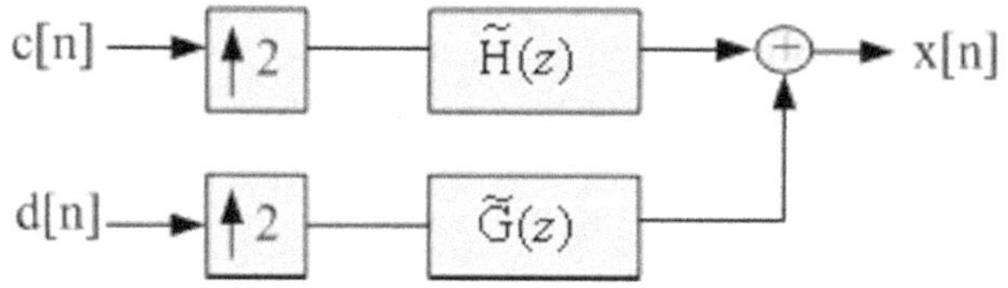

Fig. 5.2 Wavelet filter bank. With appropriate choices of $\tilde{H}$ and $\tilde{G}$, the transform will yield a perfectly reconstructed output sequence

5.3.2 Constructing a Wavelet Filter Bank

Filter bank (FB) lies at the heart of wavelet-based algorithms. The de-correlation efficiency of a wavelet FB is greatly affected by the multiplicities N_k of the zeros at π of $H(z)$. Thus, some of the main goals in the design of wavelet filters (Oraintara et al. 2003; Averbuch and Zheludev 2004) are the maintenance of the perfect reconstruction (PR) property and the proper selection of N_k. For a special choice of $H(z)$,$G(z)$, $\tilde{H}(z)$, and $\tilde{G}(z)$, the underlying wavelets and scaling functions form a biorthogonal basis and provide PR (Kovacevic and Verrerli 1992). The term "biorthogonal" refers to two different bases that are orthogonal to each other, but in which each does not form an orthogonal set. Biorthogonal wavelets (BWs) have been applied extensively to image/video processing.

Let $H(z)$ and $\tilde{H}(z)$ be the analysis and synthesis low-pass filters of a wavelet FB permitting the PR condition, respectively. If the associated high-pass filters $G(z)$ and $\tilde{G}(z)$ are defined as

$$G(z) = z^{-1}\tilde{H}(-z^{-1}), \quad \tilde{G}(z) = z^{-1}H(-z^{-1}) \tag{5.9}$$

the PR condition simplifies to equation

$$H(z)\tilde{H}(z) + H(-z)\tilde{H}(-z) = 1 \tag{5.10}$$

The polyphase representation of a filter $H(z)$ is given by

$$H(z) = H_e(z^2) + z^{-1}H_o(z^2)$$

where

$$H_e(z^2) = \frac{H(z)+H(-z)}{\sqrt{2}}, \quad H_o(z^2) = \frac{H(z)-H(-z)}{\sqrt{2}z^{-1}}$$

$H_e(z)$ and $H_o(z)$ are, respectively, obtained from the even and odd coefficients of $h(n) = Z^{-1}\{H(z)\}$, where Z^{-1} denotes the inverse zeta transform.

The analysis filters $H(z)$ and $G(z)$ (low-pass and high-pass, respectively) can thus be expressed through their polyphase matrix as

$$\boldsymbol{P}(z) = \begin{bmatrix} H_e(z) & G_e(z) \\ H_o(z) & G_o(z) \end{bmatrix}$$

The synthesis polyphase matrix $\tilde{\boldsymbol{P}}(z)$ can be analogously defined for the synthesis filters. Then the PR condition can be rewritten as

$$\mathbf{P}(z)\tilde{\mathbf{P}}^*(z) = \mathbf{I} \tag{5.11}$$

In this case, $\tilde{\mathbf{P}}^*(z)$ denotes the complex conjugated transpose of matrix $\tilde{\mathbf{P}}(z)$; $\mathbf{I}$ is the 2×2 identity matrix.

As discussed in earlier sections, the construction of BWs mainly involves the construction of their associated BWFBs, and the most commonly used construction methods fall into two categories: spectral factorization and lifting scheme (LS). In the following, we discuss spectral factorization in the following paragraph and then present the LS algorithm in detail in Section 5.3.3.

The idea of spectral factorization is first to preassign a number of vanishing moments to the BW, then to obtain a Lagrange half-band filter (LHBF) according to the PR condition, and finally to factorize the LHBF to obtain the coefficients of the corresponding synthesis filters. Many BW filters with good compression performance, for example, CDF9/7, Wingers W17/11, Villasenors V6/10 and V10/18, are constructed based upon spectral factorization. However, the disadvantage of the spectral factorization lies in the fact that, except for trivial factorization, it is hardly possible to factorize the LHBF in the rational domain. Therefore, filters obtained often have irrational coefficients and thus require infinite computational precision to implement the corresponding DWT, which increases the computational complexity.

5.3.3 Lifting Scheme

In this section, we present a short review of on the original LS algorithm as it was introduced in (Sweldens 1996). An illustration of this scheme can be found in Figs. 5.3 and 5.4.

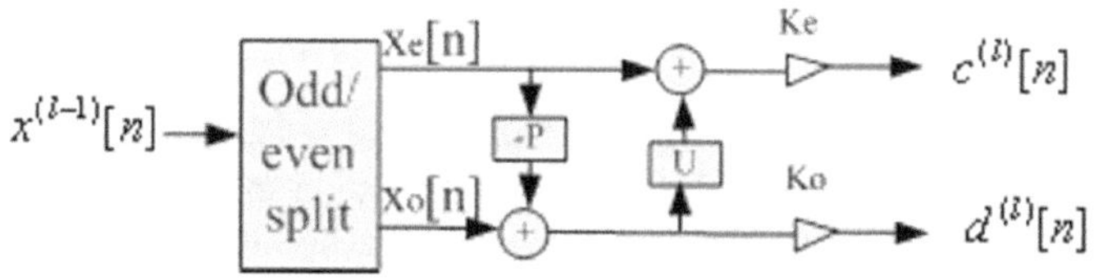

Fig. 5.3 Typical lifting scheme

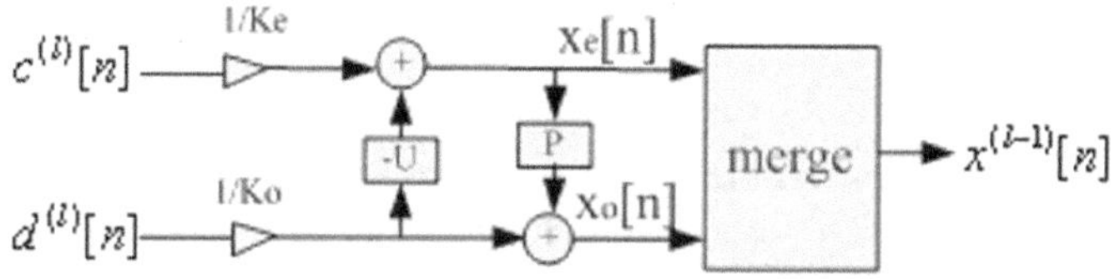

Fig. 5.4 Typical inverse lifting scheme

Constructing a DWT using the LS can be described as follows. Start with a simple wavelet transform (e.g., the lazy wavelet transform). This transform does nothing but subsample even and odd samples, and its polyphase matrix is **I**), then alternates the prediction and update steps to improve this transform, and finally implements a scaling step. As the PR property is ensured by the structure of the LS itself during the construction, other constraints need to be imposed to determine the lifting filter coefficients.

Without loss of generality, assume that the LS starts with a prediction step and consists of an even number of steps. The aforementioned procedure can be expressed as the factorization of the polyphase matrix $\tilde{\boldsymbol{P}}(z)$ or $\boldsymbol{P}(z)$, which is given by

$$\tilde{\mathbf{P}}(z) = \prod_{i=1}^{M} \left(\begin{bmatrix} 1 & -p_i(z) \\ 0 & 1 \end{bmatrix} \begin{bmatrix} 1 & 0 \\ u_i(z) & 1 \end{bmatrix} \right) \begin{bmatrix} K_e & 0 \\ 0 & K_o \end{bmatrix} \tag{5.12}$$

or

$$\mathbf{P}(z) = \prod_{i=1}^{M} \left(\begin{bmatrix} 1 & 0 \\ p_i(z^{-1}) & 1 \end{bmatrix} \begin{bmatrix} 1 & -u_i(z^{-1}) \\ 0 & 1 \end{bmatrix} \right) \begin{bmatrix} K_e & 0 \\ 0 & K_o \end{bmatrix} \tag{5.13}$$

As the factorization is not unique, several pairs of $\{p_i(z)\}$ and $\{u_i(z)\}$ filters are admissible; in case of the DWT implementation, all possible choices are equivalent.

The input signal $x^{(l-1)[n]}$ (the superscript is used to denote the current level of the DWT) is split into two signals corresponding to evenly and oddly indexed samples. Then the even signal is convolved with the lifting filter $p_i(z)$ and the result is subtracted from the odd signal. This action is called a *dual lifting step* or *prediction step*. The predicted odd signal is then convolved with the lifting filter $u_i(z)$ and added to the even signal. This is called a *prime lifting step* or *update step*. Eventually, after, say, M pairs of prediction and update steps, the even samples will become the low-pass coefficients $c^{(l)}[n]$, whereas the odd samples become the high-pass coefficients $d^{(l)}[n]$, up to two scaling factors K_e and K_o. Again, the low-pass coefficients $c^{(l)}[n]$ are regarded as the input signal to implement the next level of wavelet decomposition.

The LS is a very feasible approach for constructing BWs with their associated BWFBs (Zhang et al. 2004) having binary coefficients (i.e., the filter coefficients are sums of power of 1/2), e.g., CDFC2/6 and 5/3 Biorthogonal Interpolating Wavelets used in the JPEG2000 standard. These kinds of BWs can realize a multiplication-free DWT, so they have low computational complexity. However, the main disadvantage with wavelets of this type available in the literature lies in the fact that they exhibit poorer performance than CDFC9/7's for image compression.

5.3.4 Lifting-Based Integer Wavelet Transform

In addition to yielding a fast, in-place implementation of the wavelet transform, the LS also provides a natural framework for constructing reversible IWTs (Daubechies and Sweldens 1998; Calderbank et al. 1998) for zero loss image compression. This opens an approach to integrate lossless and lossy image compression seamlessly into a single codec (Reichel et al. 2001; Sole and Salembier 2004), and is increasingly popular, as evidenced by its use in the JPEG2000 image coding standard.

To realize the IWT, one can round the result of each lifting step to the nearest integer (Adams and Kossentini 2000). This kind of operation is nonlinear; however, the structure of the LS ensures that the PR property is still preserved after the operation. In this case, there arises the problem of how to deal with the scaling factor K, because dividing one integer by it is nonreversible. Two solutions to this issue are available: If K is close to 1, one can omit the scaling steps in the LS. Otherwise, as it has been shown in (Daubechies and Sweldens 1998), that K can always be set to 1, with at most three extra lifting steps. If the rounding operation is denoted as *Round*(), the lifting-based forward IWT can be shown as in Fig. 5.5. In addition, the inverse transform can be trivially deduced by a simple reverse procedure.

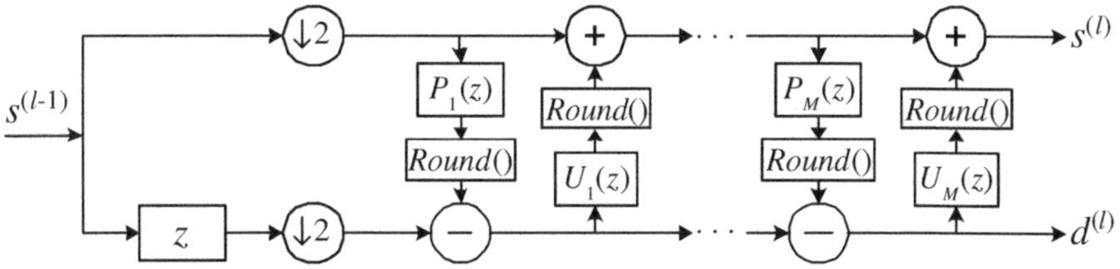

Fig. 5.5 Forward IWT based on the lifting scheme. Each lifting step is followed by a rounding to the nearest integer operation

Unlike the linearity of the DWT, due to the nonlinear operations involved, the IWT performance is heavily dependent upon the chosen factorization of the polyphase matrix of the wavelet filter, for both lossless and lossy compression. In Section 5.4, a short overview of recent advances in the optimization of IWT is presented.

5.4 Optimal Integer Wavelet Transform

The problem of deriving the optimal implementation of the IWT raises the need for criteria for the selection of the factorization that achieves the best results on the recovered images given a suitable error measure (Adams 1999, 2001; Adams and Kossentini 2000; Grangetto et al. (2002)). A trivial solution is to try all possible factorizations, seeking the one which yields the best result, according to a selected error measure (e.g., PSNR) over a set of test images (Yoo and Jeong 2002; Grangetto et al. 2002; Rioul et al. 1991; Deever and Hemami 2003).

In order to find optimal lifting coefficients (i.e., the coefficients of lifting filters) for lossless image compression, Yoo and Jeong (2002) utilize an exhaustive search. The lifting coefficients that give the minimum-weighted first-order entropy are adapted by varying the prediction coefficients from 0 to 32 and update coefficients from 0 to 16, respectively. Grangetto et al. (2002) propose several methods for the selection of the best factorizations of wavelet filters within the LS framework. These methods are based on the search for the minimally nonlinear iterated graphic functions (Rioul et al. 1991) associated with integer transforms and on the minimization of the number of lifting steps. Deever and Hemami (2003) develop a projection technique that is used to derive optimal final prediction steps for lifting-based reversible IWTs. Using this method, a transform basis vector is projected onto a subspace spanned by neighboring basis vectors (sharing some spatial support) to derive precise projection coefficients that can be used in an additional lifting step.

The aforementioned approaches have several major drawbacks. First, IWT compression performance depends on the input images (Adams 2001), making the result of the search too dependent on the data set; moreover, the exhaustive search can be computationally burdensome due to the complexity of the error metric. To overcome this limitation, a few additional efficient solutions, based on simple input-independent metrics, have been devised (Adams 1999; Grangetto et al. 2002; Boulgouris et al. 2001; Li et al. 2005).

In Adams (1999), the ratio between the lifting coefficients of maximum and minimum magnitude is suggested as a possible criterion, even if no specific factorization is proposed based on this choice. In Grangetto et al. (2002), another criterion is introduced based on a measure of minimum nonlinearity of the iterated graphic functions. The technique, which is computationally tractable and independent of the input data, relies only on the characteristics of the wavelet filter and leads to IWT implementations featuring excellent performance.

Boulgouris et al. (2001) first calculated the optimal predictors of an LS in the general 1D case and then applied these prediction filters with the corresponding update filters to the lossless compression of still images using quincunx sampling and then simple row-column sampling. In each case, the linear predictors were enhanced by directional nonlinear postprocessing in the quincunx case, and then by 6, 4, and 2 vanishing moment nonlinear postprocessing in the row-column case. In order to achieve this, the resulting six predictions were ordered according to their magnitudes and the average of the third and fourth were then taken as the prediction.

Li et al. (2005) propose a lifting-based IWT modeled on the difference correlation structure (DCCS-LIWT). First, they establish a relationship between the performance of a linear predictor and the difference correlations of an image. The obtained results provide a theoretical foundation for the construction of the optimal lifting filters. Then, the optimal prediction lifting coefficients, in the sense of least-square prediction error, are derived. DCCS-LIWT imposes heavy emphasis on image-inherent dependence. A distinct feature of this method is the use of the variance-normalized autocorrelation function of the difference image to construct a linear predictor and adapt the predictor to varying image sources. The proposed scheme also allows respective calculations of the lifting filters for the horizontal and vertical orientations. Experimental evaluation shows that the proposed method produces better results than other well-known integer transforms for lossless image compression.

Thus far, we have reviewed various construction techniques for implementing the lifting-based wavelet FBs from the standard wavelet transform. In order to evaluate the effectiveness of various lifting-based wavelet filters for lossless compression of digital images, a set of test images has been used, including natural images, computer-generated images, compound images, and different types of medical images Calderbank et al. (1998). All of these images were compressed in a lossless manner using the various transforms under evaluation. Similar performance and more filter evaluation can also be found in Adams and Kossentini (2000), Adams (1999, 2001) and Grangetto et al. (2002). Almost all of these studies declare that there is no filter that consistently performs better than all the other filters on all the test images.

Now, the focus of research is turning towards efforts to make efficient use of the lifting structure. The LS algorithm opened the way to the design of nonlinear wavelet transforms; it was originally developed to improve a given wavelet decomposition, for example, by increasing the number of vanishing moments it possesses. However, the LS increasingly is used as a tool for building wavelets on irregular grids, e.g., on a triangulation of some odd-shaped geometrical surface. The main feature of lifting is that it provides an entirely spatial domain interpretation of the transform, as opposed to the more traditional frequency domain-based constructions. The local spatial interpretation enables us to adapt the transform not only to the underlying geometry but also to the data, thereby introducing nonlinearities while retaining control of the transform's multi-scale properties. Therefore, developing new methods to construct BWs with good compression potential and low computational complexity is an important issue in the field of embedded image coding.

5.5 Introducing Adaptability into the Wavelet Transform

The success of wavelets is due to their intrinsic ability to approximate smooth signals effectively. Wavelets can act as a singularity detector, with a precise behavior across scales; while scaling functions reproduce polynomial behavior, the wavelet catches the trend in a signal. However, a classical wavelet transform doesn't do well with the discontinuities encountered in real-world signals, because wavelets are only good for point singularities (e.g., spikes, discontinuity).

5.5.1 Curve Singularities in an Image

Most images consist of regions of smoothness and texture separated by edges. The wavelet representation is efficient within locally smooth regions, where fine-scale wavelet coefficients are small and where coefficients decay rapidly from coarse to fine scales. In the neighborhood of edges, wavelet coefficients decay much more slowly, but because of local support, relatively few wavelet coefficients are affected by edges. However, even these large wavelet coefficients near edges are time-consuming to code.

Sparse coding of edges is the key to efficient image coding. Edges are piecewise smooth in 2D; they have curve singularities (Dragotti and Vetterli 2003). These singularities cannot be well represented by smooth basis functions, and they tend to give rise to large coefficients in their proximity. Large wavelet coefficients are very undesirable in compression; typically, their values and locations need to be described, which involves quantization of the coefficients and indexing their locations. At low bit rates, the quantization noise from these coefficients is clearly visible, in particular causing Gibbs artifacts at image edges with arbitrary directions.

To overcome such problems, adaptive approaches have come into practice in decomposing the signal, taking into account the signal's local properties. As we have seen so far, there exist two main ideas for how to build adaptivity into the decomposition: (1) by choosing/designing a basis that depends on the signal and (2) by making lifting-based wavelets adaptive to the geometric features in the image.

5.5.2 Anisotropic Basis

There is a long research history surrounding the choosing or designing of a wavelet basis through the minimization of a defined cost function. The best basis algorithm (Coifman and Wickerhauser 1992) selects a wavelet basis by minimizing a concave cost function such as the entropy or $l^p - norm$. Instead of changing the filter coefficients, Chan and Zhou (2002) choose to change the input signal in the proximity of discontinuities through an extrapolation procedure. By recording these changes, the original signal can be recovered at synthesis.

The inefficiency of the standard 2D wavelet transform for approximating images with rich orientated features resides in the spatial isotropy of 2D wavelet construction. In the prevailing practice, the standard wavelet transform is implemented by separable 1D filtering in the horizontal and vertical directions. The filtering and subsampling operations are applied equally along both the horizontal and vertical directions at each scale. As a result, the corresponding filters, obtained as direct products of 1D filters, are isotropic at all scales. A serious drawback to these kinds of implementations is that they are ill suited to approximate image features with arbitrary orientations that are neither vertical nor horizontal, and whose vanishing moments of the high-pass wavelet filters exist only in these two directions. They fail to provide an efficient representation for directional image features, such as edges and lines that are not aligned vertically or horizontally, since these kinds of implementations distributes the energy of these features into all subbands. In these cases, the wavelet transform results in large magnitude high-frequency coefficients.

This motivated the idea of designing anisotropic basis functions. However, ensuring an efficient matching between anisotropic basis functions and objects in an image is a nontrivial task, and how to fully exploit the directional correlation in either the image or frequency domain has been a research topic for many years. Many oriented transforms have been designed recently. These transforms are either fixed, with each subband corresponding to a specific orientation and scale, or adaptive, with the direction of analysis chosen locally.

Among the set of fixed transforms, the curvelet transform (Starck et al. 2002; Donoho and Duncan 2000) results in an NLA close to the optimum without explicit knowledge of the image geometry. Although this property is desired for compression, discrete versions of the curvelet transform are based on a finite set of the blockwise Radon transform (Deans 1983) and are highly overcomplete. Designed in the discrete domain, the contourlet transform (Do and Vetterli 2005) provides a directional analysis similar to the curvelet transform with reduced redundancy. This transform uses a fixed multi-resolution directional filterbank based on an iterated fan filter and Laplacian pyramid. Using a carefully designed directional FB, the related contourlet approach (Lu and Do 2003) even achieves critical sampling. The steerable pyramid and complex wavelet transform (Selesnick et al. 2005) are other examples of fixed directional transforms. Although the redundancy of most of these transforms is not problematic for denoising applications, the increased number of coefficients at high rates compared to critically sampled transforms is problematic for compression applications.

In contrast to these approaches in which the FB is fixed, adaptive directional transforms rely on an explicit description of the image geometry. This additional information allows them to adapt the direction of analysis to the local features of the image. Although these transforms can be viewed as highly overcomplete when considering the set of coefficients for all orientations, they are generally critically sampled, conditionally to knowledge of the additional geometric side information. This property makes them efficient for compression, provided the rate is allocated optimally in the R-D sense between the additional geometric information and the quantized transform coefficients. The bandlet transform (Peyré 2005; Peyre and Mallat 2005; LePennec and Mallat 2005), for example, was first introduced with a geometry described as a set of splines representing the image contour. To allow for easier rate allocation between the geometry and transform coefficients, a second approach was proposed in which a separable wavelet is warped along a geometric flow. By iterating the decomposition along the direction of maximal regularity, the strong correlation of the pixel intensities along the image contours is exploited. The geometric flow is described in a quad tree on which R-D optimization is performed using a bottom-up approach and an approximate model of the entropy coder.

A second adaptive approach is proposed in Velisavljevic et al. (2006), in which irrationalities are obtained by applying a separable wavelet transform along digital lines. For a given pair of directions, PR and critical sampling is guaranteed by lattice theory. By adopting the pair of chosen directions to the local features of the image, the directionlet transform provides very good NLA performance with low complexity. However, this transform has yet to be applied to image compression, by providing a practical scheme for representing and optimizing the geometry segmentation.

These methods build dictionaries of anisotropic basis functions that provide a sparse representation of edges in images. They are extensively applied in feature extraction, image enhancement, de-noising, classification, and even retrieval. However, they are not suited for compression, due to a lack of efficient entropy coding that can exploit directional information in each wavelet region. Candes and Donoho (Starck et al. 2002) further show that the parabolic scaling relation between the length and width of basis functions is a key feature to achieve good NLA behavior, but the implementation of these transforms usually requires over-sampling, having higher complexity when compared to the standard wavelet transform. Thus, parabolic scaling requires a nonseparable (convolution) filter design. Furthermore, in some of these constructions, e.g., the curvelet, the design of the associated filter is performed in the continuous domain and this makes it difficult to use them directly on discrete images to achieve PR.

Obviously, there is still a long way to go before anisotropic bases can be applied towards visual information coding, even though they show higher performance in image processing applications, such as denoising, feature extraction, etc. Detailed aspects in this direction are not discussed, and focus is given to the adaptive lifting-based wavelet in the next subsection. Readers interested in anisotropic bases can refer to Vetterli (2001) for more information.

5.5.3 Adaptive Lifting-Based Wavelet

As opposed to the traditional frequency domain-based construction of wavelet FBs, this second line of research focuses on adaptive lifting-based wavelets. The main feature of the LS is the underlying spatial domain interpretation of the wavelet transform. This local spatial interpretation enables us to adapt the transform to the data, thereby introducing nonlinearities while retaining control of the transform's multiple-scale properties.

Lifting was originally developed in order to adjust wavelet transforms to complex geometries and irregular sampling, leading to so-called second-generation wavelets. It can also be seen as an alternate implementation of the classical, first-generation wavelet transform. Wavelet bases typically employed for image compression (such as the Daubechies 9/7 system) utilize smooth scaling and wavelet functions. Such bases can be easily constructed with the predict-then-update form of lifting described earlier. Smooth basis functions correspond to lifting predictors with wide support; these predictors work poorly near edges when the discontinuities are within the data we are using for the prediction.

By relaxing the constraints used in the construction of prediction and update operators in the LS, the wavelet filter shape itself can be made according to the data it analyzes. This can be achieved by allowing the LS to adapt its update and prediction filters to the local properties of the signal. This kind of prediction or update operator can be readily incorporated into each lifting stage because it only involves a few neighboring pixels in the calculation of predicting and updating signals. Thus, the resulting lifting-based wavelet works as a locally adaptive wavelet transform while allowing filtering across block boundaries as well as regular subsampling. It also ensures PR.

The key problem in applying an adaptive lifting-based wavelet is the conflict between the global transform and local features. There are two main classes of approaches proposed to retain consistency between the global transform and local features. The first class achieves this via switching between a class of linear prediction or update operators in each lifting stage, resulting in structure adaptive LS. An overview of this is presented in Section 5.6. The second class changes the input data involved in the lifting stage and performs directional adaptive processing. It is known as the directional adaptive LS and this is reviewed in Section 5.7.

5.6 Adaptive Lifting Structure

We are aware that lifting-based wavelet filters with fixed structure filters cannot cope with sudden changes in an image. In many applications, it is desirable to have an FB that somehow determines how to shape itself according to the image.

The lifting framework allows us to incorporate nonlinearities while retaining control over the properties of the wavelet transform. In the literature, there exist two kinds of adaptive lifting structures: (1) the adaptive predictor filter (Claypoole et al. 2003; Gerek and Cetin 2005; Song et al. 2005; Ding et al. 2004) and (2) the adaptive update filter (Piella and Heijmans 2002; Tillier et al. 2004; Sole and Salembier 2006). The experimental results of both structure adaptive lifting-based filters for image coding are promising. We summarize these two kinds of adaptive lifting structures in the following two subsections.

5.6.1 Adaptive Prediction Filters

In the case of image coding, two main approaches have been proposed for the design of adaptive prediction filters in the lifting stage. The first is to choose a prediction operator from a set of candidates (Claypoole et al. 2003), and the second is to modify the prediction domain pixels according to the edge gradient (Gerek and Cetin 2005; Song et al. 2005; Ding et al. 2004). Both ideas are based on discontinuities in the signal. Since approaches that adopt the latter do not actually change the lifting structure, and because they use the geometric features in the image, we classify them as signal-dependent wavelets and discuss them in Section 5.7. Here, focus is on the former of the two approaches.

In general, the prediction filter within a lifting structure (similar to that shown in Fig. 5.3) is designed to exactly predict local polynomials up to and including degree $N-1$. In wavelet terminology, the underlying synthesis scaling function corresponding to the prediction filters can reproduce polynomials of a degree up to $N-1$, and the analysis wavelet has N zero moments. Furthermore, it can be deduced easily that the update function determines the properties of the analysis wavelet and primal scaling functions. By designing a successful prediction filter, the objective is to minimize the signal energy of the lower branch, $d^l[n]$. In the case of image/video processing, the prediction filter design can be extended to two or more dimensions.

Larger predictors (predictors that can exactly predict polynomials of a higher degree) correspond to smoother basis functions; they work well when the underlying signal is smooth. However, most images consist of regions of smoothness and texture separated by discontinuities (edges). These discontinuities cannot be well represented by smooth basis functions, because smooth basis functions correspond to lifting predictors with wide support. Larger predictors work poorly near edges when the discontinuity is within the data we are using for the prediction. Ideally, we would like to use predictors that take into account the fact that discontinuities in images tend to occur along continuous curves. Such an adaptation would allow us to exploit the additional spatial structure that exists in edges.

Claypoole et al. (2003) lower the order of the approximation near jumps to avoid prediction across discontinuities. The nonlinearity is obtained from adaptively choosing from a set of linear predictors. The choice of prediction filter depends only on the approximation signal. The main idea is to introduce a mechanism that allows us to choose the prediction operator based on the local properties of the image. This makes the operator data-dependent and thus nonlinear. However, lifting guarantees that the transform remains reversible. In regions where the image is locally smooth, the higher order predictor is used. The order of the predictor is reduced near the edges and thus the length of the predictor is reduced as well. This avoids making a prediction based on data that is separated from the point of interest by a discontinuity.

However, two problems arise when adapting prediction filters. It is difficult to maintain (1) multi-resolution properties and (2) stability and synchronization between analysis and synthesis. Regarding the first problem, when the prediction and update operators are constructed via the polynomial lifting constraints, the output of the update step is a coarse approximation (low-pass and down-sampled) version of the input image. However, if the prediction is performed with a nonlinear operator, it may not be possible to construct an update operator that satisfies the polynomial lifting constraints and provides a low-pass interpretation of the updated coefficients.

Regarding the second problem, because lossy coding schemes introduce errors into the transform coefficients, it is crucial that nonlinearities do not unduly amplify these errors. There is a need to ensure that the transform is stable. Furthermore, in the predict-then-update case, the problem of stability cannot be solved by synchronization alone.

An update-first lifting structure (see Fig. 5.6) (Claypoole et al. 2003) has been used to solve the aforementioned two problems. As shown in Fig. 5.6, it first updates the even samples based on the odd samples yielding the low-pass coefficients and then reuse these low-pass coefficients to predict the odd samples, which gives the high-pass coefficients. With this structure, the predictor operates on raw data, but the choice of the predictor is based on quantized data. This ensures that the encoder and decoder choose predictors based on the same data and eliminates the propagation of errors due to incorrect decisions on the decoder. This update-then-predict LS creates a Laplacian pyramid of the input image. To determine the appropriate prediction filters, it analyzes the data within a prediction window to implement an edge-avoiding prediction. However, all the wavelet filters to be used as candidates in the proposed lifting structure are required to be implemented with an update-first architecture. It is proposed to using $(1,N)$ branch of the Cohen–Daubenchies–Feauveau family.

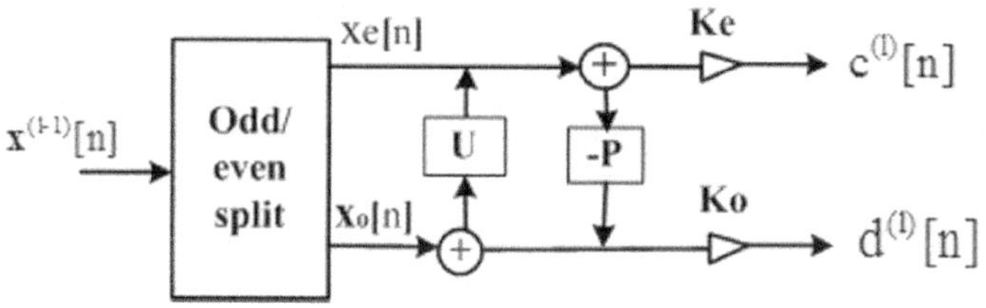

Fig. 5.6 Update-first lifting sequence (Claypoole et al. 2003)

5.6.2 Adaptive Update Filters

In the standard LS, the update operator and addition are fixed. In the adaptive update lifting in Piella and Heijmans (2002), the choice of these operations depends on the information locally available within both the approximation signal x and the detail signal y. In fact, this choice is triggered by a so-called decision map $D\colon \mathscr{X} \times \mathscr{Y} \to \mathscr{D}^{\mathscr{X}}$, where $\mathscr{D}$ is the decision set. Figure 5.7 shows a schematic representation of this version of the LS.

For every possible decision $d \in \mathscr{D}$ of the decision map, there is a different update operator U_d and addition $\oplus_d$. The decision $d_n = D(x,y)(n)$ depends on the original signal x. However, at the point of synthesis, one does not know x, only its update

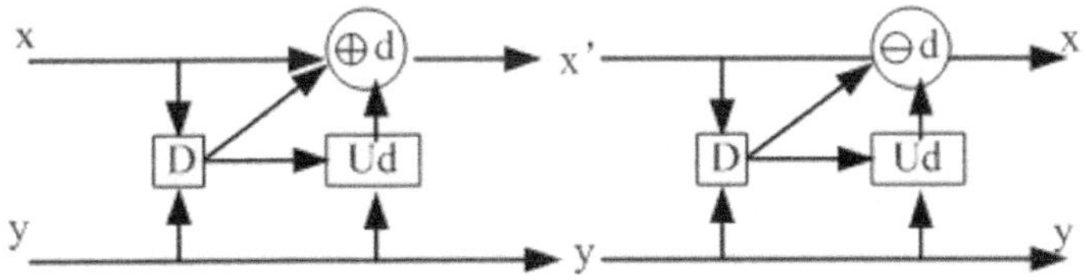

Fig. 5.7 Adaptive update lifting scheme (Claypoole et al. 2003)

x'. In general, this prohibits the computation of d_n; however, there exist a number of situations in which it is still possible to recover d_n from a posterior decision map D' that uses x' and y as inputs. D' needs to satisfy the so-called decision conservation condition: $D'(x',y) = D(x,y)$. This condition is satisfied if the decision map depends only on y.

It is assumed that the update filter utilizes local gradient information to adapt itself to the signal in the sense that smaller gradients "evoke" stronger update filters. As a result, sharp transitions in a signal will not be smoothed to the same extent as regions that are more homogeneous. No bookkeeping is required in order to acheive PR.

5.7 Adaptive Directional Lifting Scheme

Instead of making the structure adaptive to the signal, adaptive directional lifting (ADL) performs lifting-based predictions in local windows in the direction of high pixel correlation. How to fully exploit the directional correlation in either the image or frequency domains has been the major concern in this line of thinking.

Works in ADL has been reported recently and these ADL approaches generally fall into two classes. In the first class, ADLs are developed to adaptively select wavelet filtering directions (Taubman 1999; Gerek and Cetin 2006; Boulgouris et al. 2001), or the length of the wavelet filters (Boulgouris et al. 2001; Claypoole et al. 2003), such that filtering is not performed across edges in the image. These approaches eliminate the need for signaling the filter selections to the decoder by assuming lossless compression (Boulgouris et al. 2001) or knowledge of the quantization noise at the encoder (Claypoole et al. 2003; Gerek and Cetin 2006), or constraining the selection process such that it can be reliably repeated at the decoder (Taubman 1999). However, the gain of the adaptation is limited due to these assumptions and constraints. No significant improvement in objective quality measurements over conventional 2D wavelets has been reported, although a subjective improvement has been observed.

The second class chooses to explicitly signal the filtering direction selections to the decoder (Chang and Girod 2007; Ding et al. 2004; Ding et al. 2007) in order to relax the assumptions and constraints that appears in the first class. Thanks to the efficient representation of the filter selections, these approaches adapt to the image features more effectively and have demonstrated significant objective and subjective quality improvements in images with rich orientated features. Ding et al. (2004) proposed to use a simple direction estimation technique on variable blocks similar to those in H.264, which can then seamlessly integrate a directional prediction in an arbitrary orientation into the familiar framework of lifting-based 2D wavelet transforms. In each lifting stage, the prediction or update operations are carried out in the direction of image edges and textures in a local window. High angular resolution in prediction is achieved by the use of fractional pixels in the prediction and update operations. Chang et al. subsequently proposed the use of quincunx sampling in directional lifting transform (Chang and Girod 2007).

5.7.1 ADL Framework

In order to make the problem clearer, we now consider a lifting-based wavelet for image coding and adopt a similar denotation symbol as in Chang and Girod (2007). Let $\mathbf{s} = \{s[l] | l \in \Pi\}$, where $s[l] = s[l_x, l_y]$ and $l = (l_x, l_y)^T$, denote a set of image samples on a 2D orthogonal sampling gird $\Pi = \{(l_x, l_y)^T \in Z^2\}$. The grid is composed of four subgrids: $\Pi_{pq} = \{(l_x, l_y)^T \in \Pi | l_y mod2 = p, l_x mod2 = q\}$.

Without loss of generality, one can assume that the image is first decomposed into high and low subbands by a 1D wavelet in the vertical direction and then in the horizontal direction. With the LS, each 1D wavelet transform can be factored into one or multiple lifting stages. A typical lifting stage consists of three steps: split, predict, and update. More specifically, to apply the 2D DWT with lifting, a transform between the even and odd rows of the image is first applied, that is, between $\mathbf{s}_0 = \{s[l_0] | l_0 \in \Pi_0 = \Pi_{00} \cup \Pi_{01}\}$ and $\mathbf{s}_1 = \{s[l_1] | l_1 \in \Pi_1 = \Pi_{10} \cup \Pi_{11}\}$. Denote the resulting low-pass subband by $\mathbf{w}_0 = \{w_0[l_0] | l_0 \in \Pi_0\}$ and the high-pass subband by $\mathbf{w}_1 = \{w_1[l_1] | l_1 \in \Pi_1\}$. The transform on $\mathbf{s}$ can generally be expressed as

$$w_1[l_1] = g_H \cdot (s[l_1] - P_{s,l_1}(\mathbf{s}_0)), \forall l_1 \in \Pi_1 \tag{5.14}$$

$$w_0[l_0] = g_L \cdot (s[l_0] + g_H^{-1} U_{s,l_0}(\mathbf{w}_1)), \forall l_1 \in \Pi_0 \tag{5.15}$$

where the prediction function $P_{s,l_1}(\cdot)$ and the update function $U_{s,l_0}(\cdot)$ are functions of the sample values in the input with a scalar output, and g_H and g_L are scaling factors.

In the conventional 2D DWT, the prediction and update functions can be expressed as

$$P_{s,l_1}(\mathbf{s}_0) = \sum_{k=-K_p}^{K_p-1} c_{p,k} \cdot s[l_{1,x}, l_{1,y} - (2k+1)] \tag{5.16}$$

$$U_{s,l_0}(\mathbf{w}_1) = \sum_{k=-K_u}^{K_u-1} c_{u,k} \cdot w_1[l_{0,x}, l_{0,y} - (2k+1)] \quad (5.17)$$

where K_p, $c_{p,k}$, K_u, and $c_{u,k}$ are determined by the chosen wavelet kernel. Note that only samples in the same column are involved in the transform. For each sample in the high-pass subband $w_1[l_1]$, it is generally desirable to select a prediction function P_{s,l_1} that predicts $s[l_1]$ from the samples in $\mathbf{s}_0$ such that the magnitude of the residual $w_1[l_1]$ is minimized.

In directional adaptive lifting, the directional prediction filter with direction $d = (d_x, d_y)^T$ from which $P_{s,l_1}(\mathbf{s}_0)$ can be adaptively selected by

$$P_{s,l_1}^d(\mathbf{s}_0) = \sum_{k=-K_p}^{K_p-1} c_{p,k} \cdot s[l_{1,x}, l_{1,y} - (2k+1)d] \quad (5.18)$$

where d is defined such that

$$l_1 - (2k+1)d \in \Pi_0, \forall l_1 \in \Pi_1, k = -K_p, ..., K_p - 1.$$

The directional prediction filter can be thought of as performing the prediction step along direction d, where $d \in Z^2$ and d_y is always odd. The direction selected at location l_1 for $P_{s,l_1}(\mathbf{s}_0)$ is denoted as $d_{l_1}^*$. Upon completion of the prediction step of all samples, the corresponding update function is defined as

$$U_{s,l_0}(\mathbf{s}_0) = \sum_{k=-K_u}^{K_u-1} c_{u,k} \cdot \sum_{\{l_1 | l_1 - (2k+1)d_{l_1}^* = l_0\}} w_1[l_1] \quad (5.19)$$

In other words, wherever an image sample $s[l_1]$ is predicted by $c_{p,k} \cdot s[l_0]$, $s[l_0]$ is updated by $c_{u,k} \cdot w_1[l_1]$. Note that if d_0 is always selected, that is, $d_{l_1}^* = d_0, \forall l_1$, directional lifting is identical to the conventional DWT.

It should be noted that the update steps do not need to be performed at the same angle as they are in the prediction step, because the ADL framework is very general, and it does not have any restrictions on the update angle.

5.7.2 Implementation of ADL

Now that we have introduced the ADL framework, we turn our focus to three immediate problems in the practical implementation of that framework: (1) how to choose the optimal direction, (2) how to keep synchronization and stability, and (3) how to obtain the optimal $R(D)$.

Optimal prediction direction: In principle, the prediction angle can be a continuous variable. However, in practice, it has been found that nine uniformly quantized discrete angles are sufficient to reap all the coding gains of ADL. In Ding et al.

(2007), a high angular resolution in prediction is achieved by the use of fractional pixels in the prediction and update operations.

In Chang and Girod (2007), the direction d in Eq. (5.18) is constrained such that the line segment from $(0,0)^T$ to $(d_x,d_y)^T$ does not intersect with any other point in Π, that is, d_x and d_y are coprime integers. Typically, this procedure uses nine directions shown in Fig. 5.8: $d_{-4}=(-3,1)^T$, $d_{-3}=(-2,1)^T$, $d_{-2}=(-1,1)^T$, $d_{-1}=(-1,3)^T$, $d_0=(0,1)^T$, $d_1=(1,3)^T$, $d_2=(1,1)^T$, $d_3=(2,1)^T$, and $d_4=(3,1)^T$.

For the second stage of the DWT further applied to w_0 and w_1, the transform can be used along directions derived from the set of d's defined by $\check{d}=(\check{d}_x,\check{d}_y)^T=(d_y,2d_x)^T$, i.e. $\check{d}_{-4}=(1,-6)^T$, $\check{d}_{-3}=(1,-4)^T$, $\check{d}_{-2}=(1,-2)^T$, $\check{d}_{-1}=(3,-2)^T$, $\check{d}_0=(0,1)^T$, $\check{d}_1=(3,2)^T$, $\check{d}_2=(1,2)^T$, $\check{d}_3=(1,4)^T$, and $\check{d}_4=(1,6)^T$. These directions are shown in Fig. 5.8 with the dashed arrows. Consequently, $\check{d}_y$ is even, and $\check{d}_x$ is odd, and

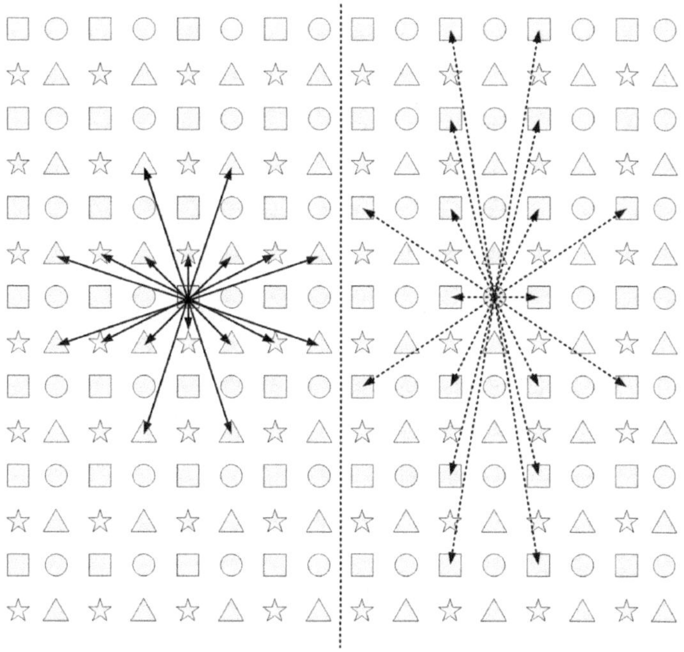

Fig. 5.8 The proposed set of directions for directional lifting in Chang and Girod (2007). The solid arrows denote d and $-d$ and the dashed arrows denote $\check{d}$ and $-\check{d}$. Stars denote Π_{00}, squares denote Π_{10}, triangles denote Π_{01}, and circles denote Π_{11}

$$l_{01} - (2k+1)\check{d} \in \Pi_{00}, l_{11} - (2k+1)\check{d} \in \Pi_{10}, \forall l_{01} \in \Pi_{01}, l_{11} \in \Pi_{11}, k = -K_p, ..., K_p - 1$$

The directions selected for the transforms on $\mathbf{w}_0$ and $\mathbf{w}_1$ may be different. The experiments in Chang and Girod (2007) show that $K_p = 3$, with $c_{p,0} = c_{p,1} = 150/256$, $c_{p,1} = c_{p,-2} = -25/256$, and $c_{p,2} = c_{p,-3} = 3/256$. $K_u = 3$, with $c_{u,0} = c_{u,1} = 150/512$, $c_{u,1} = c_{u,-2} = -25/512$, and $c_{u,2} = c_{u,-3} = -3/512$, result in the best compression performance.

To reduce the overhead needed to signal the direction selections, the selection is performed in a blockwise fashion. The best selection is obtained by minimizing the sum of the absolute values of the high-pass coefficients in a block. Additionally, the rate overhead is taken into account through a Lagrange multiplier $\lambda > 0$, similar to the rate-constrained motion estimation in H.264/AVC (Wiegand et al. 2003).

For the transform applied to $\mathbf{s}$, the original grid Π is evenly partitioned into N_b nonoverlapping blocks, each denoted by B_b, $b = 0, ..., N_b - 1$. For each block B_b, direction d_b^* is selected by minimizing a Lagrange cost function:

$$d_b^* = argmin_d \{ \sum_{l_1 \in \Pi_1 \cap B_b} |g_H(s[l_1] - P_{s,l_1}^d(\mathbf{s}_0))| + \lambda R_{b,d} \} \tag{5.20}$$

where $R_{b,d}$ denotes the number of bits spent as overhead for signaling the selection $d_b^* = d$. Given that $d_b^* = d$ for all blocks, it follows that $d_{l_1}^* = d_b^*, \forall l_1 \in B_b$, and thus that prediction and update function for every sample can be defined according to Eqs. (5.18) and (5.19). Note that although the direction is selected blockwise, filtering in the prediction and update step is carried out across block boundaries. Therefore, blocking artifacts are not observed in the reconstructed images.

To further increase the efficiency of the prediction step, each block B_b may be further partitioned into smaller subblocks. The best block partition for each block and the best direction for each subblock are then selected using the modified cost function, similar to the variable block-size motion compensation in H.264/AVC (Wiegand et al. 2003).

Coding of Direction and Block Partition Selection: The direction selection in Chang and Girod (2007) is predicted from the selections of the blocks (subblocks) in the causal neighborhood, and the residual is coded with variable length coding. Each block partition selection is independently encoded with variable length coding.

In contrast to the direction selection in Chang and Girod (2007), Ding et al. propose segmenting an image into regions of textures and edges of clear directional bias (Ding et al. 2007), in order for an image codec to benefit from the adaptability of ADL to the edge/texture orientation. The optimal direction selection is posed as the following R-D optimization problem.

R-D Optimization: For ease of implementation, this process partitions the image recursively into blocks of variable size via a quad-tree. All pixels in a quad-tree block are subject to the same ADL transform. The finer the segmentation, the greater the degree of gradient uniformity in the resulting blocks. This leads to better directional prediction of the image signal and hence lower distortion. However, the improved signal approximation of ADL is achieved at the expense of increased additional information to describe the segmentation tree and the lifting directions of individual blocks. To find the quad-tree that achieves the optimal balance between cost of coding the segmentation tree and cost of coding ADL transform coefficients, the well-known BFOS algorithm for optimal tree pruning is applied (Breiman 1984).

5.8 Motion Compensation Temporal Filtering in Video Coding

MCTF is emerging as a key technology in the coming SVC standards[ohm2005asv]. Breakthroughs associated with this approach have enabled the implementation of highly efficient scalable video codecs that provide flexible spatial, temporal, signal-to-noise ratio (SNR), and complexity scalability with fine granularity over a large range of bit rates while maintaining a very high coding efficiency.

A typical scalable video encoder structure is depicted in Fig. 5.9. Iterative temporal subband decomposition inherently allows for temporal scalability. The spatial scalability and SNR scalability can be provided by combining MCTF with spatial wavelet decomposition (2D-DWT) and embedded coding. Performing temporal decomposition in the lifting implementation allows for both subpixel accurate MC and longer filters with PR capability to be integrated into MCTF. These tools are valuable for further increasing the coding efficiency of the SVC system. In this section, focus is limited to the development of MCTF in this research field. Topics including ME, spatial subband/wavelet transform, and embedded coding have mainly been used in the areas of traditional hybrid video codecs (motion compensation (MC) +DCT) and image compression.

Fig. 5.9 Typical structure of the scalable video codec

5.8.1 Overview of MCTF

The idea of using motion-compensated temporal DWT was introduced by Ohm (1994) and then developed by Choi and Woods (1999) (Chen and Woods 2004). A motion-compensated lifting framework for MCTF is proposed in Chen and Woods (2004), Secker and Taubman (2003), Akyol et al. (2004), and Tillier et al. (2006). Given a set of motion paths, MCTF applies a temporal wavelet transform along these motion trajectories over the frames of the video sequence. Each lifting step of the MCTF consists of two steps: prediction and update. The prediction step takes the original input frames to generate the high-pass frames, and the update step uses the available high-pass frames and even frames to generate the low-pass frames. ME is performed separately for each temporal decomposition level, and then each lifting step is compensated for by the estimated scene motion to produce high-pass and low-pass frames. From the view of video compression, reducing the energy of the high temporal frame in the prediction step results in a higher coding gain. Moreover, reducing artifacts in low temporal frames results in a high-quality low-frame rate video, as required by temporal scalability. Hence, the efficiency of the prediction step relates to the choice of wavelet filters and the accuracy of motion vectors; the performance of the update step is related to noise and temporal and spatial aliasing.

Within the framework proposed by Secker and Tabuman (2003), MCTF is accomplished through a sequence of temporal lifting steps, and the MC is performed within each lifting step. Let $\mathcal{W}_{k_1 \to k_2}$ denote motion-compensated lifting steps for a 5/3 analysis by

$$h_k = f_{2k+1} - \frac{1}{2}[\mathcal{W}_{2k \to 2k+1}(f_{2k}) + \mathcal{W}_{2k+2 \to 2k+1}(f_{2k+2})] \tag{5.21}$$

$$l_k = f_{2k} - \frac{1}{4}[\mathcal{W}_{2k-1 \to 2k}(h_{k-1}) + \mathcal{W}_{2k+1 \to 2k}(h_k)] \tag{5.22}$$

Regardless of the motion model used for the $\mathcal{W}$ operator, the temporal transform can be trivially inverted by reversing the order of the lifting steps and replacing addition with subtraction as follows:

$$f_{2k} = l_k - \frac{1}{4}[\mathcal{W}_{2k-1 \to 2k}(h_{k-1}) + \mathcal{W}_{2k+1 \to 2k}(h_k)] \tag{5.23}$$

$$f_{2k+1} = h_k + \frac{1}{2}[\mathcal{W}_{2k \to 2k+1}(h_{k-1}) + \mathcal{W}_{2k+2 \to 2k+1}(f_{2k+2})] \tag{5.24}$$

A reduced temporal resolution sequence may be formed by keeping only the low-pass frame. To improve temporal scalability and exploit longer term temporal redundancy, more than one level of MCTF may be performed by subsequently applying the transform to the low-pass temporal frames. Figure 5.10 shows the lifting structure of the MCTF. The lifting structures using wavelet kernels of BT7/5 and CDF9/7 can be applied according to the structures in Figures 5.11 and 5.12, respectively. The number of consecutive frames involved in CDF9/7, BT7/5, and LG5/3 are 7, 5, and 3, respectively.

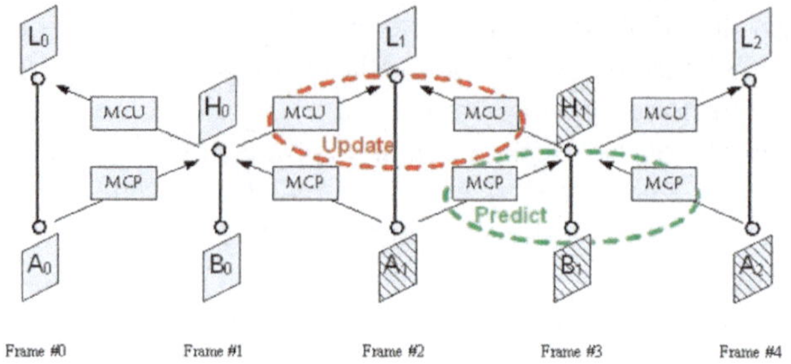

Fig. 5.10 Lifting structure of MCTF using LG5/3 wavelet. MCU, motion-compensated update; MCP, denotes motion-compensated prediction

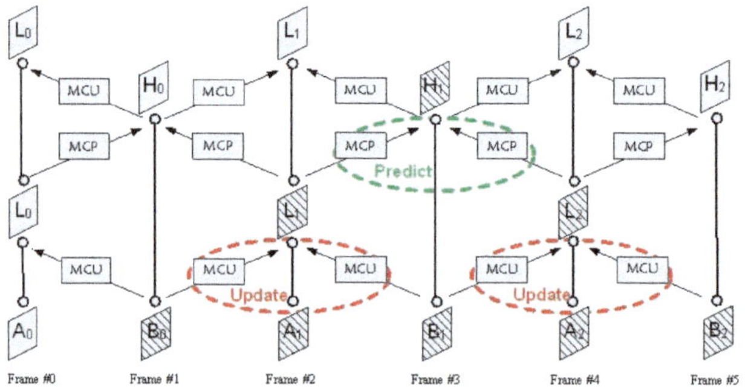

Fig. 5.11 Lifting structure of MCTF using BT7/5 wavelet. MCU, motion-compensated update; MCP, denotes motion-compensated prediction

The quality of the MCTF plays an essential role in motion-compensated nonrecursive subband/wavelet coding. It influences not only coding efficiency but also the quality of the resulting low-frame rate video. The ideal MCTF of an SVC codec should meet three primary requirements. First, the low-pass frames should present a high quality reduced frame rate video. Second, the high-pass frames should contain as little energy as possible. Third, the transform should be invertible. The invertibility of the transform can be accomplished by using an LS. The other two requirements are both closely related to the use of temporal filtering and subsampling along the motion trajectories associated with a realistic motion model. This makes the choice of a suitable wavelet kernel and estimation of the motion trajectories with high accuracy of a challenging problem.

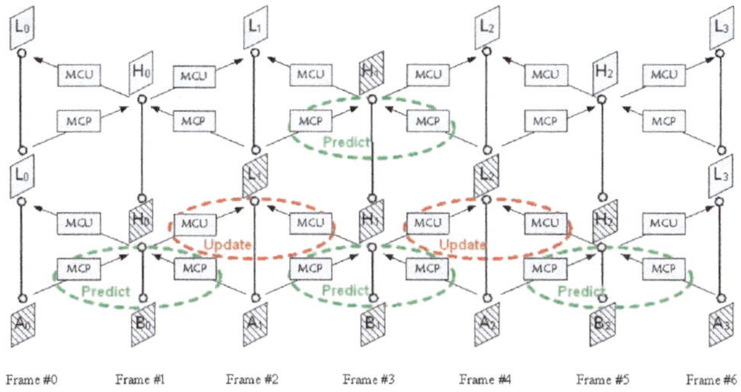

Fig. 5.12 Lifting structure of MCTF using CDF9/7 wavelet. MCU, motion-compensated update; MCP, motion-compensated prediction

5.8.2 MC in MCTF

In theory, the lifting-based MCTF can perform temporal decomposition using any desired motion model and any desired wavelet kernel with finite support. If the low-pass frames are obtained by filtering along the true scene motion trajectories, the reduced frame rate video sequence obtained by discarding high temporal frequency subbands from the compressed representation may have an even higher quality than that obtained by subsampling the original video sequence. This is because low-pass filtering along the motion trajectories tends to reduce the effects of camera noise, spatial aliasing, and scene illumination variations. If the suitable wavelet filters are used along the true motion trajectories, there should be minimal introduction of spurious spatial details, and the high-pass frame should have particularly low energy. However, there are places (e.g., scene changes and occluded/uncovered regions) where the motion model must necessarily fail. In these regions, the low-pass temporal analysis filter is effectively being applied along invalid motion trajectories. When this happens, not only does the compression performance suffer but the update steps also add ghosting to the low-pass temporal frames, significantly reducing their visual quality.

It should be emphasized that, in principle, the MC in the prediction step and the inverse motion compensation (IMC) in the update step should be independent. This still would guarantee PR by the inherent properties of the lifting structure. However, a mismatch between MC and IMC would affect a smoothing of low-pass frames and eventually deteriorate compression performance. Methods for ME as applied in existing 3D wavelet coders have mainly been developed from related hybrid coders, which are typically optimized for the prediction step, but not necessarily jointly for prediction and update steps. This is still an open problem in SVC and is discussed in Section 5.8.3.

5.8.3 Adaptive Lifting-Based Wavelets in MCTF

Due to the irregular motion of objects in the scene, or to scene changes, good matches cannot always be found using unidirectional ME as in MCTF. As a result, compensation and filtering are performed across poorly matched regions, leading to the creation of annoying visual artifacts in the low-pass frames and the reduction of coding efficiency. Another important research direction in MCTF is the adoption of the adaptive lifting-based wavelet. Similar to the mechanisms discussed in adaptive lifting-based wavelet for image compression, the mechanisms adopted in the lifting-based MCTF can also be summarized into two classes: the adaptive prediction filter and the content adaptive update filter.

Approaches in the former try to maximize the energy reduction of high-pass frames by the prediction step. Energy reduction by the prediction step is directly related to coding efficiency and exhibits varying performance with different filters and MV accuracy (Golwelkar and Woods 2003). Pau et al. (2004) discuss the optimization of the prediction operator in lifting-based MCTF. They consider the ME problem and the means for optimizing the choice of vectors involved in this prediction. Ruster et al. (2004) introduced several different block modes to allow for local adaptation of temporal filtering. They employed uni- and bi-directional block modes and optional deactivation of the temporal update step.

In contrast, UMCTF in Turaga and van der Schaar (2002) allows for flexible and efficient temporal filtering by combining the best features of MC, used in predictive coding, with the advantages of interframe scalable wavelet video coding schemes. UMTCF provides adaptive temporal filtering through a variable number of temporal decomposition levels based on video content or desired level of complexity. An adaptive choice of filters within and between temporal and spatial decomposition levels enables different temporal filtering enhancements. A variable number of successive H frames within and between levels allows flexible (non-dyadic) temporal scalability and temporal filtering enhancements and a different temporal decomposition structure.

To differentiate between the various spatial frequency components at each transform level according to their correlation noise characteristics, Xiong et al. (2006) proposed an adaptive MCTF based on the correlation noise model for SNR SVC. The strength of motion-compensated prediction is that it can be adjusted adaptively, e.g., to apply strong temporal filtering in signal components exhibiting a strong correlation and small noise, while at the same time applying weak filtering or stopping filtering altogether in signal components with a weak correlation and large noise. In this way, an adaptive MCTF scheme can be formed, not only to take advantage of temporal correlation but also to reduce the propagation of reconstruction noise. With the proposed adaptive MCTF scheme, the temporal transform filter is adjusted adaptively for each subband. Accordingly, the error propagation of each spatial temporal subband in reconstruction is changed. To achieve an optimized quantization or rate allocation, the estimated synthesis gain should be modeled based on the adaptive MCTF structure.

Alternatively, approaches in the second class, e.g., sample, content adaptive update filters, focus on the removal of annoying coding artifacts in the low-pass frames brought by the failure of ME. Li et al. (Mehrseresht and Taubman 2003) propose a new block-based update approach, which takes advantage of the chrominance information of the video sequence to further reduce ghosting artifacts in low-pass temporal frames. They adaptively weight the update steps according to the energy not only of luminance pixels but also of chrominance pixels in the high-pass temporal frames at the corresponding locations. Experimental results show that the proposed algorithm can significantly improve the quality of the reconstructed video sequence, in PSNR and visual quality. Tillier et al. (2005) proposed spatiotemporal update operators based either on weighted averages of multiple connected pixels or on nonlinear filtering of these pixels. Song et al. (2004) use content adaptive update steps based on the properties of the human vision system in lifting-based MCTF to adaptively mitigate the ghosting artifacts of low-pass temporal frames. More recently, Li et al. (Li and Ling 2006) have proposed a new scheme to improve the update steps of MCTF by analyzing the correlation of the MVs of neighboring blocks as well as the correlation of the derived update MVs in the low-pass frames. Results indicate that the proposed algorithm improves the visual quality of reconstructed video sequences at different bit rates.

5.9 Summary and Discussions

In this article, we explored emerging research on wavelet transforms and compression, which could lead to better problem domain understanding and new compression techniques. We presented a review of recent advances in constructing adaptive wavelet transforms for images and recent developments in MCTF for scalable video compression. These nonlinear wavelet transforms provide added flexibility for image and video representations and accomplish higher compression efficiency than traditional wavelets. As we have seen, there is strong interaction between representations, such as adaptive wavelets, and their performance in compression. This subtle interplay is at the heart of the success of wavelets in image and video compression. There has also been a remarkable parallel development of wavelet transformation that reduces either statistical or perceptual redundancy, beginning with the global optimal wavelet basis, then local adaptive wavelets, to most recently geometric wavelets (curvelets, ridglets, and so on).

The next generation image/video codec will encounter difficult issues such as transmitting pictures over heterogeneous networks with variable bandwidth channels, displaying images on a variety of devices, and demand for various services requiring different levels of quality. To address these issues, efforts focus primarily on improved compression efficiency, error robustness, and extended functionality, such as the scalable coding of images and videos. Enhanced motion prediction is seen by many researchers in the field as the prime means for improving video coding efficiency. To this end, novel compression strategies employ sophisticated, mid- or high-level computer vision techniques to extract and model content in image/video sequences. Examples include region-based and model-based image/video coding algorithms. Much research (Aizawa and Huang 1995; Sikora 2005; Dasu and Panchanathan 2004; Xing et al. 2001) is now focusing on the recognition of meaningful, possibly semantic information in images, and the research is moving from a blind low-level computer vision approach (no prior image knowledge) to semi-blind middle-level (employing some knowledge of underlying geometric structure) to high-level (exploiting a semantic model) computer vision strategies.

We believe that it is necessary to fuse new advances from visual pattern representation, machine learning, information theory, and computer networks to provide semantic models that can be used to develop a better representation model of visual data. As Martin Vetterli points out, the search for "true" 2D bases is only starting (Vetterli 2001).

References

Adams M (1999) Reversible Wavelet Transforms and Their Application to Embedded Image Compression. National Library of Canada – Bibliothèque nationale du Canada

Adams M (2001) The JPEG2000 Still Image Compression Standard. ISO/IEC JTC 1

Adams M, Kossentini F (2000) Reversible integer-to-integer wavelet transforms for image compression: performance evaluation and analysis. IEEE Transactions on Image Processing 9(6):1010–1024

Aizawa K, Huang T (1995) Model-based image coding advanced video coding techniques for verylow bit-rate applications. Proceedings of the IEEE 83(2):259–271

Akyol E, Tekalp A, Civanlar M (2004) Motion-compensated temporal filtering within the H. 264/AVC standard. International Conference on Image Processing 4:2291–2294

Antonini M, Barlaud M, Mathieu P, Daubechies I (1992) Image coding using wavelet transform. IEEE Transactions on Image Processing 1(2):205–220

Averbuch A, Zheludev V (2004) A new family of spline-based biorthogonal wavelet transforms and their application to image compression. IEEE Transactions on Image Processing 13(7):993

Berger T (1971) Rate Distortion Theory. Prentice-Hall, Englewood Cliffs

Boulgouris N, Tzovaras D, Strintzis M (2001) Lossless image compression based on optimal prediction, adaptivelifting, and conditional arithmetic coding. IEEE Transactions on Image Processing 10(1):1–14

Breiman L (1984) Classification and Regression Trees. Chapman & Hall/CRC, Boca Raton
Calderbank R, Daubechies I, Sweldens W, Yeo B (1998) Wavelet transforms that map integers to integers. Applied and Computational Harmonic Analysis 5(3):332–369
Candes E (1999) Ridgelets: a key to higher-dimensional intermittency? Philosophical Transactions: Mathematical, Physical and Engineering Sciences 357(1760):2495–2509
Chan T, Zhou H (2002) ENO-wavelet transforms for piecewise smooth functions. Siam Journal on Numerical Analysis 40(4):1369–1404
Chang C, Girod B (2007) Direction-adaptive discrete wavelet transform for image compression. IEEE Transactions on Image Processing 16(5):1289–1302
Chen P, Woods J (2004) Bidirectional MC-EZBC with lifting implementation. IEEE Transactions on Circus and Systems for Video Technology 14(10):1183–1194
Choi S, Woods J (1999) Motion-compensated 3-D subband coding of video. IEEE Transactions on Image Processing 8(2):155–167
Claypoole R, Davis G, Sweldens W, Baraniuk R (2003) Nonlinear wavelet transforms for image coding via lifting. IEEE Transactions on Image Processing 12(12):1449–1459
Coifman R, Wickerhauser M (1992) Entropy-based algorithms for best basis selection. IEEE Transactions on Information Theory 38(2 Part 2):713–718
Dasu A, Panchanathan S (2004) A wavelet-based sprite codec. IEEE Transactions on Circuits and Systems for Video Technology 14(2):244–255
Daubechies I, Sweldens W (1998) Factoring wavelet transforms into lifting steps. Journal of Fourier Analysis and Applications 4(3):247–269
Davis G (1994) Adaptive Nonlinear Approximations. PhD thesis, New York University
Deans S (1983) The Radon Transform and Some of Its Applications. Wiley-Interscience, New York
Deever A, Hemami S (2003) Lossless image compression with projection-based and adaptive reversible integer wavelet transforms. IEEE Transactions on Image Processing 12(5): 489–499
Ding W, Wu F, Li S (2004) Lifting-based wavelet transform with directionally spatial prediction. In: Picture Coding Symp., San Francisco, CA, December, pp 15–17
Ding W, Wu F, Xu X, Li S, Li H (2007) Adaptive directional lifting-based wavelet transform for image coding. IEEE Transactions on Image Processing 16(2):416–427
Do M, Vetterli M (2005) The contourlet transform: an efficient directional multiresolution image representation. IEEE Transactions on Image Processing 14(12):2091–2106
Donoho D, Duncan M (2000) Digital curvelet transform: strategy, implementation and experiments. Proceedings of Aerosense pp 12–29
Donoho D, Vetterli M, DeVore R, Daubechies I (1998) Data compression and harmonic analysis. IEEE Transactions on Information Theory 44(6):2435–2476
Dragotti P, Vetterli M (2003) Wavelet footprints: theory, algorithms, and applications. IEEE Transactions on Signal Processing 51(5):1306–1323
Field D (1987) Relations between the statistics of natural images and the response properties of cortical cells. Journal of the Optical Society of America A, Optics and image science 4(12): 2379–2394
Geman S, Geman D (1984) Stochastic relaxation, Gibbs distributions, and the Bayesian restoration of images. IEEE Transactions on Pattern Analysis and Machine Intelligence 6(6): 721–741
Gerek O, Cetin A (2005) Lossless image compression using an edge adapted lifting predictor. IEEE International Conference on Image Processing 2:730–733
Gerek O, Cetin A (2006) A 2-D orientation-adaptive prediction filter in lifting structures for image coding. IEEE Transactions on Image Processing 15(1):106–111
Golwelkar A, Woods J (2003) Scalable video compression using longer motion compensated temporal filters. Proceedings of SPIE 5150:1406–1416
Grangetto M, Magli E, Martina M, Olmo G, di Elettronica D (2002) Optimization and implementation of the integer wavelet transformfor image coding. IEEE Transactions on Image Processing 11(6):596–604

He Z, Mitra S (2005) From rate-distortion analysis to resource-distortion analysis. IEEE Circuits and Systems Magazine 5(3):6–18

Hyvärinen A, Hurri J, Väyrynen J (2003) Bubbles: a unifying framework for low-level statistical properties of natural image sequences. Journal of the Optical Society of America A 20(7): 1237–1252

Kim B, Pearlman W (1997) An embedded wavelet video coder using three-dimensional set partitioning in hierarchical trees (SPIHT). Proceedings of the Data Compression Conference pp 251–260

Kovacevic J, Verrerli M (1992) Nonseparable multidimensional perfect reconstruction filter banks and wavelet bases for Rłnł. IEEE Transactions on Information Theory 38(2):533–555

LePennec E, Mallat S (2005) Sparse geometric image representations with bandelets. IEEE Transactions on Image Processing 14(4):423–438

Li F, Ling N (2006) Improved update steps through motion vector correlation analysis for scalable video coding. International Conference on Consumer Electronics pp 485–486

Li H, Liu G, Zhang Z (2005) Optimization of integer wavelet transforms based on difference correlation structures. IEEE Transactions on Image Processing 14(11):1831–1847

Lu Y, Do M (2003) CRISP contourlets: a critically sampled directional multiresolution image representation. Proceedings of SPIE 5207:655–665

Mehrseresht N, Taubman D (2003) Adaptively weighted update steps in motion compensated lifting based scalable video compression. International Conference on Image Processing 2:771–774

Ohm J (1994) Three-dimensional subband coding with motion compensation. IEEE Transactions on Image Processing 3(5):559–571

Olshausen B, Field D (1996) Natural image statistics and efficient coding. Network: Computation in Neural Systems 7(2):333–339

Olshausen B, Field D (1997) Sparse coding with an overcomplete basis set: a strategy employed by V1. Vision Research 37(23):3311–3325

Oraintara S, Tran T, Nguyen T (2003) A class of regular biorthogonal linear-phase filterbanks: theory, structure, and application in image coding. IEEE Transactions on Image Processing 51:12

Ortego A, Ramchandran K (1998) Rate-distortion methods for image and video compression. IEEE Signal Processing Magazine 15(6):23–50

Pau G, Tillier C, Pesquet-Popescu B (2004) Optimization of the predict operator in lifting-based motion-compensated temporal filtering. Proceedings of SPIE 5308:712–720

Peyré G (2005) Surface compression with geometric bandelets. Proceedings of ACM SIGGRAPH 24(3):601–608

Peyre G, Mallat S (2005) Discrete bandelets with geometric orthogonal filters. IEEE International Conference on Image Processing 1:65–68

Piella G, Heijmans H (2002) Adaptive lifting schemes with perfect reconstruction. IEEE Transactions on Signal Processing 50(7):1620–1630

Reichel J, Menegaz G, Nadenau M, Kunt M (2001) Integer wavelet transform for embedded lossy to lossless imagecompression. IEEE Transactions on Image Processing 10(3): 383–392

Reichel J, Schwarz H, Wien M (2005) Scalable Video Coding – Working Draft 1. Document JVT 20

Rioul O, Vetterli M, CNET I (1991) Wavelets and signal processing. IEEE Signal Processing Magazine 8(4):14–38

Rusert T, Hanke K, Wien M (2004) Optimization for locally adaptive MCTF based on 5/3 lifting. Proceedings of the Picture Coding Symposium

Secker A, Taubman D (2003) Lifting-based invertible motion adaptive transform (LIMAT) framework for highly scalable video compression. IEEE Transactions on Image Processing 12:12

Selesnick I, Baraniuk R, Kingsbury N (2005) The dual-tree complex wavelet transform. IEEE Signal Processing Magazine 22(6):123–151

Shapiro J, Center D, Princeton N (1993) Embedded image coding using zerotrees of wavelet coefficients. IEEE Transactions on Signal Processing 41(12):3445–3462

Sheikh H, Bovik A (2006) Image information and visual quality. IEEE Transactions on Image Processing 15(2):430–444

Sikora T (2005) Trends and perspectives in image and video coding. Proceedings of the IEEE 93(1):6–17

Simoncelli E, Olshausen B (2001) Natural images statistics and neural representation. Annual Review of Neuroscience 24(1):1193–1216

Sole J, Salembier P (2004) Adaptive discrete generalized lifting for lossless compression. IEEE International Conference on Acoustics, Speech, and Signal Processing 3:57–60

Sole J, Salembier P (2006) A Common formulation for interpolation, prediction, and updat lifting design. Proceedings of International Conference on Acoustics, Speech and Signal Processing 2:13–16

Song L, Xu J, Xiong H, Wu F (2004) Content adaptive update steps for lifting-based motion compensated temporal filtering. IEEE Proc PCS

Song L, Xiong H, Xu J, Wu F, Su H (2005) Adaptive predict based on fading compensation for lifting-based motion compensated temporal filtering. IEEE International Conference on Acoustics, Speech, and Signal Processing, 2005 2

Starck J, Candes E, Donoho D (2002) The curvelet transform for image denoising. IEEE Transactions on Image Processing 11(6):670–684

Sweldens W (1996) The lifting scheme: a custom-design construction of biorthogonal wavelets. Applied and Computational Harmonic Analysis 3(2):186–200

Taubman D (1999) Adaptive, non-separable lifting transforms for image compression. IEEE International Conference on Image Processing 3:772–776

Taubman D (2000) High performance scalable image compression with EBCOT. IEEE Transactions on Image Processing 9(7):1158–1170

Tillier C, Pesquet-Popescu B, van der Schaar M (2004) Weighted average spatio-temporal update operator for subband video coding. International Conference on Image Processing 2:1305–1308

Tillier C, Pesquet-Popescu B, van der Schaar M (2005) Improved update operators for lifting-based motion-compensated temporal filtering. IEEE Signal Processing Letters 12(2): 146–149

Tillier C, Pesquet-Popescu B, van der Schaar M (2006) 3-band motion-compensated temporal structures for scalable video coding. IEEE Transactions on Image Processing 15(9): 2545–57

Turaga D, van der Schaar M (2002) Unconstrained temporal scalability with multiple reference and bi-directional motion compensated temporal filtering. doc m8388, Fairfax MPEG meeting

Velisavljevic V, Beferull-Lozano B, Vetterli M, Dragotti P (2006) Directionlets: anisotropic multidirectional representation with separable filtering. IEEE Transactions on Image Processing 15(7):1916–1933

Vetterli M (2001) Wavelets, approximation, and compression. IEEE Signal Processing Magazine 18(5):59–73

Wang Z, Bovik A, Sheikh H, Simoncelli E (2004) Image quality assessment: from error visibility to structural similarity. IEEE Transactions on Image Processing 13(4):600–612

Wiegand T, Sullivan G, Bjntegaard G, Luthra A (2003) Overview of the H. 264/AVC video coding standard. IEEE Transactions on Circuits and Systems for Video Technology 13(7):560–576

Wu Y, Zhu S, Liu X (2000) Equivalence of Julesz ensembles and FRAME models. International Journal of Computer Vision 38(3):247–265

Xing G, Li J, Li S, Zhang Y (2001) Arbitrarily shaped video-object coding by wavelet. IEEE Transactions on Circuits and Systems for Video Technology 11(10):1135–1139

Xiong R, Xu J, Wu F, Li S (2006) Adaptive MCTF based on correlation noise model for SNR scalable video coding. IEEE Conference on Multimedia Expro 1865–1868

Yoo H, Jeong J (2002) Signal-dependent wavelet transform and application to losslessimage compression. Electronics Letters 38(4):170–172

Zhang X, Wang W, Yoshikawa T, Takei Y (2004) Design of IIR orthogonal wavelet filter banks using lifting scheme. International Conference on Image Processing 4:2511–2514

Chapter 6
Supervised Learning for Visual Pattern Classification

Abstract This chapter presents an overview of the topics and major ideas of supervised learning for visual pattern classification. Two prevalent algorithms, i.e., the support vector machine (SVM) and the boosting algorithm, are briefly introduced. SVMs and boosting algorithms are two hot topics of recent research in supervised learning. SVMs improve the generalization of the learning machine by implementing the rule of structural risk minimization (SRM). It exhibits good generalization even when little training data are available for machine training. The boosting algorithm can boost a weak classifier to a strong classifier by means of the so-called classifier combination. This algorithm provides a general way for producing a classifier with high generalization capability from a great number of weak classifiers.

6.1 Introduction

Visual pattern classification is an important issue in computer vision and pattern recognition (Zheng 1998). The objective is to classify visual objects into different categories by utilizing a classification method that operates on the feature space of the visual objects. In principle, methods for visual object classification attempt to find a decision rule from the training set, so as to minimize classification error or losses on the unseen data or testing data.

When a set of training samples is obtained, a label can be assigned to every training sample to indicate its true class. By doing so, some prior or domain-specific knowledge is being incorporated into the problem of visual pattern classification. Learning from annotated data is generally called supervised learning (Heisele 2003), or learning with a teacher. The goal of the learning process is thus to adjust the parameters of a classifier using the training set with known labels, in order to make performance as high as required.

N. Zheng, J. Xue, *Statistical Learning and Pattern Analysis for Image and Video Processing*, Advances in Pattern Recognition, DOI 10.1007/978-1-84882-312-9_6,
© Springer-Verlag London Limited 2009

6.2 An Example of Supervised Learning

Here, we give an example to illustrate the process of supervised learning. Suppose we have two sets of observations, U and V. Each of them contains 100 samples, which are shown in Fig. 6.1, represented by red circles for U and blue stars for V, respectively.

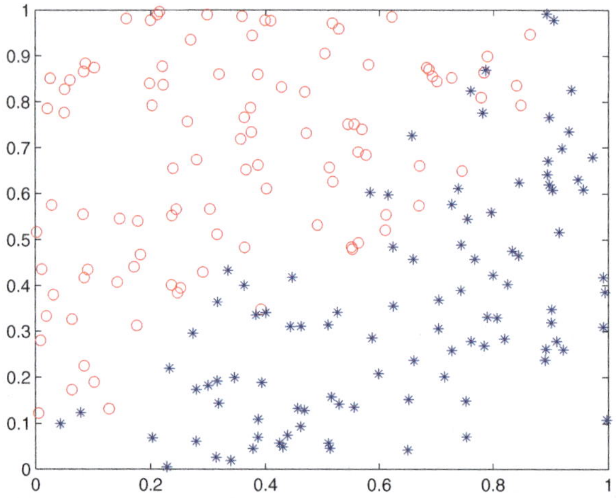

Fig. 6.1 Samples of classes U and V

We further suppose that the red circles have values of 0, and the blue stars have values of 1. Based on such labeled training samples, the process of supervised learning involves finding a classification function that can decide the classes of such points. In the simplest case, we can use the linear regression function to solve the problem.

Assume that the bivariable linear regression model has the following form:

$$y = \beta_0 + \beta_1 x_1 + \beta_2 x_2 = x\beta \tag{6.1}$$

where $y \in \{0,1\}$, $x = (1, x_1, x_2)$, $\beta = (\beta_0, \beta_1, \beta_2)^T$. We can take the minimum squared errors as the loss function, i.e.,

$$L(\beta) = \sum_{i=1}^{N} (y_i - x_i\beta)^2 \tag{6.2}$$

where N is the total number of samples.

To complete the model, first we need to estimate the unknown parameter β. For this purpose, we make N observations, resulting in N sample$(1, x_{i1}, x_{i2}; y_i)$, $i = 1, 2, \cdots, N$.

Let

$$X = \begin{pmatrix} 1 & x_{11} & x_{12} \\ 1 & x_{21} & x_{22} \\ \vdots & \vdots & \vdots \\ 1 & x_{N1} & x_{N2} \end{pmatrix}, \quad Y = \begin{pmatrix} y_1 \\ y_2 \\ \vdots \\ y_N \end{pmatrix}$$

By using the least-squares method, we can estimate the parameter as follows:

$$\hat{\beta} = (X^T X)^{-1} X^T Y \tag{6.3}$$

Then, a prediction function $\hat{y}(x_0) = x_0 \hat{\beta}$ is obtained, where x_0 is any given sample. The function is shown in Fig. 6.2. Hence, for any given x_0, its class label can be decided from the following classification function:

$$f(x_0) = \begin{cases} 0, & \text{if } \hat{y}(x_0) > 0.5 \\ 1, & \text{if } \hat{y}(x_0) \leq 0.5 \end{cases} \tag{6.4}$$

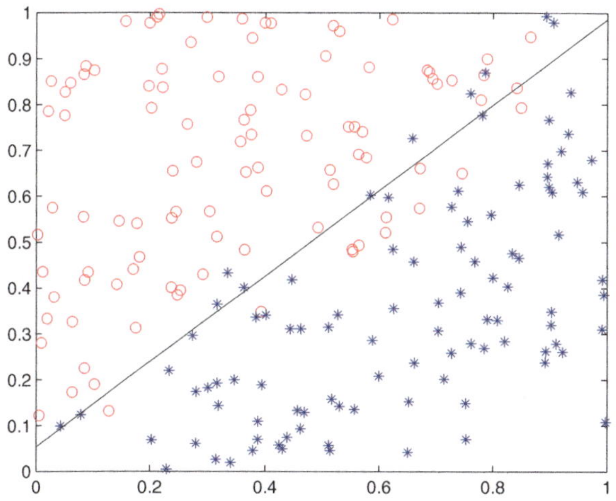

Fig. 6.2 The results of classification by linear regression

More formally, the process of supervised learning can be described as follows: given some labeled samples

$$\{(x_1, y_1), (x_2, y_2), \cdots, (x_N, y_N)\}$$

where $x_i = (x_{i1}, x_{i2}, \cdots, x_{ip}) \in \mathrm{R}^p$ is the attribute vector of the ith sample, x_{ij} is the jth attribute value of the ith sample, which can be discrete or continuous, and $y_i \in \{1, 2, \cdots, K\}$ is the class label of the ith sample. We assume there exists an inherent dependency between the input vector x and the output class label y. This dependency can generally be modeled with a function $y = f(x)$. The target of supervised learning is to learn a classifier from the labeled samples that approximates the underlying function. The classifiers can be decision trees, neural networks, Bayesian classifiers, support vector machines (SVMs), or Boosting classifiers. Once the classifier is learned, one can compute the class label for any newly observed sample.

In supervised learning, different classifiers have various learning algorithms. For example, a Bayesian classifier estimates a conditional probability density function of feature vectors by learning samples. Given the function of conditional probability and the sample set, the parameters of the probability density function can be estimated by using maximum likelihood or a Bayesian estimation method. In the general case, the decision-making rules are expressed by the classification functions, and then the loss function can be determined. Figure 6.3 gives the framework of supervised learning.

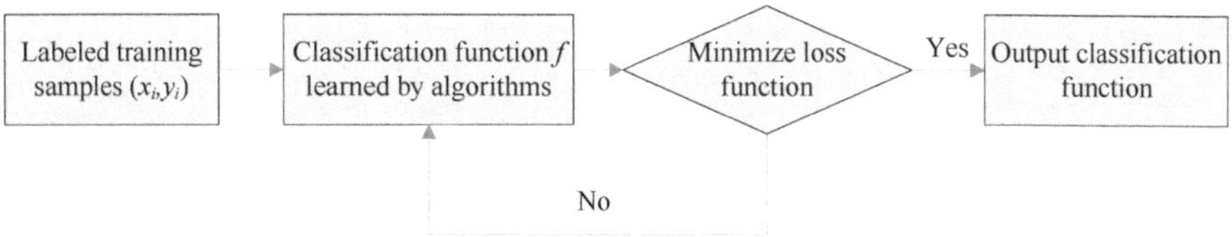

Fig. 6.3 The framework of supervised learning

In Fig. 6.3, the goal of supervised learning is to estimate the classification functions by training on labeled samples. These labeled samples are called training samples $T = \{(x_i, y_i), i = 1, 2, \cdots, N\}$, which are used to learn visual patterns. With certain learning algorithms, these labeled training samples are used to estimate a classification function. The learning algorithm can modify the classification function according to the error between estimated rules and real rules, which is known as the loss function. This modification can be implemented gradually and repeatedly, with the ultimate aim being to minimize the loss function statistically. In this way, the learning algorithm can arrive at a classification function via training samples with maximal information.

The above supervised learning approach is an error-modification method. We can use the mean squared error or the least-squares error to define the loss function. A supervised learning system can improve performance by decreasing the error iteratively, step by step. If a learning algorithm can be proposed to minimize the loss function and if the training samples and time are sufficient, the supervised learning system can well complete the task of visual pattern classification.

It is worth noting that a learning algorithm that can differentiate between some labeled samples quite well may not be adequate for many visual pattern classification problems. For example, in the exclusive-or problem ({(0,1), (1,0)} are classified as true, {(0,0), (1,1)} as false), if the training set includes only one true and one false example, the decision-making rule will misclassify two of the inputs. In the same way, choice of training samples and learning algorithm is all-important for supervised learning, that is, over-fitting samples or a lack of samples will produce a classifier with poor performance.

SVM and boosting are two hot topics in the recent supervised learning literature. In the following sections, these two algorithms are briefly reviewed.

6.3 Support Vector Machine

Statistical learning theory has been developed specially for machine learning with small volume samples (Vladimir 1992). It provides a unified framework for solving learning problems with finite samples. The SVM is such a novel general learning method that was developed on the basis of statistical learning. It shows great advantages over conventional learning methods and has seen extensive application in many fields, such as text document classification, handwriting recognition, image classification, and biological information processing. SVMs became the focus of great interest after the climax of research on artificial neutral networks. Some researchers argue that studies on SVM have led to the increased development of machine learning theories and applications (Cristianini and Shawe-Taylor 2000; Burges 1998).

From algorithmic point of view, a SVM is a data partition-based learning method. Such methods determine the class labels of unknown data by dividing the data space via a classification function (generally a hyper-plane). Representative methods include nearest neighbor classifiers, decision trees, and artificial neutral networks, among others. A nearest neighbor classifier divides the data space by Delauney triangulation, and a decision tree generally uses hyper-planes that are parallel with the coordinate axes of the data space, while artificial neutral networks use piecewise linear hyper-planes to divide the data space. Similarly, SVMs uses an optimal separating hyper-plane to partition the data. In the following sections, we will introduce some basic concepts of SVMs by considering the two-class problem.

6.3.1 Optimal Separating Hyper-plane

Assume that the training data

$$(x_1, y_1), \cdots, (x_l, y_l), x \in R^n, y \in \{+1, -1\}$$

is linearly separable, that is to say, it can be divided by a hyper-plane

$$(w \cdot x) - b = 0 \tag{6.5}$$

without any misclassifications. Among such hyper-planes, the optimal hyper-plane or the maximal margin hyper-plane is the one that has the largest geometric distance or margin (see Fig. 6.4).

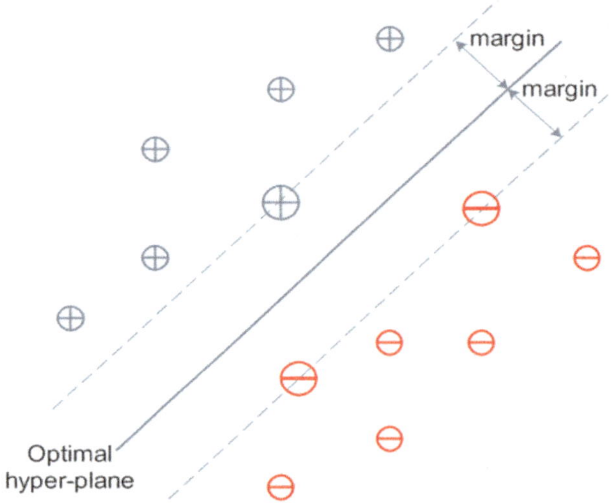

Fig. 6.4 The optimal separating hyper-plane separates the data with the maximal margin

For convenience, we take the following forms of the classification hyper-plane:

$$(w \cdot x_i) - b \geq 1, \quad \text{if } \mathrm{y_i} = 1$$
$$(w \cdot x_i) - b \leq -1, \text{ if } \mathrm{y_i} = -1$$

where $(w \cdot x^+) - b = 1$ and $(w \cdot x^-) - b = -1$ are called the standard separating hyper-plane, in which $x^+$and x^- are the positive sample and negative sample that are nearest to the classification hyper-plane, respectively. The hyper-planes above have another more compact form as follows:

$$y_i[(w \cdot x_i) - b] \geq 1, \ i = 1, \cdots, l \tag{6.6}$$

It is not difficult to calculate the geometric distance of the hyper-planes as follows:

$$\Delta = \frac{1}{2}\left(\frac{w}{\|w\|_2}, x^+ - x^-\right) = \frac{1}{2\|w\|_2}(w, x^+ - x^-) = \frac{1}{\|w\|_2}$$

Therefore, the optimal hyper-plane is the hyper-plane that satisfies the conditions (6.6) and maximizes the geometric distance of the hyper-plane. This optimal hyper-plane can be obtained by solving the following constrained convex quadratic optimization problem:

$$\begin{aligned}&\min_{w} \Phi(w) = \min_{w} \tfrac{1}{2}\|w\|^2 \\ &s.t. \quad y_i[(w \cdot x_i) - b] \geq 1, \ i = 1, \cdots, l\end{aligned} \tag{6.7}$$

By the saddle point theorem (Yuan and Sun 1997), it is known that the solution of the optimal problem corresponds to the saddle point of its Lagrange function, i.e.,

$$L(w,b,\alpha) = \frac{1}{2}(w \cdot w) - \sum_{i=1}^{l} \alpha_i \{[(x_i \cdot w) - b]y_i - 1\} \tag{6.8}$$

where α_i is the Lagrange multiplicator. The saddle point of the Lagrange function (w_0, b_0, α_0) satisfies the properties

$$\sup_{\alpha} L(w_0, b_0, \alpha) \leq L(w_0, b_0, \alpha_0) \leq \inf_{w,b} L(w, b, \alpha_0).$$

By the Kuhn–Tucker theorem (Bazaraa et al. 1992), we know that w_0, b_0 represent the optimal solution to the convex optimization problem (6.7), if and only if there exists an α_0, satisfying

(1) $\frac{\partial L(w_0,b_0,\alpha_0)}{\partial b} = 0$

(2) $\frac{\partial L(w_0,b_0,\alpha_0)}{\partial w} = 0$

(3) $\alpha_i^0 \{[(x_i \cdot w_0) - b_0]y_i - 1\} = 0, \ i = 1, \cdots, l$

(4) $\alpha_i^0 \geq 0, \ i = 1, \cdots, l.$

The third condition is the well-known Karush–Kuhn–Tucker condition, also called the KKT condition. By expanding the above equations (1) and (2), we have:

$$\sum_{i=1}^{k} \alpha_i^0 y_i = 0, \ \alpha_i^0 \geq 0, \ i = 1, \cdots, l \tag{6.9}$$

$$w_0 = \sum_{i=1}^{l} y_i \alpha_i^0 x_i, \ \alpha_i^0 \geq 0 \tag{6.10}$$

From (6.10), it is obvious that the optimal hyper-plane (vector w_0) is a linear combination of vectors in the training set. The vectors that make the constraints (6.6) tenable are called support vectors. From the KKT conditions, we can see that only the support vectors have nonzero coefficients α_i^0 in the expression of w_0, hence,

$$w_0 = \sum_{\text{support vectors}} y_i \alpha_i^0 x_i, \ \alpha_i^0 \geq 0 \tag{6.11}$$

Substituting the above equation into the Lagrange function (6.8) and applying the KKT conditions, we can get the dual version of the original optimization problem (6.7):

$$\begin{aligned}&\max_{\alpha} W(\alpha) = \max_{\alpha} \sum_{i=1}^{l} \alpha_i - \tfrac{1}{2} \sum_{i,j=1}^{l} \alpha_i \alpha_j y_i y_j (x_i \cdot x_j) \\ &s.t. \quad \sum_{i=1}^{l} \alpha_i y_i = 0, \quad \alpha_i \geq 0, \ i = 1, \cdots, l\end{aligned} \tag{6.12}$$

The dual problem generally has simple constraints in comparison with the original one and may simplify the solution process.

Once the optimal solution $\alpha_0 = (\alpha_1^0, \cdots, \alpha_l^0)$ of (6.12) is obtained, the classification rule corresponding to the optimal hyper-plane can be described with the following indicator function:

$$f(x) = sgn\left(\sum_{\text{support vectors}} y_i \alpha_i^0 (x_i \cdot x) - b_0\right) \tag{6.13}$$

where x_i is a support vector and b_0 is a constant, which can be calculated by

$$b_0 = \frac{1}{2}[(w_0 \cdot x^+) + (w_0 \cdot x^-)] \tag{6.14}$$

where x^+ and x^- are two arbitrary support vectors in the positive and negative sample set, respectively.

The training data may not be linearly separable. This commonly occurs due to the appearance of outliers, falsely labeled samples, or the overlap of probability distributions of different classes. In such cases, we can introduce a relaxation quantum $\xi_i \geq 0$ to design a soft margin classifier with the following constraints:

$$y_i((w \cdot x_i) - b) \geq 1 - \xi_i, \quad i = 1, \cdots, l \tag{6.15}$$

The soft margin classifier is also known as the generalized optimal hyper-plane. Similarly, its normal vector w can be calculated by minimizing the following function with the above constraints:

$$\Phi(w, \xi) = \frac{1}{2}(w \cdot w) + C(\sum_{i=1}^{l} \xi_i) \tag{6.16}$$

where C is a prescribed constant.

The approach to solving the above optimization problem is similar to approaches used when the data are linearly separable. By applying the Kuhn–Tucker theorem and the KKT conditions, we can obtain the corresponding dual problem as follows:

$$\begin{aligned} &\max_{\alpha} W(\alpha) = \max_{\alpha} \sum_{i=1}^{l} \alpha_i - \frac{1}{2} \sum_{i,j=1}^{l} \alpha_i \alpha_j y_i y_j (x_i \cdot x_j) \\ &s.t. \quad \sum_{i=1}^{l} \alpha_i y_i = 0, \quad 0 \leq \alpha_i \leq C, \; i = 1, \cdots, l \end{aligned} \tag{6.17}$$

As in the separable case, only some coefficients α_i, $i = 1, \cdots, l$ are nonzero, and these define the support vectors.

6.3.2 Realization of SVM

In practice, the samples to be classified are often highly nonlinear. Therefore, even if a small classification error is permitted during the classification, the generated optimal separating hyper-plane often has a very tiny interval. To deal with this problem, the SVM first maps the input vectors into a high-dimensional space by choosing a nonlinear mapping (see Fig. 6.5). In the high-dimensional space, the originally nonlinearly separable problem is often separable, and an optimal separating hyper-plane can easily be found.

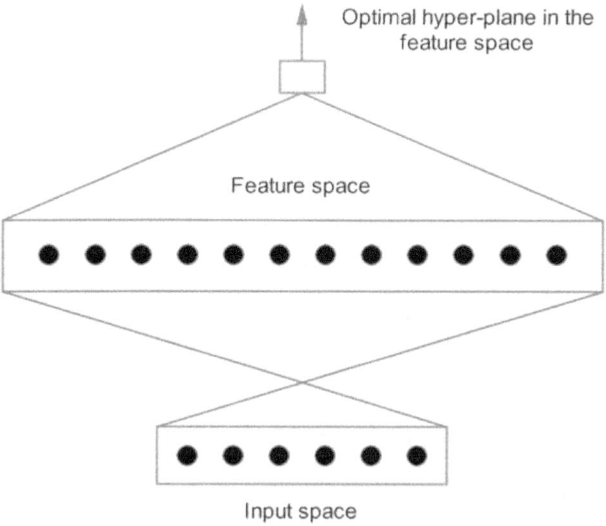

Fig. 6.5 A SVM constructs the classification hyper-plane by mapping input data into a high-dimension feature space

After mapping into a high-dimensional space, due to the sparsity of the data, it is often not difficult to find a hyper-plane to separate the training data. Such a hyper-plane corresponds to a nonlinear classification surface in the low-dimensional space. For example, to make a second-order polynomial as the decision surface, we can take the following high-dimensional space, which has $K_\gamma(\|x-x_i\|)$ coordinates, $z^1 = x^1, \cdots, z^n = x^n$, $z^{n+1} = (x^1)^2, \cdots, z^{2n} = (x^n)^2$, $z^{2n+1} = x^1x^2, \cdots, z^N = x^{n-1}x^n$, $\frac{n(n+3)}{2}$, where $x = (x^1, \cdots, x^n)$. The classification hyper-plane made in this space corresponds to a second-order polynomial in the input space.

However, calculations in the high-dimensional space may encounter the so-called curse of dimensionality. For instance, in the above mentioned example, in order to make a fourth- or fifth-order polynomial decision surface in a space with 200 dimensions, one has to construct a hyper-plane in a space with at least a billion-dimensions. Boser et al. (2003) found that to construct a hyper-plane in the high-dimensional space, it is not necessary to consider the space explicitly, but merely to define the inner product of the space (Boser et al. 2003). It is obvious from Eqs. (6.17) and (6.13) that to construct a classification hyper-plane in a high-dimensional space, we need only to define the inner product in the high-dimensional space. The solving process is exactly the same as that in the low-dimensional space.

The inner product in Hilbert space has the following form:

$$(z_i, z) = K(x, x_i) = \sum_{k=1}^{\infty} a_k \varphi_k(x) \varphi_k(x_i)$$

where $S(u)$ is the image in the feature space of the input vector x and N is the kernel function. From the Hilbert–Schmidt theorem, we know that $K(x, x_i)$ is an arbitrary symmetric function that satisfies the following Mercer condition (Courant and Hilbert 1953):

Mercer conditions:

Any symmetric function is an inner product function of a feature space if and only if for any $\Phi(u) \neq 0$ and $\int \Phi(u)^2 du < \infty$ satisfies

$$\iint K(u, v) \Phi(u) \Phi(v) du dv > 0$$

The nonlinear decision-making function of a SVM in low-dimensional space is

$$f(x) = sgn\left(\sum_{\text{support vectors}} y_i \alpha_i K(x_i, x) - b \right) \tag{6.18}$$

This function corresponds to a linear decision function made in a high-dimensional feature space $\varphi_1(x), \cdots, \varphi_N(x)$. In linearly separable cases, the coefficients α_i in the above function can be calculated by solving the following optimization problem:

$$\begin{aligned} &\max_{\alpha} W(\alpha) = \max_{\alpha} \sum_{i=1}^{l} \alpha_i - \frac{1}{2} \sum_{i,j=1}^{l} \alpha_i \alpha_j y_i y_j K(x_i, x_j) \\ &s.t. \ \sum_{i=1}^{l} \alpha_i y_i = 0, \quad \alpha_i \geq 0, \ i = 1, \cdots, l \end{aligned} \tag{6.19}$$

A learning machine that uses the decision function in (6.18) is called a SVM. It is also worth mentioning that the complexity of constructing a SVM only depends on the number of support vectors and is unrelated to the dimensions of the feature space. Figure 6.6 shows the schematic diagram of the SVM.

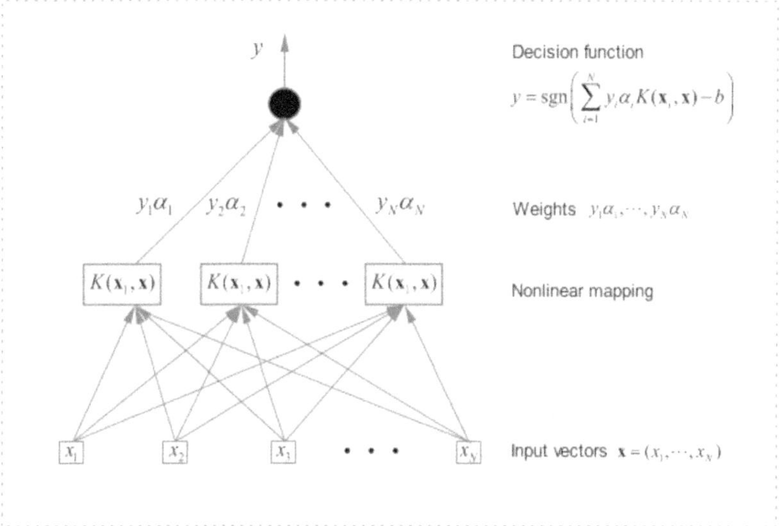

Fig. 6.6 The SVM maps the input space into a high-dimensional feature space using a kernel function to construct the optimal separating hyper-plane

6.3.3 Kernel Function

Essentially, the SVM divides two data sets by maximizing the interval between the two sets. For a nonlinear data set, it divides the data set by first mapping it into a high-dimensional space via a nonlinear mapping. During the construction of the optimal separating hyper-plane in the high-dimensional space, the SVM does not take into account the detailed descriptions of the data in the space, but only needs to define the form of the inner product of the space, i.e., to choose an appropriate kernel function. In comparison to artificial neural networks, the SVM changes the difficult problem of hidden layer parameter selection into the problem of kernel function selection, thus giving rise to a wide range of concerns.

By using different kernel functions, we can construct various types of learning machines in the input space. Here are several commonly used learning machines:

1. Polynomial Learning Machine: This type of SVM adopts a kernel function as follows:

$$K(x,x_i) = [(x \cdot x_i) + 1]^d$$

where d is the order of the polynomial. The decision function of such an SVM is

$$f(x,\alpha) = sgn\left(\sum_{\text{support vectors}} y_i\alpha_i[(x_i \cdot x) + 1]^d - b\right)$$

It is not difficult to observe that the function in fact is a factorization of the d-order polynomial in the input space R^n.

2. Radial Basis Function Machine: The traditional radial basis function machine uses a decision function as follows:

$$f(x) = sgn\left(\sum_{i=1}^{N} a_i K_\gamma(\|x - x_i\|) - b\right)$$

where $K_\gamma(\|x - x_i\|)$ depends on the distance of two vectors. For any fixed width parameter γ of the kernel function, $K_\gamma(\|x - x_i\|)$ is a nonnegative monotone function and its value converges to 0 when $\|x - x_i\|$ tends to infinity. Among this type of function, the most commonly used is

$$K_\gamma(\|x - x_i\|) = \exp\left\{-\gamma\|x - x_i\|^2\right\}$$

It is worth noting that unlike the traditional radial basis function machine, all the parameters $(N, \gamma, x_i, a_i = \alpha_i y_i)$ of the radial basis function in an SVM can be decided by minimizing an objective function.

3. Two-layer Neural Network: The kernel function used in the two-layer neural network is

$$K(x, x_i) = S[v(x \cdot x_i) + c],$$

where $S(u)$ is the sigmoid function. Thus, the corresponding decision function is

$$f(x, \alpha) = sgn\left(\sum_{i=1}^{N} \alpha_i S(v(x \cdot x_i) + c) + b\right)$$

In contrast to the construction of a neural network, the two-layer neural network SVM can automatically determine the number of hidden units N (the number of support vectors), the weight vectors of the hidden neurons $w_i = x_i$, and the weight vectors of the second layer (the value of α).

As we can see, the SVM in fact converts the problem of model selection in classification to a problem of kernel function selection. The introduction of kernel function greatly improves the ability of learning machines to deal with nonlinear problems, while maintaining the inherent linearity of learning machines in the high-dimensional space. Currently, kernel-based methods have become a general way to address the problem of nonlinearity in the field of machine learning.

However, the selection or design of an optimal kernel function is still a very complex and difficult problem and has not been well resolved yet. As with model selection approaches, the selection or design of the optimal kernel function is usually a domain-specific problem and requires that some prior be incorporated. How to select or design an optimal kernel function is an area of great interest in machine learning. Researchers have proposed various kinds of methods for kernel selection and design (Cristianini et al. 1998).

6.4 Boosting Algorithm

Since the quantity of data in visual patterns is huge, one of the critical issues in visual pattern recognition is how to combine simple patterns to form a classifier that performs well. The boosting algorithm gives us an approach to solving this problem. The principal idea behind the boosting algorithm is that combining simple rules and classifiers results in a single classifier that is better than others, thereby "boosting" performance. The principle of the boosting algorithm is that gathering a series of rules and combining them produces a stronger rule. Suppose $h_1, h_2, \ldots, h_T$ represents a set of weak or simple classifiers. The combined classifier is as follows:

$$f_T(x) = \sum_{t=1}^{T} c_t h_t(x) \tag{6.20}$$

where c_t is the combined coefficient of the simple classifier h_t. The goal of the boosting algorithm is to compute the combined parameters c_t and h_t.

The basic theory behind the boosting algorithm is the PAC (probably approximately correct) learning model which was proposed by Valiant (1984). Valiant and Kearns also put forward the conception of weak learning and strong learning. A weak learning algorithm generates a rule or hypothesis for classification which is only a little better than random guessing, and a strong learning algorithm generates a highly accurate rule or hypothesis for classification. It is easy to make a weak learning algorithm but rather difficult to produce a strong learning algorithm. It is a natural idea that a training method could be devised to improve a strong learning algorithm from a series of weak learning algorithms step by step. Based on this thought, Kearns (1990) proposed an equivalent question by looking at this approach from the opposite perspective, that is, whether weak learning algorithms could be incrementally combined into strong learning algorithms. If these perspectives are equivalent, we just need to start with some weak algorithms and then transform them into a strong learning algorithm directly. Kearns and Valiant (1994) prove that if there is enough data, a weak learning algorithm can be turned into a strong learning algorithm of arbitrarily high precision through assembled methods.

The first polynomial time boosting algorithm, proposed by (Schapire 1990), is the initial form of the boosting algorithm. This algorithm transforms a weak learning algorithm into a strong learning algorithm. In 1993, the first experiments with these early boosting algorithms were carried out by Drucker et al. (1993) on the optical character recognition (OCR) problem, in which they use a neural network as the weak learning algorithm. However, these methods have the same disadvantage: we must first know the accuracy of the weak learning algorithm. Consequently, in 1997, Freund and Schapire (1997) improved the boosting algorithm and introduced the AdaBoost algorithm. This enabled the boosting algorithm to be used in practice.

6.4.1 AdaBoost Algorithm

The AdaBoost algorithm is the most popular boosting algorithm in visual pattern classification. By using weak or base learning algorithms repeatedly, we can get a combined classification of the form (6.20) that performs well and represents a combination of weak classification functions. In the process of using weak classification repeatedly, different distributions of sample sets should be used, or a weighted sample set, to train the simple classifiers. The weight of a sample set is $d^t = \{d_1^t, d_2^t, \cdots, d_N^t\}$, $\sum_{n=1}^{N} d_n^t = 1$, $d_n^t \geq 0$. In each training, the misclassified samples will have larger weight during the next training. In general, the samples closest to the decision-making boundary will be easily misclassified. Therefore, after several iterations, these samples assume the greatest weights. As a result, if there are enough training samples and classification errors, we can obtain a stronger classifier through the AdaBoost algorithm. Figure 6.7 shows the framework of the AdaBoost algorithm.

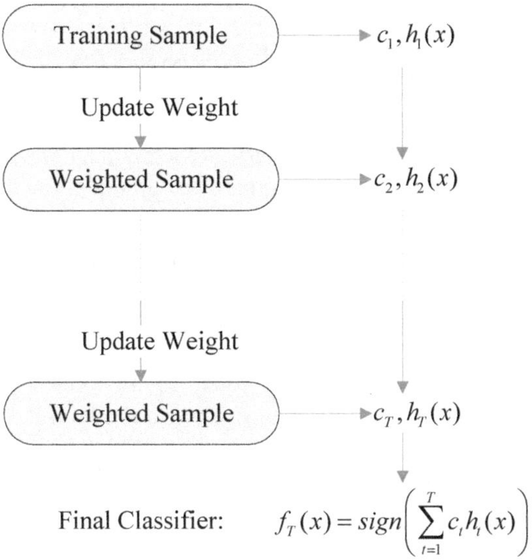

Fig. 6.7 The framework of the AdaBoost algorithm

We will now introduce the AdaBoost algorithm in detail. The algorithm can be described as follows:

1. Enter training sample set and iteration number

$$S = \{(x_1, y_1), (x_2, y_2), \cdots, (x_N, y_N)\}, T$$

2. Initialize the weights of samples

$$d_n^1 = 1/N, n = 1, 2, \cdots, N$$

3. Repeat for $t = 1, 2, \cdots, T$
   - Use weighted sample set $\{S, d^t\}$ and learning algorithm L to train the classifier. A hypothesis or simple classification function can be obtained $h_t : x \rightarrow \{-1, +1\}$, that is, $h_t \in L(S, d^t)$.
   - Compute the error of the simple classifiers ε_t:

$$\varepsilon_t = \sum_{n=1}^{N} d_n^t \cdot I(y_n \neq h_t(x_n))$$

where $I(y_n \neq h_t(x_n)) = \begin{cases} 1 \; if \; y_n \neq h_t(x_n) \\ 0 \; if \; y_n = h_t(x_n) \end{cases}$

   - Set the weight α_t of the simple classifier h_t

$$\alpha_t = \frac{1}{2} \log \frac{1 - \varepsilon_t}{\varepsilon_t}$$

   - Update the weights of training samples

$$d_n^{t+1} = \frac{d_n^t \cdot \exp\{-\alpha_t y_n h_t(x_n)\}}{Z_t}$$

where Z_t is the normalized constant, $\sum_{n=1}^{N} d_n^{t+1} = 1$

4. Output the final classifier

$$f_T(x) = \sum_{t=1}^{T} c_t h_t(x), c_t = \frac{\alpha_t}{\sum_r \alpha_r}$$

6.4.2 Theoretical Analysis of AdaBoost

As seen in Fig. 6.7, the two most important steps are the selection of the weights on the sample training set and the selection of the weights on the weak classifiers. In the following, we will give the theoretical analysis for these two steps.

To learn simple functions for classification, weak learning algorithms need to minimize empirical risk, that is, to minimize the objective function as follows:

$$\varepsilon_t(h_t, d^t) = \sum_{n=1}^{N} d_n^t I(y_n \neq h_t(x_n)) \tag{6.21}$$

After the simple classification function h_t is determined, the weights can be obtained by minimizing an exponential loss function. The AdaBoost algorithm minimizes the risk function as follows:

$$G^{AB}(\alpha) = \sum_{n=1}^{N} \exp\{-y_n(\alpha h_t(x_n) + f_{t-1}(x_n))\} \tag{6.22}$$

where $f_{t-1}(x)$ is the combination of simple classification functions that are produced by the forward iterations. That is,

$$f_{t-1}(x) = \sum_{r=1}^{t-1} \alpha_r h_r(x) \tag{6.23}$$

6.4.2.1 Compute the Weights of the Training Sample Set

In the two classes problem $h_t = \{-1, +1\}$, the distance between inputs and outputs $s_n = (x_n, y_n)$ with respect to the combined classification function $f_T(x)$ is as follows:

$$\rho(s_n, f_T) = y_n f(x_n) = y_n \sum_{t=1}^{T} \alpha_t h_t(x_n) \tag{6.24}$$

Assume that we can predict the right class of pattern and the distance of pattern is positive. If the positive distance is larger, the result of the rules will be better. The objective function (6.22) of the AdaBoost algorithm could be rewritten as follows:

$$G^{AB}(f_t) = \sum_{n=1}^{N} \exp\{-\rho(s_n, f_t)\} \tag{6.25}$$

where $\rho(s_n, f_t) = y_n \sum_{t=1}^{t} \alpha_t h_t(x_n)$

From (6.22), we know that it is essentially a loss function with respect to the interval distribution, and larger distances will have smaller values of G. To minimize the value of G, the distance between training patterns must be increased. Therefore, gradient information in the interval about the objective function can be used to compute and train the sample weights in the subsequent iteration. If training samples play a very important role in improving the interval of the training pattern, the sample weight will have a large value. Otherwise, it will have a small value. Theorem 1 tells us the relationship between the weight of a sample and objective function G.

Theorem 1 *In the* t*th iteration, the distribution calculation of sample pattern (sample weight)* d^{t+1} *equals the gradient of the normalized objective function* $G^{AB}(f_t)$ *with respect to the interval* $\rho(s_n, f_t)$*, that is,*

$$d_n^{t+1} = \frac{\nabla_{\rho(s_n, f_t)} G^{AB}(f_t)}{\sum_{n=1}^{N} \nabla_{\rho(s_n, f_t)} G^{AB}(f_t)} \tag{6.26}$$

where

$$\nabla_{\rho(s_n,f_t)} G^{AB}(f_t) = \frac{\partial G^{AB}(f_t)}{\partial \rho(s_n,f_t)}$$

See Appendix I for the proof.

6.4.2.2 Compute the Coefficient of the Simple Classifier

Given the weighted sample set $\{S,d^t\}$ and $h_t \in \{-1,+1\}$, assume that $u_n = y_n h_t(x_n)$. Then classifier f_t has the empirical risk of an exponential loss function as follows:

$$G^{AB}(f_t) = \sum_{n=1}^{N} e^{-\alpha_t u_n} e^{-y_n f_{t-1}(x_n)} \tag{6.27}$$

For $e^{-\alpha_t u_n} \leq \frac{1+u_n}{2} e^{-\alpha_t} + \frac{1-u_n}{2} e^{-\alpha_t}, u_n \in [-1,+1], \alpha_t \in R$ (the equation can be established when $h_t = \{-1,+1\}$), such that we obtain

$$G^{AB}(f_t) = \sum_{n=1}^{N} \left(\frac{1+u_n}{2} e^{-\alpha_t} + \frac{1-u_n}{2} e^{\alpha_t} \right) e^{-y_n f_{t-1}(x_n)} \tag{6.28}$$

In the following, we will compute the minimum of $G^{AB}(f_t)$ with respect to α_t. As $d_n^t = (e^{-y_n f_{t-1}(x_n)})/(\sum_{n=1}^{N} e^{-y_n f_{t-1}(x_n)})$, we obtain

$$\frac{\partial G^{AB}(f_t)}{\partial \alpha_t} = (1+\sum_{n=1}^{N} d_n^t u_n)e^{-\alpha_t} - (1-\sum_{n=1}^{N} d_n^t u_n)e^{\alpha_t} = 0 \tag{6.29}$$

From the function (6.21), we know that

$$\begin{aligned} \sum_{n=1}^{N} d_n^t u_n &= -\sum_{n=1}^{N} d_n^t I(y_n \neq h_t(x_n)) + \sum_{n=1}^{N} d_n^t I(y_n = h_t(x_n)) \\ &= -\varepsilon_t(h_t,d^t) + \sum_{n=1}^{N} d_n^t I(y_n = h_t(x_n)) \\ &= 1 - 2\varepsilon_t(h_t,d^t) \end{aligned} \tag{6.30}$$

With the functions (6.29) and (6.30), we get

$$\alpha_t = \frac{1}{2} \log \frac{1-\varepsilon_t}{\varepsilon_t} \tag{6.31}$$

6.4.3 AdaBoost Algorithm as an Additive Model

Essentially, the AdaBoost algorithm can be considered as an approach that uses a forward mode to approximate an additive model. Figure 6.8 is a typical additive model.

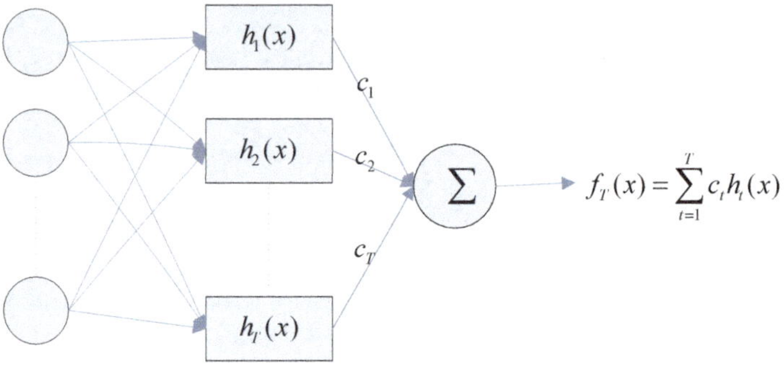

Fig. 6.8 The framework of the AdaBoost algorithm

Given a set of samples, we can use different learning methods to compute any weak classifier and its corresponding coefficient. In the visual pattern classification problem, a component of the additive model can be seen as a base classifier. By considering different base classifiers, we can derive different AdaBoost algorithms.

6.4.3.1 Discrete AdaBoost and the Real AdaBoost Algorithm

The AdaBoost algorithm can be viewed as one kind of method to construct an additive model (combined classifier). The most common AdaBoost algorithm is known as the discrete AdaBoost algorithm. In this algorithm, every simple classifier is a two-class classifier, that is, $h_t(x;\theta_t) : x \to \{-1,+1\}$. Hence, the discrete AdaBoost algorithm is described as follows:

1. Initialize: $d_i^0 = 1/N, i = 1,2,\cdots,N$
2. Repeat the training procedure, $t = 1,2,\cdots,T$
    - Use weighted sample set $\{S,d^t\}$ to train weak classifiers $h_t(x;\theta_t) \in \{-1,+1\}$
    - Compute the classification error: $\varepsilon_t = E_{d^t}\{y \neq h_t(x)\}$. In the discrete AdaBoost algorithm, the closed-form solution for the combined coefficient of weak classifiers is
$$alpha_t = \frac{1}{2}\log\frac{1-\varepsilon_t}{\varepsilon_t}$$
    - Update the sample weights:
$$d_n^t \propto d_n^{t-1}\exp\{-\alpha_t y_i h_t(x_i;\theta_t)\}, i = 1,2,\cdots,N$$

3. Output the final classifier

$$f_T(x) = \sum_{t=1}^{T} \alpha_t h_t(x; \theta_t)$$

The extension of the discrete AdaBoost algorithm is the real AdaBoost algorithm, which was proposed by Schapire. In the real AdaBoost algorithm, the weak learning algorithm forms a mapping from the feature space to the real value space, R:$\hat{h}_t(x) : x \to R$. The is in contrast to the binary mapping produced by the base classifier of discrete AdaBoost: $h_t(x) : x \to \{-1, +1\}$. The symbol $\hat{h}_t(x)$ is the classification result, and $\left|\hat{h}_t(x)\right|$ is the degree of confidence of the classification result. In the real AdaBoost algorithm, the weak learning algorithm initially returns the estimation of class probability $p_t(x) = \hat{P}_{d^t}(y = 1|x) \in [0, 1]$ and then defines its logarithmic transformation as a part of the combined classification $\hat{h}_t(x)$.

6.4.3.2 Gentle AdaBoost Algorithm

The gentle AdaBoost algorithm is a modified form of the AdaBoost algorithm. In fact, at each iteration step, the gentle AdaBoost algorithm uses Newton's method to update the weak classifiers, in contrast to the approach taken in the real AdaBoost algorithm. In the real AdaBoost algorithm, $\hat{h}_t(x) = \frac{1}{2}\log\frac{p_t(x)}{1-p_t(x)}$, whereas in the gentle AdaBoost algorithm, $\hat{h}_t(x) = P_t(y = 1|x) - P_t(y = -1|x)$. The algorithm is as follows:

1. Initialize: $d_i^0 = 1/N, i = 1, 2, \cdots, N$
2. Repeat the training procedure, $t = 1, 2, \cdots, T$

   - Minimize the risk of the squared loss function $E_d\{(y - h_t(x))^2\}$ to approximate a regression function $\hat{h}_t(x)$. This regression function can be approximated by estimating the class probability:

   $$\hat{h}_t(x) = P_t(y = 1|x) - P_t(y = -1|x)$$

   - Update the sample weights:

   $$d_n^t \propto d_n^{t-1} \exp\{-y_i \hat{h}_t(x_i)\}, i = 1, 2, \cdots, N$$

3. Output the final classifier

$$f_T(x) = \sum_{t=1}^{T} \hat{h}_t(x)$$

Compared with other AdaBoost algorithms, the gentle AdaBoost algorithm is a much simple and more stable algorithm, and it has superior performance.

6.5 Summary

We presented an overview of supervised learning techniques for visual pattern analysis in this chapter. As two important algorithms of supervised learning, the SVM and boosting algorithms were introduced. We also provided detailed derivations of the SVM and the boosting algorithm. The SVM has attracted extensive interest in recent years and has proven to be an effective and general learning method in many applications, such as handwritten character recognition and document classification. In addition, the kernel method adopted by the SVM has become a common means to deal with the problem of nonlinearity and has been widely used in pattern recognition. Boosting is a branch of ensemble learning. The approach is to boost weak classifiers into a stronger classifier. Thus, it is not necessary for us to seek a strong classifier for data classification but only to collect a group of weak classifiers that may only be marginally better than random guessing.

Appendix

The proof of Theorem 1:

Proof Let $\pi_t(s_n) = \prod_{r=1}^{t} \exp\{-y_n \alpha_r h_r(x_n)\}$. Following from the definitions of G^{AB} and ρ, we have

$$G^{AB}(f_t) = \sum_{n=1}^{N} \exp\{-\rho(s_n, f_t)\}$$

$$\frac{\partial G^{AB}(f_t)}{\partial \rho(s_n, \alpha^t)} = -\prod_{r=1}^{t} \exp\{-y_n \alpha_r h_r(x_n)\} = -\pi_t(s_n)$$

$$\begin{aligned} d_n^{t+1} &= d_n^t \exp\{-\alpha_t y_n h_t(x_n)\}/Z_t \\ &= d_n^{t-1} \exp\{-\alpha_t y_n h_t(x_n)\} \exp\{-\alpha_t y_n h_{t-1}(x_n)\}/(Z_t Z_{t-1}) \\ &= \cdots \\ &= d_n^1 \pi_t(s_n)/\tilde{Z}_t \end{aligned}$$

where $\tilde{Z}_t = \prod_{r=1}^{t} Z_r$.

$$
\begin{aligned}
d_n^{t+1} &= d_n^t \exp\{-\alpha_t y_n h_t(x_n)\}/Z_t \\
&= \frac{d_n^t \exp\{-y_n \alpha_t h_t(x_n)\}}{\sum_{n=1}^{N} d_n^t \exp\{-y_n \alpha_t h_t(x_n)\}} \\
&= \frac{d_n^1 \pi_{t-1}(s_n)/\tilde{Z}_t \exp\{-y_n \alpha_t h_t(x_n)\}}{\sum_{n=1}^{N} d_n^1 \pi_{t-1}(s_n)/\tilde{Z}_t \exp\{-y_n \alpha_t h_t(x_n)\}} \\
&= \frac{\pi_t(s_n)}{\sum_{n=1}^{N} \pi_t(s_n)} \\
&= \frac{\nabla_{\rho(s_n,f_t)} G^{AB}(f_t)}{\sum_{n=1}^{N} \nabla_{\rho(s_n,f_t)} G^{AB}(f_t)}
\end{aligned}
$$

References

Bazaraa M, Sherali D, Shetty C (1992) Nonlinear programming: theory and algorithms. Wiley-Interscience Series in Discrete Mathematics and Optimization. Wiley, New York

Boser B, Guyon I, Vapnik VN (2003) A training algorithm for optimal margin classifiers. Fifth Annual Workshop on Computational Learning Theory. pp 144–152

Burges CJC (1998) A tutorial on support vector machines for pattern recognition. Data Mining and Knowledge Discovery 2(2):121–167

Courant R, Hilbert D (1953) Methods of Mathematical Physics. John Wiley, New York

Cristianini N, Shawe-Taylor J (2000) An Introduction to Support Vector Machines. Cambridge University Press, Cambridge

Cristianini N, Shawe-Taylor J, Campbell C (1998) Dynamically adapting kernels in support vector machines. In: Advances in Neural Information Processing Systems, eds Kearns M, Solla S, Cohn D, Vol II. MIT Press, Cambridge 11

Drucker H, Schapire R, Simard P. (1993) Boosting performance in neural networks. International Journal of Pattern Recognition and Artificial Intelligence 7(4):705–719

Freund Y, Schapire R (1997) A decision-theoretic generalization of on-line learning and an application to boosting. Journal of Computer and System Sciences 55(1):119–139

Heisele B (2003) Visual object recognition with supervised learning. IEEE Intelligent Systems 18(3):38–42

Kearns M (1990) The Computational Complexity of Machine Learning. MIT Press, Cambridge

Kearns M, Valiant L (1994) Cryptographic limitations on learning boolean formulae and finite automata. Journal of the ACM 41(1):67–95

Schapire R (1990) The strength of weak learnability. Machine Learning 5(2):197–227

Valiant L (1984) A theory of the learnable. Communications of the ACM 27(11):1134–1142

Vladimir N (1992) The Nature of Statistical Learning Theory. Springer, New York

Yuan YX, Sun W (1997) Optimization Theories and Methods. Science Press, Beijing

Zheng NN (1998) Computer Vision and Pattern Recognition. Defense and Industry Press, Beijing

Chapter 7
Statistical Motion Analysis

Abstract Motion analysis involves the interpretation of image data over time. It is crucial for a range of vision tasks such as obstacle detection, depth estimation, video analysis, scene interpretation, video compression, etc. Motion analysis is difficult because it requires modeling of the complicated relationships between the observed image data and the motion of objects and motion patterns in the visual scene.
This chapter focuses on critical aspects of motion analysis, including statistical optical flow, model-based motion analysis, and joint motion estimation and segmentation. There exist many different techniques for performing various motion tasks; these techniques can be subsumed within a statistical and geometrical framework. We choose to focus on statistical approaches to classifying motion patterns in an observed image sequence.

7.1 Introduction

Motion analysis is a fundamental problem in the processing of image sequences. The goal is to compute an approximation to the two-dimensional (2D) motion field, which is actually a projection of the 3D velocities of surface points onto the imaging surface. Once computed, the measurements of image velocity can be used for a wide variety of tasks, ranging from passive scene interpretation to the autonomous detection, tracking, and recognition of objects. Of these tasks, the inference of ego motion and structure from motion requires that velocity measurements be accurate and dense, providing a close approximation to the 2D motion field.

7.1.1 Problem Formulation

Sequences of ordered images allow the estimation of objects that are apparently in motion, as well as the surfaces and edges in a visual scene caused by the relative

N. Zheng, J. Xue, *Statistical Learning and Pattern Analysis for Image and Video Processing*, Advances in Pattern Recognition, DOI 10.1007/978-1-84882-312-9_7,
© Springer-Verlag London Limited 2009

motion between an observer and the scene. With a given image sequence, the goal of motion analysis is to compute a representation of the motion that best aligns pixels in one frame of the sequence with those in the next. Accordingly, there are two components in any motion analysis technique: motion representation and a matching process. **Optical flow** is a pixel-level representation model for motion patterns, in which each point in the image is assigned a motion vector. This is illustrated in Fig. 7.1. The sphere is rotating from left to right, generating the optical flow field shown in the center. In the literature, optical flow is also known as a **motion vector field**. In the remainder of this chapter, the terms *motion vector field* and *optical flow* are interchangeable.

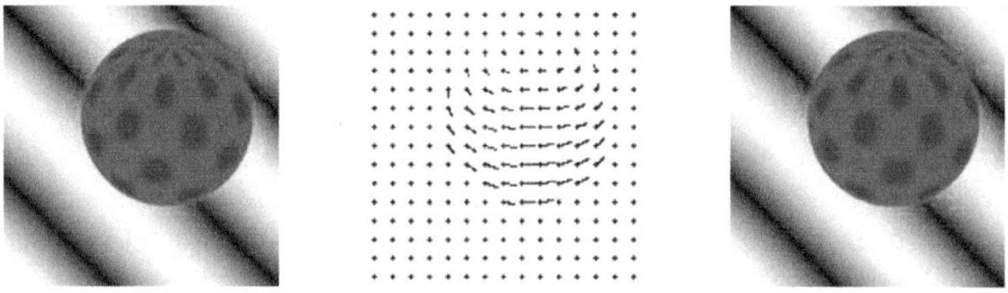

Fig. 7.1 Optical flow

We consider the estimation of motion between two given frames, $\psi(\mathbf{x},t_1)$ and $\psi(\mathbf{x},t_2)$, where $\mathbf{x} = [x,y]^T \in \Lambda_I$ denotes the coordinate of a pixel in the 2D image lattice Λ_i, and x and y represent the horizontal and vertical positions, respectively. As illustrated in Fig. 7.3, the motion vector (MV) at $\mathbf{x}$ between time t_1 and t_2 is defined as the displacement of this point from t_1 to t_2. In the motion estimation literature, when $t_1 < t_2$, the subject of study is defined as *forward motion estimation*, otherwise, it is defined as *backward motion estimation*. For notational convenience, we will use ψ_1 and ψ_2 to denote the anchor frame at time t_1 and the target frame at time t_2, respectively. The motion field is denoted as $\mathbf{d}(\mathbf{x};\mathbf{a})$, where $\mathbf{a} = [a_1,...,a_L]^T$ is a vector containing all the motion parameters.

The exact form of **a** depends on the specific representation model for the motion filed. With a given motion representation model, the motion estimation problem is equivalent to estimating the motion parameter vector **a**. As illustrated in Fig. 7.3, there are four kinds of models for representing the motion field. The *global* motion representation as shown in Fig. 7.3(a) is chosen to represent the motion field caused by the motion of the camera. The motion vector of each site in the motion field is governed by a parametric model. The affine transformation and bilinear transformation are two commonly used parametric models to describe the global motion. The vector **a** consists of coefficients of the chosen transformation. The *pixel-based* motion representation model in Fig. 7.3(b) specifies the motion vector at each site, and the vector **a** contains the vertical and horizontal components of all motion vectors. The *block-based* motion representation in Fig. 7.3(c) consists of a block partition map, and several sets of motion parameters, one for each region.

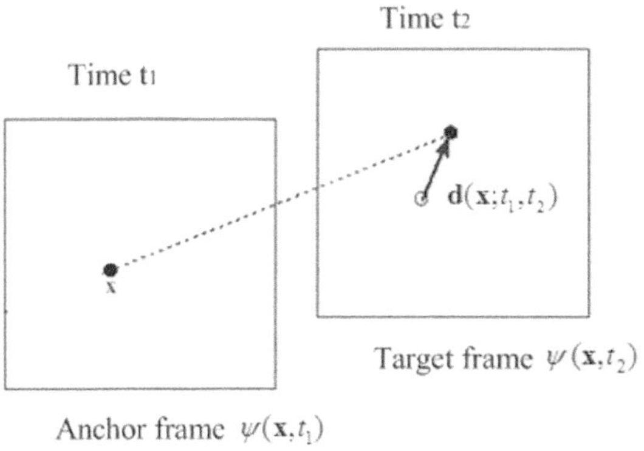

Fig. 7.2 Motion estimation

The *object-based* motion representation in Fig. 7.3(d) is an advanced version of the block-based model, in which the segmentation map replaces the block partition map. Thus, the segmentation and estimation must be accomplished jointly, which is quite a difficult problem in motion analysis.

The matching criteria for an accurate and robust optical flow estimation depends on local image constraints on motion. Several widely used constraints include local image constraints (refer to the brightness constancy) (7.1), gradient constancy (7.2),

$$\psi_1(\mathbf{x}) = \psi_2(\mathbf{x} + d(\mathbf{x})) \tag{7.1}$$

$$\nabla\psi_1(\mathbf{x}) = \nabla\psi_2(\mathbf{x} + d(\mathbf{x})) \tag{7.2}$$

and spatial coherence, which refers to the smoothness of the motion field. In estimating the optical flow, the use of just one constraint is not enough. For example, using only local image constraints can result in the "aperture problem," since we can estimate only a single flow component (normal). These constraints must be used jointly in motion estimation and often appear as regularized terms in the objective function to be optimized. Actually, most methods for computing optical flow simply represent different approaches to combining these constraints.

7.1.2 Overview of Computing Techniques

Techniques for estimating optical flow can be generally classified into three categories: (1) phase correlation, which is a fast frequency-domain approach to estimating the relative translative movement between two images (Foroosh et al.

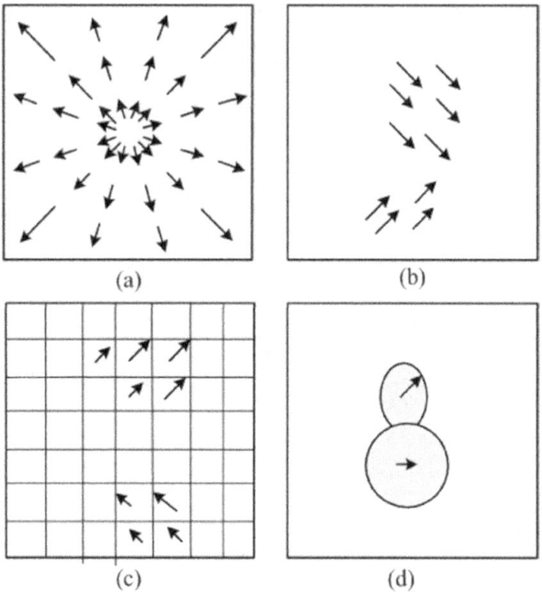

Fig. 7.3 Representation models for the motion field: (a) global motion representation, (b) pixel-based motion representation, (c) block-based motion representation, (d) object-based motion representation

2002); (2) block-based methods that minimize the sum of squared differences or the sum of absolute differences, or maximize the normalized cross-correlation, which has been widely used in video compression standards; (3) gradient-based estimation, which is a function of the partial derivatives of the image signal and/or the desired flow field and higher order partial derivatives. Additional, methods belonging to the third category include the Lucas–Kanade method (Baker and Matthews 2004), Horn–Schunck method (Bruhn et al. 2005), Black-Jepson method (Black and Jepson 1996), and general variational method (Zhao et al. 1996) (Brox et al. 2004).

To satisfy the trade-off between denoising and the preservation of motion discontinuities, most of these methods are performed on the smallest possible regions, in both the temporal domain and the spatial domain. Small regions, however, carry little motion information, and such motion computation is therefore inaccurate. Analysis of multiple moving objects based on optical flow suffers from this inaccuracy. Increasing the temporal region to more than two frames improves the accuracy of the computed optical flow. Unfortunately, the major difficulty in increasing the size of the spatial region of analysis is the possibility that larger regions will include more than a single motion, and this leads to a more difficult, motion segmentation problem.

From the perspective of motion perception, current techniques for computing motion are not satisfactory, and the computation of motion is still an open problem in the computer vision community. For example, Verri and Poggio (1987) suggested that accurate estimates of the 2D motion field are generally inaccessible due to inherent differences between the 2D motion field and intensity variations. Aloimonos and Duric (1992) argue that the measurement of optical flow is an ill-posed problem. In summary, motion computation is a challenging and complicated problem for the following reasons: (1) time-varying intensity on the retina is not necessarily caused by motion, (2) the computation must distinguish between the motion of objects in the visual field vs. its own motion, (3) motion on the retina is 2D projection of 3D object, (4) local motion often conflicts with global motion, (5) the visual scene can be complex, (6) noise and image variation limit the ability to detect change, (7) true motion is itself in a state of change. For these reasons it has been suggested that is only possible to extract qualitative information from the computed motion field.

The factors above also motivate at least two major trends in the motion analysis research community: (1) Model-based or even object-level motion representation models and constraints: it is well known that pixel-level (including block-based) motion representation models and constraints are insufficient in computing optical flow because of their disregard for the motion of neighboring picture elements. To approximate a true 2D motion field, we need a structural model along with stochastic observations and a motion field model, which incorporates prior knowledge of the motion field as well as the geometric structure of the scene. In other words, we need a priori model that relies upon high-level features of the data, such as edges, object boundaries, or complete objects, and uses them to solve the corresponding motion problem. (2) Statistical computing techniques: deterministic, iterative-improvement methods generate a sequence of motion fields that monotonically decrease the objective function. Unfortunately, these techniques can be easily trapped in local minima. Statistical computing techniques can avoid these local minima by permitting changes that increase the objective function.

This chapter concentrates on statistical approaches for learning prior knowledge of the optical flow and the estimation of the optical flow. Readers may refer to (Barron et al. 1994) for an overview and comparison of other common methods. We also recommend a good tutorial of gradient-based methods for optical flow estimation by Fleet and Weiss (2005). The rest of this chapter is organized as followings: first, we present in Section 7.2, a basic Bayesian approach to compute the pixel-level optical flow. Second, we discuss model-based motion analysis in Section 7.3. Third, we discuss approaches to motion segmentation in Section 7.4. In the last part of this chapter, Section 7.5, the statistics of optical flow are discussed, which will provide important prior knowledge about informative motion features for high-level visual perception of video.

7.2 Bayesian Estimation of Optical Flow

The problem of motion computation is ill posed, since many different vector fields can explain the same data (image). This leads to considerable computational uncertainty. Furthermore, the high dimensionality of optical flow, that is, the necessity of simultaneously computing several thousand unknowns, makes the computation complex.

In this section, we introduce the Bayesian approach to optical flow estimation (Konrad and Dubois 1992; Geman and Geman 1987). Bayesian statistics provide a conceptually simple process for updating uncertainty in the light of evidence. Specifically, we represent our initial beliefs about the motion vector field by a prior distribution. Information in the images is expressed by the likelihood function. The priori distribution and the likelihood function are then combined to obtain the posterior distribution for the motion vector. The posterior distribution expresses our revised uncertainty in light of the images.

7.2.1 Problem Formulation

In the Bayesian approach, the true motion filed $\tilde{\mathbf{d}}$ is assumed to be a sample (realization) from random field $\mathbf{D}$. Let $\hat{\mathbf{d}}$ be an estimate of $\mathbf{d}$. The motion field $\mathbf{d}$ may not be defined at all points in the image plane Λ_i, e.g., due to occlusions and may not be unique, as in the case of a rotating uniform disk. Additionally, the motion field associated with real images may contain discontinuities at the boundaries of objects with different motion. The concept of motion discontinuity is used to model sudden changes in the motion vector length and/or orientation. Actually, motion discontinuities can be viewed as curves in the image plane, defined over continuous spatiotemporal coordinates $(\mathbf{x}, t)$, and are unobservable like the true motion fields. Let the true field of such discontinuities be a sample $\mathbf{l}$ from a random field $\mathbf{L}$, which is actually a line process, and be denoted by $\tilde{\mathbf{l}}$. The objective of Bayesian estimation now is to jointly estimate the pair $(\tilde{\mathbf{d}}, \tilde{\mathbf{l}})$ at time t based on the given images $\psi_1(\mathbf{x})$ and $\psi_2(\mathbf{x})$.

In estimating a motion field, we use the maximum a posteriori (MAP) criteria. Thus the "best" or "most likely" motion field estimate $\hat{\mathbf{d}}^*$ and line field estimate $\hat{\mathbf{l}}^*$ given the observed frames $\psi_1(\mathbf{x})$ and $\psi_2(\mathbf{x})$ must satisfy the relationship:

$$(\hat{\mathbf{d}}^*, \hat{\mathbf{l}}^*) = \arg\max_{\mathbf{d},\mathbf{l}} P(\mathbf{d},\mathbf{l} | \psi_1, \psi_2) \tag{7.3}$$

where P is the conditional discrete probability distribution of the motion and line fields given the observation. Applying the Bayes' rule for discrete random variables, the above posterior distribution can be factored as follows:

$$P(\mathbf{d},\mathbf{l}|\psi_1,\psi_2) = \frac{P(\psi_2|\mathbf{d},\mathbf{l},\psi_1)P(\mathbf{d},\mathbf{l}|\psi_1)}{P(\psi_2|\psi_1)} \tag{7.4}$$

where $P(\psi_2|\mathbf{d},\mathbf{l},\psi_1)$ is the likelihood function, and $P(\mathbf{d},\mathbf{l}|\psi_1)$ is the prior distribution. The likelihood function relates motion to the observed image via a model of the observation process, while the prior characterizes our knowledge of fields $\mathbf{d}$ and $\mathbf{l}$ in the absence of some evidence. Since $P(\psi_2|\psi_1)$ is not a function of $(\mathbf{d},\mathbf{l})$, it can be ignored when maximizing the posterior probability $P(\mathbf{d},\mathbf{l}|\psi_1,\psi_2$. In order to solve the MAP estimation, both the likelihood function and the prior distribution for the motion and motion discontinuity must be known explicitly.

7.2.1.1 Likelihood Function

To facilitate the formation of the likelihood function, it is fundamental to specify a structural model that relates motion vectors and image intensity values. It is usually assumed that the image intensity or its spatial gradient is constant along motion trajectories. Recall the illustration in Fig. 7.3, applying the intensity assumption to the pixel $\mathbf{x}$ along the motion trajectories $\mathbf{d}$ in the interval $[t_1,t_2]$ results in the following relationship:

$$\psi_1(\mathbf{x}) = \psi_2(\mathbf{x}-\mathbf{d}(\mathbf{x})) \tag{7.5}$$

However, in reality, this assumption is always violated due to image sensor noise, quantization noise, and distortion due to aliasing. We can model the displaced pixel difference of each pixel in $\mathbf{x}$ using independent Gaussian random variables. Thus, we can write

$$P(\psi_2|\mathbf{d},\mathbf{l},\psi_1) = (2\pi\sigma^2)^{\frac{-M_d}{2}} \exp\left(\frac{-U_I(\psi_2|\mathbf{d},\psi_1)}{2\sigma^2}\right) \tag{7.6}$$

where M_d is the number of motion vectors contained in $\mathbf{d}$. The energy U_I is defined as

$$U_I(\psi_2|\mathbf{d},\psi_1) = \sum_{i\in\Lambda_I} [\psi_2(\mathbf{x}_i-\mathbf{d}(\mathbf{x}_i)) - \psi_1(\mathbf{x}_i)]^2 \tag{7.7}$$

7.2.1.2 Prior Model for $(\mathbf{d},\mathbf{l})$

The motion and motion discontinuity fields are jointly modeled by a pair of coupled vectors and binary MRFs. The prior model $P(\mathbf{d},\mathbf{l}|\psi_1(\mathbf{x}))$ describes the properties of the motion and motion discontinuity fields that can be factored using Bayes' rule:

$$P(\mathbf{d},\mathbf{l}|\psi_1) = P(\mathbf{d}|\mathbf{l},\psi_1)P(\mathbf{l}|\psi_1) \tag{7.8}$$

Since a single image is expected to contribute little information to the motion vector model, the conditioning on ψ_1 in $P(\mathbf{d}|\mathbf{l},\psi_1)$ is omitted as an approximation. Under assumed Markov properties, the probability governing the motion field can be expressed by the Gibbs distribution

$$P(\mathbf{d}|\mathbf{l}) = \frac{1}{Z_d}\exp\left\{\frac{-U_d(\mathbf{d}|\mathbf{l})}{\beta_d}\right\} \tag{7.9}$$

where Z_d is the partition function, β_d is a constant controlling characteristic of the motion field, and the energy function $U_d(\mathbf{d}|\mathbf{l})$ is defined as

$$U_d(\mathbf{d}|\mathbf{l}) = \sum_{c_d=\{\mathbf{x}_i,\mathbf{x}_j\}\in\mathscr{C}_d} V_d(\mathbf{d},c_d)[1-l(\mathbf{x}_i,\mathbf{x}_j)] \tag{7.10}$$

where c_d is a clique of vectors, where as $\mathscr{C}$ is a set of such cliques derived from a neighborhood system $\mathscr{N}_d$ defined over lattice Λ_I. $l(\mathbf{x}_i,\mathbf{x}_j)$ denotes a site of line elements located between vector sites $\mathbf{x}_i$ and $\mathbf{x}_j$).

The energy function U_d depicts the interaction between the motion and motion discontinuity fields. The cost $V_d(\mathbf{d},c_d)$ associated with each vector clique c_d increases if a motion field sample locally departs from the assumed a priori model characterized by β_d and V_d. If, however, the line element separating the displacement vectors from clique c_d is "turned on"($l(\mathbf{x}_i,\mathbf{x}_j)=1$), there is no cost associated with the clique c_d. In this way, there is no penalty for introducing an abrupt change in length or orientation of a motion vector. The ability to zero the cost associated with vector cliques by inserting a line element must be penalized, however. Otherwise, a line field with all elements "on" would contribute energy to the zero motion vector. This penalty is provided by the line field model.

To specify a priori motion model, the potential function V_d, the neighborhood system $\mathscr{N}_d$, and the cliques c_d have to be specified (readers may refer to the Appendix of this chapter for more detailed information about the definitions of the neighborhood system for the Markov random fields MRFs of motion and motion discontinuity). By applying the smoothness of motion field assumption, we can define the potential function V_d as follows:

$$V_d(\mathbf{d},c_d) = ||\mathbf{d}(\mathbf{x}_i)-\mathbf{d}(\mathbf{x}_j)||^2, \tag{7.11}$$

where $||\cdot||$ is a norm in $\mathbb{R}^2$. We use a first-order neighborhood system $\mathscr{N}_d^1$ for the motion field, which means every motion vector has four vector neighbors and four line neighbors.

The binary MRF field for modeling motion discontinuities is described by the Gibbs probability distribution.

$$P(\mathbf{l}|\psi_1) = \frac{1}{Z_l}\exp\left\{-\frac{U_l(\mathbf{l}|\psi_1)}{\beta_l}\right\}, \tag{7.12}$$

with Z_l and β_l as the usual constants. U_l is the line energy function and is defined as

$$U_l = \sum_{c_l \in \mathscr{C}_l} V_l(\mathbf{l}, \psi_1, c_l) \tag{7.13}$$

where c_l is a line clique, and $\mathscr{C}_l$ is the set of all line cliques derived from a neighborhood defined over the binary MRF.

The a priori probability of the line process is conditioned on the observed images. In general, a 3D scene giving rise to a motion discontinuity will also contribute to an intensity edge. The possibility that a motion discontinuity does not correspond to an edge of intensity is very low. Thus, we use the following potential function for one-element clique

$$V_{l_1}(l, \psi_1, c_l) = \begin{cases} \frac{\alpha}{(\nabla_v \psi_1)^2} l_h(< \mathbf{x}_i, \mathbf{x}_j >) & \text{for horizontal } c_l = \{\mathbf{x}_i, \mathbf{x}_j\} \\ \frac{\alpha}{(\nabla_h \psi_1)^2} l_v(< \mathbf{x}_i, \mathbf{x}_j >) & \text{for vertical } c_l = \{\mathbf{x}_i, \mathbf{x}_j\} \end{cases} \tag{7.14}$$

where l_h, l_v are horizontal and vertical line elements, ∇_h, ∇_v are horizontal and vertical components of the spatial gradient at position $(\mathbf{x}_i, \mathbf{x}_j)$, and α is a constant. The above potential introduces a penalty only if a line element is "on," and the appropriate gradient is relatively small. The total potential function for the line field can be expressed as

$$V_l(l, \psi_1, c_l) = V_{l_4}(l, c_l) + V_{l_2}(l, c_l) + V_{l_2}(l, c_l) \tag{7.15}$$

where V_{l_4} and V_{l_2} can be set empirically.

7.2.1.3 A Posteriori Probability

Combining the likelihood of Eq. (7.6), the motion a priori probability of Eq. (7.9), and the line a priori probability of Eq. (7.13) via Eq. (7.4), gives the following Gibbs form:

$$P(\mathbf{d}, \mathbf{l} | \psi_1, \psi_2) = \frac{1}{Z} \exp\{-U(\mathbf{d}, \mathbf{l}, \psi_1, \psi_2)\} \tag{7.16}$$

where Z is the new normalizing constant, and the new energy function is defined as follows:

$$U(\mathbf{d}, \mathbf{l}, \psi_1, \psi_2) = \lambda_I U_I(\psi_2 | \mathbf{d}, \psi_1) + \lambda_d U_d(\mathbf{d} | \mathbf{l}) + \lambda_l U_l(\mathbf{l} | \psi_1). \tag{7.17}$$

The conditional energies in the above relationship are defined in Eq. (7.7), (7.10), and (7.13), respectively, and $\lambda_I = \frac{1}{2\sigma^2}$, $\lambda_d = \frac{1}{\beta_d}$, $\lambda_l = \frac{1}{\beta_l}$.

Thus, it follows that the MAP estimation via Eq. (7.3) can be achieved by minimizing the energy $U(d, l, \psi_1, \psi_2)$, that is,

$$(\hat{\mathbf{d}}^*, \hat{\mathbf{l}}^*) = \arg\min_{\mathbf{d}, \mathbf{l}} \{\lambda_I U_I(\psi_2 | \mathbf{d}, \psi_1) + \lambda_d U_d(\mathbf{d} | \mathbf{l}) + \lambda_l U_l(\mathbf{l} | \psi_1)\} \tag{7.18}$$

Where the ratios λ_d/λ_I and λ_l/λ_I play an important role in weighting the confidence in the data and in the a priori model. A modification of any λ has an effect on the estimate.

7.2.2 MAP Estimation

The MAP estimation expressed in Eq. (7.18) is a very complex problem because of the number of unknowns involved and because of the multimodality of the objective function, which depends on **d** through the observations ψ_1, ψ_2. We introduce a simulated annealing algorithm proposed in Konrad and Dubois (1992) and Geman and Geman (1987) to solve this optimization problem.

In simulated annealing, the configuration of the motion and motion discontinuity fields are simulated by generating a sample configuration from the Gibbs distribution (9.29) with the energy function (7.56). A temperature parameter T is introduced into the a posteriori probability (9.29) as follows:

$$P(\mathbf{d},\mathbf{l}|\psi_1,\psi_2) = \frac{1}{Z}\exp\{-U(\mathbf{d},\mathbf{l},\psi_1,\psi_2)/T\} \tag{7.19}$$

With the annealing schedule specified by the initial and final temperatures T_0 and T_f, and the temperature change rule $T_k = \varphi(T_0,k)$ at iteration k, it has been proved that if a sufficiently high initial temperature T_0 is used, if the temperature T_k attains 0 with at most a logarithmic rate, and if every site is visited infinitely often, then with time $t \to \infty$, the estimation will converge to the global optimum for any starting configuration.

The sample configurations are produced using the Metropolis algorithm or the Gibbs sampler (Liu 2001), which is incorporated into the inhomogeneous simulated annealing algorithm. The proposal transition T(x,y) in the Metropolis sampler is often an arbitrary choice out of convenience. In many applications, the proposal is chosen so as to represent a locally uniform move. In fact, the use of symmetric and locally uniform proposals is so prevalent that these are often referred to as "unbiased proposals" in the literature. If not subjected to the Metropolis–Hastings rejection rule, this type of move leads to a form of simple random walk in the configuration space. Although such a proposal is simple both conceptually and operationally, the performance of the resulting Metropolis algorithm is often inefficient because the proposal is too "noisy." In contrast, the conditional sampling techniques discussed here enable a Markov chain Monte Carlo (MCMC) sampler to follow the local dynamics of the a posteriori distribution. A distinctive feature of these MCMC algorithms is that at each iteration, they use conditional distributions (i.e., those distributions resulting from constraining the posterior distribution on certain subspaces) to construct Markov chain moves. As a consequence, no rejection is incurred at any of its sampling steps.

We choose Gibbs sampler to produce the sample configurations. More specifically, in each iteration, the Gibbs sampler scans the motion and motion discontinuity fields and generates new states according to the Gibbs marginal probability distributions of the motion and motion discontinuity, respectively. Each iteration, a complete scan of the unknown fields (motion and motion discontinuity fields) is performed. In the following, we present the Gibbs marginal probability distributions of the motion and motion discontinuity. The Gibbs sampler for a discrete motion field is a site-replacement procedure that generates a new vector at every position $\mathbf{x}_i$ according to the following marginal conditional discrete probability distribution derived from probability (7.19):

$$P(\mathbf{d}(\mathbf{x}_i)|\mathbf{d}(\mathbf{x}_j), j \neq i, \mathbf{l}, \psi_1, \psi_2) = \frac{\exp\{-U_d^i(\mathbf{d}, \mathbf{l}, \psi_1, \psi_2)/T\}}{\sum_{\mathbf{z}} \exp\{-U_d^i(\mathbf{d}^z, \mathbf{l}, \psi_1, \psi_2)/T\}} \tag{7.20}$$

with the local motion energy function U_d^i is defined as

$$U_d^i(\mathbf{d}^z, \mathbf{l}, \psi_1, \psi_2) = \lambda_I [r(\mathbf{z}, \mathbf{x}_i)]^2 + \lambda_d \sum_{j: \mathbf{x}_j \in \eta_d(\mathbf{x}_i)} ||\mathbf{z} - \mathbf{d}(\mathbf{x}_j)||^2 [1 - l(\mathbf{x}_i, \mathbf{x}_j)] \tag{7.21}$$

where $r(\mathbf{z}, \mathbf{x}_i) = \psi_2(\mathbf{x}_i - \mathbf{z}) - \psi_1(\mathbf{x}_i)$, and $\eta_d(\mathbf{x}_j)$ is a spatial neighborhood of motion vectors at $\mathbf{x}_i$, and $\mathbf{d}^z$ denotes a motion field identical to field $\mathbf{d}$, except for spatial location $\mathbf{x}_i$, where the vector is $\mathbf{z}$.

Similarly, the Gibbs sampler for motion discontinuities can be expressed at location $\mathbf{y}$ as follows:

$$P(\mathbf{l}(\mathbf{y}_i)|\mathbf{y}_j, j \neq i, \mathbf{d}, \psi_1) = \frac{\exp\{-U_l^i(\mathbf{l}, \mathbf{d}, \psi_1)/T\}}{\sum_z \exp\{-U_l^i(\mathbf{l}^z, \mathbf{d}, \psi_1)/T\}} \tag{7.22}$$

where the local line energy function U_l^i is defined as

$$U_l^i(\mathbf{l}, \mathbf{d}, \psi_1) = \lambda_d \sum_{c_d = (\mathbf{x}_m, \mathbf{x}_n): <\mathbf{x}_m, \mathbf{x}_n> = \mathbf{y}_i} ||\mathbf{d}(\mathbf{x}_m) - \mathbf{d}(\mathbf{x}_n)||^2 [1 - z] + \lambda_l \sum_{c_l: \mathbf{y}_i \in c_l} V_l(\mathbf{l}^z, \psi_1, c_l) \tag{7.23}$$

and $\mathbf{l}^z$ denotes a line field that is identical to $\mathbf{l}$ except for spatial location $\mathbf{y}_i =< \mathbf{x}_m, \mathbf{x}_n >$, where the line element is z.

At each spatial location of random field $\mathbf{D}$ (motion field), a complete bivariate discrete probability distribution is computed (probability of all possible motion vector states). Then the 2D distribution is accumulated along one direction (e.g., horizontal) to obtain a 1D marginal cumulative distribution, and a random state is generated from this univariate distribution. The vertical state is generated by sampling the univariate cumulative distribution obtained from the 2D distribution for the known horizontal state. It should be noted that the calculation of the complete probability distribution at each location results in a high computational load per iteration of the discrete state space Gibbs sampler.

Since the random field $\mathbf{L}$ is binary, only the probability for "on" and "off" states has to be computed. A new line state is generated based on those two probability.

7.2.3 Occlusion

Optical flow can be reliably estimated between areas visible in two images, but not in areas that are occluded. Occlusion in image sequences poses a problem in dense motion field estimation since motion is not defined in the occluded regions. In order to improve the accuracy of the motion estimation process, the occlusion field must be identified and used in the motion estimation process.

One approach is to use additional views of the same scene. If such views are unavailable, an often-used alternative is to extrapolate optical flow in occlusion areas. Since the location of such areas is usually unknown prior to optical flow estimation, this is usually performed in three steps. First, occlusion-ignorant optical flow is estimated, then occlusion areas are identified using the estimated (unreliable) optical flow, and, finally, the optical flow is corrected using the computed occlusion areas. This approach, however, does not permit interaction between optical flow and occlusion estimations.

Such interaction can be permitted by modeling occlusion jointly with motion and motion discontinuity. Similar to the motion and motion discontinuity field we defined in Section 7.2.1, an occlusion field can be modeled via a binary MRF defined on the pixel lattice. Some MRF occlusion models are proposed in Tekalp (1995) and Zhang and Hanauer (1995). These models are generally based on the spatial smoothness constraint of the occluded pixels and the motion-compensated error in the occluded regions. Interaction of the occluded pixels with the line field is also considered for further improving the motion estimation process. More specifically, for the occlusion field, two types of models are generally applied. First, the presence of occlusions can be penalized. Penalizing occlusion points promotes the presence of real correspondence in an image pair. The second model for occlusions encourages connectivity of occlusion points.

The design of a joint probability model for several dense fields is by no means an easy task. In general, the modeling process is decomposed into two levels. First, via the Bayes' rule, each field can be modeled one at a time. Secondly, we can obtain the global model of each of these fields by combining many equal, simple local models. These assume independence of all entries in a field, or dependence only in a small neighborhood reflecting the Markov property.

MAP search algorithms for dense motion fields yield a large computational burden. Although stochastic methods are designed to avoid local minima, the restrictions for a feasible implementation still lead to problems with local minima. One general approach that provides faster convergence, and, at the same time, avoids local minima, is the hierarchical approach. The observed images are downsampled to lower resolution versions. The original images are at level 0; the resolution decreases with level number. At the lower resolution level the estimation starts. After estimation, the fields l are up-sampled to the resolution of level $l-1$. These fields are then used as an initial estimate for the estimation at this level. This continues until estimation is performed at full resolution level 0.

7.3 Model-Based Motion Analysis

Since optical flow computation is an underconstrained problem, all motion estimation algorithms involve additional assumptions about the structure of the motion computed. This assumption is expressed implicitly or explicitly. Previous works involving implicit assumptions treat motion structure presuppositions as a regularization term in an objective function, or describe them primarily in the context of computational issues. Methods involving explicitly model-based motion estimation include direct methods as well as methods for estimation under restricted conditions. The former use a global egomotion constraint while the latter rely on parametric motion models within local regions.

With respect to motion models, these algorithms can be divided into three categories: fully parametric, quasi-parametric, and nonparametric. Fully parametric models describe the motion of individual pixels within a region in terms of a parametric form. These include affine and quadratic flow fields. Quasi-parametric models involve representing the motion of a pixel as a combination of a parametric component that is valid for the entire region and a local component that varies from pixel to pixel. For instance, the rigid motion model belongs to this class: the egomotion parameters constrain the local flow vector to lie along a specific line, while the local depth value determines the exact value of the flow vector at each pixel. Nonparametric models are those that are commonly used in optical flow computation, i.e., those involving the use of some type of a smoothness or uniformity constraint.

The reasons for choosing one model or another are generally quite intuitive, though the exact choice of model is not always easy to make in a rigorous way. The following analysis of the properties of the three classes of motion models explains the difficulty of the problem of motion model selection: (1) In general, parametric models constrain the local motion more strongly than less parametric ones. A small number of parameters (e.g., six in the case of affine flow) are sufficient to completely specify the motion vector at every point within their region of applicability. However, they tend to be applicable only within local regions and, in many cases, are approximations to the actual optical flow field within those regions. From the point of view of motion estimation, such models allow the precise estimation of motion at locations containing no image structure, provided the region contains at least a few locations with significant image structure, (2) quasi-parametric models constrain the optical flow less, but nevertheless constrain it to some degree. For instance, for rigidly moving objects under perspective projection, the rigid motion parameters constrain the motion vector at each point to lie along a line in the velocity space. 1D image structure is generally sufficient to precisely estimate the motion of that point. These models tend to be applicable over a wide region in the image, perhaps even the entire image. If the local structure of the scene can be further parameterized, the model becomes fully parametric within that region, (3) Nonparametric models require local image structure that is 2D. However, with the use of a smoothness constraint, it is usually possible to "fill-in" where there is inadequate local information. The estimation process is typically more computationally expensive than in the other two cases. These models are more generally applicable than the other two classes.

In this section, we begin with a brief introduction to parametric motion models. We then describe the application of a statistical learning-based model selection approach to the challenging problem of estimating optimal motion models from small data sets of image measurements. Finally, we present an extended version of the parametric motion model, which can represent much more varied and complex motions.

7.3.1 Motion Models

We consider a 2D motion induced by an arbitrary 3D rigid motion, which could result from the fact that both the camera and the object are undergoing rigid motion. Therefore, without loss of generality, we assume that the camera is stationary and the object is undergoing rigid motion. A hierarchy of parametric motion models has been developed starting with pure translation, image plane rotation, 2D affine, and 2D homography. The following motion models represent the instantaneous projected image motion field generated by a moving plane. That is, as we stated in Section 7.2, these motion models are in essence a statement about the function $\mathbf{d}(\mathbf{x};\mathbf{a})$, where $\mathbf{a}$ is a vector representing the model parameters. Actually, these motion models approximate the projective mapping in different degrees.

Affine motion: When the distance between the surfaces depicted in an image and the camera is large, it is usually possible to approximate the motion of the surface as an affine transformation.

$$\begin{bmatrix} d_x(x,y) \\ d_y(x,y) \end{bmatrix} = \begin{bmatrix} a_0 + a_1 x + a_2 y \\ a_3 + a_4 x + a_5 y \end{bmatrix} \tag{7.24}$$

The affine function has six parameters, $\mathbf{a} = \{a_0, ..., a_5\}$ Additionally, the projected 2D motion of most camera motions can be described by an affine function. Affine motion can be visualized as, for example, the deformation of one triangle into another by moving the corners of the triangle. The affine parameters are completely determined by the motion vectors of the three corners.

Bilinear motion has the form of

$$\begin{bmatrix} d_x(x,y) \\ d_y(x,y) \end{bmatrix} = \begin{bmatrix} a_0 + a_1 x + a_2 y + a_3 xy \\ a_4 + a_5 x + a_6 y + a_7 xy \end{bmatrix} \tag{7.25}$$

There are eight parameters, $\mathbf{a} = \{a_0, ..., a_7\}$. Bilinear motion can be visualized, for example, as the warping of a square into a quadrangle. The parameters are determined by the motion vectors of the four corners of the original square.

Plane surface motion can be described as a second-order function of image coordinates involving eight independent parameters.

$$\begin{bmatrix} d_x(x,y) \\ d_y(x,y) \end{bmatrix} = \begin{bmatrix} a_0 + a_1x + a_2y + a_6xy + a_7x^2 \\ a_3 + a_4x + a_5y + a_6xy + a_7y^2 \end{bmatrix} \tag{7.26}$$

where the eight coefficients $\mathbf{a} = \{a_0, ..., a_7\}$ are functions of the translation, rotation, and the plane parameters. This function corresponds to the instantaneous projected motion field generated by a moving plane. The affine model (7.24) and bilinear model (7.25) can be obtained by setting some of the eight parameters to zero.

7.3.2 Statistical Model Selection

So far, we have seen that the quality of the estimated motion field depends upon making the proper assumptions about the structure of the motion field, which normally are determined by motion models. We have also seen that we can use parametric models to represent an assumption. Now, the problem becomes how to choose a proper parametric model.

We introduce a statistical learning-based model selection method for this problem (Wechsler et al. 2004). The task of motion model selection is analogous to choosing the best predictive models from a given set of linear parametric models, using a small set of noisy training data.

The training data are obtained via normal flow computation. For an image frame I, edges are found by using an implementation of the Canny edge detector. For each edge element, say at $\mathbf{x}$, we resample the image locally to obtain a small window with its rows parallel to the image gradient direction $\mathbf{n_x} = \nabla I / ||\nabla I||$. For the next image frame, we create a larger window, typically twice as large as the maximum expected value of the magnitude of the normal displacement field. We then slide the first (smaller) window along the second (larger) window and compute the difference between the image intensities. The normal flow can then be obtained by usual block-matching techniques (Barron et al. 1994).

For each edge point at $\mathbf{x}$, we have one normal flow value $\mathbf{d_x}$, that we use as an estimate of the normal displacement at that point. We also have a vector $\hat{\mathbf{d}}_x$ computed from the image coordinate of $\mathbf{x}$, and the motion model. The VC generalization bounds are then used for the selection of motion models.

$$R_{est} = \left(1 - \sqrt{(p - p\ln p + \frac{\ln n}{2n})}\right)_+^{-1} \frac{1}{n} \sum_{i=1}^{n} (\mathbf{d}_i - \hat{\mathbf{d}}_i) \tag{7.27}$$

where $p = \frac{h}{n}$, and $n \geq 8$. h denotes the VC dimension of a model and $(\cdot)_+ = 0$, for $x < 0$, $\mathbf{d}_i$ is the training data, and $\hat{\mathbf{d}}_i$ is computed from the selected motion model (7.26). The VC dimension h of a linear model is given by the number of degrees of freedom (DOF) of the model plus one.

With the problem setting above, we can choose from the following five models that can be obtained by setting various elements of $\mathbf{a}$ in (7.26) to zero.

- Pure translation, $a_1 = a_2 = a_4 = a_5 = a_6 = a_7 = 0$, $DOF = 2$, $h = 3$.

- Translation, shear, and rotation, $a_1 = a_5 = a_6 = a_7 = 0$, $DOF = 4$, $h = 5$.
- Translation and scaling, $a_2 = a_4 = a_6 = a_7 = 0$, $DOF = 4$, $h = 5$.
- Affine transformation, $a_6 = a_7 = 0$, $DOF = 6$, $h = 7$.
- Full affine, quadratic flow, $DOF = 8$, $h = 9$.

7.3.3 Learning Parameterized Models

As we discussed above, linear parameterized models of optical flow play a significant role in motion analysis. The linear model coefficients are straightforward to estimate and they provide reliable estimates of the motion flow of smooth surfaces. However, the use of such models is limited to motions for which the models represent good approximations to the actual optical flow. For example, affine models account for the motion of a planar surface under orthographic projection and provide a reasonable approximation to the motions of smooth surfaces in small image region. But they have limited applicability in complex natural scenes. For example, many image regions contain multiple image motions because of moving occlusion boundaries, transparency, reflections, or independently moving objects. Many natural scenes also contain complex local patterns of optical flow.

Much work has been devoted to extending parameterized models to cope with multiple motions. One good example is the approach proposed by Fleet et al. (2000). It explores the use of parameterized motion models that represent much more varied and complex motion. One key insight is that many complex motions can be modeled and estimated in the same way as the conventional affine model. In the rest of this section, we first introduce how to construct linear parameterized models for two broad classes of motions: (1) generic motion features such as motion discontinuities and moving bars; (2) nonrigid, object-specific motions such as the the motion of human mouths. Then we present techniques for the estimation of the coefficients of these linear models, and the recognition and classification of image motions from the estimated coefficients.

7.3.3.1 Generative Models for Generic Motion Features

Image features such as lines, edges, and junctions have been treated as primitive structures in images upon which later stages of processing, such as segmentation and object recognition, are based. Similarly, there are analogous features in image sequences and binocular image pairs. Compared to static image features, these motion and stereo features typically convey direct information about scene structure. Below, we consider the modeling of motion edges (discontinuities) and bars like those in Fig. 7.4.

The motion edge can be described by a mean motion vector $\mathbf{d}$, an edge orientation θ, and a velocity change across the motion boundary $\Delta\mathbf{d}$. Let $\mathbf{d}(\mathbf{x};\mathbf{a})$ be the corresponding flow field over spatial positions $\mathbf{x} = (x, y)$, where $\mathbf{a} = \mathbf{d}, \Delta\mathbf{d}, \theta$. We

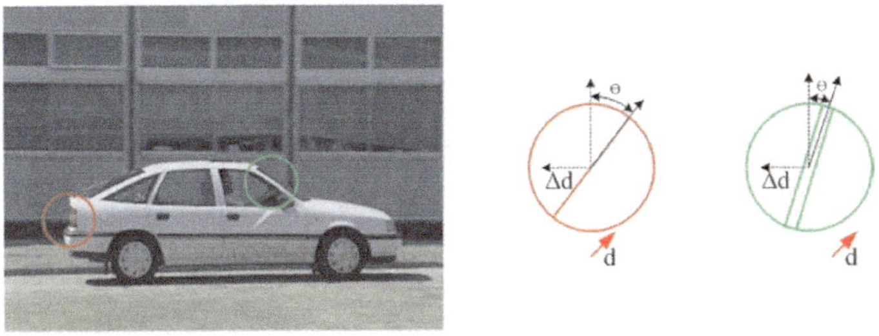

Fig. 7.4 Example of motion features and models for a motion discontinuity and a moving bar. The parameters of the idealized models are the mean translation velocity **d**, the feature orientation θ, and the velocity change across the motion feature Δd. Refer to (Fleet et al. 2000)

then approximate $\mathbf{d}(\mathbf{x};\mathbf{a})$ by projecting it onto a subspace spanned by a collection of n basis flow fields $\mathbf{b}_j(\mathbf{x})$.

$$\mathbf{d}(\mathbf{x};\mathbf{a}) = \sum_{j=1}^{n} a_j \mathbf{b}_j(\mathbf{x}) \tag{7.28}$$

The bases could be learned from examples using PCA. However, here we construct steerable sets of basis flow fields. These are similar to those learned using PCA up to rotations of invariant subspaces. The basis flow fields are steerable in orientation and velocity, and provide reasonably accurate approximations to the motion edges and motion bars.

The construction of the bases $\{\mathbf{b}_j(\mathbf{x})\}_{j=1}^{n}$ is a two-step procedure. First, we construct a basis for the spatial structure of the features. Second, these bases are then combined with a velocity basis.

The spatial structure of a motion boundary is modeled by $T(\mathbf{x})$ a generic template that is a mean-zero, unit amplitude step edge within a circular, 32 pixel diameter, window. A circular window is used to avoid orientation anisotropies in the basis set. The motion edge template, $T(\mathbf{x})$, and rotated versions of it, $T_\theta(\mathbf{x})$, are approximated by a linear combination of the basis images,

$$T_\theta(\mathbf{x}) \approx \Re\left[\sum_{k\in K} \sigma_k \alpha_k(\theta) b_k(\mathbf{x})\right] \tag{7.29}$$

where $\theta \in [0, 2\pi]$ is the rotation angle, K is the set of angular wave numbers used in the approximation, $\alpha_k(\theta)$ are the steering functions, σ_k are real-valued weights on the different harmonics, and $\Re(z)$ denotes the real part of z. $\{b_k(\mathbf{x})\}$ yields by the method in Perona (1995) a set of complex-valued basis functions. The weights, σ_k, encode the relative magnitudes of the harmonics that best approximate the spatial structure of the edge. The steering functions are angular harmonics,

$$\alpha_k(\theta) = \exp\{-ik\theta\} \tag{7.30}$$

where θ is the rotation angle. Because the template is real valued, we can rewrite Eq. (7.29) in terms of real-valued weights,

$$T_\theta(\mathbf{x}) \approx \sum_{k \in K} \sigma_k(\cos(k\theta))\Re[b_k(\mathbf{x})] + \sin(k\theta)\Im[b_k(\mathbf{x})] \tag{7.31}$$

where $\Re(b_k(\mathbf{x}))$ and $\Re(b_k(\mathbf{x}))$ are the real and imaginary parts of $b_k(\mathbf{x})$

The quality of the approximation provided by the basis (7.29) is easily characterized by the fraction of the energy in $\mathbf{T}(x)$ that is captured with the selected wave numbers. If we let $K(n)$ be the set of wave numbers that corresponds to the n largest values of σ_k^2, then the quality of the approximation, as a function of n, is given by

$$Q(n) = \frac{\sum_{k \in K(n)} \sigma_k^2}{\sum_{\mathbf{x} \in R} S(\mathbf{x})^2} \tag{7.32}$$

The basis for velocity is the two vectors $(1,0)^T$ and $(0,1)^T$. The basis flow fields for the motion features are then formed by combining this basis with the basis for the spatial structure of the features. The horizontal and vertical components of the motion features are therefore given by

$$\mathbf{b}_k^h = \begin{pmatrix} b_k(\mathbf{x}) \\ 0 \end{pmatrix}$$

$$\mathbf{b}_k^v = \begin{pmatrix} 0 \\ b_k(\mathbf{x}) \end{pmatrix}$$

For each angular wave number, k, there are four real-valued flow fields. These are the real and imaginary parts of $b_k(\mathbf{x})$, each multiplied by the horizontal and the vertical components of the velocity basis.

7.3.3.2 PCA-Based Motion Model

A more general way to construct a model for a particular class of motion is to learn the basis flow fields from a training set that contains representative samples of the class. Below, we introduce a PCA-based approach to learn the linear parameterized model for object-specific complex motion.

Let the training ensemble be a set of p optical flow fields, $\{\mathbf{d}_j(\mathbf{x})\}_{j=1}^p$. For images with s pixels, each flow field contains $2s$ quantities. We form a vector of $2s$ components for each flow field by collecting the horizontal components of the flow in the standard lexicographic order, followed by vertical components. These vectors become the columns of a $2s \times p$ matrix $\mathbf{C}$. Let $\mathbf{c}_l$ be the lth column of C, corresponding to the flow field $\mathbf{d}_l(\mathbf{x})$ from the training set. In practice, we take $\mathbf{c}_l$ to be $\mathbf{d}_l(\mathbf{x}-\bar{\mathbf{d}}(\mathbf{x}))$ where $\bar{\mathbf{d}}(\mathbf{x})$ is the mean (flow field) of the training set.

PCA can then be used to compute a low-dimensional model for the structure of the flow fields. The singular value decomposition (SVD) of C can be written as $C = U\Sigma V^T$, where $U = [\mathbf{u}_1, \mathbf{u}_2, ..., \mathbf{u}_p]$ is a $2s \times p$ matrix. The columns, $\mathbf{u}_j$, comprise an orthonormal basis for the range of C, Σ is a $p \times p$ diagonal matrix containing the singular values $\lambda_1, ..., \lambda_p$ sorted in decreasing order along the diagonal, and V^T is a $p \times p$ orthonormal matrix.

We can approximate each training flow field as a linear combination of the n basis flow fields.

$$\mathbf{d}_l(x) \approx \sum_{j=1}^{n} a_j \mathbf{b}_j(\mathbf{x}), \mathbf{b}_j = \mathbf{u}_j \tag{7.33}$$

where a_j are the linear coefficients. Because the basis vectors, $\mathbf{u}_j$, are orthonormal, the optimal approximation to $\mathbf{c}_l$ in the least-squares sense is obtained using the coefficients that equal the projection of $\mathbf{c}_l$ onto the basis vector. Each column of M corresponds to a flow field, and these columns form the basis flow field; i.e., $a_j = \mathbf{c}_l^T \mathbf{u}_j$

The quality of the approximation provided by the first n columns of U is easily characterized as the fraction of the training set that is accounted for by the n coefficients:

$$Q(n) = \frac{\sum_{j=1}^{n} \lambda_j^2}{\sum_{j=1}^{p} \lambda_j^2} \tag{7.34}$$

7.3.3.3 Estimating the Coefficients

Within an image region R, we wish to find the linear coefficients $\mathbf{a}$ of a parameterized motion model that satisfy the brightness constancy assumption,

$$\psi_1(\mathbf{x}) = \psi_2(\mathbf{x} - \mathbf{d}(\mathbf{x};\mathbf{a})), \forall \mathbf{x} \in R \tag{7.35}$$

where $\mathbf{d}(\mathbf{x};\mathbf{a}) = \sum_{j=1}^{n} a_j \mathbf{b}_j(\mathbf{x})$. Equation (7.35) states that the image ψ_2 is a warped version of the image ψ_1.

The estimation of the model coefficients can be formulated as minimizing the objective function

$$E(\mathbf{a}) = \sum_{\mathbf{x} \in R} \rho(\psi_1(\mathbf{x}) - \psi_2(\mathbf{x} - \mathbf{d}(\mathbf{x};\mathbf{a})), \sigma) \tag{7.36}$$

where σ is a scaling parameter, and $\rho(r, \sigma)$ is a robust error function applied to the residual error $\triangle\psi(\mathbf{x};\mathbf{a}) = \psi_1(\mathbf{x}) - \psi_2(\mathbf{x} - \mathbf{d}(\mathbf{x};\mathbf{a}))$. Because of the continuous nature of the motion models used here and the expected violations of the brightness constancy, it is important that the estimator be robust with respect to these outliers. The robust error function can take the form

$$\rho(r,\sigma) = \frac{r^2}{\sigma^2 + r^2} \tag{7.37}$$

The parameter σ controls the shape of $\rho(\cdot,\sigma)$ to minimize the influence of large residual errors on the solution.

There are a number of ways to minimize the objective function (7.36). Here we present a coarse-to-fine, iterative coordinate descent method. We first rewrite the model coefficient vector in terms of an initial guess $\mathbf{a}$, and an update $\triangle\mathbf{a}$. This allows us to rewrite Eq. (7.36) as:

$$E(\mathbf{a}) = \sum_{\mathbf{x}\in R} \rho(\psi_1(\mathbf{x}) - \psi_2(\mathbf{x} - \mathbf{d}(\mathbf{x};\mathbf{a} + \triangle\mathbf{a})), \sigma) \tag{7.38}$$

The problem now becomes: given an estimate, $\mathbf{a}$, of the motion coefficients, the goal is to estimate the update, $\triangle\mathbf{a}$, that minimizes Eq. (7.38); $\mathbf{a}$ then becomes $\mathbf{a} + \triangle\mathbf{a}$.

To minimize Eq. (7.38), we first approximate it by linearizing the residual, $\triangle\psi(\mathbf{x};\mathbf{a} + \triangle\mathbf{a})$, with respect to the update vector $\triangle\mathbf{a}$ to give

$$E_1(\triangle\mathbf{a};\mathbf{a}) = \sum_{\mathbf{x}\in R} \rho(\mathbf{d}(\mathbf{x};\triangle\mathbf{a})^T \nabla\psi_2(\mathbf{x} - \mathbf{d}(\mathbf{x};\mathbf{a})) + \triangle\psi(\mathbf{x};\mathbf{a}), \sigma) \tag{7.39}$$

where $\nabla\psi_2(\mathbf{x} - \mathbf{d}(\mathbf{x};\mathbf{a}))$ denotes the spatial image gradient, warped by the current motion estimate $\mathbf{d}(\mathbf{x};\mathbf{a})$ using bilinear interpolation.

The coarse-to-fine control strategy with a continuation method is used to minimize Eq. (7.39). First, we construct a Gaussian pyramid for the images ψ_1 and ψ_2. The motion coefficients, $\mathbf{a}_l$, determined at a coarse scale, l, are used in the minimization at the next finer scale, $l+1$. In particular, the motion coefficients, $\mathbf{a}_l + \triangle\mathbf{a}_l$, from the coarse level are first multiplied by a factor of two to produce the initial guess $\mathbf{a}_{l+1}$ at level $l+1$. These coefficients are then used in Eq. (7.39) to warp the image ψ_2 toward the image ψ_1, from which $E_1(\triangle\mathbf{a};\mathbf{a})$ is minimized to compute the next update $\triangle\mathbf{a}_{l+1}$.

7.3.3.4 Detecting and Recognizing Motion Types

The problem of detecting and recognizing the motion bars and motion edges using the estimated linear coefficients can be formulated as a nonlinear least-squares estimation: Given the estimated flow field $F(\mathbf{x};\mathbf{a})$, we wish to estimate the parameters that produce the idealized flow filed $T(\mathbf{x};\mathbf{d},\triangle\mathbf{d},\theta)$, namely, the two components of the mean velocity $\mathbf{d} = (d_x, d_y)$, the two components of the velocity changes $\triangle\mathbf{d} = (\triangle d_x, \triangle d_y)$, and the feature orientation θ. In other words, with the estimated parameters, $T(\mathbf{x};\mathbf{d},\triangle\mathbf{d},\theta)$ should be closest to the given flow field, $\mathbf{d}(\mathbf{x};\mathbf{a})$.

To solve this problem, we first project the idealized flow $T(\mathbf{x};\mathbf{d},\triangle\mathbf{d},\theta)$ onto the basis flow fields:

$$T^p(\mathbf{x};\mathbf{d},\triangle\mathbf{d},\theta) = \mathbf{d} + \Re\left[\sum_{k\in K} \sigma_k e^{-ik\theta}(\triangle d_x \mathbf{b}_k^h(\mathbf{x}) + \triangle d_y \mathbf{b}_k^v(\mathbf{x}))\right] \tag{7.40}$$

For a region R and the estimated flow field $F(\mathbf{x},\mathbf{a})$, we search for the five parameters $(\mathbf{d},\triangle\mathbf{d},\theta)$ that minimize $E(\mathbf{d},\triangle\mathbf{d},\theta) = \sum_{\mathbf{x}\in R} ||T^p(\mathbf{x};\mathbf{d},\triangle\mathbf{d},\theta) - F(\mathbf{x},\mathbf{a})||^2$.

Then, let $F(\mathbf{x},\mathbf{a})$ be explicitly expressed using same the basis field as in Eq. (7.40):

$$F(\mathbf{x},\mathbf{a}) = \mathbf{d}_{dc} + \Re\left[\sum_{k\in K} (\alpha_k \mathbf{b}_k^h(\mathbf{x}) + \beta_k \mathbf{b}_k^v(\mathbf{x}))\right] \tag{7.41}$$

where $\mathbf{d}_{dc}$ is a two-vector that corresponds to the coefficients associated with the DC basis flow fields, and α_k and β_k are the estimated coefficients that correspond to the horizontal and vertical components of the basis flow fields with wave numbers k.

Finally, we formulate the estimation into a least-squares minimization problem. Since the basis flow $\{\mathbf{b}_k^h(\mathbf{x}),\mathbf{b}_k^v(\mathbf{x})\}_{k\in K}$ is orthogonal, the mean velocity is given directly by $\mathbf{d} = \mathbf{d}_{dc}$. In addition, minimizing $E(\mathbf{d},\triangle\mathbf{d},\theta)$ is equivalent to minimizing $\sum_{k\in K} ||(\alpha_k,\beta_k) - \sigma_k e^{-ik\theta}(\triangle d_x,\triangle d_y)||^2$ given a sufficiently good initial guess.

To obtain an initial guess for $\triangle\mathbf{d}$ and θ, we must first decouple the constraints on them. The minimization enforces two constraints on the parameters $\triangle\mathbf{d}$ and θ. First, $\triangle\mathbf{d}$ must be consistent over all angular harmonics. Second, θ must be consistent over all angular harmonics and both components of flow.

With the first constraint, we can initially collect the complex-valued coefficients of the model flow in (7.40) into an matrix

$$M = \triangle\mathbf{d}(\sigma_{k_1} e^{-ik_1\theta}, \ldots, \sigma_{k_1} e^{-ik_n\theta}) \tag{7.42}$$

Then we construct $MM^{*T} = (\sigma_{k_1}^2 + \ldots + \sigma_{k_n}^2)\triangle\mathbf{d}\triangle\mathbf{d}^T$, which is a set of transformed model coefficients that depend solely on $\triangle\mathbf{d}$, where M^* is the conjugate transpose of M. Then the singular vector associated with the largest singular value e_1 of MM^{*T} should give the direction of the velocity. The estimate of the velocity change, $\triangle\mathbf{d}$, is obtained by scaling this singular vector by $sqrte_1/(\sigma_{k_1}^2 + \ldots + \sigma_{k_n}^2)$.

To obtain an initial orientation estimate θ, we form the product $A = \triangle\mathbf{d}^T M$, with the estimated velocity change $\triangle\mathbf{d}$ and the matrix of estimated coefficients M. θ can then be obtained by first dividing the phase of each component of A according to its corresponding wave number, and then taking their average. According to the model, ignoring the noise, the resulting phase values should then be equal, and computing their average yields the orientation estimation θ.

7.4 Motion Segmentation

The problem of motion segmentation can be formulated as follows: given a sequence of images and the optical flow field (output of standard motion estimation algorithms), the goal is to find a small number of moving objects in the sequence of images. In the output of segmentation, each pixel in each image is associated with the object to which it belongs. In segmentation, the algorithm combines motion and spatial data. A segmented object can contain parts with different static parameters, which is a quite different problem from static image segmentation. Also, the object representation in an image can be noncontinuous when there are occlusions or only parts of the object are captured.

Motion segmentation is difficult because of (1) motion estimation, (2) the integration vs. segmentation dilemma, and (3) the fact that smoothing inside the model while keeping models independent is desired. The first difficulty stems from limitations in current motion estimation techniques. Motion estimation cannot be done from local measurements only, because of the aperture problem. Therefore, many motion estimation algorithms have focused on conditions of texture, where junctions or corner-like image structures are assumed to be reliable for tracking. But under some conditions, these local measurements are unreliable and can generate spurious motions. For example, T-junctions caused by occlusion can move in an image very differently than either of the objects involved in the occlusion event. The second difficulty arises from the dilemma of finding the consistency between integration and segmentation. To accurately estimate motion in textureless regions, we need a motion representation beyond the pixel level. Thus integrating corners, lines, and flat regions (textureless) to represent motion is appropriate. However, in reality we will not be able to make a clear distinction between corners and lines. In addition, boundary motion is typically analyzed locally, which can again lead to spurious junction tracking. If we integrate without segmentation, when there are multiple motions, we may get false intersection points of velocity constraints at T-junctions. The third difficulty is how to use the smoothness constraint. Flat regions do not always move smoothly (discontinuities at illusory boundaries). Most pixels inside an object do not supply movement information, and they move with the whole object. Thus smoothness constraints should be added inside objects, not between objects.

There is a rich literature on motion segmentation. In the following, we choose to introduce the layered motion model, which can represent moving images with sets of overlapping layers. We also show how the above-mentioned difficulties are addressed by different approaches.

7.4.1 Layered Model: Multiple Motion Models

Parameterized optical flow methods assume that spatial variation in the image motion within a region can be represented by a low-order polynomial (e.g., affine motion). With many motion constraints and few parameters to estimate, these approaches can recover accurate motion estimates when the motion model is a good approximation to the image motion. The problem with these methods is that those large image regions are typically not well modeled by a single parametric motion due to the complexity of the motion or the presence of multiple motions. The selection of a region size has been referred to as the generalized aperture problem. One solution to addressing this problem is to assume that motion within a patch can be represented by a small number of affine motions that can be thought of as "layers."

With the layered model, a sequence of moving images can be represented with a set of overlapping layers. Each layer contains an intensity map that defines the additive values of each pixel, along with an alpha map that serves as a mask indicating the transparency. Velocity maps define how the layers are to be warped over time. The layered model relies on the understanding that images are not made up of random collections of pixels. Rather, the world consists of objects present at different depths and hence an image can be understood as a collection of different layers with an associated depth ordering. Pixels are grouped into these layers. Pixels that belong to the same layer share a common model for their motion.

Layer extraction and optimization over the possible parameters in each layer make this a chicken and egg problem. Many approaches have been proposed to address this problem. In general, these approaches fall into three sets. The first set of approaches estimates a fixed number of parametric motions within a given image region using a variety of regression techniques including robust statistics (Darrell and Pentland 1995) and mixture models (Jepson and Black 1993). These approaches can cope with a small number of motions within a region but not with general flow fields. These area-based approaches do not address how to select appropriate image regions in which to apply the parametric models nor how to select the appropriate number of motions or layers. The second set of approaches apply parametric models to coarse flow fields by grouping flow vectors into consistent regions (Adiv 1985; Wang and Adelson 1994). These approaches, like the regression approaches above, assume that image motion can be represented by a small number of layers within an image region. Still, they do not address problems such as how to estimate the correct number of layers and how to deal with motions that are significantly more complex than simple polynomials. The third set of methods addressed these problems (Ayer et al. 1994; Darrell and Pentland 1995; Black and Jepson 1996; Weiss 1997). Both Ayer et al. (1994) and Darrell and Pentland (1995) solve this problem by using a minimum description length encoding principle to strike a balance between accurate encoding of the motion and the number of layers needed to represent it. Black et al. first segment an image using brightness information and then hypothesize that these regions correspond to planar patches in the scene, and then apply parameterized motion models to smaller, more local image regions. To model complex motions in single layer, Weiss (1997) proposes a layered mixture model in which the motion in each layer is modeled with a smooth flow field. This method shows promise as it combines many of the features of the layered models and regularization approaches.

In the following, we first present Wang and Adelson's (1994) work as a starting point for examining the layered motion model. Then we introduce a unified mixture framework that can segment image sequences by fitting multiple smooth flow fields to the spatiotemporal data (Weiss and Adelson 1996; Weiss 1997).

7.4.2 Clustering Optical Flow Field into Layers

Nonprobabilistic approaches to layer extraction usually involve iterations between region creation and motion model estimation. For example, Wang and Adelson's (1994) algorithm consists of two steps: motion segmentation and then synthesis of the layered representation. The segmentation is based upon the assumption that optical flow in an image can be described as a set of planar patches in velocity space, and the pixels that lie on these best-fit planes basically define a region to which one affine motion model can be ascribed. The synthesis stage involves combining information from all multiple frames to get more reliable values of the intensity map and also to find the relative depth ordering of the regions extracted by motion segmentation.

Optical flow serves as the input to layer extraction. Here we introduce a gradient-based approach. Optical flow is calculated using a coarse-to-fine pyramid approach in a local setting. The pixel velocity is given by

$$\begin{bmatrix} \sum \psi_{1x}^2 & \sum \psi_{1x}\psi_{1y} \\ \sum \psi_{1x}\psi_{1y} & \sum \psi_{1y}^2 \end{bmatrix} \begin{bmatrix} \mathbf{d}_x \\ \mathbf{d}_y \end{bmatrix} = \begin{bmatrix} -\sum \psi_{1x}(\psi_2 - \psi_1) \\ -\sum \psi_{1y}(\psi_2 - \psi_1) \end{bmatrix} \tag{7.43}$$

where ψ_{1x} denotes the components of the gradient of the target image ψ_1. The summation is done over a small window. Taking all the velocities within the window, we can compute robust estimates of the affine parameters for motion. The reliability of an affine motion hypothesis is computed by taking the mean squared error (MSE). Hypotheses with a residual greater than a threshold are ignored. In order to avoid object boundaries, the region size is kept to minimum.

Motion segmentation consists of two steps: (1) affine model fitting and (2) parameter clustering. Given the optical flow, the global distortion function for the affine model fitting is defined as $\sum_{(x,y)}(\mathbf{d}(x,y) - \mathbf{d}_{aff}(x,y))$, which gives the error between the velocity estimated by optic flow and the velocity described by the ith affine motion model. To minimize this distortion function, a greedy per pixel minimization is done by picking the affine motion model that best describes the estimated velocity. Secondly, the algorithm then groups pixels into the motion-segmented regions by applying an adaptive k-means algorithm to the affine motion parameters. The distance metric between two sets of parameters corresponding to two affine motion models is defined as $[(\mathbf{a}_i - \mathbf{a}_j)^T M(\mathbf{a}_i - \mathbf{a}_j)]^{\frac{1}{2}}$, where $M = diag\; 1\; r^2\; r^2\; 1\; r^2\; r^2$, and r is roughly the dimensions of the image.

Intensity and alpha values are obtained by first applying inverse affine warping to apply motion compensation to the layers. Then median filtering is done on those pixels that become stationary as a result of the motion compensation.

$$Layer_i(x,y) = median\{M_{i,1}(x,y), \ldots, M_{i,n}(x,y)\} \tag{7.44}$$

where $M_{i,k}(x,y)$ is the motion-compensated image obtained by warping frame k of the original sequence by the affine transformation for layer i. Each layer is therefore derived by a number of pixels from the different frames that become stationary after motion compensation. To determine occlusion relationships, a layer derived from more pixels occludes one derived from fewer points. A layer with more observable pixels after motion compensation is less likely to have been occluded.

We show one of the results obtained by Wang and Adelson's (1994) algorithm in Fig. 7.5. The top row shows three frames of the flower garden MPEG video sequence. In this sequence, the tree, the flower bed, and the row of houses move toward the left at different velocities. The bottom row shows the extracted layers corresponding to the tree, the flower bed, and the house. The layer extraction on the 30 frame sequence took several dozens of minutes. The initial segmentation was done by taking 75 nonoverlapping regions. The approach shown works well when the motion regions in the image can be described by the affine motion model.

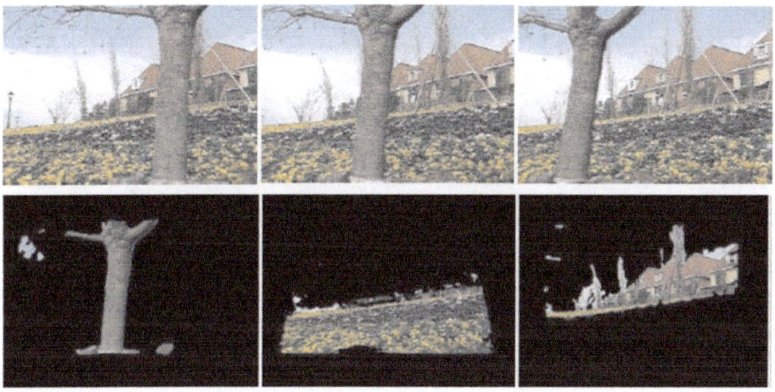

Fig. 7.5 *Top*: frames 0, 15, 30 of MPEG flower garden sequence. *Bottom*: the layers corresponding to the tree, the flower bed, and the house

7.4.3 Mixture Estimation for Layer Extraction

Alternatively, the grouping of optical into layers can be well formulated in a mixture estimation framework. However, previous work using only motion data will fail since it does not make use of static cues when segmenting the sequence. Furthermore, the number of models is either specified in advance or estimated outside the mixture model framework. In the following, we show how to add spatial constraints to the mixture model framework and introduce a variant of the expectation maximization (EM) algorithm that makes use of both form and motion constraints.

We can assume that the image data (the spatial and temporal derivatives of the sequence) were generated by K smooth motion groups. The velocity of each group is drawn from a distribution where smooth velocities are more probable.

$$P(\mathbf{d}) = \frac{1}{Z_d} \exp\left\{ -\sum_{\mathbf{x}} \frac{||\Phi\mathbf{d}(\mathbf{x})||}{\sigma^2} \right\} \tag{7.45}$$

where $\Phi\mathbf{d}$ is a differential operator that penalizes fields that have strong derivatives:

$$\Phi\mathbf{d} = \sum_{n=0}^{\infty} a_n \mathbf{d}^{(n)} \tag{7.46}$$

where $a_n = \frac{\sigma^{2n}}{n! 2^n}$ and $\mathbf{d}^{(n)}$ denotes the n-order derivative.

The optimal velocity field $\mathbf{d}(\mathbf{x})$ guaranteeing the coherence of motion is a linear combination of basis flow fields, $B_i(\mathbf{x})$:

$$\mathbf{d}(\mathbf{x}) = \sum_i \alpha_i \mathbf{b}_i(\mathbf{x}) \tag{7.47}$$

There is a basis flow field centered at every pixel where the image gradient is nonzero:

$$\mathbf{b}_i(\mathbf{x}) = G(\mathbf{x} - \mathbf{x}_i) \nabla \psi(\mathbf{x}) \tag{7.48}$$

where the scalar value function $G(\mathbf{x} - \mathbf{x}_i)$ is a 2D Gaussian. $\nabla \psi$ denotes the image gradient $\nabla \psi(\mathbf{x}) = \left[\frac{\partial \psi_1}{\partial x}, \frac{\partial \psi_1}{\partial y} \right]^T$. If w denoted by N the number of basis fields in the reduced expansion, then the N coefficients are a solution to the linear system:

$$(M^T W M + \lambda R)\alpha = M^T W Y \tag{7.49}$$

where $\alpha = [\alpha_1, ..., \alpha_N]$, M_{ij} is given by the scalar product of the basis field centered on pixel i and the gradient at pixel j. R is an $N \times N$ submatrix of M in which only the pixels that have basis functions centered on them are used, and W is a diagonal matrix whose diagonal elements determine the weight of a pixel in estimating model parameters $W_{ii} = \sqrt(L(\mathbf{x}_i))$. Y_i is simply the temporal derivative at pixel i. The solution of the system gives the flow field spanned by the reduced basis set that best satisfies the gradient constraints at all pixels.

The labels of the image are drawn from an MRF distribution:

$$P(L) = \frac{1}{Z_l} \exp\left\{ \sum_{\mathbf{x}_i, \mathbf{x}_j} w_{ij} L^T(\mathbf{x}_i) L(\mathbf{x}_j) \right\} \tag{7.50}$$

where $L(\mathbf{x}) = [l_1(\mathbf{x}), ..., l_K(\mathbf{x})]$ is a vector at every location such that $l_k(\mathbf{x}) = 1$ if and only if position $\mathbf{x}$ is assigned to group k. The link w_{ij} determines the distribution of the labelings.

Given the labelings and the velocity field of each group, the probability of observing $\nabla \psi$, $\Delta \psi = \psi_2(\mathbf{x}) - \psi_1(\mathbf{x})$ at location $\mathbf{x}$ is given by

$$P(\nabla\psi,\Delta\psi|L(\mathbf{x}),\mathbf{d}(\mathbf{x})) = \exp\left\{-\sum_k l_k(\mathbf{x})(\nabla\psi^T\mathbf{d}_k+\Delta\psi)^2/\sigma_N^2\right\} \tag{7.51}$$

where $\mathbf{d}_k$ indicates that motion vector $\mathbf{d}(\mathbf{x})$ is a member of the kth group. For clarity's sake, we have omitted the dependence of $\nabla\psi, \Delta\psi, l_k(\mathbf{x})$, and $\mathbf{d}(\mathbf{x})$ on $\mathbf{x}=(x,y)$.

We obtain the posterior probability $P(L(\mathbf{x}),\mathbf{d}(\mathbf{x})|\nabla\psi,\Delta\psi)$ with Bayes' rule by combining the priors of the velocity field in Eq. (7.45) and labeling field Eq. (7.50), with the observation model Eq. (7.51). Then we find the MAP estimation of L via an EM algorithm. The energy function of the EM algorithm is:

$$J_k(\mathbf{d}) = \sum_{\mathbf{x}} l_k(\mathbf{x})((\nabla\psi^T(\mathbf{x})\mathbf{d}(\mathbf{x})+\Delta\psi)/\sigma_N)^2 + \lambda_d\sum_{\mathbf{x}}||\Phi\mathbf{d}(\mathbf{x})|| - \lambda_l\sum_{\mathbf{x}_i,\mathbf{x}_j} w_{ij}L^T(\mathbf{x}_i)L(\mathbf{x}_j) \tag{7.52}$$

where the statistical assumptions about the generative model are characterized by five parameters: σ, the assumed level of noise in the optical flow; σ_N, the assumed level of noise in the sequence; w_{ij}, which specifies the probability that a pixel will belong to a different model than its four neighbors; and λ_d and λ_l, which embody the smoothness assumption of the optical flow.

The EM algorithm iterates over two steps: (1) the expectation step (E step) in which the hidden labels are replaced with their conditional expectations and (2) the maximization step (M step) in which the velocity fields are found by maximizing their posterior probabilities. In the E step, the algorithm calls for replacing $l_k(\mathbf{x})$ at each iteration with its conditional expectation based on the current parameter estimates. We denote the conditional expectation of $l_k(\mathbf{x})$ as $g_k(\mathbf{x})$. Although $l_k(\mathbf{x})$ is binary valued, $g_k(\mathbf{x})$ takes on continuous values between 0 and 1 and $g_k(\mathbf{x})$ sums to 1 for fixed $\mathbf{x}$. Actually, $g_k(\mathbf{x})$ is a kind of soft segmentation of the image. In the M step, it uses current values of $g_k(\mathbf{x})$ to maximize the likelihood of the parameters, θ_k, of motion model k(θ_k can be thought of as a parametric description of the motion predicted by model k). In summary, the algorithm can be characterized as assigning each pixel to the model that minimizes the residual between the observed and the predicted measurements, assuming the motion of model k (E step), and then updating model parameters based upon these assignments (M step).

There are two important considerations that make the algorithm computationally feasible. First, the use of Green's functions enables the estimation of a single smooth flow field in closed form and thus increases the efficiency of the multiple model estimation. Secondly, the algorithm uses segmented images instead of nonsegmented images. The spatial constraint in terms of the MRF prior on L introduces intensive computation in the E step. These calculations must be carried out at every iteration. One possible solution to reduce the computation is to use an incremental algorithm based on mean field approximation. Another alternative is to use segmented images. With segmented images based on static intensity cues, the E step reduces to assigning pixels to models based on their summed deviation from the model prediction for all pixels in the same fragment. Again, the assignment can be soft or hard depending upon the assumed probability distribution of the deviations.

Finally, the number of models can be estimated automatically by initializing the algorithm with more models than will be needed. The algorithm merges redundant models and the final number of models found depends on the parameter σ_N.

7.5 Statistics of Optical Flow

In this section, we study the statistics of optical flow in natural imagery and exploit recent advances in machine learning to obtain a rich probabilistic model of the optical flow field. This extends to the domain of image motion work that has already been done on the analysis of image statistics in nature scenes and range images. The expected output of this approach relates well to previous robust statistical formulations of optical flow smoothness prior.

7.5.1 Statistics of Optical Flow

The statistics of realistic motion fields can lead to a more accurate prior of flow fields and help to improve flow estimation algorithms. The formulation of smoothness constraints for optical flow estimation has its Bayesian formulation in terms of MRF. Such formulations of optical flow estimate the flow using Bayesian inference based on a suitable posterior distribution. Using Bayes' rule, the posterior can be broken down into a likelihood term and an optical flow prior. The likelihood term enforces the brightness constancy assumption, which underlies most flow estimation techniques; the prior term enforces spatial smoothness, for example using an MRF model. A large class of techniques makes use of spatial regularization terms derived from the point of view of variational methods, PDEs, and nonlinear diffusion. However, most of these spatial terms are very local prior models that are typically formulated in terms of the first differences in the optical flow. They can model piecewise constant- or smooth flow but not more complex spatial structures. They are limited in capturing the statistics of the real optical flow.

However, compared with the intensive study of natural image statistics, the spatial and temporal statistics of optical flow are relatively unexplored because databases of natural scene motions cannot be directly measured. Thus, it is important to have a ground-truth motion database with diverse examples. Recently, preliminary success has been obtained. Roth and Black (2007) construct training flow fields using range images of nature scenes and 3D camera motions recovered from handheld and car-mounted video devices. They also develop a machine learning method to learn an MRF model of optic flow. Liu et al. (2008) design a system to allow the user to specify layer configurations and motion hints. Their human-in-loop methodology can create a ground-truth motion database for videos taken with ordinary cameras in both indoor and outdoor scenes. Based on the obtained motion field, these two research groups have obtained similar statistics surrounding optical flow.

Marginal and joint statistics surrounding ground-truth flow in motion databases have been computed. Their log histograms are displayed in Fig. 11.4. In (a) and (b), the marginal of u (horizontal flow) is flatter than that of v (vertical flow), indicating that horizontal motion dominates the vertical. As shown in (b) and (i), the marginal of v is asymmetric, and there are more pixels moving down than going up (due to gravity). The marginals of the 1st-order derivatives of the flows are sparse, as shown in (c) to (f). Unlike the marginals of synthetic flow fields in (Roth and Black 2007), the statistics in the realistic motion database in (Liu et al. 2008) show that vertical flow is sparser than horizontal flow, consistent with the fact that horizontal motion has a larger range. The temporal derivatives of the flow are not as sparse as the spatial derivatives, as depicted in (g) and (h). The joint histogram in (j) suggests that horizontal and vertical motions are likely to increase or decrease together temporally. The joint histograms in (k) and (l) reveal that the discontinuities of the flow are isotropic. At motion discontinuities, the change in vertical motion may dominate the change in horizontal motion, and vice versa, as shown in (m) and (n).

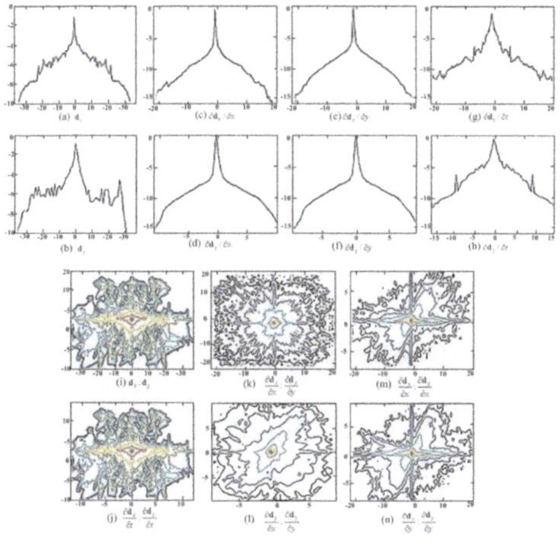

Fig. 7.6 Velocities and spatial derivative histograms of the optical flow in the database discussed in the text. Figures refer to (Liu et al. 2008)

7.5.2 Motion Prior Modeling

Spatial regulation of optical flow benefits from prior models that capture interactions beyond adjacent pixels. Roth and Black's (2007) experimental results have shown clearly that high-order MRFs are quite powerful for certain low-level vision applications. They formulate the prior probability of a flow field as a field-of-experts (FoE) model that captures the spatial statistics in overlapping patches and train it using contrastive divergence. The learned flow prior quantitatively improves flow accuracy, and captures the spatial structure found in natural scene motion.

The FoE approach models the probability of an optical field using an MRF (Roth and Black 2007). In contrast to many previous MRF models, it uses larger cliques of, for example, 3×3 or 5×5 motion patches (motion vectors within a rectangular region with a defined size), and allows learning the appropriate clique potentials from training data. In this formulation, motion vectors of a flow field are assumed to be represented by nodes V in a graph $G = (V, E)$, where E are the links connecting the nodes. The links are typically defined through a neighborhood system that connects all nodes in a square $m \times m$ region. Every such neighborhood centered on a node $k = 1, \ldots, K$ defines a maximal clique $\mathbf{x}_k$ in the graph. The probability of a flow field component $\mathbf{x}$ under the MRF is

$$p(\mathbf{x}) = \frac{1}{Z} \prod_{k=1}^{K} \varphi(\mathbf{x}_k) \tag{7.53}$$

where $\varphi(\mathbf{x}_k$ is the so-called potential function for clique $\mathbf{x}_k$, and Z is a normalization term.

The potential function is modeled with an FoE model. The FoE approach models a high-dimensional probability distribution by taking the product of several expert distributions, where each expert works on a low-dimensional subspace that is relatively easy to model. Usually, the experts are defined in linear 1D subspaces. Since the responses of linear filters applied to flow components in the optical flow database show histograms that are typically well fit by t-distributions, The potential function can be written as:

$$\varphi(\mathbf{x}_k) = \prod_{i=1}^{N} \phi(\mathbf{J}_i^T \mathbf{x}_k; \alpha_i) \tag{7.54}$$

where $\mathbf{J}_i$ is a linear filter which is expressed as a vector. Each expert is a t-distribution with parameter α_i:

$$\phi(\mathbf{J}_i^T \mathbf{x}_k; \alpha_i) = \left(1 + \frac{1}{2}(\mathbf{J}_i^T \mathbf{x}_k)\right)^{-\alpha_i} \tag{7.55}$$

One important property of the potential function is that all parameters can be automatically learned from training data, i.e., both the α_i and the filters $\mathbf{J}_i$. The number N in Eq. (7.55) is not necessarily equal to the number of dimensions m^2.

In the context of optical flow estimation, the prior knowledge about the flow field is typically expressed in terms of an energy function $E(\mathbf{x}) = -\log p(\mathbf{x})$. Accordingly, we can express the energy for the FoE prior model as

$$E_{FoE} = -\sum_{k=1}^{K}\sum_{i=1}^{N} \log\phi(\mathbf{J}_i^T \mathbf{x}_k; \alpha_i) + \log Z \tag{7.56}$$

Note that for fixed parameters α and $\mathbf{J}$, the partition function Z is constant, and can thus be ignored when estimating flow.

7.5.3 Contrastive Divergence Learning

By maximizing the likelihood of the FoE model, the parameters α_i as well as the linear filters $\mathbf{J}_i$(a vector) can be learned from a set of M training optical flows $O^{(1)}, \ldots, O^{(M)}$. Maximizing the likelihood for the FoE model is equivalent to minimizing the Kullback–Leibler divergence between the model and the data distribution, and so guarantees the model distribution to be as close to the data distribution as possible.

The maximizing can be performed by a gradient descent on the log likelihood. If we denote the parameters α and $\mathbf{J}$ as Θ_i, and the update as Θ_i be $\Delta\Theta_i$, then we have

$$\Delta\Theta_i = \rho\left[\left\langle \frac{\partial E_{FoE}}{\partial \Theta_i} \right\rangle_p - \left\langle \frac{\partial E_{FoE}}{\partial \Theta_i} \right\rangle_O\right] \tag{7.57}$$

where ρ is a user-defined learning rate, $\langle\cdot\rangle_p$ denotes the expectation value with respect to the model distribution $p(\mathbf{x})$, and $\langle\cdot\rangle_O$ the average over the training data O. The expectation over the model distribution is computed approximately using Monte Carlo integration by repeatedly drawing samples from $p(\mathbf{x})$ using MCMC sampling. The average over the training data is easy to compute.

The gradient of the energy can be written as

$$\nabla_{\mathbf{x}} E_{FoE}(\mathbf{x}) = -\sum_{i=1}^{N} \mathbf{J}_i^- * \zeta_i(\mathbf{J}_i * \mathbf{x}) \tag{7.58}$$

where $\mathbf{J}_i * \mathbf{x}$ denotes the convolution of the image velocity component with filter $\mathbf{J}_i$. Also we define $\zeta_i(y) = \frac{\partial}{\partial y} log\phi(y; \alpha_i)$, and let $\mathbf{J}_i^-$ denote the filter obtained by mirroring $\mathbf{J}_i$ around its center pixel.

7.6 Summary

In this chapter, we have discussed motion analysis within the Bayesian estimation framework. We covered five important topics of motion analysis. First, we formulated optical flow estimation with the MRF model, and introduced a stochastic approach to obtain the MAP estimate. Second, we focused on linear parametric models for motion estimation and discussed the model selection problem based upon statistical learning theory. Third, we introduced generative models for handling motion discontinuities and specific motion, which are used as an extension of linear parametric models. Fourth, we discussed the layered model and mixture framework for motion estimation. Finally, we presented recent advances in the statistics of optical flow, which leads to more accurate motion estimation algorithms.

Appendix

Graph and Neighborhood

Let $S = s_1, ..., s_N$ be a set of motion vector sites and let $\mathcal{N} = N_s, s \in S$ be a neighborhood system for S, meaning any collection of subsets of S for which (1) $s \notin N_s$ and (2) $s \in N_r \Leftrightarrow r \in N_s$. Obviously, N_s is the set of neighbors of s and the pair $S, \mathcal{N}$ is a graph in the usual way. A subset $C \subseteq S$ is a clique if every pair of distinct sites in C are neighbors.

There are three cases involved in the Bayesian approach to motion estimation discussed in this chapter:

Case 1: S is the set of motion vector sites in the motion field F; N is the number of pixels in the image lattice. We are interested in homogenous neighborhood systems of the form

$$N = N^c = \{F_{i,j}\}; F_{i,j} = \{(k,l) : 0 < (k-i)^2 + (l-j)^2 \leq c\} \tag{7.59}$$

Notice that sites at or near the boundary of the field have fewer neighbors than interior sites. Figure 7.7 shows the neighborhood configuration for $c = 1, 2, 8$. In each case, (i, j) is at the center, and the symbol "$\circ$" stands for neighboring sites. The cliques for $c = 1$ are all subsets of the form $\{(i, j)\}, \{(i, j+1)\}$, or $\{(i, j), (i+1, j)\}$ are shown in Fig. 7.7(d). For $c = 2$, we have the cliques in Fig. 7.7(d) as well as those in Fig. 7.7(e). Obviously, the number of the clique types grows rapidly with c.

Case 2: Think of sites as being placed midway between each vertical and horizontal pair of motion vector sites and as representing the possible locations of motion discontinuity (boundary). Figure 7.8(a) shows six motion vector sites together with seven sites denoted by an $\times$. The six surrounding $\times$ s are the neighbors of the middle $\times$ for the neighborhood system. Figure 7.8(b) is a segment of realization of a binary line process for which, at each line site, there may or may not be a line element.

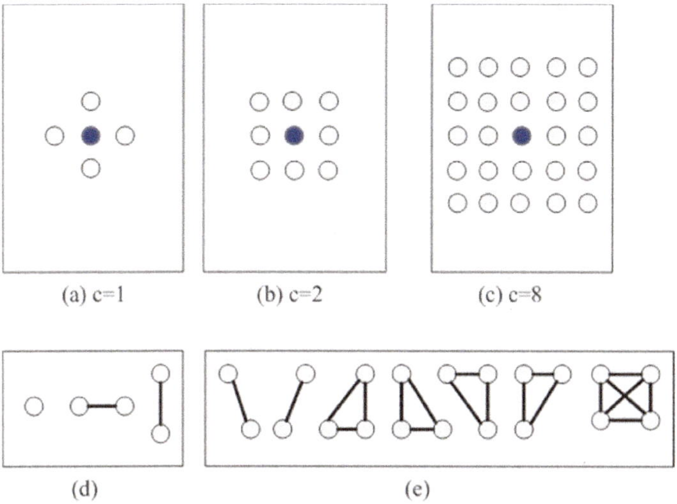

Fig. 7.7 Neighborhood and cliques

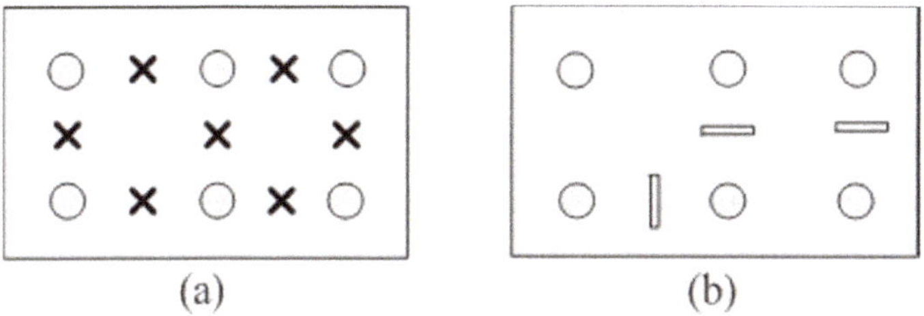

Fig. 7.8 Neighborhood and cliques for the dual sampling structure

Steerable Filter Design

The steerable filter is a class of filters in which a filter of arbitrary orientation is synthesized as a linear combination of a set of "basis filters." The key point of design in a steerable filter is to find the right basis filters. This problem can be formulated as follows: Given a kernel $F:\mathbb{R}^2 \to \mathbb{C}^2$, define the family of "rotated" copies of F as: $F_\theta = F \circ R_\theta$, $\theta \in S^1$, where S is the circle and R_θ is a rotation. The F_θ can be expressed as

$$F_\theta(\mathbf{x}) = \sum_{i=1}^{n} \alpha(\theta)_i G_i(\mathbf{x}), \forall\theta \in S^1, \forall\mathbf{x} \in \mathbb{R}^2 \tag{7.60}$$

a finite linear combination of functions $G_i : \mathbb{R}^2 \to \mathbb{C}^2$. The quality of approximation of $G_\theta^{[n]} \approx F_\theta$ is measured by an L^2-normal distance D_n.

$$D_n(F_\theta, G_\theta^{[n]}) = \left|\left| F_\theta - G_\theta^{[n]} \right|\right|_L^2 (\mathbb{R}^2 \times S^1) \tag{7.61}$$

We call $F_\theta^{[n]}$ the n-terms sum:

$$F_\theta^{[n]} = \sum_{i=1}^{n} \sigma_i \alpha_i(\mathbf{x}) b_i(\theta) \tag{7.62}$$

with σ_i,α_i and b_i defined in the following way: let $\hat{h}(v)$ be the Fourier series expansion of the function $h(\theta)$ defined by

$$h(\theta) = \int_{\mathbb{R}^2} F_\theta(\mathbf{x}) \overline{F_{\theta'=0}(\mathbf{x})} d\mathbf{x} \tag{7.63}$$

Let v_i be the frequencies on which $\hat{h}(v)$ is defined, ordered in such a way that $\hat{h}(v_i) \geq \hat{h}(v_j)$ if $i \leq j$. Call $N \leq \infty$ the number of nonzero terms $\hat{h}(v_i)$. Finally, for $i \leq N$ define the quantities:

$$\sigma_i = \sqrt{\hat{h}(v_i)} \tag{7.64}$$

$$b_i(\theta) = \exp\{j2\pi v_i \theta\} \tag{7.65}$$

$$\alpha_i(\mathbf{x}) = \sigma_i^{-1} \int_{S^1} \overline{F_\theta(\mathbf{x})} \exp\{j2\pi v_i \theta\} d\theta \tag{7.66}$$

Then $F_\theta^{[n]}$ is an optimal n-dimensional approximation to F_θ with respect to the distance D_n. The approximation error is

$$D_n(F_\theta, F_\theta^{[n]}) = \sqrt{\left(\sum_{i=n+1}^{N} \sigma_i^2 \right)} \tag{7.67}$$

References

Adiv G (1985) Determining three dimensional motion and structure from optical flow generated by several objects. IEEE Transactions on Pattern Analysis and Machine Intelligence 7:384–401

Aloimonos Y, Duric Z (1992) Active egomotion estimation: a qualitative approach. In: Proceedings of European Conference on Computer Vision Ligure, Italy, Springer, pp 497–510

Ayer S, Schroeter P, Bigun J (1994) Segmentation of moving objects by robust motion parameter estimation over multiple frames. In: Proceedings of European Conference on Computer Vision, Springer, Berlin, pp 316–327

Baker S, Matthews I (2004) Lucas-Kanade 20 Years On: a unifying framework. International Journal of Computer Vision 56(3):221–255

Barron J, Fleet D, Beauchemins (1994) Performance of optical flow techniques. International Journal of Computer Vision 12(1):43–77

Black M, Jepson A (1996) Estimating optical flow in segmented images using variable-orderparametric models with local deformations. IEEE Transactions on Pattern Analysis and Machine Intelligence 18(10):972–986

Brox T, Bruhn A, Papenberg N, Weickert J (2004) High accuracy optical flow estimation based on a theory for warping. Lecture Notes in Computer Science pp 25–36

Bruhn A, Weickert J, Schnörr C (2005) Lucas/Kanade meets Horn/Schunck: combining local and global optic flow methods. International Journal of Computer Vision 61(3):211–231

Darrell T, Pentland A (1995) Cooperative robust estimation using layers of support. IEEE Transactions on Pattern Analysis and Machine Intelligence pp 474–487

Fleet D, Weiss Y (2005) Optical flow estimation. In: Mathematical Models for Computer Vision: The Handbook, ed O Faugeras, Springer, Newyork, pp 239–258

Fleet D, Black M, Yacoob Y, Jepson A (2000) Design and use of linear models for image motion analysis. International Journal of Computer Vision 36(3):171–193

Foroosh H, Zerubia J, Berthod M (2002) Extension of phase correlation to subpixel registration. IEEE Transactions on Image Processing 11(3):188–200

Geman S, Geman D (1987) Stochastic relaxation, Gibbs distributions and the Bayesian restoration of images. Readings in Computer Vision: Issues, Problems, Principles, and Paradigms pp 564–584

Jepson A, Black M (1993) Mixture models for optical flow computation. In: IEEE Conference on Computer Vision and Pattern Recognition, pp 760–761

Konrad J, Dubois E (1992) Bayesian estimation of motion vector fields. IEEE Transactions on Pattern Analysis and Machine Intelligence 14(9):910–927

Liu C, Freeman W, Adelson E, Weiss Y (2008) Human-assisted motion annotation. In: Proceedings of IEEE Conference on Computer Vision and Pattern Recognition, pp 1–8

Liu J (2001) Monte Carlo Strategies in Scientific Computing. Springer, New york

Perona P (1995) Deformable kernels for early vision. IEEE Transactions on Pattern Analysis and Machine Intelligence pp 488–499

Roth S, Black M (2007) On the spatial statistics of optical flow. International Journal of Computer Vision 74(1):33–50

Tekalp A (1995) Digital Video Processing. Prentice Hall, Upper Saddle River, NJ

Verri A, Poggio T (1987) Against quantitative optical flow. In: Proceedings of the First Internaional Conference on Computer Vision, pp 171–180. Computer Society Press, New york

Wang J, Adelson E (1994) Representing moving images with layers. IEEE Transactions on Image Processing 3(5):625–638

Wechsler H, Duric Z, Li F, Cherkassky V (2004) Motion estimation using statistical learning theory. IEEE Transactions on Pattern Analysis and Machine Intelligence pp 466–478

Weiss Y (1997) Smoothness in layers: motion segmentation using nonparametricmixture estimation. In: Proceedings of IEEE Conference on Computer Vision and Pattern Recognition, pp 520–526

Weiss Y, Adelson E (1996) A unified mixture framework for motion segmentation: incorporatingspatial coherence and estimating the number of models. In: Proceedings of IEEE Conference on Computer Vision and Pattern Recognition, pp 321–326

Zhang J, Hanauer G (1995) The application of mean field theory to image motion estimation. IEEE Transactions on Image Processing 4(1):19–33

Zhao H, Chan T, Merriman B, Osher S (1996) A variational level set approach to multiphase motion. Journal of Computational Physics 127(1):179–195

Chapter 8
Bayesian Tracking of Visual Objects

Abstract Tracking objects in image sequences involves performing motion analysis at the object level, which is becoming an increasingly important technology in a wide range of computer video applications, including video teleconferencing, security and surveillance, video segmentation, and editing. In this chapter, we focus on sequential Bayesian estimation techniques for visual tracking. We first introduce the sequential Bayesian estimation framework, which acts as the theoretic basis for visual tracking. Then, we present approaches to constructing representation models for specific objects.

8.1 Introduction

Visual tracking of objects in image sequences is becoming an increasingly important technology in the computer vision, video surveillance, and virtual reality communities. In recent years, development is this area has resulted in the availability of products on the market capable of tracking isolated or a small number of targets. This technology has a wide range of applications.

Visual tracking can be thought of as the problem of performing motion analysis on the object level, which in turn address temporal and spatial correspondence belonging to specific objects within the input image sequence. Whether one tries to track (1) objects of a given nature, e.g., cars, people, faces; (2) object of a given nature with a specific attribute, e.g., moving cars, walking people, talking heads, the face of a given person; or (3) objects of an a priori unknown nature but of specific interest, e.g., moving objects, objects of semantic interest manually labeled in the first frame. In each case, part of the input video is searched against a reference model describing the appearance of the objects. As shown in Fig. 8.1, two major components can be distinguished in a typical visual tracker: (1) object representation and object localization, which must cope with changes in the appearance of the target, and (2) filtering and data association (i.e., the addressing of dynamics of the tracked object, the learning of scene priors, and the evaluation of different hypothesizes).

N. Zheng, J. Xue, *Statistical Learning and Pattern Analysis for Image and Video Processing*, Advances in Pattern Recognition, DOI 10.1007/978-1-84882-312-9_8,
© Springer-Verlag London Limited 2009

Prior knowledge of the object is inserted into the object model, which involves both the processing and measurement of the spatial and dynamic representation. While filtering and data association have their roots in control theory, algorithms for target representation and localization are specific to images and are related to registration methods. The way in which the two components are combined and weighted is task dependent and plays a decisive role in the robustness and efficiency of the tracker.

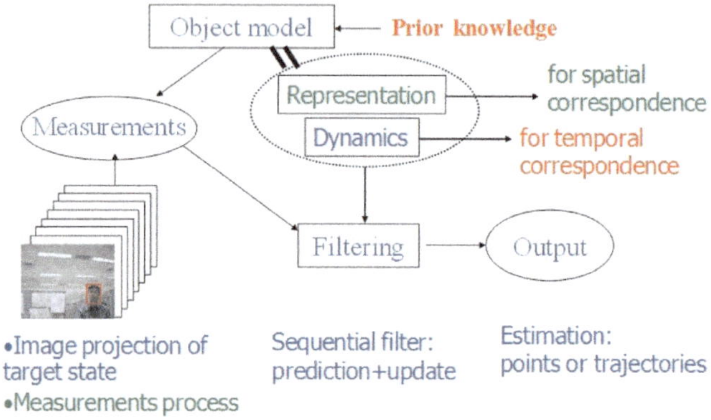

Fig. 8.1 The structure a visual tracker

The object representation describes the possible appearance of the target in the image sequence, which determines the accuracy of the matching of the object's location in the spatial-temporal domain. Since no single cue is robust and general enough to deal with a wide variety of environmental conditions, combining multiple visual cues promises to increase robustness and generality. In general, there are two types of methods. One is known as the adaptive tracking approach, and the other consists of the methods for multiple visual cue integration. In adaptive tracking, different tracking algorithms are selected with respect to the actual conditions: whenever conditions are good, an accurate and precise tracking algorithm is employed. When conditions deteriorate more robust but less accurate algorithms are chosen. Using multiple simultaneous cues not only allows the use of complementary and redundant information at all times, but also enables the more robust detection of failures, thus facilitating recovery. In multiple visual cue integration, there exist two main strategies for fusing the output of multiple cues: voting and the use of a probabilistic approach. In the former, all visual cues contribute simultaneously to the overall results and none of the cues have greater relevance than the others. That is, each cue makes an independent decision without regard to other cues, and then the decision that gains the most support in the voting is chosen as the final decision. In the latter, more care must be taken in designing the object representation model so that the different cues combine in the desired manner. However, there also lies the strength of these probabilistic methods, since it forces the user to be explicit in terms of designing the model and specifying what parameters are used and what assumptions are made.

Filtering and data association are formulated so as to be able to estimate the state of a dynamic system that changes over time by using a sequence of noisy measurements made on the system. The state vector contains all relevant information required to describe the system under investigation. In the context of visual tracking, the state may be the location, shape, or other parameters of the object of interest. The measurement vector represents observations that are related to the state vector. The measurement vector generally is of a lower dimension than the state vector. In order to analyze and make inferences about a dynamic system, at least two models are required. First, a model is needed to describe the evolution of the state over time (state equation), and second, a model is needed that relates the noisy measurements to the state (observation equation). We shall assume that these models are available in a probabilistic form. The probabilistic state space formulation and the additional requirement information is updated upon receipt of new measurements make this model well suited for a Bayesian approach. With a Bayesian approach, one attempts to construct the posterior probability density function (pdf) of the state based upon all available information. In principle, an optimal estimate of the state (with respect to any criterion) may be obtained from the pdf. A measurement of the accuracy of the estimate may also be obtained. For many problems an estimate is required every time that a measurement is received.

In this chapter, we introduce a general systematic framework for visual tracking. First, we introduce a sequential Bayesian estimation framework and sequential Monte Carlo filtering in Sections 8.2 and 8.3, respectively. These two form the theoretic basis for statistical visual tracking. In Section 8.4, we introduce how to construct an object representation model that uses color, shape, and exemplar images.

8.2 Sequential Bayesian Estimation

Visual tracking can be formulated as a sequential Bayesian estimation problem in a dynamic system, in which the state is estimated over time using a sequence of noisy measurements made on the object. In this case a recursive filter is a convenient solution. Such a filter consists of essentially two stages: prediction and update. The prediction stage uses the system model to predict the pdf of the state, forward from one measurement time to the next. The update operation uses the latest measurement to modify the predicted pdf. This is achieved by using Bayes' theorem, which provides a mechanism for updating knowledge about the target state in light of new information from the most recent measurement.

8.2.1 Problem Formulation of Bayesian Tracking

Consider the evolution of the state sequence $\{\mathbf{x}_k, k \in \mathbb{N}\}$ of a target, given by

$$\mathbf{x}_k = f(\mathbf{x}^{k-1}, \mathbf{v}_k) \tag{8.1}$$

where $f : \mathbb{R}^{n_x} \times \mathbb{R}^{n_v} \mapsto \mathbb{R}^{n_x} \times$ is a possibly nonlinear function of the state $\mathbf{x}^{k-1} = (\mathbf{x}_1, ..., \mathbf{x}_{k-1})$, $\{\mathbf{v}_k, k \in \mathbb{N}\}$ is an i.i.d process noise sequence, n_x and n_v are dimensions of the state and process noise vector, respectively. The objective of tracking is to recursively estimate $\mathbf{x}_k$ from measurement sequence $\mathbf{z}^k = (\mathbf{z}_1, ..., \mathbf{z}_k)$, where the measurement at time k is generated by the measurement process:

$$\mathbf{z}_k = h(\mathbf{x}_k, \mathbf{n}_k) \tag{8.2}$$

where $h : \mathbb{R}^{n_x} \times \mathbb{R}^{n_n} \mapsto \mathbb{R}^{n_z} \times$ is a possibly nonlinear function of the state $\mathbf{x}_k$, $\{\mathbf{n}_k, k \in \mathbb{N}\}$, is an i.i.d. process noise sequence, and n_n and n_z are dimensions of the measurement and process noise vectors, respectively. In particular, we seek a filtered estimate of $\mathbf{x}_k$ based upon the set of all available measurements $\mathbf{z}^k$ up to time k.

From a Bayesian perspective, the tracking problem is to recursively calculate some degree of belief in the state $\mathbf{x}_k$ at time k, taking different values, given the data up to time k, $\mathbf{z}^k$. In other words, the objective is to construct the pdf $p(\mathbf{x}_k|\mathbf{z}^k)$. This can be done by first modeling the state and measurement processes probabilistically, and then using Bayes' rule: (1) we can describe the state equation as a state transition density $f_k(\mathbf{x}_k|\mathbf{x}_{k-1}, \mathbf{v}_k)$, and the measurement process as $h_k(\mathbf{z}_t|\mathbf{x}_k), \mathbf{n}_k$; (2) It is assumed that the initial pdf $p(\mathbf{x}_0|\mathbf{z}_0)$, of the state vector, also known as the prior, is available, that in principle, the pdf may be obtained recursively in two stages: a prediction step and followed by an update step.

In the prediction step, we can suppose that the required pdf $p(\mathbf{x}_{k-1}|\mathbf{z}^{k-1})$ at time $k-1$ is available. Thus, the prediction step involves using the system model, Eq. (8.1), to obtain the prior pdf of $\mathbf{x}_{k-1}$ via the Chapman–Kolmogorov equation:

$$p(\mathbf{x}_k|\mathbf{z}^{k-1}) = \int p(\mathbf{x}_k|\mathbf{x}_{k-1})p(\mathbf{x}_{k-1}|\mathbf{z}^{k-1})d\mathbf{x}_{k-1} \tag{8.3}$$

Note, here we assume that $p(\mathbf{x}_k|\mathbf{x}_{k-1}, \mathbf{z}^{k-1}) = p(\mathbf{x}_k|\mathbf{x}_{k-1})$.

In the update step, with the available measurement $\mathbf{z}_k$, the prior $p(\mathbf{x}_k|\mathbf{z}^{k-1})$ can be updated via Bayes' rule:

$$p(\mathbf{x}_k|\mathbf{z}^k) = \frac{p(\mathbf{z}_k|\mathbf{x}_k)p(\mathbf{x}_k|\mathbf{z}^{k-1})}{p(\mathbf{z}_k|\mathbf{z}^{k-1})} \tag{8.4}$$

Where the normalized constant

$$p(\mathbf{z}_k|\mathbf{z}^{k-1}) = \int p(\mathbf{z}_k|\mathbf{x}_k)p(\mathbf{x}_k|\mathbf{z}^{k-1})d\mathbf{x}_k \tag{8.5}$$

depends on the likelihood function $p(\mathbf{z}_k|\mathbf{x}_k)$, defined by the measurement model in Eq. (8.2) and the known statistics of the measurement noise $\mathbf{n}$. The recurrent relations (8.3) and (11.15) form the basis for the optimal Bayesian solution.

For many problems an estimate is required every time that a measurement is received. In this case, the recursive filter above is a convenient solution. In practice, the recursive filter will take different forms depending upon the task. In the following sections, we introduce several typical recursive filters.

8.2.2 Kalman Filter

In the case of linear dynamical systems, both the state equation and measurement process are linear operators with Gaussian noise mixed in. That is, the state equation and measurement process can be written as

$$\mathbf{x}_k = F_k\mathbf{x}_k + \mathbf{v}_k \tag{8.6}$$

$$\mathbf{z}_k = H_k\mathbf{x}_k + \mathbf{n}_k \tag{8.7}$$

where F_k and H_K are known matrices defining the linear operators. The covariance of $\mathbf{v}_k$ and $\mathbf{n}_k$ are, respectively, Q_k and R_K. Here we consider the case in which $\mathbf{v}_k$ and $\mathbf{n}_k$ have a zero mean and are statistically independent.

The Kalman filter assumes that the posterior density at every time step is a Gaussian and hence parameterized by a mean and a covariance. If $p(\mathbf{x}_{k-1}|\mathbf{z}^{k-1})$ is Gaussian, it can be proved that $p(\mathbf{x}_k|\mathbf{z}^k)$ is also Gaussian. Thus the Kalman filter algorithm, derived using (8.3) and (11.15), can be viewed as having the following recursive relationship:

$$p(\mathbf{x}_{k-1}|\mathbf{z}^{k-1}) = N(\mathbf{x}_{k-1};\mathbf{m}_{k-1|k-1},P_{k-1|k-1}) \tag{8.8}$$

$$p(\mathbf{x}_k|\mathbf{z}^{k-1}) = N(\mathbf{x}_k;\mathbf{m}_{k|k-1},P_{k|k-1}) \tag{8.9}$$

$$p(\mathbf{x}_k|\mathbf{z}^k) = N(\mathbf{x}_k;\mathbf{m}_{k|k},P_{k|k}) \tag{8.10}$$

where

$$\mathbf{m}_{k|k-1} = F_k\mathbf{m}_{k-1|k-1} \tag{8.11}$$

$$P_{k|k-1} = Q_k + F_kP_{k-1|k-1}F_k^T \tag{8.12}$$

$$\mathbf{m}_{k|k} = \mathbf{m}_{k|k-1} + K_k(\mathbf{z}_k - H_k\mathbf{m}_{k|k-1}) \tag{8.13}$$

$$P_{k|k} = P_{k|k-1} - K_kH_kP_{k|k-1} \tag{8.14}$$

$$K_k = P_{k|k-1}H_k^TS_k^{-1} \tag{8.15}$$

$$S_k = H_kP_{k|k-1}H_k^T + R_k \tag{8.16}$$

where $N(\mathbf{x};\mathbf{m},P)$ is a Gaussian density with argument $\mathbf{x}$, mean $\mathbf{m}$, and covariance P. S_k and K_k are the covariance and the Kalman gain of the innovation term $\mathbf{z}_k - H_k\mathbf{m}_{k|k-1}$, respectively.

8.2.3 Grid-Based Methods

Grid-based methods provide the optimal recursion of the filtered density, $p(\mathbf{x}_k|\mathbf{z}^k)$ if the state space is discrete and consists of a finite number of states. Suppose the state space at time $k-1$ consists of discrete states $\mathbf{x}_{k-1}^{(i)}$, $i = 1, ..., N_s$. For each state $\mathbf{x}_{k-1}^{(i)}$, let the conditional probability of that state, given measurements up to time $k-1$ be denoted by $w_{k-1|k-1}^{(i)}$. Then, the posterior pdf $p(\mathbf{x}_{k-1}|\mathbf{z}^{k-1})$ at $k-1$ can be written as

$$p(\mathbf{x}_{k-1}|\mathbf{z}^{k-1}) = \sum_{i=1}^{N_s} w_{k-1|k-1}^{(i)}\delta(\mathbf{x}_{k-1} - \mathbf{x}_{k-1}^{(i)}) \tag{8.17}$$

So the prediction and update equations are as follows:

$$p(\mathbf{x}_k|\mathbf{z}^{k-1}) = \sum_{i=1}^{N_s} w_{k|k-1}^{(i)}\delta(\mathbf{x}_k - \mathbf{x}_k^{(i)}) \tag{8.18}$$

$$p(\mathbf{x}_k|\mathbf{z}^k) = \sum_{i=1}^{N_s} w_{k|k}^{(i)}\delta(\mathbf{x}_k - \mathbf{x}_k^{(i)}) \tag{8.19}$$

where

$$w_{k|k-1}^{(i)} = \sum_{j=1}^{N_s} w_{k-1|k-1}^{(j)} p(\mathbf{x}_k^{(i)}|\mathbf{x}_{k-1}^{(j)}) \tag{8.20}$$

$$w_{k|k}^{(i)} = \frac{w_{k|k-1}^{(i)} p(\mathbf{x}_k|\mathbf{x}_k^{(i)})}{\sum_{j=1}^{N_s} w_{k|k-1}^{(j)} p(\mathbf{z}_k|\mathbf{x}_k^{(j)})} \tag{8.21}$$

8.2.4 Sub-optimal Filter

In fact, in many applications, the posterior density will be non-Gaussian, and the space model are nonlinear, so the Kalman filter and grid-based methods cannot be used as described. Therefore, three approximate nonlinear Bayesian filters are proposed: (1) the extended Kalman filter, (2) approximate grid-based methods, and (3) the particle filter. We will introduce the first two suboptimal filters in the following. The particle filter will be specifically introduced in Section 8.3.

The extended Kalman filter (EKF) is based on a local linearization to approximate the state and observation equation in Eq. (8.1) and (8.2). We have

$$p(\mathbf{x}_{k-1}|\mathbf{z}^{k-1}) \approx N(\mathbf{x}_{k-1}; \mathbf{m}_{k-1|k-1}, P_{k-1|k-1}) \tag{8.22}$$
$$p(\mathbf{x}_k|\mathbf{z}^{k-1}) \approx N(\mathbf{x}_k; \mathbf{m}_{k|k-1}, P_{k|k-1}) \tag{8.23}$$
$$p(\mathbf{x}_k|\mathbf{z}^k) \approx N(\mathbf{x}_k; \mathbf{m}_{k|k}, P_{k|k}) \tag{8.24}$$

where

$$\mathbf{m}_{k|k-1} = \hat{F}_k(\mathbf{m}_{k-1|k-1}) \tag{8.25}$$
$$P_{k|k-1} = Q_k + \hat{F}_k P_{k-1|k-1} \hat{F}_k^T \tag{8.26}$$
$$\mathbf{m}_{k|k} = \mathbf{m}_{k|k-1} + K_k(\mathbf{z}_k - h(\mathbf{m}_{k|k-1})) \tag{8.27}$$
$$P_{k|k} = P_{k|k-1} - K_k \hat{H}_k P_{k|k-1} \tag{8.28}$$
$$K_k = P_{k|k-1} \hat{H}_k^T S_k^{-1} \tag{8.29}$$
$$S_k = \hat{H}_k P_{k|k-1} \hat{H}_k^T + R_k \tag{8.30}$$

where and $\hat{F}_k$ and $\hat{H}_k$ are local linearization of are now nonlinear functions $f(\cdot)$ and $h(\cdot)$:

$$\hat{F}_k = \frac{df(\mathbf{x})}{d\mathbf{x}}|_{\mathbf{x}=\mathbf{m}_{k-1|k-1}} \tag{8.31}$$
$$\hat{H}_k = \frac{dh(\mathbf{x})}{d\mathbf{x}}|_{\mathbf{x}=\mathbf{m}_{k|k-1}} \tag{8.32}$$

The EKF as described above utilizes the first term in a Taylor expansion of the nonlinear functions $f(\cdot)$ and $h(\cdot)$. A higher order EKF that retains further terms in the Taylor expansion exists, but the additional complexity has prohibited its widespread use. Recently, the "Unscented Kalman Filter," considers a set of points that are deterministically selected from the Gaussian approximation of $p(\mathbf{x}_k|\mathbf{z}^k)$. These points are propagated through the true nonlinearity and the parameters of the Gaussian approximation are then reestimated. For some applications, this filter has achieved better performance than a standard EKF since it better approximates the nonlinearity; the parameters of the Gaussian approximation are improved.

Approximate grid-based methods are used when the state space is continuous, but can be decomposed into cells $\{\mathbf{x}_k^i, i = 1, ..., N_s\}$, in which case a grid-based method can be used to approximate the posterior pdf.

$$p(\mathbf{x}_{k-1}|\mathbf{z}^{k-1}) \approx \sum_{i=1}^{N_s} w_{k-1|k-1}^{(i)} \delta(\mathbf{x}_{k-1} - \mathbf{x}_{k-1}^{(i)}) \tag{8.33}$$

The prediction and update equation can be written as:

$$p(\mathbf{x}_k|\mathbf{z}^{k-1}) \approx \sum_{i=1}^{N_s} w_{k|k-1}^{(i)} \delta(\mathbf{x}_k - \mathbf{x}_k^{(i)}) \tag{8.34}$$
$$p(\mathbf{x}_k|\mathbf{z}^k) \approx \sum_{i=1}^{N_s} w_{k|k}^{(i)} \delta(\mathbf{x}_k - \mathbf{x}_k^{(i)}) \tag{8.35}$$

where

$$w_{k|k-1}^{(i)} = \sum_{j=1}^{N_s} w_{k-1|k-1}^{(j)} \int p(\mathbf{x}_k|\bar{\mathbf{x}}_{k-1}^{(j)})d\mathbf{x} \tag{8.36}$$

$$w_{k|k}^{i} = \frac{w_{k|k-1}^{(i)} \int p(\mathbf{z}_k|\mathbf{x}_k^{(i)})dx}{\sum_{j=1}^{N_s} w_{k|k-1}^{(j)} \int p(\mathbf{z}_k|\mathbf{x}_k^{(j)})dx}. \tag{8.37}$$

Here $\bar{\mathbf{x}}_{k-1}^{(j)}$ denotes the center of the $j-1$st cell at time step $k-1$. The integral here is due to the fact that grid points $\{\mathbf{x}_k^{(i)}, i = 1,...,N_s\}$, represent regions of continuous state space, and thus the probabilities must be integrated over these regions. In practice, to simplify computation, a further approximation is made by computing these weights at the center of the cell corresponding to $\mathbf{x}_k^{(i)}$:

$$w_{k|k-1}^{(i)} \approx \sum_{j=1}^{N_s} w_{k-1|k-1}^{(j)} p(\bar{\mathbf{x}}_k^{(i)}|\bar{\mathbf{x}}_{k-1}^{(j)}) \tag{8.38}$$

$$w_{k|k}^{(i)} \approx \frac{w_{k|k-1}^{(i)} p(\mathbf{z}_k|\bar{\mathbf{x}}_k^{(i)})}{\sum_{j=1}^{N_s} w_{k|k-1}^{(j)} p(\mathbf{z}_k|\bar{\mathbf{x}}_k^{(j)})} \tag{8.39}$$

The grid must be sufficiently dense in order to arrive at a good approximation of the continuous state space. Another disadvantage of grid-based methods is that the state space must be predefined and therefore cannot be partitioned unevenly to give greater resolution in regions with a high probability density, unless prior knowledge is used.

8.3 Monte Carlo Filtering

In visual tracking, most dynamic systems are in practice nonlinear and non-Gaussian. Therefore, it is a significant challenge to find efficient methods for online (real time) estimation and prediction (filtering) of ever-changing system characteristics. Along with issues surrounding the processing of the continuous flow of the system information (observation), this has spawned great research interest in nonlinear filtering methods. In this section, we focus on sequential Monte Carlo filtering techniques.

8.3.1 Problem Formulation

Definition 1: The probabilistic definition of a dynamic system is: A sequence of evolving probability distributions $\pi_k(\mathbf{x}_k)$, indexed by discrete time intervals $k = 1,2,3,$ is called a probabilistic dynamic system. The state variable $\mathbf{x}_k$ can evolve in the following three ways: (1) increasing dimension: $\mathbf{x}_{k+1} = (\mathbf{x}^k, \mathbf{x}_{k+1})$, where $\mathbf{x}_{k+1}$ can be multidimensional component, (2) discharging: $\mathbf{x}_k = (\mathbf{x}_{k+1}, \mathbf{d}_k)$, and (3) no change $\mathbf{x}_{k+1} = \mathbf{x}_k$. In most applications, the difference between π_k and π_{k+1} is caused by the incorporation of new information in the analysis.

In order to analyze and make inference about a dynamic system, at least two models are required. This is the starting point of the state–space model. As shown in Fig. 8.2, the model consists of two parts: (1) a measurement (observed) process, which is formulated as $\mathbf{z}_k \sim h_k(\cdot|\mathbf{x}_k, \phi)$, and (2) state (unobserved or hidden) process, which is represented by a Markov process: $\mathbf{x}_k \sim f_k(\cdot|\mathbf{x}_{k-1}, \theta)$. The $\mathbf{z}_k$ represents observations and the $\mathbf{x}_k$ refers to the state. ϕ and θ denote parameters of the state and measurement processes, respectively. Of interest at any time k is the posterior distribution of the state $\mathbf{x}_k = (\phi, \theta, \mathbf{x}_1, \mathbf{x}_2 ..., \mathbf{x}_k)$, hence the target distribution is

$$\pi_k(\mathbf{x}_k) = \pi_k(\phi, \theta, \mathbf{x}_1, \mathbf{x}_2 ..., \mathbf{x}_k|\mathbf{z}^k) \propto p(\phi, \theta) \prod_{s=1}^{k} h_s(\mathbf{z}^s|\mathbf{x}_s, \phi) f_s(\mathbf{x}_s|\mathbf{x}_{s-1}, \theta) \quad (8.40)$$

where $\mathbf{z}^k = (\mathbf{z}_1, \mathbf{z}_2, ..., \mathbf{z}_k)$, and $\mathbf{z}_t$ can be multidimensional component.

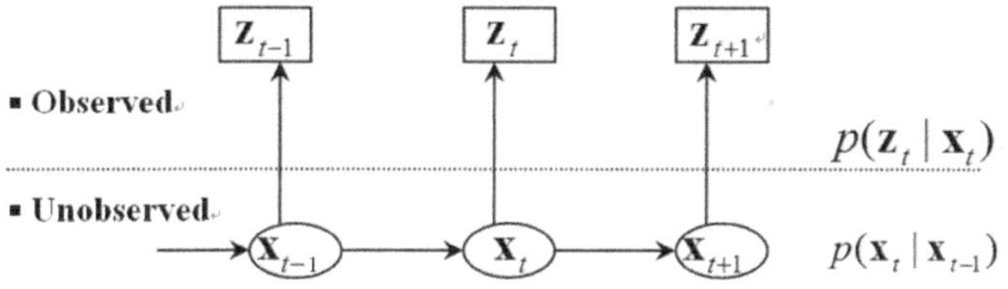

Fig. 8.2 The state space model of a probabilistic dynamic model

The primary object of study is the Markov process, $\mathbf{x}$, whose probability law is known but cannot be observed directly. It serves as a model for the true state of the system under study. Of interests in these systems is usually (a) prediction: $\pi(\mathbf{x}_{k+1}|\mathbf{x}^k)$, that is, when π_k can be extended to a new component $\mathbf{x}_{k+1}$, the best prediction of $\mathbf{x}_{k+1}$ before new information arrives is via π_k, (b) smoothing: $\pi_{k+1}(\mathbf{x}_k)$, that is, the revision of the previous state given new information, (c) filtering: $\pi_{k+1}(\mathbf{x}_{k+1})$, that is, what we know in light of the new information. The solution of the sequential estimation problem is given by posterior density $p(\mathbf{x}^k|\mathbf{z}^k)$, by recursively computing a marginal of the posterior, the filtering density $p(\mathbf{x}_k|\mathbf{z}^k)$, one need not to keep track of the complete history of the state. Given the filtering density, a number of estimates of the system state can be calculated: mean, mode, median, confidence intervals, kurtosis, etc.

Obviously, nonlinear filtering represents the computation of a conditional probability measure. Since computational resources are finite, one must choose how to give a finite representation of the probability measure. To date, there has yet to be developed a universally effective algorithm for dealing with nonlinear and non-Gaussian systems. Depending upon the features of individual problems, some generalization of the Kalman methodology for nonlinear systems can be effective. However, in the context of visual tracking, these Kalman-based methods may fail. Monte Carlo filtering techniques are proposed for nonlinear non-Gaussain filtering problems.

Monte Carlo filtering (MCF) can be loosely defined as a set of methods that use Monte Carlo simulation to solve online estimation and prediction problems in a dynamic system. Compared with traditional filtering methods, simple, flexible, yet powerful MCF techniques provide an effective means to overcome computational difficulties in dealing with nonlinear dynamic models. To implement Monte Carlo for a dynamic system, we need, at any given time, random samples drawn from $\pi_k(\mathbf{x}_k)$. In those cases where directly generating independent samples from $\pi_k(\mathbf{x}_k)$ is not possible, we must either opt for an importance sampling strategy, in which random samples are generated from a trial distribution different from, but close to, the target distribution and then weighted according to an importance ratio; or produce statistically dependent samples based upon a Markov Chain Monte Carlo sampling, which runs a Markov chain whose stationary distribution is π.

Roughly speaking, two types of methods can be used to achieve this end: (1) static Monte Carlo methods, which treat the sample of each time separately and repeat same kind of iterative process. In other words, all of the results obtained at time k are discarded when the system evolves from π_k to π_{k+1}, and (2) sequential Monte Carlo methods, which take a different approach by reusing the sample $S_k = \{\mathbf{x}^{k(i)}, i = 1, ...m\}$ from π_k and attaching to each sample one or several $\mathbf{x}_{k+1}$ draw from some appropriate distribution $g_{k+1}(\cdot|\mathbf{x}_k^{(i)})$, and in which the evolved sample $\mathbf{x}^{k+1(i)} = (\mathbf{x}^{k(i)}, \mathbf{x}_{k+1}^{(i)})$ often needs to be re-weighted or re-sampled to accommodate π_{k+1}. Sequential Monte Carlo techniques achieve the filtering task by recursively generating Monte Carlo samples of the state variables or some other latent variables. These methods are often more adaptive to features of the target system because of the flexible nature of the Monte Carlo simulations. One of the key elements among all the MCF techniques is a recursive use of the importance sampling principle, which leads to a more precise name, sequential importance sampling (SIS).

8.3.2 Sequential Importance Sampling

The notion behind importance sampling is that one should focus on the regions of "importance" so as to save computation resources. This is essential for Monte Carlo computation in high-dimensional models in computer vision. In high-dimensional problems, the region in which the target function is meaningfully nonzero compared with the whole space is like a needle in a haystack. Sampling uniformly is bound to fail in these problems. Another reason for importance sampling is that it is usually infeasible to generate an i.i.d. random sample from the target distribution π directly in many real applications. In this case, we may generate random samples from a different, but similar, trivial distribution $g(\cdot)$, and then correct the bias by using the importance sampling procedure.

Suppose one is interested in computing $\mu = E_{\pi}\{h(\mathbf{x})\}$. Using importance sampling, we can first generate independent samples $\mathbf{x}^1,...,\mathbf{x}^m$ from an easy-to-sample trial distribution, $g(\cdot)$, and then correcting the bias by incorporating the importance weight $w^{(i)} \propto \pi(\mathbf{x}^{(i)})/g(\mathbf{x}^{(i)})$ for $i = 1,...,m$. Finally, we can approximate μ by

$$\hat{\mu} = \frac{\sum_{i=1}^{m} w^{(i)}\mathbf{x}^{(i)}}{\sum_{i=1}^{m} w^{(i)}} \tag{8.41}$$

In this way, we need to only know the ratio $\pi(\mathbf{x})/g(\mathbf{x})$ up to a multiplicative constant. An idealized sampling distribution g should be reasonably close to π; in particular, that g must have a longer tail than π. Note that finding a good trial distribution g can be a major undertaking in high-dimensional problems.

SIS techniques build up the trial sampling distribution sequentially and compute the importance weights recursively. More precisely, we first decompose the random variable $\mathbf{x}$ into a number of components, $\mathbf{x} = (x_1,...,x_d)$, and then build up the trial distribution as

$$g(\mathbf{x}) = g_1(x_1)g_2(x_2|x_1)...g_d(x_d|x_1,...,x_{d-1}) \tag{8.42}$$

where g_t are chosen by the investigator so as to make the joint sampling distribution of $\mathbf{x}$ as close as to the target distribution, $\pi(\mathbf{x})$, as possible. When this recursion is repeated independently m times, we obtain m i.i.d. random samples $\mathbf{x}^{(1)},...,\mathbf{x}^{(m)}$ from the trial distribution $g(\mathbf{x})$, which can be used to estimate integrals related to the target distribution π. The importance weight of the sample simulated from $g(\mathbf{x})$ can be evaluated either at the end when all the parts of $\mathbf{x}$ are in place, or recursively

$$w_t = w_{t-1}\frac{\pi_t(x_1,...,x_t)}{g_t(x_t|x_1,...,x_{t-1})\pi_{t-1}(x_1,...,x_{t-1})}, t = 1,...,d \tag{8.43}$$

in which case the sequence of distributions $\pi_1,...\pi_d$ is referred as a sequence of auxiliary distributions. A necessary condition for these distributions is that $\pi_d(x_1,...,x_d) = \pi(x_1,...,x_d)$. The π can be thought of as an approximation to the marginal distribution

$$\pi(x_1,...x_t) = \int \pi(\mathbf{x})dx_{t+1}\cdots dx_d \tag{8.44}$$

of the partial sample $\mathbf{x}_t = (x_1,...x_d)$.

In the following, we introduce some concepts and techniques of sequential importance sampling.

8.3.2.1 Basic Concepts

Definition 2: A random variable $\mathbf{x}$ drawn from a distribution g is said to be properly weighted by a weighting function $w(\mathbf{x})$ with respect to the distribution π if for any integrable function $h(\cdot)$:

$$E_g\{w(\mathbf{x})h(\mathbf{x})\} = E_\pi\{h(\mathbf{x})\} \tag{8.45}$$

where E_g denotes expectation with respect to the distribution g. A set of random draws and weights, $\{x^{(i)}, w^{(i)} i = 1, 2...\}$, is said to be properly weighted with respect to π if for any integrable function h

$$\lim_{m \to \infty} \frac{\sum_{i=1}^{m} w^{(i)} h(x^{(i)})}{\sum_{i=1}^{m} w^{(i)}} = E_\pi(h(x)) \tag{8.46}$$

In a practical sense, we can think of π as being approximated by the discrete distribution supported on $\mathbf{x}^{(i)}$ with probabilities proportional to the weights $w^{(i)}$. In other words, a probability distribution π, no matter how complicated it is, can be represented, at least conceptually, by any set of properly weighted samples. This is also the key concept in all Monte Carlo computations.

If $\mathbf{x}$ has a "natural decomposition" $\mathbf{x} = (x_0, ..., x_N)$, we can imagine building up $\mathbf{x}$ sequentially by adding one component a time. Let $S_t = \{x_t^{(i)}, i = 1, ..., m\}$ denote a set of random draws that are properly weighted by the set of weights $W_t = \{w_t^{(i)}, i = 1, ..., m\}$ with respect to π_t. Let H_{t+1} be the sample space of x_{t+1}, and let g_{t+1} be a trial distribution. Then the sequential importance sample procedure consists of recursive application of the following steps:

1. For $i = 1, \ldots, m$
2. Draw $x_{t+1}^{(i)}$ from $g_{t+1}(x_{t+1}|\mathbf{x}_t^{(i)})$; attach it to $\mathbf{x}_t^{(i)}$ to form a $\mathbf{x}_{t+1}^{(i)} = (\mathbf{x}_t^{(i)}, x_{t+1}^{(i)})$.
3. Compute

$$w_{t+1}^{(j)} = w_t^{(i)} \frac{\pi_{t+1}(\mathbf{x}_{t+1}^{(i)})}{\pi_t(\mathbf{x}_t^{(i)}) g_{t+1}(x_{t+1}^{(i)}|\mathbf{x}_t^{(i)})} \tag{8.47}$$

It is easy to show that $(x_{t+1}^{(i)}, w_{t+1}^{(i)})$ is a properly weighted sample of π_{t+1}. Thus SIS can be applied recursively for $t = 1, 2, \cdots$ to accommodate an evolving dynamic system. It is often fruitful to construct the trial distribution sequentially. Indeed, in many real problems hints are available for how to go about choosing those g_t's. More formally, these hints can be formulated as an evolving probabilistic dynamic system. So we can let $g_{t+1}(x_{t+1}|\mathbf{x})$ be the same as or at least close to $\pi_{t+1}(x_{t+1}|\mathbf{x})$.

8.3.2.2 Sampling Strategies

Simple application of this sequential built-up strategy is still not good enough to simulate π. Several strategies such as resampling, reweighting, and rejection have been proposed to improve the performance of SIS.

In a probabilistic dynamic system with SIS, resampling helps one steer in the right direction. Suppose at time t we have a set of random samples $S_t = \{\mathbf{x}_t^{(i)}, w_t^{(i)}, i = 1, \cdots, m\}$ properly weighted with respect to π. Then, we can generate another discrete representation as follows:

1. For $j = 1, \cdots, \tilde{m}$, let $\tilde{\mathbf{x}}_t^{(j)}$ be $\mathbf{x}_t^{(i)}$ independently with probability proportional to $\alpha^{(i)}$, and let the new weight associated with this sample be $\tilde{w}_t^{(j)} = w_t^{(i)}/\alpha^{(i)}$.
2. Return the new representation $\tilde{S}_t = \{\tilde{\mathbf{x}}_t^{(i)}, \tilde{w}_t^{(i)}, i = 1, \cdots, \tilde{m}\}$.

A few heuristics support this view: (a) resampling can prune away those hopelessly bad samples by giving them a small $\alpha^{(i)}$, and (b) resampling can produce multiple copies of the good samples by assigning them a large $\alpha^{(i)}$ to help generate better future samples in the SIS setting. A general choice of $\alpha^{(i)}$ is $\alpha^{(i)} = [w_t^{(i)}]^{\alpha}$, where α can vary according to the coefficient of variation of the w_t, ζ_t.

$$\zeta_t^2 = \frac{var(w_t^{(i)})}{(E(w_t^{(i)}))^2} \tag{8.48}$$

It should be noted that extra variance is introduced by resampling.

Instead of resampling, a more efficient approach is partial deterministic reallocation, which can be implemented so as to generate $\tilde{S}_t$ from S_t.

1. For $j = 1, \cdots, \tilde{m}$
   - If $\alpha^j \geq 1$, retain $k_j = \lfloor \alpha^j \rfloor$ copies of the samples $\mathbf{x}_t^{(j)}$; then assign weight $\tilde{w}_t^{(j)} = w_t^{(j)}/k_j$ to each copy.
   - If $\alpha^j < 1$, remove the sample with probability $1 - \alpha^j$, and then assign weight $\tilde{w}_t^{(j)} = w_t^{(j)}/\alpha_j$ to the surviving sample.
2. Return the set $\tilde{S}_t$, consisting of the new set of x_t's and $\tilde{w}_t$.

The above scheme tends to slightly decrease the total sample size when applied. Alternatively, one can choose $k_j = \lfloor \alpha^j \rfloor + 1$, which will tend to slightly increase the sample size.

Another useful technique for rejuvenating a sequential importance sampler is the rejection control (RC) method, which can be understood as a combination of the rejection method and importance sampling. In RC, one monitors the coefficient of variation of the importance weights for $\mathbf{x}_t^{(i)}$. This can be used to derive a heuristic criterion, i.e., the effective sample size:

$$ESS_t = \frac{m}{1 + \zeta_t^2} \tag{8.49}$$

which is heuristically understood as the equivalent number of i.i.d samples at time t. Once ESS_t drops below a threshold, say $ESS_t \leq \alpha_0 m, (0 < \alpha_0 \leq 1)$, we refer to this time as a (dynamic) "checkpoint." The checkpoint sequence can also be prescribed in advance, in which case the checkpoints are called static checkpoints.

When encountering a new checkpoint, we compute a control threshold c_k, which may be a quantity given in advance, or the median, or a quantile of the $w_{t_k}^{(i)}$. Then we check through every sample and decide whether to accept it according to the probability $\min\{1, w_{t_k}^{(i)}/c_k\}$. In other words, those samples with weights greater than or equal to c_k are automatically accepted, whereas those with weights less than c_k are accepted only with a certain probability. All accepted samples are given a new weight $\tilde{w}_{t_k}^{(i)} = \max\{c_k, w_{t_k}^{(i)}\}$, whereas. Rejected samples are restarted from $t = 0$ and rechecked at all previous checkpoints. One problem with RC is that its computation cost increases rapidly as t increases, although the threshold c_k can be adjusted by the user to compromise between computation cost and the ESS_t.

To overcome the computational difficulties associated with RC, PRC (partial RC) was proposed in Liu et al. (1999), which combines RC with resampling and can be understood as a sort of delayed resampling. More precisely, if t is the kth checkpoint, do the following:

1. Compute the control threshold c_k as either the median or a quantile of the weights $\{w_t^{(j)}, j = 1, \cdots, m\}$.
2. For $j = 1, \cdots, m$, accept the jth sample with probability $w_t^{(j)}$. If accepted, update its weights to $\max\{w_t^{(j)}, c_k\}$.
3. For any rejected sample at time t_k , go back to the previous check-point t_{k-1} to draw a previous partial sample $\mathbf{x}_{t_{k-1}}^{(j)}$. This partial sample is drawn from the set $S_{t_{k-1}}$ with probability proportional to its weights at time t_{k-1} (i.e., $w_{t_{k-1}}^{(j)}$) and give an initial weight of $W_{t_{k-1}}$, where $W_{t_{k-1}} = \sum_{j=1}^{m} w_{t_{k-1}}^{(j)}$. Apply the SIS recursion to this partial sample until the current time t_k; conduct the same RC in step 1 and 2.
4. Repeat Step 3 until acceptance.

When doing inference with the samples, several issues concerning the statistical efficiency of the estimates are worth mentioning:

- Estimation should be done before a resampling step, because resampling introduces extra random variation in the current sample.
- Rao-Blackwellization can improve the accuracy of the estimation. This reflects a basic principle in Monte Carlo computation: one should carry out analytical computation as much as possible. When weight (8.47) does not depend upon $\mathbf{x}_{t+1}$, such as is the case when using the optimal trial distribution $g_{t+1} = \pi(\mathbf{x}_{t+1}|\mathbf{x}^t)$, the current state should be estimated before it is drawn from g_{t+1}, by using

$$\hat{E}_{\pi_{t+1}}(h(x_{t+1})) = \frac{\sum_{j=1}^{m} w_{t+1}^{(j)} E_{\pi_{t+1}}(h(\mathbf{x}_{t+1}|\mathbf{x}^{t(j)}))}{\sum_{j=1}^{m} w_{t+1}^{(j)}} \tag{8.50}$$

provided that $E_{\pi_{t+1}}(h(\mathbf{x}_{t+1}|\mathbf{x}^{t(j)}))$ can be calculated easily.

- Delayed estimation (i.e., estimation of $E_{\pi_t}(h(\mathbf{x}_{t-k}))$) usually is more accurate than concurrent estimation (estimation of $E_{\pi_{t-k}}(h(\mathbf{x}_{t-k}))$ at time $t-k$), since the estimation is based upon more information.

8.3.3 Sequential Monte Carlo Filtering

As discussed above, the key idea behind SIS is to represent the target distribution by a set of random samples with associated weights and to compute estimates based upon these samples and weights. This forms the basis for most sequential Monte Carlo (SMC) filters developed over recent decades. Now we turn to the problem of nonlinear, non-Gaussian filtering using sequential importance sampling techniques.

Consider the dynamic system in Fig. 8.2. Suppose that the posterior distribution of state $\mathbf{x}_{k-1}$ is given by $p(\mathbf{x}_{k-1}|\mathbf{z}^{k-1})$. Then the predictive distribution for $\mathbf{x}_k$ is

$$p(\mathbf{x}_k|\mathbf{z}^{k-1}) \int f_t(\mathbf{x}_k|\mathbf{x}_{k-1})p(\mathbf{x}_{k-1}|\mathbf{z}^{k-1})d\mathbf{x}_k \tag{8.51}$$

Since analytical computation with this distribution is often difficult, a possible alternative is a Monte Carlo approximation. More precisely, if we can draw $\mathbf{x}_{k-1}^{(i)}$ from $p(\mathbf{x}_{k-1}|\mathbf{z}^{k-1})$, then we can approximate $p(\mathbf{x}_k|\mathbf{z}^{k-1})$ by

$$\hat{p}(\mathbf{x}_k|\mathbf{z}^{k-1}) = \frac{1}{N}\sum_{i=1}^{N} f_k(\mathbf{x}_k|\mathbf{x}_{k-1}^{(i)}) \tag{8.52}$$

In many cases, however, directly sampling from $p(\mathbf{x}_k|\mathbf{z}^k)$ is infeasible, but drawing from a trial $g(\mathbf{x}_k|\mathbf{z}^k)$ distribution is easy. If this is the case, we need to modify Eq. (8.52) by adjusting the weight of each sample $\mathbf{x}_{k-1}^{(i)}$ drawn from $g(\mathbf{x}_k|\mathbf{z}^k)$:

$$\tilde{p}(\mathbf{x}_k|\mathbf{z}_{k-1}) = \frac{1}{W_{k-1}}\sum_{i=1}^{N} w_{k-1}^{(i)} f_k(\mathbf{x}_k|\mathbf{x}_{k-1}^{(i)}) \tag{8.53}$$

where $w_{k-1}^{(i)} = \frac{p(\mathbf{x}_{k-1}^{(m)}|\mathbf{z}^{k-1})}{g(\mathbf{x}_{k-1}|\mathbf{z}^{k-1})}$ and $W_{t-1} = \sum_{i=1}^{N} w_{t-1}^{(i)}$. The $w_{t-1}^{(i)}$ are usually called "importance weights."

In the update step, when new data $\mathbf{z}_t$ is observed, the posterior distribution of $\mathbf{x}_k$ is updated as

$$\tilde{p}(\mathbf{x}_k|\mathbf{z}^k) \propto \frac{1}{W_k}\sum_{i=1}^{N} w_k^{(i)} f_k(\mathbf{x}_k|\mathbf{x}_{k-1}^{(i)}) \tag{8.54}$$

where the importance weights $w_t^{(i)}$ are updated as $w_k^{(i)} = w_{k-1}^{(i)} h_t(\mathbf{z}_k|\mathbf{x}_k)$.

From this approximation, one can conduct an SIS step to obtain an approximate sample from Eq. (8.54), which forms the basis for the bootstrap filter Gordon et al. (1993). Many improvements upon this basic algorithm have been proposed, Liu and

Chen (2001) rewrite Eq. (8.54) as

$$\tilde{p}(\mathbf{x}_k|\mathbf{z}^k) \propto \frac{1}{W_k}\sum_{i=1}^{N} w_k^{(i)} p(\mathbf{x}_k|\mathbf{z}_k, \mathbf{x}_{k-1}^{(i)}) \tag{8.55}$$

where $w_k^{(i)} = \mu_k^{(i)} \times w_{k-1}^{(i)}$ and $W_k \sum_{i=1}^{N} w_k^{(i)}$,

$$\mu_k^{(i)} = \int h_k(\mathbf{z}_k|\mathbf{x}_k) f_k(\mathbf{x}_k|\mathbf{x}_{k-1}^{(i)}) d\mathbf{x}_k \tag{8.56}$$

$$p(\mathbf{x}_k|\mathbf{z}_k, \mathbf{x}_{k-1}^{(i)}) = \frac{1}{\mu_k^{(i)}} h_k(\mathbf{z}_k|\mathbf{x}_k) f_k(\mathbf{x}_k|\mathbf{x}_{k-1}^{(i)}) \tag{8.57}$$

Thus, we can draw an exact sample from (8.55) instead of an approximate one from (8.54).

Generally, under the SIS framework, we proceed from a discrete representation $S_{k-1} = \{\mathbf{x}_{k-1}^{(i)}, w_{k-1}^{(i)}, i = 1, \cdots, N\}$ of the posterior distribution $p(\mathbf{x}_{k-1}|\mathbf{z}^{k-1})$ to the discrete representation $S_k = \{\mathbf{x}_k^{(i)}, w_k^{(i)}, i = 1, \cdots, N\}$ of $p(\mathbf{x}_k|\mathbf{z}^k)$ as follows: draw a sample from $g_k(\mathbf{x}_k|\mathbf{x}^{k-1})$ to form $\mathbf{x}^{k(i)} = (\mathbf{x}^{k-1(i)}, \mathbf{x}_k^{(i)})$; attach to it a weight computed recursively according to

$$w_k^{(i)} = w_{k-1}^{(i)} \times \frac{f_k(\mathbf{x}_k^{(i)}|\mathbf{x}^{k-1(i)}) h_k(\mathbf{z}_k|\mathbf{x}_k^{(i)})}{g_k(\mathbf{x}_k^{(i)}|\mathbf{x}^{k-1(i)})} \tag{8.58}$$

Then S_t is proper with respect to π_t. If the weights are too skewed (as measured by ESS_t), we can do resampling, or RC or both as described in Section 8.3.2.2.

8.3.4 Particle Filter

Particle filters are sequential Monte Carlo methods based upon point mass (or particle) representations of probability densities. Let $\{\mathbf{x}^{k(i)}, w_k^{(i)}, i = 1 \cdots N_s\}$ characterize the posterior pdf $p(\mathbf{x}^k|\mathbf{z}^k)$, where $\{\mathbf{x}^{k(i)}\}$ is a set of support points with associated weights $\{w_k^{(i)}\}$ and $\mathbf{x}^k = (\mathbf{x}_1, \cdots, \mathbf{x}_k)$ is the set of all state up to time k. Then the posterior density at time k can be approximated as follows:

$$p(\mathbf{x}^k|\mathbf{z}^k) \approx \sum_{i=1}^{N_s} w_k^{(i)} \delta(\mathbf{x}^k - \mathbf{x}^{k(i)}) \tag{8.59}$$

We therefore have a discrete weighted approximation to the true posterior, $p(\mathbf{x}^k|\mathbf{z}^k)$. The weights are chosen using the principle of importance sampling. So if the samples $\mathbf{x}^{k(i)}$ were drawn from an importance density $q(\mathbf{x}^k|\mathbf{z}^k)$, then the weights are defined as

$$w_k^{(i)} \propto \frac{p(\mathbf{x}^{k(i)}|\mathbf{z}^k)}{q(\mathbf{x}^k|\mathbf{z}^k)} \tag{8.60}$$

In the sequential case, at each iteration, one could have samples constituting an approximation to the $p(\mathbf{x}^{k-1}|\mathbf{z}^{k-1})$, and want to approximate $p(\mathbf{x}^k|\mathbf{z}^k)$ with a new set of samples. If the importance density chosen to factorize is such that:

$$q(\mathbf{x}^k|\mathbf{z}^k) = q(x^k|\mathbf{x}^{k-1},\mathbf{z}^k)q(\mathbf{x}^{k-1}|\mathbf{z}^{k-1}) \tag{8.61}$$

Then one can obtain samples $\mathbf{x}^{k(i)} \sim q(\mathbf{x}^k|\mathbf{z}^k)$ by augmenting each of the existing samples $\mathbf{x}^{k-1(i)} \sim q(\mathbf{x}^{k-1}|\mathbf{z}^{k-1})$ with the new state $\mathbf{x}_k^i \sim q(\mathbf{x}_k|\mathbf{x}^{k-1},\mathbf{z}^k)$. To derive the weight update equation, $p(\mathbf{x}^k|\mathbf{z}^k)$ is expressed in terms of $p(\mathbf{x}^{k-1}|\mathbf{z}^{k-1})$, $p(\mathbf{z}_k|\mathbf{x}_k)$ and $p(\mathbf{x}_k|\mathbf{x}_{k-1})$ via Bayes' rule,

$$\begin{aligned}
p(\mathbf{x}^k|\mathbf{z}^k) &= \frac{p(\mathbf{z}_k|\mathbf{x}^k,\mathbf{z}^{k-1})p(\mathbf{x}^k|\mathbf{z}^{k-1})}{p(\mathbf{z}_k|\mathbf{z}^{k-1})} \\
&= \frac{p(\mathbf{z}_k|\mathbf{x}^k,\mathbf{z}^{k-1})p(\mathbf{x}_k|\mathbf{x}^{k-1},\mathbf{z}^{k-1})p(\mathbf{x}^{k-1}|\mathbf{z}^{k-1})}{p(\mathbf{z}_k|\mathbf{z}^{k-1})} \\
&= \frac{p(\mathbf{z}_k|\mathbf{x}_k)p(\mathbf{x}_k|\mathbf{x}_{k-1})p(\mathbf{x}^{k-1}|\mathbf{z}^{k-1})}{p(\mathbf{z}_k|\mathbf{z}^{k-1})} \\
&\propto p(\mathbf{z}_k|\mathbf{x}_k)p(\mathbf{x}_k|\mathbf{x}_{k-1})p(\mathbf{x}^{k-1}|\mathbf{z}^{k-1})
\end{aligned} \tag{8.62}$$

By substituting Eqs. (8.62) and (8.61) into Eq. (8.60), the weight update equation can then be shown to be

$$w_k^{(i)} \propto \frac{p(\mathbf{z}_k|\mathbf{x}_k^{(i)})p(\mathbf{x}_k^{(i)}|\mathbf{x}_{k-1}^{(i)})p(\mathbf{x}^{k-1(i-1)}|\mathbf{z}^{k-1})}{q(\mathbf{x}^k|\mathbf{x}^{k-1},\mathbf{z}^k)q(\mathbf{x}^{k-1}|\mathbf{z}^{k-1})} = w_{k-1}^i \frac{p(\mathbf{z}_k|\mathbf{x}_k^{(i)})p(\mathbf{x}_k^{(i)}|\mathbf{x}_{k-1}^{(i)})}{q(\mathbf{x}_k^{(i)}|\mathbf{x}^{k-1(i)},\mathbf{z}^k)} \tag{8.63}$$

Furthermore, if $q(\mathbf{x}_k|\mathbf{x}^{k-1},\mathbf{z}^k) = q(\mathbf{x}_k|\mathbf{x}_{k-1},\mathbf{z}^k)$, then the importance density only depends on $\mathbf{x}_{k-1}$ and $\mathbf{z}_k$. This is particularly useful in the common case in which only a filtered estimate of $p(\mathbf{x}_k|\mathbf{z}^k)$ is required at each time step. In this case, only $\mathbf{x}_k^{(i)}$ needs to be stored, and so one can discard the path $\mathbf{x}^{k-1(i)}$, and the history of observations $\mathbf{z}^{k-1}$. The modified weight is then

$$w_k^{(i)} \propto w_{k-1}^i \frac{p(\mathbf{z}_k|\mathbf{x}_k^{(i)})p(\mathbf{x}_k^{(i)}|\mathbf{x}_{k-1}^{(i)})}{q(\mathbf{x}_k^{(i)}|\mathbf{x}_{k-1}^{(i)},\mathbf{z}_k)} \tag{8.64}$$

and the posterior filtered density $p(\mathbf{x}_k|\mathbf{z}^k)$ can be approximated as

$$p(\mathbf{x}_k|\mathbf{z}^k) \approx \sum_{i=1}^{N_s} w_k^{(i)} \delta(\mathbf{x}_k - \mathbf{x}_k^{(i)}) \tag{8.65}$$

So the SIS particle filter is given in Table 8.1.

Table 8.1 SIS Particle filter

Generate weighted samples $\{\mathbf{x}_k^{(i)}, w_k^{(i)}, i = 1, \cdots, N_s\}$ from $\{\mathbf{x}_{k-1}^{(i)}, w_{k-1}^{(i)}, i = 1, \cdots, N_s\}$.

1. For $i = 1, \cdots, N_s$;
2. Draw samples $\mathbf{x}_k^{(i)} \sim q(\mathbf{x}_k|\mathbf{x}_{k-1}^{(i)}, \mathbf{z}_k)$;
3. Assign the sample a weight $w_k^{(i)}$, according to Eq. (8.64);
4. END.

However, a common problem with the SIS particle filter is the degeneracy phenomenon, in which, all but one particle has negligible weight after a few iterations. It has been shown that the variance of the importance weights can only increase over time, and it is impossible to avoid this problem. So we can use techniques described in Section 8.3.2.2 to solve this problem. In addition, the choice of importance density is very important.

The optimal importance density function which minimizes the variance of the true weights $w_k^{*(i)} = p(\mathbf{x}_k^{(i)}|\mathbf{z}^k)/q(\mathbf{x}_k^{(i)}|\mathbf{x}_{k-1}^{(i)}, \mathbf{z}_k)$ is conditioned on $\mathbf{x}_k^{(i)}$ and $\mathbf{z}_k$ given by the following:

$$q(\mathbf{x}_k|\mathbf{x}_{k-1}^{(i)}, \mathbf{z}_k)_{opt} = \frac{p(\mathbf{z}_k|\mathbf{x}_k, \mathbf{x}_k^{(i)})p(\mathbf{x}_k|x_{k-1}^{(i)})}{p(\mathbf{z}_k|\mathbf{x}_{k-1}^{(i)})} \tag{8.66}$$

Thus, we obtain the optimal weight update

$$w_k^{(i)} \propto w_{k-1}^{(i)} p(\mathbf{z}_k|\mathbf{x}_{k-1}^{(i)}) = w_{k-1}^{(i)} \int p(\mathbf{z}_k|\mathbf{x}_k)p(\mathbf{x}_k|\mathbf{x}_{k-1}^{(i)}) \tag{8.67}$$

This choice of importance density is optimal since for a given $\mathbf{x}_{k-1}^{(i)}$, $w_k^{(i)}$ takes the same value regardless of which sample is drawn from $q(\mathbf{x}_k|\mathbf{x}_{k-1}^{(i)}, \mathbf{z}_k)_{opt}$. Hence conditional on $\mathbf{x}_{k-1}^{(i)}$, $var(w_k^{(i)}) = 0$. However this optimal importance density suffers from two major drawbacks. It requires the ability to sample from $p(\mathbf{x}_k|\mathbf{x}_{k-1}^{(i)}, \mathbf{z}_k)$ and to evaluate the integral over the new state. There are two cases in which use of the optimal importance density is possible: (1) $\mathbf{x}_k$ is a member of a finite state, so the integral becomes a sum and sampling from $p(\mathbf{x}_k|\mathbf{x}_{k-1}^{(i)}, \mathbf{z}_k)_{opt}$ is possible. An example of this case is the jump Markov linear system (Doucet et al. 2001) and (2) when $p(\mathbf{x}_k|\mathbf{x}_{k-1}^{(i)}, \mathbf{z}_k)_{opt}$ is Gaussian. This can occur if the dynamics are nonlinear and the measurement linear. Finally, it is often convenient to choose the importance density to be the prior $q(\mathbf{x}_k|\mathbf{x}_{k-1}^{(i)}, \mathbf{z}_k) = p(\mathbf{x}_k|\mathbf{x}_{k-1}^{(i)})$. This is the most common choice and it is easy to implement.

In Table 8.2, we present a generic particle filter which considers both the resampling and the importance sampling density.

Table 8.2 Generic particle filter

Generate weighted samples $\{\mathbf{x}_k^{(i)}, w_k^{(i)}, i = 1, \cdots, N_s\}$ from $\{\mathbf{x}_{k-1}^{(i)}, w_{k-1}^{(i)}, i = 1, \cdots, N_s\}$ with predefined effective sample size threshold N_T.

1. For $i = 1, \cdots, N_s$
   a. Draw $\tilde{\mathbf{x}}_k^{(i)} \sim p(\mathbf{x}_k|\mathbf{x}_{k-1}^{(i)})$;
   b. Assign the sample a weight $\tilde{w}_k^{(i)} = w_{k-1}^{(i)} p(\mathbf{z}_k|\tilde{\mathbf{x}}_k^i)$.
2. Normalize $\tilde{w}_k^{(i)}$;
3. Calculate $\hat{N}_{eff} = \frac{1}{\sum_{i=1}^{N_s} \tilde{w}_k^{(i)}}$;
4. If $\hat{N}_{eff} < N_T$, do resampling as
   a. Initialize the cumulative distribution function (CDF): $c_1 = 0$;
      - For $i = 2, \cdots, N_s$, $c_i = c_{i-1} + \tilde{w}_k^{(i)}$.
   b. Start at the bottom of the CDF: $i = 1$;
   c. Draw a start point:$u_1 \sim U(0, N_s^{-1})$;
   d. For $j = 1, \cdots, N_s$
      i. Move along the CDF: $u_j = u_1 + N_s^{-1}(j-1)$;
      ii. While $u_j > c_i$, $i = i+1$.
   e. Assign sample $\mathbf{x}_k^j = \tilde{\mathbf{x}}_k^i$.
   f. Assign weight $w_k^j = N_s^{-1}$.
5. Do next iteration.

8.4 Object Representation Model

The object representation problem is a fundamental and common problem for several visual tasks including object detection, recognition, and tracking. In these visual tasks, the object representation consists of selecting features of the object and defining a measure of visual similarity in order to discriminate the object of interest from other objects and the background in the video frame image. When suitable representations of a moving object are available, they can be matched effectively to image data, though usually at considerable computational cost (in detection). Once an object has been located approximately, tracking it in subsequent images becomes more efficient computationally, especially if motion is modeled as well as represented. In Bayesian tracking, object representation including geometry, motion, appearance and characterizes the object in a state space either explicitly or implicitly. For example, parameterized shapes and color distributions are often used as object representations. To provide a more constrained description of the object, some methods employ both shape and color. With a chosen representation, the observation likelihood function determines the probabilities of all object candidates within the search region. These are predicted from estimates at previous time step and are formulated in terms of visual similarity using a variety of metrics ranging from simple template matching scores to more sophisticated measures, for example, robust statistics for image correlation.

The representation model can also be based on the image patches, thus describing how the tracked region should look pixelwise. To add uniqueness to the object representation, many methods even employ object appearance, such as image templates or eigen-space values as the object representation. Motion can also be taken into account in constructing object representation, since different objects can be discriminated by the differences in their motions. If two objects share the same appearance, it is difficult to correctly track either of them when they are close to each other in the state space. For instance, tracking a person in a crowd is a challenging visual task. Object localization is implemented by observation likelihood, which defines the image evidence of the object representation. For example, if the object is represented by its contour, we expect to observe edges of the contour in the image.

Object representation modeling is still a challenge problem, since the same object can look incredibly different in different images due to differences in view point, view distance illumination, color, occlusion, etc. The learning and modeling of the visual appearance of the object from a set of training imagery (suitably normalized and preprocessed) provides an efficient way to build the representation model of an object. In this section, we cover several well-known object representation models for visual tracking as well as the corresponding probabilistic visual learning techniques. First, we briefly review an unsupervised technique for the visual learning example, and then we introduce three major object representation models based upon that visual learning method: contour (or shape) tracking, appearance-based object representation for tracking.

8.4.1 Visual Learning for Object Representation

Normalized correlation or template matching represent the standard paradigm in defining an observation likelihood function in the modeling of object representation. However, this approach is only optimal in the simplistic case of a deterministic signal embedded in additive white Gaussian noise. When we begin to consider a target class tracking problem – e.g., tracking a generic human face or hand in a scene, we must incorporate the underlying probability distribution of the object. Subspace methods and eigenspace decompositions (Zhang et al. 1997) are particularly well suited to such a task since they provide a compact and parametric description of the object's appearance and also automatically identify the degrees of freedom in the underlying statistical variability. The reconstruction error (or residual) of the eigenspace decomposition is an effective indicator of similarity.

Learning an object representation based on eigenspace decomposition estimates the complete probability distribution of the object's appearance using an eigenvector decomposition of the image space (Moghaddam and Pentland 1997). Specially, given a set of training images $\{\mathbf{x}_t\}_{t=1}^{N_t}$, from an object class Ω, we wish to estimate the likelihood function for a new image $\mathbf{x}$, i.e., $P(\mathbf{x}|\Omega)$. This density is decomposed into two components: the density in the principal subspace (containing the traditionally defined principal components) and its orthogonal complement (which is usually discarded in standard PCA). Then we can derive the optimal density for the case of Gaussian data and a near-optimal estimator for arbitrary complex distributions in terms of a mixture-of-Gaussian density model. And finally, with the density estimate $\hat{P}(\mathbf{x}|\Omega)$, we can compute a local measure of target saliency at each spatial position (i, j) in an input image based on the vector obtained by the lexicographic ordering of the pixel values in a local neighborhood.

In most applications, it is customary to simply work with the principal subspace but discard the orthogonal complement density. However, the use of the complement density is critically important in formulating the likelihood of an observation $\mathbf{x}$ since there are an infinity of vectors which are not members of Ω which have likely principal projections, and this leads to a significant number of false measurement in tracking.

8.4.2 Active Contour

Effective methods have arisen in computer vision for modeling the shape of a class of object. One important task is the modeling of curve segments which interact with images or image sequences. This is more general problem than modeling entire objects, but more clutter resistant than applying signal processing to low-level corners or edges. With this formulation, the problem of tracking outlines and features of foreground objects becomes the problem of tracking curves in visual clutter (Blake et al. 1993).

8.4.2.1 Shape-Space for Parametric Curves

The B-spline is a good choice for representing a curve parameterized by its control points. However, in practice this results in too many degrees of freedom for stable tracking. Thus, it is necessary to restrict the curve to a low-dimensional shape-space defined by a few parameters. We represent the state of a tracked object as a vector of the shape-space. The tracking problem is now to estimate the motion of some curves. The tracker generates estimates of the control points, and the aim is that the estimates should represent a curve that, at each time step, matches the underlying curve as closely as possible. In accordance with the practice in temporal filtering, the tracker is based on two models: (1) a state model specifying the likely dynamics of the curve over time, relative to a template and (2) a measurement model specifying the positions along the curve at which measurements are made and how reliable they are.

Objects are modeled as a curve, or a set of curves, and represented at time t by a parameterized image curve $\mathbf{c}(s,t) = (c_x(s,t), c_y(s,t))$ (Isard and Blake 1998; Blake et al. 1995); Curves are represented as parametric B-splines with N spans and N_c control points.

$$\begin{cases} c_x(s,t) = \mathbf{B}(s)Q_x(t) \\ c_y(s,t) = \mathbf{B}(s)Q_y(t) \end{cases}, \qquad 0 \leq s \leq N \tag{8.68}$$

where $Q = (Q_x, Q_y)$ are vectors of the B-spline control point coordinates. The number of control points is equal to the number of spans ($N_c = N$) for closed curves, whereas $N_c = N + d$ for open curves. The vector $B(s)$ consists of blending coefficients defined by $\mathbf{B}(s) = (B_1(s), \cdots, B_{N_c}(s))$, where $B_m(s)$ is a B-spline basis function appropriate for the order of the curve and its set of knots.

Complex shapes usually require many control points to describe them, and this leads to instability in tracking. Provided that perspective effects are not strong, a shape-space vector is used to approximate the curve shape as it changes over time. A shape-space vector $\mathbf{x}$ is defined by

$$\begin{pmatrix} Q_x \\ Q_y \end{pmatrix} = W\mathbf{x} + \begin{pmatrix} \bar{Q}_x \\ \bar{Q}_y \end{pmatrix} \text{ and } \qquad \mathbf{x} = M \begin{pmatrix} Q_x - \bar{Q}_x \\ Q_y - \bar{Q}_y \end{pmatrix} \tag{8.69}$$

where the matrix W is a matrix of rank N_x considerably lower than the $2N_c$ degree of freedom of the unconstrained spline. The relationships $\mathbf{x} \leftrightarrow Q$ are expressed in terms of two matrices M, W, which are defined in terms of the shape template $\bar{Q}$. Typically, the shape-space may allow affine deformations of the template shape $\bar{Q}$, or more generally a space of rigid and nonrigid deformations. The space of possible $\mathbf{x}$ is expressible as a six-dimensional (6D) linear subspace of the shape-space vector $\mathbf{x}$. In this case, the matrices M, W converting B-spline control points Q to and from $\mathbf{x}$ can be defined, in terms of the template, as follows:

$$W = \begin{pmatrix} \mathbf{1} & \mathbf{0} & \bar{Q}_x & \mathbf{0} & \mathbf{0} & \bar{Q}_y \\ \mathbf{0} & \mathbf{1} & \mathbf{0} & \bar{Q}_y & \bar{Q}_x & \mathbf{0} \end{pmatrix} \tag{8.70}$$

where $\mathbf{0}$ and $\mathbf{1}$ are N_c-vectors of elements of 0 and 1, respectively. Also, we have $M = (W^T H W)^{-1} W^T H$ where $H = \int_0^N \begin{pmatrix} 1 & 0 \\ 0 & 1 \end{pmatrix} \otimes (\mathbf{B}(s)\mathbf{B}(s))^T ds$, in which $\otimes$ denotes the "Kronecker product" of two matrices.

The parametric B-spline can be fully reconstructed from the compact representation of a curve in terms of the configuration-space vector $\mathbf{x}$. The reconstruction formula is

$$\mathbf{c}(s,t) = U(s)\mathbf{x}(t) \tag{8.71}$$

where

$$U(s) = \left[\begin{pmatrix} 1 & 0 \\ 0 & 1 \end{pmatrix} \otimes \mathbf{B}(s) \right] W \tag{8.72}$$

Object dynamics are modeled as a second-order process represented in discrete time as a second-order linear difference equation. This provides the basis for the computation of prior $p(\mathbf{x}_t|\mathbf{x}_{t-1})$ in the Bayesian tracking.

8.4.2.2 Observation Likelihood Function

Given an estimator $\mathbf{c}(\hat{s},t)$ for the contour $\mathbf{c}(s,t)$, generated by the hypothesized state $\mathbf{x}$, the visual measurement process at time t consists of casting rays along normal $\mathbf{n}(\hat{s},t)$ to the estimated curve and, simultaneously, at certain points s along the curve. These rays are called measurement lines; typically they will space equally around the contour, with between 1 and 5 measurement points per span of the B-spline. Often the length of the measurement line is fixed in advance, and it is almost always assumed that the measurement line is symmetric about the measurement point. Next, a 1D feature detector is applied to the image intensity along each measurement line. For a given line, the result is a list of numbers describing the distance from each feature found to the measurement point; these numbers are called the feature innovations. The method is demonstrated in Fig. 8.3.

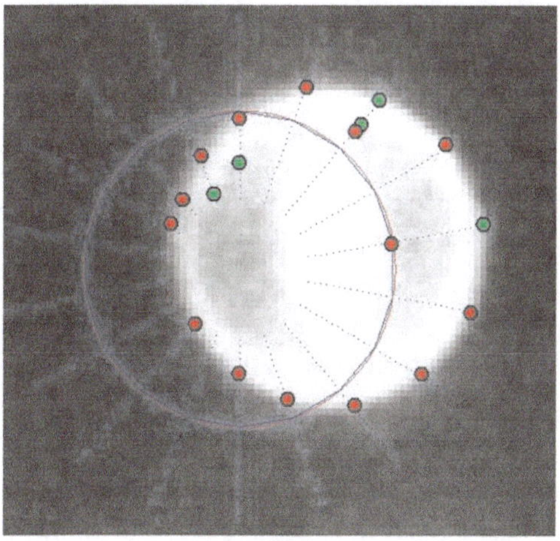

Fig. 8.3 Contour observation construction. The *blue dashed line* denotes the measurement line, and *blue* and *red points* are edge points that lie along measurement lines. The *blue point* in *red* indicates true contour point, while the *red circle* is the generated contour by a shape-space vector

Consider the one-dimensional problem of observing, along a single measurement line, the set of feature positions $\mathbf{z} = (z_1, ..., z_M)$ reduced to a set of scalar position in which the observation density has the form $p(\mathbf{z}|x)$, and where x is 1D position.

Assuming a uniform distribution of background clutter and a Gaussian model of the error in the measurement of the true position of the object edge, we can obtain a multimodal observation density. This leads to the calculation of the likelihood that is so critical for contour tracking. We give a detailed discussion as follows.

Given L, the length of the ith measurement line, we denote the predicted contour point position by x, so that the contour is discretized by the set of $\{x_i\}$. After applying a 1D edge detector to the pixels along the measurement line, we obtain the locations of the edge points $\mathbf{z}_i = \{z_i^{(1)}, ..., z_i^{(m_i)}\}$, where m_i is the number of detected feature points on the ith measurement line. Since different measurement lines may have different numbers of such feature points, the likelihoods for different contour hypotheses may not be comparable. However, since at most one of the $\{z_i^{(k)}\}$ is generated by the target contour points x_i, it is the position of that $\{z_i^{(k)}\}$ that of interest. We can then associate other edge points with the clutter, which is modeled by a Poisson process. We only need be concerned about the numbers of the feature points, rather than their actual positions. Therefore, the observations for calculating the likelihood consist of (1) the position of the one edge point (which is not known yet) and (2) the number of the detected feature points.

Assume that the detected features points associated with the clutter distribution along the measurement line bear a Poisson process $\beta(m;\lambda)$, where m is the number of features. If m feature points are associated with clutter, then we have

$$p(m(L)|clutter) = \frac{\lambda L^m}{m!} e^{-\lambda L} \tag{8.73}$$

where $m(L)$ is the number of feature points along the measurement line.

We also assume that the feature points associated with the target contour point x_i are produced by a Gaussian distribution $G(z;x_i,\sigma)$ within a window Win. These feature points are denoted as $z_i(Win) = \{z_i^{(1)}, \cdots, z_i^{(m(Win))}\}$, where $m(Win)$ denotes the number of feature points within the window. At most one of these features is associated with the target, which we denoted by $z_i^{(*)}$. The ith measurement line as illustrated in Fig. 8.4, in which the observation $z_i(Win)$ consists of $m(Win)$ detected features.

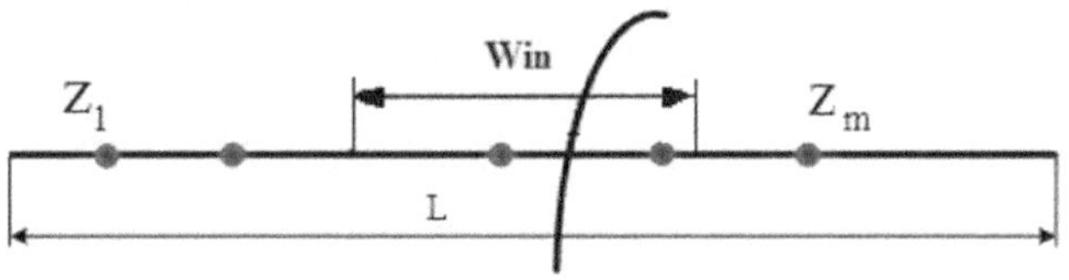

Fig. 8.4 Edge points on measurement lines

Since we cannot determine which feature inside Win should be associated with the target contour, we must integrate all the possibilities. In addition, since accommodating the missing detection of the feature associated with the target can make the tracker more robust, we denote events $\phi_0 = \{z_i^{(*)}$ incorrectly detected$\}$ and $\phi_1 = \{z_i^{(*)}$is detected$\}$. Conditioned on ϕ_0, the likelihood is set as

$$p(\mathbf{z}_i|x_i, clutter, \phi_0) = G(Win/4; 0, \sigma)\beta(m(L); \lambda) \tag{8.74}$$

Similarly, the likelihood conditioned on ϕ_1 is

$$p(\mathbf{z}_i|x_i, clutter, \phi_1) = \begin{cases} G(Win/2; 0, \sigma)\beta(m(L)), & m(Win) = 0 \\ \frac{\sum_{z_i^k \in Win} G(z_i^k; x_i, \sigma)}{m(Win)}\beta(m(L)-1), & m(Win) \neq 0 \end{cases} \tag{8.75}$$

Therefore, we have

$$p(\mathbf{z}_i|x_i, clutter) = p(\mathbf{z}_i|x_i, clutter, \phi_0)p(\phi_0) + p(\mathbf{z}_i|x_i, clutter, \phi_1)p(\phi_1) \tag{8.76}$$

Since we assume that the measurement lines are independent, the target observation models are

$$p(Z|x, clutter) = \prod_{i=1}^{n} p(\mathbf{z}_i|x_i, clutter) \tag{8.77}$$

8.4.3 Appearance Model

The use of the parametric appearance models to characterize the PDF of an object's appearance in the image is related to the idea of a view-based representation which describes the spatial structure of the target object by interpolating between the previously seen views. Because of the fact that the natural objects displays a wide range of structural and nonrigid variations, it is necessary to extend the notion of "view" to include the characterization of the range of the geometric and feature variation. Such density-based techniques are referred to as appearance-based model. To obtain such an appearance-based representation, one must first transform the image into a low-dimensional coordinate system that preserves the general perceptual quality of the target object's image. The necessity for such a transformation stems from "curse of dimensionality" and the need to address it. Typical methods of dimensionality reduction include the Karhunen–Loeve transform (also called PCA) or the Ritz approximation (Birkhoff et al. 1966) (also known as example-based representation). Other dimensionality reduction methods are also employed, including sparse filter representation (e.g., Gabor jets (Phillips et al. 1998), wavelet transforms), feature histograms, independent components analysis, blobs, and so forth. These methods have in common the property that they allow an efficient characterization of a low-dimensional subspace within the overall space of raw image measurements. Once a low-dimensional representation of the target class has been obtained, standard statistical parameter estimation methods can be used to learn the range of appearances that target exhibits in the new low-dimensional coordinates. Because of the lower dimensionality, relatively few examples are required to obtain a useful estimate of either the PDF or the inter-class discriminant function.

8.4.3.1 Color Appearance Model

Recently, trackers using a global color reference model have been shown robust and versatile at a modest computational cost. They have proved in particular to be very useful for tracking tasks where the objects of interest can be of any kind and can exhibit drastic changes in spatial structure through the sequence, due to pose changes, partial occlusions, etc. This type of tracking problem arises, for instance, in the context of video analysis and manipulation. For such applications, most trackers based on a space-dependent appearance reference may break down very fast. In contrast, using a global, though sufficiently discriminant model of the color distribution within the region of interest, is an appealing way to address such complex tracking task.

This technique is based upon the following principle: the current frame is searched for a region, a fixed-shape variable-size window, whose color content best matches a reference color model. The search is deterministic. Starting from the final location in the previous frame, it proceeds iteratively at each frame so as to minimize a distance measure to the reference color histogram. However, this deterministic search can run into problems when parts of the background nearby exhibit similar colors, or when the tracked object is temporarily, but completely occluded.

In Bayesian tracking, a variety of parametric and nonparametric statistical techniques have been used to model the color distribution of homogeneous colored regions. The use of a single Gaussian to model the color of a blob restricts us to a single color which is not a sufficiently general assumption to model regions with mixtures of colors. For example, people's clothing and surfaces with texture usually contain patterns and mixtures of colors. Fitting a mixture of Gaussian using the EM algorithm provides a way to model color blobs with a mixture of colors. The mixture of Gaussian techniques faces the problem of choosing the right number of Gaussian components for the assumed model (model selection). Nonparametric techniques using histograms have been widely used for modeling the color of objects, in order to overcome the previously mentioned problems with parametric models for different applications. The major drawback with a color histogram is the lack of convergence to the right density function if the data set is small. Another drawback is that, in general, color histograms are not suitable for higher dimensional features.

The kernel density estimation technique (Elgammal et al. 2002, Elgammal et al. 2003)is a particular nonparametric technique that estimates the underlying density, while avoiding having to store the complete data set. Using kernel density estimation for color modeling has many motivations. Unlike histograms, even with a small number of samples, kernel density estimation leads to a smooth, continuous, and differentiability density estimate. Since kernel density estimation does not assume any specific underlying distribution and the estimate can converge to any density shape with enough samples, this approach is suitable for modeling the color distribution of regions with patterns and mixture of colors. If the underlying distribution is a mixture of Gaussians, kernel density estimation converges to the right density with a small number of samples. Unlike parametric fitting, if the underlying distribution is a mixture of Gaussians, kernel density estimation is a more general approach that does not require the selection of the number of Gaussians to be fitted. Another important advantage of using kernel density estimation is that the adaptation of the model is trivial and can be achieved by adding new samples. Since color spaces are low in dimensionality, efficient computation of kernel density estimation can be achieved using the fast Gauss transform algorithm (Greengard and Strain 1991).

Given a sample $S = \{x_i\}$ taken from an image region, where $i = 1, \cdots, N$ and x_i is a d-dimensional vector representing color, we can estimate the density function at any point y of the color space directly from S using the product of 1D kernels as

$$\hat{p}(y) = \frac{1}{N}\sum_{i=1}^{N}\prod_{j=1}^{d} K_{\sigma_i}(y_j - x_{ij}) \tag{8.78}$$

where the same kernel function K_{σ_i} is used in each dimension with a different bandwidth σ_j for each dimension of the color space,

$$K_{\sigma_i}(t) = \frac{1}{\sigma_i} K\left(\frac{t}{\sigma_i}\right). \tag{8.79}$$

The kernel function K should satisfy $K(t) \geq 0$ and $\int K(t)dt = 1$.

Usually in color modeling 2D or 3D color spaces are used. 2D chromaticity spaces, $r = R/(R+G+B)$, $g = G/(R+G+B)$, and a, b from the Lab color space, are used when model invariance to illumination geometry is desired. 3D color spaces are widely used because of their greater suitability for discrimination, since brightness information is preserved. The use of different bandwidths for kernels in different color dimensions is desirable since the variances in each color dimensions are different. For example, the luminance variable usually has more variance than the chromaticity variables, and therefore wider kernels should be used in that dimension.

8.5 Summary

Visual tracking is a kind of motion analysis at the object level, which consists of two major components: object representation modeling and temporal filtering. We have focused on stochastic approaches, e.g., sequential Bayesian estimation techniques for visual tracking. We first introduced the sequential Bayesian estimation framework which acts as the theoretic basis for visual tracking. Then, we introduced several methods for constructing representation models of objects of interest.

References

Birkhoff G, de Boor C, Swartz B, Wendroff B (1966) Rayleigh-Ritz approximation by piecewise cubic polynomials. SIAM Journal on Numerical Analysis 3:188

Blake A, Curwen R, Zisserman A (1993) A framework for spatiotemporal control in the tracking of visual contours. International Journal of Computer Vision 11(2):127–145

Blake A, Isard M, Reynard D (1995) Learning to track the visual motion of contours. Artificial Intelligence 78(1–2):179–212

Doucet A, Gordon N, Kroshnamurthy V (2001) Particle filters for state estimation of jump Markov linear systems. IEEE Transactions on Signal Processing 49(3):613–624

Elgammal A, Duraiswami R, Harwood D, Davis L (2002) Background and foreground modeling using nonparametric kernel density estimation for visual surveillance. Proceedings of the IEEE 90(7):1151–1163

Elgammal A, Duraiswami R, Davis L (2003) Efficient Kernel density estimation using the fast gauss transform with applications to color modeling and tracking. IEEE Transactions on Pattern Analysis and Machine Intelligence pp 1499–1504

Gordon N, Salmond D, Smith A (1993) Novel approach to nonlinear/non-Gaussian Bayesian state estimation. In: IEE Proceedings of Radar and Signal Processing, vol 140, pp 107–113

Greengard L, Strain J (1991) The fast Gauss transform. SIAM Journal on Scientific and Statistical Computing 12(1):79–94

Isard M, Blake A (1998) Condensation conditional density propagation for visual tracking. International Journal of Computer Vision 29(1):5–28

Liu J (2001) Monte Carlo Strategies in Scientific Computing. Springer, New York

Liu J, Chen R, Wong W (1999) Rejection control and importance sampling. Journal of the American Statistical Association 93:1022–1301

Moghaddam B, Pentland A (1997) Probabilistic visual learning for object representation. IEEE Transactions on Pattern Analysis and Machine Intelligence 19(7):696–710

Phillips P, Wechsler H, Huang J, Rauss P (1998) The FERET database and evaluation procedure for face-recognition algorithms. Image and Vision Computing 16(5):295–306

Zhang J, Yan Y, Lades M (1997) Face recognition: Eigenface, elastic matching, and neural nets: Automated biometrics. Proceedings of the IEEE 85(9):1423–1435

Chapter 9
Probabilistic Data Fusion for Robust Visual Tracking

Abstract Developing robust visual tracking algorithms for real-world application is a major challenge even today. In this chapter, we focus on visual tracking with data fusion using sequential Monte Carlo filtering techniques, and present a tracking framework with a four-layer probabilistic fusion. The framework consists of four layers: a cue fusion layer, a model fusion layer, a tracker fusion layer, and a sensor fusion layer, in a bottom-up fusion process. These layers are defined as follows: the cue layer fuses visual modalities via an adaptive fusion strategy, the model layer fuses prior motion information via an interactive multi-model method (IMM), the tracker layer fuses results from multiple trackers via an adaptive tracking mode that switches between model associations, and the sensor layer fuses multiple sensors in a distributed way. Only state distributions in the input and output of each layer are required to ensure consistency of so many visual modules within the framework. Furthermore, the proposed framework is general and allows augmenting and pruning of fusion layers according to the visual environment at hand. The proposed framework is tested and satisfactory results obtained in various complex scenarios in which many existing trackers are inclined to fail.

9.1 Introduction

Robustness in a visual tracking system means the ability to track accurately and precisely during or after visual circumstances that are less than ideal. In biological systems, this robustness is taken for granted; yet in computer vision, it is at present a difficult issue that has received much more attention than ever before. Developing a robust object tracking system for real-world applications remains a major challenge, owing to the existence of complex and unexpected visual events, including background clutter, distractions, varying illumination, and deformations of the tracked object.

One major characteristic expected of a robust visual tracking system is the ability to recover from tracking failures. Tracking failures of any tracking system can

N. Zheng, J. Xue, *Statistical Learning and Pattern Analysis for Image and Video Processing*, Advances in Pattern Recognition, DOI 10.1007/978-1-84882-312-9_9,
© Springer-Verlag London Limited 2009

arise from two different error sources: measurement errors and algorithmic failures. Measurement errors occur when a target is tracked properly, but its new position cannot be determined with perfect precision. Measurement errors are well behaved in the sense that they can be largely accounted for by employing filtering techniques and propagating confidence values throughout the system (Liu and Chen 1998). Algorithmic failures occur when the system generates an incorrect trajectory for a target; correspondence mistakes are a typical example. These errors will usually have much more serious consequences on any subsequent processing because they are unbounded. Recovery is impossible using only local filtering. Errors produced by algorithmic failures are a major obstacle to the design of robust vision systems. The easiest way of reducing algorithmic errors is to reject a larger portion of unlikely potential matches. However, in practice, this is not an easy job. For example, algorithmic errors can be reduced by improving individual tracking algorithms, but it is unlikely that any one single algorithm will be successful in all situations.

Many research results indicate that data fusion is a feasible approach to achieving robust visual tracking (Bar-Shalom and Li 1995; McCane et al. 2002; Spengler and Schiele 2003).The first reason stems from findings in biological vision research, in which the human visual system exhibits an amazing robustness in the face of complex and unexpected visual events. Ongoing cognitive processes can continually integrate incoming sensory data to constrain inferences about the external world and thereby limit the set of possible interpretations. The second reason is that video contains an extraordinary wealth of information, although, despite the large body of literature on visual tracking, the potential for harnessing this information remains largely unrealized, and many useful algorithms remain confined to the laboratory. The third reason has to do with the generalized concept of data fusion. Traditionally, data fusion for tracking (or estimation fusion) focuses on the problem of how to best utilize the valuable information contained in multiple sets of data for the purposes of estimating an unknown measurable attribute of the interested object – a parameter or process (at a given time). The multiple data sets in data fusion are usually obtained from multiple sources (e.g., multiple sensors). However, with the generalized concept of data fusion, the multiple sets of data may also be collected from a single source over a time period or be generated by multiple tracking algorithms or multiple measurement processes. With this wider view of data fusion, the conventional problems of filtering, prediction, and smoothing of an unknown process are special cases of fusion for estimation problems. The integration of multiple visual tracking modules, i.e., organizing multiple tracking algorithms and search heuristics into a single tracking system becomes of increasing importance as research progress on individual tracking modules approaches performance ceilings.

In the context of generalized data fusion for robust visual tracking, many results have been obtained in both research analysis and experimentation, including in both civilian and military applications (Siebel and Maybank 2002; Toyama and Hager 1999; Leichter et al. 2006). While these results do represent some major progress, to the best of our knowledge, they are still limited in several aspects. First, most of the existing object tracking systems designed for day and night vision in visible infrared- and thermal-spectrum are built on fundamental building blocks, and are obtained by ingenious, nonsystematic manipulations. Compared to this body of literature, data fusion for visual tracking is still a hot research topic in its early stages, and a systematic approach to the development of system for visual tracking with data fusion is still lacking. Second, combining different visual tracking modules requires a common framework that ensures consistency. The sequential Monte Carlo (SMC) framework provides a principled approach to fusing information from different measurement sources. Although this has been acknowledged before, it has not been fully exploited within a visual tracking context, where a host of cues are available to increase the reliability of the tracking algorithm (Perez et al. 2004).

We present a four-layer probabilistic fusion framework for visual tracking within an SMC framework. To make a real tracking system with data fusion easy to implement, a bottom-up fusion procedure is divided into three different layers with their corresponding fusion algorithms. Layer 1 is the visual cue fusion layer which fuses multiple visual modalities via adaptive fusion strategies. Layer 2 is the model fusion layer, which fuses prior motion information via interactive multiple models (IMM) (Li and Jilkov 2005). Layer 3 is the tracker fusion layer, which fuses results from multiple trackers via an interactive multiple tracking algorithm. To ensure consistency among these three sequential fusion layers, the state distributions for the input and output of each layer are defined. Sequentially, for every input image, each layer provides a probability distribution function (PDF) of the target state within a state space. One complete data fusion procedure thus consists of propagating the probability distribution of the state through three stages, each of which corresponds to one of the three layers defined here. This framework can be depicted as Fig. 9.1. This work is a refined version of the conference papers (Xue and Zheng 2006; Zhong et al. 2006a, b), along with some new results not found therein.

The probabilistic framework proposed in this chapter differs from previous related works in several aspects: (1) the four consecutive layers form a bottom-up fusion procedure, (2) only state distributions in the input and output of each layer are required to ensure consistency of visual modules within the framework, and (3) it provides a general methodology for the design of a robust visual tracking system with data fusion. Furthermore, there are three distinguished components in this framework:

- A novel adaptive fusion strategy in the visual cue fusion layer. At each time step, the strategy switches back and forth between a product fusion rule and a weighted sum fusion rule, according to the predefined reliability of each visual cue.
- The definition of a pseudo measurement via fusing the measurements predicted by multiple motion models. The fusing coefficients are built set by combining both the image-based likelihood and the motion-based association probability.
- The adoption of a novel concept, model association, with which we propose an interactive multiple tracker tracking framework that cooperatively fuses multiple motion models and multiple observation models in a general and adaptive way.

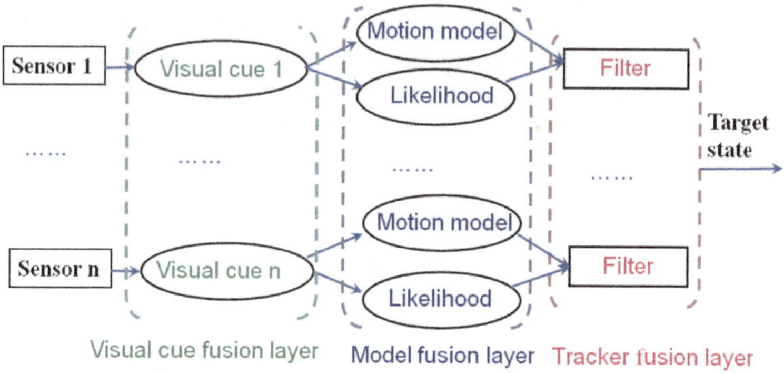

Fig. 9.1 The three-layer data fusion framework for object tracking

The rest of this chapter is organized as follows. We start with a brief survey of the earlier work on robust visual tracking in Section 9.2. Then the proposed framework is defined in Section. 9.3, and the four fusion layers are presented in Sections 9.4, 9.5, 9.6, and 9.7 in greater detail. Finally, implementation issues and experimental results are discussed in Section 9.8. Section 9.9 concludes with a summary of this work.

9.2 Earlier Work on Robust Visual Tracking

There is a rich literature on robust tracking. The approaches to robust tracking can be categorized into research that contributes to either ante-failure or post-failure robustness (Toyama and Hager 1996). Ante-failure robust systems seek to avoid tracking failure altogether through specialized algorithms that anticipate visual disturbances and attempt tracking despite of them. Post-failure systems, on the other hand, accept the inevitability of mistracking and are designed to recover from failure once it happens. In the following paragraphs, a brief survey is presented on these two different error-handling mechanisms.

Advances in ante-failure robustness have generally been achieved through data fusion, robust statistics, temporal filtering, or ad hoc methods for handling specific types of visual perturbations. Two basic fusion architectures are widely used to enhance the robustness of the tracking systems: feature combination and tracker fusion (corresponding to centralized and distributed fusion in data fusion literature, respectively). Which architecture is used depends on whether or not features are used directly for fusion. Feature combination is performed explicitly in a single tracker(i.e., the features themselves are fused), usually in the observation phase. In contrast, tracker fusion is performed implicitly by combining trackers that use different features(i.e., the trackers are fused, rather than the features).

Examples of the first type of architecture include (Zhong et al. 2006a); (Vermaak et al. 2002; Jepson et al. 2003; Roth et al. 2004; Collins et al. 2005; Wu and Yu 2006). In (Zhong et al. 2006a), a visual cue dependency model is constructed via a graphical model, and nonparametric belief propagation is used for cue integration (Xue et al. 2006) to achieve tracker robustness. In (Vermaak et al. 2002), the tracker uses an observation model that combines color and motion from a fixed filter bank and uses motion information for initialization via a Monte Carlo proposal distribution. In (Jepson et al. 2003), to track a complex natural object, an adaptive appearance model is constructed, which integrates a learned mixture of stable image structure and two-frame motion information, along with an outlier process. The method in (Roth et al. 2004) uses various filter responses at multiple scales and orientations as image measurements, and then models the likelihood function of the Bayesian-based tracker using Gibbs learning. In (Collins et al. 2005), the tracker performs online switching between different features, according to their ability to discriminate between object and background pixels. In (Wu and Yu 2006), a new approach based on a two-layer statistical field model is presented. This model characterizes the prior of the complex shape variations as a Boltzmann distribution and embeds this prior and the complex image likelihood into a Markov random field. These approaches have achieved practical robustness to some degree; however, they usually heavily rely on the discriminability of their well-designed observation models. The increase of the tracking performance is achieved at the cost of the computational complexity.

The second type of architecture follows a sort of "the whole is greater than the sum of the parts" philosophy. Rather than simply trying to make small, incremental improvements in the way features are combined in existing trackers (each of which may be quite effective within a narrow slice of the visual tracking problem), it is better to focus research on fusing these trackers together for a much broader approach in the face of the general visual tracking problem. This has been investigated for several decades (Siebel and Maybank 2002; McCane et al. 2002; Toyama and Hager 1999; Spengler and Schiele 2003; Leichter et al. 2006) (Wu and Huang 2001). In (Siebel and Maybank 2002), a system containing three cooperating detection and tracking modules is devised for tracking people in an indoor environment. In (McCane et al. 2002), a framework using a classification approach for merging the results of independent feature-based motion trackers is presented. In (Toyama and Hager 1999), multiple window-based trackers simultaneously track the same feature. Different situations where mistracking occurs are categorized and dealt with by the appropriate trackers. In (Spengler and Schiele 2003), a democratic integration scheme is used to combine multiple cues for visual tracking. In

(Leichter et al. 2006), a probabilistic framework for combining multiple tracking algorithms allows the user to treat separate tracking algorithms as "black boxes," in which only the state distributions in the input and output are needed for the combination process. In (Wu and Huang 2001), two co-inference tracking algorithms are developed, combining trackers of different modalities.

None of the efforts mentioned that use feature combination and tracker fusion to achieve robust tracking mentioned here are error-free. Feature combination and tracker fusion have pros and cons in terms of performance, channel requirements, reliability, survivability, information sharing, and so on. They cannot eliminate failures entirely. Most often, the limitations are a reflection not of poor algorithmic design, but rather of the impossibility of perfect vision-based tracking in complex circumstance.

To deal with such situations, some researchers have incorporated post-failure schemes to recover tracking when mistracking does occur. One milestone in this kind of thinking is the incremental focus of attention mechanism presented in (Toyama and Hager 1999). It controls the transitions between layers and executes algorithms appropriate to the visual environment at hand. It seems clear that both ante-failure and post-failure are necessary for reliable tracking.

In this chapter, we consider that both ante-failure and post-failure are necessary for reliable tracking and present a three-layer robust visual tracking framework. The proposed framework differs from previous related work in the following aspects:

- First, the three consecutive layers form a bottom-up fusion procedure, and this differs from the layer composition of the layered hierarchy of vision-based tracking algorithms in (Toyama and Hager 1999) where all layers are sorted by output precision. In our framework, each layer contains tracking algorithms (the particle filter or kalman filter is used as the basic form of these tracking algorithms) with different tracking performance, and efficient fusion strategies are developed to meet the requirement of each individual layer. For example, the visual cue fusion layer tackles the measurement uncertainty, while the model fusion layer deals with uncertainty in motion modeling. The tracker fusion layer is used to combine the output of multiple trackers.
- Second, only state distributions in the input and output of each layer are required to ensure consistency of visual modules within the framework. A similar idea can be found in (Leichter et al. 2006), in which the proposed framework combines synchronous trackers via their state distribution. However, using the same feedback to reinitialize the trackers makes the tracker with the worst estimation affect the tracker with the better estimation. In our framework, the state distribution is not only for the purpose of the fusing trackers in the same layer, but also for the purpose of propagating estimated target state of different precisions through different layers.
- Furthermore, the proposed framework provides a general methodology for the design of a data fusion for robust visual tracking system. The framework allows augmenting and pruning of fusing layers according to visual environment at hand. Each layer can work independently or cooperatively with other layers.

The robustness of the proposed framework is illustrated in the experiments and obtains satisfying tracking results in various complex scenarios where most existing trackers may fail or obtain inaccurate output.

9.3 Data Fusion-Based Visual Tracker

Visual tracking entails the detection and recursive localization of objects, or more generally features, in a video sequence. Within this context, data fusion utilizes a combination of physical models (such as differential equations of motion and observation models) and statistical assumptions about observation noise processes to map observational data to a state vector. The state vector is an independent set of variables such as position and velocity, which, if known, would allow accurate prediction of the future behavior (e.g., dynamical motion) of the object of interest.

Visual tracking algorithms calculate a series of estimates $\hat{\mathbf{x}}_k$ of the actual state $\mathbf{x}_k^*$, of the target at time k. The domain of the target state is denoted as $\mathbf{X}$. The input to a tracking algorithm is an input configuration set, or a set of candidate target states $\mathbf{x}^{in} \subseteq \mathbf{X}$, together with an image, $\mathbf{I}$. The output at each time step consists of an output configuration set, $\mathbf{x}^{out} \subseteq \mathbf{X}$, where $\mathbf{x}^{out}$ should include $\hat{x}$. In this chapter, both the input set, $\mathbf{x}^{in}$, and the output set, $\mathbf{x}^{out}$, of an algorithm represent a statistical distribution over states.

In the following subsections, the sequential Bayesian estimator (SBE) is first briefly introduced, which acts as the basic unit in our data fusion-based visual tracker. Then several forms of the SBE in different layers of a general data fusion visual tracker are introduced. And finally, an overview of the proposed data fusion framework is presented.

9.3.1 Sequential Bayesian Estimator

The objective of visual tracking is to estimate the unknown motion state $\mathbf{x}_k$ of an object of interest given observations till time k, $\mathbf{z}^k = \{\mathbf{z}_1, ..., \mathbf{z}_k\}$ with each observation arriving in sequential fashion. A state space model is often employed to accommodate the visual tracking problem. Two important components of a tracker are the state and measurement models whose most general forms can be defined as follows:

- State model: $\mathbf{x}_k = F_k(\mathbf{x}_{k-1}, \mathbf{u}_k)$
- Measurement model: $\mathbf{z}_k = H_k(\mathbf{x}_k, \mathbf{v}_k)$

where $\mathbf{u}_k$ is a dynamic noise process, $F_k(.,.)$ characterizes the dynamic of the state process, $\mathbf{v}_k$ is the observation process noise, and $H_k(.,.)$ models the measurement process. For tracking, the distribution of interest is the posterior $p(\mathbf{x}_k|\mathbf{z}^k)$, also known as the filtering distribution. The estimate of state $\mathbf{x}_k$ can be either the minimum mean squared error (MMSE) estimate

$$\mathbf{x}_k^{mmse} = E[\mathbf{x}_k|\mathbf{z}^k] = \int \mathbf{x}_k p(\mathbf{x}_k|\mathbf{z}^k) d\mathbf{x}_k \tag{9.1}$$

or the maximum a posterior (MAP) estimate

$$\mathbf{x}_k^{map} = arg \max_{\mathbf{x}_k} p(\mathbf{x}_k|\mathbf{z}^k) \tag{9.2}$$

or other forms based on $p(\mathbf{x}_k|\mathbf{z}^k)$.

In the sequential Bayesian estimation, the filtering distribution can be computed according to a two-step recursion.

- Prediction step: $p(\mathbf{x}_k|\mathbf{z}^{k-1}) = \int p(\mathbf{x}_k|\mathbf{x}_{k-1}) p(\mathbf{x}_{k-1}|\mathbf{z}^{k-1}) d\mathbf{x}_{k-1}$
- Filtering step:$p(\mathbf{x}_k|\mathbf{z}^k) \propto p(\mathbf{z}_k|\mathbf{x}_k) p(\mathbf{x}_k|\mathbf{z}^{k-1})$

where the prediction step follows from marginalization, and the new filtering distribution is obtained through a direct application of Bayes rule. $p(\mathbf{x}_k|\mathbf{x}_{k-1})$, which describes the state transition, can be derived by the state model $\mathbf{x}_k = F_k(\mathbf{x}_{k-1}, \mathbf{u}_k)$, and, $p(\mathbf{z}_k|\mathbf{x}_k)$, which defines the likelihood of any state in light of the current observation, can be derived from the measurement model $\mathbf{z}_k = H_k(\mathbf{x}_k, \mathbf{v}_k)$.

The particle filter keeps a representation of $p(\mathbf{x}_k|\mathbf{z}^k)$ by means of a set of weighted samples, the particles $\{\mathbf{x}_k^{(n)}, w_k^{(n)}\}_{n=1}^N$, and $\sum_{n=1}^N w_k^{(n)} = 1$. An optimal estimate $\hat{\mathbf{x}}_k$ is obtained by applying an optimality criterion, for example, MMSE, or MAP, and so on, and finding the $\mathbf{x}_k$ that maximizes that criterion. The n-th sample $\mathbf{x}_k^{(n)}$ is drawn from the so-called proposal density function. The many forms of particle filtering differ in their choice of this function.

An important aspect of the design of a state estimator is the selection of a suitable state space model describing the underlying physical state process and the sensory system. Errors in the model lead inevitably to (unforeseen) estimation errors and an overoptimistic error covariance matrix. Modeling errors can never be avoided since real physical systems are more complex than mathematical models can describe. The crux is to find a model with a degree of accuracy such that the influence of modeling errors is negligible when compared with the (foreseen) errors due to process noise and measurement noise. If the model is too coarse, with only a few parameters and states, larger modeling errors give rise to biased estimates. If the model is too fine, many parameters must be determined during system identification. The risk of over-fitting then emerges. The more parameters the model contains, the more sensitive the estimator becomes to small deviations in these parameters. Finding a systematic way of selecting the target and sensor parameters to cover the problem space is highly desirable. We believe that the data fusion for visual tracking provides a possible promising way.

9.3.2 The Four-Layer Data Fusion Visual Tracker

A typical tracking algorithm consists of two major components. One is for target representation and measurement generation and the other is for filtering and data association. The former is a bottom-up process that tries to cope with changes in appearance by exploring every visual unique of the target. The latter is a top-down process dealing with the dynamics of the tracked object, learned scene priors, and evaluation of different hypotheses. Tracking algorithms begin with an a priori estimate of an object's state and update the estimated state to the time of each new observation.

Similarly, the process of data fusion for robust visual tracking may be partitioned into three layers: (1) visual cue fusion, (2) model fusion, and (3) tracker fusion. Obviously, the design of a data fusion system for visual tracking begins with an inventory of the tracking algorithms that are available for tracking a particular target. The raw material for each fusion layer is existing tracking algorithms, visual search heuristics and fusion strategies.

The visual cue fusion layer tackles the problem of measurement uncertainty. A visual cue represents one of measurable attributes of the target. The measurement model relating a visual cue and the measurement often exhibits nonlinearities. The visual cue fusion layer sorts or correlates into groups of observations from multiple filters (within the state space defined by a single visual cue) or multiple visual cues, with each group representing data related to a single distinct attribute of the target. A novel adaptive fusion strategy is used in visual cue fusion layer. At each time instant, the strategy switches between the product fusion rule and the weighted sum fusion rule according to the predefined reliability of each visual cue.

The model fusion layer deals with uncertainty in the modeling of dynamics. Even when there is measurement-origin certainty, target-tracking faces two fundamental and interrelated main challenges: target motion uncertainty and nonlinearity. Multi-model methods (MM) (Li and Jilkov 2005) have been generally considered to be the mainstream approach to maneuvering target tracking under motion (model) uncertainty. The model fusion layer uses multiple motion models simultaneously to approximate the dynamics of the target, and these models are fused by adopting a multiple-model method.

The tracker fusion layer provides an interactive mechanism to fuse multiple trackers. Different from the tracking algorithm combination approach in (Leichter et al. 2006), this tracking layer fuses multiple tracking algorithms in a cooperative framework, and is more flexible than the probabilistic approach in (Leichter et al. 2006). This is implemented by an interactive multiple tracking algorithm that considers the multiple trackers to be a jump Markov linear system, and estimate the state via the sequential Monte Carlo filtering technique.

Additionally, in order to increase the application domain of the system, a sensor fusion layer can be added directly. Readers refer to (Bar-Shalom and Li 1995) for more detail.

This four-layer structure provides a general framework for visual tracking with data fusion. It can act as a general guideline in designing a very robust visual tracking system. Each algorithm in a given set of visual searching and tracking algorithms must be placed within the three layers of the framework with careful consideration to their role in tracking. Fig. 9.2 presents a typical data fusion for visual tracking system, which inputs from a CCD Camera, a visible infrared and a thermal-spectrum sensor. To make it easy to implement, only layers 1–3 within the channel of a single sensor are considered. Sensor fusion ultimately outputs the final fusion result via a weighted sum fusion rule. The data flow of the system is also presented in Fig. 9.2. In Sections 9.4, 9.5, 9.6, and 9.7, more details of each layer are presented.

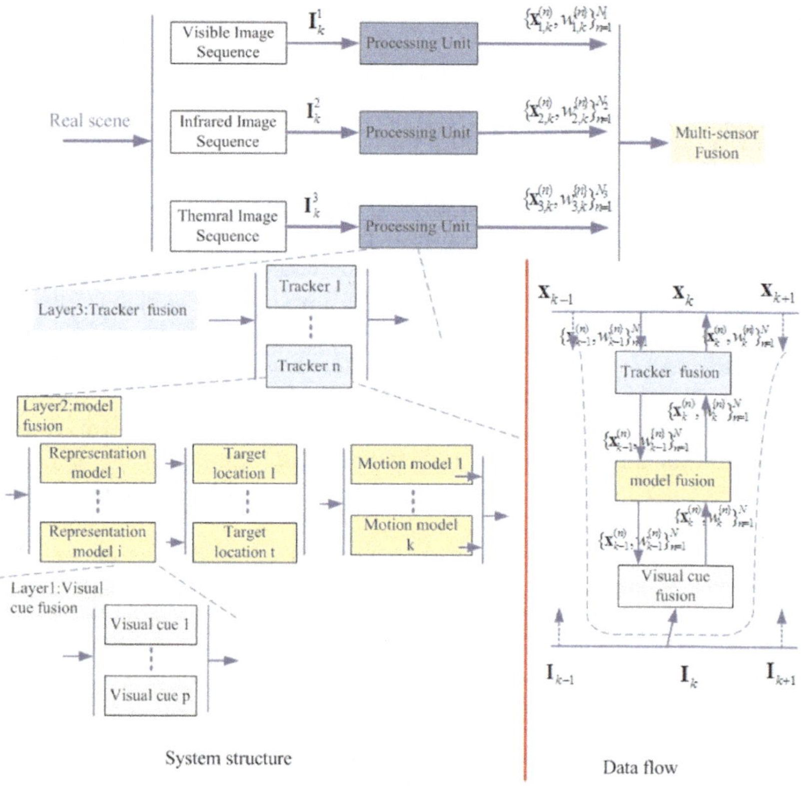

Fig. 9.2 An overview of the fusion process of a typical tracking system with multiple imaging sensors

To ensure consistency among these three sequential fusion layers, a weighted sample set or an explicit PDF is used to represent the PDF of the input and output of each layer. Mapping functions are defined for transformations between two state spaces with different dimensions. The idea of PDF propagating has its roots in the techniques of the sequential Monte Carlo techniques framework (Liu and Chen 1998; Isard and Blake 1998). Data fusion with particle filters has been mostly confined to visual cues (Wu and Huang 2001; Vermaak et al. 2002). Another similar idea can be found in (Leichter et al. 2006), in which combining tracking algorithms in a probabilistic framework is considered, which allows the combining of any set of separate tracking algorithms that output either an explicit PDF, or a weighted sample set. However, using the same feedback to reinitialize the trackers makes the tracker with the worst estimation affect the tracker with the better estimation. This work extends this idea. The state distribution is not only for the purpose of the fusing trackers in the same layer, but also for the purpose of propagating estimated target state of different precisions through different layers.

9.4 Layer 1: Visual Cue Fusion

In context of tracking, visual cues for target representation include attributes such as geometry, motion, appearance, and so on. A visual cue represents one of measurable attributes of the target, and characterizes the target in a state space either explicitly or implicitly. A visual can be expressed in a variety of forms: raw data output by the imaging sensors, the response of a specified filter, or a model or method which describes the visual pattern. Visual cues are different from each other in their application domain, discriminability for the object under different imaging conditions, and the degree of correlations. No single cue is robust and general enough to deal with a wide variety of environmental conditions, thus their combination promises to increase robustness and the generality of the representation model of the target. Using multiple cues simultaneously allows us not only to use complementary and redundant information at all times but also to detect failures more robustly, thus enabling recovery.

The visual cue fusion layer considers the combination of multiple visual cues. Two coupled problems are taken into consideration: (i) choosing visual cues, e.g., how to select cues for the fusion and (ii) the fusion strategies, e.g., how to integrate cues selected efficiently.

9.4.1 Fusion Rules: Product Versus Weighted Sum

Overall system performance may be improved in two main ways, either by enhancing each individual cue, or by improving the scheme for integrating the information from the different modalities. This leads to two primary schemes for fusing the output of multiple cues: voting and the probabilistic approach.

The voting scheme can be stated without ambiguity as weighted sum rule since it can be depicted as a mixture distribution density of the form (9.3).

$$p(\mathbf{x}|\mathbf{z}_1,\cdots\mathbf{z}_K) = \sum_{i=1}^{K} \alpha_i p(\mathbf{x}|\mathbf{z}_i) \tag{9.3}$$

where $\mathbf{z}_i$ denotes the i-th visual cue, K denotes the number of cues, $\mathbf{x}$ denotes the target state, and α_i is the weight of the i-th visual cue and with $\sum_i \alpha_i = 1$.

With the voting scheme, all visual cues contribute simultaneously to the overall result and none of the cues has an outstanding relevance when compared with others. That is, each cue makes an independent decision before these decisions are combined using the weighted sum rule. Robustness and generality are two major contributions of the weighted sum rule over nonfusion methods.

Probabilistic methods take more care in designing the model of each cue so that the different cues combine in the desired manner. However, their strength also lies there since it forces the user to be explicit in terms of designing the model and specifying what parameters are used and what assumptions are made. In real applications, integrating visual cues with probabilistic methods often ignores correlations among visual cues, and assumes that each visual cue works independently. With this independence assumption, probabilistic visual cues integration can be stated as product rule, and can be depicted as

$$p(\mathbf{x}|\mathbf{z}_1,\cdots\mathbf{z}_K) = \prod_{i=1}^{K} p(\mathbf{x}|\mathbf{z}_i). \tag{9.4}$$

Even though the independence assumption is sometimes violated, it can still achieve better tracking performance than simply using a single visual cue. Figure. 9.3 shows the simulation result of fusing two cues by the product rule. For simplicity, the conditional likelihood density for each cue is assumed to be a 1-D Gaussian. Obviously, the fused estimation, $p(\mathbf{x})$, has a small variance compared with that of the estimation using any an individual cue.

The product rule and weighted sum rule have their own advantages and disadvantages. The product rule has wide application because it is optimal under the independence assumption. However, it is sensitive to noise. For example, when the tracked target approaches distractions that are similar to it, use of product rule results in failure. On the other hand, the weighted sum rule will not amplify the noise contained in the visual cues, but it cannot increase the belief in the estimate, and cannot be used for a long period of time. These can be depicted as Fig. 9.4. We present the estimated state distributions by four trackers in case of an occlusion. These four trackers include one using edge cue, one using color cue, one fusing two cues via product rule, and one fusing via the weighted sum rule. The state distribution from the tracker using product rule has highest peak among other three trackers, but it decrease quickly when it is affected by occlusion. Even the tracking performance of

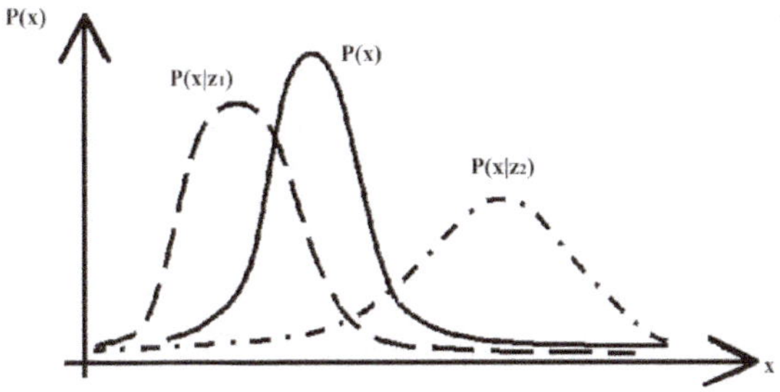

Fig. 9.3 Fusion by product rule. Two *dashed curves* show the estimated PDFs by using two individual cues, respectively. The *solid-line curve* shows the resulting PDF by using the product rule

the weighted sum rule is also affected by occlusion, but the it works better than the product rule.

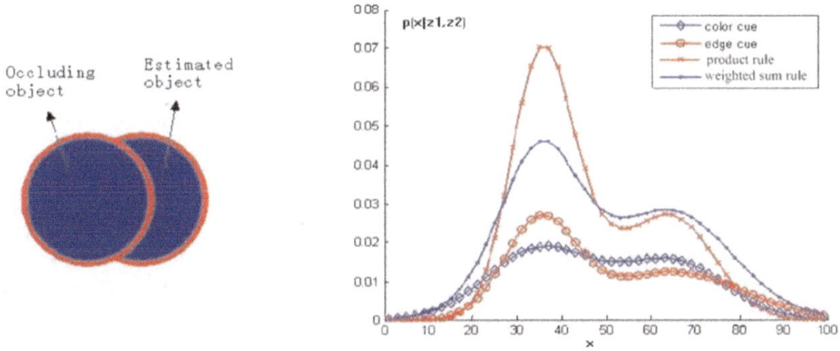

Fig. 9.4 *Left*: an occlusion occurs between two similar objects. *Right*: The resulted horizontal direction marginal densities of the tracked object from four trackers in dealing with occlusion are shown. One uses edge only and one uses color only. The other two fuse color and edge via the product rule and the weighted sum rule, respectively

9.4.2 Adaptive Fusion Rule

Since the max rule, min rule, median rule, and majority vote rule have been shown to be special cases of the sum and the product rules (Kittler et al. 1998), we just focus on the product rule and weighted sum rule for tracking in this section.

In the context of visual tracking, the weighted sum rule and the product rule can be complementary to each other especially when occlusion occurs during tracking. This finding forms the basis of the adaptive fusion strategy: when all cues used are reliable, fusion with the product rule can increase the belief of the estimate. When one visual cue degenerates, the fusion scheme should switch to using the weighted sum rule. The uncertainty of the state estimated by the cue can be used to determine whether this cue is degenerate or not.

Using the weighted sample set belonging to the i-th cue, we first estimate second moment of the sample set, and then compute its Frobenius norm as the measure of the uncertainty of the i-th cue. We denote Δ_i as the Frobenius norm, which is defined as

$$\Delta_i = \|Cov(C_i)\|_F = \left(\sum_{m=1}^{dim(\mathbf{x})} \sum_{n=1}^{dim(\mathbf{x})} |Cov(C_i)_{m,n}|^2 \right)^{1/2}, \tag{9.5}$$

where C_i denotes the weighted sample set of the i-th cue and $\|\cdot\|_F$ denotes the Frobenius norm. We denote $Cov(C_i)$ as the second moment of the sample set and $Cov(C_i)_{m,n}$ as the element of the $Cov(C_i)$. Given the particle set $\{\mathbf{x}^{(n)}, \omega_n\}_{n=1}^{N}$ of the i-th cue, $Cov(C_i)$ is then calculated as

$$Cov(C_i) = E[(\mathbf{x}-\mathbf{m}_i)\cdot(\mathbf{x}-\mathbf{m}_i)^T|C_i] = \sum_{n=1}^{N} \omega_n \cdot (\mathbf{x}^{(n)}-\mathbf{m}_i)\cdot(\mathbf{x}^{(n)}-\mathbf{m}_i)^T, \tag{9.6}$$

where N is the number of sample, ω_n is the weight of the n-th particle by computing the defined likelihood function $p(\mathbf{z}_i|\mathbf{x}^{(n)}, C_i)$. $\mathbf{m}_i$ is the mean of the sample set of the i-th cue, which can be calculated as $\mathbf{m}_i = \sum_{n=1}^{N} \omega_n \cdot \mathbf{x}^{(n)}$.

Finally, the reliability of each cue is defined as $r_i = \Delta_i^{-1}$. More specifically, this strategy employs a particle filtering technique, estimating the second-order moment of the weighted sample set and computing its Frobenius norm to denote how reliable cues are, and then switch between the product rule and the weighted sum rule adaptively. A threshold t_i for each cue is set to determine whether it is degenerate or not. The weight of the i-th cue, α_i in (9.3), can be computed according to the formula (9.7). Detailed steps of the adaptive fusion algorithm are shown in Table 9.1.

$$\alpha_i = \Delta_i^{-1} / \sum_{j=1}^{K} \Delta_j^{-1} \tag{9.7}$$

9.4.3 Online Approach to Determining the Reliability of a Visual cue

In the above section, the threshold for each cue is determined empirically. Here we introduce an online approach to determine the threshold for eachcue. This approach

Table 9.1 Detailed steps of the adaptive fusion rule

Assume that there are K visual cues available for the fusion.

1. Initialization: for $k=1$, initialize the particle set $\{\mathbf{x}_k^{(n)}, \frac{1}{N}, n=1,...,N\}$
2. For $k=2,...,N_f$, where N_f is the length of the input video sequence, do

- Prediction: $\tilde{\mathbf{x}}_k^{(n)} = p(\mathbf{x}_k|\mathbf{x}_{k-1}^{(n)}),\ n=1,...,N$;
- Calculate particle weight for each cue, and then normalize them, respectively. $\omega_{i,k}^{(n)} \propto p(\mathbf{z}_{i,k}|\mathbf{x}_k^{(n)}),\ i=1,...,K$, and $n=1,...,N$. $\mathbf{z}_{i,k}$ is the measurement corresponding to the i-th cue.
- Determine reliability of each cue according to Eqs. (9.5) and (9.6), and then fuse them;
  a. If any one cue degenerates, $\tilde{\omega}_{i,k}^{(n)} = \sum_{j=1}^{K} \alpha_j \omega_{j,k}^{(n)}$, where α_j is calculated according to Eq. (9.7), and then normalize $\tilde{\omega}_{i,k}^{(n)}$ to obtain $\omega_{i,k}^{(n)}$.
  b. Otherwise, $\tilde{\omega}_{i,k}^{(n)} = \prod_{j=1}^{K} \omega_{j,k}^{(n)}$, and then normalize $\tilde{\omega}_{i,k}^{(n)}$ to obtain $\omega_{i,k}^{(n)}$.
- Output: $\hat{\mathbf{x}}_k = \sum_{i=1}^{N} \omega_{i,k}^{(n)} \cdot \tilde{\mathbf{x}}_k^{(n)}$;
- Resample the particle set $\{\mathbf{x}_k^{(n)}, \omega_{i,k}^{(n)}\}$.

is based on detecting changes in the sequence of the recent observed measurement for the cue. If the sequence of the observed measurement does not follow the statistical properties prescribed by the measurement distribution, then the cue is degenerated.

Suppose that, for a visual cue $\mathbf{z}$, the PDF of the predicted state $\hat{\mathbf{x}}_k$ is $p(\mathbf{x}_k|\mathbf{z}^{k-1})$, then the probability of $\mathbf{z}_k$ can be calculated as

$$p(\mathbf{z}_k|\mathbf{z}^{k-1}) = \int p(\mathbf{z}_k, \mathbf{x}_k|\mathbf{z}^{k-1})d\mathbf{x} = \int p_z(\mathbf{z}_k|\mathbf{x}_k)p(\mathbf{x}_k|\mathbf{z}^{k-1})d\mathbf{x}. \tag{9.8}$$

where $p_z(\mathbf{z}_k|\mathbf{x}_k)$ is the measurement model of the visual cue. Since $p(\mathbf{x}_k|\mathbf{z}^{k-1})d\mathbf{x}$ is represented by a set of particles, Eq. (9.8) can be calculated online. If a sequence of the observed measurement $\mathbf{z}_k$ for the cue does not follow the statistical properties prescribed by $p(\mathbf{z}_k|\mathbf{z}^{k-1})$, then the cue is degenerated.

However, testing whether a sequence of $\mathbf{z}_k$ complys with $p(\mathbf{z}_k|\mathbf{z}^{k-1})$ is not an easy job, because $p(\mathbf{z}_k|\mathbf{z}^{k-1})$ depends on k and it evolves with time. In Andrieu et al. (2004), test variables are defined by treating each scalar component of the measurement, $\mathbf{z}_k$, separately. However, this leads to a set of dependent test variables.

To guarantee these variables following identical and independent distributions, we define the test variables as $u_{m,k} = g_m(z_{m,k}|z_{1,k},...,z_{m-1,k},z_{m+1,k},...,\mathbf{z}^{k-1})$, where $z_{m,k}$ is the m-th scalar components of the measurement $\mathbf{z}_k$, $g_m(\cdot)$ is the cumulative distribution of $z_{m,k}$ conditioning on $z_{1,k},...,z_{m-1,k},z_{m+1,k},...,z_{D,k}),\mathbf{z}^{k-1}$, where D denotes the dimension of $\mathbf{z}_k$.

We need access to $p(\mathbf{z}_k|\mathbf{z}^{k-1})$ to evaluate test variables $u_{m,k}$. Since $p(\mathbf{x}_k|\mathbf{z}^{k-1})$ is represented by a set of particles, $p(\mathbf{z}_k|\mathbf{z}^{k-1})$ can be represented as

$$p(\mathbf{z}_k|\mathbf{z}^{k-1}) \cong \frac{1}{N}\sum_{n=1}^{N} p_z(\mathbf{z}_k|\mathbf{x}_k^{(n)}). \tag{9.9}$$

If $p_z(\mathbf{z}_k|\mathbf{x}_k)$ admits analytic evaluations, then distribution $p(\mathbf{z}_k|\mathbf{z}^{k-1})$ can be expressed analytically. If $p_z(\mathbf{z}_k|\mathbf{x}_k)$ is too complex to allow for an analytical expression, we still can obtain a nonparametric expression for $p(\mathbf{z}_k|\mathbf{z}^{k-1})$ by first sampling from $p_z(\mathbf{z}_k|\mathbf{x}_k)$ to obtain a set sample, $\{\mathbf{z}_{s,k}^{(n)}\}_{n=1}^{N}$, for $p(\mathbf{z}_k|\mathbf{z}^{k-1})$, and then using a smooth Parzen estimator (Parzen 1961) to calculate

$$p(\mathbf{z}_k|\mathbf{z}^{k-1}) \cong \frac{1}{N}\sum_{n=1}^{N} H(\mathbf{z}_k - \mathbf{z}_{s,k}^{(n)}), \tag{9.10}$$

where $H(\cdot)$ is a separable Gaussian kernel, i.e., $h(\mathbf{z}) = \prod_m h(z_m)$.

With these definitions, test variables can be evaluated as

$$u_{m,k} = \frac{\sum_{n=1}^{N}\sum_{i=1}^{m-1} s(z_{i,k} - z_{s,i,k}^{(n)}) \int_{-\infty}^{z_{m,k}} h(\alpha - z_{s,m,k}^{(n)})d\alpha}{\sum_{n=1}^{N}\sum_{i=1}^{m-1} h(z_{m,k} - z_{s,i,k}^{(n)})}, \tag{9.11}$$

where $z_{s,m,k}^{(n)}$ is the m-th component of $\mathbf{z}_{s,k}^{(n)}$. The density of the vectors $\mathbf{u}_k = \{u_{1,k},\ldots,u_{D,k}\}$ will be a D-dimensional hypercube.

The statistical test finally boils down to the application of a distribution test to the set of $\{\mathbf{u}_j|j \in MW(i)\}$, where $MW(i)$ is a moving window that contains the recent I past time steps. This can be done as a chi-square test:

1. Divide the D-dimensional hypercube into L equally sized containers, and count the number of occurrence that the elements of the set $\{\mathbf{u}_j|j \in MW(i)\}$ fall into the l-th container. This number is denoted as b_l, and we have $\sum_{l=1}^{L} b_l = I$ (L must be such that $b_l > 5$ for each l). The expectation of b_l, e, is defined as $e = \frac{I}{L}$;
2. Calculate the test variable $\chi_{\mathbf{u}_k} = \sum_{l=1}^{L} \frac{(b_l-e)^2}{e}$.

If the cue is not degenerate, then the test variable $\chi_{\mathbf{u}_k}$ should has a χ_{L-1}^2 distribution.

9.5 Layer 2: Model Fusion

In contrast to the amount of research focused on target representation model, research efforts on modeling motion in visual tracking has received relatively little attention. However, the agile motion of a target often exceeds the prediction ability of simple motion models in real applications. This leads to very poor tracking with only one fixed dynamic model. A principled choice of motion model in a tracking system is essential for good results.

Recently, in visual tracking, considerable efforts have been undertaken in adopting hybrid system estimation techniques (Bar-Shalom et al. 2001), which are popular in the field of radar tracking. One well-known example is the multiple model approaches that provide a systematic method for using several motion models simultaneously to characterize the motion of agile targets. The IMM algorithm (Li and Jilkov 2005) is a well-known example, which has been proven to be one of the best compromises between optimal filtering and computational complexity in the radar target tracking literature. There appears some applications of IMM in visual tracking. For example, in (Tissainayagam and Suter 2003), an IMM algorithm has been embedded in a contour-tracking application.

In the models fusion layer, we propose a pseudo measurement-based IMM algorithm to address the uncertainties in motion modeling. We employ the prediction of the so-called pseudo measurement to fuse the motion information from multiple motion models. Furthermore, the fusing coefficients are set by combining both the image-based likelihood and the motion-based association probability. Since when the target approaches a distraction with similar appearance, it is reasonable that motion information plays a more important role than the appearance information in discriminating the target from the distraction.

9.5.1 Pseudo-Measurement-Based Multiple Model Method

The framework of the pseudo measurement-based IMM algorithm is depicted as Fig. 9.5. As shown in Fig. 9.5, there are J motion models for an IMM filter. The i-th motion model and its corresponding measurement model are

$$\mathbf{x}_k^i = F_k^i \mathbf{x}_{k-1}^i + \mathbf{w}_{k-1}^i \tag{9.12}$$

$$\mathbf{z}_k^i = H_k^i \mathbf{x}_k^i + \mathbf{v}_k^i \tag{9.13}$$

where $\mathbf{x}_k^i$ and $\mathbf{z}_k^i$ are the state vector and measurement vector at time k, respectively. Matrix F_k^i relates the state at the previous time step $k-1$ to the state at the current step k, in the absence of process noise $\mathbf{w}_{k-1}^i$. Matrix H_k^i relates the state $\mathbf{x}_k^i$ to the measurement $\mathbf{z}_k^i$. $\mathbf{w}^i$ and $\mathbf{v}^i$ are process noise and measurement noise, respectively. They are assumed to be independent (of each other), white, and with normal probability distributions. In the following, we denote the process noise covariance and measurement noise covariance matrices as R_k^i and Q_k^i, respectively.

The so-called pseudo measurement is obtained by combining the image-based and motion-based likelihood functions together. As shown in Fig. 9.5, $J(J \geq 1)$ measurements are involved in estimating the state of the target. Each of them is obtained from two sources: image information, and motion information. Let $\{\mathbf{z}_k^i\}_{i=1}^J$ denote J measurements at time k. The pseudo measurement $\bar{\mathbf{z}}_k$ is used to drive the IMM filter, and is defined as follows:

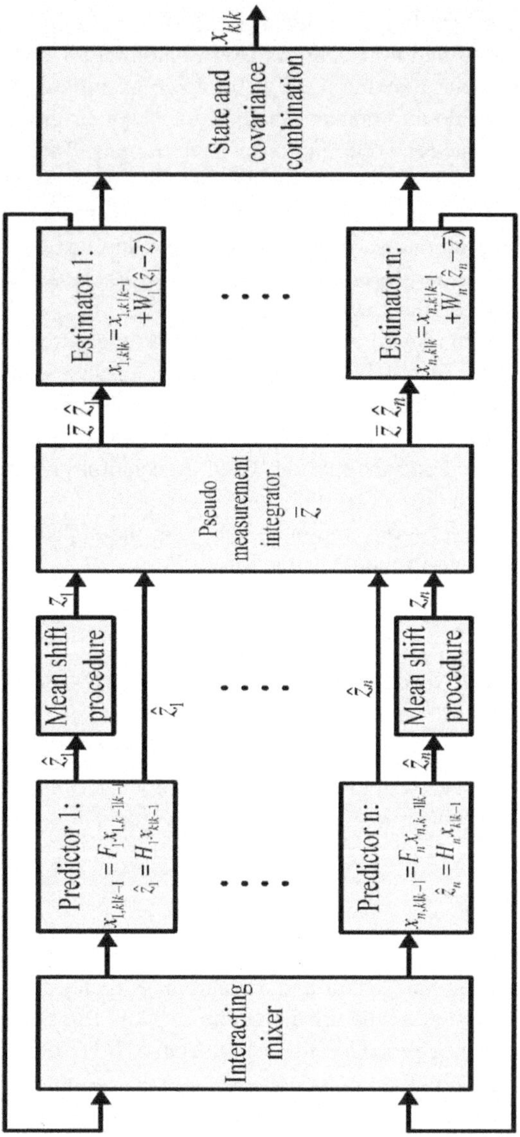

Fig. 9.5 Pseudo Measurement-based MM Filtering Framework. There are J motion models involved. For simplicity, each estimator is assumed to be a Kalman filter, and $W_i, i = 1, \ldots, J$ are the Kalman gain matrices

$$\bar{\mathbf{z}}_k = \sum_{i=1}^{J} \omega_k^i \cdot \mathbf{z}_k^i \tag{9.14}$$

$$\omega_k^i = \frac{p_k^i(\mathbf{z}_k^i|\mathbf{x}_k^i)}{\sum_{i=1}^{J} p_k^i(\mathbf{z}_k^i|\mathbf{x}_k^i)}.$$

where ω_k^i is the weight determined by $p_k^i(\cdot)$, the likelihood function of each candidate measurement belonging to the real target. The details of the likelihood function are presented in Section 9.5.2.

Let m_k^j be the j-th motion model at time k. Then the model probability conditioned on history measurements is

$$p(m_k^j|\mathbf{z}^{k-1}) = \sum_{i=1}^{J} p(m_k^j|m_{k-1}^i, \mathbf{z}^{k-1}) \cdot p(m_{k-1}^i|\mathbf{z}^{k-1}) \tag{9.15}$$

Where $\mathbf{z}^{k-1}$ is the history measurement up to time $k-1$. $p(m_k^j|m_{k-1}^i, \mathbf{z}^{k-1})$ indicates the predefined model transition probability, and $p(m_{k-1}^i|\mathbf{z}^{k-1})$ is the previous model probability conditioned on the history measurements. For each model, its corresponding filter (e.g., standard Kalman filter, or Particle filter) can calculate a measurement prediction, denoted by $\tilde{\mathbf{z}}_k^j$. Then, the pseudo measurement prediction is achieved by

$$\tilde{\mathbf{z}}_k = \sum_{j=1}^{J} p(m_k^j|\mathbf{z}^{k-1}) \cdot \tilde{\mathbf{z}}_k^j \tag{9.16}$$

This pseudo measurement prediction is crucial in the case of occlusion.

9.5.2 Likelihood Function

The likelihood function $p_k^i(\mathbf{z}_k^i|\mathbf{x}_k^i)$ in Eq. (9.14) , which uses appearance information as well as motion information, can be calculated as follows:

$$p_k^i(\mathbf{z}_k^i|\mathbf{x}_k^i) = (La_i(\mathbf{z}_k^i|\mathbf{x}_k^i))^{\alpha} \cdot (Lm_i(\mathbf{z}_k^i|\mathbf{x}_k^i))^{\beta}. \tag{9.17}$$

Where $La_i(\cdot)$ and $Lm_i(\cdot)$ denote the image-based likelihood and the motion-based likelihood, respectively. α and β are the weights corresponding to the reliability of the image-based and the motion-based information respectively, satisfying $0 \leq \alpha, \beta \leq 1$, and $\alpha + \beta = 1$.

Equation (9.17) indicates that the likelihood p_k^i becomes more rigorous when considering both the target representation and the motion model. For real applications, if there is frequent occlusions presented in the video, β should be set bigger than α and vice versa. Furthermore, to build a general adaptive likelihood model, one can treat the motion model and appearance model as two different cues, and then adopt the method in Section 9.4.3 to evaluate their reliability online. With this method, α and β can be adjusted adaptively.

There are many choices of functions for the image-based likelihood $La_i(\cdot)$, such as the image-based template matching function, the feature-based template matching function, and even the statistics-based likelihood function. We adopt the Bhattacharyya coefficient, and define $La_i(\cdot)$ as

$$La_i(\mathbf{z}_k^i|\mathbf{x}_k^i) = \exp\left(-\gamma\sum_l \sqrt{p_l(\mathbf{z}_k^i)q_l}\right) \tag{9.18}$$

where p and q are color histogram of the appearance of the target and that of measurement $\mathbf{z}_k^i$; γ is an adjustable parameter, which has a similar function as α and β. Thus in experiment, for simplicity, we fix α and β, and adjust γ only.

When occlusion occurs, the contribution of appearance information of the target fades out while the motion information plays an increasingly important role in the tracker. It is assumed that the measurement innovation, which is obtained via the pseudo measurement prediction, obeys a Gaussian distribution. Similar to the likelihood definition of IMM (Li and Jilkov 2005), Lm_i is defined as

$$Lm_i(\mathbf{z}_k^i|\mathbf{x}_k) = \frac{1}{\sqrt{2\pi|S_k^i|}}\exp\left[-\frac{(\mathbf{z}_k^i-\tilde{\mathbf{z}}_k)^T\cdot(S_k^i)^{-1}\cdot(\mathbf{z}_k^i-\tilde{\mathbf{z}}_k)}{2}\right] \tag{9.19}$$

where $\tilde{\mathbf{z}}_k$ is the predicted pseudo measurement defined in Eq. (9.16), S_k^i is the innovation covariance, which is calculated with the measurement covariance R_k^i in a standard Kalman filter. The motion-based likelihood function $Lm_i(\cdot)$ indicates that the pseudo measurement is biased towards motion prediction, controlled by the parameter α and β.

The detailed steps of the fusing algorithm in model fusion layer are presented in Table 9.2. We denote the model probability of the i-th model at time k as μ_k^i, the pre-defined model transition probability as $p(i,j)$, and mixing probability at time k as $\mu_k^{i,j}$, respectively. It seems that the algorithm still works within the IMM framework (Li and Jilkov 2005). However, we use a global pseudo measurement, which combines the motion-based likelihood and image-based likelihood, to calculate the novel information which flows into the filter of each model. These local adjustments finally result in a global improvement through the initialization step 2 and the final estimation steps 11 and 12.

9.6 Layer 3: Tracker Fusion

Both the appearance and motion of a target in an image will vary when it approaches the camera or vice versa. When the target is far away from the camera, it appears

Table 9.2 The detailed steps of the pseudo-measurement-based MM filtering algorithm for model's fusion in one circle

1. Calculate the mixing probabilities: $\mu_{k-1}^{i,j} = \frac{p(i,j)\cdot\mu_{k-1}^{i}}{\sum_i p(i,j)\cdot\mu_{k-1}^{i}}$
2. Redo the filters' initialization

$$\tilde{\mathbf{x}}_{k-1}^{j} = \Sigma_i \hat{\mathbf{x}}_{k-1}^{i}\mu_{k-1}^{i,j}$$
$$v_{k-1}^{i,j} = \hat{\mathbf{x}}_{k-1}^{i} - \tilde{\mathbf{x}}_{k-1}^{j}$$
$$P_{k-1}^{j,0} = \Sigma_i \mu_{k-1}^{i,j}\cdot\{P_{k-1}^{i} + v_{k-1}^{i,j}\cdot {v_{k-1}^{i,j}}^{T}\}$$

3. Filters' prediction: $\tilde{\mathbf{z}}_k^j = H_k^j\cdot\tilde{\mathbf{x}}_k^j = H_k^j\cdot F_k^j\cdot\tilde{\mathbf{x}}_{k-1}^j$
4. Calculate pseudo-measurement prediction $\tilde{\mathbf{z}}_k$ in (9.16);
5. Obtain $\mathbf{z}_k^j$ by starting Mean shift procedure from $\tilde{\mathbf{z}}_k^j$, and obtain R_k^j by SSD;
6. Get the appearance likelihood La_i via certain localization method;
7. Obtain the motion-based likelihood Lm_i by (9.19);
8. Calculate measurement likelihood p_k^i in (9.17);
9. Combine pseudo measurement $\tilde{\mathbf{z}}_k$ via (9.14);
10.Run each filter (particle filter or Kalman filter) to obtain $\hat{\mathbf{x}}_k^i$ and covariance P_k^i for each model;
11. Update model likelihood and probabilities as follows:

$$\Lambda_k^j = \mathcal{N}(\tilde{\mathbf{z}}_k - H_j\tilde{\mathbf{x}}_k^j; 0, S_k^j);$$
$$\eta_k^j = \Lambda_k^j \Sigma_i p(i,j)\cdot\mu_{k-1}^i;\quad \mu_k^j = \frac{\eta_k^j}{\Sigma_i \eta_k^i}$$

12. Obtain final estimate and covariance

$$\hat{\mathbf{x}}_k = \Sigma_i \hat{\mathbf{x}}_k^i\mu_k^i;\quad P_k = \Sigma_i \mu_k^i\{P_k^i + [\hat{\mathbf{x}}_k^i - \hat{\mathbf{x}}_k]\cdot[\hat{\mathbf{x}}_k^i - \hat{\mathbf{x}}_k]^T\}$$

like a spot; the nearer the target approaches, the bigger is the size of the spot. Eventually, its shape features become stronger, and finally, the texture and geometry of its surface become clear. This causes great difficulty for a tracking system that uses only one tracker based on a specific representation and a specific motion model. This fact must be considered in designing a robust tracker. To address this problem, a tracker fusion layer is presented.

9.6.1 Problem Formulation

Since an object may switch between different modes, e.g., from motion mode to representation mode, a specific filter may only be accurate for one type of mode. Even using multiple model approaches, the tracker with a single feature-based measurement model cannot completely eliminate the tracking failure owing to the varying appearance of the target. One feasible approach for robust tracking is to fuse trackers suitable for different object modes. Thus the tracking problem becomes a hybrid estimation problem if one has to simultaneously consider the discrete mode and continuous state processes.

We formulate the tracker fusion as a hybrid estimation problem. Let t_k, $k = 1,2,...,$ denote a discrete time Markov chain with known transition probabilities $p(t_{k+1}|t_k) = T_{t_k t_{k+1}}$. The fused tracker is a hybrid system, which is then defined as

$$\mathbf{x}_k = F(t_k, \mathbf{x}_{k-1}) + G(t_k, \mathbf{w}(t_{k+1})) \tag{9.20}$$

$$\mathbf{z}_k = H(t_k, \mathbf{x}_k) + \mathbf{v}(t_k) \tag{9.21}$$

where t_k indicates the system mode at time k. The parameter set $(F(\cdot), G(\cdot), H(\cdot))$ evolves with time according to the finite state Markov chain t_k. Moreover, neither the continuous variable $\mathbf{x}_t$ nor the discrete variable t_k is observable. Only the noisy measurement process $\mathbf{z}_t$ is observable. For simplicity, we assume

$$E[\mathbf{w}(t_k)] = 0, COV[\mathbf{w}(t_k)] = Q(t_k), \tag{9.22}$$

$$E[\mathbf{v}(t_k)] = 0, COV[\mathbf{v}(t_k)] = R(t_k). \tag{9.23}$$

The model space is extended in the tracker fusion layer. In the model fusion layer, the model space consists of the set of possible motion models in target tracking, as well as the measurement models. However, from the perspective of the tracker-estimator, the model space should consist of both motion models and measurement models, for representing the motion prior and for relating the state to the observation, respectively. In the tracker fusion layer, the model space is extended to include both the set of motion models and the set of the representation models.

The tracker t_k is composed by the m_k-th motion model and the r_k-th measurement model, where $m_k \in \{1,...,J\}$ and $r_k \in \{1,...,K\}$. Thus, there are JK different trackers available at each time step. The problem of the tracker fusion can be then described as estimating the optimal $\mathbf{x}_k$ from $p(\mathbf{x}_k|\mathbf{z}^k)$ according to the MMSE or MAP criterion, with the given JK trackers. In Section 9.6.2, Bayesian filtering is applied to suboptimally solving the hybrid estimation of the pair $(\mathbf{x}_k, t_k)$ given the history observations $\mathbf{z}^k$. It is worth noting that if $J = 1$, this problem reduces to a multiple model problem; if $K = 1$, then the problem degenerates to a multiple cue fusion problem.

9.6.2 Interactive Multiple Trackers

Brute-force implementation of the optimal MMSE and MAP estimators by fusing JK trackers is infeasible, since the number of possible tracker sequences (hypotheses) increases exponentially with time (more precisely, geometrically increases with discrete time). One straightforward means for reducing the hypothesis tree is to have a fixed memory depth, such that all hypotheses that are the same in the latest n time steps are merged. In this case, each of the JK trackers runs $(JK)^{n-1}$ times at each recursion. Motivated by the merging strategies of

IMM (Li and Jilkov 2005), we consider merging different estimates based on same tracker pair $t^{(i)}$ and $t^{(j)}$ at time $k-1$ and k, respectively. The recursive conditional filtering at time k consists of $(JK)^k$ conditional filtering operations, which may be approximated by only $(JK)^2$ conditional filtering operations.

First, the branched prior densities are merged into JK tracker-conditional prior densities.

$$p(\mathbf{x}_k|t_{k+1},\mathbf{z}^k) = \sum_{t_k} p(\mathbf{x}_k|t_k,\mathbf{z}^k)p(t_k|t_{k+1},\mathbf{z}^k) \tag{9.24}$$

where the mixing probability $p(t_k|t_{k+1},\mathbf{z}^k)$ can be obtained by

$$p(t_k|t_{k+1},\mathbf{z}^k) = \frac{p(t_{k+1}|t_k)p(t_k|\mathbf{z}^k)}{\sum_{t_k} p(t_{k+1}|t_k)p(t_k|\mathbf{z}^k)} \tag{9.25}$$

Then, after tracker-conditioned filtering,

$$p(\mathbf{x}_{k+1}|t_{k+1},\mathbf{z}^{k+1}) \leftarrow p(\mathbf{x}_k|t_{k+1},\mathbf{z}^k) \tag{9.26}$$

and tracker probability updating,

$$p(t_{k+1}|\mathbf{z}^{k+1}) \propto p(\mathbf{z}_{k+1}|t_{k+1},\mathbf{z}^k)p(t_{k+1}|\mathbf{z}^k) \tag{9.27}$$

$$p(t_{k+1}|\mathbf{z}^k) = \sum_{m_k}\sum_{r_k} p(t_{k+1}|t_k)p(t_k|\mathbf{z}^k) \tag{9.28}$$

the posterior density is obtained by the weighted sum fusion,

$$p(\mathbf{x}_{k+1}|\mathbf{z}^{k+1}) = \sum_{t_{k+1}} p(\mathbf{x}_{k+1}|t_{k+1},\mathbf{z}^{k+1})p(t_{k+1}|\mathbf{z}^{k+1}) \tag{9.29}$$

Equations (9.24), (9.25), (9.26), (9.27), (9.28) and (9.29) form the interactive multiple trackers (IMT)fusing framework. As shown in Fig. 9.6, the IMT framework clearly shows that this tracker fusion layer fuses multiple tracking algorithms in a more cooperative and flexible way than other brute-force fusion methods, for example, the black box approach in (Leichter et al. 2006).

9.6.3 Practical Issues

Multiple trackers can work cooperatively within framework aforementioned. However, the number of trackers (filters) is still large if JK is not small. Thus, the model association is introduced to reduce the number of tracker candidates. Furthermore, there still need some preprocessing before fusing these trackers fusion with the IMM framework. Thus, we introduce the rectification of prediction in the preprocessing.

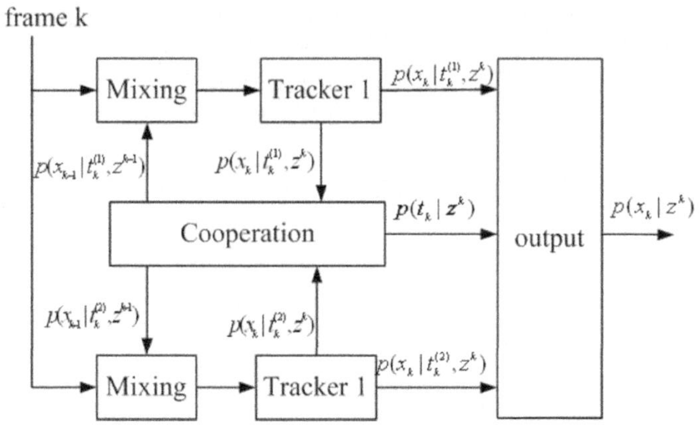

Fig. 9.6 The framework of the interactive multiple tracker

9.6.3.1 Model Association

Since the representation models in a tracker do not work in the prediction step of filtering, they can be wrapped into one filtering process as follows.

$$p(\mathbf{x}_k|m_k,\mathbf{z}^k) = \sum_{r_k} p(\mathbf{x}_k|t_k,\mathbf{z}^k)p(r_k|m_k) \tag{9.30}$$

where $p(r_k|m_k)$ is the association probability of the r_k-th representation model with the m_k-th motion model.

Different representation models have different observation noise R_{r_k}. However, how they match the base process noise Q_0 hasn't been investigated. To be more reliable, the tracker should sharpen the posterior distribution, which is proportional to the product of the prior and the likelihood function. In the Gaussian case, using a Kalman filter, the covariance of posterior $\mathcal{N}(\mu,C)$ can be obtained by (9.31)

$$C_{r_k}^{-1} = R_{r_k}^{-1} + Q_0^{-1}. \tag{9.31}$$

In the non-Gaussian case, using a particle filter, the covariance of the posterior can be calculated based on the set of particles by using equation (9.6).

Under the same noise level $det(R_{r_k})$, the tracker will pick model r_k with a smaller C_{r_k} with a greater probability. Therefore, one can define the model association probability as

$$\mathcal{L}_{r|m} = det(\bar{C}_r^{-1}) = \frac{1}{det(R_r)}R_r^{-1} + \frac{1}{det(Q)}Q_m^{-1}, \tag{9.32}$$

$$p(r|m) = \frac{\mathscr{L}_{r|m}}{\sum_r \mathscr{L}_{r|m}}. \tag{9.33}$$

where the terms $\frac{1}{det(R_r)}$ and $\frac{1}{det(Q)}$ are used to maintain the same noise level.

9.6.3.2 Rectification of Prediction

In the prediction step of a standard SMC filter, noise samples $\{\tilde{w}^{(i)}\}_{i=1}^{n}$ are drawn independently from dynamic processes. However, they ignore the correlation of different components in noise, that is, the covariance Q is a diagonal matrix, which is not true in real scene images. Thus, prediction must be rectified via multiplying a projection matrix formed by the eigenvectors of Q, that is,

$$w^{(i)} = (\frac{\lambda_1 \mathbf{v}_1}{||\mathbf{v}_1||}, \frac{\lambda_2 \mathbf{v}_2}{||\mathbf{v}_2||}, \ldots, \frac{\lambda_{dim} \mathbf{v}_{dim}}{||\mathbf{v}_{dim}||})^T \tilde{w}^{(i)} \tag{9.34}$$

where $\mathbf{v}_j$ is the j-th eigenvector of Q , λ_j denotes the corresponding eigenvalue, and dim is the number of eigenvectors. Moreover, the components are divided by the norm to preserve the ellipsoidal shape of uncertainty.

9.6.3.3 IMT Algorithm

To adapt to the non-Gaussian case, we adopt particle filtering techniques to achieve an interactive multiple tracker algorithm. Each recursion of the IMT particle filter consists of six steps which are presented in Table 9.3. In the algorithm, we use $t_k|t_k^m = \mu$ to denote the tracker whose component of motion model is μ, and $n(t_k)$ to denote the number of samples using tracker t_k at time k. There are N_s samples in the conditioned sample set for each tracker.

9.7 Sensor Fusion

A distributed fusion structure can be chosen as the additional sensor fusion layer. The objective of fusing the individual outputs of multiple sensors is to achieve a higher accuracy than that of the best of the individual sensors.

There is a consensus among researchers in multiple sensor fusion that the major factor for higher accuracy is the diversity of the sensor team, and so, the fusion method is of secondary importance. However, the configuration of multiple sensors is an application specified problem. Given a set of sensors, the only way to extract the maximum potential from that set is to pick a good fusion method. In the following and in Fig. 10.3, a typical data fusion system is presented, for tracking with and going beyond visible spectrum imaging sensors is presented. The system is equipped with three kinds of sensors: a CCD camera, a visible infrared-spectrum

Table 9.3 Detailed steps of interactive multiple model filtering

For all trackers, get $\{\mathbf{x}_{k,t_k}^{(i)}\}_{i=1}^{n(t_k)}$ from $\{\mathbf{x}_{k-1,t_{k-1}}^{(i)}\}_{i=1}^{n(t_{k-1})}$, where $t_k, t_{k-1} \in \{1,...,J\} \times \{1,...,K\}$;

1. Get mixing probability $p(t_{k-1}|t_k, \mathbf{z}^{k-1})$ from Eq. (9.25);
2. Perform particle set mixing:
   Draw $n(t_{k-1})$ samples $\bar{\mathbf{x}}_{k-1,t_{k-1}}$ from integrated sample set
   $\bar{p}(\mathbf{x}_{k-1}|t_k, \mathbf{z}^{k-1}) = \sum_{t_{k-1}} \sum_{i=1}^{n(t_{k-1})} p(t_{k-1}|t_k, \mathbf{z}^{k-1}) \frac{1}{n(t_{k-1})} \delta(\mathbf{x}_{k-1}, \mathbf{x}_{k-1,t_{k-1}}^{(i)})$
   to represent $p(\mathbf{x}_{k-1}|t_k, \mathbf{z}^{k-1})$;
3. Filter prediction: draw noise $w_{k,t_k}^{(i)}$ from dynamic process to obtain $\tilde{\mathbf{x}}_{k,t_k}^{(i)}$;
4. Filtering update:

   - Given observation $\mathbf{z}_k$, re-weight the samples:
     $\tilde{\pi}_{k,t_k}^{(i)} = p(\mathbf{z}_k|\tilde{\mathbf{x}}_{k,t_k}^{(i)}, t_k, \mathbf{z}^{k-1}) p(r_k|m_k)$
   - Normalize in the same motion model:
     $\alpha_k^{t_k} = \sum_{i=1}^{n(t_k)} \tilde{\pi}_{k,t_k}^{(i)}$, $\beta_k^u = \sum_{t_k|t_k^m=u} \alpha_k^{t_k}$,
     $\pi_{k,t_k|t_k^m=u}^{(i)} = \tilde{\pi}_{k,t_k|t_k^m=u}^{(i)} / \beta_k^u$
   - Get $\{\mathbf{x}_{k,t_k|t_k^m=u}^{(i)}\}_{i=1}^{N_s}$ by resampling N_s times from
     $\{\tilde{\mathbf{x}}_{k,t_k|t_k^m=u}^{(i)}, \pi_{k,t_k|t_k^m=u}^{(i)}\}_{i=1}^{N_s}$
   - Gather the samples belonging to the same tracker to obtain $\{\mathbf{x}_{k,t_k}^{(i)}\}_{i=1}^{n(t_k)}$;

5. Update the tracker probability: $p(t_k|\mathbf{z}^{k-1}) = \sum_{t_{k-1}} p(t_k|t_{k-1}) p(t_{k-1}|\mathbf{z}^{k-1})$,
   $p(t_k|\mathbf{z}^k) = \alpha_k^{t_k} p(t_k|\mathbf{z}^{k-1}) / \sum_{t_k} \alpha_k^{t_k} p(t_k|\mathbf{z}^{k-1})$;
6. Output: $p(\mathbf{x}_k|\mathbf{z}^k) = \sum_{t_k} \sum_{i=1}^{n(t_k)} p(t_k|\mathbf{z}^k) \frac{1}{n(t_k)} \delta(\mathbf{x}_k, \mathbf{x}_{k,t_k}^{(i)})$

sensor, and a thermal-spectrum sensor for the 24-h surveillance of an open space. In the experiment, a weighted sum fusion rule is used in the sensor fusion layer.

Data from sensors is often preprocessed before fusion with other data. Examples of source processing include image processing, signal processing or conditioning, alignment of the data in time or space, filtering of data, and other operations to prepare the data for the subsequent fusion. We do not address preprocessing in detail in this section for two reasons: (1) the first three fusion layers within the channel of a single sensor have been defined and (2) the pre-processing is specific to individual sensors and data types.

Since there already exists a mature theoretical framework in the distributed fusion of multiple sensors, we do not present much additional detail here. Interested readers can refer to (Bar-Shalom and Li 1995) and (Hall and McMullen 2004) for more further information.

9.8 Implementation Issues and Empirical Results

In this section, some implementation issues with respect to the three-layer robust visual tracking system are discussed and some empirical results are presented. The performance of each layer is tested with visible or infrared video sequence containing several challenging situations. Since the first three layers of the fusion framework are handled within a single sensor channel, only visible video or infrared video are used in the experiments on these three layers. It should be noted that experiments in this section deal only with general object tracking, without explicit prior knowledge about the object, so no model-based features are involved.

9.8.1 Visual Cue Fusion Layer

9.8.1.1 Two-Hand Tracking

We test the visual cue fusion algorithm with a video sequence containing two hands on opposite sides of an image that switch positions, overlapping paths in the process. The occluded hand is selected as the target. Two visual cues are fused, the color cue and the edge cue. Since the particle filer is being applied, the likelihood for each cue must be defined. In this experiment, a likelihood function for the color cue is adopted, similar to the likelihood function in (Pérez et al. 2002). For the edge cue, a Hausdorff distance-based likelihood is defined in the following formula:

$$p(\mathbf{z}|\mathbf{x}) = p_0 + k_s \exp^{-HD^2(M,P(\mathbf{x}))/2\sigma^2}. \tag{9.35}$$

where HD denotes Hausdorff distance, M_t is the edge-template, and $P(\mathbf{x})$ is edge set of the candidate $\mathbf{x}$. $p_0 = 0.1$ is a constant to make the likelihood bigger than zero even in the worst case.

Figure 9.7 shows some key frames from the tracking results when two hands are switched. Frames in the top row show some tracking results using the product fusion rule. More results are available from the attached video clip "demo-prod-only-02.avi". Frames in the middle row show tracking results using the weighted sum rule, and more results are available from the attached video clip "demo-sum-only-02.avi". Tracking results using adaptive fusion rule are presented in the bottom row, and more results can be available from the attached video clip "longtime-01.avi". Figure. 9.8 shows the Frobenius norm value of the covariance of the two cues when using the three different fusion rules. Empirical results show in comparison to the weighted sum rule and the product rule, the adaptive strategy in the fusion layer for visual cues increases the compactness of the weighted sample efficiently, as well as increasing the accuracy and robustness of the tracker.

Figure 9.8 shows the Frobenius norm value of the covariance of the estimated target state conditioned on a visual cue when using three different fusion rules. Theoretically, at a fixed time instant and in a specified scenario, the uncertainty (or reliability) of a visual cue for tracking should be a constant. The reason why curves

Fig. 9.7 Tracking results from the visual cue fusion layer. The estimated tracked hand position is marked with a *red box* attached with particles from each cue. The *left* column displays the tracking result of the product rule. The *middle* column shows the results of the weighted sum rule. And the results generated by the adaptive strategy are shown in the right colum. The *bottom left* of each frame contains a label indicating the method used

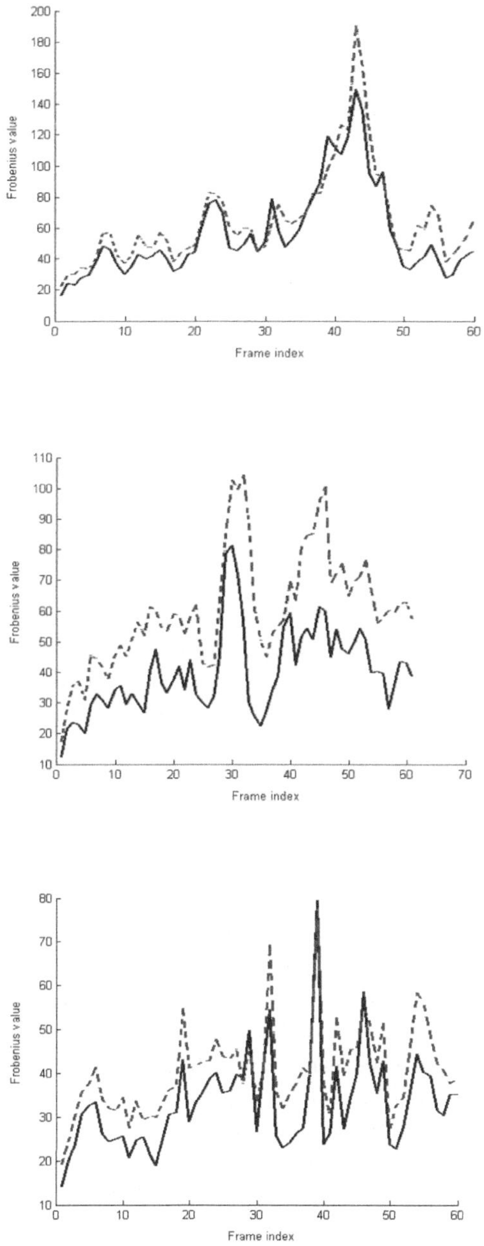

Fig. 9.8 The Frobenius norm of each cue at each frame. The *dashed-line* denotes the color cue, and the *solid-line* denotes the edge cue. The top figure shows the results of the product rule. The middle graph shows the results of the weighted sum rule, and the *bottom* shows the results of the adaptive strategy

produced by these three trackers are different is due to the way of evaluating the uncertainty of the visual cue. In this chapter, the uncertainty of a visual cue is evaluated by the Frobenius norm of the covariance of the estimated target state which is now the estimation of fusing two cues, not the estimation of the individual cue. However, by comparing these three sets of curves in Fig. 9.9, we have at least two findings: (1) change trends of these curves are almost same, this indicates the method of evaluating the uncertainty of the visual cue still make sense and (2) the adaptive fusion rule is the most efficient in reducing the uncertainties of these cues. This also shows that the adaptive fusion rule outperforms the product rule and the weighted sum rule.

Furthermore, we tested the nonparametric approach for measuring reliability presented in Section 9.4.3 by comparing two trackers: one tracker use nonparametric approach, another tracker use Frobenius norm of the covariance matrix to determine the reliability. Experimental results show that the two trackers has almost the same performance.

9.8.2 Model Fusion Layer

9.8.2.1 Tracking a Soccer Player

We tested the algorithm with a real video sequence from a soccer game, and compared it to two other algorithms in several phases (the mean shift procedure, and mean shift (Comaniciu and Meer 2002) in conjunction with the constant velocity (CV) motion model, which is based upon Kalman filtering). Three motion models are used to characterize the ballplayer's motion: constant velocity model (CA), constant acceleration model with small noise (LowCA), and constant acceleration model with large noise (HighCA). α and β in Eq. (9.17) are both set to 0.5.

Figure 9.9 presents some tracking results of these three trackers. The estimated position marked with a red cross. Only frames ♯6, ♯10, ♯27, ♯28, ♯29 are shown. Additional results from these three methods are available from the attached three video clips: "MeanShift tracking.mpg" for mean shift-based tracker, "MeanShift+Kalman.mpg" for the second method, and "psdMsmMM tracking.mpg" for the model fusion layer. Obviously, the mean shift method fails when two players of the same team are very close to each other, as in Frame 6 to Frame 10, because mean shift cannot differentiate well based only upon the player's appearance. From Frame 27 to Frame 29, the mean shift + Kalman method also fails since the player's position predicted in the Kalman filter drops into the region of another similar player. However, this approach is such a robust tracking method for player tracking that it can still succeed in many hard cases. For the proposed algorithm, several tracking failures occurs in the case when the target is occluded by another ball player wearing same clothes over five frames and the overlap area is over 70%.

The left graph in Fig. 9.10 shows the history of the motion model probabilities for the player selected by the model fusing algorithm. Obviously, the motion model probability is not as stable as that in the radar literature because the mean shift procedure is not stable for player localization. Moreover, we redo our method only under the modification of parameter γ, comparing the square root error in position with the actual position, as marked by hand (the right graph in Fig. 9.10). These experimental results have demonstrate that image based likelihood does improve player tracker. We found that the variations of γ do not affect the performance of the tracker fused tracker very much.

Fig. 9.9 Tracking results of the model fusion layer. The estimated tracked player position is marked with a *red* cross. The *left* column displays the mean shift only tracking result. The middle column shows the result of the Kalman + mean shift method. The results of the pseudo measurement-based multiple model approach is shown in the *right* column

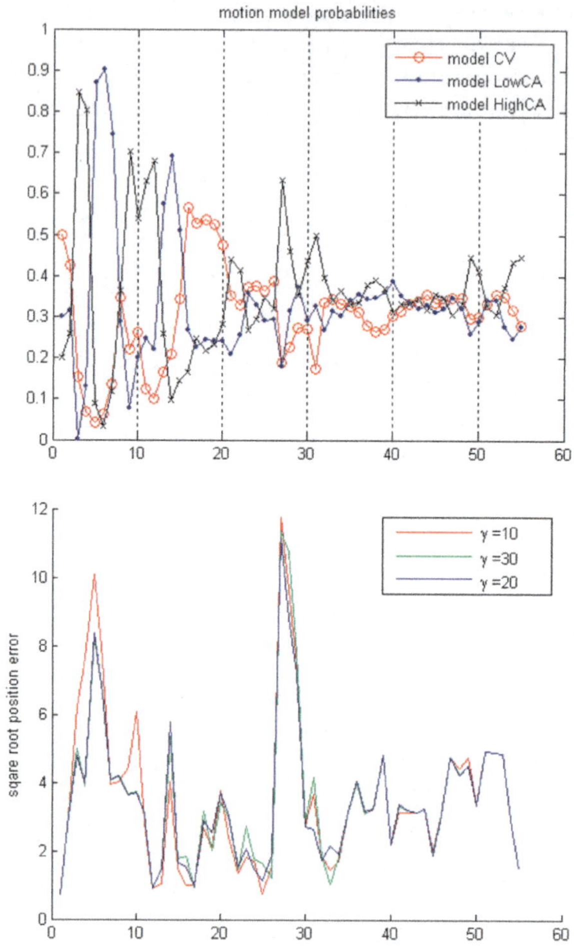

Fig. 9.10 The *left* graph shows the motion model probability of the selected player. The right graph demonstrates the square root position error of the tracking results by adjusting γ in the image-based likelihood

9.8.3 Tracker Fusion Layer

This section presents the experimental results of testing the tracker fusion layer. The multiple tracker fusion algorithm is first tested with an infrared video sequence, and then tested with a real video sequence.

9.8.3.1 Tracking in Infrared Video

The test video contains challenging situations that target approaches and moves away from the camera, and the range of target appearance changes beyond the describing power of the appearance model available. In the experiment, we adopted an adaptive window algorithm in Sung et al. (1997) to determine the search region.

According to the appearance change within the search region, four appearance modes are defined: (1) point target, (2) target with weak-shape, (3) target with salient shape, and (4) large target. In each mode, a set of specified tracking algorithms for robust tracking is selected. More specifically, in the point target mode, only intensity information is available, and only the intensity-based tracker can be used. When the target appears to have a weak shape, both the intensity-based tracker and the template-based tracker are used. As more information is available, more types of trackers may be employed. for example, the contour-based appearance model and the shape model are adopted for target with salience shape and large target. For each appearance model, three motion models, CA, LowCA, and HighCA, are available. Thus we have 12 trackers in the tracker fusion layer.

Figure 9.11 presents some frames from the tracking results. More results are available from the video clip "Tracker fusion1.avi". Experimental results show that a single tracker cannot track the boat reliably through the test video, while the fused tracker can. We also found that fusion of multiple tracker increases not only the reliability of tracking, but also its accuracy in comparison to using only a single tracker.

9.8.3.2 Robust Head Tracking in Video

To further test the tracker fusion algorithm, it is used track a head in a real video sequence. Three representation models for head are selected. They are color, ellipse shape, and intensity-change-based representation models. For simplicity, the head's projection on the image is approximated by an ellipse. Furthermore, to make tracker fusion approach clear, all trackers are set in the same state space, which is a 4D upright elliptical space. In other words, we are modeling the head configuration as an ellipse parameterized by $\mathbf{x}_i = (x_0, y_0, a, b)$, $i = 1, \ldots, M$, where coordinate (x_0, y_0) is the center of the ellipse with a and b being the lengths of the two axes, respectively. Without ambiguity, all the time subscripts of the states are omitted in this subsection. Also, three motion models, CA, LowCA, and HighCA, are used to characterize the dynamics of the head configuration.

Color Based Tracker: Color has proven to be a simple but effective feature in computer vision. Owing to a statistical characteristic, a MoG (Mixture of Gaussians) is often used to model color distribution and is easy to train via the EM (Expectation-Maximization) algorithm. Therefore, MoG is employed to model head color which mainly consists of face(skin) color and hair color. Given the parameter Θ, the probability of the color $\mathbf{c}$ belonging to a particular head is formulated as

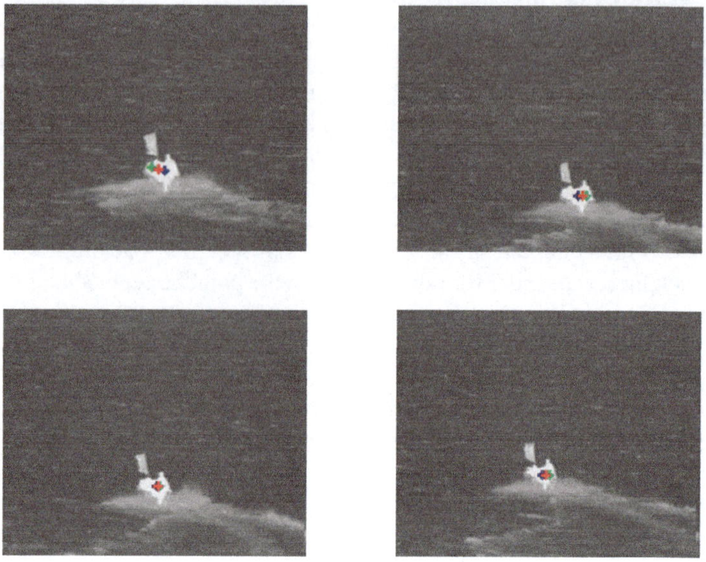

Fig. 9.11 Tracking results of the tracker fusion layer. From *left* to *right*, *top* to *bottom*, frames 2, 15, 25, 40 of the input video are chosen to present the tracking results. *Green, blue* and *red* crosses denote the output of the peak-based tracker, the correlation-based tracker, and the final fusion results, respectively

$p_c(\mathbf{c}|head,\Theta) = \sum_{i=1}^{M_c} \alpha_{c,i}\mathcal{N}(\mathbf{c};\mu_{c,i},\Sigma_{c,i})$, where $\Theta = \{\alpha_{c,i},\mu_{c,i},\Sigma_{c,i}\}_{i=1}^{M_c}$ is an EM-trained parameter set with the number of Gaussians M_c.

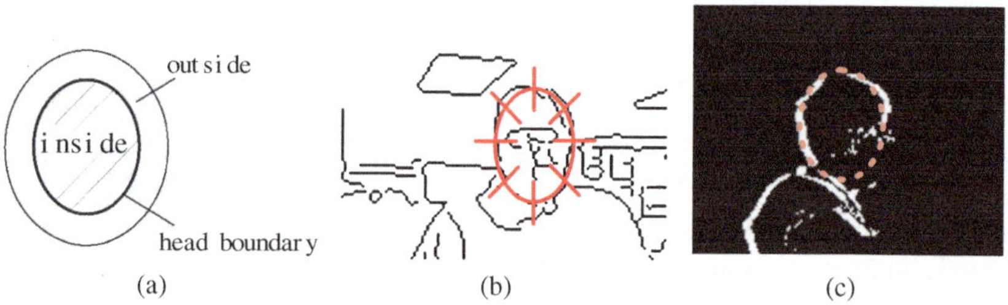

Fig. 9.12 (**a**) Two concentric elliptical areas are used to locate the head. The elliptical area *inside* indicates the head area, and the elliptical area *outside* is the transition area from head to background. (**b**) Measurement line of ellipse shape. (**c**) Measurement point of intensity-change

Further, we model the likelihood of observing an image given a head configuration $\mathbf{x}_i$ in the following way. First, the area inside the head and the area outside the head are defined along the boundary of the head as in Fig. 9.12(a). Then, the average foreground probability of the inside area is calculated as

$$f_{in}(\mathbf{x}_i) = \frac{1}{N_{in}} \sum_{k=1}^{N_{in}} p_{c_k}(\mathbf{c}_k | head, \Theta) \tag{9.36}$$

where N_{in} is the number of pixels in the inside area and $\mathbf{c}_k$ is the color value of the kth pixel. The average foreground probability of the outside area is similarly defined as $f_{out}(\mathbf{x}_i) = \frac{1}{N_{out}} \sum_{k=1}^{N_{out}} p_{c_k}(\mathbf{c}_k | head, \Theta)$.

Finally, a likelihood function for the head configuration yields,

$$p_{cl}(\mathbf{z}_i | \mathbf{x}_i) \propto \exp\{-\lambda_{c,1} \cdot \frac{(f_{out})^{\lambda_{c,2}}}{f_{in}}\}, \tag{9.37}$$

where $\lambda_{c,1}$ is used for adjusting sensitivity to the head configuration and $\lambda_{c,2}$ for tuning the impact of the outside area.

Ellipse-Shape-Based Tracker: The second representation mdoel is the ellipse-shape-based model, following the model introduced by MacCormick (2000). Unlike the complicated B-Spline contour model introduced earlier, we draw N_{nl} measurement lines normal to the elliptical head contour directly (see Fig. 9.12(b)).

An edge detector is applied on each measurement line, such that there are $n_l (l = 1, ..., N_{nl})$ edge points which can be used for the features on the lth measurement line. The distance between the jth feature and the ellipse contour is denoted by z^l_j, $j = 1, ..., n_l$. In addition, this distance is assumed to be Gaussian, with zero mean and variance σ_s^2. Let the probability of no feature being detected on the measurement line be p_0 and the number of features generated by clutter obey a Poisson process with density λ_s. Then, the likelihood of an observation on lth measurement line is defined as

$$\mathcal{L}_s(z^l | \mathbf{x}_i) \propto p_0 + \frac{1 - p_0}{\sqrt{2\pi}\sigma_s \lambda_s} \sum_{j=1}^{n_l} exp\{-\frac{(z^l_j)^2}{2\sigma_s^2}\}. \tag{9.38}$$

Consequently, we take the independent assumption of likelihoods on each measurement line. Thus the overall ellipse shape likelihood is

$$p_{sh}(\mathbf{z}_i | \mathbf{x}_i) = \prod_{l=1}^{N_{nl}} \mathcal{L}_s(z^l | \mathbf{x}_i). \tag{9.39}$$

Intensity-Change-Based Tracker: The last representation model is intensity-change-based, which is based on the differences between neighboring frames. Without a doubt, the intensity-change-based tracker provides a single target's motion because it is always assumed that the camera motion is trivial.

We introduce a new likelihood function for the ellipse state as follows. First, the motion area (white area in Fig. 9.12(c)) is obtained by set of threshold of the difference of neighboring frames. Then a number of points, called measure points, are put at equidistance on the ellipse boundary. The number of measure points that have been covered by motion area, which is denoted by $N_{e,co}$, are counted, as well as the number of pixels covered by motion area inside the ellipse, which is denoted by $N_{p,co}$. Further, the total number of measure points is denoted by $N_{e,to}$ and the total number of pixels inside the ellipse by $N_{p,to}$. Intutively, the likelihood could be defined as $exp\{-\lambda_{in,1}\frac{N_{e,co}}{N_{e,to}}\}$; however, pixels inside the object area should not be included in the motion area due to their slight motion. Thus, a penalty is needed such that the likelihood function can be written as

$$p_{in}(\mathbf{z}_i|\mathbf{x}_i) \propto \exp\{-\lambda_{in,1}(\frac{N_{e,co}}{N_{e,to}} - \lambda_{in,2}\frac{N_{p,co}}{N_{p,to}})\}, \quad (9.40)$$

where the parameter $\lambda_{in,1}$ adjusts the sensitivity to the intensity-change cue and $\lambda_{in,2}$ adjusts the penalty for only slight motion.

In Fig. 9.13 and 9.14, the red ellipse is used to indicate the MMSE estimate of the color-based observation model, green is used for the shape-based observation model, and yellow for the intensity-change-based observation model.

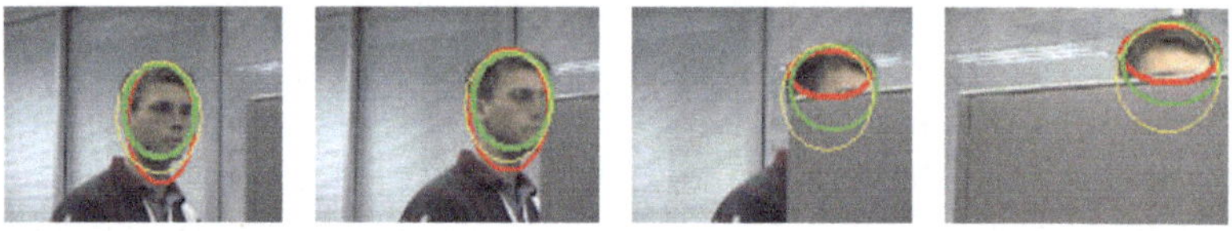

Fig. 9.13 Head tracking results in the sequence "seq_cubicle.avi". From left to right, frame number 52, 56, 60 and 68 are shown, respectively. The thickness of the ellipse represents the mixing probability of each tracker

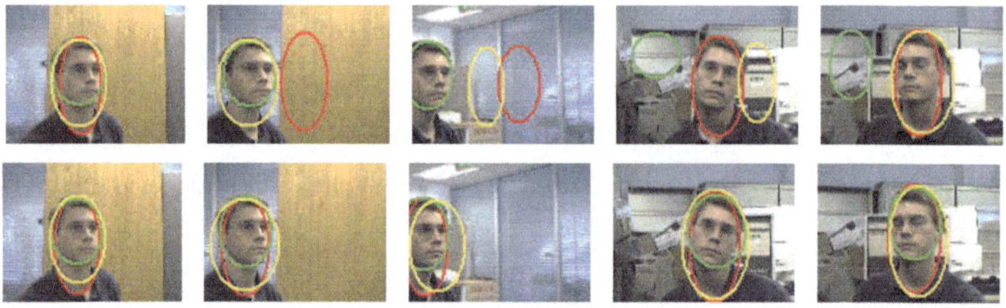

Fig. 9.14 Head tracking results in the sequence "seq_sb.avi". Figures in the *top* row show results produced by three independent trackers without fusion. Figures in the *bottom* show results produced by our IMT method. From *left* to *right*, the frames 116, 123, 133, 164 and 183 are shown, respectively

Figure 9.13 shows the results of head tracking with occlusion in the sequence "seq_cubicle.avi".[1] We use the thickness of the ellipse to represent the mixing probability of the tracker.

A portion of the head tracking results in the sequence "seq_sb.avi" are shown in Fig. 9.14 for performance comparison. When tracking without (top row) fusion, the color, shape, and intensity-change-based trackers all fail in frames 123, 164 and 133

[1] The test sequence is available at http://robotics.standard.edu/birch/headtracker/seq/.

respectively. In contrast, the IMT tracker is able to robustly and flexibly track the head at all time (bottom row) .

9.8.4 Bottom-Up Fusion with a Three-Layer Structure

To fully evaluate the performance of the proposed framework, the tracker consisting of first three layers of fusion, that is, the visual cue fusion layer, the model fusion layer and the tracker fusion layer, is tested by tracking head in a real video sequence. The input and output of each layer are either an explicit PDF, or a weighted sample set. The test video contains many challenging situations for visual trackers. For example, the cluttered background, varying illuminations, and variable appearance of the target.

Figure 9.15 shows tracking results for the three-layer fusion system. Firstly, the tracker is built by using the visual cue fusion layer only. There are three cues involved in the fusion: color, ellipse-shape, and intensity-change. The likelihood functions for cues are same as that have been defined in Section 9.8.3.2. The top row in Fig. 9.15 shows some results of the tracker using visual cue fusion only. Obviously, using visual cue fusion layer only is not enough to achieve robust tracking. Then, taking the visual cue fusion layer as the first layer, the tracker is augmented with the model fusion layer and the tracker fusion layer. The motion models for the model fusion layer are CA, LowCA, and HighCA. In addition to these three motion models, the same representation models for the target as that in Section 9.8.3.2 are also used in the tracker fusion layer. Some tracking results are presented in bottom row of Fig. 9.15. More experimental results are available from the video file three-layer.mpg. From the experiment, we found that because the output of the tracker fusion layer acts as initialization of the visual cue fusion layer, thus the visual cue fusion layer can easily recover from the tracking failures, and further improve the quality of the input to the model fusion layer. The tracker with three fusion layers can track the head reliable through the video sequence of 3245 frames.

9.8.5 Multi-Sensor Fusion Tracking System Validation

We also test the tracking the system presented in Fig. 10.3. This system is equipped with a CCD Camera, a visible infrared-spectrum sensor, and a thermal-spectrum sensor. Figure 9.16 presents the tracking results of a typical three-layer fusion system with three sensors at a single instance in time. Extensive empirical results show that fusion of these three sensors not only increases the accuracy and robustness of the system, but also extends areas of application. More extensive experimental results are available at http://www.aiar.xjtu.edu.cn/videocomputing.html.

Fig. 9.15 From *left* to *right*, the frame numbers are 24, 159, 201, 212, 221. Left column: Tracking results of the visual cue fusion layer. The ellipse indicates the estimated position of the head. Right column: Tracking results of the three-layer-fusion. Ellipse with *solid-line*, *short dashed-line*, and *long dashed-line* is the output of the tracker fusion layer, the model fusion layer and visual cue fusion layer, respectively

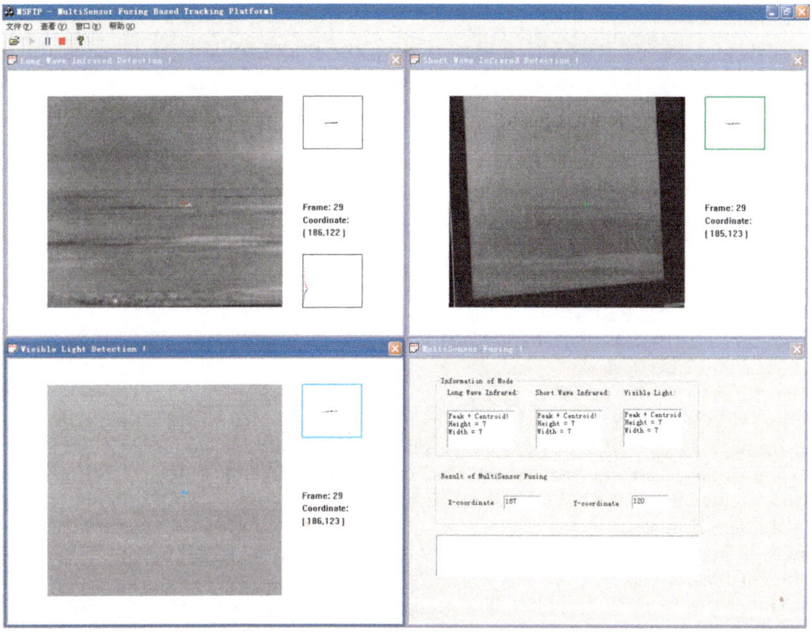

Fig. 9.16 Data fusion tracking system with three sensors. From *left* to *right*, *top* to *bottom*, the four overlaid views present tracking results of an infrared-spectrum sensor, a thermal-spectrum sensor, a CCD camera, and their final fusion results, respectively

9.9 Summary

In this chapter, we have discussed the design of a robust visual tracking system. A three-layer probabilistic fusion framework for visual tracking that employs visible spectrum sensors was proposed, but is not limited to these. Three different layers were defined in a bottom-up data fusion process for visual tracking. We demonstrated how the visual cue layer fuses multiple visual the modalities via adaptive fusion strategies, how the model layer fuses prior motion information via the IMM, and how the tracker layer fuses multiple trackers cooperatively and adaptively. State distributions are used as the interface between each pair of consequential layers to ensure consistency throughout the framework. Furthermore, the proposed framework is general and allows the augmentation and pruning of fusing layers according to the specifics of the visual environment at hand. The proposed framework has been tested extensively under various complex scenarios in which a single sensor-based tracker may fail, and satisfying tracking results have been obtained.

References

Andrieu C, Doucet A, Singh S, Tadic V (2004) Particle methods for change detection, system identification, and control. Proceedings of the IEEE 92(3):423–438

Bar-Shalom Y, Li X (1995) Multitarget-multisensor tracking: Principles and techniques. University of Connecticut Storrs, CT:

Bar-Shalom Y, Li X, Kirubarajan T (2001) Estimation with Applications to Tracking and Navigation. Wiley, New York

Collins R, Liu Y, Leordeanu M (2005) Online selection of discriminative tracking features. IEEE Transactions on Pattern Analysis and Machine Intelligence 27(10):1631–1643

Comaniciu D, Meer P (2002) Mean shift: a robust approach toward feature space analysis. IEEE Transactions on Pattern Analysis and Machine Intelligence 24(5):603–619

Hall D, McMullen S (2004) Mathematical Techniques in Multisensor Data Fusion. Artech House Publishers, London

Isard M, Blake A (1998) CONDENSATION–Conditional density propagation for visual tracking. International Journal of Computer Vision 29(1):5–28

Jepson A, Fleet D, El-Maraghi T (2003) Robust online appearance models for visual tracking. IEEE Transactions on Pattern Analysis and Machine Intelligence 25(10):1296–1311

Kittler J, Hatef M, Duin R, et al. (1998) On combining classifiers. IEEE Trans Pattern Analysis and Machine Intelligence 20(3):226–239

Leichter I, Lindenbaum M, Rivlin E (2006) A general framework for combining visual trackers–The Black Boxes? Approach. International Journal of Computer Vision 67(3):343–363

Li X, Jilkov V (2005) Survey of maneuvering target tracking. Part V: multiple-model methods. IEEE Transactions on Aerospace and Electronic Systems 41(4):1255

Liu J, Chen R (1998) Sequential monte carlo methods for dynamic systems. Journal of the American Statistical Association 93(443):1032–1044

MacCormick J (2000) Probabilistic exclusion and partitioned sampling for multiple object tracking John MacCormick and Andrew Blake. International Journal of Computer Vision, 39(1): 57–71, 2000. Abstract. International Journal of Computer Vision 39(1):57–71

McCane B, Galvin B, Novins K (2002) Algorithmic fusion for more robust feature Tracking. International Journal of Computer Vision 49(1):79–89

Parzen E (1961) On estimation of a probability density function and mode

Pérez P, Hue C, Vermaak J, Gangnet M (2002) Color-based probabilistic tracking. In: Proceedings of Europe Conference on Computer Vision, pp 661–675

Perez P, Vermaak J, Blake A (2004) Data fusion for visual tracking with particles. Proceedings of the IEEE 92(3):495–513

Roth S, Sigal L, Black M (2004) Gibbs Likelihoods for Bayesian Tracking. Proceedings of IEEE Conference on Computer Vision and Pattern Recognition 1:886–893

Siebel N, Maybank S (2002) Fusion of multiple tracking algorithms for robust people tracking. Proceedings of the 7th European Conference on Computer Vision pp 373–387

Spengler M, Schiele B (2003) Towards robust multi-cue integration for visual tracking. Machine Vision and Applications 14(1):50–58

Sung S, Chien S, Kim M, Kim J (1997) Adaptive window algorithm with four-direction sizing factors for robust correlation-based tracking. IEEE Conference on Tools with Artificial Intelligence, pp 208–215

Tissainayagam P, Suter D (2003) Contour tracking with automatic motion model switching. Pattern Recognition 36(10):2411–2427

Toyama K, Hager G (1996) Incremental focus of attention for robust visual tracking. Proceedings IEEE Conf on Computer Vision and Pattern Recognition pp 189–195

Toyama K, Hager G (1999) Incremental focus of attention for robust vision-based tracking. International Journal of Computer Vision 35(1):45–63

Vermaak J, Perez P, Gangnet M, Blake A (2002) Towards improved observation models for visual tracking: selective adaptation. European Conference on Computer Vision 1:645–660

Wu Y, Huang T (2001) A co-inference approach to robust visual tracking. Proceedings of the International Conference on Computer Vision

Wu Y, Yu T (2006) A Field Model for Human Detection and Tracking. IEEE Transactions on Pattern Analysis and Machine Intelligence 28(5):753–765

Xue J, Zheng N (2006) Robust tracking with and beyond visible spectrum: a four-layer data fusion framework. The International Workshop on Intelligent Computing in Pattern Analysis/Synthesis 1:1–16

Xue J, Zheng N, Zhong X (2006) Sequential stratified sampling belief propagation for multiple targets tracking. Science in China Series F 49(1):48–62

Zhong X, Xue J, Zheng N (2006a) Graphical model based Cue integration strategy for head tracking. In Proceedings of 17th British Machine Vision Conference

Zhong X, Zheng N, Xue J (2006b) Pseudo Measurement Based Multiple Model Approach for Robust Player Tracking. In Proceedings of Asian Conference on Computer Vision

Chapter 10
Multitarget Tracking in Video-Part I

Abstract Multitarget tracking in video (MTTV) presents a technical challenge in video surveillance applications. In this chapter, we formulate the MTTV problem using dynamic Markov network (DMN) techniques. Our model consists of three coupled Markov random fields: (1) a field for the joint state of multiple targets; (2) a binary random process for flagging the existence of each individual target; and (3) a binary random process for flagging occlusion in each dual adjacent targets. To make inference tractable, we introduce two robust functions that eliminate the two binary processes. We then propose a novel belief propagation algorithm, called Particle-based belief propagation, and embed it into a Markov chain Monte Carlo approach to obtain the maximum a posteriori (MAP) estimation in the DMN. With a stratified sampler, we incorporate the information obtained from a learned bottom-up detector (e.g., support vector machine (SVM) based classifier) and the motion model of the target into a message propagation framework. Other low-level visual cues, such as motion and shape, can be easily incorporated into our framework to obtain better tracking results. We have performed extensive experimental verification, and results suggest that our method is comparable to the state-of-art multitarget tracking methods in all cases we tested.

10.1 Introduction

In recent years, multitarget tracking in video (MTTV) has emerged as a very active research topic due to its widespread applications in many areas, including intelligent surveillance, intelligent transportation systems, visual human–computer interfaces, and smart conference rooms. The goal of MTTV is to determine specifically measurable attributes of multiple targets given a sequence of temporally ordered images. There has been considerable work in MTTV, in which isolated objects or a small number of objects with transient occlusions can be tracked with acceptable performance (Isard and Blake 1998, Perez et al. 2002, Isard and MacCormick 2001, Rasmussen and Hager 2001). However, the MTTV problem still remains

N. Zheng, J. Xue, *Statistical Learning and Pattern Analysis for Image and Video Processing*, Advances in Pattern Recognition, DOI 10.1007/978-1-84882-312-9_10,
© Springer-Verlag London Limited 2009

challenging when many targets are moving in close proximity or their paths present occlusions.

In tracking targets with a less-than-unity probability of detection as well as the presence of false alarms (FAs) (clutter), it is crucial to decide which measurements to use, among multiple candidates, to update each track. Traditional multitarget tracking (MTT) approaches (e.g., in radar target tracking) usually consist of two core components: data association and state estimation, working in consecutive order to accomplish the tracking task (Bar-Shalom and Li 1995; Cox et al. 1996). While explicit association of measurements with targets is a useful pragmatic device, it is difficult to find the exact solution due to uncertainties in modeling state dynamics and the measurement process. Many strategies have been proposed to solve the data association problem (Bar-Shalom and Li 1995; Cox et al. 1996; Fortmann et al. 1983; Reid 1979). These can be broadly categorized as follows:

(1) Single frame assignment methods: These types of methods (such as the joint probabilistic data association (JPDA) algorithm (Fortmann et al. 1983)) consider measurements at the current time step. They track a fixed number of targets by evaluating the measurement-to-track (or track-to-measurement) association probabilities and combining them to find the state estimate.
(2) Multiframe assignment methods: These types of methods (such as multiple hypothesis tracking (MHT) (Reid 1979)) consider measurements across several time steps. Compared with the JPDA algorithm, MHT is usually more effective in tracking a varying number of targets, since it involves a more complicated algorithm to initiate new tracks or terminate old tracks.

    Theoretically, MHT can solve increasingly difficult data association tasks with the increasing availability of measurements. However, construction of a new hypothesis requires an enumeration of all possibilities and the total number of association hypotheses can grow exponentially with the increase in the number of targets. The joint probabilistic data association filter (JPDAF) is a sequential tracker, and can solve data association faster than the deferred logic tracker of MHT. However, there are two sides to the coin and JPDAF has the following limitations (Bar-Shalom and Li 1995):

(1) It is prone to making erroneous associations, and it cannot initiate or terminate tracks, since only measurements at the current time step are considered.
(2) It assumes a fixed number of targets and requires a good initial state for each target.
(3) The exact calculation of data association in JPDAF is also theoretically NP-Hard when tracking numerous targets.

Unlike the point-like measurements in traditional MTT, image measurements in MTTV are fundamentally fraught with the presence of a cluttered background, a variable number of targets, and complicated inter-target interactions (occlusions or crosses). Due to these difficulties, a probabilistic framework is required to adequately address uncertainties in the measurement and state processes. Bayesian sequential estimationis such a framework, and is widely used in single target tracking in video (STTV). This framework maintains the recursive estimation of a time-evolving posterior distribution that describes the target state conditioned on all input measurements. It handles data association implicitly, since it samples data association hypotheses from the predictive distribution (which is constructed by propagating the posterior distribution of the target state at the previous time step) and then updates the posterior distribution using measurements assigned by these data association hypotheses. Thus, the data association and state estimation problems can be solved jointly. However, when applied to real world MTTV problems, the Bayesian sequential estimation framework faces two problems: nonlinear and non-Gaussian models, and difficult data association.

First, realistic motion models of targets and their measurement models are often nonlinear and non-Gaussian; thus, no closed-form analytic expression can be obtained for tracking recursion. Particle filtering provides a Monte Carlo (MC) based solution to this problem, and has achieved huge success in STTV (Isard and Blake 1998; Perez et al. 2002). If the objects to be tracked are distinctive from each other, they can be tracked independently with the least confusion by using multiple independent particle filters. However, a chief shortcoming of particle filtering and other MC methods in general, when applied to MTTV, is their poor ability to consistently maintain the multimodality of the filtering distribution (Vermaak et al. 2003). For example, in practice, when applying a particle filter with a multimode filtering distribution, all the particles will quickly migrate to the mode with the highest likelihood, subsequently discarding all other modes. This does not work in the MTTV case, because all modes in a filtering distribution for MTTV must continue to be tracked, since each mode may correspond to a target.

Second, measurements of targets yielded by image sensors are unlabeled, leading to a very challenging combinatorial data association problem, particularly when targets have a little separation compared with the measurement errors. This is especially problematic when multiple tracks compete for measurements. When occlusions occur, or the sudden disappearance or appearance of targets, or a cluttered background exists, etc., measurements may be incomplete or totally absent. In combination these lead to a formidable state estimation task.

Recently, many approaches have been proposed (Isard and MacCormick 2001; Vermaak et al. 2003; Tao et al. 1999; Zhao and Nevatia 2004; Li et al. 2004a; Xu and Xu 2004) to partially alleviate the difficulties in MTTV. However, within a dynamic background, the problems of how to model a variable number of potentially occluded targets and occlusions still remains unsolved.

In this chapter, we present a novel MTTV approach to modeling occlusion and a variable number of targets, and solve these problems using particle-based belief propagation (Xue et al. 2008). We have made two contributions: (1) an MTTV model derived from three coupled Markov random fields (MRFs); and (2) a novel particle-based belief propagation algorithm. First, we explicitly model the joint state of targets by using three coupled MRFs, and subsequently approximate them with a Markov network. When applied to tracking, the Markov network becomesan ad hoc dynamic Markov network (DMN). Second, we apply a novel belief propagation technique, called the particle-based belief propagation (BP) algorithm, to obtain the maximum a posterior (MAP) estimation in the DMN. By using a stratified sampler, we incorporate information both from a bottom-up learned detector (e.g., Support Vector Machine (SVM) detector (Suykens and Vandewalle 1999)) and a top-down target motion model into the belief propagation. Other low-level visual cues (e.g., motion and shape) can be easily combined into our framework to obtain a better tracker (Zhong et al. 2006). This chapter presents a refined version of two conference proceedings papers (Xue et al. 2006c; Xue et al. 2006b), along with some new results not found therein.

The remainder of this chapter is organized as follows: after reviewing related work in Section 11.2, we present a distributed graph to model the existence, occlusion, and state of each target in Section 10.3, and then propose a stratified sampling belief propagation algorithm in Section 10.4. In Section 10.5, we then extend the model to integrate other cues such as temporal information from the target motion model and bottom-up information from a learned detector. Empirical results shown in Section 10.6 demonstrate that our model is effective and efficient. Finally, we summarize and suggest future work in Section 10.7.

10.2 Overview of MTTV Methods

As discussed above, most previous works in MTTV deal with implicitly the problem of data association. We present here a brief survey of that work. Readers interested in handling data association explicitly are referred to (Rasmussen and Hager 2001; Xue et al. 2006a).

In general, data association in MTTV is handled implicitly through sequential Bayesian estimation, and can be classified into two categories: (1) solving MTTV by estimating joint target states through a single tracker (Hue et al. 2002; Isard and MacCormick 2001; Tao et al. 1999); and (2) solving MTTV by estimating individual target states through multiple trackers (Tweed and Calway 2002; Yu and Wu 2004; MacCormick and Blake 2000; Okuma et al. 2004; Vermaak et al. 2003).

The first category clearly reduces the problem of MTTV to that of STTV, and overcomes at least theoretically, the limitation that single target state based sequential Monte Carlo filters (e.g., particle filters) cannot properly handle multimodality distributions. In addition, dynamic changes in the number of targets to be tracked can be easily accommodated either by varying the dimension of the state space, or by using a set of indices for target presence or absence (called assignment vectors).

Unfortunately, such a straightforward implementation suffers severely from the curse of dimensionality. As the number of targets increases, an exponentially increasing number of particles in a sequentialMonte Carlo filter are required to exploit the joint state space in order to maintain the same level of estimation accuracy. To overcome this problem, Tao et al. presented an efficient hierarchical sampling algorithm to approximate the inference process in a high dimensional space (Tao et al. 1999). In the context of surveillance, Isard et al. proposed a Bayesian multiblob tracker to perform inference by a single particle filter and a well-designed likelihood function that takes hypotheses on a varying number of targets into consideration (Isard and MacCormick 2001). For a changing number of targets, Hue et al. described an extension of the classical particle filter in which the stochastic assignment vector is estimated by a Gibbs sampler (Hue et al. 2002).

Another problem with these kinds of approaches is that the good estimates in some components are penalized later by possibly bad estimates in other components within the same joint state estimation in the sequential Monte Carlo filtering process. Quantitative results indicate that this could lead to a rapid degeneration in the estimation performance. Recently, Kan et al. developed a joint tracker that includes a Markov chain Monte Carlo (MCMC)-based particle filter and a sophisticated motion model to maintain the identity of targets throughout an interaction (Khan et al. 2004). Research on the exploitation of efficient sampling techniques is still called for approaches in the first category.

The second category of approaches to implicit data association obviously avoids the curse of dimensionality. However, one inevitable but challenging problem in this category is the occlusion of targets and the background. Strategies of various levels of sophistication have been developed to interpret outputs of multiple trackers when occlusion occurs. Tweed et al. introduced bindings among particles (Tweed and Calway 2002) of a standard Condensation algorithm (Isard and Blake 1998), and this enabled the modified algorithm to handle multiple occlusions in a natural way. But the computation of occlusion detection between every two particles becomes intensive when the number of particles increases. For the coalescence problem in which one measurement is shared by two targets at the same time, Yu et al. presented a collaborative approach of linear complexity (Yu and Wu 2004).

In addition, the occurrence of a variable number of targets represents another challenge in technique. Recently, several slightly different approaches have been proposed (Yu and Wu 2005; Okuma et al. 2004; Cai 2004; Zhao and Nevatia 2004; Li et al. 2004b). A decentralized approach (Yu and Wu 2005) was proposed, in which the individual trackers are autonomous in the sense that they can select targets to track and evaluate themselves. They are also collaborative in the sense that they need to compete, and ultimately agree with those trackers close to them upon which tracker will be responsible for tracking a particular target. To track a varying number of hockey players, Okuma et al. proposed a boosted particle filter (BPF) (Okuma et al. 2004) based upon the mixture particle filter (Vermaak et al. 2003). Actually, a single particle filter tracking framework was used by Okuma et al. (2004) and Vermaak et al. (2003) to address MTTV with the help of a mixture density model. However, in this framework, multiple trackers are likely to become confused with each other or migrate onto only one target when measurements are indistinguishable or absent because of occlusion. (Cai 2004) suggests using data association techniques as a complement to maintain the accurate identity of each track. In our recent work (Xue et al. 2006a), we proposed integrating JPDAF with belief propagation (BP) to solve the data association problem in MTTV. For surveillance with a stationary camera, Zhao et al. have developed a method of detecting and tracking multiple people (Zhao and Nevatia 2004). To address the self-occlusion problem in tracking a three-dimensional geometric hand, Sudderth et al. proposed inferring these occlusions in a distributed fashion (Sudderth et al. 2004).

Based on this previous work, this chapter presents a probabilistic model for the MTTV problem with a moving camera in a DMN (Xue et al. 2008). Estimation of the joint states for multiple targets can be conveniently obtained by a sequential particle-based belief propagation algorithm.

10.3 Static Model for Multitarget

We present in this section a distributed MTTV model as shown in Fig. 10.1, which explicitly models a varying number of targets and occlusions among them.

10.3.1 Problem formulation

We assume that the total number of targets varies but is bounded by a known maximum number M. At each time step t, $x_{i,t}$ denotes the state of an individual target, where $i = 1,...,m_t$, and m_t is the number of targets, $1 \leq m_t \leq M$. $\mathbf{X}_t = \{x_{i,t}, i = 1,...,m_t\}$ denotes the joint state of m_t targets, $y_{i,t}$ denotes the image observation of state $x_{i,t}$, and $\mathbf{Y}_t$ denotes the joint observation of $\mathbf{X}_t$. We define $x_{i,t} = (p_{i,t}, v_{i,t}, a_{i,t}, l_{i,t})$ for each single target, where $p_{i,t}$ is the image location, $v_{i,t}$ is the two-dimensional (2D) velocity of the target, $a_{i,t}$ is the appearance, and $s_{i,t}$ is the scale. $p_{i,t}$ and $v_{i,t}$ use continuous image coordinates. The appearance $a_{i,t}$ is the color histogram computed within a bounding box, and the scale $l_{i,t}$ defines the size of the box. Given image observations $\mathbf{Y}_t$ at time t and $\mathbf{Y}_{1:t}$ through time t, the tracking problem is to obtain the maximum a posterior probability of the joint state $P(\mathbf{X}_t|\mathbf{Y}_{1:t})$. According to Bayes' rule and the Markovian assumption of the joint state dynamics, we have the filtering distribution $P(\mathbf{X}_t|\mathbf{Y}_{1:t})$ as follows:

$$P(\mathbf{X}_t|\mathbf{Y}_{1:t}) \propto P(\mathbf{Y}_t|\mathbf{X}_t) \int P(\mathbf{X}_t|\mathbf{X}_{t-1})P(\mathbf{X}_{t-1}|\mathbf{Y}_{1:t-1})d\mathbf{X}_{t-1}, \tag{10.1}$$

where $P(x_{i,t}|\mathbf{Y}_{1:t})$ for the i-th target can be obtained by marginalizing $P(\mathbf{X}_t|\mathbf{Y}_{1:t})$.

To avoid the curse of dimensionality in estimating the joint state $\mathbf{X}_t$, we factorize the joint dynamics $P(\mathbf{X}_t|\mathbf{X}_{t-1})$ and the joint likelihood $P(\mathbf{Y}_t|\mathbf{X}_t)$ in order to decompose the difficult joint-target state estimation problem into a number of easier single-target state estimation problems. It is generally assumed that targets are moving according to independent Markov dynamics. However, when targets move in close proximity or cause occlusions, it is quite difficult to associate them with these spatially adjacent image observations, since the joint observation cannot be segmented easily. Thus, the components of $\mathbf{X}_t$ are coupled, and the curse of dimensionality remain unsolved.

For clarity of notation, the time instant index t is omitted in the rest of this section. At each time step, the joint state is modeled by three coupled MRFs: a continuous MRF $\mathbf{X} = \{x_i\}$ for the joint state, in which each node denotes a target, a binary process $\mathbf{D} = \{D_i\}$ representing the existence of each target ($D_i = 0$ indicating for nonexistence and $D_i = 1$ indicating existence), and another binary process $\mathbf{O} = \{O_{i,j}, i \neq j\}$ for representing occlusions between targets, in which $O_{i,j}$ flags the existing of an occlusion between target i and j ($O_{i,j} = 0$ indicating occlusion and $O_{i,j} = 1$ indicating for no occlusion). In order to be able to model mutually occluding targets, we do not specify which target is the occluded and which is causing the occlusion.

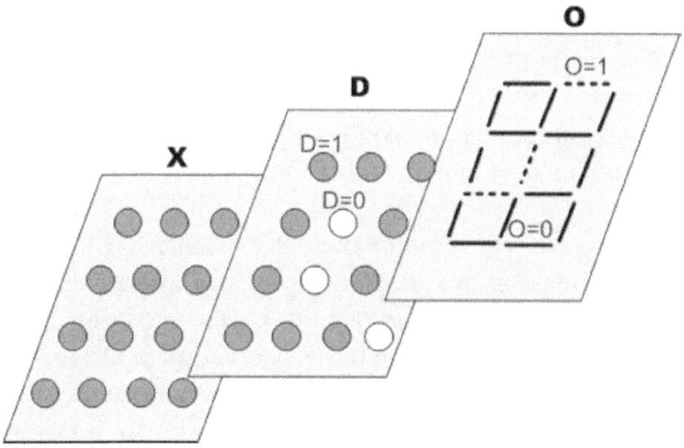

Fig. 10.1 The distributed MTT model, MRF **X** for the joint state, each node indicates a target; **D** for a binary random process, each node represents the absence of a target, $D = 0$ for absence and $D = 1$ for existence; **O** for a binary line process, $O = 1$ for no occlusion, and $O = 1$ for occlusion

With an MRF, a joint probability distribution can be factored as a product of local potential functions defined at each node and interactive potential functions defined on neighborhood cliques. These potential functions afford us the opportunity to incorporate domain knowledge into the model. According to Bayes' rule, the joint posterior probability over $\mathbf{X}$,$\mathbf{D}$, and $\mathbf{O}$ given image observation $\mathbf{Y}$ can be computed as (10.2).

$$P(\mathbf{X},\mathbf{D},\mathbf{O}|\mathbf{Y}) = P(\mathbf{Y}|\mathbf{X},\mathbf{D},\mathbf{O})P(\mathbf{X},\mathbf{D},\mathbf{O})/P(\mathbf{Y}) \tag{10.2}$$

10.3.2 Observation Likelihood Function

The probability $P(\mathbf{Y}|\mathbf{X},\mathbf{D},\mathbf{O})$ describes how the underlying state $\{\mathbf{X},\mathbf{D},\mathbf{O}\}$ of the system fits the observation $\mathbf{Y}$, and one ought to assign a comparable likelihood to hypotheses of the joint state that contain different numbers of targets. However, uncertainties in modeling the mapping between targets and their image projection make $P(\mathbf{Y}|\mathbf{X},\mathbf{D},\mathbf{O})$ a rather complicated distribution. To approximate it, image-based likelihood (Isard and MacCormick 2001; Zhao and Nevatia 2004) and target-based likelihood (Tweed and Calway 2002; Vermaak et al. 2003; Okuma et al. 2004; Yu and Wu 2004; MacCormick and Blake 2000) are widely used.

Image-based likelihood tries to explain every pixel of the image observation with the given joint state. Usually, the raw image contains more information than necessary for the tracking task. In order to reduce the computational burden, a certain amount of pre-processing, such as background modeling, is often required to emphasize the salient features of the target (Zhao and Nevatia 2004).

Target-based likelihood computes the matching score of the object representation and the image patch that possibly contains the target, so it need not explain the image observation pixel by pixel. However, background clutter or similar scene elements nearby make target-based likelihood a function with multiple modalities, and the search for the maximal modality may sometimes be trapped at a local optimum.

We focus on target-based likelihood in this chapter. To deal with the multimodality likelihood function, we adopt stochastic sampling techniques in the computation. Specifically, a set of discrete samples is generated from a mixture proposal which combines a learned detector and the target motion model together to represent the possible states of each target, and then computes the likelihood for each sample (refer to Section 10.5 for more details). Since observation $\mathbf{Y}$ is target-based, we can assume that $P(\mathbf{Y}|\mathbf{X},\mathbf{O},\mathbf{D})$ is independent of targets absent from the scene; that is, we have $P(\mathbf{Y}|\mathbf{X},\mathbf{O},\mathbf{D}) = P(\mathbf{Y}|\mathbf{X},\mathbf{O})$. We also assume that observation noise follows an independent identical distribution (i.i.d), and hence the target-based likelihood can be defined as follows:

$$P(\mathbf{Y}|\mathbf{X},\mathbf{O}) \propto \prod_{i\in\mathbf{O}} \exp[-L(i,x_i,\mathbf{Y})] \tag{10.3}$$

The likelihood (10.3) considers only targets not involved with occlusions, $\{i \in \mathbf{O}\}$, because targets with occlusions cannot be well defined. The function $L(i,x_i,\mathbf{Y})$ can be chosen from observation models based on shape (Isard and Blake 1998), color-histogram (Vermaak et al. 2003; Okuma et al. 2004; Perez et al. 2002), learning (Isard 2003), or the integration of multiple visual cues (Zhong et al. 2006). In the experiment, we use a color histogram–based observation model. Given the target state $x_i = (p_i, v_i, a_i, l_i)$, we obtain the color histogram H_{x_i} which is computed within a bounding box of size l_i at position p_i, for example, $\mathbf{Y} = \{y_i = H_{x_i}\}$. The Bhattacharyya similarity coefficient $D(H_i, H_{x_i})$ (Comaniciu and Ramesh 2003) is adopted to measure the distance between the reference histogram H_i of the i-th target and the obtained histogram H_{x_i}. We then define the likelihood function as (10.4).

$$L(i, x_i, \mathbf{Y}) = \lambda_d D(H_i, H_{x_i})^2 \tag{10.4}$$

$$D(H_i, H_{x_i}) = \sqrt{1 - \sum_{u=1}^{m} \sqrt{H_i(u) H_{x_i}(u)}} \tag{10.5}$$

where λ_d is a constant which can be adjusted as necessary in practice, and H_i, H_{x_i} are two $m-bin$ histograms, respectively.

10.3.3 Prior Model

Although there are no simple statistical relationships between the coupled fields $\mathbf{X}, \mathbf{O}$ and $\mathbf{D}$, to simplify the problem, we ignore the statistical dependence between $\mathbf{D}$ and $\mathbf{X}, \mathbf{O}$, and assume the prior as follows:

$$P(\mathbf{X}, \mathbf{O}, \mathbf{D}) = P(\mathbf{X}, \mathbf{O}) P(\mathbf{D}) \tag{10.6}$$

Given the assumption that $\mathbf{X}, \mathbf{O}$ and $\mathbf{D}$ follow the Markov property, the specification of the first-order neighborhood system $\Theta(i)$ and $\Gamma(i) = \{j | d(x_i, x_j) < \delta, j \in \Theta(i)\}$ for target i, where $d(x_i, x_j)$ is the distance between targets i and j in the state space, and denoting δ as the threshold that determines the neighborhood, we can expand the prior as:

$$P(\mathbf{X}, \mathbf{O}, \mathbf{D}) = \prod_i \prod_{j \in \Gamma(i)} \exp[-\eta(D_i) - \varphi(x_i, x_j, O_{i,j})] \tag{10.7}$$

where $\eta(D_i)$ is the clique potential function of the single site D_i, and $\varphi(x_i, x_j, O_{i,j})$ is the interactive potential function between sites x_i, x_j (neighbor of x_i) and $O_{i,j}$. Since we can customize the potential functions $\varphi(x_i, x_j, O_{i,j})$ and $\eta(D_i)$ to enforce contextual constraints for state estimation, we define $\varphi(x_i, x_j, O_{i,j})$ to enforce the spatial interaction between x_i and x_j.

$$\varphi(x_i, x_j, O_{i,j}) = \varphi_c(x_i, x_j)(1 - O_{i,j}) + \gamma(O_{i,j}) \tag{10.8}$$

where $\varphi_c(x_i,x_j)$ penalizes the sharing of one common measurement with two neighboring sites when occlusion occurs between them. The term $\gamma(O_{i,j})$ penalizes the occurrence of occlusion between sites i and j. Typically, we set $\gamma(0)=0$.

Similarly, we define $\eta(D_i)$ as (10.9)

$$\eta(D_i) = \eta_c(D_i)(1-D_i) + \varphi_s(x_i)D_i \tag{10.9}$$

$$\varphi_s(x_i) = \ln\{1-\exp[-\lambda_s A(x_i)]\} \tag{10.10}$$

where $\eta_c(D_i)$ encodes the probability of targets being absent from the scene, and $\varphi_s(x_i)$ defines the prior probability of target i with the size $A(x_i)$. The term $\varphi_s(x_i)$ penalize targets of very small size, since they are more likely to be noise. λ_s is a constant, we set $\lambda_s = 2.6$ in our experiment.

Following from formulas (10.3), (10.4), (10.5), (10.6), (10.7), (10.8) and (10.9), our basic model (10.2) becomes:

$$\begin{aligned} &P(\mathbf{X},\mathbf{D},\mathbf{O}|\mathbf{Y}) \propto \\ &\prod_i \exp\{-[L(i,x_i,\mathbf{Y})+\varphi_s(x_i)]D_i - \eta_c(D_i)(1-D_i)\} \\ &\times \prod_i \prod_{j\in\Gamma(i)} \exp[-\varphi(x_i,x_j)(1-O_{i,j}) - \gamma(O_{i,j})] \end{aligned} \tag{10.11}$$

10.4 Approximate Inference

To find the MAP solution of (10.11), we need to first determine the forms and parameters of $\varphi_c(x_i,x_j)$, $\gamma(O_{i,j})$ and $\eta_c(D_i)$, and then provide a tractable inference algorithm. It is, however, nontrivial to specify or learn appropriate forms and parameter values for $\varphi_c(x_i,x_j)$, $\gamma(O_{i,j})$ and $\eta_c(D_i)$. Even if the forms and parameters are given, it is still difficult to find the MAP of a composition of a continuous MRF $\mathbf{X}$ and two binary MRFs $\mathbf{O}$ and $\mathbf{D}$. Although the MCMC technique provides an effective way to explore a posterior distribution, computational complexity makes MCMC impractical for multitarget tracking because of the curse of dimensionality. That is why we need to make some approximations of both the model and the algorithm.

10.4.1 Model Approximation

Maximization of the posterior (10.11) can be rewritten as:

$$\max_{\mathbf{X},\mathbf{D},\mathbf{O}} P(\mathbf{X},\mathbf{D},\mathbf{O}|\mathbf{Y}) = \max_{\mathbf{X}}\{\max_{\mathbf{D}}\prod_i \exp\{-\{L(i,x_i,\mathbf{Y}) + \ln[1-\exp(-\lambda_s A(x_i))]D_i\} - \eta_c(D_i)(1-D_i)\} \times \max_{\mathbf{O}}\prod_i\prod_{j\in\Gamma(i)} \exp\{-[\varphi_c(x_i,x_j)(1-O_{i,j}) + \gamma(O_{i,j})]\}\} \tag{10.12}$$

because the first two factors on the r.h.s of (10.12) are independent of **O** and the last factor on the r.h.s of (10.12) is independent of **D**.

Next we relax the binary processes $O_{i,j}$ and D_i to become analog processes $O'_{i,j}$ and D'_i, respectively, by allowing $0 \le O'_{i,j} \le 1$ and $0 \le D'_i \le 1$. Now we can use the two robust estimators proposed in Black and Rangarajan (1996) to approximate the two terms on the r.h.s of (10.12).

For the first term

$$\max_{\mathbf{D}}\prod_i \exp\{-\{L(i,x_i,\mathbf{Y}) + \ln[1-\exp(-\lambda_s A(x_i))]\}D_i - \eta_c(D_i)(1-D_i)\} \approx \exp\{-\min_{\mathbf{D}'}\sum_i\{[L(i,x_i,\mathbf{Y}) + \ln(1-\exp(-\lambda_s A(x_i)))]D'_i + \eta_c(D'_i)(1-D'_i)\}\} \tag{10.13}$$

where the r.h.s of (10.13) is the objective function of a robust estimator (Black and Rangarajan 1996), of which the robust function is

$$\psi_d(x_i) = \min_{D'_i}\{\{L(i,x_i,\mathbf{Y}) + \ln[1-\exp(-\lambda_s A(x_i))]D'_i\} + \eta_c(D'_i)(1-D'_i)\} \tag{10.14}$$

Similarly, we obtain a robust function $\psi_p(x_i,x_j)$ for the second term in (10.12):

$$\psi_p(x_i,x_j) = \min_{O'_{i,j}}[\varphi_c(x_i,x_j)(1-O'_{i,j}) + \gamma(O'_{i,j})] \tag{10.15}$$

Leading us to the posterior probability over **X** defined by the robust functions $\psi_d(x_i)$ and $\psi_p(x_i,x_j)$:

$$P(\mathbf{X}|\mathbf{Y}) \propto \prod_i \exp[-\psi_d(x_i)] \prod_i\prod_{j\in\Gamma(i)} \exp[-\psi_p(x_i,x_j)] \tag{10.16}$$

Thus, we eliminate two analog processes via two robust functions and explicitly convert the task of modeling the prior terms $\varphi(x_i,x_j)$, $\gamma(O_{i,j})$, and $\eta_c(D_i)$ into the task of defining the robust functions $\psi_p(x_i,x_j)$ and $\psi_d(x_i)$ that model occlusion and the existence of targets implicitly. In this chapter, these two robust functions are chosen to be derived from the total variance (TV) model (Rudin et al. 1992) with the potential function $\rho(z) = |z|$ because of its attractive property of preserving discontinuity. We truncate this potential function so that it can serve as our robust function:

$$\psi_d(x_i) = -\ln\left\{(1-e_d) \times \exp\left[-\frac{|L(i,x_i,\mathbf{Y}) + \ln[1-\exp(-\lambda_s \mathrm{A}(\mathrm{x_i}))]|}{\sigma_d}\right] + e_d\right\} \tag{10.17}$$

$$\psi_p(x_i,x_j) = -\ln[(1-e_p)\exp(-\frac{|\Omega(x_i,x_j)|}{\sigma_p}) + e_p] \tag{10.18}$$

where $\Omega(x_i,x_j)$ merely depends upon the number of pixels overlapping between the two targets; this function is maximized when two targets coincide and gradually falls off as targets move apart. e_p and σ_p are two adjustable parameters to control the shape of the robust function. Figure 10.2 shows the shapes of our robust function with different parameters.

An upside-down Gaussian model has been used in Yu and Wu (2004) and Yu and Wu (2005) to model occlusion, in which the distance between the two targets in state space is used as an input variable. It has a parameter that characterizes the competition region in the state space. Our robust function $\psi_p(x_i,x_j)$ differs from this approach by using the absolute size of the overlap as an input variable, and exploiting the two adjustable parameters e_p and σ_p to control the shape of the robust function and, therefore, the posterior distribution.

Moreover, our robust functions are capable of preserving the discontinuity, which is very important in preventing particles associated with occluded targets from degenerating in the sequential estimation. This is because, in estimating states of the occluded target, the prior information from target dynamics plays a more important role than does the incomplete image evidence. Particles attributed to the occluded target will be depleted rapidly within several frames, since these particles lack support from image evidence. By controlling the shape of the robust function, we can slow down the depletion speed of these particles. Furthermore, the eliminated processes can be recovered from these two robust functions by identifying an occlusion between two targets or the disappearance of a target when one of them reaches an upper bound.

Currently, we lack a theoretical approach on how to choose these adjustable parameters optimally. However, in experiments, we found that parameters e_p and σ_p can be chosen according to the duration of the occlusion events. The longer the duration, the less the sharpness of the robust function, and the better the performance in handling occlusion will be. The exact relationship between the adjustable parameters and duration is worthy of research, as are approaches to the detection of occlusion.

After approximating the model, the next task is to provide an effective and efficient inference algorithm. In Section 10.4.2, we present how the particle-based belief propagation algorithm is used to compute the MAP of the posterior distribution (10.16).

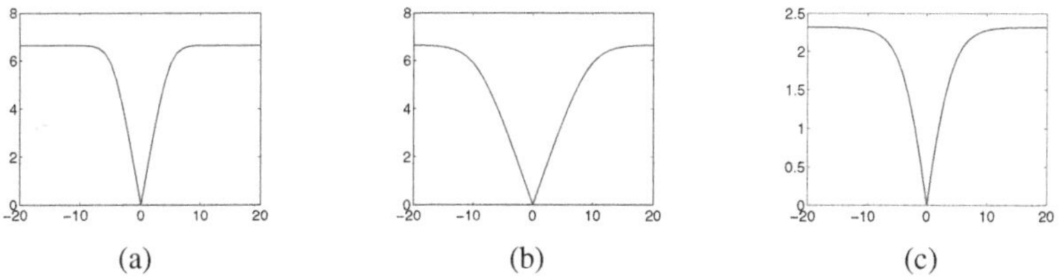

Fig. 10.2 (**a**) $e = 0.01$; $\sigma = 1.0$. (**b**) $e = 0.01$; $\sigma = 2.0$, (**c**) $e = 0.1$; $\sigma = 2.0$. The robust function $\rho(x) = -\ln[(1-e)\exp(-\frac{|x|}{\sigma}) + e]$ is derived from the TV model. Parameters e and σ, respectively, control the sharpness and the upper-bound of the function

10.4.2 Algorithm Approximation

Consider a Markov network **G = (V,E)**, where **V** denotes the node set and **E** denotes the edge set in an undirected graph as shown in Fig. 10.3.

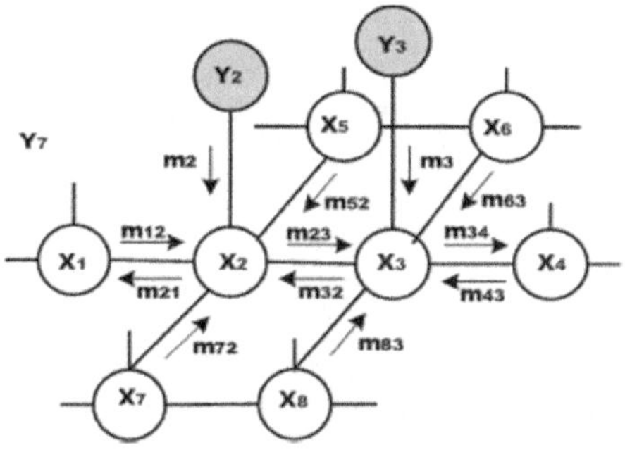

Fig. 10.3 Local message passing in a Markov network. *Gray* nodes are observable variables, and *white* nodes are hidden variables. Messages propagate in the network in the belief propagation algorithm

Nodes $\{x_i, i \in \mathbf{V}\}$ are hidden variables and nodes $\{y_i, i \in \mathbf{V}\}$ are observed variables. By denoting $\mathbf{X} = \{x_i\}$ and $\mathbf{Y} = \{y_i\}$, the posterior $P(\mathbf{X}|\mathbf{Y})$ can be factorized as

$$P(\mathbf{X}|\mathbf{Y}) \propto \prod_i \rho_i(x_i, y_i) \prod_i \prod_{j \in \Gamma(i)} \rho_{i,j}(x_i, x_j) \tag{10.19}$$

where $\rho_{i,j}(x_i, x_j)$ is the interactive potential function between nodes x_i and x_j , and $\rho_i(x_i, y_i)$ is the local evidence for node x_i. It can be observed that the form of our posterior (10.16) and (10.19) are the same if we define $\rho_{i,j}$ and $\rho_i(x_i, y_i)$ as (10.20) and (10.20), respectively.

$$\rho_{i,j}(x_i, x_j) = \exp[-\psi_p(x_i, x_j)] \tag{10.20}$$

$$\rho_i(x_i, y_i) = \exp[-\psi_d(x_i)] \tag{10.21}$$

Therefore, inferring the joint state in our framework can be defined as estimating the beliefs of nodes in the graphical model.

BP is an iterative inference algorithm for the MRF network. At the n-th iteration of the BP algorithm, each node $i \in \mathbf{V}$ calculates a message $m_{ij}^n(x_j)$ to be sent to its neighboring node $j \in \Gamma(i)$, where $\Gamma(i) \equiv \{j|(i,j) \in \mathbf{E}\}$ is the set of all nodes that are directly connected to node i.

$$m_{ij}^n(x_j) = \kappa \int_{x_i} \rho_{i,j}(x_i, x_j)\rho_i(x_i, y_i) \times \prod_{u \in \Gamma(i)\setminus j} m_{ui}^{n-1}(x_i)dx_i \tag{10.22}$$

where κ denotes a proportionality constant that puts m_{ij} in the form of a probability. At the n-th iteration, each node can produce an approximation $\hat{p}^n(x_i|\mathbf{Y})$ to the marginal distribution $p(x_i|\mathbf{Y})$ by combining the incoming messages with the local observation potential.

$$\hat{p}^n(x_i|\mathbf{Y}) = \kappa_1 \rho_i(x_i, y_i) \prod_{j \in \Gamma(i)} m_{ji}^n(x_i) \tag{10.23}$$

where κ_1 denotes a proportionality constant.

However, the discrete approximation obtained by BP cannot be applied to the graphical model, which contains hidden variables of continuous, non-Gaussian distributions. To cope with these difficulties, we adopt an MC approximation to the integral in (10.22). Each message passing from x_i to x_j is then represented by a set of weighted samples, that is, $m_{ij}(x_j) \sim \{s_j^{(n)}, w_j^{(i,n)}\}_{n=1}^N, i \in \Gamma(j)$, where $s_j^{(n)}$ and $w_j^{(i,n)}$ denote the sample and its weight, respectively. Finally, the message updating process is based on these sets of weighted samples, and the marginal posterior probability of each node can also be represented by a set of weighted samples, that is, $P(x_j|\mathbf{Y}) \sim \{s_j^{(n)}, \pi_j^{(n)}\}_{n=1}^N$.

The efficiency of MC algorithms is strongly dependent on sampling positions. Therefore, we would like to use all the available information possible when choosing these positions. We use a stratified sampler to sample $(1-\nu)N$ particles (where $0 \leq \nu \leq 1$) from the estimated current belief distribution, and νN particles from the conditional distribution that combines incoming messages. Our implementation is a slightly different version of similar ideas in Hua and Wu (2004) and Sudderth et al. (2003) and Yu and Wu (2005) Okuma et al. (2004). The message passing framework is illustrated in Fig. 10.3, and our algorithm in Table 10.1 presents a propagation loop consisting of message updating and belief computation at each iteration.

Generate $\{s^{(n)}_{j,t,k+1}, w^{(i,n)}_{j,t,k+1}, \pi^{(n)}_{j,t,k+1}\}_{n=1}^{N}$ *from* $\{s^{(n)}_{j,t,k}, w^{(i,n)}_{j,t,k}, \pi^{(n)}_{j,t,k}\}_{n=1}^{N}$, $j = 1,\ldots,m_t$ *and* $i \in \Gamma(j)$

1. *Stratified Sampling*

   a. *For* $1 \le n \le \nu N$, *sample* $s^{(n)}_{j,t,k+1}$ *from a suitable proposal function* $B(x_{j,t})$, *set weight* $\tilde{w}^{(i,n)}_{j,t,k+1} = 1/B(s^{(n)}_{j,t,k+1})$

   b. *For* $\nu N \le n \le N$, *sample* $s^{(n)}_{j,t,k+1}$ *from* $\hat{P}(x_{j,t}|Y_t) \sim \{s^{(n)}_{j,t,k}, \pi^{(n)}_{j,t,k}\}_{n=1}^{N}$, *set* $\xi^{(i,n)}_{j,k+1} = 1/\pi_{j,t,k}$

   c. *For* $1 \le n \le \nu N$, *weight correction for re-sampling*

   $$\tilde{w}^{(i,n)}_{j,,t,k+1} = \nu \tilde{w}^{(i,n)}_{j,t,k+1} / \left(\sum\nolimits_{l=1}^{\nu N} \tilde{w}^{(i,l)}_{j,t,k+1}\right)$$

   d. *For* $\nu N \le n \le N$, *weight correction for re-sampling*

   $$\tilde{w}^{(i,n)}_{j,,t,k+1} = (1-\nu)\xi^{(i,n)}_{j,t,k+1} / \left(\sum\nolimits_{l=\nu N}^{N} \xi^{(i,l)}_{j,t,k+1}\right)$$

2. *Applying importance correction: for* $1 \le n \le N$ $w^{(i,n)}_{j,t,k+1} = \tilde{w}^{(i,n)}_{j,t,k+1} \times m_{ij}(s^{(n)}_{j,t,k+1})$

   $$m_{ij}(s^{(n)}_{j,t,k+1}) = \sum_{m=1}^{N} \{\rho_i(y^{(m)}_{i,t,k}, s^{(m)}_{i,t,k})$$

   $$\times \prod_{l \in \Gamma(i)\setminus j} w^{(l,m)}_{i,t,k} \times [\sum_{r=1}^{N} p(s^{(m)}_{i,t,k} | s^{(r)}_{i,t-1})]$$

   $$\times \rho_{ij}(s^{(m)}_{i,t,k}, s^{(n)}_{j,t,k+1})\}$$

3. *Normalization:normalize* $w^{(i,n)}_{j,t,k+1}$, $i \in \Gamma(j)$ $\pi^{(n)}_{j,t,k+1} = \rho_j(y^{(n)}_{j,t,k+1}, s^{(n)}_{j,t,k+1}) \prod_{u \in \Gamma(j)} w^{(u,n)}_{j,k+1} \times \sum_r p(s^{(n)}_{j,t,k+1} | s^{(r)}_{j,t-1})$, *and normalize, then obtain* $\{s^{(n)}_{j,t,k+1}, w^{(i,n)}_{j,t,k+1}\}_{n=1}^{N}$ *and* $\{s^{(n)}_{j,t,k+1}, \pi^{(n)}_{j,t,k+1}\}_{n=1}^{N}$.
4. $k \leftarrow k+1$, *iterate step 1*$\rightarrow$*4 until convergence.*

Table 10.1 Algorithm 1—One iteration of the stratified sampling, message updating and belief computation

In Table 10.1, steps 1(a) and 1(b) perform stratified sampling from a proposal density and belief nodes separately, and step 1(c) and 1(d) normalize weights of these sampled particles. The proposal distribution $B(x)$ can be constructed based on prior knowledge of the application domain. In this chapter, we use a target motion model mixed with an SVM-based detector as the proposal distribution, which is presented in Section 10.5.

Our method samples from the messages with a stratified sampler that incorporates the information obtained from a learned bottom-up detector (e.g. SVM classifier) and the dynamic motion model of target into message propagation, and speeds up convergence. In contrast, PAMAPS (Isard 2003) and NBP (Sudderth et al. 2003) approximate messages with a Gaussian mixture, which results in sampling from the product of Gaussian mixtures, and requires a Gibbs sampler. The idea of approximating messages in BP using importance sampling was also presented in Hua and Wu (2004) for multiscale visual tracking of an object, but it did not use a stratified sampler, and there was no information mixed between the forward and backward directions.

It should be noted that, despite loops in the network, BP has been applied successfully to some vision tasks (Murphy et al. 1999). Although we have not obtained rigorous results on convergence rates, we have observed empirically that convergence is generally achieved in less than four iterations.

10.5 Fusing Information from Temporal and Bottom-Up Detectors

Thus far, our discussion has focused solely on joint state estimation in a single time step. In order to track targets, however, we must have a motion model that allows us to build a temporal correspondence between the joint state at the current time step and that of previous time steps. Thus, the Markov network in Fig. 10.3 becomes a DMN as shown in Fig. 10.4.

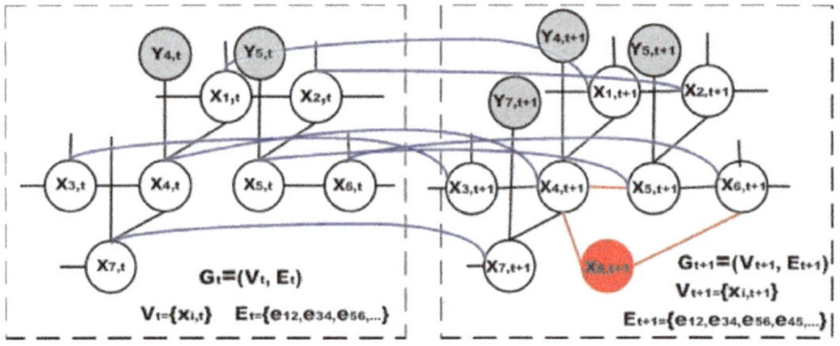

Fig. 10.4 Dynamic Markov network for multiple targets. The link between each pair of hidden nodes indicates the occurence of a possible occlusion. Graphs G_{t-1} and G_t describe the joint state of multiple targets at two consecutive points in time. Links and nodes in *red* indicate new occlusions and the addition of a new target

We describe the joint state at time t and $t-1$ by two Markov networks G_t and G_{t-1}, where $G_t = (V_t, E_t)$, V_t is the set of nodes that represent active targets at time step t(i.e., all targets in the current frame), and E_t is the set of links which indicates all possible occlusions. The evolution of G_t reflects the change in motion correlation due to changes in the spatial relationships between the targets, as well as the appearance of new targets and disappearance of old ones.

By assuming independent motion of each object, $P(\mathbf{X}_t|\mathbf{X}_{t-1})$ can be factorized as:

$$P(\mathbf{X}_t|\mathbf{X}_{t-1}) \propto \Psi_1\Psi_2\Psi_3 \tag{10.24}$$

Where:

$$\Psi_1 = \prod_{i\in V_t\cap V_{t-1}} P(x_{i,t}|x_{i,t-1}) \tag{10.25}$$

$$\Psi_2 = \prod_{i\in V_t\backslash V_{t-1}} P_{add}(p_{i,t}) \tag{10.26}$$

$$\Psi_3 = \prod_{i\in V_{t-1}\backslash V_t} P_{delete}(p_{i,t-1}) \tag{10.27}$$

Ψ_1 represents the state transition dynamics:

$$x_{i,t} = \phi x_{i,t-1} + \Sigma w_{t-1} \tag{10.28}$$

where ϕ is a state transition matrix, Σ is a disturbance matrix, and w_t is normal random noise with zero mean and covariance Λ. The parameters $\{\phi,\Sigma,\Lambda\}$ can be specified empirically. In the experiment, we adopt a constant acceleration model as the target state dynamics model Ψ_1. Ψ_2 and Ψ_3 describe the initiation of a new track and the termination of an existing track, respectively. P_{add} and P_{delete} are set empirically according to the distance of the target location from the boundaries of the image (Tao et al. 1999).

As G_t evolves, the solution space may consist of subspaces with different dimensions, corresponding to a different number of targets. To make sampling more efficient, we embed algorithm 1 into an MCMC framework. All MCMC methods work by generating a sequence of states. In our case, we hope the collection of generated states approximates the filtering distribution (10.1). In this chapter, we use a random-scan Gibbs sampler (Hastings 1970), and the key to the efficiency of this sampler rests upon the informed proposal density. We use a mixture of factorized motion model (10.25), (10.26) and (10.27) as the proposal function, and only change the state of one target at a time.

In the case of state transition dynamics (10.25), the proposal density $B(\cdot)$ in Table 10.1 is based upon (10.28). For each active target, given the inference results $P(x_{i,t-1}|\mathbf{Y}_{1:t-1})$ at the previous time step $t-1$, the message updating at time t is

$$\begin{aligned} m_{ij}^{n}(x_{j,t}) = \kappa \int \rho_{i,j}(x_{i,t},x_{j,t})\rho_i(x_{i,t},y_{i,t}) \\ \times \int P(x_{i,t}|x_{i,t-1})P(x_{i,t-1}|\mathbf{Y}_{1:t-1})dx_{i,t-1} \\ \times \prod_{u\in\Gamma(i)\backslash j} m_{ui}^{n-1}(x_{i,t})dx_{i,t} \end{aligned} \tag{10.29}$$

and the belief of target i can be computed as:

$$\hat{P}_{i,t}(x_{i,t}|\mathbf{Y}_{1:t}) = \kappa_1 \rho_i(x_{i,t}, y_{i,t}) \prod_{j \in \Gamma(i)} m_{ji}(x_{i,t})$$
$$\times \int P(x_{i,t}|x_{i,t-1})\hat{P}_{i,t-1}(x_{i,t-1}|\mathbf{Y}_{1:t-1})dx_{i,t-1} \tag{10.30}$$

Comparing (10.30) with (10.23), we can see clearly that at each time step t , the belief in target i is determined by three factors: (1) the local evidence $\rho_i(x_i, y_i)$, (2) the prediction $\int P(x_{i,t}|x_{i,t-1})\hat{P}_{i,t-1}(x_{i,t-1}|\mathbf{Y}_{1:t-1})dx_{i,t-1}$ from the previous frame, and (3) the incoming messages from sites in the neighborhood. When occlusion occurs, the state of the occluded target can still be predicted by the motion model, and the robust compatibility functions introduced in Section 10.3 will slow down the depletion speed of particles corresponding to the occluded targets.

In the case of (10.26) and (10.27), the proposal density makes use of bottom-up information from a learned SVM classifier; other detectors can also be adopted in the same way. One expects detectors to be noisy in that they sometimes fail to detect targets or find spurious targets, but even this noisy information can provide valuable cues in handling the varying number targets problem in MTTV. The proposal based on the learned SVM classifier is

$$P(\mathbf{X}_t|\ \mathbf{X}_{0:t-1}, \mathbf{Y}_{1:t}) = R(Q_{svm}(\mathbf{Y}_t), \mathbf{X}_{t-1}) \tag{10.31}$$

where $R(\cdot)$ defines a probability density function, and Q_{svm} is the set of Gaussian distributions centered around the detected targets by the trained SVM classifier at time step t. If there is an overlap between clusters (each Gaussian distribution forms a cluster) in Q_{svm} and in $P(\mathbf{X}_t|\mathbf{X}_{t-1})$, we sample from Q_{svm} and $P(\mathbf{X}_t|\mathbf{X}_{t-1})$ proportionately, or else we sample from $P(\mathbf{X}_t|\mathbf{X}_{t-1})$ only. By doing this, the mixed proposal distributions can determine where to start a new track or which track to terminate.

Similar to algorithm 1 in Table 10.1 , we represent messages and marginal posterior probabilities (beliefs) at each time step t as a set of weighted samples, that is, $m_{ij}(x_{j,t}) \sim \{s^n_{j,t}, w^{i,n}_{j,t}\}^N_{n=1}$ and $P(x_{j,t}|\mathbf{Y}) \sim \{s^n_{j,t}, \pi^n_{j,t}\}^N_{n=1}$. Following (10.24), (10.29), and (10.30), we can easily extend algorithm 1 to its sequential version. The detailed steps of the particle-based BP are summarized in algorithm 2 in Table 10.2.

10.6 Experiments and Discussions

The experiment consists of two parts. In the first part, we validated the proposed algorithms, and in the second part we compared our tracker with the multiple independent trackers (M.I.Tracker). In the validation step, two video sequences are used: (1) a synthesized video sequence, in which the stratified sampler is not used, and parameter v in algorithm 1 is set to 1; and, (2) a real video sequence of a hockey game,[1] in which a stratified sampler is used, and the parameter v is set as 0.8.

---

[1] The authors acknowledge Mr. Kenji Okuma for providing the test video sequence on the website.

Generate $\{s_{j,t}^{(n)}, \pi_{j,t}^{(n)}\}_{n=1}^{N}$ *from* $\{s_{j,t-1}^{(n)}, \pi_{j,t-1}^{(n)}\}_{n=1}^{N}$ *,V be the hidden nodes set in current graph G*
1. *Initialization:* a. *Re-sampling: for each* $j \in V, i \in \Gamma(j)$, *sample* $\{s_{j,t-1}^{(n)}\}_{n=1}^{N}$ *according to the weights* $\pi_{j,t-1}^{(n)}$ *to obtain* $\{s_{j,t-1}^{(n)}, 1/N\}_{n=1}^{N}$ b. *Prediction: for each j, for each sample in* $\{s_{j,t-1}^{(n)}, 1/N\}_{n=1}^{N}$, *sampling from* $p(x_{j,t}\|x_{j,t-1})$ *to obtain* $\{s_{j,t}^{(n)}\}_{n=1}^{N}$ c. *Belief and message initialization: for each* $j = 1,..,M$, *assign weight* $w_{j,t,k}^{(i,n)} = 1/N, \pi_{j,t,k}^{(n)} = p_j(y_{j,t,k}^{(n)}\|s_{j,t,k}^{(n)})$ *and normalize, where* $i \in \Gamma(j)$.
2. *Iterates L times:* a. *Do one of following three steps randomly with probabilities 0.8,0.1 and 0.1 to obtain a new graph* G' i. *Randomly select a target* $j \in V$ *to move, obtain* G' ii. *Randomly select a particle cluster from* $R(Q_{svm}(\mathbf{Y}_t, \mathbf{X}_{t-1}))$, *delete the corresponding node from V to obtain* G' iii. *Randomly select a particle cluster from* $R(Q_{svm}(\mathbf{Y}_t, \mathbf{X}_{t-1}))$,*add the corresponding node into V to obtain* G' b. *Do algorithm 1 on* G'
3. *Inference result* $p(x_{j,t}\|\mathbf{Y_t}) \sim \{s_{j,t}^{(n)}, \pi_{j,t}^{(n)}\}_{n=1}^{M}$, *where* $s_{j,t}^{(n)} = s_{j,t,k+1}^{(n)}$ *and* $\pi_{j,t}^{(i,n)} = \pi_{j,t,k+1}^{(i,n)}$.

Table 10.2 Algorithm 2—particle-based belief propagation

In the second part, we chose three trackers, including an MHT tracker (Cox et al. 1996), the boosted particle filter (BPF) (Okuma et al. 2004), and the netted collaborative autonomous trackers (NCAT) (Yu and Wu 2005), to compare with our tracker, respectively. The comparison results are presented in Section 10.6.2. The test video sequences used in this part include one synthesized video sequence and one real video sequence. In the final part of this section, we discuss the convergence rate of the random-scan Gibbs sampler used in our algorithm.

10.6.1 Proof-of-Concept

10.6.1.1 Synthesized Video

In the synthesized video, there are five identical balls in motion with a noisy background. Each ball presents an independent constant velocity motion and is bounded by the image borders. The synthesized sequence challenges many existing methods due to the frequent presence of occlusions.

We use a colored box to display the estimated position of the tracked ball. An index is attached to the box to denote the identifier of each ball. We compare our results with those obtained by M.I.Tracker, which consists of color-based probabilistic trackers for all targets (Perez et al. 2002). Figure 10.5 shows some examples, where the results of M.I.Tracker are in the left column and ours are in the right column. We use 20 particles for each target in both. The experimental results clearly shows that M.I.Tracker cannot produce satisfactory results in the case of occlusion, while our algorithm can obtain much more satisfying results. The red lines in Fig. 10.5 linking different targets are the visual illustration of the structure of the Markov network in our algorithm. By observing the changing structure of the network over frames, we can evaluate the performance of our algorithm in handling occlusion. Some statistical values concerning performance of the M.I.T tracker are listed in Table 10.4, from which we find that our approach can track targets with occlusion with only 9 failures out of 133 occlusions in a 1000 frame test video sequence.

10.6.1.2 Multiple Hockey Player Tracking

Our algorithm and M.I.Tracker were tested on the real video sequence of a hockey game for further comparison. For the first frame of the video sequence, a trained SVM classifier (Cristianini and Shawe-Taylor 2000) is executed to obtain the initial prior for both trackers. In order to train the SVM-based detector, a total of 1300 examples of hockey players collected from other video segments are used in training samples. Ultimately the training arrived at 34 support vectors. In Figure 10.6, the tracking results of M.I.Tracker are shown on the top, and our final and intermediate results are shown in the middle and on the bottom, respectively. Frames #55, #70, #80, #90 in Figure 10.6 show four occlusions among targets 1, 2, and 3. These results show that our algorithm can handle occlusions as expected, while M.I.Tracker fails to do so. As new targets 7, 8, and 9 appear, our algorithm assigns particles to them and starts new tracks, whereas M.I.Tracker is unable to generate new tracks.

To fully test our algorithm, we also applied it to the switching problem, which can be easily validated by the subjective evaluation of the tracking sequence. Note that a set of fixed parameters $e_p = 0.05, e_d = 0.03, \sigma_p = \sigma_d = 1$ is used in our algorithm in both synthesized and real video. Obviously, this set of parameters is not optimal for both video sequences, because their occlusion situations are quite different.

The experimental results show that our algorithm can improve tracking accuracy, especially in the case of occlusion, compared with the M.I.Tracker. However, it

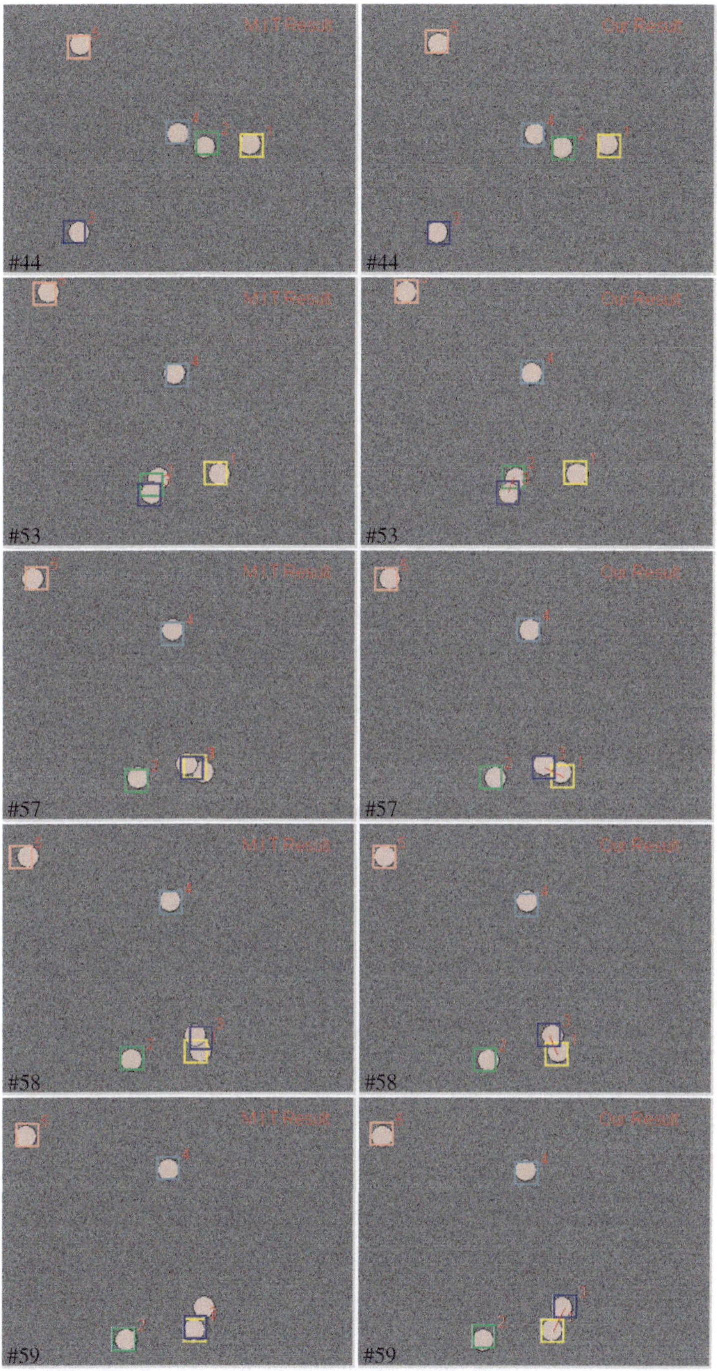

Fig. 10.5 Tracking balls by M.I.Tracker and our algorithm. The *left column* shows results obtained with M.I.Tracker, and the *right column* shows results from our algorithm. Frames 53 to 59 present an occlusion event, in which M.I.Tracker produces incorrect identities whereas our algorithm produces correct results

should be noted that our algorithm cannot find all the new targets as they appear because of the limited detection performance on the part of the SVM-based detector. Figure 10.7 shows four detection results produced by the SVM detector. The SVM detector cannot locate targets accurately, and it sometimes even detects spurious targets. Moreover, we chose no to implement the target ID (identifier) management component, because it sometimes causes errors in tracking. For example, in Figure 10.6(b), the target attached to *ID*9 in frame #80 was lost because of its sudden disappearance. When it did reappear in frame #92, it was attached to *ID*10, because ID9 was no longer available; it has been assigned to a new target that appeared in two frames earlier, in frame #90.

10.6.2 Comparison with Other Trackers

To establish a comparative context with representative previous work, we chose to compare our tracker with an MHT tracker based on the Bayesian approach by (Cox 1996), the BPF (Okuma et al. 2004), and the NCAT (Yu and Wu 2005). These four trackers were all tested with the hockey game video sequence and the synthesized video sequence. First, we compared our tracker with MHT, BPF, and NCAT, respectively, using the hockey game video sequence. Second, we compared these four trackers with several quantitative measures in handling occlusion and tracking a variable number of targets, using one synthesized video sequence.

10.6.2.1 Comparison with MHT Tracker

We implemented the MHT tracker based on Cox et al. (1996). The measurements of the MHT tracker are supplied by the same SVM classifier we trained for our tracker, and each target was then tracked with a standard Kalman filter. Figure 10.8 illustrates the manner in which multiple hypotheses are generated and managed in the MHT tracker.

For each input frame, targets were automatically extracted by the SVM classifier to supply the MHT tracker, and the threshold for detection was set to locate approximately 10 targets in each frame.

Table 10.3 Parameter values for the MHT tracker

Parameters of MHT tracker	Values
Probability of detection	$P_D = 0.99$
Mean rate of false alarm	$\lambda_f = 0.01$
Termination likelihood	$\lambda_t = 34$
Mean rate of new tracks	$P_{new} = 0.02$
Depth of tree	$N_{scan} = 3$
Maximum number of hypotheses	$N_{hyp} = 100$

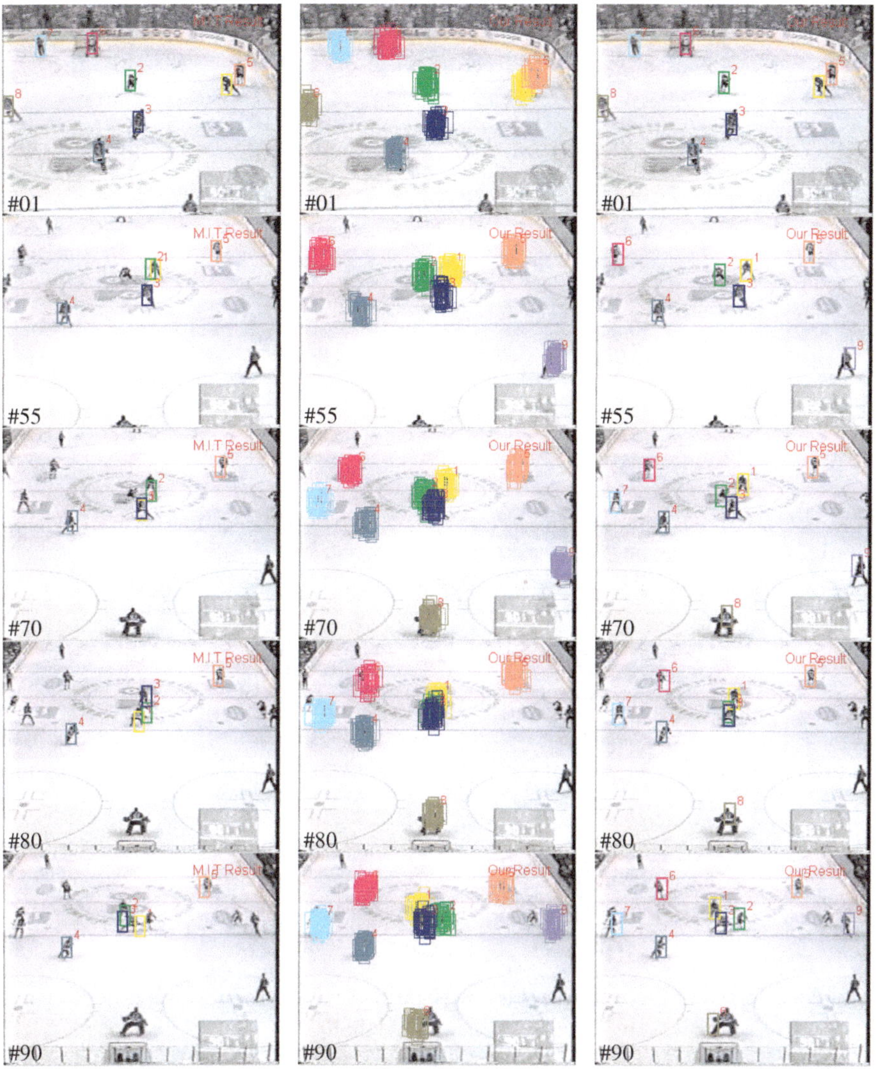

Fig. 10.6 Tracking hockey players: 20 particles were used for each target in both algorithms. *Left column:* results from M.I.Tracker; *Middle column:* intermediate results from our tracker; *Left column:* final results from our tracker

It is tedious to obtain the exact values of P_D, λ_f,λ_t, and P_{new} in the MHT algorithm, and thus these parameters in Table 10.3 are specified empirically. The MHT tracker is very attractive in theory since it not only models track initiation and termination explicitly, but it also enforces exclusion rules by disjoint constraints. The MHT tracker indeed works well in motion analysis in Cox et al. (1996). However, tracking hockey players represents quite a different situation. Figure 10.10 shows the X and Y coordinates of the trajectories of targets 1, 2, and 3

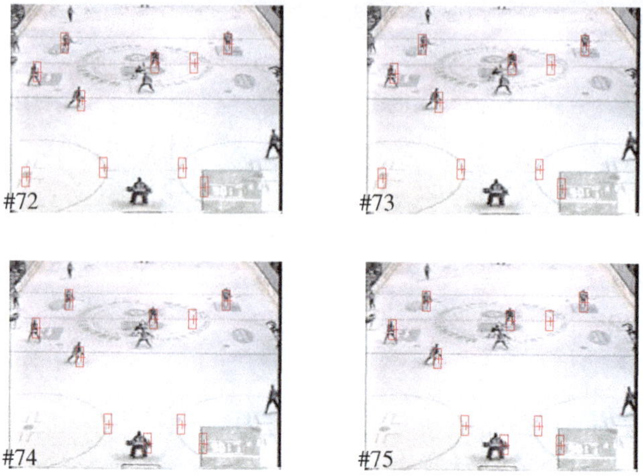

Fig. 10.7 Detected targets by the trained SVM detector: the threshold for decision of SVM classifier is 1.45, the *red cross* indicates the detected position of the target

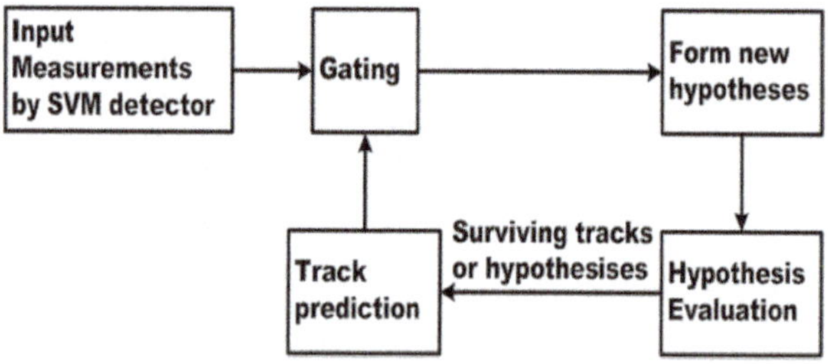

Fig. 10.8 Framework of the MHT tracker

obtained from our algorithm and the MHT tracker. The ground-truth trajectories of targets 1, 2, and 3 were obtained via manual labeling. It was shown that the MHT tracker failed in tracking targets 2 and 3 when occlusion occured between targets 1, 2, and 3.

Two reasons may account for the failure of the MHT tracker. The first is that the hypotheses surrounding the formation and validation of data association depends heavily on predicted measurements, and hence the accumulated prediction error caused by uncertainties in dynamics modeling causes the tracker to drift away, especially when the target engages in particularly agile motion. The second is that the MHT tracker lacks a mechanism to make use of image observations directly, and therefore its performance is affected by the noisy measurements provided by the detector.

10.6.2.2 Comparison with BPF

We compared our algorithm to BPF, which we also implemented ourselves. Figure 10.9 shows the X and Y coordinates of the trajectories of targets 1 and 2 obtained by our algorithm and BPF. It shows that both trackers have almost the same performance in tracking accuracy and can track a variable number of targets when there is no occlusion. However, when occlusion occurs, our algorithm performs better than BPF in tracking accuracy (illustrated in Fig. 10.9), and with a lower frequency of failure (this could be seen in Table 4).

In our implementation, BPF used a multiple sub-region color-histogram based representation model for the target. The target appearance was defined as the sum of multiple sub-regions, and the likelihood was defined as the sum of the reference histograms associated with each sub-region. Compared with the single region color-histogram based representation model used in our algorithm, the multiple sub-region color-histogram is a better approximation to the color density of the target appearance, since the spatial layout of the color distribution is considered. As for the ability to handle occlusion, in the experiment, we found that BPF depends mainly on the discriminability of its likelihood function, while our tracking algorithm relies on the modeling of interactions between multiple targets. When we substituted a multiple sub-region color-histogram model for the single region model, the tracking accuracy of BPF deteriorated in presence of occlusions.

Obviously, our algorithm has a slightly higher computational complexity than BPF when both algorithms use the same observation likelihood function and dynamics model. However, the additional computation in our algorithm is worthwhile when higher tracking accuracy is required in the case of tracking multiple targets with frequent occlusions.

10.6.2.3 Comparison with NCAT

We also compared our algorithm with the latest NCAT (Yu and Wu 2005) which we implemented ourselves. Using the hockey game video, our implementation of NCAT can obtain nearly the same tracking results as reported in Yu and Wu (2005). Comparing the tracking results of our algorithm with those of NCAT, we found that both algorithms can track players in the presence of occlusions and a varying number of the targets.

However, our algorithm surpasses NCAT in at least two respects. First, whether initializing a new track for a just appeared player or deleting the existing track of a just disappeared target, our algorithm is in many such cases faster than NCAT. Second, in handling occlusion, NCAT is sometimes sensitive to the parameter that characterizes the size of competition region in the state space, while our algorithm robustly follows most of the hockey players and handles the occlusions satisfactorily. This can also be validated by the designed experiment using the synthesized video sequence discussed in Section 10.6.2.4.

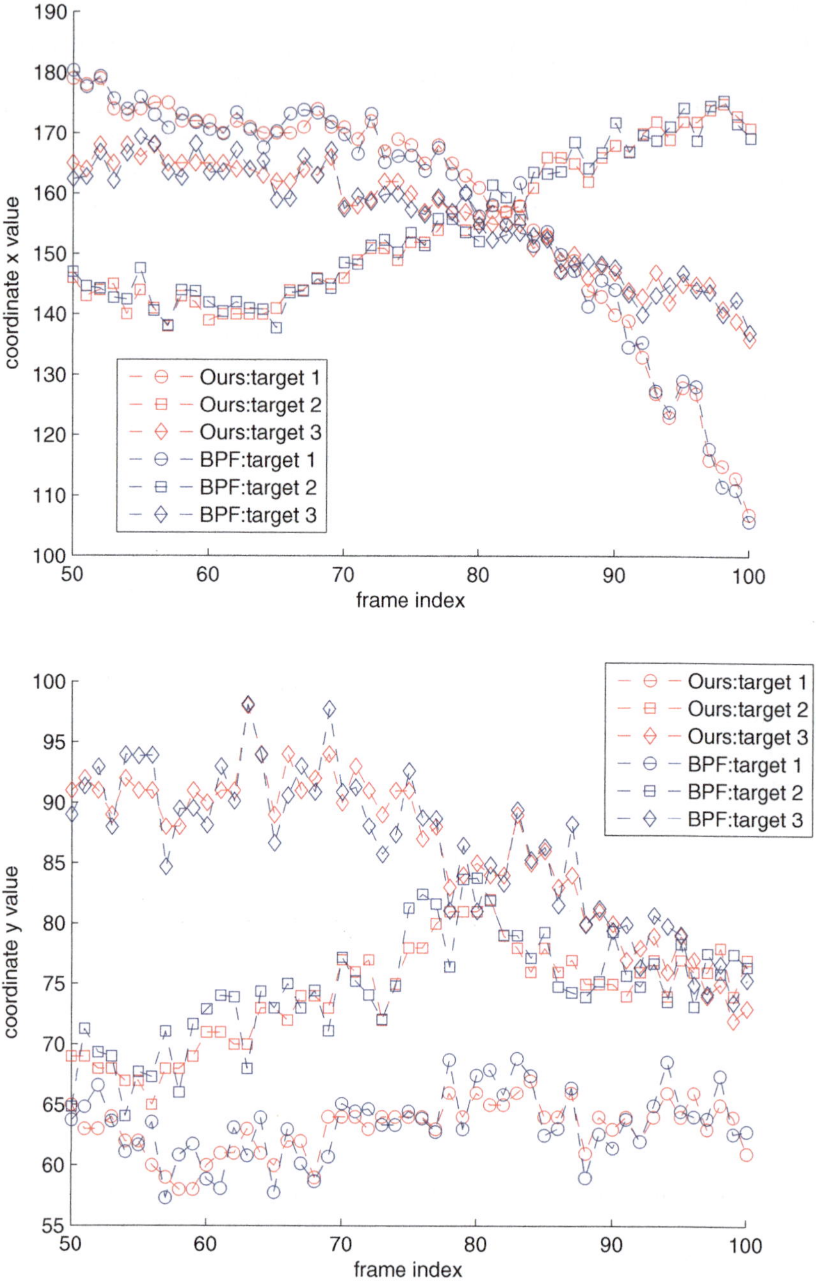

Fig. 10.9 *X* direction and *Y* coordinates of the trajectories of targets 1, 2, and 3, obtained by our algorithm and BPF

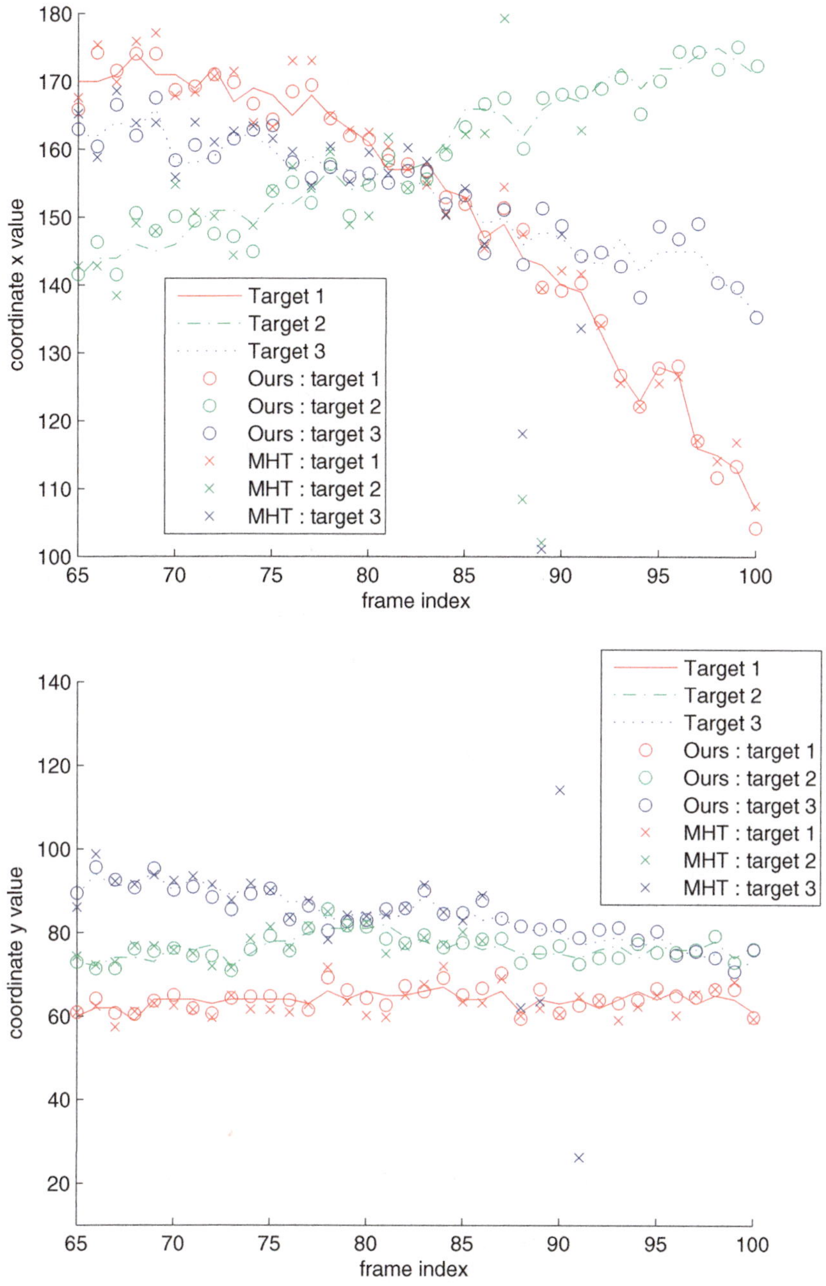

Fig. 10.10 X direction and Y direction component of the trajectories of targets 1, 2, and 3 : hand-labeled ground-truth, plus tracked trajectories generated by our algorithm and MHT tracker

We further compared the theories behind the particle-based belief propagation and NCAT. First, our DMN-based model differs from that of NCAT in the use of the compatibility functions, which are two robust functions derived by eliminating two binary MRFs. Second, we approximate the posterior distribution over the DMN using particle-based belief propagation. NCAT uses a mean-field approximation to the posterior of each target. Theoretically, the fully factorized variational density used to approximate the posterior is only a function of the one-node beliefs (Yedidia et al. 2005). In contrast, the fixed points of the BP algorithm correspond to the stationary points of Bethe free energy, which is a function of both one-node beliefs and two-node beliefs. This can explain why our particle-based belief propagation outperforms NCAT in handling occlusions.

10.6.2.4 In Handling Occlusion and the Varying Number of Targets Problem

To compare the performance of MHT, BPF, NCAT, and our tracker in handling occlusion and tracking a variable number of targets, we evaluated these four trackers with respect to a baseline ground-truth test sequence. The test sequence is a synthesized video sequence that contains a varying number of randomly moving balls. We recorded the correct number of target appearances, disappearances, and occurrences of occlusion present in the 2000 frame test video, and used these statistics as the ground-truth. Statistics for each tracker were obtained by running that tracker on the synthesized sequence. The results are illustrated in Table 10.4. We can see that our algorithm outperforms MHT, BPF, and NCAT in handling occlusions and tracking a variable number of targets.

Table 10.4 Results from four trackers: MHT, BPF, NCAT, and our algorithm. These values are obtained by running these four trackers on the 2000-frame synthesized test sequence. The ground truth of the test sequence contains counts of new appearances, disappearances, and the number of occurrences of occlusion

Trackers	MHT	BPF	NCAT	Ours	Ground-truth
Number of track failures	21	27	12	9	
Number of correct track initiations	43	38	51	56	62
Number of track swaps	25	28	16	9	133 (occlusions)
Number of false track drops	18	15	19	23	23 (disappearances)

In our view, the fact that our algorithm outperforms the other three trackers can be attributed to two factors: (1) our algorithm explicitly models the state of occlusion and the existence of each target, and (2) our algorithm employs a collaborating mechanism implemented via particle-based belief propagation. The second factor also explains NCAT outperforms MHT and BPF.

10.6.3 The Efficiency of the Gibbs Sampler

In the experiments, we found that the Gibbs sampler chain converges geometrically, and its convergence rate is heavily related to how the variables were correlated with each other. Based upon the fact that a Gibbs sampler's convergence rate is controlled by the maximal correlation between the states of two consecutive Gibbs iterations, Liu (1994) argued that grouping highly correlated components together (updating them jointly) in the Gibbs sampler can greatly improve efficiency. Applying this argument to our situation, the problem becomes how to determine which targets are involved in interaction, then group them together, and change their state simultaneously. This will be a focal point of our future work.

10.7 Summary

This chapter proposed to model MTTV problems by using a DMN. The DMN consisted of three coupled MRFs: an MRF for joint states of multiple targets, a binary random process for flagging the existence of each individual target, and another binary random process for flagging occlusion between every two adjacent targets. We showed how the particle-based BP algorithm obtains the maximum a posteriori (MAP) estimation in the DMN. We also described a method for incorporating bottom-up information from a learned detector (e.g., SVM classifier) and lay out a framework that employs belief propagation by using stratified sampler. The method we proposed was able to track multiple targets and handle their complex interactions, including occlusion and the sudden appearance or disappearance of target. We empirically validated this method by applying it to a synthetic and a real world tracking problem. Our experimental results showed that the proposed method is comparable to representative previous work, such as the MHT tracker and BPF. Our future work will include improvement of the current inference algorithm and the development of a target ID management technique for MTTV problems.

References

Bar-Shalom Y, Li X (1995) Multitarget-Multisensor Tracking: Principles and Techniques. Yaakov Bar-Shalom, Storrs

Black M, Rangarajan A (1996) On the unification of line processes, outlier rejection, and robust statistics with applications in early vision. International Journal of Computer Vision 19(1):57–91

Cai Y (2004) Maintaining accurate multi-target tracking under frequent occlusion. European Conference on Computer Vision

Comaniciu D, Ramesh V (2003) Real-time tracking of non-rigid objects using mean shift. US Patent 6,590,999

Cox I, Hingorani S, et al. (1996) An efficient implementation of Reid's multiple hypothesis tracking algorithm and its evaluation for the purpose of visual tracking. IEEE Transactions on Pattern Analysis and Machine Intelligence 18(2):138–150

Cristianini N, Shawe-Taylor J (2000) An introduction to Support Vector Machines: And Other Kernel-Based Learning Methods. Cambridge University Press, Cambridge, Cambridge

Fortmann T, Bar-Shalom Y, Scheffe M (1983) Sonar tracking of multiple targets using joint probabilistic data association. IEEE Journal of Oceanic Engineering 8(3):173–184

Hastings W (1970) Monte Carlo sampling methods using Markov chains and their applications. Biometrika 57(1):97

Hua G, Wu Y (2004) Multi-scale visual tracking by sequential belief propagation. IEEE International Conference on Computer Vision and Pattern Recognition 1

Hue C, Le Cadre J, Perez P, IRISA R (2002) Tracking multiple objects with particle filtering. IEEE Transactions on Aerospace and Electronic Systems 38(3):791–812

Isard M (2003) PAMPAS: real-valued graphical models for computer vision. IEEE International Conference on Computer Vision and Pattern Recognition 1

Isard M, Blake A (1998) CONDENSATIONłConditional Density Propagation for Visual Tracking. International Journal of Computer Vision 29(1):5–28

Isard M, MacCormick J (2001) BraMBLe: A Bayesian multiple-blob tracker. International Conference on Computer Vision 2(5)

Khan Z, Balch T, Dellaert F (2004) An MCMC-based particle filter for tracking multiple interacting targets. Europe Conference on Computer Vision

Li B, Meng Q, Holstein H (2004a) Articulated Pose Identification With Sparse Point Features. IEEE Transactions on Systems, Man, and CyberneticsłPart B: Cybernetics 34(3):1412–1422

Li B, Meng Q, Holstein H (2004b) Articulated Pose Identification With Sparse Point Features. IEEE Transactions on System, Man, and Cybernetics-Part B:Cybernetics 34(3)

Liu J (1994) The collapsed gibbs sampler in bayesian computations with applications to a gene regulation problem. Journal of the American Statistical Association 89(427):958–966

MacCormick J, Blake A (2000) A probabilistic exclusion principle for tracking multiple objects. International Journal of Computer Vision 39(1):57–71

Murphy K, Weiss Y, Jordan M (1999) Loopy belief propagation for approximate inference: An empirical study. Proceedings of Uncertainty in AI pp 467–475

Okuma K, Taleghani A, de Freitas N, Little J, Lowe D (2004) A boosted particle filter: Multitarget detection and tracking. European Conference on Computer Vision 1:28–39

Perez P, Hue C, Vermaak J, Gangnet M (2002) Color-based probabilistic tracking. European Conference on Computer Vision 1:661–675

Rasmussen C, Hager G (2001) Probabilistic data association methods for tracking complex visual objects. IEEE Transactions on Pattern Analysis and Machine Intelligence 23(6):560–576

Reid D (1979) An algorithm for tracking multiple targets. IEEE Transactions on Automatic Control 24(6):843–854

Rudin L, Osher S, Fatemi E (1992) Nonlinear total variation based noise removal algorithms. Physica D 60(1–4):259–268

Sudderth E, Ihler A, Freeman W, Willsky A (2003) Nonparametric belief propagation. IEEE Conf on Computer Vision and Pattern Recognition pp 605–612

Sudderth E, Mandel M, Freeman W, Willsky A (2004) Distributed occlusion reasoning for tracking with nonparametric belief propagation. Advances in Neural Information Processing Systems 17:1369–1376

Suykens J, Vandewalle J (1999) Least squares support vector machine classifiers. Neural Processing Letters 9(3):293–300

Tao H, Sawhney H, Kumar R (1999) A sampling algorithm for tracking multiple objects. Workshop on Vision Algorithms 99:53–68

Tweed D, Calway A (2002) Tracking many objects using subordinate Condensation. British Machine Vision Conference (BMVC)

Vermaak J, Doucet A, Perez P (2003) Maintaining multimodality through mixture tracking. IEEE International Conference on Computer Vision, 2003 pp 1110–1116

Xu J, Xu J (2004) On iterative learning from different tracking tasks in the presence of time-varying uncertainties. IEEE Transactions on Systems, Man, and CyberneticsłPart B: Cybernetics 34(1):589–597

Xue J, Zheng N, Zhong X (2006a) An integrated Monte Carlo data association framework for multi-object tracking. Proceedings of the 18th International Conference on Pattern Recognition 01:703–706

Xue J, Zheng N, Zhong X (2006b) Sequential stratified sampling belief propagation for multiple targets tracking. Science in China Issue F(01)

Xue J, Zheng N, Zhong X (2006c) Tracking Targets Via Particle Based Belief Propagation. Lecture Notes in Computer Science, Proceeding of ACCV'06 3851:348

Xue J, Zheng N, Geng J, Zhong X (2008) Tracking multiple visual targets via particle-based belief propagation. IEEE Transactions on System, Man, and Cybernetics, Part B: Cybernetics 38(1):196–209.

Yedidia J, Freeman W, Weiss Y (2005) Constructing free-energy approximations and generalized belief propagation algorithms. IEEE Transactions on Information Theory 51(7):2282–2312

Yu T, Wu Y (2004) Collaborative tracking of multiple targets. IEEE International Conference on Computer Vision and Pattern Recognition 1

Yu T, Wu Y (2005) Decentralized multiple target tracking using netted collaborative autonomous trackers. IEEE International Conference on Computer Vision and Pattern Recognition 1:939–946

Zhao T, Nevatia R (2004) Tracking multiple humans in crowded environment. IEEE International Conference on Computer Vision and Pattern Recognition 2:406–413

Zhong X, Xue J, Zheng N (2006) Graphical Model based Cue Integration Strategy for Head Tracking. British Machine Vision Conference'06

Chapter 11
Multi-Target Tracking in Video – Part II

Abstract This chapter presents a sequential Monte Carlo data association algorithm for tracking a varying number of interacting objects in a dynamic scene. The algorithm is based on a computational framework that consists of a hybrid measurement process, a Monte Carlo joint probabilistic data association filter, and a particle-based belief propagation algorithm. The hybrid measurement process addresses problems associated with having a varying number of objects. It does so by mixing target-driven measurements provided by a prior model of target dynamics and data-driven measurements based on a discriminative model; the Monte Carlo joint probabilistic data association filter combats the curse of dimensionality by providing a marginal posterior distribution for each individual target; and particle-based belief propagation is used to deal with occlusions among objects. Within this framework, the learning of discriminative model, the Monte Carlo joint data association filtering, and belief propagation are realized as different levels of approximation to the 'ideal' generative model inherent in the problem of tracking multiple visual objects. Together, these result in an efficient sequential Monte Carlo data association algorithm. The algorithm is illustrated via the tracking of multiple pedestrians in several real-life test videos. Empirical results demonstrate the algorithm's efficiency in a number of test situations.

11.1 Introduction

In a traditional multi-target tracking (MTT) system for use in conjunction with a radar or laser signal, data association and state estimation are two core consecutive steps (Bar-Shalom and Li 1995). The data association step outputs a partition of measurements such that each element of a partition represents a collection of measurements generated by a single target or clutter; the tracks are updated with the assigned measurements during the filtering process. While explicit association of measurements to targets is a useful pragmatic device, theoretically, the data association is an NP-hard problem. To minimize the difficulty of the data association

N. Zheng, J. Xue, *Statistical Learning and Pattern Analysis for Image and Video Processing*, Advances in Pattern Recognition, DOI 10.1007/978-1-84882-312-9_11,
© Springer-Verlag London Limited 2009

problem, much work has been done (Bar-Shalom and Li 1995). The joint probabilistic data association filter (JPDAF) (Fortmann et al. 1983) and multiple hypothesis tracker (MHT) (Reid 1979) are two landmarks in the literature. JPDAF considers measurements at the current time step, while MHT considers measurements for several time steps. However, whether in MHT or in JPDAF, the construction of a new data association hypothesis requires an enumeration of all possibilities, and the total number of association hypotheses can grow exponentially with the increase in the number of targets (Cox et al. 1996).

In the context of MTT in video (MTTV), data association becomes more difficult when densely distributed visual objects move in close proximity or pass by each other. Moreover, MTTV is fraught with uncertainties, such as background clutter and inter-object as well as object-background occlusion. Instead of handling data association explicitly, some MTTV methods (Zhao and Nevatia 2004; Isard and MacCormick (2001)) use track-driven measurements generated from the predictions of a model of target dynamics. However, in these methods, ambiguities arise when the distance between objects is small compared to errors in the measurement processes and their dynamics models.

It seems feasible to augment the joint state space of objects with data association, and then use a sequential Monte Carlo (SMC) filter (Liu 2001) to estimate the joint state. Some work has addressed this feasibility (Vermaak and Pérez 2005). However, in MTTV, the direct implementation of an SMC filter for the purpose of estimating the augmented joint state suffers greatly from the curse of dimensionality, as well as the existence of the occlusions among objects and background. In addition, it can also be difficult to generate measurements from an observed image in the presence of occlusions.

First, models of an object's motion and measurement are often nonlinear and non-Gaussian. Thus, no closed-form analytic expression can be obtained for tracking recursion. Particle filtering techniques provide an efficient solution to the nonlinear/ non-Gaussian problem, and have achieved a great success in tracking single objects (Isard and Blake 1998; Perez et al. 2002). If the objects to be tracked are distinctive from each other, they can be tracked independently with the least confusion by using multiple independent particle filters. However, a chief shortcoming of particle filtering and other MC methods in general is their poor ability to consistently maintain the multi-modality of the filtering distribution (Vermaak et al. 2003). For example, in practice, when applying a particle filter with a multi-mode filtering distribution, the mode with the highest likelihood will quickly attract almost all the particles, leaving other modes to be subsequently discarded. This does not work in MTTV, in which modes cannot be discarded; all modes in an MTTV filtering distribution must continue to be tracked since each mode may correspond to a potential object.

Second, measurements of objects yielded by image sensors are often unlabeled, which leads to a very challenging combinatorial data association problem when objects have a small separation compared with the measurement errors, especially when multiple tracks compete for measurements. For example, in situations such as occlusion, or a varying number of objects, or a cluttered background, it is quite difficult to associate objects with these spatially adjacent image measurements, since the joint image measurements cannot be segmented easily. Even if segmentation is possible, the resulting measurements may be incomplete or totally absent for some occluded objects.

However, we believe that the problem of accurately identifying targets in visual tracking requires a probabilistic framework to address the aforementioned difficulties, and should take the following three observations into consideration.

First, data association techniques are needed in order to maintain a unique identifier for each track when visual information is indistinguishable or temporarily unavailable due to occlusion. Confusion due to occlusion can be resolved by exploiting continuity of motion or appearance. However, it is not possible to reliably maintain a target's identifier using only continuity of appearance or motion, because in many applications there is a significant likelihood that multiple tracks will be confused with each other or migrate onto only a single track.

Second, target existence should be treated jointly with the target state and data association processes. The problem of a varying number of targets in MTT can be solved if information on target appearance and disappearance is available from some external source. Even the appearance and disappearance of targets are themselves uncertain events. One possible way to address this uncertainty is to associate with each target a binary existence variable indicating whether the target is active or inactive (Xue et al. 2008, 2006a). A suitable prior process can then be specified for existence variables, which facilitates joint inference with the state and data association processes. This is in essence an important component of the approach described in this chapter.

Third, the tasks of detecting and tracking of targets should be combined rather than being separated into two independent procedures. A detector can act as an useful information source for the varying number of targets problem in MTT, although it may be weak when detecting targets in the presence of occlusions. Similarly, a sequential filters-based tracker can solve the occlusion problem by exploiting the continuity of the motion, but such trackers always fail in dealing with the varying number of targets problem. Thus, we propose an interactive mechanism that combines the detection and tracking of objects. This not only allows the detection to make use of temporal consistency, but also facilitates robust tracking of multiple targets.

Building on previous work (Xue et al. 2008, 2006a), we propose to achieve these goals via an SMC data association algorithm. We model data association explicitly within the SMC framework, and present an integrated Monte Carlo data association filtering framework for tracking a varying number of interacting objects in dynamic scene. There are three contributions in this chapter: (1) the modeling of target state, data association, target existence, and interaction between targets explicitly and jointly within a probabilistic framework, (2) the approximation of the (MAP) estimation of the joint target state by maximizes a posterior an SMC data association algorithm within a two-level computing framework, and (3) the development of an interaction mechanism using a hybrid measurement process. The hybrid measurement process mixes both the target-driven measurements provided by a model of the target motion prior and the data-driven measurements from a learned discriminative model. The framework integrates discriminative model learning, MC joint data association filtering, and a belief propagation algorithm. These methods are realized as different levels of approximations to an 'ideal' generative model of multiple visual target tracking, and result in a novel sequential MC data association algorithm. Parts of our work have been previously described in Xue et al. 2006a, b. This chapter presents several enhancements, and provides a unified and detailed presentation, as well as additional results.

The rest of this chapter is organized as follows: In Section 11.2, we present an overview of the data association mechanism in MTTV. In Section 11.3, we introduce the proposed generative model for MTTV. In Section 11.4, we introduce an improved MC JPDAF for the data association. Section 11.5 presents a distributed joint state model and the particle-based belief propagation algorithm. The hybrid measurement process is described in Section11.6. Empirical results and discussion are given in Section 11.7.

11.2 Overview of the MTTV Data Association Mechanism

The literature on MTTV is abundant, and we have provided a brief survey in Chapter 10. We do not attempt to give an exhaustive summary again in this section, but rather highlight some of the key observations in handling data association within the SMC framework. We also describe several techniques for detecting multiple, partially occluded objects in a static image, since these works are relevant to the hybrid measurement process in this chapter.

11.2.1 Handing Data Association Explicitly

In a typical automatic MTTV system, based on a given set of measurements, data association must address three main problems: (1) how to assign measurements to each individual track? (2) when to initialize a track? and (3) when to terminate a trajectory.

Approaches to data association can be broadly categorized as either single frame assignment methods, which only consider observations at the current time step, or multi-frame assignment, which defers difficult data association decision until more data are received. The JPDAF (Fortmann et al. 1983) and the multiple hypothesis tracker (MHT) (Reid 1979) may be the most notable example of these two categories, respectively. The MHT attempts to keep track of all possible hypotheses over time. Each hypothesis associates past observations with a target, and as a new set of observations arrives, a new set of hypotheses is formed from previous hypotheses. JPDAF is a widely applied strategy in the single-frame assignment method. JPDAF enumerates all possible associations between the most recent set of observations and known tracks and clutter, and computes each association weight. A filtering estimate is then computed for each of the hypotheses, and combined in proportion to the corresponding posterior hypothesis probabilities. However, these heuristics are used at the expense of optimality and the algorithms can still suffer from the combinatoric explosion in a dense environment. As we mentioned in Chapter 10, the construction of a new data association hypothesis in both the MHT and the JPDAF theoretically requires an enumeration of all possibilities, and the total number of association hypotheses can grow exponentially with the increase in the number of targets. Several heuristics, such as pruning, gating clustering, and N-scan-back logic (Bar-Shalom and Li 1995) have been proposed in the initial implementations and later extensions of MHT and JPDAF to reduce the number of association hypotheses.

Recently, strategies have been proposed to accommodate the data association problem in the context of SMC filtering techniques. The feasibility of multi-target tracking with particle filters was first claimed by (Gordon 1997), but the examples in those works deal only with a single target. In Hue et al. (2002), a method is described that computes the distribution of the association hypotheses using a Gibbs sampler (Liu 2001) at each time step. The method is similar in spirit to one described in Dellaert et al. (2000), which uses Markov chain Monte Carlo (MCMC) techniques (Liu 2001) to compute the correspondences between image points within the context of stereo reconstruction. The main problem with these MCMC strategies is that they are iterative in nature and take an unknown number of iterations to converge. They are thus not entirely suitable for online applications. To address this problem, a method is presented in Hue et al. (2002) in which associations are sampled from an optimally designed importance distribution. The method is intuitively appealing, since the association hypotheses are treated in a similar fashion to the target state, such that the resulting algorithm is noniterative. It is, however, restricted to jump Markov linear systems (JMLS), in which samples of the association hypotheses are generated from an efficient proposal distribution based on the notion of a soft gating of the measurements.

More recently, some MC versions of JPDAF and MHT have been proposed. In Vermaak and Pérez (2005), an MC-based JPDAF is described, in which the marginal filtering distributions for each of the targets is approximated with particles rather than with a Gaussian. Correspondingly, a Markov chain Monte Carlo MCMC-based MHT is described in Oh et al. (2004), which takes a data-driven, combinatorial optimization approach to the data association problem but avoids the enumeration of tracks by applying MCMC sampling; this method can be taken as an MC-based MHT, since the decision about whether to form a track is based on current and past observations.

In some SMC-based approaches to MTTV, data association has also been explicitly addressed. For efficient tracking, these SMC approaches requires informative proposal distribution, and thus, some bottom-up detection approaches are introduced. In MTTV, a target may return more than one measurement per target and interacting targets may return multiple merged measurements between targets. To deal with this problem, an MCMC-based particle filter is proposed in Khan et al. (2004) to simulate the distribution of the association hypotheses. Data association in this approach allows multiple temporal associations between observations and targets, but cannot deal with a varying number of targets. In Yu et al. (2006), the MTTV is formulated as finding the best partition of a measurement graph containing all detected moving regions, and the posterior distribution is augmented with an Adaboost image likelihood. The method presented in Cai et al. (2006) suggests using data association techniques as a complement to the boosted particle filter (Okuma et al. 2004) to accurately maintain the identity of each target in the field.

11.2.2 Handing Data Association Implicitly

For MTTV, much work has been done within a Bayesian sequential estimation framework. However, most of this work has not explicitly tackled the data association issue.

Some early methods, e.g., (Tao et al. 1999; Isard and MacCormick 2001) track motion blobs and assume that each individual blob corresponds to one human. These early methods usually do not consider multiple objects jointly and tend to fail when blobs merge or split. Some more recent methods (Zhao and Nevatia 2004; Rittscher et al. 2005) try to fit multiple object hypotheses to explain the foreground or motion blobs. These methods deal with occlusions by computing the joint image likelihood of multiple objects. Because the joint hypothesis space is usually of high dimension, an efficient optimization algorithm, such as MCMC (Zhao and Nevatia 2004) or EM (Rittscher et al. 2005) is used. All of these methods have only been applied in experiments with a stationary camera, where background subtraction provides relatively robust object motion blobs. The foreground blob-based methods are not discriminative. They assume all moving pixels are from objects. Although this is true in some environments, it is not true in more general situations. Moreover, none of the above tracking methods deals with occlusion by scene objects explicitly.

Recently, discriminative methods, e.g., (Paul and Michael 2001; Viola et al. 2005), have been incorporated into the SMC framework to provide informative proposal distribution for MC sampling. Works in this line of thinking include (Okuma et al. 2004; Cai et al. 2006; Khan et al. 2004), Yu and Wu (2005). In (Okuma et al. 2004), a boosted particle filter (BPF) based on the mixture particle filter (Vermaak et al. 2003) is described, in which the proposal of the particle filter combines the information of a trained AdaBoost detector (Paul and Michael 2001) and a model of targets' dynamics. However, in this method, multiple tracks can become confused with each other or migrate onto only one track when measurements are indistinguishable or absent because of occlusion. To solve this problem, a method proposed in Cai et al. (2006) suggests using data association techniques as a complement to the boosted particle filter (Okuma et al. 2004) to accurately maintain the identity of each target in the field. In Khan et al. (2004), a joint tracker that includes an MCMC-based particle filter and a sophisticated motion model is developed to maintain the identity of targets throughout an interaction. A decentralized approach is proposed in Yu and Wu (2005), in which the individual trackers are autonomous in the sense that they can select targets to track and evaluate themselves, and they are also collaborative, since they must compete against targets in close proximity to be the 'owner' of a target.

To address the occlusion problem in MTTV, a pair-wise Markov random field (MRF) motion prior is introduced to model the interaction between targets in (Khan et al. 2004; Yu and Wu 2005). However, these MRFs are built only on simultaneous observations, and therefore require good detection of moving regions. To address the self-occlusion problem in tracking a three-dimensional geometric hand, it is proposed in Sudderth et al. (2004) to infer these occlusions in a distributed fashion. In Nillius et al. (2006), a method is presented that assumes a track graph exists. The graph denotes when targets are isolated and describes how they interact. The identities of the isolated tracks are then associated by exploiting the graph constraints and the defined similarity measures between isolated tracks.

11.2.3 Detection and Tracking

Objects to be tracked must be first detected. The process of detection provides measurements for the tracking task. There is an extensive literature on object detection in the field of computer vision. See Gavrila (1999) for a survey. The detection task is not difficult for moving, isolated objects viewed with a fixed camera and fixed or slowly varying illumination. However, in the presence of multiple complex, moving objects (eg., pedestrians) with inter-object occlusion as well as object-scene occlusion and/or a moving camera, reliable detection becomes a difficult problem.

The general guideline to design a specific object detector is discussed in Chapter 6. Here we review just a few papers (Dalai et al. 2005; Viola et al. 2005; Leibe et al. 2005; Wu and Nevatia 2005) relevant to the human detector we adopted in this chapter. It was shown empirically in Dalai et al. (2005) that grids of histograms of oriented gradient (HOG) descriptors significantly outperform existing feature sets for human detection. In Viola et al. (2005), a method is described which builds an efficient moving person detector, using AdaBoost to train a chain of progressively more complex region rejection rules based on Haar-like wavelets and space–time differences. In Leibe et al. (2005), a pedestrian detector is described, in which the core of the method is the combination of local and global cues via a probabilistic top-down segmentation. Altogether, this approach enables the examination and comparison of object hypotheses with high precision down to the pixel level. Recently, a pedestrian detector based on the Bayesian combination of edgelet part detectors was proposed in Wu and Nevatia (2005). It can detect multiple, partially occluded humans in a single image.

In previous work (Xue et al. 2006a), we proposed the integration of JPDAF with belief propagation (BP) to solve the data association in MTTV. In this chapter, we extend the integrated MC data association framework by combining several efficient part-based human detectors. We also introduce an interactive mechanism that can also be used. With this mechanism, tracking can be used to facilitate detection.

11.3 The Generative Model for MTT

Most MTTV techniques are model based, i.e., they rely explicitly upon two descriptions: a description of the behavior of the objects, usually in the form of a motion (or dynamics) model, and a description of the measurements of the object, known as the measurement model. In general, we would like to represent the object concisely with a parametric model, and define the state of the object with the parameters of the object model. We would also like to define the measurements as the coherent visual patterns in the observed image that may be used for state estimation. What an MTTV algorithm can accomplish depends crucially upon how much it knows about the dynamics and measurements of the objects, and whether this knowledge can be mathematically represented by general and parsimonious models that can realistically characterize both the visual patterns and motion of the objects.

In general, mathematically representing knowledge about the dynamic and measurement processes of the target is an essential step leading to an efficient MTT algorithm. However, this is not always a success story. Information about the working environment sometimes also plays an important role in an efficient MTT algorithm. In this section, we first formulate the MTT problem, and then model the problem via a generative model.

11.3.1 Problem Formulation

In an MTT problem, one is interested in recursively estimating the state of each target $\mathbf{x}_{i,t}$ and its existence variable $e_{i,t}$ based on a sequence of measurements $\mathbf{Y}_{1:t} = \{\mathbf{Y}_1,..\mathbf{Y}_t\}$, where $i = 1,...,K$ and K is the maximum number of targets to track, and $e_{i,t} \in \{0,1\}$. The full joint state space of $\mathbf{X}_t$ is the union of spaces $\{\mathbf{x}_{i,t}|e_{i,t} = 1\}_{i=1}^{K}$. The number of targets present at time t is denoted by k_t, which can be determined by $k_t = \sum_i^K e_{i,t}$.

A typical MTT problem is shown in Fig. 11.1. At each time t, the measurements comprise m_t detections, which is denoted by $\mathbf{Y}_t = \{\mathbf{y}_{j,t}, j = 1,...,m_t\}$. A target may disappear with probability P_{de}, and appear with probability P_{re}. More specifically, we assume that the target state can be measured with a detection probability P_d less than unity, and the number of false alarms follows a Poisson distribution parameterized by $\lambda_f V$, where V is the volume of a surveillance region in the view of the camera. The measurements are unlabeled and may come from the target or even clutter. To represent this uncertainty, a target to measurement association variable $r_{i,t}$ is defined as

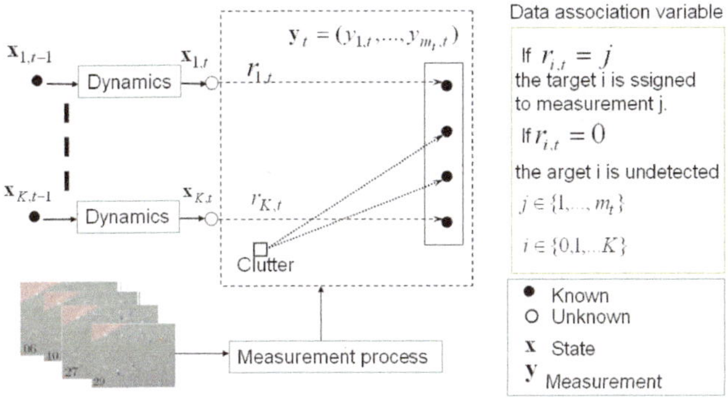

Fig. 11.1 The MTT problem formulation: tracking k_t targets with the given m_t measurements, with the defined association variable of target to measurement association

$$r_{i,t} = \begin{cases} 0 & \text{if target } i \text{ is undetected,} \\ j \in \{1,...,m_t\} & \text{if target } i \text{ generated measurement } j. \end{cases} \tag{11.1}$$

Thus far, the complete set of unknowns at time t can be summarized as $\{\mathbf{X}_t, \mathbf{r}_t, \mathbf{e}_t\}$, where $\mathbf{r}_t = \{r_{i,t}\}_{i=1}^K$ is the data association vector and $\mathbf{e}_t = \{e_{i,t}\}_{i=1}^K$ is the binary vector that describes the existence of each individual target. From the viewpoint of Bayesian theory, an MTT tracker is expected to estimate the joint state $\mathbf{X}_t$ that MAP $P(\mathbf{X}_t, \mathbf{r}_t, \mathbf{e}_t|\mathbf{Y}_{1:t})$, and to maintain a unique identifier for each target that persists throughout tracking. At each time t, the MAP estimation $\mathbf{X}_t$ partitions the input image into at least $k_t + 1$ regions corresponding to different targets and the background, along with the estimated $\mathbf{e}_t$.

11.3.2 The Generative Model

Ideally, a generative model for MTT is the posterior $p(\mathbf{X}_t|\mathbf{Y}_{1:t})$, which is also known as a filtering distribution, and can be computed according to

$$p(\mathbf{X}_t|\mathbf{Y}_{1:t}) = \sum_{(\mathbf{e}_t, \mathbf{r}_t)} p(\mathbf{X}_t|\mathbf{r}_t, \mathbf{e}_t, \mathbf{Y}_{1:t}) p(\mathbf{r}_t, \mathbf{e}_t|\mathbf{Y}_{1:t}) \tag{11.2}$$

.

It is difficult to find the MAP estimation of the composition of a continuous stochastic variable $\mathbf{X}_t$ and two discrete stochastic variables $\mathbf{e}_t$ and $\mathbf{r}_t$, even if the forms and parameters of the joint distributions of $\mathbf{e}_t$ and $\mathbf{r}_t$ are given. The computational complexity may increase exponentially with the number of targets. However, if the set of valid data association hypotheses is given, this computation becomes the task of estimating the state of each individual target independently. It turns out that the number of tracks itself may not make the MTT problem more difficult if the tracks are scattered apart, but the difficulty arises when there are many tracks that are moving closely and crossing each other. Thus, modeling interactions between targets is necessary for an MTT tracker.

We use a pairwise MRF to model the joint state of the targets. In the MRF, each target is treated as a node in the graph. The interaction between every two targets is modeled by a clique function defined on two neighboring nodes. Thus we obtain a more realistic model of $p(\mathbf{X}_t|\mathbf{r}_t,\mathbf{e}_t,\mathbf{Y}_{1:t})$

$$p(\mathbf{X}_t|\mathbf{r}_t,\mathbf{e}_t,\mathbf{Y}_{1:t}) = \prod_{i=1}^{K} p(\mathbf{x}_{i,t}|r_{i,t},e_{i,t},\mathbf{Y}_{1:t}) \prod_{i,k\in\mathbf{C}_2} \psi(\mathbf{x}_{i,t},\mathbf{x}_{k,t}) \tag{11.3}$$

where $\mathbf{C}_2$ is the set of cliques of two neighboring targets. The clique function ψ defined on $\mathbf{C}_2$ affords us the possibility of specifying domain knowledge governing the joint behavior of interacting targets. A similar idea can also be found in Khan et al. (2004); Yu and Wu (2005).

Substituting Equation (11.3) into Equation (11.2), the generative model can then be rewritten as

$$p(\mathbf{X}_t|\mathbf{Y}_{1:t}) = \underbrace{\sum_{(\mathbf{e}_t,\mathbf{r}_t)} p(\mathbf{r}_t,\mathbf{e}_t|\mathbf{Y}_{1:t}) \prod_{i=1}^{K} p(\mathbf{x}_{i,t}|r_{i,t},e_{i,t},\mathbf{Y}_{1:t})}_{\text{marginal}} \underbrace{\prod_{i,k\in\mathbf{C}_2} \psi(\mathbf{x}_{i,t},\mathbf{x}_{k,t})}_{\text{interactive}} \tag{11.4}$$

Thus, we obtain a model that consists of two terms: the marginal term and the interactive term.

The marginal term corresponds to the marginal filtering distribution of each individual target. Since the origins of the measurements are unknown, the existence and association variables for the individual targets are coupled. Thus, in computing $P(\mathbf{r}_t,\mathbf{e}_t|\mathbf{Y}_{1:t})$, the existence and association variables must be treated jointly. Once this joint relationship is known, the state filtering of each individual target can proceed in a similar manner as in the JPDAF (Vermaak and Pérez 2005), and the required marginal and conditionals for the individual targets are easily obtained by summation.

The interactive term characterizes the joint behavior of the targets involved in an interaction. This means that the estimation of the state of an individual target is not only determined by its own observation and dynamics, but also through interaction and collaboration with the estimates of its adjacent targets. Thus, an iterative message propagation mechanism is needed to ensure consistency between these marginal filtering distributions.

Although the MCMC technique provides an efficient way to explore the solution space, the computational requirements of Equation (11.4) make MCMC impractical because of the curse of dimensionality. Therefore, we propose the two-level approximation framework illustrated in Fig. 11.2. The first-level approximation uses an improved MCJPDAF. The filter recursively updates the marginal distribution for each individual target, while simultaneously considering the joint hypothesis of the existence and association variables. The second-level approximation uses a particle-based BP algorithm to facilitate interaction between objects. With the initial state of each node supplied by the first level, the second level can produce a more accurate estimation at a fast convergence rate for a target involved in occlusion. Furthermore, a hybrid measurement process is used to mix the track-driven measurements provided by the target dynamics prior model and data-driven measurements based on a discriminative model.

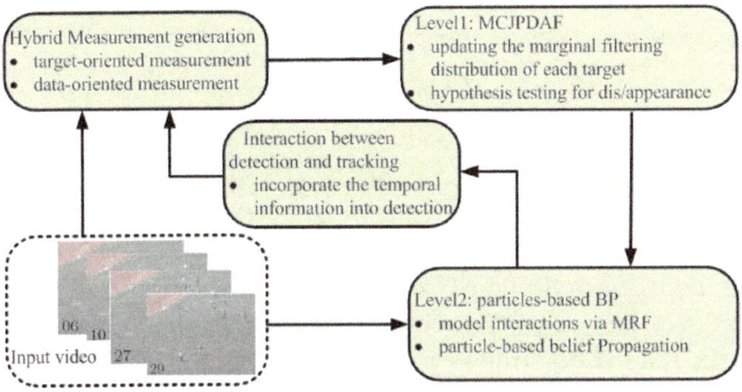

Fig. 11.2 The two-level computing framework

11.4 Approximating The Marginal Term

With the concept of data association, the marginal term of Equation (11.4) represents a collaboration between the filtering distributions of each individual target. Actually, this collaboration is performed through the soft assignment of the same set of measurements $\mathbf{Y}_t$ to each track. This observation motivates us to approximate the marginal term by recursively updating these filtering distributions $p(\mathbf{x}_{i,t}|E_{i,t},\mathbf{Y}_{1:t})$, where $E_{i,t}$ denotes the event $\{e_{i,t}=1\}$.

The filtering distribution of each individual target can be computed according to

$$p(\mathbf{x}_{i,t}|E_{i,t},\mathbf{Y}_{1:t})=\sum_{r_{i,t}}p(r_{i,t}|E_{i,t},\mathbf{Y}_{1:t})p(\mathbf{x}_{i,t}|r_{i,t},E_{i,t},\mathbf{Y}_{1:t}) \tag{11.5}$$

where $p(r_{i,t}|E_{i,t},\mathbf{Y}_{1:t})$ is the posterior of the association variable $r_{i,t}$ and $p(\mathbf{x}_{i,t}|r_{i,t}, E_{i,t},\mathbf{Y}_{1:t})$ is the posterior of the target that is present at time t under the given association. Using Bayes' rule and the fact that the measurements at a given time step are independent conditional on the target state, existence, and association variables, the last term of Equation (11.5) can be computed as

$$p(\mathbf{x}_{i,t}|r_{i,t},E_{i,t},\mathbf{Y}_{1:t}) = \frac{p_T(\mathbf{y}_{r_{i,t},t}|\mathbf{x}_{i,t})p(\mathbf{x}_{i,t}|E_{i,t},\mathbf{Y}_{1:t-1})}{\int_{\mathbf{x}_{i,t}} p_T(\mathbf{y}_{r_{i,t},t}|\mathbf{x}_{i,t})p(\mathbf{x}_{i,t}|E_{i,t},\mathbf{Y}_{1:t-1})} \tag{11.6}$$

where $p_T(\mathbf{y}_{j,t}|\mathbf{x}_{i,t})$ is the likelihood function of the measurement $\mathbf{y}_{j,t}$ with the given state $\mathbf{x}_{i,t}$.

At each time step t, one can assume that there are M_C clutter measurements and M_T target measurements in the m_t measurements, i.e., $m_t = M_C + M_T$. We denote $P(r_{i,t} = j|E_{i,t},\mathbf{Y}_{1:t})$ as β_{ij}, which defines the association probability that the jth measurement is associated with the ith target at time t, where $i \in \{1,...,K\}, j \in \{1,...,m_t\}$. Similarly, the association probability β_{i0} indicates that the ith target goes undetected. The association probability β_{ij} can then be computed according to

$$\begin{aligned}\beta_{ij} &= \sum_{\{\mathbf{r}_t \in \Lambda_t : r_{i,t}=j\}} P(\mathbf{r}_t|E_{i,t},\mathbf{Y}_{1:t}) \\ &\propto \sum_{\{\mathbf{r}_t \in \Lambda_t : r_{i,t}=j\}} p(\mathbf{r}_t)\frac{(\lambda_f V)^{M_C}}{M_C!}e^{-\lambda_f V}\prod_{j\in I_t} p_i(\mathbf{y}_{j,t}|\mathbf{Y}_{1:t})\end{aligned} \tag{11.7}$$

where Λ_t is the set of all valid association hypotheses and $p(\mathbf{r}_t)$ is the joint association prior as discussed in Section 11.4.2; I_t is the subset of measurements associated with the ith target; and $p_i(\mathbf{y}_{j,t}|\mathbf{Y}_{1:t})$ is the predictive likelihood for the jth measurement using the information from the ith target.

$$p_i(\mathbf{y}_{j,t}|\mathbf{Y}_{1:t}) = \int p_T(\mathbf{y}_{j,t}|\mathbf{x}_{i,t})p(\mathbf{x}_{i,t}|\mathbf{Y}_{1:t-1}) \tag{11.8}$$

Thus far, to recursively update the filtering distribution for each target, we must compute the state prediction distribution $p(\mathbf{x}_{i,t}|E_{i,t},\mathbf{Y}_{1:t-1})$ and the joint posterior distribution of the existence and association $p(\mathbf{r}_{i,t},\mathbf{e}_{i,t}|\mathbf{Y}_{1:t-1})$.

11.4.1 The State Prediction

By introducing the previous state and the previous existence variables, and using the total probability, the state prediction can be computed as

$$\begin{aligned}p(\mathbf{x}_{i,t}|E_{i,t},\mathbf{Y}_{1:t-1}) &= \int_{\mathbf{x}_{i,t-1}} p(\mathbf{x}_{i,t}|\mathbf{x}_{i,t-1},E_{i,t},e_{i,t-1}) \\ &\times p(\mathbf{x}_{i,t-1}|e_{i,t-1},\mathbf{Y}_{1:t-1})\sum_{e_{i,t-1}} p(e_{i,t-1}|E_{i,t},\mathbf{Y}_{i:t-1})\end{aligned} \tag{11.9}$$

Applying Bayes' rule and the assumption that $p(E_{i,t}|e_{i,t-1},\mathbf{Y}_{1:t-1}) = p(E_{i,t}|e_{i,t-1})$, we have

$$p(e_{i,t-1}|E_{i,t},\mathbf{Y}_{i:t-1}) = \frac{p(E_{i,t}|e_{i,t-1})p(e_{i,t-1}|\mathbf{Y}_{1:t-1})}{\sum_{e_{i,t-1}} p(E_{i,t}|e_{i,t-1})p(e_{i,t-1}|\mathbf{Y}_{1:t-1})} \tag{11.10}$$

Using the probability terms defined in Section 11.3, the state prediction distribution follows as

$$p(\mathbf{x}_{i,t}|E_{i,t},\mathbf{Y}_{1:t-1}) = \frac{1}{P_{re}+P_{E_{i,t-1}}(1-P_{re}-P_{de})} \times [P_{re}(1-P_{E_{i,t-1}})p_0(\mathbf{x}_{i,t})+(1-P_{de})P_{E_{i,t-1}}p(\mathbf{x}_{i,t}|\mathbf{Y}_{1:t-1})], \quad (11.11)$$

where $p_0(\mathbf{x}_{i,t})$ is the initial state distribution of the ith target, and where $P_{E_{i,t-1}} = p(e_{i,t-1}=1|\mathbf{Y}_{1:t-1})$.

The probability $p(\mathbf{x}_{i,t}|\mathbf{Y}_{1:t-1})$ is calculated as follows:

$$p(\mathbf{x}_{i,t}|\mathbf{Y}_{1:t-1}) = \int_{\mathbf{x}_{i,t-1}} p(\mathbf{x}_{i,t}|\mathbf{x}_{i,t-1})p(\mathbf{x}_{i,t-1}|\mathbf{Y}_{1:t-1}). \quad (11.12)$$

We assume that a set of samples $\{w_{i,t-1}^{(n)},\mathbf{x}_{i,t-1}^{n}\}_{n=1}^{N}$ for the ith target at time $t-1$ is available, and approximately distributed according to $p(\mathbf{x}_{i,t-1}|E_{i,t-1},\mathbf{Y}_{1:t-1})$. New samples of $\mathbf{x}_{i,t}$ may then be sampled from a suitable proposal distribution.

Instead of using a traditional transition distribution modeled by autoregressive state dynamics, we sample from a mixture proposal to integrate information from both the target dynamics and the current detections. The mixture proposal is

$$p(\mathbf{x}_{i,t}|\mathbf{x}_{i,t-1},\mathbf{Y}_t) = \alpha Q_{ada}(\mathbf{x}_{i,t}|\mathbf{x}_{i,t-1},\mathbf{Y}_t)+(1-\alpha)p(\mathbf{x}_{i,t}|\mathbf{x}_{i,t-1}) \quad (11.13)$$

where Q_{ada} is a multi-modality probability distribution constructed by the output of a learned AdaBoost detector (Viola et al. 2005). Each mode of the distribution centers around one detection, and is modeled by a Gaussian distribution approximated by a cluster of samples. Other kinds of detectors can also be adopted. The parameter $0 \leq \alpha \leq 1$ can be set dynamically without affecting the convergence of the method. By decreasing α, one can place more importance on the prediction than on the detector (Fig. 11.3).

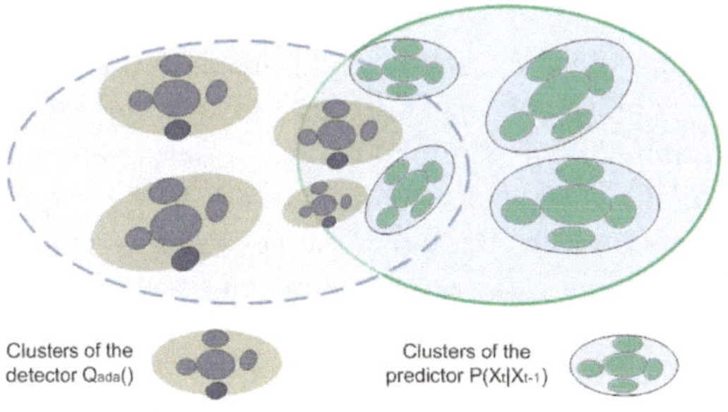

Fig. 11.3 The clusters produced by the detector and the predictor. Each cluster contains many particles. The weight of each particle is illustrated by its size

Sampling from the mixture proposal, we obtain a set of samples for each target. These samples approximate the predictive likelihood Equation (11.8), which can be expressed in a straightforward manner as follows:

$$p_i(\mathbf{y}_{j,t}|\mathbf{Y}_{1:t}) \approx \sum_{n=1}^{N} w_{i,t-1}^{(n)} \frac{p(\mathbf{x}_{i,t}^{(n)}|\mathbf{x}_{i,t-1}^{(n)})}{p(\mathbf{x}_{i,t}^{(n)}|\mathbf{x}_{i,t-1}^{(n)}, \mathbf{Y}_t)} p_T(\mathbf{y}_{j,t}|\mathbf{x}_{i,t}^{(n)}). \tag{11.14}$$

Substituting Equation (11.14) into Equation (11.7), we obtain the association probabilities β_{ij}, which can in turn be used in Equation (11.5) to compute the filtering distribution of each target. Thus, the filtering distribution $p(\mathbf{x}_{i,t}|E_{i,t}, \mathbf{Y}_{1:t})$ can be approximated by the particles $\{w_{i,t}^{(n)}, \mathbf{x}_{i,t}^{(n)}\}_{n=1}^{N}$ and by setting the weights as follows:

$$w_{i,t}^{(n)} \propto w_{i,t-1}^{(n)} \frac{p_i(\mathbf{x}_{i,t}^{(n)}|\mathbf{x}_{i,t-1}^{(n)})}{p(\mathbf{x}_{i,t}^{(n)}|\mathbf{x}_{i,t-1}^{(n)}, \mathbf{Y}_t)} p_i(\mathbf{Y}_t|\mathbf{x}_{i,t}^{(n)}), \sum_{n=1}^{N} w_{i,t}^{(n)} = 1. \tag{11.15}$$

11.4.2 Existence and Association Posterior

The joint posterior of existence and association $p(\mathbf{e}_t, \mathbf{r}_t|\mathbf{Y}_{1:t})$ can be expressed as

$$p(\mathbf{e}_t, \mathbf{r}_t|\mathbf{Y}_{1:t}) = p(\mathbf{r}_t|\mathbf{e}_t, \mathbf{Y}_{1:t})p(\mathbf{e}_t|\mathbf{Y}_{1:t}) \tag{11.16}$$

We adopt a soft-gating procedure to reduce the number of valid data association hypotheses. For each target, a validation region is constructed, and only measurements that fall within the target validation region are considered as possible candidates to be associated with the target. The validated set of measurements for the ith target can be defined as $\mathbf{Y}_i = \{y_j : d_i^2(y_j) \leq \xi\}$, where $d_i^2(y_j)$ is the squared distance between the measurement and the center of the validation region of the target i and ξ is a parameter that determines the size of the validation region.

The validation region of a target can be calculated by first assuming the particle set as the Gaussian mixture model, then approximating the Gaussian mixture as a single Gaussian, and finally computing the mean and covariance matrix of the particle set. With the mean and the covariance matrix, the validation region of the target can be determined. It is straightforward to derive the set of valid target to measurement associations for the target i: $r_i = \{y_j : d_i^2(y_j) \leq \xi\} \cup \{0\}$.

Once a pair $(\mathbf{e}_t, \mathbf{r}_t)$ is given, M_C and M_T are deterministically calculated. For the time being, we assume that association vectors take a form that factorizes sequentially over the individual associations.

$$q(\mathbf{r}_t) = p_c(M_C) \prod_{k=1}^{k_t} q(r_{k,t}|r_{1:k-1,t}) \tag{11.17}$$

$$p_c(M_C) = \frac{(\lambda_f V)^{M_C}}{M_C!} e^{-\lambda_f V} \tag{11.18}$$

where p_C denotes the clutter likelihood. It should be noted that sequential factorization can be performed over any permutation of the individual targets.

Since Equation (11.17) depends only on information available at the current time step, the components of an association vector can be sampled sequentially conditional on each other, and the proposal for the kth component is conditional on all the components sampled earlier in the sequence. We make use of this property to ensure that the measurements associated with targets earlier in the sequence are not considered as candidates for association with the current target. In this way, the algorithm is guaranteed to generate only valid association hypotheses. Thus we have

$$q(r_{i,t} = j | r_{1:i-1,t}) \propto \begin{cases} 1 - P_d & \text{if } j = 0 \\ 0 & \text{if } j > 0 \text{ and } j \in \{r_1, ..., r_{i-1}\} \\ \frac{P_d}{M_i} & \text{otherwise} \end{cases} \tag{11.19}$$

where $M_i = m_t - \sharp\{l : r_l \neq 0, l = 1, ..., i-1\}$ is the number of unassigned measurements, taking into account the assignments of the previous $i-1$ associations.

Thus, the joint posterior for the existence and association variables can be calculated as

$$\begin{aligned} p(\mathbf{e}_t, \mathbf{r}_t | \mathbf{Y}_{1:t}) &\propto p(M_C) p_C(\mathbf{y}_t^{g(\mathbf{e}_t, \mathbf{r}_t)}) \\ &\times \prod_{i=1}^{K} [q(r_{i,t} | r_{1:i-1}, t) p(e_{i,t} | \mathbf{Y}_{1:t-1}) p(\mathbf{y}_{r_{i,t},t} | e_{i,t}, \mathbf{Y}_{1:t-1})] \end{aligned} \tag{11.20}$$

where $g(\mathbf{e}_t, \mathbf{r}_t)$ is the set of indices of clutter measurements under the joint existence-association hypothesis$(\mathbf{e}_t, \mathbf{r}_t)$.

Now, we have $p(e_{i,t} | \mathbf{Y}_{1:t-1}) = \sum_{e_{i,t-1}} p(e_{i,t} | e_{i,t-1}) p(e_{i,t-1} | \mathbf{Y}_{1:t-1})$. With the particles $\{w_{i,t}^{(n)}, \mathbf{x}_{i,t}^{(n)}\}_{n=1}^{N}$, we can further compute the probability of the disappearance and reappearance of a target as follows:

$$p(e_{i,t} = 0 | e_{i,t-1} = 1, \mathbf{Y}_{1:t-1}) = \sum_{j=1}^{m_t} \beta_{ij} = 1 - \beta_{i0} \tag{11.21}$$

$$p(e_{i,t} = 1 | e_{i,t-1} = 0, \mathbf{Y}_{1:t-1}) = \sum_{i=1}^{k_t} \beta_{ij} \tag{11.22}$$

Each mode in the proposal distribution may correspond to a possible target. By comparing the distances between modes in $Q_a da(\cdot)$ and in $P(\mathbf{X}_t | \mathbf{X}_{t-1})$, we can classify modes in the mixture into three sets: (1) existing targets (EO: these matched modes between $Q_a da()$ and $p(\mathbf{X}_t | \mathbf{X}_{t-1})$), (2) newly appeared targets (NO: modes in $Q_a da(\cdot)$ which cannot find their correspondences in $p(\mathbf{X}_t | \mathbf{X}_{t-1})$), and (3) objects that have disappeared (DO:modes in $p(\mathbf{X}_t | \mathbf{X}_{t-1})$, which have no corresponding mode in $Q_a da(\cdot)$). Only when sampling from a mode $i \in$ NO, can we replace k_t by $k_t + 1$ and initialize a new set of particles for the new object.

The marginal term can be computed directly after the joint existence–association probabilities are computed.

11.5 Approximating the Interactive Term

For each target, the filtering distribution $p(\mathbf{x}_{i,t}|\mathbf{Y}_{1:t})$ output by the first-level approximation is purely local, since interactions between targets are not taken into consideration. To obtain more better estimation, we then run a particle-based BP algorithm (Xue et al. 2008) on the MRF which models $p(\mathbf{X}_t|\mathbf{Y}_{1:t})$.

We define the interactive potential function $\Psi(\mathbf{x}_i,\mathbf{x}_j)$ as a robust function

$$\Psi(\mathbf{x}_i,\mathbf{x}_j) = (1-e_p)\exp\{-\frac{|\Omega(\mathbf{x}_i,\mathbf{x}_j)|}{\sigma_p}\}+e_p \tag{11.23}$$

where $\Omega(\mathbf{x}_i,\mathbf{x}_j)$ is maximal when two objects coincide and gradually falls off as they move apart. $|\Omega(\mathbf{x}_i,\mathbf{x}_j)|$ denotes the number of pixels overlapping between two targets.

The use of MRF to model interaction between targets is also adopted in Yu and Wu (2005); Khan et al. (2004). In contrast to the upside-down Gaussian in Yu and Wu (2005); Khan et al. (2004), we derived Ψ from the total variance (TV) model (Rudin et al. 1992) with a potential function $\rho(z) = |z|$ because of its discontinuity preserving property. We truncate this potential function as our compatibility function. By varying the parameters e_p and σ_p, one can control the shape of $\rho_{ij}(\mathbf{x}_i,\mathbf{x}_j)$ and, therefore, the final posterior probability. This is important in preventing particles for occluded targets from being to rapidly a depleted.

The local evidence $\rho_i(\mathbf{x}_i,\mathbf{y}_i)$ is defined as the matching cost function of state $\mathbf{x}_i$ given observation $\mathbf{y}_i$. In the experiment, we use a color histogram to represent the target appearance, and the matching cost is a function of the Bhattacharyya distance, which takes a same form as that in Perez et al. (2002).

After the local evidence and interactive potential functions are defined, and the belief of each node is initialized with the filtering distribution obtained in the first level, the messages and believes can be computed in each iteration of the particle-based BP algorithm (refer to Xue et al. 2008 for more details) as follows: $m_{ij}(\mathbf{x}_{j,t}) \sim \{\mathbf{x}_{j,t}^{(n)}, w_{j,t}^{i,(n)}\}_{n=1}^{N}$ and $P(\mathbf{x}_{j,t}|\mathbf{Y}) \sim \{\mathbf{x}_{j,t}^{(n)}, \pi_{j,t}^{(n)}\}_{n=1}^{N}$. Given the particles at the kth iteration, $m_{ij}(\mathbf{x}_{j,t,k+1}^{(n)})$ and $\pi_{j,t,k+1}^{(n)}$ in next iteration are computed according to

$$m_{ij}(\mathbf{x}_{j,t,k+1}^{(n)}) = \sum_{m=1}^{N}\{\pi_{i,t,k}^{(m)}\rho_i(\mathbf{y}_{i,t,k}^{(m)},\mathbf{x}_{i,t,k}^{(m)}) \prod_{l\in\Gamma(i)\backslash j} w_{i,t,k}^{(l,m)}[\sum_{r=1}^{N} p(\mathbf{x}_{i,t,k}^{(m)}|\mathbf{x}_{i,t-1}^{(r)})]\} \tag{11.24}$$

$$\pi_{j,t,k+1}^{(n)} = \rho_j(\mathbf{y}_{j,t,k+1}^{(n)},\mathbf{x}_{j,t,k+1}^{(n)}) \prod_{u\in\Gamma(j)} w_{j,k+1}^{(u,n)} \sum_{r} p(\mathbf{x}_{j,t,k+1}^{(n)}|\mathbf{x}_{j,t-1}^{(r)}) \tag{11.25}$$

11.6 Hybrid Measurement Process

We propose a hybrid measurement process which is implemented via two mechanisms: (1) the factored sampling procedure and (2) an update strategy for target appearance. These two mechanisms enhance the interaction between the detection and tracking.

The factored sampling procedure, which is implemented by sampling from the mixture proposal Equation (11.13), is used to find nonlocal maxima of multi-modal image likelihoods. The mixture proposal integrates measurements from the learned AdaBoost detector and the predicted measurements of particle filtering. After eliminating low-fitness samples in every process, each remaining sample $\mathbf{x}_i$ is then refined via the mean shift algorithm to obtain a local maximum $\mathbf{x}_i'$.

Starting with the fittest sample $\mathbf{x}_{best}$, all less fit samples $\mathbf{x}_i$ such as $|\mathbf{x}_{best} - \mathbf{x}_i| \leq \triangle$ are eliminated. The purpose of $\triangle$, the threshold, is to compensate for any lack of precision in the mean-shift algorithm. The thinning process is repeated for the next fittest sample and so on, yielding a set of m_t measurements. The value of m_t may vary due to the randomness of the sampling procedure and whether the image actually has only m_t target-like features.

As to the mutual occlusion problem, we perform a sequential factorization of the data association, as described in Section 11.4. Each permutation of the individual target association provides an occlusion relationship hypothesis. Under each permutation, the target in the front of the sequence is measured first from the measurements, then the target in the second can be matched from the masked measurements, and so on. In this way, measurement results of nonoverlapping objects are equivalent for different depth ordering permutations.

The update strategy for object appearance is used to enhance the robustness of the search process. In the mean-shift algorithm, the appearance model for a visual object is a color histogram. The histogram is updated only when the Kullback–Leibler (KL) distance between the reference histogram and the target histogram is less than a small threshold. This update strategy can avoid the potential for appearance model to drift away from the object that it was initialized to track.

11.7 Experiments and Discussion

We evaluate the performance of the proposed algorithm on a challenging people tracking problem. The implemented tracker is tested in two scenes: (1) tracking soccer players in video sequences and (2) tracking pedestrians in a dynamic scene. Due to target and camera movement in both scenes, the number of targets in view varies continuously, and occlusion occurs frequently.

We trained an AdaBoost pedestrian detector (Viola et al. 2005) in the experiment. A set of 2250 positive samples and 2250 negative samples was collected. Each positive sample is a pair of 20×15 pedestrian images taken from two consecutive frames of a video sequence. Negative examples are similar image pairs that do not contain any pedestrians. The resulting detector contains 457 features nested in an 11-layer structure, which has a detection rate 88.7% and a false alarm rate of 10^{-4}.

In the experiments, we compare our tracker with the MCJPDAF tracker proposed in Vermaak and Pérez (2005) and the integrated tracker proposed in Xue et al. (2006a). All three trackers are configured with the trained pedestrian detector.

The color histogram model for each individual target is sampled in the first frame at which it appears. In both experiments, we assign 50 particles to each target. Other parameters are assigned the following values: $\alpha = 0.3$ (in Equation 11.13), $\lambda_f = 20$, $e_p = 0.1$, and $\sigma_p = 432$. It should be noted that these parameter settings are not optimal. However, variations in the parameter settings have little impact on our tracker's performance.

11.7.1 Tracking Soccer Players

The video sequence in this experiment has 3234 frames with a resolution of 223 × 153. The number of players in a frame ranges from 6 to 9.

Figure 11.4 shows the number of targets in about 400 frames estimated by our tracker, MCJPDAF tracker, and the integrated tracker. The MCJPDAF tracker failed

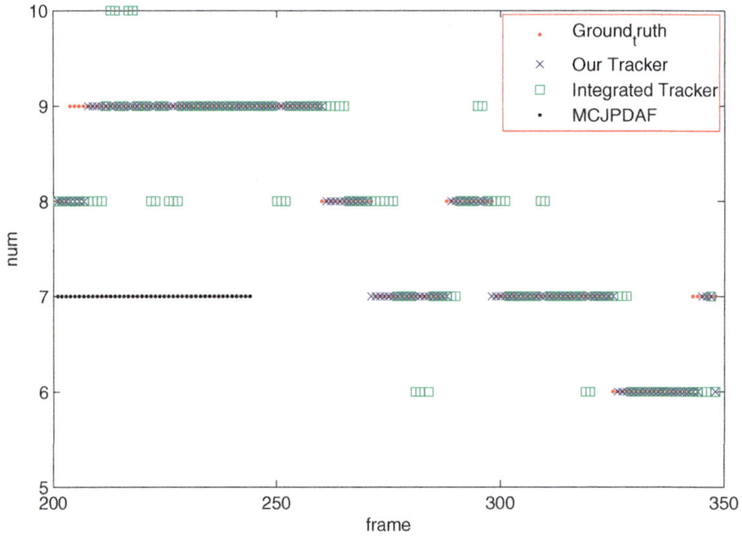

Fig. 11.4 The comparison between the groundtruth and the number of players estimated by our tracker, the MCJPDAF tracker, and the integrated tracker

when the first occlusion occurred in the video. There are some errors in the output of the integrated tracker. Furthermore, there is always at least a five-frame lag between the time a change in the number of targets occurs and the integrated trackers recognizes this fact. Our tracker, on the other hand, can output the right number of players almost immediately (with at most a 1–2 frame delay) throughout the entire video sequence.

Figure 11.5 shows some tracking results produced by our tracker and the MCJPDAF tracker.

11.7.2 Tracking Pedestrians in a Dynamic Scene

The video sequence in the second experiment contains 2000 frames with a resolution of 223×153. The number of pedestrians in a frame ranges from 3 to 5. The video was taken in the plaza of a university campus by a handheld camera. The camera sometimes shakes during the video sequence. This makes the detection and tracking difficult. The detection rate of the trained detector in this video drops to 67% according to our statistics. Figure 11.6 shows two frames of the detections by the detector.

Our tracker can track pedestrians and maintain their identifiers through most of the video clip, while the MCJPDAF tracker failed within the first 20 frames, and the integrated tracker failed in managing the identifiers of all targets, and can only maintain two tracks less than 300 frames. Our tracker failed in tracking some targets in a few frames because the failure of the detector in finding these targets lasts more than 15 frames. Some tracking results of our tracker are illustrated in Fig. 11.7.

11.7.3 Discussion

In the above experiments, we implemented the tracker in Matlab code without optimization, and the tracking process runs on a $P4$, 3.0 GHz PC. The speed is around 8 fps in tracking soccer players and 14 fps in tracking pedestrians.

Several advantages of our tracker (shown in both experiments) are worth highlighting. First, because of the hybrid measurement process, the tracker can integrate information from both the detection and the tracking processes, and it works well in tracking a varying number of targets. Second, because of the MC data association, even given a detector with a low detection rate, ambiguities due to occlusion can be resolved, and the tracker can still maintain identifiers of targets. We found empirically that the number of tracks itself does not make the problem more difficult if they are scattered apart. The difficulty arises when there are many targets that are moving closely and crossing each other's paths. Also, solving the occlusion problem is the most time-consuming part in our tracker; even the BP can converge

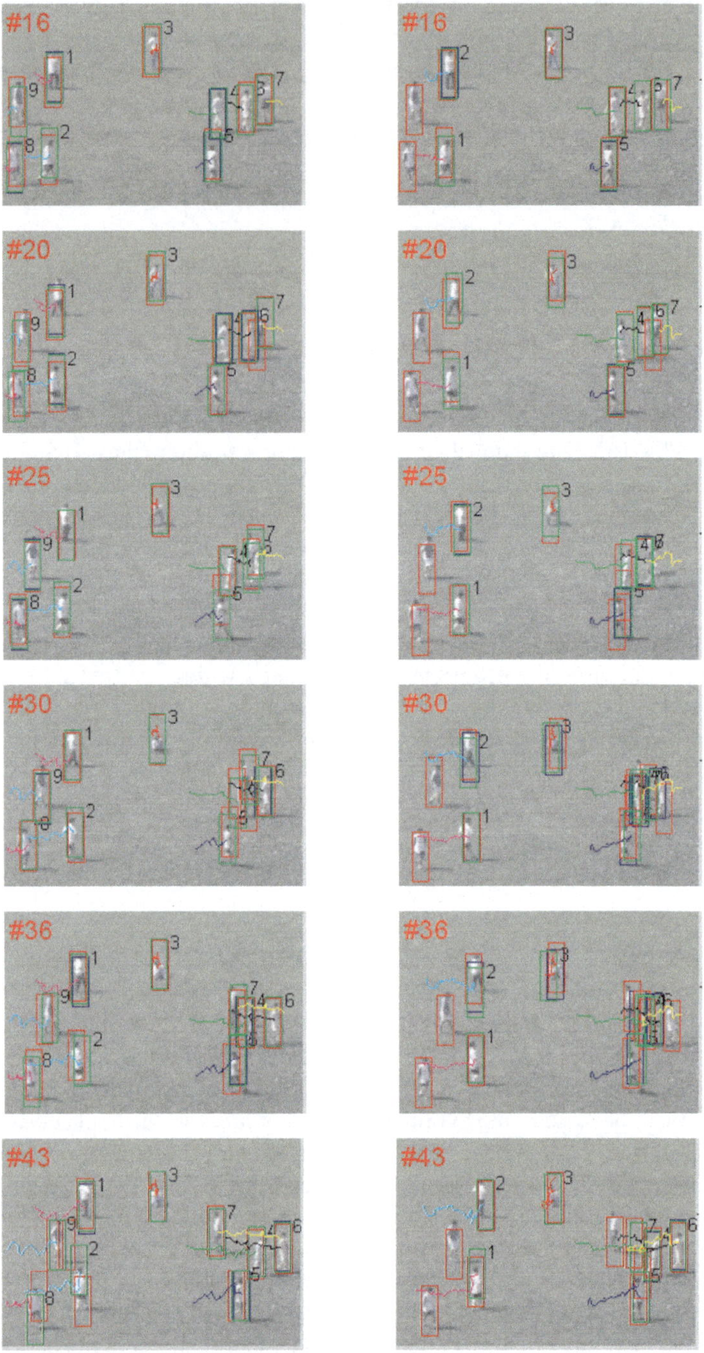

Fig. 11.5 Tracking performance comparison in dealing with occlusion. *Left column*: results from our tracker; *Right column:* results from the MCJPDAF tracker. In each frame, the *red, blue* and *green boxes* represent the results of the detector, the predicted measurement, and our tracker, respectively

Fig. 11.6 Detection results of the learned AdaBoost detector

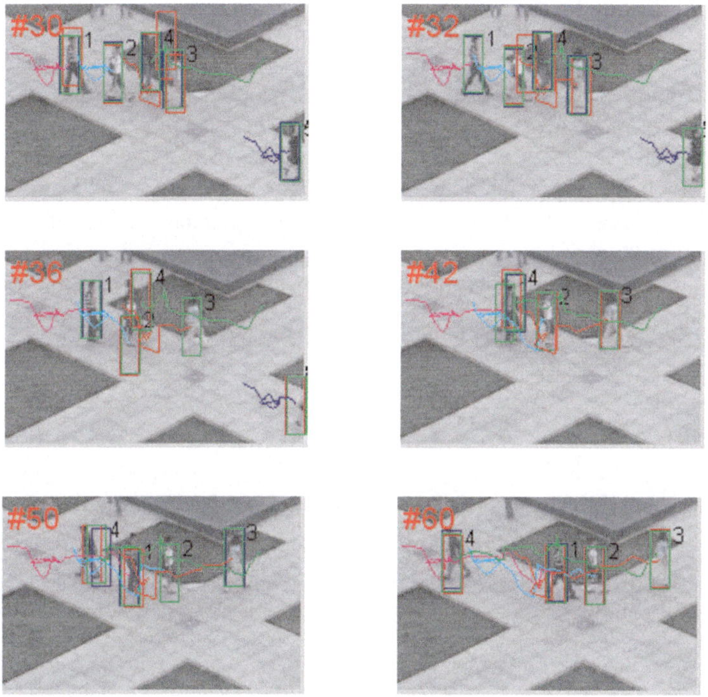

Fig. 11.7 Tracking results of our tracker. In each frame, the *red, blue* and *green boxes* represent the result of the detector, the predicted measurement, and our tracker, respectively

within four iterations. Third, the complexity of the MTT problem can be measured by the relationship between several of the metrics, including the intensity of the false alarm rate λ_f, the detection probability P_d, the number of tracks k_t, and the density of tracks. The problem gets more and more challenging with an increase in the values of λ_f and k_t, a decrease in P_d, and a increase in the density of tracks (Fig. 11.7).

11.8 Summary

We have proposed a sequential MC data association algorithm for the detecting and tracking of a varying number of interactive targets in a dynamic scene. The algorithm unifies detection and tracking via sequential MC data association. The algorithm consists of three major components: (1) an ideal generative model of the state, existence, data association, and interactions among targets; (2) an algorithm approximating the 'ideal' generative model of the tracking problem with a two-level computing framework; and (3) an interactive mechanism that uses a hybrid measurement process and update strategy for the target model. The algorithm was tested by tracking many people in several real video sequences. Despite a constantly varying number of targets and frequent occlusion, the proposed tracker can reliably track many people. Future work will focus on implementations of real-time MTT applications.

References

Bar-Shalom Y, Li X (1995) Multitarget-Multisensor Tracking: Principles and Techniques. Yaakov Bar-Shalom, Storrs

Cai Y, de Freitas N, Little J (2006) Robust visual tracking for multiple targets. ECCV

Cox I, Hingorani S, et al. (1996) An efficient implementation of Reid's multiple hypothesis tracking algorithm and its evaluation for the purpose of visual tracking. IEEE Transactions on PAMI 18(2):138–150

Dalai N, Triggs B, Rhone-Alps I, Montbonnot F (2005) Histograms of oriented gradients for human detection. In: IEEE Conference on Computer Vision and Pattern Recognition, vol 1

Dellaert F, Seitz S, Thorpe C, Thrun S (2000) Structure from motion without correspondence. In: IEEE Conference On Computer Vision And Pattern Recognition, IEEE Computer Society; 1999, vol 2

Fortmann T, Bar-Shalom Y, Scheffe M (1983) Sonar tracking of multiple targets using joint probabilistic data association. IEEE Journal of Oceanic Engineering 8(3):173–184

Gavrila D (1999) The visual analysis of human movement: a survey. Computer Vision and Image Understanding 73(1):82–98

Gordon N (1997) A hybrid bootstrap filter for target tracking in clutter. IEEE Transactions on Aerospace and Electronic Systems 33(1):353–358

Hue C, Le Cadre J, Perez P, Irisa R (2002) Tracking multiple objects with particle filtering. IEEE Transactions on Aerospace and Electronic Systems 38(3):791–812

Isard M, Blake A (1998) CONDENSATIONł Conditional density propagation for visual tracking. International Journal of Computer Vision 29(1):5–28

Isard M, MacCormick J (2001) BraMBLe: A Bayesian multiple-blob tracker. ICCV 2(5):34–41

Khan Z, Balch T, Dellaert F (2004) An MCMC-based particle filter for tracking multiple interacting targets. ECCV 2004

Leibe B, Seemann E, Schiele B (2005) Pedestrian detection in crowded scenes. In: IEEE Conference on Computer Vision and Pattern Recognition, IEEE Computer Society; 1999, vol 1, p 878

Liu J (2001) Monte Carlo Strategies in Scientific Computing. Springer, New York

Nillius P, Sullivan J, Carlsson S (2006) Multi-target tracking-linking identities using Bayesian network inference. IEEE CVPR 2:2187–2194

Oh S, Russell S, Sastry S (2004) Markov chain Monte Carlo data association for general multiple-target tracking problems. IEEE CDC, 2004 1:735–742

Okuma K, Taleghani A, de Freitas N, Little J, Lowe D (2004) A boosted particle filter: multitarget detection and tracking. ECCV 2004 1:28–39

Paul V, Michael JJ (2001) Rapid object detection and a boosted cascade of simple features. In: ICCV 2001, pp 511–518

Perez P, Hue C, Vermaak J, Gangnet M (2002) Color-based probabilistic tracking. ECCV 2002 1:661–675

Reid D (1979) An algorithm for tracking multiple targets. IEEE Trans on Automatic Control 24(6):843–854

Rittscher J, Tu P, Krahnstoever N (2005) Simultaneous estimation of segmentation and shape. IEEE CVPR 2:486–493

Rudin L, Osher S, Fatemi E (1992) Nonlinear total variation based noise removal algorithms. Physica D 60(1–4):259–268

Sudderth E, Mandel M, Freeman W, Willsky A (2004) Distributed occlusion reasoning for tracking with nonparametric belief propagation. Advances in Neural Information Processing Systems 17:1369–1376

Tao H, Sawhney H, Kumar R (1999) A sampling algorithm for tracking multiple objects. Workshop on Vision Algorithms 1:53–68

Vermaak J, Pérez P (2005) Monte carlo filtering for multi-target tracking and data association. IEEE Transactions on Aerospace and Electronic Systems 41(1):309–332

Vermaak J, Doucet A, Perez P (2003) Maintaining multimodality through mixture tracking. IEEE ICCV, 2003 pp 1110–1116

Viola P, Jones M, Snow D (2005) Detecting pedestrians using patterns of motion and appearance. International Journal of Computer Vision 63(2):153–161

Wu B, Nevatia R (2005) Detection of multiple, partially occluded humans in a single image by Bayesian combination of edgelet part detectors. In: IEEE Conference on Computer Vision, vol 1

Xue J, Zheng N, Zhong X (2006a) An integrated Monte Carlo data association framework for multi-object tracking. ICPR 1:703–706

Xue J, Zheng N, Zhong X (2006b) Tracking targets via particle based belief propagation. ACCV 3851:348

Xue J, Zheng N, Geng J, Zhong X (2008) Multiple targets tracking via particle-based belief propagation. IEEE Transactions on System, Man, and Cybernetics, Part B: Cybernetics 38(1):96–209

Yu Q, Cohen I, Medioni G, Wu B (2006) Boosted Markov chain Monte Carlo data association for multiple target detection and tracking. ICPR 2:675–678

Yu T, Wu Y (2005) Decentralized multiple target tracking using netted collaborative autonomous trackers. IEEE CVPR 1:939–946

Zhao T, Nevatia R (2004) Tracking multiple humans in crowded environment. IEEE CVPR 2:406–413

Chapter 12
Information Processing in Cognition Process and New Artificial Intelligent Systems

Abstract In this chapter, we discuss, in depth, visual information processing and a new artificial intelligent (AI) system that is based upon cognitive mechanisms. The relationship between a general model of intelligent systems and cognitive mechanisms is described, and in particular we explore visual information processing with selective attention. We also discuss a methodology for studying the new AI system and propose some important basic research issues that have emerged in the intersecting fields of cognitive science and information science. To this end, a new scheme for associative memory and a new architecture for an AI system with attractors of chaos are addressed.

12.1 Introduction

The human brain is now the most effective biometric intelligent system for information processing (Palricia and Terrence 1992). It has many important abilities, such as perception, recognition, learning, association, memory, and reasoning. Studying these basic functions of the human brain and realizing a machine implementation of them has always been a very significant yet challenging problem in the development of science. The structure of the cerebral cortex has the ability to perform complicated and accurate analysis and synthesis and can adaptively meet the requirements of human logical thinking. An in-depth study of information processing based upon human perception and cognitive mechanisms will have a great impact on the natural sciences and technology. Due to the demands of social production and practice, people are showing an increased interest in the problems that occur during the cognitive process. Cognitive science is the study of all mental states and processes from an even greater variety of methodologically distinct fields including not only psychology, neuroscience, linguistics, and computer science, but also philosophy, anthropology, sociology, and others. Vision science is the single most coherent integrated and successful branch of cognitive science (Palmer 1999).

N. Zheng, J. Xue, *Statistical Learning and Pattern Analysis for Image and Video Processing*, Advances in Pattern Recognition, DOI 10.1007/978-1-84882-312-9_12,
© Springer-Verlag London Limited 2009

With the development of brain science, information science, neural computing, and neurophysiology, the combination of cognitive science and information science is now increasingly possible, and research in these fields is beginning to exhibit all the characteristics of their intersecting agendas. A breakthrough in the theories and methods of cognitive-based intelligent information processing, may trigger an explorative development on the further technologies of intelligent visual information processing and this in turn contributes further to the realization of the new AI system alluded to above.

Empirical and rationalistic models and interpretation of these models often dominates our understanding of the process of human cognition (Roediger 1991). Hence, to reveal the relationship between intelligence and machines, humans should make reasonable use of their experiences and view intelligence, from an evolutionary viewpoint, as a dynamic process. The problems that are encountered in theories of intelligence often have a form of "environment problem goal solving." By combining the three major research areas, i.e., connectionist-based neural network theory (Kohonen 1991), symbolic expert systems, and cognitive mechanisms-based modeling, we may achieve a new kind of artificial intelligent (AI) system and a new methodology for intelligent information processing.

The study and application of new generation media and network-based intelligent communication systems will be a cornerstone of information science and technology in the twenty-first century. Human language, facial expression, body language, etc., will be understood by machines and then converted into a series of command orders for information acquisition and transmission. With the improving performance of machine approaches to language and image recognition, new security technologies are being developed for information systems. Theoretical research in the technologies of cognitive information processing, which is the basis for natural language processing and image understanding, has attracted wide attention among many scientists and research institutions.

In the past decade, the international scientific community has paid a great deal of attention to the study of cognitive science and intelligent information processing. Many researchers have been made the studies of the relationship between consciousness and neural networks, and the theories and methodologies of perception and cognitive-based intelligent signal processing. For example, in October 1997, a special issue of *IEEE Transaction on Circuits and Systems* was published to discuss the theory of nonlinear chaos and methods for chaotic signal processing and control. In October 1999, the *IEEE Transaction on Neural Networks* published an issue to discuss intelligent hybrid computing approaches that combine several models and methods, such as neural networks, fuzzy reasoning and representation, and probabilistic reasoning. Moreover, some Nobel laureates, such as Francis H. Crick, Sir John C. Eccles, Gerald M. Edelman, and Briad D. Josephson, and the prominent father of AI, Marvin Minsky, also showed great interests in the problems of consciousness and cognition in their research.

12.2 Cognitive Model: A Prototype of Intelligent System

The development of human intelligence is a hypercyclical process, in which existing cognitive structures interact with evolving cognition and where each is the cause of the other. Some studies show that the structure of the human cerebral cortex facilitates the accurate analysis and synthesis of complex information and can adapt to the requirements of logical human thinking. The cognitive process of human interaction with the external world is by nature a process of information fusion from multiple sensors. The human brain acquires knowledge of the outside through learning, which is constrained by the supervision of multiple information channels upon each other. By fusing information from multiple sensors, the human brain can recognize and understand objects. Furthermore, the human brain can also control each sensor according to previously gained knowledge. The perfect combination of such feedforward and feedback processes endows the human brain with a very high level of intelligence. Even in very noisy environments or circumstances under which sensory information is unreliable, the human brain can still perform very effectively. Thus, it provides a perfect example for designing an intelligent system. Cognitive modeling itself can be taken as the prototype of an intelligent system. It can also provide a new scientific basis and theoretical direction for researchers engaged in designing a new AI system.

For decades, numerous efforts have been made in the study of cognitive modeling and perception-based intelligent information processing. Though great achievements have been made, these have still fallen short expectations. This is largely due to the great disparity between the methods used by researchers and the approach to cognitive information processing used by the human brain. Statistical methods and syntactic analysis, as well as traditional methods of artificial intelligence, can merely be applied to specific, well-defined applications. They have achieved limited success due to an inability to generalize to novel situations, and because they lack the dynamics and flexibility that are possessed by truly intelligent information processing systems.

Currently, the achievements that cognitive science has made are focused primarily on the theories of cognitive psychology and on the basic process of cognition. In the theory of cognitive psychology, the human brain is viewed as a computer system for information processing, and mental processes are regarded as computations on symbol sequences. Based on this point of view, the notions of a physical symbol system and parallel distributed processing are proposed. Such viewpoints have greatly promoted research on the computational theory of information science. Generally speaking, cognition consists of three basic parts, namely memory, attention, and consciousness. As for "memory," Baddeley and Tulving have suggested the ideas of "working memory" (Baddeley 1992) and "multiple memory system" (Tulving and Thomson 1973); for "attention," Treisman has proposed the "features binding theory" (Treisman 1996, 1998); and for "consciousness," Baars has presented the Global Workspace Theory, also called the theater model of consciousness (Baars 1997).

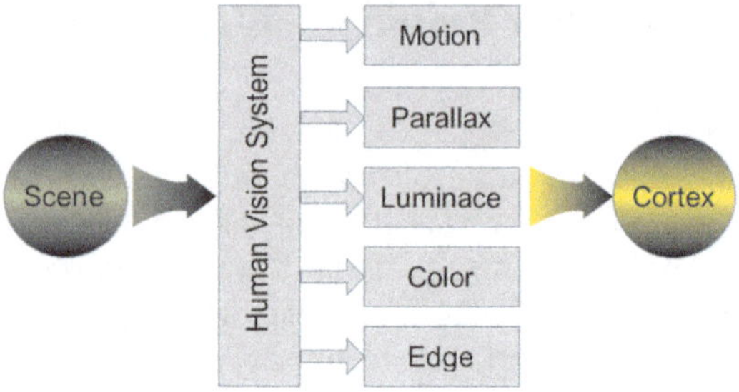

Fig. 12.1 Simulated data in the plane is clustered into three groups by the K-means clustering algorithm. The three colors indicate the cluster memberships

Human brain is a very complicated system that also happens to be the vehicle of cognition (Francis and Jen 1993) (Fred et al. 1999) (Daniel 1993). The complexity of human brain is not only due to its huge number of neurons (about 100 billion neurons), but also due to the more important complicated connections between them. Such connections have diversified forms. With respect to direction, they include both multiple feedforward and feedback connections. They are distributed in both convergent and divergent fashion. Together they ultimately form a complex network – the brain. Not only is the overall physical structure complex, so are its functions. In the structure, there are molecules, subcellulars, cells, nuclei, and systems. With respect to function, neurons on different levels and in different brain areas are responsible for different processing tasks. For example, in the vision system, different neurons respond to different features of visual images, which range from simple to increasingly complicated stimuli such as movement, edges, shapes, colors, and textures. The stimuli are ultimately synthesized in the cerebral cortex to form descriptive images of the outside world (see Fig. 12.1). Cells with such differing functions in the biometric vision system have been revealed in animal experiments. For humans, there are also cells that can respond to different levels of abstract concepts. The highly sophisticated visual system possessed by humans can instantly perceive the external world in the context of these abstract concepts. This has served as a good example of an intelligent system in the research being done in the field of visual information processing. The material basis of the example consists of the perfectly attuned organs of vision and the complicated yet sophisticated central nervous system, in which neurons are the atomic units.

The basic function of the brain, i.e., cognitive information processing, involves appropriately processing and storing environmental data and then making decisions or responses upon that data. The implementation of this brain function depends upon the joint activities and integration of many independent neurons in multiple brain areas, all acting in conjunction as a single system. There is a notable difference between the human brain and brains of other animals in this respect. For example, the human brain is highly consistent with the brain of mouse on the molecular level, but shows great differences in higher levelfunctions. Such differences are due to the organization of connections across levels of neurons; this organization can be thought of as belonging to the system level. Therefore, it is very difficult for us, using molecular biology to interpret such advanced functions as perception, memory, and thinking. Currently, although studies in brain science and cerebral function imaging have made great progress, we are still faced with many difficulties, both in theory and practice, when we try to understand the diversity and flexibility of the brain and, in particular, reveal its performance and how it works as an information processing system.

12.3 Issues in Theories and Methodologies of Current Brain Research and Vision Science

In order to facilitate the development of a new AI system in a cognitive information processing framework, it is of great theoretical and practical importance to have a clear understanding of the problems associated with the theories and methodologies of current brain research. Traditional AI research has achieved many results in the simulation of the intelligent activities of humans. In the 1980s, Professor Marr of MIT proposed the first well-defined framework for a vision system from an information processing perspective by integrating achievements made in image processing, psychophysics, and neurophysiology (Marr 1982). In recent years, many efforts have been devoted to the study of the various functional modules of the primary, sensor, and advanced stages of the visual system proposed in the basic theoretical framework. Though much evidence has shown that the theory is not perfect, it is reluctantly accepted in practice by many researchers in computer vision.

The basic theories of the cognitive functions of brain thus far can be summarized as follows: (1) theories regarding cognitive functions related to specific areas of the brain, as have been verified through experimental results from imaging of cerebral function, (2) theories surrounding the features of the external world as detected through an elaborate division of work between individual brain cells, represented in a sort of frequency-modulated coding, (3) theories that attempt to explain how information represented in discrete signals is processed, level by level and in a bottom-up fashion. Here feature integration is implemented in higher level centers. The initial detection of a huge number of features is in parallel, while the integration of features is serial. The switch between parallel and serial modes is controlled by the mechanism of selective attention, (4) theories about how the brain is different in structure from the computer, but similar in function. Despite enormous differences in structure and materials, the task of signal processing for intelligent activities is similar and thus computable, and (5) theories of cognitive science, which can be categorized as theories of physical symbol processing, sub-symbolic processing, and modularity.

Recently, based on new developments in the study of cognitive functions of the brain, some researchers have proposed different viewpoints on the above theories, e.g., Gibson's theory of psychological ecology. He argues that the process of visual cognition is not passive but rather active in response to the environment. Under the stimuli of environmental information, people extract invariance from the dynamic information flow using ocular movement, or relocation of viewpoint, and then generate perception through this interaction. This point of view has been applied to the active visual system proposed recently (see Fig. 12.2). Ecological theory or the environmental dependent theory of cognition views human cognitive endeavors not as a function of signal processing that occurs only in the brain of each individual. The possibilities and limits of human cognition are not only a function of the evolution of the biological world, but also the development of civilization and human society. As a result, the human brain is very different from the computer, regardless of its structure or its functional processes. We cannot reveal the full nature of human cognitive activities by using any current Turing computation or simple parallel distributed processing mechanism. Thus the ecological theory, which emphasizes the essential differences between the human brain and the computer, has had great impact on the theory of cognitive science.

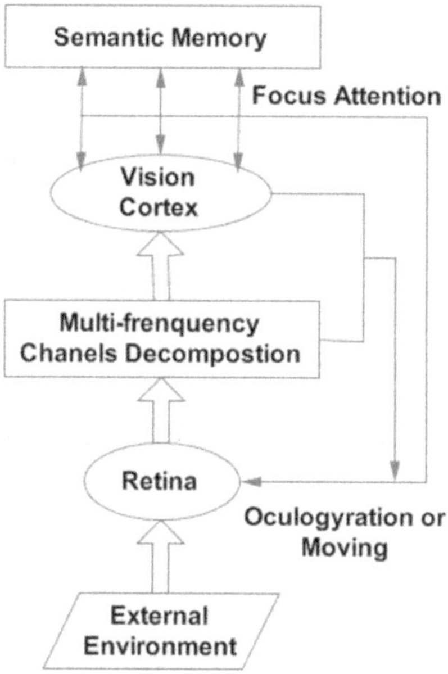

Fig. 12.2 The channels and feedback structure of vision information processing

The human brain is a nonholonomic information processing system. This fact becomes evident by looking at visual perception. For example, the distribution of photoreceptors on the retina is not uniform. Most photoreceptors are located at the center of the macular area, and its density decreases dramatically with the increase of eccentricity, showing a form of shape spreading (see Fig. 12.3(a), from Porat and Zeevi 1988). Meanwhile, study of the transmission path from the retina to the cortex also shows that the retina is projected onto the visual cortex in a topological form, that is, each specific area of the cortex has its own receptive field. The large area of the cortex is correlated with the central visual cortex. From Fig. 12.3(a), it is clear that (1) the pyramidal cells in the macular area of the fovea centralis have the largest distribution density and the maximum luminance sampling density, (2) with the increase in eccentricity, the distribution density of pyramidal cells decreases and the ability to process visual information, like shape and color, also decreases. This shows that the visual perception sampling in advanced animals is nonuniform and forms a nonholonomic information processing system. Figure 12.3(b) shows the nonuniform sampling realized by using a wavelet transformation. This method of sampling makes early visual computing models more consistent with the actual mechanisms of biometric vision. It also facilitates a lively simulation of the nonuniform sampling process of visual information on a biometric retina, as well as the selective attention mechanism possessed by many biometric vision systems. On the other hand, nonuniform sampling can further reduce the complexity of vision computing. This method is being developed on the basis of observations and experiments in biometric vision.

Actually, many human scientific achievements come from observations and in-depth studies of the corresponding objects in the natural world. For example, airplanes were invented and refined by studying the flight of birds. Similarly, nature also provides us a perfect example of information pocessing – the human brain. Therefore, studies of intelligent information processing systems cannot proceed without an overall and in-depth study of the cognitive functions of the human brain. Ever since AI became a subject of research, scientists have been following a definite guideline – the study of the general laws of human thinking, simulating it on the computer. The study of intelligent information processing need not be constrained to a direct copy of the cognition of the human brain, just as the airplane was not invented by simply copying the flight of birds.

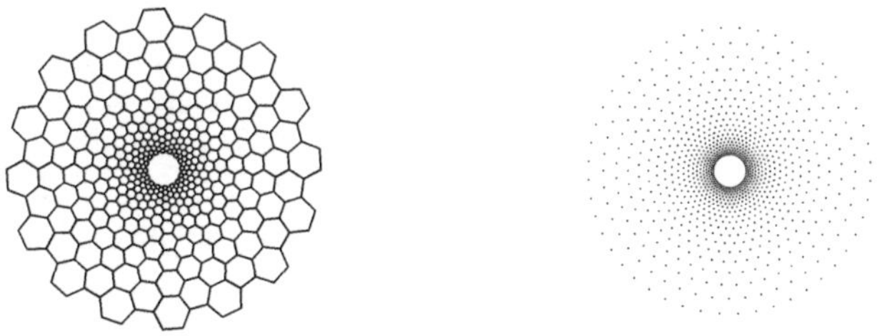

(a) (b)

Fig. 12.3 The distribution of photoreceptors of vision system and its nonuniform sampling. **(a)** The distribution of photoreceptors on the retina. **(b)** biometric nonuniform sampling

The human brain even exhibits special performance when processing information on a single perceptual path. For example, in visual information processing, humans can accurately master objects in the visual perceptive field through top-down logical reasoning, given some abstract descriptions and conceptual symbols, as well as the incorporation of prior knowledge. Such a binding mechanism, which realizes object perception through the integration of object features, enables the selective processing of vision information (Burt 1988) (Bajcsy 1988) (Wechsler 1990). Vision is a kind of computation, and during the task of visual information processing, the human brain exhibits the ability to compute with a high degree of parallelism. Though the parallelism inherent in visual information processing may be very different from the normal meaning of the word, the human brain can effectively partition the visual task and integrate local information in both the time and space domain, i.e., integrate receptive fields level by level, to realize vision perception. This is a bottom-up process, and exhibits the obvious property of multiple scaling. Meanwhile, serial computing plays an important role in the integration of local features and logical reasoning. The selective attention mechanism of the brain guides the vision system to the most interesting part of a scene and overlooks irrelevant information, such as background. Furthermore, the attention mechanism also enables the vision system to remain focused on the same object as it appears in a series of varying scenes. The information processing mechanism of human cognition is a multilayer, closed-loop feedback system that integrates the bottom-up and top-down (see Fig. 12.4), fuses information from multiple sensors, and intertwines parallel and serial threads of processing. This mechanism ensures the effectiveness and accuracy of the human brain in perception of the outside world.

Today, we still have little understanding of our own intelligent activities. However, with the growth in development of neurobiology and neurophysiology, many material bases and information processing mechanisms are being revealed that may help with the study of machine intelligence. Human sensory mechanisms, such as vision, hearing, and touch, receive various streams of information from the outside world. After being processed by the human brain, a scene is understood. Different sensory systems have varying sensitivities to different information. For example, the vision system is sensitive to object location, shape, and color. The auditory system is sensitive to the frequency of signals, while the tactile system is sensitive to the textural and surface structure of materials. Different streams of information also inform and constrain each other in the cognitive process. How to process and integrate information from multiple sensors in an intelligent system is a very important issue in the current intelligent information processing literature.

The process of thinking is tantamount to performing creative information processing and generating new information and knowledge. Human cognition is a developing process, from concrete to abstract, from simple to complex, and from low level to high level. This view helps us to explore how to use the computer to mine knowledge in the enormous and ubiquitous environment of the web.

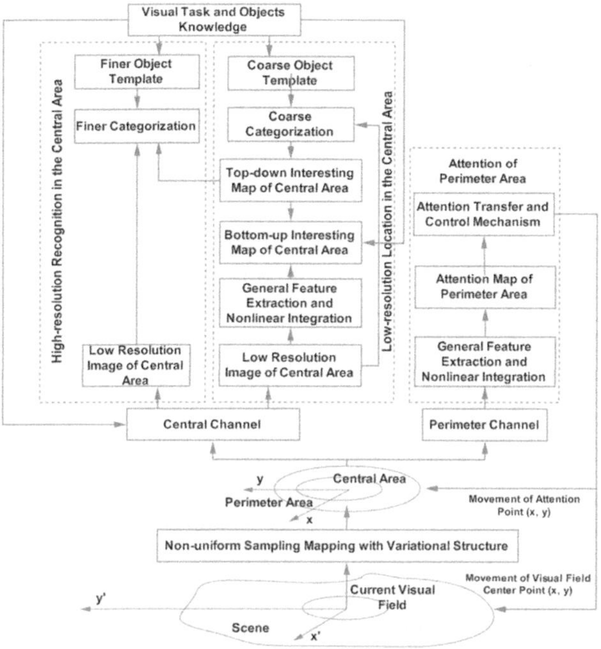

Fig. 12.4 The framework of information processing model of vision system with a form of *bottom-up and top-down* multilayer closed-loop feedback

12.4 Interactive Behaviors and Selective Attention in the Process of Visual Cognition

Empirical evidence of human visual perception shows that people can search for a specific object in a complicated environment and process selective information regarding that object. This search and selection process is called focus of attention. In this age of information explosion, acquiring the necessary information in the most effective and efficient manner represents a significant problem. Examinimg the human vision system may provide a potential solution to the problem. For example, we might apply the mechanism for environmental and self focus possessed by the human perception system to learning in a system of multiple modules, or we might determine the input of an attention network according to the nature of the information processing task, so as to make the entire system complete the task more effectively under the supervision of the attention subsystem.

In active vision system, selective attention can be divided into two levels: (1) data-driven, that is, bottom-up low-level visual attention that is independent of content and semantics, and (2) knowledge-driven, top-down, content- and semantics-based high-level visual attention. For purely data-driven based visual attention, the selection of interesting regions is related to theextraction and integration of features, such as edges, corners, curvature, and symmetry. In contrast, high-level visual attention is related to the knowledge of the vision task, representation of objects and environment, and is also highly relevant to pattern recognition and matching. High-level visual attention is developed on the basis of low-level attention and has a feedback effect on low-level attention. However, previous relevant studies of artificial vision are mainly focused on low-level visual attention, and pay little attention to high-level visual attention and the interaction between low-level and high-level attention. The mechanism of visual attention must be a function of the interaction between low-level and high-level attention, and must be realized in the bottom-up and top-down simultaneously. Basic related issues include the mechanisms of selective attention and attention focus, the feedback mechanism of the visual cortex, the receptive field, and nonlinear vision processing.

The theory of interactive behaviors views vision problems from the following perspective: first, vision is not an independently acting function, but is rather just one component of a complicated behavioral system; second, the computation of vision is dynamic and generally does not clearly compute all problems at one time, but computes the necessary ones; third, vision computation must be adaptive, the characteristics of a vision system must be variable with respect to the interacting process between the system and its environment. Therefore, the interactive behavior theory takes the view that vision computation is the joint outcome of the interaction between the external environment and the visual perception, and both are indispensable. Once behavior is accepted as a basic element of the computation of vision, the exact details of the representation are generally not so important. With the inclusion of behavior, some computation problems, such as the computation of optic flow, surface direction, and depth, can be constrained by behavioral assumptions and thus can be easily addressed.

Local and global perceptions in primary vision are also subject to interactive behaviors. An important controversial and open issue in biometric visual perception is whether the perception of global structures comes prior to that of local structures or vice versa, during the perceptual process in living beings. Researchers who believe global perception comes first often take a great number of examples from texture perception experiments. For instance, when we observe Fig. 12.5(a), we see "a patch with a large area of textured background" without directly perceiving the local texture itself. The coarse-to-fine multiresolution analysis in vision processing also reveals this view. On the other hand, vision researchers who view local perception as coming first hold that vision perception starts with feature extraction on local regions, and finally gains the global feature image through the analysis and synthesis of local regions. This idea is demonstrated in the construction of the 2.5-dimensional element map in Marr's theory of the computation of vision (Marr 1982). In addition, it is also embodied in the feature integration theory of Treisman (1996).

Actually, globality and locality are the reflections of different perceptual scales. The two viewpoints both find evidence in successful biometric examples. As the Gestalt school of thought holds, globality restricts the characteristics and interpretation of locality, and locality thus becomes more accurate due to the restrictions. As a result, it is reasonable to believe that global perception and local perception are intertwined, and perceptions on a small and large scale are parallel and interactive. On the other hand, biometric vision possesses the property of competition on a small scale and cooperation on a large scale. For example, when we observe Fig. 12.5(b), ∩ and ∪ are distinguished from each other by local competition, while the "H shape" consisting of ∩ is extracted from the background by large-scale cooperation. Studies of physiology find that in the visual cortex of the cat and monkey, the receptive field of a simple cell has the shape of a central positive petal. On both sides there are two small negative petals and there are also two smaller positive petals. Figure 12.5(c) shows the response surface of a competitive and cooperative filter, which is obtained by adding three 2D Gaussian filters with the same shape but different scales. The structure of such a competitive and cooperative mechanism reflects the interaction between different scales and also illustrates the competition on a small scale and cooperation on a large scale. The perceptual organization theory of Grossberg takes the view that competition on a small scale and cooperation on a large scale are two important principles of neural computing. Competition on a small scale includes two cases: (1) competition between neurons with adjacent positions and identical orientations and (2) competition between neurons with identical positions but different orientations. While being processed through competition on a small scale, signals are also input into a large-scale cooperative process. By cooperation, global features, such as shape, i.e., the entire boundary of objects, are eventually perceived.

12.5 Intelligent Information Processing and Modeling Based on Cognitive Mechanisms

12.5.1 Cognitive Modeling and Behavioral Control in Complex Systems in an Information Environment

Many researchers are pursuing the systemic and holistic study of the human cognitive process and attempting to construct a similar network model of the complicated background in a real scene. The capacity of a network model for information processing is limited by its topological structure as well as system size. The first question encountered is how to realize the automatic growth of a network structure and construct a multimodule system on a moderate scale. The second question is how to control the communication and integration of each functional module, so as to make the whole system operate in unison. The problem of how to adapt to the uncertainty and dynamics of the outside world widely arises in many systems. Some examples are dealing with rapid faults in complex industrial systems, system reconstruction and restoration, the design and manufacture of humanoid robots for operation in complex environments, emergency command and organization systems for major social events (such as wars, disasters, and economic crises). Traditional AI methods fail to address the above – mentioned problems of environmental adaptation, while the characteristics of human behavior fully reflects its ability to respond and adapt to environments. This directs us to study the principles and methods of information processing based on the characteristics of human behavior, that is, to study the ability of a system to respond to an uncertain and dynamic environment and its ability to fully perceive external objects.

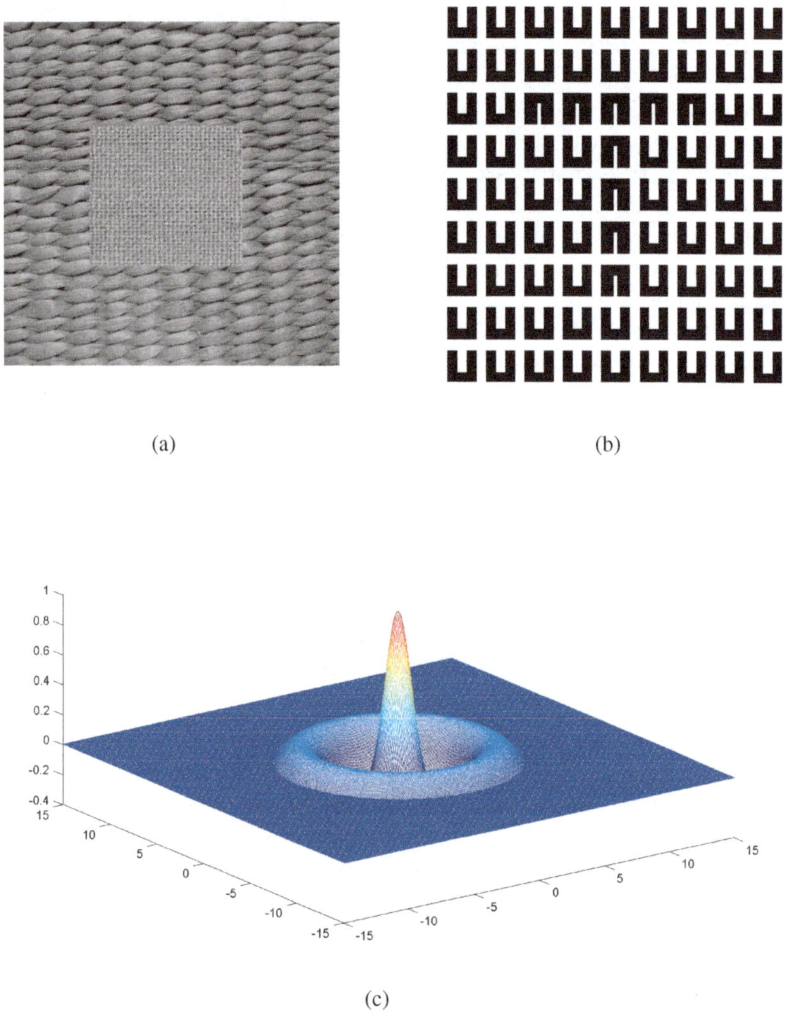

Fig. 12.5 **(a)** The distribution of photoreceptors on retina. **(b)** Biometric nonuniform sampling. **(c)** Two-dimensioal competitive and cooperative filter

12.5.1.1 Behavioral Control

The automatic execution of a complicated system requires an effective control mechanism. Control strategies based on conventional AI methods are no longer adaptable to the real autonomous system. The studies of humanoid robots that have sensory ability and are capable of cognition have aroused extensive concern in the international community. Such a system can take on a task from a human operator through some kind of human computer interaction (HCI). Human language, gestures, and facial expressions, etc., can be understood by the machine and converted into a series of commands. A better understanding of the interaction between system, human, and environment will be a breakthrough in the development of this field. Studies of the cognitive basis for the control of movement in human limbs will provide valuable references for the construction of an autonomous system.

12.5.1.2 Adaptation and Trans-Dimensional Learning

Adaptive mechanisms for information processing and trans-dimensional learning algorithms are the rapidly developing branches of AI. When applying neural networks to the problem of pattern recognition, it is often essential to determine which network structure best suits the given problem. Meanwhile, deriving the minimum structure of network is also necessary. Autonomous pattern recognition algorithms must know how to represent knowledge and how to acquire new knowledge without any human intervention.

12.5.1.3 Natural Language Processing in the Brain

The ability to learn language (or recognize a human face) is one of advanced human cognitive functions. There must be a set of very complicated general grammar rules in the human brain, which are internalized in the brain's structure in some form and constitute the basis of human cognition. The creation and use of natural language again demonstrates the advanced intelligence of the human being. Studies of natural language understanding will help to exploit the nature of human intelligence and thought processes.

12.5.1.4 Inverse Problems-Solving the Ill-Posed Problem

By perceiving the outside world through sensory organs, the human brain acquires appropriate knowledge of the world. On the other hand, based upon limited knowledge, the human brain also supervises the process of perception via certain conceptual mechanisms, such as analysis, discrimination, and decision-making. Inference of the world based on limited knowledge, in fact, is an ill-posed problem. People can find an optimal or semi-optimal solution to a problem according to additional constraints or heuristic rules derived from the surrounding environment. Problems of data restoration, that is, filling in ambiguous or missing data, which commonly occur in the study of machine intelligence, pattern recognition, and so on, are all ill posed. Finding a knowledge-based algorithm for solving these inverse problems will improve research on the theory of intelligent information processing and its technological implementation.

12.5.1.5 Ecological Problems in the Information Environment

With the popularity of the Internet, copyright protection of digital media has become an urgent problem. In addition, the exponential growth of useful and useless information demands higher retrieval, storage, and processing efficiency of multimedia data. Research topics in this area include the programming of intelligent software based upon perception and machine learning, retrieval of desired multimedia information distributed over the Internet, automated assessment of environment, interactive processing and understanding of information through vision and auditory processing, automatic removal of harmful information on the Internet, information hiding, knowledge-based image understanding, natural language understanding, and the basic theory of knowledge base management through automatic learning.

12.5.2 Distributed Cognition

The concept of distributed cognition originates from situated cognition and information-processing theory. Its basic idea is that the processing and representation of cognition system of human brain can be extended to the processing and representation of external world. This is a process of interaction with environment. Malsburg has speculated from the theoretical view that the connections between neurons that are distributed in different areas of brain are probably based on the form of synchronous oscillations. Neurons that are sensitive to the different features of the same object in sensory channel, especially vision channel, are maybe integrated or bound by synchronous oscillations with low frequency to generate an overall concept of the object. Similarly, the problem we often encounter in information processing is how to combine or integrate the feature information with different attributes to produce a unified perception experience of the scene. The object features provided by every information sensing system have their own independent structures. How to extract object knowledge from a feature set with a distributed representation so as to generate its high-level semantics to interpret the object correctly is a very necessary ability that should be possessed by an effectively intelligent information processing system. There is another problem during the study of such binding mechanism. If a description about an object is given, whether there is another object that also accords with the same description? For this problem, it should be especially concerned that how to solve the representation and binding problem of content-sensitive multimode features, such as image and sound. The distance measurement in the conventional pattern recognition theory cannot be used to treat with this problem. Thus, novel pattern recognition theory that is different from the traditional analysis methods has to be proposed.

12.5.2.1 Feature Binding and Information Fusion

In visual perception understanding, the combining of information is implemented in the spatial or temporal domain. Therefore, there are two possible methods for information combination: (1) combine the information of every channel at some position along the processing path of the vision system and (2) information binding in the time domain. In practice, "binding" embodies two notions in information processing. One is how the information is bound; the other is how the information processing methods themselves are bound. The study of biometric-based authentication systems is an example of one such attempt. In such systems, biometric data describing a face, voice, iris, or fingerprint, etc., are captured by different sensors. After being processed, they are integrated for identification recording and authentication.

12.5.2.2 Methods for Information Coding

The survival and development of human and other living beings depend upon the coding, storing, and transmission of genetic information. Attempts to develop a theory and methodology for biometric feature-based information coding, storage, and transmission, and attempts to exploit rules inherent in the nonlinear mechanisms of biometric feature-based information coding, copying, and decoding, as well attempts to exploit the nonlinear nature of information compression and amplification will have a significant impact on the prospects for success in theoretical studies and engineering applications, and even lead to a revolution in information science. Nervous discharge frequency, gene sequential expression, evolution, and meridian mapping demonstrate the perfect encoding processes of biometric information. Such processes entirely contain the highly complicated information inherent in biometric activities and their nonlinearities. It is a lofty and great scientific task to attempt to unveil the correspondence between the characteristics of biometric activities and information encoding mechanisms. In this task, one of the most important steps is to exploit the relationship between biometric nonlinear behaviors and nonlinear encoding mechanisms inherent in biometric information processing. This relationship can be used for more robust and effective intelligent information processing.

12.5.3 *Neurophysiological Mechanism of Learning and Memory and Information Processing Model*

Learning is the ability to respond to experiences and then adapt the corresponding behaviors, whereas memory is the ability to save the learned information. The two are different, but correlated to each other. Regardless of whether one looks at the human brain from the viewpoint of Pavlov's two signal systems, or from the viewpoint of experimental studies on the anatomic structure and channels of learning and memory, there do exist several important areas in the brain that have a close relationship with learning and memory. Research achievements in this area have greatly inspired the study of artificial intelligence networks (ANNs) with the capacity to learn (Kohonen 1989).

Learning from the environment and improving performance through learning are the main features of ANNs. In brief, learning is an adjustment process of free parameters of an ANN, which is driven by environmental stimuli, namely network inputs. The learning rule is defined according to the method of updating free parameters. Therefore, a learning algorithm represents a predefined rule set used for finding the solution to a problem. There are many learning algorithms that have been defined for ANNs. Convergence rate and global convergence are two major measures for evaluating the quality of different kinds of learning algorithms. Most studies on learning algorithms are focused on these measures.

12.5.3.1 Learning

The theories and algorithms of unsupervised learning include Bayesian methods for self-organized network learning, variations on the principles of unsupervised learning, active learning with a lateral inhibition and a competition mechanism, vector quantization of terrain structure, and the auto-programming machine.

Stochastic learning theories include the simulated annealing algorithm, the deterministic annealing method, the Boltzmann machine, the Belief machine, the Helmholtz machine, and the mean field theory.

Learning models of information theory include independent component analysis, independent factor analysis, natural gradient learning theory, and information geometry.

Statistical learning theory includes support vector machines, kernel learning, sparse approximation, and regularization networks.

12.5.3.2 Associated Memory

Information transmission and processing in the nervous system of humans are highly nonlinear. The process of human memory and association are two such examples. The procedure of human memory can be briefly divided into three stages: encoding, storage, and retrieval. They are also the main steps in machine-based associative memory. We can borrow some ideas from the group encoding mechanisms of biometric information processing to study new pattern encoding schemes. By storing encoding results in a nonlinear system (neural network) with biometric characteristics, and controlling the nonlinear system to realize automatic association, there is a strong likelihood that we may be able to develop a novel theory of pattern recognition.

12.5.3.3 Chaotic Neural Network and the Associated Memory Machine Model in the Cognitive Process

(Li and Zheng 1998a) (Li and Zheng 1998c) and (Li and Zheng 1998b)

Chaos is reflected in a set of human perceptions and cognitive processes. The chaotic state of perception also fully reflects biometric features in the cognitive process. Therefore, it is promising to realize a kind of pattern information processing with biometric characteristics, by incorporating chaos theory into the design of a new associative memory model and mimicking the biometric structures upon which human perception is based. Recently, many researchers have begun to discuss cognitive models with complex dynamic properties. Some are devoted to the study of bifurcation and chaos that appears in nonlinear networks; others are focused on the application of pseudorandom chaos. Some researchers also regard the chaotic system as a black box. However, none of them take advantage of the plentiful structures inherent in chaos, pay too little attention to its intensive physical meanings in information processing, and fail to take into account its connections with the uncertainties in the process of human perception and cognition. Using chaos attractors for pattern storage or information fusion so as to realize an automatic associative machine memory is a novel idea. But many theoretical and practical difficulties must be addressed before its realization, such as computability and computational complexity.

12.6 Cognitive Neurosciences and Computational Neuroscience

How electrical signals and chemical signals in the nervous system influence information processing is a major issue that has beset researchers for some time. Using methods from computational neuroscience to exploit the laws of information processing in the human nervous system is of far-reaching significance for revealing the working principles of the human brain.

12.6.1 Consciousness and Intention Reading

Consciousness is one basic state of the human brain. As the foundation for executing high-level, complex functions, it is a prerequisite for us in our thinking and behavior. With the invention of some advanced noninvasive apparatuses, such as PET, MRI, EG, and MEG, the problem of consciousness has been a frontier issue of cognitive neuroscience and has thus inspired some good ideas and laid a solid foundation for the development of new information processing techniques. For example, a machine-based system might be used to interpret a human subject's intentions and then infer the subject's needs, in order to take the appropriate actions to ensure that those needs are met.

12.6.2 The Core of Computational Neuroscience Is to Compute and Interpret the States of Nervous System

The state of a nervous system reflects events and states in the internal and external world. Computational neuroscience attempts to map such states of the brain to an informative state in an abstract algorithm for solving a computational problem.

Achievements in the fields of brain cognition neuroscience and computational neuroscience will lay a theoretical and practical foundation for the development of biometric feature-based vision and hearing information processing methods.

12.7 Soft Computing Method

With the appearance of the digital computer based upon the Turing machine and the conceptual framework of Von Neumann, artificial intelligent information processing based on symbolic computing and inference has made great progress, including artificial apparatuses, automatic tracing and monitoring systems, automatic control and guidance systems, and automatic diagnose systems. In conventional AI systems, there are functions that mimic or partially replace people in some tasks that are related to human thinking. Following inference rules in a logical symbol processing system, automatic diagnosis, problem-solving, and intelligent robots or expert systems can sometimes be realized. This approach reflects the style of logical reasoning in humans, that is, to compute and operate step by step according to some rules in a serial program. Serial computers can process numbers and symbols. They are widely applicable, at least in principle, but in fact have many limitations. The limitations are most distinct when such computers are used to fulfill certain specific tasks. For example, in the problem of vision, if real-time processing is implemented, the computer has to process a huge quantity of binary digits. Even the fastest computer today may be too slow, rendering this problem essentially intractable. This has greatly limited the intelligence of information processing systems and their real-time applicability. The development of the serial computer alone can no longer keep pace of the increasing needs of society for the processing of huge amounts of information. However, it is obvious that biology has successfully overcome this obstacle. Although the processing speed of a neuron is low and the time for order processing is on the millisecond level, we can recognize patterns quickly in less than 1s. This is because the human brain is a complex and huge system, and its information processing is in a style neither totally parallel nor totally serial, but rather takes on intertwining each other. This endows the human brain with a very high capacity for intelligent information processing. This has compelled researchers to pay much more attention to the perspective of human cognition in designing the appearance and structure of new intelligent information processing systems.

There are generally two ways to improve the intelligence of a system. One is to accelerate speed by increasing parallelism based on the classical model of computational logic. The other is to develop new forms of logic that possess higher intelligence. The former focuses mainly on computational speed. With respect to computational speed there are also two approaches toward improvement: to develop corresponding parallel computing method based upon the original algorithms, or to design more effective and highly parallel algorithms. The latter upgrades intelligence mainly from the improvement of the structure of system itself, its main techniques are developed by drawing inspiration from the study of human or the advanced animal or the nature. Therefore, the human brain and natural systems have provided us with good insights into solving the problems of intelligence and the real-time implementation of information processing. Parallel and distributed neural network processing and expert system-based artificial intelligence, with its symbolic and logical reasoning, will be two important basic formulations in comprehensive intelligent information processing. These will also be integrated with fuzzy logic, chaotic dynamics, soft computing, i.e., neural networks and probabilistic reasoning, uncertainty reasoning and self-organization, biologically inspired approaches, such as evolutionary computation and simulated annealing.

Some new approaches have been proposed, including the study of intelligence simulation, information processing based upon the combination of man and machine, and situated cognition based upon interaction with the environment, which departs from the conventional view about cognition, i.e., the assumption of physical symbol system, the study of the representation of mechanisms of perception and selective attention, and information processing and integration in the process of learning and memory. But they rely much more heavily on what is now known about the human brain and human cognition and less on the Aristotelian, rationalist, "brain as a computer" metaphor – this is why they will have a great impact on the development of information science and technology in the coming years.

12.8 Summary

We discuss the relationship between a general model of intelligent visual information processing systems and cognitive mechanisms in this chapter. In particular, we explore approaches to visual information processing with selective attention. We also discuss a methodology for studying the new AI system and propose some important basic research issues that have emerged in the intersecting fields of cognitive science and information science. To this end, a new scheme for associative memory and a new architecture for an AI system with attractors of chaos are addressed.

References

Baars B (1997) In the Theater of Consciousness: The Workspace of the Mind. Oxford University Press, USA

Baddeley A (1992) Working memory. Science 255(5044):556–559

Bajcsy R (1988) Active perception. Proceedings of the IEEE 86(8):996–1005

Burt PJ (1988) Attention mechanisms for vision in a dynamic world. Proceedings 9th Int Conf on Pattern Recognition pp 977–987

Daniel G (1993) Neurobiology of Neural Networks. The MIT Press, Cambridge, MA

Francis MC, Jen Y (1993) Brain mechanisms. Annals of The New York Academy of Science 151:968–976

Fred R, David W, Rob D, William B (1999) Spikes: Exploring the Neural Code. The MIT Press, Cambridge, MA

Kohonen T (1989) Self Organization and Associative Memory. Springer-Verlag, New York

Kohonen T (1991) The Perception of Multiple Objects: A Connectionist Approach. The MIT Press, Cambridge, MA

Li YY, Zheng NN (1998a) Controlling the chaotic neural network. Chinese Journal of Computers 21(S1):142–146

Li YY, Zheng NN (1998b) Improved dynamical model for neural network and the stabilization of associative memory. Progress in Natural Science 8(5):610–618

Li YY, Zheng NN (1998c) The unstable space pattern and its stabilization of neural networks with the applications in associative memory. Chinese Journal of Computers 8(2):228–236

Marr D (1982) Vision: A Computational Investigation into the Human Representation and Processing of Visual Information. W. H. Freeman, San Francisco

Palmer S (1999) Vision science: Photons to phenomenology. MIT press Cambridge, MA

Palricia SC, Terrence JS (1992) The Computational Brain. The MIT Press, Cambridge, MA

Porat M, Zeevi Y (1988) The generalized Gabor scheme of image representation in biological and machine vision. IEEE Transactions on Pattern Analysis and Machine Intelligence 10(4):452–468

Roediger MH (1991) Psychology, 3rd ed. Harper Collins Publishers, New York

Treisman A (1996) The binding problem. Current Opinion in Neurobiology 6(2):171–178

Treisman A (1998) Feature binding, attention and object perception. Philosophical Transactions of the Royal Society B: Biological Sciences 353(1373):1295–1306

Tulving E, Thomson D (1973) Encoding specificity and retrieval processes in episodic memory. Psychological Review 80(5):352–373

Wechsler H (1990) Computational Vision. Academic Press New York

Index

N. Zheng, J. Xue, *Statistical Learning and Pattern Analysis for Image and Video Processing*, Advances in Pattern Recognition, DOI 10.1007/978-1-84882-312-9_BM2,

© Springer-Verlag London Limited 2009

GPSR Compliance

The European Union's (EU) General Product Safety Regulation (GPSR) is a set of rules that requires consumer products to be safe and our obligations to ensure this.

If you have any concerns about our products, you can contact us on ProductSafety@springernature.com

In case Publisher is established outside the EU, the EU authorized representative is:

Springer Nature Customer Service Center GmbH
Europaplatz 3
69115 Heidelberg, Germany

Batch number: 10771042

Printed by Printforce, the Netherlands